AMERICA

A NARRATIVE HISTORY

Brief Eighth Edition

GEORGE BROWN TINDALL

DAVID EMORY SHI

W · W · NORTON & COMPANY · NEW YORK · LONDON

W. W. Norton & Company has been independent since its founding in 1923, when William Warder Norton and Mary D. Herter Norton first published lectures delivered at the People's Institute, the adult education division of New York City's Cooper Union. The firm soon expanded its program beyond the Institute, publishing books by celebrated academics from America and abroad. By mid-century, the two major pillars of Norton's publishing program—trade books and college texts—were firmly established. In the 1950s, the Norton family transferred control of the company to its employees, and today—with a staff of four hundred and a comparable number of trade, college, and professional titles published each year—W. W. Norton & Company stands as the largest and oldest publishing house owned wholly by its employees.

Editor: Jon Durbin
Manuscript editor: Abby Winograd
Project editor: Melissa Atkin
Emedia editor: Steve Hoge
Print ancillary editor: Rachel Comerford
Production manager: Christine D'Antonio
Book design by Antonina Krass
Editorial assistant: Jason Spears
Composition by TexTech, Inc.
Manufacturing by Worldcolor, Taunton

Library of Congress Cataloging-in-Publication Data

Tindall, George Brown.
 America : a narrative history / George Brown Tindall,
David Emory Shi.—8th ed.
  p.   cm.
 Includes bibliographical references and index.
 ISBN 978-0-393-93408-3
 1. United States—History.   I.   Shi, David E.   II.   Title.
 E178.1 .T55 2009   2009024625
 973—dc22
 ISBN 978-0-393-93410-6

W. W. Norton & Company, Inc., 500 Fifth Avenue, New York, NY 10110
www.wwnorton.com

W. W. Norton & Company Ltd., Castle House, 75/76 Wells Street, London W1T 3QT

2 3 4 5 6 7 8 9 0

FOR BRUCE AND SUSAN
AND FOR BLAIR

FOR
JASON AND JESSICA

GEORGE B. TINDALL late of the University of North Carolina, Chapel Hill, was an award-winning historian of the South with a number of major books to his credit, including *The Emergence of the New South, 1913–1945* and *The Disruption of the Solid South.*

DAVID E. SHI is a professor of history and the president of Furman University. He is the author of several books on American cultural history, including the award-winning *The Simple Life: Plain Living and High Thinking in American Culture* and *Facing Facts: Realism in American Thought and Culture, 1850–1920.*

CONTENTS

Part Five / GROWING PAINS

Part Six / MODERN AMERICA

MAPS

PREFACE

This edition of *America: A Narrative History* marks the twenty-fifth anniversary of the book. I very much regret that George Tindall is not alive to celebrate with me. He died on December 2, 2006, in Chapel Hill, North Carolina. He was eighty-five. George was a meticulous, pathbreaking, award-winning scholar. He was also an eloquent writer, an engaging teacher, and a caring mentor. And, of course, he wrote a wonderful history of America!

George Tindall developed the idea for a distinctive American history textbook nearly four decades ago. He set out to write a compelling narrative history of the American experience, a succinct narrative that would be animated by colorful characters, informed by balanced analysis and social texture, and guided by the unfolding of events. Those classic principles, combined with the book's handy format and low price, have helped make *America: A Narrative History* a book students like to read and teachers like to teach. It was my good fortune to join George in this worthy endeavor beginning with the second edition.

My duty as the new co-author on *America* at that time was to create the first brief edition. Making sure that the very first brief edition remained a coherent narrative was my overriding concern. Up to that time, most instructors complained about the choppy and incoherent nature of all the brief histories of America. Many of us still do today. We want to do the right thing for our students by purchasing a briefer, more affordable text, but too often we feel like we sacrifice quality to gain those other advantages. This is not the case when you choose the Brief Edition of *America*. We overcame that criticism by bringing it in at a length that gave us a workable balance between breadth and depth in the way we covered the topics and periods. The first brief edition was a big success!

The new Brief Eighth Edition of *America: A Narrative History* is better positioned than ever to meet the needs of today's teachers and students. *America*'s briefer, coherent narrative voice provides a clear path through the complexities of American history. New, carefully crafted pedagogical features have been added to the Eighth Edition to further help guide students through the narrative. New focus questions and chapter summaries work together seamlessly to highlight core content. Other text features include easy-to-read, full-color maps, new chapter chronologies, and new lists of key terms. Even with all these noteworthy improvements, we remain the lowest priced brief edition in full color in the marketplace!

We also continue our tradition with the new Brief Eighth Edition of creating thematic based revisions that are designed to show how politics, economics, culture, and society interact to shape the American experience. New themes in previous editions have included the role of immigration, the western experience, work, and the environment. This Brief Eighth Edition of *America* features the theme of religion and its myriad effects on history and society. Religion, of course, is one of the most powerful forces in human life, and it has played a crucial role in the development of the United States. Americans have always been a peculiarly religious people. Native American cultures centered their societies on spiritual life. And most of the first European colonists saw themselves as "a chosen people," agents of divine providence with a mission to spread the gospel to the so-called New World. In 1831 and 1832 the astute Frenchman Alexis de Tocqueville toured the United States and reported that there "is no country in the world where the Christian religion retains a greater influence over the souls of men than in America."

Yet Christianity in America has always assumed many forms. Religious freedom has been as valued a principle as religious belief. And in recent years the United States has witnessed a surge in non-Christian religions. "We are a religious people," said Supreme Court Justice William O. Douglas in 1952. Yet thirteen years later he added that America had become "a nation of Buddhists, Confucianists, and Taoists." Islam, in fact, is the nation's fastest-growing faith; there are more Muslims in America than Episcopalians. The United States is fast becoming a pluralistic, multireligious nation in which toleration is an ever-important outlook. More than the members of any other industrialized society, the vast majority of Americans (90 percent) believe in God, pray, and attend religious services at churches, synagogues, temples, and mosques. To a remarkable degree, many Americans fashion their personal conduct upon their religious principles and their social relationships upon their religious beliefs. Thus diversity characterizes American religious life. There are many different faiths and also quite different expressions of the same faith. Although the U.S. Constitution creates a "wall of separation" between religion and government, Americans are also more apt to mix faith and politics than citizens of other countries. In other words, religion continues to be one of the most dynamic—and most contested—elements of American life.

Some of the additions to the Eighth Edition relating to religious history are outlined here:

- Chapter 1 includes discussions of Aztec religious beliefs and rituals, sixteenth-century European religious life, and Spanish efforts to convert Native Americans to Catholicism.
- Chapter 2 examines the English Reformation and the distinctive characteristics of Anglicanism (the faith of the Church of England), the Native Americans' reverence for nature, and Judaism in British North America.
- Chapter 3 describes the important role of women in colonial religious life, the popularity of Deism among many key Revolutionary leaders, and the social aspects of the Great Awakening.
- Chapter 4 details the impact of the Jesuit missionaries in New France.
- Chapter 8 analyzes the logic of the First Amendment's emphasis on the separation of church and state.
- Chapter 13 explores the changes in religious life during the early nineteenth century.
- Chapter 15 includes new material on religious life in the Old South.
- Chapter 16 features the religious revival of 1857–1859.
- Chapter 17 shows that the armies fighting the Civil War engaged in frequent religious services and revivals.
- Chapter 18 details the role played by religious life in the Reconstruction of the South after the Civil War.
- Chapter 22 summarizes the role that religious fervor played in the populist movement of the 1890s.
- Chapter 23 discusses the role of religion in justifying American imperialism at the end of the nineteenth century.
- Chapter 24 highlights the role of religion in the motives of "progressive" social reformers.
- Chapter 32 describes the efforts of Congress and President Dwight Eisenhower to reaffirm America's belief in God.
- Chapter 33 stresses the crucial role played by religion in the development of the civil rights movement of the 1950s and 1960s.
- Chapter 36 explains the rise of the Republican conservatives and the role that the major revival of evangelical religion played in the conservative ascendancy in American politics.

As a thank you to our adopters and to highlight our new theme on religion, we are pleased to offer adopters the *Norton American History Digital Archive,* a 7-DVD set, including a new DVD on religion.

Beyond those explorations of religious history, I have introduced other new material throughout the Eighth Edition, including new segments on Native Americans, African Americans, women, and minorities. In addition, I have incorporated fresh insights from important new scholarly works.

Also revised is the outstanding support package that supplements the text. *For the Record: A Documentary History of America,* Fourth Edition, by David E. Shi and Holly A. Mayer (Duquesne University), is the perfect companion reader for *America: A Narrative History.* The new edition has been brought into closer alignment with the main text, and the price has been reduced by nearly 50 percent. *For the Record* now has 225 primary-source readings from diaries, journals, newspaper articles, speeches, government documents, and novels, including a number of readings that highlight the new theme of religion in *America.* If you haven't looked at *For the Record* in a while, now would be a good time.

America's StudySpace (http://wwnorton.com/studyspace) provides a proven assignment-driven plan for each chapter. Highlights include chapter outlines, quizzes in the the new Quiz Plus format, iMaps and new iMap quizzes, map worksheets, flashcards, interactive timelines, new U.S. History Tours powered by Google Earth map technology, research topics, and several hundred multimedia primary-source documents. The *Norton Instructor's Resource Disk* provides enhanced PowerPoint lecture outlines with images from the text, four-color maps, the U.S. History Tours in a slide-show format, additional images from the Library of Congress archives, and audio files of historic speeches.

The *Instructor's Manual and Test Bank,* by Stephen Davis (Kingwood College), Edward Richey (University of North Texas), Michael Krysko (Kansas State University), Brian McKnight (Angelo State University), and David Dewar (Angelo State University), includes a test bank of short-answer and essay questions, as well as detailed chapter outlines, lecture suggestions, and bibliographies. Finally, Norton coursepacks deliver all the instructor materials in a ready-to-use format for your course management system (Blackboard, WebCT, Angel, Moodle, and so on).

It's easy now to see why *America* continues to set the standard, even after twenty-five years, when it comes to providing a low-cost book with high-value content. Your students will read it, and they will save money when you use it.

In preparing the Eighth Edition, I have benefited from the insights and suggestions of many people. Some of those insights have come from student readers of the text, and I encourage such feedback. I'd particularly like to thank Eirlys Barker (Thomas Nelson Community College), who was a reviewer for us and worked on the wonderful new pedagogy in the text. Likewise, I'd like to thank Stephen Davis for his work on the *Instructor's Manual and Test Bank*. I'd like to give special thanks to Brandan Franke (Blinn College, Bryan) for his work on the new PowerPoint lectures. Numerous scholars and survey instructors advised me on the new edition:

Heather Abdelnur (Augusta State University), Alan Autrey (Lamar University), Frank Bagolione (Tallahassee Community College), Mario Bennekin (Georgia Perimeter College), William Bush (University of Nevada, Las Vegas), David Castle (Ohio University, Eastern), Craig Coenen (Mercer County Community College), Alice Colbert (University of Arkansas, Fort Smith), Alice Connally (Purdue University, North Central), Scott Cook (Motlow State Community College), Amy Darty (University of Central Florida), Wade Derden (Pulaski Technical College), Mark Goldman (Tallahassee Community College), James Good (North Harris College), Shane Hamilton (University of Georgia), Yolanda Orizando-Harding (University of Central Florida), George Hatfield (Clayton State University), Marc Horger (Ohio State University), Charles Killinger (Valencia Community College), Margaret (Peggy) Lambert (Lone Star College, Kingwood), Pat Ledbetter (North Central Texas College), Robby Luckett (University of Georgia), Lisa Morales (North Central Texas College, Corinth), Bret Nelson (San Jacinto College, North), Michael Nichols (Tarrant County College, Northwest), George Pabis (Georgia Perimeter College), Thomas Price (State University of New York, Ulster County Community College), Brooks Simpson (Arizona State University), John M. Wegner (Eastern Michigan University), Joe Whitehorne (Lord Fairfax Community College).

Once again, I thank my friends at W. W. Norton, especially Steve Forman, Jon Durbin, Steve Hoge, Karl Bakeman, Nicole Netherton, Melissa Atkin, Christine D'Antonio, Rachel Comerford, Abigail Winograd, Stephanie Romeo, and Jason Spears for their care and attention along the way.

AMERICA

18
RECONSTRUCTION: NORTH AND SOUTH

FOCUS QUESTIONS   wwnorton.com/studyspace

- What were the different approaches to Reconstruction?
- How did white southerners respond to the end of the old order in the South?
- To what extent did blacks function as citizens in the reconstructed South?
- What were the main issues in national politics in the 1870s?
- Why did Reconstruction end in 1877?

In the spring of 1865, the wearying war was finally over. At a frightful cost of over 630,000 lives and the destruction of the southern economy and much of its landscape, the Union had emerged triumphant, and some 4 million enslaved African Americans were freed. Now the nation faced the imposing task of reuniting, providing for the freed slaves, and "reconstructing" a ravaged and resentful South.

THE WAR'S AFTERMATH

In the war's aftermath the victors faced difficult questions: Should the Confederate leaders be tried for treason? How should new governments be formed? How and at whose expense was the South's economy to be rebuilt? Should debts incurred by the Confederate state governments be honored? Who should pay to rebuild the South's railroads and public buildings, dredge the clogged southern harbors, and restore damaged levees? What was to be done for the freed slaves? Were they to be given land? social equality? education? voting rights? Such complex questions required sober reflection and careful planning, but policy makers did not have the luxury of time or the benefit of consensus. Some northerners wanted the former Confederate states returned to the Union with little or no changes in the region's social, political, and economic life. Others wanted southern society punished and transformed. At the end of 1865, the editors of the nation's foremost magazine, *Harper's Weekly,* expressed this vengeful attitude when they declared that "the forgive-and-forget policy . . . is mere political insanity and suicide."

DEVELOPMENT IN THE NORTH   To some Americans the Civil War was more truly a social revolution than the War of Independence, for it reduced the once-dominant influence of the South's planter elite in national politics and elevated that of the northern "captains of industry." Government, both federal and state, grew more friendly to business leaders and more unfriendly to those who would probe into their activities. The wartime Congress had delivered on the party's major platform promises of the 1860 campaign, which had cemented the allegiance of northeastern businessmen and western farmers to the Republican party.

In the absence of southern members, the wartime Congress had centralized national power and enacted the Republican economic agenda. It passed the Morrill Tariff, which doubled the average level of import duties. The National Banking Act created a uniform system of banking and bank-note currency and helped finance the war. Congress also decided that the first transcontinental railroad would run along a north-central route, from Omaha to Sacramento, and donated public land and sold bonds to ensure its financing. In the Homestead Act of 1862, moreover, Congress provided free federal homesteads of 160 acres to settlers, who had only to occupy the land for five years to gain title. The Morrill Land Grant Act of the same year conveyed to each state 30,000 acres of federal land per member of Congress from the state, the proceeds from the sale of which went to create colleges of "agriculture and mechanic arts." Such measures helped stimulate the North's economy in the years after the Civil War.

DEVASTATION IN THE SOUTH   The postwar South offered a sharp contrast to the victorious North. Along the path of General William T. Sherman's Union army, one observer reported in 1866, the countryside of Georgia and South Carolina "looked for many miles like a broad black streak of ruin and desolation." Columbia, South Carolina, said another witness, was "a wilderness of ruins"; Charleston, a place of "vacant houses, of widowed

A street in the "burned district"

Ruins of Richmond, Virginia, in the spring of 1865.

women, of rotting wharves, of deserted warehouses, of weed-wild gardens, of miles of grass-grown streets, of acres of pitiful and voiceless barrenness."

Throughout the South, property values had collapsed. Confederate bonds and paper money were worthless; most railroads were damaged or destroyed. Cotton that had escaped destruction was seized as Confederate property or in forfeit of federal taxes. Emancipation wiped out $4 billion invested in human flesh and left the labor system in disarray. The great age of expansion in the cotton market was over. Not until 1879 would the cotton crop again equal the record harvest of 1860; tobacco production did not regain its prewar level until 1880; the sugar crop of Louisiana did not recover until 1893; and the old rice industry of the Tidewater and the hemp industry of the Kentucky Bluegrass never regained their prewar status.

A TRANSFORMED SOUTH   The defeat of the Confederacy transformed much of southern society. The liberation of slaves, the destruction of property, and the free fall in land values left many planters destitute and homeless. After the Civil War many former Confederates were so embittered that they abandoned their native region rather than submit to "Yankee rule." Some migrated to Canada, Europe, Mexico, South America, or Asia. Others preferred the western territories and states. Still others moved to northern and midwestern cities on the assumption that their educational and economic opportunities would be better among the victors.

Most of those who remained in the South found their farms, homes, and communities transformed. One Confederate army captain reported that on his father's plantation "our negroes are living in great comfort. They were delighted to see me with overflowing affection. They waited on me as before, gave me breakfast, splendid dinners, etc. But they firmly and respectfully informed me: 'We own this land now. Put it out of your head that it will ever be yours again.'"

LEGALLY FREE, SOCIALLY BOUND In the former Confederate states the newly freed slaves suffered most of all. A few northerners argued that what the ex-slaves needed most was their own land. In 1865, Representative George Washington Julian of Indiana and Senator Charles Sumner of Massachusetts proposed to give freed slaves forty-acre homesteads carved out of Confederate lands taken under the Confiscation Act of 1862. But their plan for outright grants was replaced by a program of rentals, since confiscation was effective under the law only for the lifetime of the Confederate property owner. Discussions of land distribution fueled rumors, however, that freed slaves would get "forty acres and a mule," a slogan that swept the South at the end of the war. But even abolitionists shrank from taking land

Freed slaves in Richmond, Virginia

According to a former Confederate general, freed slaves had "nothing but freedom."

from whites to give to the freed slaves. Citizenship and legal rights were one thing, wholesale confiscation of property and land redistribution quite another. Instead of land or material help, the freed slaves more often got advice about proper behavior.

THE FREEDMEN'S BUREAU   On March 3, 1865, while the war was still raging, Congress set up within the War Department the Bureau of Refugees, Freedmen, and Abandoned Lands to provide "provisions, clothing, and fuel" to relieve "destitute and suffering refugees and freedmen and their wives and children." It was the first federal experiment in social welfare, albeit temporary. Agents of what came to be called the Freedmen's Bureau negotiated labor contracts (a new practice for both African Americans and planters), provided medical care, and set up schools. The bureau had its own courts to deal with labor disputes and land titles, and its agents were authorized to supervise trials involving blacks in other courts. White intransigence and racial prejudice thwarted the efforts of Freedmen's Bureau agents to protect and assist the former slaves, however.

THE BATTLE OVER RECONSTRUCTION

The question of how to reconstruct the South's political structure centered on deciding which governments would constitute authority in the defeated states. As Union forces advanced into the South, President Lincoln in 1862 named military governors for conquered Tennessee, Arkansas, and Louisiana. By the end of the following year, he had formulated a plan for regular civilian governments in those states and any others that might be liberated from Confederate rule.

LINCOLN'S PLAN AND CONGRESS'S RESPONSE   In late 1863, President Lincoln had issued a Proclamation of Amnesty and Reconstruction, under which any former Confederate state could form a Union government whenever a number equal to 10 percent of those who had voted in 1860 took an oath of allegiance to the Constitution and the Union and had received a presidential pardon. Participants also had to swear support for laws and proclamations dealing with emancipation. Excluded from the pardon, however, were certain groups: Confederate officials and officers; judges, congressmen, and military officers of the United States who had left their federal posts to aid the rebellion; and those accused of failure to treat captured African American soldiers and their officers as prisoners of war.

Under this plan, governments loyal to the Union appeared in Tennessee, Arkansas, and Louisiana, but Congress refused to recognize them. In the absence of specific provisions for Reconstruction in the Constitution, politicians disagreed as to where authority to restore Rebel states properly rested. A few conservative and most moderate Republicans supported Lincoln's program of immediate restoration. A small but influential group, known as Radical Republicans, demanded a sweeping transformation of southern society that would include making the freed slaves full-fledged citizens. The Radicals hoped to reconstruct southern society so as to dismantle the planter elite and the Democratic party.

The Radical Republicans were talented, earnest leaders who maintained that Congress, not the president, should supervise the Reconstruction program. To this end in 1864 they helped pass the Wade-Davis Bill, sponsored by Senator Benjamin Franklin Wade of Ohio and Representative Henry Winter Davis of Maryland. In contrast to Lincoln's 10 percent plan, the Wade-Davis Bill required that a *majority* of white male citizens declare their allegiance and that only those who swore an "ironclad" oath that they had always remained loyal to the Union could vote or serve in the state constitutional conventions. The conventions, moreover, would have to abolish slavery, deny political rights to high-ranking civil and military officers of the Confederacy, and repudiate Confederate war debts. Passed during the closing days of the 1864 session, the bill was vetoed by Lincoln. The bill's sponsors then issued the Wade-Davis Manifesto, a blistering statement accusing the president of usurping power and attempting to use readmitted states to ensure his reelection.

Lincoln made his final statement on Reconstruction in his last public address, on April 11, 1865. Speaking from the White House balcony, he dismissed the theoretical question of whether the Confederate states had technically remained in the Union as "good for nothing at all—a mere pernicious abstraction." Those states were simply "out of their proper practical relation with the Union," and the object was to get them back "into their proper practical relation" as quickly as possible. Lincoln hoped to get new southern state governments in operation before Congress met in December. He worried that Congress might push through a harsher Reconstruction program. Lincoln wanted "no persecution, no bloody work," no dramatic restructuring of southern social and economic life.

On the evening of April 14, 1865, Lincoln went to Ford's Theatre and his rendezvous with death. Shot in the head by John Wilkes Booth, a crazed actor and Confederate zealot, the president died the next morning. Pursued into Virginia, Booth was trapped and shot in a burning barn. His last words were "Tell mother I die for my country. I thought I did for the best." Three collaborators were tried and hanged, along with Mary Surratt, at whose boardinghouse they had plotted. Three other conspirators received life sentences, including a Maryland doctor who set the leg Booth had broken when he jumped from Lincoln's box onto the stage.

JOHNSON'S PLAN   Lincoln's death elevated to the White House Vice President Andrew Johnson of Tennessee, a combative man who lacked most presidential virtues. Essentially illiterate, Johnson was provincial and bigoted, short-tempered and impetuous. At the inaugural ceremonies in early 1865, he had drunkenly slurred his vice-presidential address, embarrassing Lincoln and the nation. Johnson was a war (pro-Union) Democrat who had been put on the National Union ticket in 1864 as a gesture of unity. Of origins as humble as Lincoln's, Johnson had moved as a youth from his birthplace in Raleigh, North Carolina, to Greeneville, Tennessee, where he became the proprietor of a tailor shop. Self-educated with the help of his wife, Johnson grew prosperous, acquiring several slaves in the process.

Beginning in the 1830s, Johnson emerged as a leading Jacksonian Democrat. A bitter critic of the "swaggering" planter aristocracy "who are too lazy and proud to work," he promoted free land for the poor, defended slavery, and championed white supremacy. A notoriously stubborn man, he became a self-righteous, hot-tempered orator who enjoyed strong drink and employed abusive language to belittle his opponents. His fiery speeches and firm principles helped him win election as mayor, congressman, governor, and senator.

Like many other whites living in mountainous eastern Tennessee, Johnson ardently believed in the Union. In 1861 he was the only southern senator from a Confederate state to vote against secession, leading critics to denounce him as a "traitor" to the region. Yet his devotion to the Union did not include opposition to slavery. He hated the Confederacy because he hated the planter elite. "Damn the Negroes," Johnson bellowed to a friend during the war, "I am fighting those traitorous aristocrats, their masters."

Some Radical Republicans at first thought President Johnson, unlike Lincoln, was one of them. Johnson had, for example, asserted that treason "must be made infamous and traitors must be impoverished." But the Radicals would soon find Johnson to be as unsympathetic as Lincoln had been to their sweeping agenda, if for different reasons. Johnson's loyalty to the Union sprang from a strict adherence to the Constitution and a fervent belief in limited government. He held that the rebellious states should be quickly brought back into their proper relation to the Union because the states and the Union were indestructible. In 1865, Johnson declared that "there is no such thing as Reconstruction. Those states have not gone out of the Union. Therefore Reconstruction is unnecessary."

Johnson's plan to restore the Union thus closely resembled Lincoln's. A new Proclamation of Amnesty, issued on May 29, 1865, excluded from pardon not only those Lincoln had excluded but also everybody with taxable property worth more than $20,000. Those wealthy planters and merchants were the people Johnson believed had led the South to secede. Those in the excluded groups might make special applications for presidential pardon, and before the year was out Johnson had issued some 13,000 pardons.

Andrew Johnson

A pro-Union Democrat from Tennessee.

In each of the Rebel states not already organized by Lincoln, Johnson named a native Unionist provisional governor with authority to call a convention of men elected by loyal voters. Lincoln's 10 percent requirement was omitted. Johnson called upon the conventions to invalidate the secession ordinances, abolish slavery, and repudiate all debts incurred to aid the Confederacy. Each state, moreover, was to ratify the Thirteenth Amendment, which ended slavery. Like Lincoln, Johnson endorsed limited voting rights for blacks. The state conventions for the most part met Johnson's requirements. Emboldened by the president's indulgence, however, southern whites ignored his advice to move cautiously in restoring their political and social traditions. Suggestions of black suffrage were scarcely raised in the state conventions and promptly squelched when they were.

SOUTHERN INTRANSIGENCE When Congress met in December 1865, for the first time since the end of the war it faced the fact that the new state governments in the former Confederacy were remarkably like the old ones. Among the new members presenting themselves to Congress were Georgia's Alexander Stephens, former vice president of the Confederacy, four Confederate generals, eight colonels, and six cabinet members. The Congress forthwith denied seats to all such officials. It was too much to expect, after four bloody years, that the Unionists in Congress would welcome back ex-Confederate leaders.

Furthermore, the new southern state legislatures, in passing repressive "black codes" restricting the freedom of African Americans, baldly revealed that they intended to preserve the trappings of slavery as nearly as possible. As one southerner stressed, the "ex-slave was not a free man; he was a free Negro," and the black codes were intended to highlight the distinction.

The black codes varied from state to state, but some provisions were common. Existing black marriages, including common-law marriages, were recognized (although interracial marriages were prohibited), and testimony by blacks was accepted in legal cases involving them—and in six states in all cases. Blacks could own property. They could sue and be sued in the courts. On the other hand, in Mississippi they could not own farmland, and in South Carolina they could not own city lots. Blacks who worked for whites were required to enter into labor contracts with their employers, with provision for punishment in case of violation. Their dependent children were subject to compulsory apprenticeship and corporal punishment by the employer. "Vagrant" (unemployed) blacks were punished with severe fines, and if unable to pay they were forced to work in the fields of whites who paid the courts for their cheap labor. Slavery was thus revived in another guise.

THE RADICAL REPUBLICANS Faced with such southern intransigence, moderate Republicans drifted more and more toward the Radical camp. The new Congress set up a Joint Committee on Reconstruction, with nine members from the House and six from the Senate, to gather evidence and submit proposals for reconstructing the southern states. As a parade of witnesses testified to the Rebels' impenitence, initiative on the committee fell to determined Radicals: Benjamin Wade of Ohio, George Julian of Indiana, Henry Wilson of Massachusetts, and most conspicuously of all, Thaddeus Stevens of Pennsylvania and Charles Sumner of Massachusetts.

Stevens, a crusty old bachelor with a chiseled face, thin, stern lips, and brooding eyes, was the domineering floor leader in the House. Driven by a genuine if at times fanatic idealism, he angrily insisted that the "whole fabric of southern society *must* be changed." Sumner, Stevens's counterpart in the Senate, agreed. Now recovered from "Bully" Brooks's 1856 assault, Sumner strove to see the South *reconstructed* rather than simply restored. This aim put him at odds with President Johnson. After visiting the White House, Sumner found the president "harsh, petulant, and unreasonable." He was especially disheartened by President Johnson's "prejudice, ignorance, and perversity" regarding the treatment of African Americans. Sumner, along with other Radicals, now grew determined to take matters into their own hands. He argued that "Massachusetts could govern Georgia better than Georgia could govern herself." The southern plantations, seedbeds of aristocratic pretension and secession, he later added, "must be broken up, and the freedmen must have the pieces."

Most of the Radical Republicans had long been abolitionists, and they approached the question of African American rights with a sincere humanitarian impulse. Yet the Republicans also had political reasons for promoting civil rights. They needed black votes to maintain their control of Congress and the White House. They also needed to disenfranchise former Confederates to keep them from helping to elect Democrats who would restore the old ruling class to power. In public, however, the Radical Republicans rarely disclosed such partisan self-interest. Instead, they asserted that the Republicans, the party of Union and freedom, could best guarantee the fruits of victory and that extending voting rights to African Americans would be the best way to promote their welfare.

The growing conflict of opinion over Reconstruction policy brought about an inversion in constitutional reasoning. Secessionists—and Andrew Johnson—were now arguing that the Confederate states had in fact technically remained in the Union, and some Radical Republicans were contriving arguments that they had left the Union after all. Thaddeus Stevens argued that the Confederate states had indeed seceded and were now conquered provinces, subject to the absolute will of the victors. He added that the "whole fabric of southern society must be changed." Most congressmen, however, held that the Rebel states continued to exist but by the acts of secession and war had forfeited "all civil and political rights under the Constitution." And Congress, not the president, was the proper authority to determine how and when such rights might be restored.

JOHNSON'S BATTLE WITH CONGRESS   A long year of political battling remained, however, before this idea triumphed. By the end of 1865, the Radical Republicans' views had gained only a slight majority in Congress, insufficient to override presidential vetoes. The critical year of 1866 saw the gradual waning of Andrew Johnson's power, much of which was self-induced. Johnson first challenged Congress in February, when he vetoed a bill to extend the life of the Freedmen's Bureau. The measure, he said, violated the Constitution. For the moment, Johnson's prestige remained sufficiently intact that the Senate upheld his veto.

Three days after the veto, however, on George Washington's Birthday, Johnson undermined his authority by launching an intemperate assault

"The Cruel Uncle and the Vetoed Babes in the Wood"

A cartoon depicting Andrew Johnson leading two children, "Civil Rights" and "Bureau," into the "Veto Wood."

upon the Radical Republican leaders during an impromptu speech. From that point, moderate Republicans abandoned the president, and Radical Republicans went on the offensive.

In mid-March 1866 the Radical-led Congress passed the Civil Rights Act. A direct response to the black codes created by unrepentant state legislatures in the South, it declared that "all persons born in the United States . . . excluding Indians not taxed" were citizens entitled to "full and equal benefit of all laws." The granting of citizenship to native-born blacks, Johnson claimed, exceeded the scope of federal power. It would, moreover, "foment discord among the races." He vetoed the measure, but this time, in April, Congress overrode his veto. Then in July it enacted a revised Freedmen's Bureau Bill, again overturning a veto. From that point on, Johnson's public and political support steadily eroded.

THE FOURTEENTH AMENDMENT   To remove all doubt about the validity of the new Civil Rights Act, the joint committee recommended a new constitutional amendment, which passed Congress in 1866 and was ratified by the states in 1868. The Fourteenth Amendment went far beyond the Civil Rights Act, however. The first section asserts four principles: it reaffirms the state and federal citizenship of all persons—regardless of race—born or naturalized in the United States, and it forbids any state (the word *state* would be important in later litigation) to "abridge the privileges or immunities of citizens," to deprive any *person* (again an important term) "of life, liberty, or property, without due process of law," or to "deny any person . . . the equal protection of the laws."

These clauses have been the subject of lawsuits resulting in applications not foreseen at the time. The "due-process clause" has come to mean that state as well as federal power is subject to the Bill of Rights, and it has been used to protect corporations, as legal "persons," from "unreasonable" regulation by the states. Other provisions of the amendment had less far-reaching effects. One section specified that the debt of the United States "shall not be questioned" but declared "illegal and void" all debts contracted in aid of the Confederate rebellion. The final sentence specified the power of Congress to pass laws enforcing the amendment.

Johnson's home state was among the first to ratify the Fourteenth Amendment. In Tennessee, which had harbored more Unionists than any other Confederate state, the government had fallen under Radical Republican control. The rest of the South, however, steadfastly resisted the Radical challenge to Andrew Johnson's lenient program. In 1866 bloody race riots in Memphis and New Orleans added fuel to the flames. Both incidents sparked indiscriminate massacres of blacks by local police and white mobs. The rioting, Radical Republicans argued, was the natural fruit of Johnson's foolish policy.

RECONSTRUCTING THE SOUTH

THE TRIUMPH OF CONGRESSIONAL RECONSTRUCTION As 1866 drew to an end, the November congressional elections promised to be a referendum on the growing split between Johnson and the Radical Republicans. The president embarked on a speaking tour of the Midwest, a "swing around the circle," which sparked undignified shouting contests between the president and his audiences. In Cleveland he described the Radical Republicans as "factious, domineering, tyrannical" men. Various incidents tended to confirm his image as a "ludicrous boor," which Radical Republican newspapers eagerly promoted. When the election returns came in, the Republicans had more than a two-thirds majority in each house, a comfortable margin with which to override presidential vetoes.

Congress actually enacted a Reconstruction program even before the new members took office. On March 2, 1867, two days before the old Congress expired, it passed three basic laws of congressional Reconstruction over Johnson's vetoes: the Military Reconstruction Act, the Command of the Army Act, and the Tenure of Office Act.

The first of these acts prescribed conditions under which new southern state governments should be formed. The other two sought to block any effort by the president to obstruct the process. The Command of the Army Act required that all orders from the president as commander in chief go through the headquarters of the general of the army, then Ulysses Grant. The Tenure of Office Act required the Senate's permission for the president to remove any federal officeholder whose appointment the Senate had confirmed. In large measure it was intended to retain Secretary of War Edwin

Stanton, the one Radical Republican sympathizer in Johnson's cabinet. But an ambiguity had crept into the wording of the act. Cabinet officers, it said, should serve during the term of the president who appointed them—and Lincoln had appointed Stanton, although, to be sure, Johnson was serving out Lincoln's term.

The Military Reconstruction Act was hailed—or denounced—as the triumphant victory of Radical Reconstruction. Originally intended by the Radical Republicans to give military commanders in the South ultimate control over law enforcement and to leave open indefinitely the terms of restoration, it was diluted by moderate Republicans until it boiled down to little more than a requirement that southern states accept African American suffrage and ratify the Fourteenth Amendment.

Tennessee, which had already ratified the Fourteenth Amendment, was exempted from the application of the act. The other ten states were divided into five military districts, and the commanding officer of each was authorized to keep order and protect the "rights of persons and property." The Johnson governments remained intact for the time being, but new constitutions were to be framed "in conformity with the Constitution of the United States," in conventions elected by male citizens aged twenty-one and older "of whatever race, color, or previous condition." Each state constitution had to provide the same universal male suffrage. Then, once the constitution was ratified by a majority of voters and accepted by Congress, the state legislature had ratified the Fourteenth Amendment, and the amendment had become part of the Constitution, any given state would be entitled to renewed representation in Congress. Persons excluded from officeholding by the proposed amendment were also excluded from participation in the process. Before the end of 1867, new elections had been held in all the states but Texas.

Having clipped the president's wings, the Republican Congress moved a year later to safeguard its Reconstruction program from possible interference by the Supreme Court. On March 27, 1868, Congress simply removed the power of the Supreme Court to review cases arising under the Military Reconstruction Act, which Congress clearly had the constitutional right to do under its power to define the Court's appellate jurisdiction. The Court accepted this curtailment of its authority on the same day it affirmed the notion of an "indestructible Union" in *Texas v. White* (1869). In that case the Court also acknowledged the right of Congress to reframe state governments, thus endorsing the Radical Republican point of view.

THE IMPEACHMENT AND TRIAL OF JOHNSON   By 1868, Radical Republicans were convinced not only that the power of the Supreme

Court and the president needed to be curtailed but also that Andrew Johnson himself had to be removed from office. Johnson, though hostile to the congressional Reconstruction program, had gone through the motions required of him. He continued to pardon former Confederates, however, and transferred several of the district military commanders who had displayed Radical Republican sympathies. Johnson lacked Lincoln's resilience and pragmatism, and he allowed his temper to get the better of his judgment. He castigated the Radical Republicans as "a gang of cormorants and bloodsuckers who have been fattening upon the country." During 1867, newspapers reported that the differences between Johnson and the Republicans had grown irreconcilable.

The Radical Republicans unsuccessfully tried to impeach Johnson early in 1867, alleging a variety of flimsy charges, none of which represented an indictable crime. Then Johnson himself provided the occasion for impeachment when he deliberately violated the Tenure of Office Act in order to test its constitutionality. Secretary of War Edwin Stanton had become a thorn in Johnson's side, refusing to resign despite his disagreements with the president's Reconstruction policy. On August 12, 1867, during a congressional recess, Johnson suspended Stanton and named General Ulysses Grant in his place. When the Senate refused to confirm Johnson's action, however, Grant returned the office to Stanton.

The Radical Republicans now saw their chance to remove the president. On February 24, 1868, the House passed eleven articles of impeachment by a party-line vote of 126 to 47. Eight of the articles focused on the charge that Johnson had unlawfully removed Secretary of War Stanton. Article 9 accused the president of issuing orders in violation of the Command of the Army Act. The last two articles in effect charged him with criticizing Congress by "inflammatory and scandalous harangues." Article 11 also accused him of "unlawfully devising and contriving" to violate the Reconstruction Acts, contrary to his obligation to execute the laws. At the very least, it stated, Johnson had tried to obstruct Congress's will while observing the letter of the law.

The Senate trial began on March 5, 1868, and continued until May 26, with Chief Justice Salmon P. Chase presiding. Debate eventually focused on Stanton's removal, the most substantive impeachment charge. Johnson's lawyers argued that Lincoln, not Johnson, had appointed Stanton, so the Tenure of Office Act did not apply to him. At the same time they claimed (correctly, as it turned out) that the law was unconstitutional.

As the five-week trial ended and the voting began in May 1868, seven moderate Republicans and all twelve Democrats voted to acquit. The final tally was 35 to 19 for conviction, one vote short of the two thirds needed for removal from office.

Although the Senate failed to remove Johnson, the trial crippled his already weak presidency. During the remaining ten months of his term, he initiated no other clashes with Congress. In 1868, Johnson sought the Democratic presidential nomination but lost to New York governor Horatio Seymour, who then lost to the Republican, Ulysses Grant, in the general election. The impeachment of Johnson was in the end a great political mistake, for the failure to remove the president damaged Radical Republican morale and support. Nevertheless, the Radical cause did gain something: Johnson's agreement not to obstruct the process of Reconstruction. Thereafter Radical Reconstruction began in earnest.

REPUBLICAN RULE IN THE SOUTH   In June 1868, Congress agreed that seven southern states, all but Virginia, Mississippi, and Texas, had met the more stringent conditions for readmission to the Union. Congress rescinded Georgia's admission, however, when the state legislature expelled twenty-eight African American members and seated former Confederate leaders. The federal military commander in Georgia then forced the legislature to reseat the black members and remove the Confederates, and the state was compelled to ratify the Fifteenth Amendment before being readmitted in July 1870. Mississippi, Texas, and Virginia had returned earlier in 1870, under the added requirement that they, too, ratify the Fifteenth Amendment. That amendment, ratified in 1870, forbids the states to deny any citizen the right to vote on grounds of "race, color, or previous condition of servitude."

Long before the new governments were established, partisan Republican groups had begun to spring up in the South, promoted by the Union League, an organization founded in 1862 to rally support for the federal government. Its representatives enrolled blacks and loyal whites as members, initiated them into the secrets and rituals of the order, and instructed them "in their rights and duties." The Union Leagues became a powerful source of Republican political strength in the South and as a result drew the ire of unreconstructed whites.

THE RECONSTRUCTED SOUTH

Throughout the South during Reconstruction, many former Confederates continued to harbor deeply ingrained racial prejudices. They adopted a militant stance against federally imposed changes in southern society.

Whites used terror, intimidation, and violence to suppress black efforts to gain social and economic equality. In July 1866, for instance, a black woman in Clinch County, Georgia, was arrested and given sixty-five lashes for "using abusive language" in an encounter with a white woman. A month later another black woman suffered the same punishment. The Civil War had brought freedom to the enslaved, but it did not bring protection against exploitation or abuse.

THE FREED SLAVES   Southern blacks were active agents in affecting the course of Reconstruction. Many former slaves found themselves liberated but destitute after the fighting ended. The mere promise of freedom, however, had raised their hopes for biracial democracy, equal justice, and economic opportunity. "Most anyone ought to know that a man is better off free than as a slave, even if he did not have anything," said the Reverend E. P. Holmes, a black Georgia preacher and former domestic servant. "I would rather be free and have my liberty."

Participation in the Union army or navy had provided many freedmen with training in leadership. Black military veterans would form the core of the first generation of African American political leaders in the postwar South. Military service provided many former slaves with the first opportunities to learn to read and write. Army life also alerted them to alternative social choices and to new opportunities for economic advancement and social respectability. Fighting for the Union cause also instilled a fervent sense of nationalism. A Virginia freedman explained that the United States was "now *our* country—made emphatically so by the blood of our brethren."

Former slaves established independent churches after the war, which quickly formed the foundation of African American community life. Blacks preferred Baptist churches over other denominations, in part because its decentralized structure allowed each congregation to worship in its own way. By 1890 over 1.3 million African Americans were worshipping in Baptist churches in the South, nearly three times as many as had joined any other denomination. In addition to forming viable new congregations, freed African Americans organized thousands of fraternal, benevolent, and mutual-aid societies, as well as clubs, lodges, and associations. Memphis, for example, had over 200 such organizations; Richmond boasted twice that number.

Freed slaves also hastened to reestablish and reaffirm their families. Marriages that had been prohibited were now legitimized through the assistance of the Freedmen's Bureau. By 1870 most former slaves were living in two-parent households.

Former slaves had little money or technical training and were thus faced with the prospect of becoming wage laborers to support themselves. To avoid this alternative and retain as much autonomy as possible over their productive energy and that of their children, many freed slaves chose to become sharecroppers, tenant farmers who gained access to separate plots of land owned by whites. In payment for the use of the land and a cabin, and sometimes even the tools, seed, and fertilizer needed to farm the land, they were required to give between one half and two thirds of the harvested crops to the landowner. This arrangement gave them higher status than they would have had as wage laborers. It also gave them the freedom to set their own hours and work as much or as little as they pleased, and it enabled mothers and wives to devote time to domestic responsibilities while contributing to the family's income.

African American communities in the postwar South also sought to establish schools. The antebellum planter elite had denied education to blacks because they feared that literate slaves would organize uprisings. After the war the white elite worried that formal education would encourage poor whites and poor blacks to leave the South in search of better social and economic opportunities. Economic leaders wanted to protect the competitive advantage afforded by the region's low-wage labor market. Yet white opposition to education for blacks made education all the more important to African Americans. South Carolina's Mary McLeod Bethune, the seventeenth child of former slaves and one of the first children in the household born after the Civil War, reveled in the opportunity to gain an education: "The whole world opened to me when I learned to read." She walked five miles to school as a child, earned a scholarship to college, and went on to become the first black woman to found a school that became a four-year college, Bethune-Cookman, in Daytona Beach, Florida.

AFRICAN AMERICANS IN SOUTHERN POLITICS   In the postwar South the new role of African Americans in politics caused the most controversy. If largely illiterate and inexperienced in the rudiments of politics, southern blacks were little different from the millions of whites enfranchised in the age of Jackson or immigrants herded to the polls by political bosses in New York and other cities after the war. Some freedmen frankly confessed their disadvantages. Beverly Nash, a black delegate to the South Carolina convention of 1868, told his colleagues: "I believe, my friends and fellow-citizens, we are not prepared for this suffrage. But we can learn. Give a man tools and let him commence to use them, and in time he will learn a trade. So it is with voting."

Several hundred African American delegates participated in the statewide political conventions. Most had been selected by local political meetings or churches, fraternal societies, Union Leagues, or black Federal army units, although a few simply appointed themselves. The African American delegates "ranged all colors and apparently all conditions," but free mulattoes from the cities played the most prominent roles. At Louisiana's Republican state convention, for instance, nineteen of the twenty black delegates had been born free.

By 1867 former slaves had begun to gain political influence and vote in large numbers, and this development revealed emerging tensions within the African American community. Some southern blacks resented the presence of northern brethren who moved south after the war, while others complained that few ex-slaves were represented in leadership positions. Northern blacks and the southern black elite, most of whom were urban dwellers, opposed efforts to redistribute land to the rural freedmen, and many insisted that political equality did not mean social equality. As a black Alabama leader stressed, "We do not ask that the ignorant and degraded shall be put on a social equality with the refined and intelligent." In general, however,

Freedmen voting in New Orleans

The Fifteenth Amendment, ratified in 1870, guaranteed at the federal level the right of citizens to vote regardless of "race, color, or previous condition of servitude." But former slaves had been registering to vote—and voting in large numbers—in state elections since 1867, as in this scene.

unity rather than dissension prevailed, and African Americans focused on common concerns such as full equality under the law.

Brought suddenly into politics in times that tried the most skilled of statesmen, many African Americans served with distinction. Nonetheless, the derisive label "black Reconstruction," used by later critics, exaggerates African American political influence, which was limited mainly to voting, and overlooks the political clout of the large number of white Republicans, especially in the mountain areas of the Upper South, who supported the congressional plan for Reconstruction. Only one of the new state conventions, South Carolina's, had a black majority, seventy-six to forty-one. Louisiana's was evenly divided racially, and in only two other conventions were more than 20 percent of the members black: Florida's, with 40 percent, and Virginia's, with 24 percent.

In the new state governments any African American participation was a novelty. Although some 600 blacks—most of them former slaves—served as state legislators, no black was ever elected governor, and few served as judges. In Louisiana, however, Pinckney Pinchback, a northern black and former Union soldier, won the office of lieutenant governor and served as acting governor when the white governor was indicted for corruption. Several African Americans were elected lieutenant governor, state treasurer, or secretary of state. There were two black senators in Congress during Reconstruction, Hiram Revels and Blanche K. Bruce, both from Mississippi, and fourteen black members of the House. Among them were some of the ablest congressmen of the time.

CARPETBAGGERS AND SCALAWAGS The top positions in postwar southern state governments went for the most part to white Republicans whom the opposition labeled carpetbaggers and scalawags, depending upon their place of birth. Northerners who allegedly rushed south with all their belongings in carpetbags to reap political spoils were more often than not Union veterans who had arrived as early as 1865 or 1866, drawn south by the hope of economic opportunity. Others were lawyers, businessmen, editors, teachers, social workers, or preachers who came on sincere missionary endeavors.

The scalawags, or southern white Republicans, were even more reviled and misrepresented. A Nashville newspaper editor called them the "merest trash." Most scalawags had opposed secession, forming a Unionist majority in mountain counties as far south as Georgia and Alabama and especially in the hills of eastern Tennessee. Though many were indeed crass opportunists who indulged in corruption at the public's expense, several were distinguished figures. They included the former Confederate general James Longstreet, who decided after Appomattox that the Old South must change its ways. To that end he became a successful cotton broker in New Orleans, joined the Republican party, and supported the Radical Reconstruction program. Others were former Whigs who supported the Republican party's expansive industrial and commercial program in keeping with Henry Clay's earlier efforts to use the government to promote economic growth and industrial development.

THE RADICAL REPUBLICAN RECORD Former Confederates not only resented carpetbaggers and scalawags, but they also objected to the new state constitutions, primarily because of their provisions allowing for black voting and civil rights. Nonetheless, most of those state constitutions remained in effect for some years after the end of Radical Republican control, and later constitutions incorporated many of their features. Conspicuous among the Radical innovations were steps toward greater democracy, such as requiring universal male suffrage, reapportioning legislatures more nearly according to population, and making more state offices elective.

Given the hostile circumstances under which the Radical Republican governments operated, their achievements were remarkable. They established the first state-supported public school systems, in which some 600,000 black pupils were enrolled by 1877. State governments under the Radical Republicans also paid more attention to the poor and to orphanages, asylums, and institutions for the disabled of both races. Public roads, bridges, railroads, and buildings were repaired or rebuilt. African Americans achieved rights and opportunities that would never again be taken away, at least in principle: equality before the law and the right to own property, carry on business, enter professions, attend schools, and learn to read and write.

Yet several of the Republican state regimes also engaged in systematic corruption. Public money and public credit were often awarded to privately owned corporations, notably railroads, under conditions that invited influence peddling. Still, corruption was not invented by the Radical Republican regimes, nor did it die with them. In Mississippi the Republican Reconstruction governments were quite honest compared with those of their Democratic successors.

RELIGION AND RECONSTRUCTION The religious community played a critical role in the implementation and ultimate failure of Radical Reconstruction. And religious commentators offered quite different interpretations of what should be done with the defeated South. Thaddeus

Stevens and many other Radical Republican leaders who had spent their careers promoting the abolition of slavery and racial equality were motivated primarily by religious ideals and moral fervor. They wanted no compromise with racism. Likewise, most of the Christian missionaries who headed south after the Civil War brought with them a progressive vision of a biracial "beloved community" emerging in the reconstructed South, and they strove to promote social and political equality for freed slaves. For these crusaders, civil rights was a sacred cause. They used Christian principles to challenge the prevailing theological and "scientific" justifications for racial inferiority. They also promoted Christian solidarity across racial and regional lines.

At the same time, the Protestant denominations, all of which had split into northern and southern branches over the issues of slavery and secession, struggled to reunite after the war. A growing number of northern ministers promoted reconciliation between the warring regions after the Civil War. These "apostles of forgiveness" prized white unity over racial equality. For example, the Reverend Henry Ward Beecher, the powerful New York minister whose sister Harriet Beecher Stowe wrote *Uncle Tom's Cabin*, wanted white southern planters—rather than federal officials or African Americans themselves—to oversee Reconstruction. Not surprisingly, Beecher's views gained widespread support among evangelical ministers in the South.

The "white republic"

This cartoon illustrates white unity over racial equality.

The collapse of the Confederacy did not prompt southern whites to abandon their belief that God was on their side. In the wake of defeat and emancipation, white southern ministers reassured their congregations that they had no reason to question the moral foundations of their region or their defense of white racial superiority. For African Americans, the Civil War and emancipation demonstrated that God was on their side. Emancipation was in their view a redemptive act through which God wrought national regeneration. African American ministers were convinced that the United States was indeed a divinely inspired nation and that blacks had a providential role to play in its future. Yet neither black nor idealistic white northern ministers could stem the growing chorus of whites who were willing to abandon goals of racial equality in exchange for national religious reconciliation. By the end of the nineteenth century, mainstream American Protestantism promoted the image of a "white republic" that conflated whiteness, godliness, and nationalism.

THE GRANT YEARS

THE ELECTION OF 1868   Ulysses S. Grant, who served as president during the collapse of Republican rule in the South, brought to the White House little political experience. But in 1868 northern voters supported the Lion of Vicksburg because of his brilliant record as a war leader. Both parties wooed Grant, but his falling-out with President Johnson had pushed him toward the Republicans and had built trust in him among the Radicals.

The Republican party platform of 1868 endorsed Radical Reconstruction, cautiously defending black suffrage as a necessity in the South but a matter that each northern state should settle for itself. It also urged payment of the nation's war debt in gold rather than in the new "greenback" paper currency printed during the war. More important than the platform were the great expectations of a soldier-president, whose slogan was "Let us have peace."

The Democrats opposed the Republicans on both Reconstruction and the debt. The Republican Congress, the Democratic platform charged, had subjected ten states, "in the time of profound peace, to military despotism and Negro supremacy." As for the public debt, the party endorsed the "Ohio idea" of Representative George H. Pendleton: since most war bonds had been bought with depreciated greenbacks, they should be paid off in greenbacks rather than in gold. With no conspicuously available candidate in sight, the convention turned to Horatio Seymour, wartime governor of New York. The Democrats ran a closer race than expected, attesting to the strength of traditional party loyalties. Although Grant swept the Electoral College by 214 to 80, his popular majority was only 307,000 out of 5.7 million votes. Over 500,000 African American voters accounted for Grant's margin of victory.

Grant had proved himself a great military leader, but in the White House he was often blind to the political forces and influence peddlers around him. Shy and withdrawn, he was uncomfortable around intellectuals and impatient with idealists. Grant preferred watching horse races to reading about complex issues. Although personally honest, he was dazzled by men of wealth and unaccountably loyal to greedy subordinates who betrayed his trust. In the formulation of policy, he passively followed the lead of Congress. This approach initially endeared him to Republican party leaders, but it left him ineffective and caused others to grow disillusioned with his leadership. At the outset, Grant consulted nobody on his cabinet appointments. Some of his choices indulged personal whims; others simply reflected bad judgment. Secretary of State Hamilton Fish of New York turned out to be a fortunate exception; he was a master in guiding foreign policy throughout the Grant presidency. Other than Fish, however, Grant's cabinet overflowed with incompetents.

THE GOVERNMENT DEBT　Financial issues dominated Grant's presidency. After the war the Treasury had assumed that the $432 million in greenbacks issued during the conflict would be retired from circulation and that the nation would revert to a "hard-money" currency—gold coins. Congress in 1866 granted the Treasury discretion to do so gradually. Many agrarian and debtor groups resisted this contraction of the money supply, believing that it would mean lower farm prices and harder-to-pay debts. They were joined by a large number of Radical Republicans who thought that a combination of high tariffs and inflation would generate more rapid economic growth. In 1868 "soft-money" supporters in Congress halted the retirement of greenbacks, leaving $356 million outstanding. There matters stood when Grant took office.

The "sound-money" (or hard-money) advocates, mostly bankers, merchants, and other creditors, claimed that Grant's election was a mandate to save the country from the Democrats' "Ohio idea" of using greenbacks to repay government bonds. Quite influential in Republican circles, the hard-money advocates also had the benefit of agreeing with the deeply ingrained popular assumption that gold coins were morally preferable to paper currency. Grant agreed as well, and in his inaugural address he endorsed payment of the national debt in gold as a point of national honor.

SCANDALS　Within less than a year of his election, Grant had fallen into a cesspool of scandal. In the summer of 1869, two unscrupulous financial buccaneers, Jay Gould and James Fisk, connived with the president's brother-in-law to corner the nation's gold market. That is, they would create a public craze for gold by purchasing massive quantities of the precious metal and convincing traders that the price would keep climbing. As more buyers joined the frenzy, the value of gold would soar. The only danger lay in the federal Treasury's selling large amounts of gold.

Grant apparently smelled a rat from the start, but he was seen in public with the speculators. As the rumor spread on Wall Street, gold rose from $132 to $163 an ounce. Finally, on Black Friday, September 24, 1869, Grant ordered the Treasury to sell a large quantity of gold, and the bubble burst. Fisk got out by repudiating his agreements and hiring thugs to intimidate his creditors. "Nothing is lost save honor," he said.

The plot to corner the gold market was only the first of several scandals that rocked the Grant administration. In 1872 the public learned about the financial crookery of the Crédit Mobilier, a construction company that had milked the Union Pacific Railroad for exorbitant fees to line the pockets of insiders who controlled both firms. Union Pacific shareholders were left holding the bag. This chicanery had transpired before Grant's election in 1868, but it now touched a number of prominent Republicans who had been given shares of Crédit Mobilier stock in exchange for favorable votes. Of the thirteen congressmen involved, only two were censured.

Even more odious disclosures soon followed, some involving the president's cabinet. Grant's secretary of war, it turned out, had accepted bribes from merchants who traded with Indians at army posts in the West. He was impeached, but he resigned in time to elude trial. Post-office contracts, it was revealed, went to carriers who offered the highest kickbacks. In St. Louis a "whiskey ring" bribed tax collectors to bilk the government of millions of dollars in revenue. Grant's private secretary was enmeshed in that scheme, taking large sums of money and other valuables in return for inside information. There is no evidence that Grant himself participated in any of the scandals, but his poor choice of associates and his gullibility earned him widespread censure.

WHITE TERROR President Grant initially fought hard to enforce the federal efforts to reconstruct the postwar South. By the time he became president, southern resistance to "Radical rule" had turned violent as unrepentent whites organized vigilante groups to terrorize blacks. Most white southerners remained so conditioned by the social prejudices embedded in the institution of slavery that they were unable to conceive of blacks as citizens. In some places, hostility to the new regimes turned violent. Said one unreconstructed Mississippian in 1875, "Carry the election peaceably if we can, forcibly if we must."

The prototype of all the terrorist groups was the Ku Klux Klan (KKK), organized in 1866 by some young men of Pulaski, Tennessee, as a social club, with the costumes and secret rituals common to fraternal groups. At first a

"Worse Than Slavery"

This Thomas Nast cartoon chides the Ku Klux Klan and the White League for promoting conditions "worse than slavery" for southern blacks after the Civil War.

group of pranksters, its members soon began to intimidate blacks and white Republicans, and the KKK spread rapidly across the South in answer to the Republican party's Union League. Klansmen rode about the countryside, hiding behind masks and under robes, spreading horrendous rumors, harassing blacks, and wreaking violence and destruction. "We are going to kill all the Negroes," a white supremacist declared during one massacre.

At the urging of President Grant, Congress struck back with three Enforcement Acts (1870–1871) to protect black voters. The first of these measures levied penalties on anyone who interfered with any citizen's right to vote. A second placed the election of congressmen under surveillance by federal election supervisors and marshals. The third (the Ku Klux Klan Act) outlawed the characteristic activities of the Klan—forming conspiracies, wearing disguises, resisting law officers, and intimidating government officials. In 1871 the federal government singled out nine counties in up-country South Carolina and pursued mass prosecutions that brought an abrupt halt to Klan terrorism. In general, however, the federal acts designed to protect African Americans suffered from weak and inconsistent enforcement. Moreover, the South's strong tradition of states' rights and local autonomy, as well as racial prejudice, resisted federal force. The unrelenting efforts of white racists to use violence to thwart Reconstruction continued into the 1870s. On Easter Sunday in 1873 in Colfax, Louisiana, a mob of white vigilantes attacked a group of black Republicans, slaughtering eighty-one. White southerners had lost the war, but during the 1870s they were winning the peace with their reactionary behavior. In the process, the goals of racial justice and civil rights were blunted.

REFORM AND THE ELECTION OF 1872 Long before President Grant's first term ended, Republicans broke ranks with the administration.

"What I Know about Raising the Devil"

With the tail and cloven hoof of the devil, Horace Greeley (center) leads a small band of Liberal Republicans in pursuit of incumbent president Ulysses S. Grant and his supporters in this 1872 cartoon.

Their alienation was a reaction to Radical Reconstruction and the incompetence and corruption in the administration. A new faction, called Liberal Republicans, favored free trade, the redemption of greenbacks with gold, the removal federal troops from the South, the restoration of the rights of former Confederates, and civil service reform.

In 1872 the Liberal Republicans held their own national convention, which produced a compromise platform condemning the Republican party's "vindictive" southern policy and favoring civil service reform but remaining silent on the protective tariff. The delegates stampeded to endorse an anomalous presidential candidate: Horace Greeley, editor of the *New York Tribune* and an enthusiastic reformer. During his long career in journalism, Greeley had promoted vegetarianism, freethinking, socialism, and spiritualism. His image as a visionary eccentric was complemented by his open hostility to the Democrats, whose support the Liberals needed. The Democrats gave the nomination to Greeley as the only hope of beating Grant and the Radical Republicans. Greeley's promise to end Radical Reconstruction and restore "self-government" to the South won over Democrats who otherwise despised the man and his beliefs.

The 1872 election results surprised no one. Republican regulars duly endorsed Grant, Radical Reconstruction, and the protective tariff. Grant still had seven southern states in his pocket, generous aid from business and banking interests, and the stalwart support of the Radical Republicans. Above all he still evoked the glory of military heroism. Greeley carried only six southern and border states, none in the North. Devastated by his crushing defeat and the death of his wife, Greeley entered a sanatorium and died three weeks later.

CONSERVATIVE RESURGENCE   The Klan in fact could not take credit for the overthrow of Republican control in any state. Perhaps its most important effect was to weaken the morale of African Americans and Republicans in the South and strengthen in the North a growing weariness

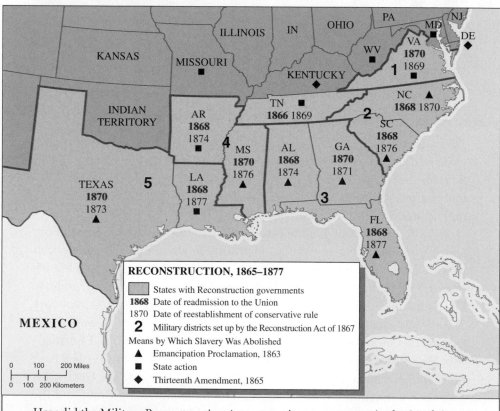

RECONSTRUCTION, 1865–1877

States with Reconstruction governments
1868 Date of readmission to the Union
1870 Date of reestablishment of conservative rule
2 Military districts set up by the Reconstruction Act of 1867
Means by Which Slavery Was Abolished
▲ Emancipation Proclamation, 1863
■ State action
◆ Thirteenth Amendment, 1865

How did the Military Reconstruction Act reorganize governments in the South in the late 1860s and 1870s? What did the former Confederate states have to do to be readmitted to the Union? How did "Conservative" parties gradually regain control of the South from the Republicans in the 1870s?

with the whole "southern question." Republican control in the South gradually loosened as "Conservative" parties—a name used by Democrats to mollify former Whigs—mobilized the white vote. Scalawags and many carpetbaggers drifted away from the Radical Republican ranks under pressure from their white neighbors. Few of them had joined the Republicans out of concern for African American rights in the first place. And where persuasion failed to work, Democrats were willing to use chicanery. As one enthusiastic Democrat boasted, "The white and black Republicans may outvote us, but we can outcount them."

Such factors led to the collapse of Republican control in Virginia and Tennessee as early as 1869 and in Georgia and North Carolina in 1870. Reconstruction lasted longest in states with the largest black population, where whites abandoned Klan hoods for barefaced intimidation in paramilitary groups like the Mississippi Rifle Club and the South Carolina Red Shirts. In the 1873 elections in Yazoo County, Mississippi, the Republicans cast 2,449 votes and the Democrats 638; two years later the Democrats polled 4,049 votes, the Republicans 7. By 1876, Radical Republican regimes survived only in Louisiana, South Carolina, and Florida, and those collapsed after the elections of that year.

The erosion of northern interest in promoting civil rights in the postwar South reflected weariness as well as interest in other activities. Western expansion, Indian wars, new economic opportunities, and political debates over the tariff and the currency distracted attention from southern outrages. In addition, a business panic in 1873 led to a sharp depression and created both social problems and new racial tensions in the North and the South that helped undermine already inconsistent federal efforts to promote racial justice in the former Confederacy.

PANIC AND REDEMPTION   A paralyzing economic panic followed closely upon the public scandals besetting the Grant administration. A contraction of the nation's money supply resulting from the Treasury's postwar withdrawal of greenbacks and the reckless overexpansion of the railroads into sparsely settled areas helped precipitate a financial panic. During 1873 some twenty-five strapped railroads defaulted on their interest payments. A financial panic in Europe forced many financiers to unload American stocks and bonds. Caught short of cash, the prominent investment bank of Jay Cooke and Company went bankrupt on September 18, 1873. The event so frightened investors that the New York Stock Exchange had to close for ten days. The panic of 1873 set off a depression that lasted six years. It was the longest and most severe contraction that Americans had yet suffered, marked by widespread bankruptcies, chronic unemployment, and a drastic slowdown in railroad building.

Hard times and political scandals hurt Republicans in the midterm elections of 1874, allowing the Democrats to win control of the House of Representatives and gain seats in the Senate. The new Democratic House launched inquiries into the Grant scandals and unearthed further evidence of corruption in high places. The financial panic, meanwhile, focused attention once more on greenback currency. Since the value of greenbacks was lower than that of gold, paper money had become the chief circulating medium. Most people spent greenbacks first and held their gold or used it to settle foreign accounts, thereby draining much gold out of the country. To relieve this deflationary spiral and stimulate business expansion, the Treasury issued more greenbacks.

For a time the advocates of paper money were riding high. But Grant vetoed an attempt to issue more greenbacks in 1874, and in his annual message he called for the redemption of greenbacks in gold. Congress obliged the president by passing the Specie Resumption Act of 1875. The resumption of payments in gold to customers who turned in greenbacks began on January 1, 1879, after the Treasury had built a gold reserve for the purpose and reduced the value of the greenbacks in circulation. This act infuriated those promoting an inflationary monetary policy and led to the formation of the Greenback party. The much debated and very complex "money question" would remain one of the most divisive issues in American politics through the end of the century.

THE COMPROMISE OF 1877   Grant yearned to run for a third term in 1876, but his scandal-ridden administration cost him Republican support. James Gillespie Blaine of Maine, a former Speaker of the House, emerged as the Republican front-runner, but he, too, bore the taint of scandal. Letters in the possession of James Mulligan of Boston linked Blaine to dubious railroad dealings. Newspapers soon published the "Mulligan letters," and Blaine's candidacy was dealt a hefty blow.

The Republican Convention therefore eliminated Blaine and several other hopefuls in favor of Ohio's favorite son, Rutherford B. Hayes. Three-time governor of Ohio and an advocate of hard money, Hayes had a sterling reputation and had been a civil service reformer. But his chief virtue, as a journalist put it, was that "he is obnoxious to no one."

The Democratic Convention was abnormally harmonious from the start. The nomination went on the second ballot to Samuel J. Tilden, a millionaire

The Compromise of 1877

This illustration represents the compromise between Republicans and southern Democrats that ended Radical Reconstruction.

corporation lawyer and reform governor of New York who had directed a campaign to overthrow the corrupt Tweed ring that controlled New York City politics.

The 1876 election campaign generated no burning issues. Both candidates favored the trend toward relaxing federal authority and restoring white conservative rule in the South. In the absence of strong differences, Democrats aired the Republicans' dirty linen. In response, Republicans waved "the bloody shirt," which is to say that they linked the Democratic party to secession and the outrages committed against Republicans in the South.

Early election returns pointed to a Tilden victory. Tilden had a 254,000-vote edge in the popular vote and won 184 electoral votes, just one short of a majority. Hayes had only 165 electoral votes, but Republicans also claimed 19 disputed votes from Florida, Louisiana, and South Carolina. The Democrats laid a counterclaim to 1 of Oregon's 3 votes. The Republicans had clearly carried Oregon, but the outcome in the South was less certain, and given the fraud and intimidation perpetrated on both sides, nobody will ever know the truth of the matter. In all three of the disputed southern states, rival canvasing boards sent in different returns. The Constitution offered no guidance in this unprecedented situation. Even if Congress had been empowered to sort things out, the Democratic House and the Republican Senate would have proved unable to reach an agreement.

The impasse dragged on for months, and there was even talk of partisan violence. Finally, on January 29, 1877, Congress set up a special Electoral Commission to investigate and report its findings. Its fifteen members, five each from the House, the Senate, and the Supreme Court, were chosen such that there were seven from each major party, with Justice David Davis of Illinois as the swing vote. Davis, though appointed to the Court by Lincoln, was no party regular and in fact was thought to be leaning toward the Democrats. Thus the panel appeared to be stacked in favor of Tilden.

As it turned out, however, the panel got restacked the other way. Shortsighted Democrats in the Illinois legislature teamed up with minority Greenbackers to name Davis their senator. Davis accepted, no doubt with a sense of relief. From the remaining justices, all Republicans, the panel chose Joseph P. Bradley to fill the vacancy. The decision on each disputed state then went by a vote of 8 to 7 along party lines, in favor of Hayes. After much bluster and the threat of a filibuster by the Democrats, the House voted on March 2 to accept the report and declared Hayes elected by an electoral vote of 185 to 184.

Critical to this outcome was the defection of southern Democrats, who had made several informal agreements with the Republicans. On February 26, 1877, a bargain was struck at Wormley's Hotel in Washington, D.C., between prominent Ohio Republicans (including James A. Garfield) and powerful southern Democrats. The Republicans promised that if elected, Hayes would withdraw federal troops from Louisiana and South Carolina, letting the Republican governments there collapse. In return, the Democrats pledged to withdraw their opposition to Hayes, accept in good faith the Reconstruction amendments, and refrain from partisan reprisals against Republicans in the South.

Southern Democrats could now justify deserting Tilden. This so-called Compromise of 1877 brought a final "redemption" from the Radicals and a return to "home rule," which meant rule by white Democrats. As a former slave observed in 1877, "The whole South—every state in the south—has got [back] into the hands of the very men that held us as slaves." Other, more informal promises, bolstered the secret agreement. Hayes's friends pledged more support for rebuilding Mississippi River levees and other internal improvements, including a federal subsidy for a transcontinental railroad along a southern route. Southerners extracted a further promise that Hayes would name a white southerner as postmaster general, the cabinet position with the most patronage jobs to distribute. In return, southerners would let the Republicans make James Garfield the Speaker of the new House. Such a deal illustrates the relative weakness of the presidency compared with Congress during the postwar era.

THE END OF RECONSTRUCTION   In 1877 the new president withdrew federal troops from Louisiana and South Carolina, and the Republican governments there soon collapsed—along with Hayes's claim to legitimacy. Hayes chose a Tennessean as postmaster general. But most of the other promises made at Wormley's Hotel were renounced or forgotten. As for southern promises to protect the civil rights of African Americans, only a few Democratic leaders remembered them for long. Over the next three decades the federal protection of civil rights crumbled under the pressure of restored white rule in the South and the force of Supreme Court decisions narrowing the application of the Fourteenth and Fifteenth Amendments.

Radical Reconstruction never offered more than an uncertain commitment to racial equality. Yet it left an enduring legacy—the Thirteenth, Fourteenth, and Fifteenth Amendments—not dead but dormant, waiting to be revived. If Reconstruction did not provide social equality or substantial economic opportunities for African Americans, it did create the opportunity for future transformation. It was a revolution, sighed former North Carolina governor Jonathan Worth, and "nobody can anticipate the action of revolutions."

End of Chapter Review

CHAPTER SUMMARY

- **Reconstruction** Abraham Lincoln and his successor, the southerner Andrew Johnson, wanted a lenient and quick plan for Reconstruction. Lincoln's assassination made many northerners favor the Radical Republicans, who wanted to end the grasp of the old planter class on the South's society and economy. Congressional Reconstruction included the stipulation that in order to reenter the Union, former Confederate states had to ratify the Fourteenth and Fifteenth Amendments. Congress also passed the Military Reconstruction Act, which attempted to protect the voting rights and civil rights of African Americans.

- **Southern Violence** Many white southerners blamed their poverty on freed slaves and Yankees. White mobs attacked blacks in 1866 in Memphis and New Orleans. That year the Ku Klux Klan was formed as a social club; its members soon began to intimidate freedmen and white Republicans. Despite government action, violence continued and even escalated in the South.

- **Freed Slaves** Newly freed slaves suffered economically. Most did not have the resources to succeed in the aftermath of the war's devastation. There was no redistribution of land; former slaves were given their freedom but nothing else. The Freedmen's Bureau attempted to educate and aid freed slaves and reunite families. Many former slaves found comfort in their families and the independent churches they established. Some took part in state and local governments under the last, radical phase of Reconstruction.

- **Grant Administration** During Ulysses Grant's administration fiscal issues dominated politics. Paper money (greenbacks) was regarded as inflationary; and agrarian and debtor groups opposed its withdrawal from circulation. Many members of Grant's administration were corrupt; scandals involved an attempt to corner the gold market, construction of the intercontinental railroad, and the whiskey ring's plan to steal millions of dollars in tax revenue.

- **End of Reconstruction** Most southern states had completed the requirements of Reconstruction by 1876. The presidential election returns of that year were so close that a special commission was established to count contested electoral votes. A decision hammered out at a secret meeting gave the presidency to the Republican, Rutherford B. Hayes; in return, the Democrats were promised that the last federal troops would be withdrawn from Louisiana and South Carolina, putting an end to the Radical Republican administrations in the southern states.

CHRONOLOGY

1862	Congress passes the Morrill Land Grant Act
	Congress guarantees the construction of a transcontinental railroad
	Congress passes the Homestead Act
1864	Lincoln refuses to sign the Wade-Davis Bill
1865	Congress sets up the Freedmen's Bureau
April 14, 1865	Lincoln is assassinated
1866	Ku Klux Klan is organized
	Congress passes the Civil Rights Act
1867	Congress passes the Military Reconstruction Act
	Congress passes the Tenure of Office Act
1868	Fourteenth Amendment is ratified
	Congress impeaches President Andrew Johnson; the Senate fails to convict him
1877	Compromise of 1877 ends Reconstruction

KEY TERMS & NAMES

Freedmen's Bureau p. 524

John Wilkes Booth p. 525

Andrew Johnson p. 526

black codes p. 528

Thaddeus Stevens p. 528

scalawags p. 538

carpetbaggers p. 538

greenbacks p. 541

Crédit Mobilier scandal p. 543

Horace Greeley p. 545

Compromise of 1877 p. 548

Fourteenth Amendment p. 551

Fifteenth Amendment p. 551

Part Five

GROWING

PAINS

he Federal victory in 1865 restored the Union and in the process helped accelerate America's transformation into a modern nation-state. A distinctly national consciousness began to displace the sectional emphases of the antebellum era. During and after the Civil War the Republican-led Congress pushed through legislation to foster industrial and commercial development and western expansion. In the process the United States abandoned the Jeffersonian dream of a decentralized agrarian republic and began to forge a dynamic new industrial economy generated by an increasingly national market.

After 1865 many Americans turned their attention to the unfinished business of settling a continent and completing an urban-industrial revolution begun before the war. Huge corporations based upon mass production and mass marketing began to dominate the economy. As the prominent social theorist William Graham Sumner remarked, the process of industrial development "controls us all because we are all in it. It creates the conditions of our own existence, sets the limits of our social activity, and regulates the bonds of our social relations."

The Industrial Revolution was not only an urban phenomenon; it transformed rural life as well. Those who got in the way of the new emphasis on large-scale, highly mechanized commercial agriculture and ranching were brusquely pushed aside. The friction between new market forces and traditional folkways generated political revolts and social unrest during the last quarter of the nineteenth century.

The clash between tradition and modernity peaked during the 1890s, one of the most strife-ridden decades in American history. A deep depression, agrarian unrest, and labor violence provoked fears of class warfare. This turbulent situation transformed the presidential election campaign of 1896 into a clash between rival visions of America's future. The Republican candidate, William McKinley, campaigned on behalf of modern urban-industrial values. By contrast, William Jennings Bryan, the nominee of the Democratic and Populist parties, was an eloquent defender of America's rural past. McKinley's victory proved to be a watershed in political and social history. By 1900 the United States would emerge as one of the world's greatest industrial powers, and it would thereafter assume a new leadership role in world affairs.

19

THE SOUTH AND THE WEST TRANSFORMED

wwnorton.com/studyspace

FOCUS QUESTIONS

- How did life in the South change for blacks and whites politically, economically, and socially after the Civil War?
- What happened to Native Americans as whites settled the West?
- What were the experiences of farmers, cowboys, and miners in the West?
- How did mining affect the development of the West?
- How important was the concept of the frontier to America's political and diplomatic development?

After the Civil War the South and the West provided enticing opportunities for pioneers and entrepreneurs. The two regions were ripe for development. The devastated South had to be rebuilt; the trans-Mississippi West beckoned entrepreneurs and farmers. In both cases, undeveloped regions would prove to be fertile catalysts for urbanization and industrialization. This was particularly true of the West, where before 1860 most Americans had viewed the region between the Mississippi River and California as a barren landscape unfit for human habitation or cultivation, an uninviting land suitable only for Indians and animals. Half the state of Texas, for instance, was still not settled at the end of the Civil War. After 1865, however, the federal government encouraged western settlement and economic development. The construction of transcontinental railroads, the military conquest of the Indians, and a liberal land-distribution policy combined to help lure thousands of pioneers and expectant capitalists westward.

Although the first great wave of railroad building occurred in the 1850s, the most spectacular growth took place during the quarter century after the Civil War. From about 35,000 miles of track in 1865, the national rail network grew to nearly 200,000 miles by 1897. The transcontinental rail lines led the way, and they helped populate the plains and the Far West. Meanwhile, southern rail lines were rebuilt and supplemented with new branches. The defeated South, although not a frontier in the literal sense of the term, attracted investment and industrial development. After 1865, proponents of a "New South" argued that the region must abandon its single-minded preoccupation with agriculture and pursue industrial and commercial development. As a result, the South also West experienced dramatic social and economic changes during the last third of the nineteenth century. By 1900 the South and the West had been transformed in ways that few could have predicted, and twelve new states were created out of the western territories.

THE NEW SOUTH

A FRESH VISION   After the Civil War many southerners looked wistfully to the plantation life that had characterized their region before the firing on Fort Sumter in 1861. A few prominent leaders, however, insisted that the postwar South must liberate itself from nostalgia and create a new society of small farms, thriving industries, and bustling cities. The major prophet of this New South was Henry W. Grady, the young editor of the *Atlanta Constitution*. Grady's compelling vision of a New South attracted many supporters, who preached the gospel of industry with evangelical fervor. The Confederacy, they reasoned, had lost because it had relied too much upon King Cotton. In the future the South must follow the North's example and industrialize. From that central belief flowed certain implications: that a more diversified and a more efficient agriculture would be a foundation for economic growth and that more widespread education, especially vocational training, would promote material success. By the late 1870s, with Reconstruction over and the panic of 1873 forgotten, a mood of progress permeated the editorials and speeches of the day.

ECONOMIC GROWTH   The chief accomplishment of the New South movement was a dramatic expansion of the region's textile production. From

1880 to 1900, the number of cotton mills in the South grew from 161 to 400, and the number of mill workers (among whom women and children outnumbered men) increased fivefold. By 1900 the South had surpassed New England as the nation's largest producer of cotton cloth.

Tobacco growing also increased significantly after the Civil War. Essential to the rise of the tobacco industry was the Duke family of Durham, North Carolina. At the end of the Civil War, the story goes, Washington Duke took a load of tobacco and, with the help of his two sons, beat it out with hickory sticks, stuffed it into bags, hitched two mules to his wagon, and set out across the state, selling tobacco in small pouches as he went. By 1872 the Dukes had a factory producing 125,000 pounds of tobacco annually, and Washington Duke prepared to settle down and enjoy success.

His son Buck (James Buchanan Duke) wanted even greater success, however. He recognized that the tobacco industry was "half smoke and half ballyhoo," so he poured large sums into advertising schemes and perfected the mechanized mass production of cigarettes. Duke also undersold competitors in their own market and cornered the supply of ingredients. In 1890, Duke brought most of his competitors into the American Tobacco Company, which controlled nine tenths of the nation's cigarette production. In 1911 the Supreme Court ruled that the massive company was in violation of the anti-trust laws and ordered it broken up, but by then Duke had found new worlds to conquer, in hydroelectric power and aluminum.

Systematic use of other natural resources helped revitalize the region along the Appalachian Mountain chain from West Virginia to Alabama. Coal production in the South grew from 5 million tons in 1875 to 49 million tons by 1900. At the southern end of the mountains, Birmingham, Alabama, sprang up during the 1870s as a major steel-producing center and soon tagged itself the Pittsburgh of the South.

Industrial growth created a need for wood-framed housing, and after 1870 lumbering became a thriving industry in the South. By the turn of the century, it had surpassed textiles in value. Tree cutting seemed to know no bounds, despite the resulting ecological devastation. In time the industry would be saved only by the warm climate, which fostered quick growth of replanted forests, and the rise of scientific forestry.

Two forces that would impel an even greater industrial revolution were already on the southern horizon at the turn of the century: petroleum in the Southwest and hydroelectric power in the Southeast. In 1901 the Spindletop oil gusher in Texas brought a huge bonanza. Electric power proved equally profitable, and local power plants dotted the South by the 1890s. Richmond, Virginia, developed the nation's first electric streetcar system in 1888, and

Columbia, South Carolina, boasted the first electrically powered cotton mill in 1894. The greatest advance would begin in 1905, when Buck Duke's Southern Power Company set out to electrify entire river valleys in the Carolinas.

AGRICULTURE OLD AND NEW At the start of the twentieth century, however, most of the South remained undeveloped, at least by northeastern standards. Despite the optimistic rhetoric of Henry Grady and other New South spokesmen, the typical southerner was less apt to be tending a textile loom than, as the saying went, facing the eastern end of a westbound mule. King Cotton survived the Civil War and expanded over new acreage even as its export markets leveled off. Louisiana cane sugar, probably the most war-devastated of all crops, was flourishing again by the 1890s.

The majority of southern farmers were not flourishing, however. A prolonged deflation in crop prices affected the entire Western world during the last third of the nineteenth century. Sagging prices for farm crops made it more difficult than ever to own land. Sharecropping and tenancy among poor blacks and whites became the norm. By 1890 most southern farms were worked by people who did not own the land.

How did the system work? Sharecroppers, who had nothing to offer the landowner but their labor, worked the owner's land in return for supplies and a share of the crop, generally about half. Tenant farmers, hardly better off, might have their own mule, a plow, and credit with the country store. They were entitled to claim a larger share of the crops. The sharecropper-tenant system was horribly inefficient; it was essentially a form of land slavery, and tenants and owners developed an intense suspicion of each other. The folklore of the rural South was replete with tales of tenants who remained stubbornly shiftless and scheming landlords who swindled farmworkers by not giving them a fair share of the crops.

The postwar South suffered an acute shortage of capital; people had to devise ways to operate without cash. One innovation was the crop-lien system: merchants furnished supplies in return for liens (or mortgages) on farmers' crops. To a few tenants and small farmers who seized the chance, such credit offered a way out of dependency, but to most it offered only a hopeless cycle of perennial debt. The merchant, who assumed great risks, generally charged interest that ranged, according to one journalist, "from 24 percent to grand larceny." The merchant required his farmer clients to grow a cash crop, which could be readily sold at harvesttime. Thus the routines of tenancy and sharecropping were geared to a staple crop, usually cotton. The resulting stagnation of rural life held millions, white and black, in bondage to privation and ignorance.

TENANCY AND THE ENVIRONMENT   The pervasive use of tenancy and sharecropping unwittingly caused profound environmental damage. Growing commercial row crops like cotton on the same land year after year leached the nutrients from the soil. Tenants had no incentive to take care of farmland by manuring fields or rotating crops because it was not their own. They used fertilizer to accelerate the growing cycle, but the extensive use of phosphate fertilizers only accelerated soil depletion, by enabling multiple plantings each year. Fertilizer, said an observer, seduced southern farmers into believing that there was a "short cut to prosperity, a royal road to good crops of cotton year after year. The result has been that their lands have been cultivated clean year after year, and their fertility has been exhausted."

Once the soil had lost its fertility, the tenants moved on to another farm, leaving behind rutted fields whose topsoil washed away with each rain. The

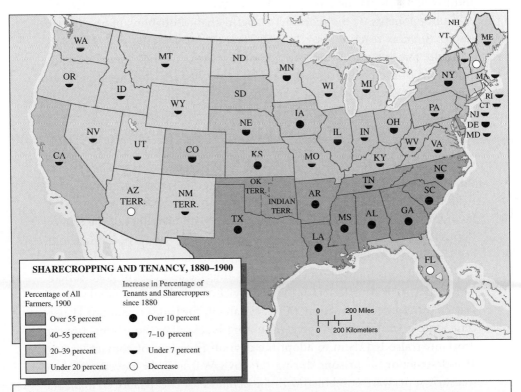

SHARECROPPING AND TENANCY, 1880–1900

Percentage of All Farmers, 1900
- Over 55 percent
- 40–55 percent
- 20–39 percent
- Under 20 percent

Increase in Percentage of Tenants and Sharecroppers since 1880
- ● Over 10 percent
- ◗ 7–10 percent
- ◞ Under 7 percent
- ○ Decrease

Why was there a dramatic increase in sharecropping and tenancy in the late nineteenth century? Why did the South have more sharecroppers than other parts of the country? Why, in your opinion, was the rate of sharecropping low in the western territories of New Mexico and Arizona?

silt and mud flowed into creeks and rivers, swamping many lowland fields and filling millponds and lakes. By the early twentieth century much of the rural South resembled a ravaged land: deep gullies sliced through, bare eroded hillsides, and streams and deep lakes were clogged with silt. As far as the eye could see, red clay devoid of nutrients dominated the landscape.

THE BOURBONS AND THE REDEEMERS   In post-Civil War southern politics, habits of social deference and elitism still prevailed. After Reconstruction ended, in 1877, an elite group of planters, lawyers, merchants, and entrepreneurs dominated southern politics. The supporters of these postwar Democratic leaders referred to them as redeemers because they supposedly saved the South from Yankee domination, as well as from the limitations of a purely rural economy. The redeemers included a rising class of entrepreneurs eager to promote a more diversified economy based upon industrial development and railroad expansion.

The opponents of the redeemers labeled them Bourbons in an effort to depict them as reactionaries. Like the French royal family that, Napoléon had said, forgot nothing and learned nothing in the ordeal of revolution, the Bourbons of the postwar South were said to have forgotten nothing and to have learned nothing in the ordeal of the Civil War.

The Bourbons of the New South perfected a political alliance with northeastern conservatives and an economic alliance with northeastern capitalists. They generally pursued a government policy of frugality, except for the tax exemptions and other favors they offered business. They slashed expenditures and avoided political initiatives, making the transition from Republican rule to Bourbon rule less abrupt than is often assumed. The Bourbons' favorable disposition toward the railroads was not unlike that of the Radical Republicans. And despite their reputation for honesty, Bourbon officeholders were occasionally caught with their fingers in the till.

The Bourbons focused on cutting back the size and cost of government. This policy spelled austerity for public services, including the school systems started during Reconstruction. Illiteracy rates at the time were about 12 percent among whites and 50 percent among blacks. The Bourbons' urge to economize also led them to adopt the degrading system of convict leasing. The destruction of prisons during the Civil War and the poverty of state treasuries afterward combined with the demand for cheap labor to make the leasing of convict workers a way for southern states to avoid penitentiary expenses and generate revenue.

The Bourbons reduced not only state expenditures but also a vast amount of government debt. The corruption and extravagance of Radical Republican rule were commonly advanced as justification for the process, but repudiation of debts was not limited to those incurred during Reconstruction. Altogether, nine states repudiated more than half of what they owed bondholders and other creditors.

The penny-pinching Bourbon regimes did respond to the demand for commissions to regulate the rates charged by railroads for commercial transport. They also established boards of agriculture and public health, agricultural and mechanical colleges, teacher-training schools and women's colleges, and even state colleges for African Americans. Nor can any simplistic interpretation encompass the variety of Bourbon leaders. The Democratic party was then a mongrel coalition that threw old Whigs, Unionists, secessionists, businessmen, small farmers, hillbillies, planters, and even some Republicans together in an alliance against the Reconstruction Radicals. Democrats, therefore, even those who bore the Bourbon label, often marched to different drummers, and the Bourbon regimes never achieved complete unity in philosophy or government.

Perhaps the ultimate paradox of the Bourbons' rule was that these paragons of white supremacy tolerated a lingering black voice in politics and showed no haste to raise legal barriers of racial separation in public places. African

The effects of Radical and Bourbon rule in the South

This 1880 cartoon shows the South staggering under the oppressive weight of military Reconstruction (left) and flourishing under the "Let 'Em Alone Policy" of President Rutherford B. Hayes and the Bourbons (right).

Americans sat in Virginia's state legislature until 1890, in South Carolina's until 1900, and in Georgia's until 1908; some of them were Democrats. The South sent black congressmen to Washington in every election except one until 1900, though they always represented gerrymandered districts into which most of a state's black voters had been thrown. Under the Bourbons the disenfranchisement of black voters remained inconsistent, a local matter brought about mainly by fraud and intimidation, although it occurred often enough to ensure white control of the southern states.

A like flexibility applied in other aspects of race relations. The color line was drawn less strictly immediately after the Civil War than it would be in the twentieth-century South. In some places, to be sure, racial segregation appeared before the end of Reconstruction, especially in schools, churches, hotels, and rooming houses and in private social relations. In other public places, such as trains, depots, theaters, and diners, however, segregation was more sporadic.

DISENFRANCHISING AFRICAN AMERICANS   During the 1890s the attitudes that had permitted moderation in race relations evaporated. A violent "Negrophobia" swept across the South and much of the nation at the end of the century. Many whites had come to resent signs of black success and social influence. An Alabama newspaper editor declared that "our blood boils when the educated Negro asserts himself politically."

Education did bring enlightenment—as it was supposed to do. A new generation of young African Americans born and educated since the end of the Civil War was determined to gain true equality. This generation was more assertive and less patient than their parents. A growing number of young white adults, however, were equally determined to keep "Negroes in their place."

Racial violence and repression surged to the fore during the last decade of the nineteenth century and the first two decades of the twentieth. By the end of the nineteenth century, the so-called New South had come to resemble the racially segregated Old South. Ruling whites ruthlessly imposed their will over all areas of African American life. They prevented blacks from voting and enacted "Jim Crow" laws mandating public separation of the races. This development was not the logical culmination of the Civil War and emancipation but rather the result of a calculated campaign by white elites and racist thugs to limit African American political, economic, and social life.

The political dynamics of the 1890s exacerbated racial tensions. The rise of Populism, a farm-based protest movement that culminated in the creation of a third political party in the 1890s, divided the white vote to such an extent that in some places the African American vote became the balance of power. Some Populists courted black votes. In response the Bourbons revived the race issue, which they exploited with seasoned finesse, all the while controlling for their ticket a good part of the black vote in plantation areas. Nevertheless, during the 1890s the Bourbons began to insist that the black vote be eliminated completely from southern elections. Some farm leaders hoped that the disenfranchisement of African Americans would make it possible for whites to divide politically without raising the specter of "Negro domination."

But since the Fifteenth Amendment made it illegal simply to deny blacks the vote, racists accomplished their purpose indirectly, through such devices as poll taxes (or head taxes) and literacy tests. Mississippi led the way to near-total disenfranchisement of blacks—and many poor whites as well. The state called a constitutional convention in 1890 to change the suffrage provisions of the Radical Republican constitution of 1868. The resulting Mississippi plan set the pattern that seven more states would follow over the next twenty years. First, a residence requirement—two years in the state, one year in an election district—struck at those black tenant farmers who were in the habit of moving yearly in search of better opportunities. Second, voters were disqualified if convicted of certain crimes, many of them petty. Third, all taxes, including a poll tax, had to be paid by February 1 of each year. This proviso fell most heavily on the poor, most of whom were black. Finally, all voters had

"Jim Crow" laws

In this wood engraving, African Americans are depicted leaving Mississippi from the wharves of Vicksburg.

to be literate. The alternative, designed as a loophole for otherwise-disqualified whites, was an "understanding" clause. The voter, if unable to read the Constitution, could qualify by "understanding" it—to the satisfaction of the registrar. Fraud was thus institutionalized by "legal" disenfranchisement.

Other states added variations on the Mississippi plan. In 1898, Louisiana invented the "grandfather clause," which allowed illiterates to register to vote if their fathers or grandfathers had been eligible to vote on January 1, 1867, when African Americans were still disenfranchised. By 1910, Georgia, North Carolina, Virginia, Alabama, and Oklahoma had adopted the grandfather clause. Every southern state, moreover, adopted a statewide Democratic primary, which became the only meaningful election outside isolated areas of Republican strength. With minor exceptions the Democratic primaries excluded African American voters altogether. The effectiveness of these measures can be seen in a few sample figures: Louisiana in 1896 had 130,000 registered black voters and in 1900, 5,320. In Alabama in 1900, 121,159 black men over twenty-one were literate, according to the census, but only 3,742 were registered to vote.

THE SPREAD OF SEGREGATION   What came to be called Jim Crow social segregation followed disenfranchisement and in some states came first. From 1875 to 1883, in fact, any racial segregation violated a federal Civil Rights Act, which forbade discrimination in places of public accommodation. But in 1883 the Supreme Court ruled on seven civil rights cases involving discrimination against blacks by corporations or individuals. The Court held, with only one dissent, that the force of federal law could not extend to individual action because the Fourteenth Amendment, which provided that "no State" could deny citizens equal protection of the law, stood as a prohibition only against state action; individuals were free to discriminate as they saw fit.

This interpretation left as an open question the validity of state laws *requiring* separate public facilities under the rubric of "separate but equal," a slogan popular with the New South prophets. In 1888, Mississippi required railway passengers to occupy the car set aside for their race. When Louisiana followed suit in 1890, the law was challenged in the case of *Plessy v. Ferguson,* which the Supreme Court decided in 1896.

The test case originated in New Orleans when Homer Plessy, an octoroon (a person of one-eighth African ancestry), refused to leave a whites-only railroad car when asked to do so. He was convicted of violating the segregation statute, and the case rose on appeal to the Supreme Court. The Court ruled in 1896 that segregation laws "have been generally, if not universally recognized as within the competency of state legislatures in the exercise of their police power." Soon the principle of statutory racial segregation extended to every area of southern life, including streetcars, hotels, restaurants, hospitals, parks, and places of employment.

Violence accompanied the Jim Crow laws. From 1890 to 1899, lynchings in the United States averaged 188 per year, 82 percent of which occurred in the South; from 1900 to 1909, they averaged 93 per year, of which 92 percent occurred in the South. Whites constituted 32 percent of the victims during the former period but only 11 percent in the latter. By the end of the nineteenth century, legalized racial discrimination—segregation of public facilities, political disenfranchisement, and vigilante justice punctuated by brutal public lynchings and race riots—had elevated government-sanctioned bigotry to an official way of life in the South. South Carolina senator Benjamin Tillman, an outspoken racist, declared in 1892 that blacks "must remain subordinate or be exterminated."

How did African Americans respond to the resurgence of racism and statutory segregation? Some left the South in search of equality and opportunity, but the vast majority stayed in their native region. In the face of overwhelming force and prejudicial justice, survival in the South required blacks to wear a mask of deference and apply discretion. "Had to walk a quiet life," explained James Plunkett, a Virginia black. "The least little thing you would do, they [whites] would kill ya."

Yet accommodation did not mean total submission. Excluded from the dominant white world and eager to avoid confrontations, black southerners after the 1890s increasingly turned inward and constructed their own culture and nurtured their own pride. A young white visitor to Mississippi in 1910 noticed that nearly every black person he met had "two distinct social selves, the one he reveals to his own people, the other he assumes among the whites."

African American churches continued to serve as the hub for black community life. Often the only public buildings available for blacks, churches were used not only for worship but also for activities that had nothing to do with religion: social gatherings, club meetings, and political rallies. For men especially, churches offered leadership roles and political status. Serving as a deacon was often one of the most prestigious roles an African American man could achieve. Churches enabled African Americans of all classes to interact and exercise roles denied them in the larger society. Religious life provided great comfort to people worn down by the daily hardships and abuses associated with segregation.

One irony of state-enforced segregation is that it opened up new economic opportunities for blacks. A new class of African American entrepreneurs emerged to provide services—insurance, banking, funeral, barbering—to the black community in the segregated South. At the same time, African

Americans formed their own social organizations, all of which helped bolster black pride and provide fellowship and opportunities for service.

Middle-class black women formed a network of thousands of racial-uplift-organizations around the nation. The women's clubs were engines of social service in their communities. Members cared for the aged and the infirm, the orphaned and the abandoned. They created homes for single mothers and provided nurseries for working mothers. They sponsored health clinics and classes in home economics for women. In 1896 the leaders of such women's clubs converged to form the National Association of Colored Women, an organization meant to combat racism and segregation.

IDA B. WELLS   One of the most outspoken African American activists of the time was Ida B. Wells. Born into slavery in 1862 in Mississippi, she attended a school staffed by white missionaries. In 1878 yellow fever killed her parents and infant brother. At age sixteen, Wells assumed responsibility for her five younger siblings. In search of economic security and opportunity, Wells moved to nearby Memphis.

In 1883 after being denied a seat on a railroad car because she was black, she became the first African American to file suit against such discrimination. The circuit court decided in her favor and fined the railroad, but the Tennessee Supreme Court overturned the ruling. Wells thereafter discovered "[my] first and [it] might be said, my only love"—journalism—and, through it, a weapon

Ida B. Wells

While raising four children, Wells sustained her commitment to ending racial and gender discrimination.

with which to promote civil rights. She became a prominent editor of *Memphis Free Speech,* a newspaper focusing on African American issues.

In 1892, when three of her friends were lynched by a white mob, Wells launched a lifelong crusade against lynching. Angry whites responded by destroying her newspaper office and threatening to lynch her. She moved to New York and continued to use her fiery journalistic talent to criticize Jim Crow laws and demand that African Americans have their voting rights restored. Wells helped found the National Association for the Advancement of Colored People (NAACP) in 1909 and promoted women's suffrage.

WASHINGTON AND DU BOIS
Booker T. Washington, born in Virginia of a slave mother and a white father, fought extreme adversity to get an education at Hampton Institute, one of the postwar missionary schools, and went on to build at Tuskegee, Alabama, a leading college for African Americans. By 1890, Washington had become the nation's foremost black educator.

Booker T. Washington

Founder of the Tuskegee Institute.

Washington argued that blacks should not antagonize whites by demanding social or political equality; instead, they should concentrate on establishing an economic base for their advancement. In a speech at the Cotton States and International Exposition in Atlanta in 1895 that propelled him to fame, Washington advised African Americans: "Cast down your bucket where you are—cast it down in making friends . . . of the people of all races by whom we are surrounded. Cast it down in agriculture, mechanics, in commerce, in domestic service, and in the professions." He conspicuously omitted politics from that list and implied an endorsement of segregation: "In all things that are purely social we can be as separate as the five fingers, yet one as the hand in all things essential to mutual progress."

Some people bitterly criticized Washington, in his lifetime and after, for making a bad bargain: the sacrifice of broad educational and civil rights for the dubious acceptance of white conservatives and the creation of economic opportunities for blacks. W. E. B. Du Bois led this criticism. A native of Great Barrington, Massachusetts, and the son of free blacks, Du Bois first experienced southern racial practices as an undergraduate at Fisk University in Nashville. Later he was the first African American to earn a doctoral degree from Harvard (in history) and afterward attended the University of Berlin. In addition to an active career in racial protest, he left a distinguished record as a teacher and scholar. Trim and dapper in appearance, sporting a goatee, carrying a cane, and often wearing gloves, he possessed a combative, fiery spirit. Not long after he began his teaching career, at Atlanta University in 1897, he began to assault Booker T. Washington's accommodationist philosophy and put forward his own program of "ceaseless agitation." He became the architect of the twentieth-century civil rights movement.

W. E. B. Du Bois

A fierce advocate for black education.

Washington, Du Bois argued, preached "a gospel 'of Work and Money to such an extent . . . as to over shadow the higher aims of life." The education of African Americans, Du Bois maintained, should not be merely vocational but should nurture bold leaders willing to challenge segregation and discrimination through political action. He demanded that disenfranchisement and legalized segregation cease and that the laws of the land be enforced. Du Bois castigated Washington's "Atlanta Compromise" philosophy: "We refuse to surrender the leadership of this race to cowards."

THE NEW WEST

Like the South, the vast region west of the Mississippi River has become wrapped in myths and constricting stereotypes. It is a diverse land of extremes—majestic mountains, roaring rivers, searing deserts, dense forests, sprawling grasslands, and fertile plains. For vast reaches of western America, the great epics of the Civil War and Reconstruction were remote events hardly touching the lives of Indians, Mexicans, Asians, and white trappers, miners, cowboys, traders, and Mormons scattered through the plains and mountains. There the march of settlement and exploitation continued, propelled by a lust for land and a passion for profit. Between 1870 and 1900, Americans settled more land in the West than had been occupied by all Americans up to 1870. On one level the settlement of the West beyond the Mississippi River constitutes a colorful drama of determined pioneers and cowboys overcoming all obstacles to secure their vision of freedom and opportunity amid the region's awesome vastness. On another level, however, the colonization of the Far West involved shortsighted greed and irresponsible behavior, a story of reckless exploitation that scarred the land, decimated its wildlife, and nearly exterminated the culture of Native Americans.

In the second tier of trans-Mississippi states—Iowa, Kansas, Nebraska—and in western Minnesota, farmers began spreading out onto the Great Plains after the Civil War. From California, miners spread east through the mountains as scattered enclaves sprang up at one new strike after another. From

Texas nomadic cowboys migrated northward onto the plains and across the Rocky Mountains into the Great Basin. As settlers moved west, they encountered climates and landscapes markedly different from those they had left behind. The scarcity of water and timber on the Great Plains rendered obsolete the ax, the log cabin, the rail fence, and the usual methods of tilling the soil. For a long time the region had been called the Great American Desert; it was thought of only as a barren barrier to cross on the way to the Pacific, unfit for human habitation and therefore, to white Americans, the perfect refuge for Indians. But that view changed in the last half of the nineteenth century as a result of newly discovered deposits of gold, silver, and other minerals, the completion of the transcontinental railroads, the destruction of the buffalo, the rise of the range-cattle industry, and the dawning realization that the arid region need not be a sterile desert. With the use of what water was available, techniques of dry farming and irrigation could make the land fruitful after all.

THE MIGRATORY STREAM   During the second half of the nineteenth century, an unrelenting stream of migrants flowed into the largely Indian and Hispanic West. Millions of Anglo-Americans, African Americans, Mexicans, and European and Chinese immigrants transformed the patterns of western society and culture. Because of the expense of transportation, land, and supplies, the very poor could not afford to relocate. Three quarters of the western migrants were men. The largest number of foreign immigrants came from northern Europe and Canada. In the northern plains, Germans, Scandinavians, and Irish were especially numerous.

AFRICAN AMERICAN MIGRATION   In the aftermath of the collapse of Radical Republican rule in the South, thousands of African Americans began migrating west from Kentucky, Tennessee, Louisiana, Arkansas, Mississippi, and Texas. Some 6,000 southern blacks arrived in Kansas in 1879 alone, and as many as 20,000 may have come the following year. These migrants came to be known as Exodusters, because they were making their exodus from the South—in search of a haven from racism and poverty.

The foremost promoter of African American migration to the West was Benjamin "Pap" Singleton. Born a slave in Tennessee in 1809, he escaped to Detroit. After the Civil War he returned to Tennessee, convinced that God was calling him to rescue his brethren. When Singleton learned that land in Kansas could be had for $1.25 an acre, he began distributing a recruiting pamphlet, *The Advantage of Living in a Free State,* to former slaves. In 1878, Singleton led his first party of 200 colonists to Kansas, bought 7,500 acres that had been an Indian reservation, and established the Dunlop community.

Nicodemus, Kansas

A colony founded by southern blacks in the 1860s.

Over the next several years, thousands of African Americans followed Single-ton into Kansas, causing many southern leaders to worry about the loss of black laborers. In 1879 white Mississippians closed access to the river and threatened to sink all boats carrying black colonists from the South to the West.

The African American exodus to the West died out by the early 1880s. Many of the settlers were unprepared for life on the plains. Their Kansas homesteads were not large enough to allow self-sufficiency, and most of the farmers were forced to supplement their income by hiring themselves out to white ranchers. Drought, grasshoppers, prairie fires, and dust storms led to crop failures. The sudden influx of so many people taxed resources and patience. Many of the black pioneers in Kansas soon abandoned their land and moved to the few cities in the state. Life on the frontier was not always the "promised land" that setters had been led to expect. Nonetheless, by 1890 some 520,000 African Americans lived west of the Mississippi River. As many as 25 percent of the cowboys who participated in the Texas cattle drives were African Americans.

In 1866, Congress passed legislation establishing two "colored" cavalry units and dispatched them to the western frontier. Nicknamed buffalo sol-diers by the Indians, the men were mostly Civil War veterans from Louisiana and Kentucky. They built and maintained forts, mapped vast areas of the Southwest, strung hundreds of miles of telegraph lines, protected railroad construction crews, subdued hostile Indians, and captured outlaws and rustlers. For this they were paid $13 a month. Eighteen of the buffalo soldiers won Congressional Medals of Honor for their service.

MINING THE WEST   Valuable mineral deposits continued to lure people to the West after the Civil War. The mass migration of miners to California in 1849 (the forty-niners) set the typical pattern, in which the disorderly rush of prospectors was quickly joined by camp followers, a motley array of saloon keepers, prostitutes, cardsharps, hustlers, and assorted desperadoes eager to mine the miners. An era of lawlessness eventually gave way to vigilante rule and, finally, to a stable community.

The drama of the 1849 gold rush was reenacted time and again in the following three decades. While nearly 100,000 early rushers were crowding around Pikes Peak in Colorado in 1859, miners discovered the Comstock Lode at Gold Hill, Nevada. The lode produced gold and silver and within twenty years had yielded more than $300 million from shafts that reached hundreds of feet into the mountainside. Yet in Arizona and Montana the most important mineral proved to be neither gold nor silver but copper.

The growing demand for orderly government in the West led to the hasty creation of new territories and eventually the admission of a host of new states. In 1861, Nevada became a territory, and in 1864 it was admitted to the Union in time to give two electoral votes to Abraham Lincoln (their third electoral voter got caught in a snowstorm). After Colorado's admission in 1876, however, no new states entered the union for over a decade because of party divisions in Congress: Democrats were reluctant to create states out of territories that were heavily Republican. After the sweeping Republican victory in the 1888 legislative races, however, Congress admitted the Dakotas, Montana, and Washington in 1889 and Idaho and Wyoming in 1890, completing a tier of states from coast to coast. Utah entered the union in 1896 (after the Mormons abandoned the practice of polygamy) and Oklahoma in 1907, and in 1912 Arizona and New Mexico rounded out the forty-eight continental states.

MINING AND THE ENVIRONMENT   During the second half of the nineteenth century, the nature of mining changed drastically. It became a mass-production industry as individual prospectors gave way to large companies. The first wave of miners who rushed to California in 1849 sifted gold dust and nuggets out of riverbeds by means of "placer" mining, or "panning." But once the placer deposits were exhausted, efficient mining required large-scale operations and huge investments. Companies shifted from surface digging to hydraulic mining, dredging, or deep-shaft "hard-rock" mining. Hydraulic mining used a powerful jet of water to excavate whole hillsides, washing the gravel through sluices that caught gold nuggets and disposed of the tailings (dirt and gravel debris). Dredging carved out whole riverbeds in order to sift gold from the surrounding sand and gravel.

Hydraulicking, dredging, and shaft mining transformed vast areas of vegetation and landscape. Huge hydraulic cannons shot enormous streams of water under high pressure, stripping the topsoil and gravel from the bedrock and creating steep-sloped barren canyons that could not sustain plant life. The tons of dirt and debris unearthed by the water cannons covered rich farmland downstream and created sandbars that clogged rivers and killed fish. All told, some 12 billion tons of earth were blasted out of the Sierra Nevadas and washed into local rivers.

Irate California farmers in the fertile Central Valley bitterly protested the damage done downstream by the industrial mining operations. In 1878 they formed the Anti-Debris Association, with its own militia, to challenge the powerful mining companies. Efforts to pass state legislation restricting hydraulic mining repeatedly failed because mining companies controlled the votes. The Anti-Debris Association then turned to the courts. On January 7, 1884, the farmers won their case when federal judge Lorenzo Sawyer, a former miner, outlawed the dumping of mining debris where it could reach farmland or navigable rivers. Thus *Woodruff v. North Bloomfield Gravel Mining Company* became the first major environmental ruling in the nation. As a result of the ruling, hydraulic mining dried up, leaving a legacy of abandoned equipment, ugly ravines, ditches, gullies, and mountains of discarded rock and gravel.

THE INDIAN WARS   As settlers pressed in from east and west, the Native Americans were forced into what was supposed to be their last refuge. Perhaps 250,000 Indians on the Great Plains and in the mountain regions lived mainly off the buffalo herds, which provided food and, from their hides, clothing and shelter. The 1851 Fort Laramie Treaty, in which the chiefs of the Plains tribes agreed to accept definite tribal borders and allow white settlers to travel on their trails unmolested, worked for a while, with wagon trains passing safely through Indian lands and the army building roads and forts without resistance. Fighting resumed, however, as the emigrants began to encroach upon Indian lands rather than merely pass through them. From 1850 to 1860, for example, 150,000 whites moved into Sioux territory in violation of treaty agreements.

From the early 1860s until the late 1870s, the frontier raged with Indian wars. In 1864, Colonel John Chivington's poorly trained militia assaulted an Indian camp along Sand Creek in Colorado Territory. Although the Indian

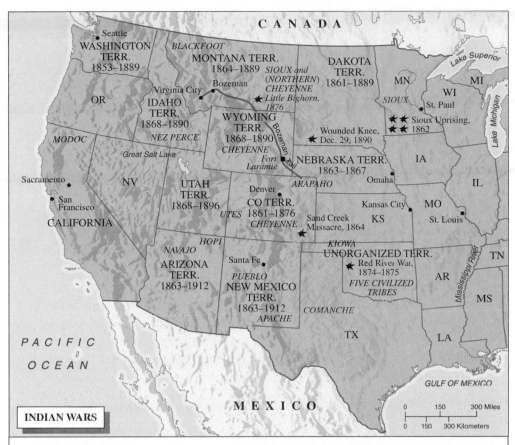

What was the Great Sioux War? What happened at Little Bighorn, and what were the consequences? Why were hundreds of Indians killed at Wounded Knee?

camp displayed a white flag of truce, the soldiers slaughtered 200 Indians—men, women, and children. One general called the Sand Creek Massacre the "foulest and most unjustifiable crime in the annals of America."

With other scattered battles erupting, a congressional committee gathered evidence on the grisly Indian wars and massacres. Its 1867 "Report on the Condition of the Indian Tribes" led to an act to establish an Indian Peace Commission charged with removing the causes of Indian wars in general. Congress decided that this would be best accomplished at the expense of the Indians, by persuading them to take up life on out-of-the way reservations, a solution that perpetuated the encroachment on Indian hunting grounds. In 1870, Indians outnumbered whites in the Dakota territory by two to one; in 1880, whites outnumbered Indians by more than six to one.

In 1867 a conference at Medicine Lodge, Kansas, ended with the Kiowas, Comanches, Arapahos, and Cheyennes reluctantly accepting land m western Oklahoma. The following spring the Sioux agreed to settle within the Black Hills Reservation in Dakota Territory. But Indian resistance on the southern plains continued until the Red River War of 1874-1875, when soldiers led by General Philip Sheridan, a hard-charging Civil War cavalryman, forced the Indians to disband in the spring of 1875. Seventy-two Indian chiefs were imprisoned for three years.

Meanwhile, trouble was brewing again in the north. In 1874, Lieutenant Colonel George A. Custer, a reckless, glory-seeking officer, led an exploratory expedition into the Black Hills. Miners were soon filtering onto the Sioux hunting grounds despite promises that the army would keep them out. The army had done little to protect Indian land, but when ordered to move against wandering bands of Sioux hunting on the range according to their treaty rights, it moved vigorously.

What became the Great Sioux War was the largest military event since the end of the Civil War. It lasted fifteen months and entailed some fifteen battles in present-day Wyoming, Montana, South Dakota, and Nebraska. The Sioux were ably led by chief Sitting Bull. After several indecisive encounters, Custer found the main encampment of Sioux and their Northern Cheyenne allies on the Little Bighorn River. Separated from the main body of his men and surrounded by 2,500 warriors, Custer and 210 soldiers were annihilated.

Instead of following up their victory, the Indians threw away their advantage in celebration and renewed hunting. The army quickly regained the offensive, and the Sioux were forced to give up their hunting grounds and the goldfields in return for payments. Forced onto reservations situated on the least valuable lands in the region, the Indians soon found themselves struggling to subsist under harsh conditions. Many died of starvation or disease.

In the Rocky Mountains and to the west, the same story of hopeless resistance was repeated. Indians were the last obstacle to white expansion, and they suffered as a result. In Idaho the peaceful Nez Perce bands refused to surrender land along the Salmon River, and prolonged fighting erupted there and in eastern Oregon. In 1886 a generation of Indian wars virtually ended with the capture of Geronimo, a chief of the Chiricahua Apaches, who had fought encroachments in the Southwest for fifteen years.

The epilogue, too, would be tragic. Late in 1888, Wovoka (or Jack Wilson), a Paiute in western Nevada, fell ill and in a delirium imagined he had visited the spirit world, where he learned of a deliverer coming to rescue the Indians

The Battle of Little Bighorn, 1876

A painting by Amos Bad Heart Bull, an Oglala Sioux.

and restore their lands. To hasten their deliverance, he said, they had to take up a ceremonial dance at each new moon. The Ghost Dance craze fed upon old legends of a coming messiah and spread rapidly. In 1890 the Lakota Sioux adopted it with such fervor that it alarmed white authorities. They banned the Ghost Dance on Lakota reservations, but the Indians defied the order, and a crisis erupted. On December 29, 1890, a bloodbath occurred at Wounded Knee, South Dakota. An accidental rifle discharge led nervous soldiers to fire into a group of Indians who had come to surrender. Nearly 200 Indians and 25 soldiers died in the Battle of Wounded Knee. The Indian wars had ended with characteristic brutality and misunderstanding.

THE DEMISE OF THE BUFFALO Over the long run the collapse of Indian resistance in the face of white settlement on the Great Plains resulted as much from the decimation of the buffalo herds as from the actions of federal troops. In 1750 there were an estimated 30 million buffalo on the plains; by 1850 there were less than 10 million; by 1900 only a few hundred were left. What happened to them? The conventional story focuses on intensive harvesting of buffalo by white hunters after the Civil War. Americans east of the Mississippi River developed a voracious demand for buffalo robes and buffalo leather. The average white hunter killed 100 animals a day, and the hides and bones (to be ground into fertilizer) were shipped east on railroad cars. Some army officers encouraged the slaughter. "Kill every buffalo you can!" Colonel Richard Dodge told a sport hunter in 1867. "Every buffalo dead is an Indian gone."

This conventional explanation tells only part of a more complicated story, however. The buffalo disappeared from the western plains for a variety of environmental reasons, including a significant change in climate; competition with other grazing animals; and cattle-borne disease. A prolonged drought on the Great Plains during the late 1880s and 1890s, the same drought that would help spur the agrarian revolt and the rise of populism, also devastated the buffalo herds by reducing the grasslands upon which the animals depended. At the same time, the buffalo had to compete for forage with an ever-increasing number of horses, cattle, and sheep. By the 1880s over 2 million horses were grazing on buffalo lands. In addition, the Plains Indians themselves, empowered by horses and guns and spurred by the profits reaped from selling hides and meat to white traders, accounted for much of the devastation of the buffalo herds after 1840. White hunters who killed buffalo by the millions in the 1870s and 1880s played a major role in the animals' demise, but only as the final catalyst. If there had been no white hunters, the buffalo would probably have lasted only another thirty years because their numbers had been so greatly reduced by other factors.

INDIAN POLICY   Most white westerners had little tolerance for moralizing on the Indian question, but many easterners decried the slaughter and mistreatment of Indians. Well-intentioned reformers sought to "Americanize" Indians by dealing with them as individuals rather than tribes. The Dawes Severalty Act of 1887 proposed to introduce the communal Indians to individual land ownership and agriculture. Sponsored by Senator Henry Dawes of Massachusetts, the act permitted the president to divide the land of any tribe and grant 160 acres to each head of a family and lesser amounts to others. To protect the Indians' property, the government held it in trust for twenty-five years, after which the owner won full title and became a U.S. citizen. In 1901, citizenship was extended to the Five Civilized Tribes of Oklahoma and, in 1924, to all Indians.

But the more it changed, the more Indian policy remained the same. Although well intended, the Dawes Act created new chances for more plundering of Indian land and disrupted what remained of the traditional culture. The Dawes Act broke up reservations and often led to the loss of Indian land to whites. Land not distributed to Indian families was sold, and some of the land the Indians did receive was lost to speculators because of the Indians' inexperience with private ownership or simply because of their powerlessness in the face of fraud. Between 1887 and 1934, Indians lost an estimated 86 million of their 130 million acres. Most of what remained was unsuited for agriculture.

CATTLE AND COWBOYS   While the West was being taken from the Indians, cattle entered the grasslands where the buffalo had roamed. Much of the romance of the open-range cattle industry derived from its Mexican roots. The Texas longhorns and the cowboys' horses had in large part descended from stock brought to America by the Spaniards, and many of the industry's trappings had been worked out in Mexico first: the cowboy's saddle, chaps *(chaparreras)* to protect the legs, spurs, and lariat.

For many years wild cattle competed with the buffalo in the Spanish borderlands. Natural selection and contact with Anglo-American cattle produced the Texas longhorns: lean and rangy, they were noted more for speed and endurance than for yielding a choice steak. They had little value, moreover, because the largest markets for beef were too far away. At the end of the Civil War, as many as 5 million longhorns roamed the grasslands of Texas, still neglected—but not for long. In the upper Mississippi Valley, where herds had been depleted by the war, cattle were in great demand, and the Texas cattle could be had just for the effort of rounding them up.

New opportunities arose as railroads pushed farther west, where cattle could be driven through relatively vacant lands. Joseph G. McCoy, an Illinois livestock dealer, encouraged railroad executives to run a line from the prairies to Chicago, the meatpacking center. The Kansas Pacific Railroad liked McCoy's vision, and with its help he made Abilene, Kansas, the western terminus of a new line. In 1867 the first shipment of Texas cattle went to Chicago.

During the twenty years after the Civil War, some 40,000 cowboys roamed the Great Plains. They were young—the average age was twenty-four—and from diverse backgrounds. Some 30 percent were Mexican or African American, and hundreds were Indians. Many others were Civil War veterans from the North and the South, and still others were immigrants from Europe. The life of a cowboy, for the most part, was rarely as exciting as has been depicted by motion pictures and television shows. Working as a ranch hand involved grueling wage labor interspersed with drudgery and boredom.

The thriving cattle industry spurred rapid growth, however. The population of Kansas increased from 107,000 in 1860 to 365,000 ten years later and reached almost 1 million by 1880. Nebraska witnessed similar increases. During the 1860s, cattle would be delivered to rail depots, loaded onto freight cars, and shipped east. By the time the animals arrived in New York

The cowboy era

Cowboys herd cattle near Cimarron, Colorado, 1905.

or Massachusetts, some would be dead or dying, and all would have lost significant weight. The secret to higher profits for the cattle industry was to devise a way to slaughter the cattle in the Midwest and ship the dressed carcasses east and west. That process required refrigeration to keep the meat from spoiling. In 1869, G. H. Hammond, a Chicago meat packer, shipped the first refrigerated beef in an air-cooled railcar from Chicago to Boston. Eight years later Gustavus Swift developed a more efficient system of mechanical refrigeration, an innovation that earned him a fortune and provided the cattle industry with a major stimulus.

The flush times of the cowtowns soon faded, however. The long cattle drives played out because they were economically unsound. The dangers of the trail, the wear and tear on men and cattle, the charges levied on drives that crossed Indian territory, and the advance of farms across the trails combined to persuade cattlemen that they could function best near railroads. As railroads spread out into Texas and across the plains, the cattle business spread with them as far as Montana and on into Canada.

In the absence of laws governing the open range, cattle ranchers at first worked out their own arrangements when rights and uses conflicted. As cattle wandered onto other ranchers' property, cowboys would "ride the line" to keep the strays off the adjoining ranches. In the spring they would "round up" the herds and sort out ownership by identifying the distinctive mark "branded" into the cattle. All that changed in 1873, when Joseph Glidden, an Illinois farmer, invented the first effective barbed wire, which ranchers used to fence off their claims at relatively low cost. Orders for the new fence poured in, and soon the open range was no more.

THE END OF THE OPEN RANGE   Yet a combination of factors put an end to the open range. Farmers kept crowding in and laying out homesteads. The boundless range was being overstocked by 1883, and expenses mounted as stock breeders formed associations to keep intruders off overstocked ranges, establish and protect land titles, deal with railroads and buyers, fight prairie fires, and cope with rustlers and wolves. The rise of sheepherding by 1880 caused still another conflict with the ranchers. A final blow to the open-range industry came with two unusually severe winters, in 1886 and 1887, followed by ten long years of drought.

Surviving the hazards of the range required ranchers to establish legal title, fence in the land, limit the herds to a reasonable size, and provide shelter and hay during the rigors of winter. Moreover, as the long cattle drives gave way to more rail lines and refrigerated railcars, the cowboy settled into a more sedentary existence. Within merely two decades, from 1866 to 1886, the era of the cowboy had come and gone.

RANGE WARS   Conflicting claims over land and water rights triggered violent disputes between ranchers and farmers. Ranchers often tried to drive off neighboring farmers, and farmers in turn tried to sabotage the cattle barons, cutting their fences and spooking their herds. The cattle ranchers also clashed with sheepherders over access to grassland. A strain of ethnic and religious prejudice heightened the tension between ranchers and. herders. In the Southwest, shepherds were typically Mexican Americans; in Idaho and Nevada, they were from the Basque region of Spain, or they were Mormons. Many Anglo-American cattlemen and cowboys viewed those ethnic and religious groups as un-American and inferior, an attitude that helped them rationalize the use of violence against sheepherders. Conflict faded, however, as the sheep for the most part found refuge in the high pastures of the mountains, leaving the grasslands of the plains to the ranchers.

Yet there also developed a perennial tension between large and small cattle ranchers. The large ranchers fenced in huge tracts of public land, leaving the smaller ranchers with too little pasture. To survive, the smaller ranchers cut the fences. In central Texas this practice sparked the Fence-Cutters' War of 1883-1884. Several ranchers were killed and dozens wounded before the state ended the conflict by passing legislation outlawing fence cutting.

FARMERS AND THE LAND   Among the legendary figures of the West, farmers projected an unromantic image in contrast to that of the cowboys, cavalrymen, and Indians. Yet farmers were the mainstay of the western economy. After 1865, on paper at least, the federal land laws offered farmers favorable terms. Under the Homestead Act of 1862, a farmer could gain title to federal land either by simply staking out a claim and living on it for five years or by buying the land at $1.25 an acre after six months.

As so often happens, however, environmental forces more than government policy shaped development. The unchangeable fact of aridity, rather than land laws, influenced institutions in the West after the Civil War. Where farming was impossible, ranchers simply established dominance by control of the water, regardless of the law. Belated legislative efforts to develop irrigable land finally achieved a major success when the 1901 Newlands Reclamation Act (after the aptly named Senator Francis G. Newlands of Nevada) set up the Bureau of Reclamation. The proceeds of public land sales in sixteen states created a fund for irrigation works, and the Reclamation Bureau set about building such major projects as the Boulder (later the Hoover) Dam on the Nevada-Arizona line, the Roosevelt Dam in Arizona, and the Elephant Butte Dam in New Mexico.

The lands of the New West, like those on previous frontiers, passed to their ultimate owners more often from private hands than directly from the government. Many of the 274 million acres claimed under the Homestead Act passed quickly to cattle ranchers or speculators and thence to settlers. The land-grant railroads got some 200 million acres of the public domain between 1851 and 1871 and sold much of it to build towns along the lines. The West of ranchers and fanners was in fact largely the product of the railroads.

The first arrivals on the sod-house frontier of the Plains faced a grim struggle against danger, adversity, and monotony. Though land was relatively cheap, horses, livestock, wagons, wells, fencing, seed, and fertilizer were not. Freight rates and interest rates on loans seemed criminally high. As in the South, declining crop prices produced chronic indebtedness, leading strapped western farmers to embrace virtually any plan to inflate the money

The construction of Hoover Dam

When completed in 1936, Hoover Dam was the world's largest concrete structure.

supply. The land itself, although fertile, resisted planting; the heavy sod broke many a plow. Since wood was almost nonexistent on the prairie, pioneer families used buffalo chips (dried dung) for fuel.

Farmers and their families also fought a constant battle with the elements: tornadoes, hailstorms, droughts, prairie fires, blizzards, and pests. Swarms of locusts would often cloud the horizon, occasionally covering the ground six inches deep and consuming everything in their path. A Wichita newspaper reported in 1878 that the grasshoppers devoured "everything green, stripping the foliage off the bark and from the tender twigs of the fruit trees, destroying every plant that is good for food or pleasant to the eyes, that man has planted."

As time passed and farmers were able to lay aside some money from their labor, farm families could leave their sod houses and build frame houses with lumber carried from Chicago by the railroads. New machinery also provided fresh opportunities for farmers. In 1868, James Oliver, a Scottish immigrant living in Indiana, made a successful chilled-iron plow. With further improvements his "sodbuster" plow greatly eased the task of breaking the shallow but tough grass roots of the Plains. Improvements and new inventions lightened the burden of labor but added to the farmers' capital outlay.

While the overall value of farmland and farm products increased in the late nineteenth century, small farmers did not keep up with the march of progress. Their numbers grew but decreased in proportion to the population at large. The wheat produced on the eastern plains from Minnesota and North Dakota down to Texas, like cotton in the antebellum period, was the great export crop that evened America's balance of payments and spurred economic growth. For a variety of reasons, however, few small farmers prospered. And by the 1890s many were in open revolt against "greedy" bankers, railroads, and grain processors who seemed to thwart their efforts and deny their dreams.

PIONEER WOMEN   The West remained a largely male society throughout the nineteenth century. Women were not only a minority; they also continued to face traditional legal barriers and social prejudice. A wife could not sell property without her husband's approval for example. Texas women could not sue except for divorce, nor could they serve on juries, act as lawyers, or witness a will. But the fight for survival in the West often made husbands and wives more equal partners in everyday life than were their eastern counterparts. Prairie life also allowed women more independence than could be had by leading a domestic life back East.

"THE FRONTIER HAS GONE"   American life reached an important juncture in the last decade of the nineteenth century. After the 1890 population count the superintendent of the national census noted that he could no longer locate a continuous frontier line beyond which population thinned out to fewer than two people per square mile. This fact inspired the historian Frederick Jackson Turner to develop the influential frontier thesis, first outlined in "The Significance of the Frontier in American History," a paper delivered to the American Historical Association in 1893. "The existence of an area of free land," Turner wrote, "its continuous recession, and the advance of American settlement westward, explain American development." The frontier, he added, had shaped the national character in striking ways. It was

> to the frontier [that] the American intellect owes its striking characteristics. That coarseness and strength combined with acuteness and acquisitiveness; that practical, inventive turn of mind, quick to find expedients; that masterful grasp of material things, lacking in the artistic but powerful to effect great ends; that restless, nervous energy; that dominant individualism, working for good and for evil, and with all that buoyancy and exuberance which comes with freedom—these are traits of the frontier, or traits called out elsewhere because of the existence of the frontier.

Women of the frontier

A woman and her family in front of their sod house. The difficult life on the prairie led to more egalitarian marriages than were found in most other regions of the country.

But, Turner ominously concluded in 1893, "the frontier has gone and with its going has closed the first period of American history."

Turner's "frontier thesis" guided several generations of scholars and students in their understanding of the distinctive characteristics of American history. His view of the frontier as the westward-moving source of the nation's democratic politics, open society, unfettered economy, and rugged individualism, far removed from the corruptions of urban life, gripped the popular imagination as well. But it left out much of the story. Turner's description of the frontier experience exaggerated the homogenizing effect of the environment and virtually ignored the role of women, African Americans, Indians, Mormons, Hispanics, and Asians in shaping the diverse human geography of the western United States. Turner also implied that the West would be fundamentally different after 1890 because the frontier experience was essentially over. In many respects, however, that region has retained the qualities associated, with the rush for land, gold, timber, and water rights during the post-Civil War decades. The mining frontier, as one historian has recently written, "set a mood that has never disappeared from the West: the attitude of extractive industry—get in, get rich, get out."

CHAPTER SUMMARY

- **Southern Segregation** By 1900 elite southern whites had regained control of state governments; prominent black Republicans had been squeezed out of political positions; and black men were being kept from exercising their right to vote. Segregation became the social norm. Some African American leaders, most prominently Booker T. Washington, believed that by showing deference to whites, blacks could avoid violence while quietly acquiring an education and property. Others, like Ida B. Wells and W. E. B. Du Bois, wanted to fight segregation and lynching through the courts.

- **Indian Wars and Policies** By 1900, Native Americans in the West were no longer free to roam the plains. Disease and the influx of farmers and miners reduced their numbers and curtailed their way of life. Instances of resistance, such as the Great Sioux War, were dealt with harshly. Initially, Indian tribes were forced to sign treaties and were confined to reservations. From 1887 the American government's Indian policy was aimed at forcing Indians to relinquish their traditional culture and adopt individual land ownership, settled agriculture, and Christianity.

- **Life in the West** Life in the West was harsh and violent, but the promise of cheap land or wealth from mining drew settlers from the East. Most cowboys and miners did not acquire wealth, however, because raising cattle and mining became large-scale enterprises that enriched only a few. Although most westerners were white Protestant Americans or northern European immigrants, Mexicans, African Americans, and Chinese contributed to the West's diversity. As a consequence of the region's rugged isolation, women achieved greater equality in everyday life than did most women elsewhere in the country.

- **Growth of Mining** Mining lured settlers to largely uninhabited regions, thereby hastening the creation of new territories and the admission of new states into the Union. By the 1880s, when mining became a big business employing large-scale equipment, its environmental impact could be seen in the blighted landscape.

- **The American Frontier** The historian Frederick Jackson Turner believed that the enduring presence of the frontier was responsible for making Americans individualistic, materialistic, practical, democratic, and energetic. In 1893 he declared that the closing of the frontier had ended the first stage of America's history.

CHRONOLOGY

1859	Comstock Lode is discovered
1862	Congress passes the Homestead Act
1864	Sand Creek Massacre
1873	Joseph Glidden invents barbed wire
1876	Battle of Little Bighorn
1877	With the Compromise of 1877, Rutherford B. Hayes becomes president and Reconstruction comes to an end
1886	Surrender of Geronimo marks the end of the Indian wars
1887	Congress passes the Dawes Severalty Act
1890	Battle of Wounded Knee
1890	Mississippi plan
1895	Booker T. Washington delivers his Atlanta Compromise speech
1896	Supreme Court issues *Plessy v. Ferguson* decision
1909	National Association for the Advancement of Color People is created

KEY TERMS & NAMES

New South p. 560

sharecropping p. 562

Bourbons p. 564

Redeemers p. 564

"Jim Crow" laws p. 566

Mississippi plan p. 567

"separate but equal" p. 568

Ida B. Wells p. 570

Booker T. Washington p. 571

W. E. B. Du Bois p. 571

panning p. 575

George A. Custer p. 578

Great Sioux War p. 578

Ghost Dance movement p. 579

range wars p. 583

20

BIG BUSINESS AND ORGANIZED LABOR

FOCUS QUESTIONS wwnorton.com/studyspace

- What fueled the growth of the post–Civil War economy?
- What roles were played by leading entrepreneurs like John D. Rockefeller, Andrew Carnegie, and J. Pierpont Morgan?
- Who composed the labor force of the period, and what were labor's main grievances?
- What led to the rise of labor unions?

America emerged as an industrial and agricultural giant in the late nineteenth century. Between 1869 and 1899 the nation's population nearly tripled, farm production more than doubled, and the value of manufactures grew sixfold. Within three generations after the Civil War, the predominantly rural nation had became an urban-industrial society buffeted by the imperatives of mass production, mass consumption, and time-clock efficiency. Bigness became the prevailing standard of corporate life, and social tensions worsened with the rising scale of business enterprise.

THE RISE OF BIG BUSINESS

The Industrial Revolution created huge corporations that came to dominate the economy—as well as political and social life—during the late nineteenth century. As businesses grew, their owners sought to integrate all the processes of production and distribution into single companies, thus producing even larger firms. Others grew by mergers, joining forces with

their competitors in "pools" or "trusts" in an effort to dominate entire industries. This process of industrial combination and concentration transformed
the nation's social order. It also aroused widespread dissent and the emergence of an organized labor movement.

Many factors converged to help launch the dramatic economic growth
after the Civil War. The nation's unparalleled natural resources—forests,
mineral wealth, rivers—along with a rapidly expanding population, were
crucial ingredients. At the same time, inventors and business owners developed more efficient, labor-saving machinery and mass-production techniques that spurred dramatic advances in productivity and efficiency. As the
volume and efficiency of production increased, the larger businesses and
industries expanded into numerous states and in the process developed
standardized machinery and parts, which became available nationwide.
Innovative, bold leadership was crucial. A group of shrewd, determined, and
energetic entrepreneurs took advantage of fertile business opportunities to
create huge enterprises. Federal and state officials after the Civil War actively
encouraged the growth of big business by imposing high tariffs on foreign
manufacturers as a means of blunting foreign competition and by providing
government land and cash to finance railroads and other internal improvements. At the same time that the federal government was issuing massive
land grants to railroads and speculators, it was also distributing land to
farmers through the Homestead Act of 1862.

The American agricultural sector, by 1870 the world's leader, fueled the
rest of the economy by providing wheat and corn to be milled into flour
and meal. With the advent of the cattle industry, the processes of slaughtering and packing meat themselves became major industries. So the farm
sector directly stimulated the industrial sector of the economy. A national
government-subsidized network of railroads connecting the East and West
Coasts played a crucial role in the development of related industries and in
the evolution of a national market for goods and services. Industry in the
United States also benefited from an abundance of power sources—water,
wood, coal, oil, and electricity—that were inexpensive compared with those
of the other nations of the world.

THE SECOND INDUSTRIAL REVOLUTION   The Industrial Revolution "controls us all," said Yale sociologist William Graham Sumner,
"because we are all in it." Sumner and other Americans living during the second half of the nineteenth century experienced what economic historians
have termed the Second Industrial Revolution. The First Industrial Revolution
began in Britain during the late eighteenth century. It was propelled by

the convergence of three new technologies: the coal-powered steam engine, textile machines for spinning thread and weaving cloth, and blast furnaces to produce iron.

The Second Industrial Revolution began in the mid–nineteenth century and was centered in the United States and Germany. It was sparked by three related developments. The first was the creation of an interconnected national transportation and communication network, which facilitated the emergence of new national and even international markets for American goods and services. Contributing to this development were the completion of the national telegraph and railroad systems, the emergence of steamships, and the laying of the undersea telegraph cable, which spanned the Atlantic Ocean and connected the United States with Europe.

During the 1880s a second major breakthrough—the use of electric power—accelerated the pace of industrial change. Electricity created dramatic advances in the power and efficiency of industrial machinery. It also spurred urban growth through the addition of electric trolleys and subways, and it greatly enhanced the production of steel and chemicals.

The third major aspect of the Second Industrial Revolution was the systematic application of scientific research to industrial processes. Laboratories staffed by graduates of new research universities sprouted up across the country, and scientists and engineers discovered dramatic new ways to

"The Hand of Man" (1902)

Photogravure by Alfred Stieglitz.

improve industrial processes. Researchers figured out, for example, how to refine kerosene and gasoline from crude oil and how to improve steel production. Inventors developed new products—telephones, typewriters, adding machines, sewing machines, cameras, elevators, and farm machinery—that resulted in lower consumer prices. These advances in turn expanded the scope and scale of industrial organizations. Capital-intensive industries such as steel and oil, as well as processed food and tobacco, took advantage of new technologies to gain economies of scale that emphasized maximum production and national as well as international marketing and distribution.

BUILDING THE TRANSCONTINENTAL RAILROADS Railroads were the first big business, the first magnet for the great financial markets, and the first industry to develop a large-scale management bureaucracy. The railroads opened the trans-Mississippi West to economic development and transported raw materials to factories, and in so doing they created an interconnected national market for the country's goods and produce. At the same time, the railroads were themselves gigantic consumers of iron, steel, lumber, and other capital goods.

Transcontinental railroads

Using picks, shovels, wheelbarrows, and horse-drawn carts, Chinese laborers largely helped to construct the Central Pacific track.

The renewal of railroad building after the Civil War filled out the railway network east of the Mississippi River, but the most spectacular exploits were the transcontinental lines built across the Great Plains and the Rocky Mountains. Running through sparsely settled land, they served the purpose of binding the country together. The buccaneering executives and financiers directing the transcontinental railroads were shrewd entrepreneurs so driven by dreams of great wealth that they often cut corners and bribed legislators. They also ruthlessly used federal troops to suppress the Plains Indians. But their shenanigans do not diminish the heroic efforts of the workers and engineers who built the rail lines, erected the bridges, and gouged out the tunnels under terrible conditions. Building the transcontinental railroads was an epic feat of daring engineering that tied a nation together, changed the economic and political landscape, and enabled the United States to emerge as a world power.

Before the Civil War, sectional differences over routes had delayed the start of a transcontinental line. Secession and the departure of southerners from Congress finally permitted passage of the Pacific Railroads Act, which Abraham Lincoln signed into law in 1862, authorizing a 2,000-mile line along a north-central route, to be built jointly by the Union Pacific Railroad westward from Omaha, Nebraska, and by the Central Pacific Railroad eastward from Sacramento, California.

Both railroads began construction during the war, but most of the work was done after 1865. The Union Pacific pushed across the plains at a rapid pace, avoiding the Rocky Mountains by going through Evans Pass in Wyoming. The work crews, including large numbers of ex-soldiers and Irish immigrants, had to cope with bad roads, water shortages, rugged weather, Indian attacks, and frequent accidents and injuries.

The Central Pacific construction crews were mainly composed of Chinese workers lured to America first by the California gold rush and then by railroad jobs. Thousands of Chinese had emigrated, raising their numbers in the United States from 7,500 in 1850 to 105,000 in 1880. Most of these "coolie" laborers were single men intent upon accumulating money and returning to their homeland, where they could then afford to marry and buy a parcel of land. Their temporary status and dream of a good life back in China apparently made them more willing than American laborers to endure the dangerous working conditions and low pay of railroad work. By 1867 the Central Pacific Railroad's 12,000 Chinese laborers represented 90 percent of its workforce.

Clearing trees, handling explosives, operating power drills, and working in snowdrifts were dangerous activities, and many Chinese died on the job. Fifty-seven miles east of Sacramento the construction crews encountered

The Union Pacific meets the Central Pacific

The celebration of the completion of the first transcontinental railroad, Promontory, Utah, May 10, 1869.

the towering Sierra Nevadas, through which they had to cut before reaching more level country in Nevada. The Union Pacific had built 1,086 miles to the Central Pacific's 689 when the race ended on the salt plains of Promontory, Utah, near Ogden. There, on May 10, 1869, Leland Stanford, former governor of California and one of the organizers of the Central Pacific, drove a gold spike symbolizing the railroad's completion.

The next transcontinental line, completed in 1881, linked the Atchison, Topeka, and Santa Fe Railroad with the Southern Pacific Railroad in southern California. The transcontinentals soon sprouted numerous trunk lines, which in turn encouraged the building of other transcontinentals. The result was a massive railroad-building boom that lasted into the 1890s and stimulated the rest of the economy.

FINANCING THE RAILROADS The railroads were built by private companies that raised money for construction primarily by selling bonds to U.S. and foreign investors. While constitutional scruples over state sovereignty initially constrained the granting of federal aid for internal improvements, many states had subsidized the building of railroads within their borders. Finally, in 1850, Illinois senator Stephen Douglas secured from Congress a federal grant of public lands to subsidize a north-south railroad connecting Chicago and Mobile, Alabama. Over the next twenty years, transcontinental railroad companies received generous government aid in the form of federal land grants, as well as loans and tax breaks from federal, state, and local governments.

In the long run, the federal government recovered much if not all of its investment. As farms, ranches, and towns sprouted up around the rail lines, the value of the government land along the tracks skyrocketed. The railroads also hauled government freight, military personnel and equipment, and the mail. Moreover, by helping to accelerate the creation of a national market,

TRANSCONTINENTAL
RAILROAD LINES, 1880s

What was the route of the first transcontinental railroad, and why was it not in the South? Who built the railroads? How were they financed?

the railroads spurred economic growth and thereby increased government tax revenues.

But that is only part of the story. The vast sums of money used to finance the building of the transcontinental lines generated shameless profiteering. Prince of the railroad robber barons was Jay Gould, a secretive trickster who mastered the art of buying rundown railroads, making cosmetic improvements, and selling out at a profit while using corporate funds for personal gain and bribes for politicians and judges. Nearly every enterprise he touched was compromised or ruined; Gould, meanwhile, built a fortune that amounted to $100 million upon his death.

Few railroad fortunes were amassed in those freewheeling times by purely ethical methods, but compared with opportunistic rogues such as Gould, most railroad entrepreneurs were giants of honesty. They at least took some interest in the welfare of their companies, if not always in that of the public. Cornelius Vanderbilt, called Commodore by virtue of his early exploits in steamboating, stands out among the railroad barons. Already rich before the Civil War, he decided to give up the hazards of wartime shipping and move his money into land transport. His great achievement was consolidating separate trunk lines into a single powerful rail network led by the New York Central. After the Commodore's death, in 1877, his son William Henry extended the Vanderbilt lines to include more than 13,000 miles in the Northeast. The consolidation trend was nationwide: about two thirds of the nation's railroad mileage were under the control of only seven major groups by 1900.

INVENTIONS SPUR MANUFACTURING   Like the railroad industry, the story of manufacturing after the Civil War shows much the same pattern of expansion and merger in old and new industries. Technological innovations spurred phenomenal increases in productivity. The U.S. Patent Office, which had recorded only 276 inventions during its first decade of existence, the 1790s, registered 234,956 in the 1890s. The list of innovations after the Civil War can be extended nearly indefinitely: barbed wire, farm implements, the air brake for trains (1868), steam turbines, gas distribution and electrical devices, the typewriter (1867), the vacuum cleaner (1869), and countless others. Before the end of the century, the internal-combustion engine and the motion picture were spawning new industries that would blossom in the twentieth century.

These technological advances transformed daily life. In no field was this truer than in the application of electricity to communications and power. Few if any inventions of the time could rival the importance of the telephone, which Alexander Graham Bell patented in 1876. To promote the new device, the inventor and his supporters formed the Bell Telephone Association, out of which grew in 1877 the Bell Telephone Company. In 1885 the Bell interests organized the American Telephone and Telegraph Company, which by 1899 was a huge holding company controlling forty-nine licensed subsidiaries and an operating company for long-distance lines.

In the development of electrical industries, the name Thomas Alva Edison stands above those of other inventors. Edison invented the phonograph in 1877 and the first lightbulb in 1879. At his laboratories in Menlo Park, New Jersey, he created or perfected hundreds of new devices and processes, including the storage battery, Dictaphone, mimeograph, electric motor, electric transmission, and the motion picture.

Until 1880 or so the world was lit by flickering oil or gas lamps. In 1882, with the backing of the financier J. P. Morgan, the Edison Electric Illuminating Company began to supply current to eighty-five customers in New York City, beginning the great electric utility industry. A number of companies making lightbulbs merged into the Edison General Electric Company in 1888. But the use of direct current limited Edison's lighting system to a radius of about two miles. To cover greater distances required an alternating current, which could be transmitted at high voltage and then stepped down by transformers. George Westinghouse, inventor of the air brake for railroads, developed the first alternating-current electric system in 1886 and set up the Westinghouse Electric Company to manufacture the equipment. Edison considered the new method too dangerous, but just as Edison's instrument supplanted Bell's first telephone, the Westinghouse system won the "battle of the currents," and the Edison companies had to switch over. After the invention of the alternating-current motor in 1888, Westinghouse improved upon it. This invention enabled factories to locate wherever they wished. Capable now of using electricity as a power source, they no longer had to cluster around waterfalls and coal deposits for a ready supply of energy.

ENTREPRENEURS

Thomas Edison and George Westinghouse were rare examples of inventors with the luck and foresight to get rich from the industries they created. Most of the architects of industrial growth—the great captains of industry—were not inventors but pure entrepreneurs, men skilled mainly in organizing and promoting industry. Called robber barons by critics because of their greed and ruthlessness, they helped create thousands of new jobs and supplied the nation with an array of new goods and services. Three post Civil War business titans stand out for their enterprise: John D. Rockefeller, Andrew Carnegie, and J. Pierpont Morgan. Each of them in different ways replaced the small-scale economy of the early republic with vast new industries that forever altered the size and scope of the nation's business. Two other entrepreneurs, Richard Sears and Alvah Roebuck, perfected mail-order retailing.

ROCKEFELLER AND THE OIL TRUST   Born in New York State, the son of a flamboyant con-man father and a devout Baptist mother, John D. Rockefeller moved as a youth to Cleveland, Ohio. Soon thereafter his father abandoned the family and started a new life under an assumed name with a second wife. Raised by his mother, John Rockefeller developed a passion for systematic organization and self-discipline. He was obsessed with precision, order, and tidiness. And early on he decided to bring order and rationality to the chaotic oil industry.

Cleveland's railroad and shipping connections made that city a strategic location for servicing the oil fields of western Pennsylvania. In economic importance the Pennsylvania oil rush of the 1860s far outweighed the California gold rush of just ten years earlier. Well before the end of the Civil War, derricks checkered the area around Titusville, Pennsylvania, where the first oil well had been struck, and refineries sprang up in Pittsburgh and Cleveland.

Of the two cities, Cleveland had the edge in transportation, and John Rockefeller made the most of the fast-growing commercial city's advantages. A man of icy efficiency and tenacious daring, Rockefeller moved aggressively into the oil business. In 1870 he incorporated his various interests, naming his enterprise the Standard Oil Company of Ohio. His goal was to eliminate all of his competitors. To do that, he hatched an ingenious scheme. In the early 1870s, Rockefeller created the South Improvement Company, which he made the marketing agent for a large percentage of his oil shipments. By controlling this traffic, he gained clout with the railroads, which in turn gave him large rebates (or secret refunds) on the standard freight rates in order to keep his high-volume business. In some cases they even gave

John D. Rockefeller

His Standard Oil Company dominated the oil industry.

him information on competitors' shipments. Rockefeller then approached his Cleveland competitors and pressured them to sell out at his price. Most of them complied. Those who resisted were forced out. In less than six weeks, Rockefeller had taken over twenty-two of his twenty-six rivals. By 1879, Standard Oil was controlling 90 to 95 percent of the oil refined throughout the country.

Much of Rockefeller's success reflected his determination to "pay nobody a profit." Instead of depending upon the products or services of other firms, known as middlemen, Standard Oil started making its own barrels, cans, and whatever else it needed—in economic terms this is called vertical integration. The company kept large cash reserves to make it independent of banks in case of a crisis. Rockefeller also set out to control his transportation needs. With Standard Oil owning most of the pipelines leading to railroads, as well as the railroad tank cars and the oil-storage facilities, it was able to dissuade the railroads from serving its eastern competitors. Those rivals that had insisted upon holding out then faced a giant marketing organization capable of driving them to the wall with price wars.

To consolidate their scattered business interests under more efficient control, Rockefeller and his advisers resorted to the new legal device of the trust. In 1882, Rockefeller organized the Standard Oil Trust. All thirty-seven stockholders in various Standard Oil enterprises conveyed their stock to nine trustees, getting "trust certificates" in return. The nine trustees thereby controlled all the varied Standard Oil companies.

But the trust device, widely copied by other corporations in the 1880s, proved legally vulnerable to prosecution under state laws against monopoly or restraint of trade. In 1892, Ohio's supreme court ordered the Standard Oil Trust dissolved. For a while the company managed to unify control by the simple device of interlocking directorates, through which the board of directors of one company was made identical or nearly so to the boards of the others. Gradually, however, Rockefeller perfected the idea of the holding company: a company that controlled other companies by holding all or at least a majority of their stock. In 1899, Rockefeller brought his empire under the direction of the Standard Oil Company of New Jersey, a holding company. Though less vulnerable to prosecution under state law, some holding companies were broken up by the Sherman Anti-Trust Act of 1890.

Rockefeller not only made a colossal fortune, but he also gave much of it away, mainly to support advances in education and medicine. A man of simple tastes who opposed the use of tobacco and alcohol and believed his fortune was a public trust awarded by God, Rockefeller became the world's leading philanthropist. He donated more than $500 million during his ninety-eight-year lifetime. "I have always regarded it as a religious duty," Rockefeller said late in life, "to get all I could honorably and to give all I could."

CARNEGIE AND THE STEEL INDUSTRY   Andrew Carnegie, like Rockefeller, experienced the atypical rise from poverty to riches that came to be known in those days as the typical American success story. Born in Scotland, he migrated with his family to Allegheny County, Pennsylvania, in 1848. Then thirteen, he started work in a textile mill at wages of $1.20 per week. Quick-witted, shrewd, and brilliant, he worked hard, and in 1853 he became personal secretary and telegrapher to the district superintendent of the Pennsylvania Railroad. When the superintendent became president of the line, Carnegie took his place, and the pace of his career accelerated. During the Civil War, Carnegie went to Washington, D.C., where he developed a military telegraph system.

Carnegie kept on moving—from telegraphy to railroading to bridge building, then to iron- and steelmaking and investments. In 1872 he netted $150,000 on a trip to Great Britain, during which he met Sir Henry Bessemer, who in 1855 had invented what became known as the Bessemer converter, a process by which steel could be produced directly and quickly from pig iron (crude iron made in a blast furnace) by using forced air to heat the metal. The next year, 1873, Carnegie resolved to concentrate on steel, the miracle material of the post–Civil War era, not because it was new but because Bessemer's process had made it suddenly cheap. As more steel was produced, its price dropped and uses soared. In 1860 the United States had produced only 13,000 tons of steel. By 1880, production had reached 1.4 million tons.

Carnegie was never a technical expert on steel. He was a promoter, salesman, and organizer with a gift for hiring men of expert ability. Fiercely competitive and obsessed with efficiency and innovation, he insisted on up-to-date machinery and equipment. Carnegie retained a large portion of his annual profits during good times. During business depressions,

Andrew Carnegie

Steel magnate and business icon.

when construction costs were low and competitors were forced to the wall, he used his surplus capital to buy out competitors and expand. He preached to his employees a philosophy of continual innovation in order to reduce operating costs.

Carnegie stood out from other business titans as a thinker who publicized a philosophy of big business, a conservative rationale that became deeply ingrained in the conventional wisdom of some Americans. Carnegie argued that the captains of industry were on the whole public benefactors. He believed that the best way to dispense a fortune was to donate it during one's lifetime to causes promoting the public good: "The man who dies rich dies disgraced." Carnegie insisted that by supporting universities, libraries, hospitals, parks, halls for meetings and concerts, and church buildings, the wealthy should provide means for the less fortunate to help themselves. Carnegie spent some $60 million on public libraries and another $60 million on higher education.

J. P. MORGAN, FINANCIER   Unlike Carnegie and Rockefeller, J. Pierpont Morgan was born to wealth, in Hartford, Connecticut, and increased it enormously through his bold financial innovations. Morgan's father was a partner in a London banking house, and his wealth enabled him to send young Pierpont to schools in Switzerland and Germany. After a brief apprenticeship, Morgan in 1857 began work in a New York firm that represented his father's London bank, and in 1860 he set himself up as its New York agent under the name J. Pierpont Morgan and Company. This firm, under various names, channeled European capital into the United States and grew into a financial power in its own right.

J. Pierpont Morgan

A famous portrait by Edward Steichen (1903).

As an investment banker, Morgan bought corporate stocks and bonds wholesale and sold them at a profit. The growth of large corporations put investment firms such as Morgan's in an increasingly strategic position in the economy. Since the investment business depended upon the health of client companies, investment bankers became involved in the operation of their clients' firms, demanding seats on boards of directors so as to influence company policies.

Like John Rockefeller, J. P. Morgan sought to consolidate rival firms into giant trusts. Morgan realized that railroads were the key to the times, so he bought and reorganized one rail line after another. After the panic of 1893, when hard times gutted the net worth of many railroads, Morgan bought many of them. By the 1890s he controlled a sixth of America's railway system.

Yet Morgan's crowning triumph was the consolidation of the steel industry. In 1901 he bought out Andrew Carnegie's huge steel and iron holdings. Carnegie set the price, nearly $500 million, of which Carnegie's personal share was nearly $300 million. After closing the deal, Morgan told the steel king, "Mr. Carnegie, I want to congratulate you on being the richest man in the world." Morgan's new United States Steel Corporation, a holding company for various steel interests, was a marvel of the new century, the first billion-dollar corporation, the climactic event in the age of relentless corporate consolidation.

SEARS AND ROEBUCK American inventors helped manufacturers after the Civil War produce a vast number of new products, but the most important challenge was extending the reach of modern commerce to the millions of people who lived on isolated farms and in small towns. In the aftermath of the Civil War, a traveling salesman from Chicago named Aaron Montgomery Ward decided that he could reach more people by mail than on foot and in the process could eliminate the middlemen whose services increased the retail price of goods. Beginning in the early 1870s, Montgomery Ward and Company began selling goods at a 40 percent discount through mail-order catalogs.

Cover of the 1897 Sears, Roebuck and Company catalog

Sears, Roebuck's extensive mail-order business and discounted prices allowed its many products to reach customers in cities and in the backcountry.

By the end of the century, a new retailer had come to dominate the mail-order industry: Sears, Roebuck and Company, founded by two young midwestern entrepreneurs, Richard Sears and Alvah Roebuck, who began offering a cornucopia of goods by mail in the early 1890s. The Sears, Roebuck catalog in 1897 was 786 pages long and was published in German and Swedish as well as English. It included groceries, drugs, tools, bells, furniture, iceboxes, stoves, household utensils, musical instruments, farm implements, boots and shoes, clothes, books, and sporting goods.

The Sears catalog helped create a truly national market and in the process transformed the lives of millions of people. With the advent of free rural mail delivery in 1898 and the widespread distribution of Sears catalogs, families on farms and in small towns and villages could purchase by mail the products that heretofore were either prohibitively expensive or available only to city dwellers. By the turn of the century, 6 million Sears catalogs were being distributed each year, and the catalog had become the single most widely read book in the nation after the Bible.

Labor Conditions and Organization

SOCIAL TRENDS   Accompanying the spread of giant corporations during the Gilded Age was a rising standard of living for most people. If the rich were still getting richer, a lot of other people were at least better off. The continuing demand for workers, meanwhile, was filled by new groups entering the workforce at the bottom: immigrants above all, but also growing numbers of women and children. Because of a long-term decline in prices and the cost of living, real wages and earnings in manufacturing went up about 50 percent between 1860 and 1890 and another 37 percent from 1890 to 1914. By latter-day standards, however, working conditions were dreary—and dangerous. At the turn of the century, the average hourly wage in manufacturing was about $3.50 in 2009 dollars. The average workweek was fifty-nine hours, which amounted to nearly six ten-hour workdays, but that was only an average. Most steelworkers put in a twelve-hour workday, and as late as the 1920s a great many worked a seven-day, eighty-four-hour workweek.

CHILD LABOR   A growing number of wage laborers in the late nineteenth century were children—boys and girls who worked full-time for meager wages under unhealthy conditions. Young people had always worked in America: farms required everyone to pitch in. After the Civil War, however, many children took up work outside the home, operating machines, sorting coal, stitching clothes, shucking oysters, peeling shrimp, canning food, blowing glass, and tending looms. Parents desperate for income believed they had no choice but to put their children to work. By 1880 one out of every six children was working full-time. By 1900 there were almost 2 million child laborers in the United States. In southern cotton mills, where few African Americans were hired, a fourth of the employees were below the age of fifteen, with half of the children below age twelve. Children as young as eight were laboring alongside adults twelve hours a day, six days a week. This meant they received little or no education and had little time for play or parental nurturance.

Factories, mills, mines, and canneries were dangerous places, especially for children. Throughout Appalachia, soot-smeared boys worked deep in the coal mines. In New England and the South, thousands of young girls worked in dusty textile mills. Children suffered three times as many accidents as adult workers, and respiratory diseases were common in the unventilated buildings. A child working in a textile mill was only half as likely to reach age twenty as a child outside a mill. Although some states passed laws limiting the number of hours children could work and establishing minimum-age requirements, they were rarely enforced and often ignored. By 1881 only seven states, mostly in New England, had laws requiring children to be at least twelve before they worked for wages. Yet the only proof required by employers in such states was a statement from a child's parents. Working-class and immigrant parents were often so desperate for income that they forged work permits for their children or taught them to lie about their age to keep a job.

DISORGANIZED PROTEST   Under these circumstances it was difficult for workers to organize unions. Civic officials and business leaders respected property rights more than the rights of labor. Among workers recently removed from an agrarian world of independent farmers, the idea of permanent labor unions was slow to take hold. And much of the workforce was made up of immigrant workers from a variety of cultures. They spoke different languages and harbored ethnic animosities. Nonetheless, with or without unions, workers often staged impromptu strikes protesting long working hours and wage cuts. During the 1870s, however, such action often led to violent incidents, which colored much of the public's view of labor unions thereafter.

The decade's early years saw a reign of terror in the eastern Pennsylvania coalfields, attributed to an Irish group called the Molly Maguires. The Mollies took their name from an Irish patriot who had directed violent resistance against the British. They were motivated by the dangerous working conditions in the mines and the owners' brutal efforts to suppress union activity. Convinced of the justness of their cause, the Mollies aimed to right perceived wrongs against Irish workers by such methods as intimidation, beatings, and killings. Their terrorism reached its peak in 1874–1875. At trials in 1876, twenty-four of the Molly Maguires were convicted, and ten of them were hanged. The trials also resulted in a wage reduction in the mines.

THE RAILROAD STRIKE OF 1877   A more widespread labor incident was the Great Railroad Strike of 1877, the first major interstate strike in American history. After the financial panic of 1873 and the ensuing depression, the major rail lines in the East had cut wages. In 1877 they made another 10 percent cut, which provoked most of the railroad workers at Martinsburg, West Virginia, to walk off the job and block the tracks. Without organized direction, however, the group of picketers degenerated into a mob that burned and plundered railroad property.

Walkouts and sympathy demonstrations spread spontaneously from Maryland to San Francisco. The railroad strike engulfed hundreds of cities and towns, leaving in its wake over 100 people dead and millions of dollars in property destroyed. Public sympathy for the strikers was so great at first that local militiamen, called out to suppress them, joined the workers instead. Militiamen from Philadelphia managed to disperse one crowd at the cost of twenty-six lives but then found themselves besieged in the railroad's roundhouse, where they disbanded and shot their way out. Federal troops finally quelled the violence, but the looting, rioting, and burning went on for another day until the frenzy wore itself out. A reporter described the scene as "the most horrible ever witnessed, except in the carnage of war." Eventually the strikers, lacking organized bargaining power, had no choice but to drift back to work. Everywhere, the strikes failed.

For many Americans the Great Railroad Strike raised the specter of a worker-based social revolution. As a Pittsburgh newspaper warned, "This may be the beginning of a great civil war in this country between labor and capital." From the point of view of organized labor, however, the Great Railroad Strike demonstrated potential union strength and the need for tighter organization.

THE SAND-LOT INCIDENT   In California the railroad strike indirectly gave rise to a working-class political movement. At a San Francisco sand lot, a meeting to express sympathy for the railroad strikers ended with attacks on some passing Chinese. Within a few days sporadic anti-Chinese riots had led to a mob attack on Chinatown. The depression of the 1870s had hit the West

The rise of oil

Wooden derricks crowd the farm of John Benninghoff in Oil Creek, Pennsylvania, in the 1860s.

Coast especially hard, and the Chinese were handy scapegoats for white laborers' frustrations.

Soon an Irish immigrant, Denis Kearney, had organized the Workingmen's Party of California, whose platform called for an end to further Chinese immigration. A gifted agitator, himself only recently naturalized, Kearney harangued the "sand lotters" about the "foreign peril" and assaulted the rich railroad barons for exploiting the poor. In 1878 his new party won a hefty number of seats to a state constitutional convention. The Workingmen's movement peaked in 1879, when it elected many members to the state legislature and the mayor of San Francisco. Kearney lacked the gift for building a durable movement, but as his party went to pieces, his anti-Chinese theme became a national issue—in 1882, Congress voted to prohibit Chinese immigration for ten years.

TOWARD PERMANENT UNIONS Meanwhile, efforts to build a permanent labor-union movement were gaining momentum. Earlier efforts, in the 1830s and 1840s, had largely been dominated by reformers with schemes that ranged from free homesteads to utopian socialism. But the 1850s witnessed the beginning of "job-conscious" unions in selected skilled trades.

By 1860 there were about twenty such unions, and during the Civil War, because of the demand for labor, those craft unions grew in strength and number.

There was no overall federation of such groups until 1866, when the National Labor Union convened in Baltimore. The NLU comprised delegates from labor and reform groups more interested in political and social change than in bargaining with employers. The groups espoused such ideas as the eight-hour workday, workers' cooperatives, paper money, and equal rights for women and African Americans. But the organization lost momentum after the death of its president in 1869, and by 1872 it had entirely collapsed. The NLU was not a total failure, however. It was influential in persuading Congress to enact an eight-hour workday for federal employees and to repeal the 1864 Contract Labor Act, which allowed employers to bind immigrant (contract) laborers by paying for their passage from Europe. That those immigrants were willing to work for low wages made them unpopular with American workers.

THE KNIGHTS OF LABOR   Before the National Labor Union collapsed, another labor group of national standing had emerged: the Noble Order of the Knights of Labor, a name that evoked the aura of medieval guilds. The founder of the Knights of Labor, Uriah S. Stephens, a Philadelphia tailor, was a habitual joiner involved with several secret orders, including the Masons. Secrecy, he felt, along with a semireligious ritual, would protect members from retaliation by employers and create a sense of solidarity.

The Knights of Labor, started in 1869, grew slowly, but during the years of depression after 1873, as other unions collapsed, it spread more rapidly. Throughout its existence the Knights emphasized reform measures and preferred boycotts to strikes as a way to put pressure on employers. It also had a liberal membership policy, welcoming all who had ever worked for wages, except lawyers, doctors, bankers, and those who sold liquor. Theoretically it was one big union of all workers, skilled and unskilled, regardless of race, color, creed, or sex. In the 1880s membership in the Knights grew rapidly, from about 100,000 to more than 700,000 in 1886. But the organization peaked in 1886 and went into rapid decline after the failure of a railroad strike.

ANARCHISM   The tensions between labor and management during the late nineteenth century in the United States and Europe helped generate interest in the doctrine of anarchism. Anarchists believed that government— any government—was in itself an abusive device used by the rich and powerful to oppress and exploit the working poor. Anarchists dreamed of the eventual

Members of the Knights of Labor

This national union was more egalitarian than most of its contemporaries.

disappearance of government altogether, and many of them believed that the transition to this stateless society could be hurried along by promoting revolutionary action among the masses. One favored tactic was the use of dramatic acts of violence against representatives of the government. A number of European anarchists emigrated to the United States during the last quarter of the nineteenth century, bringing with them their belief in the impact of "propaganda of the deed."

THE HAYMARKET AFFAIR Labor-related violence had been increasing during the 1880s, and on May 3, 1886, Chicago's International Harvester plant was the site of a clash between strikers and policemen in which one striker was killed. Leaders of a minuscule anarchist movement in Chicago scheduled an open meeting the following night at Haymarket Square to protest the killing. Under a light drizzle the crowd listened to long speeches promoting socialism and anarchism and was beginning to break up when a group of policemen arrived and called upon the activists to disperse. At that point someone threw a bomb at the police, killing one officer and wounding others. The police fired on the demonstrators, killing four. Six more policemen were also killed. Subsequently, in a trial marked by prejudice and hysteria, seven anarchist leaders were sentenced to death despite the lack of any evidence linking them to the bomb thrower, whose identity was never established. Of the seven, two were reprieved, one committed suicide in prison, and four were hanged. All but one of the group were German speaking, and that one held a membership card in the Knights of Labor.

By the turn of the century, the Knights were but a memory. Several factors accounted for their decline: a leadership devoted more to ideas than to pragmatic organization, the failure of the Knights' cooperative enterprises, and a preoccupation with politics rather than negotiations with management. The Knights nevertheless attained some lasting achievements, among them the creation of the federal Bureau of Labor Statistics and the Foran Act of 1885, which penalized employers who imported contract laborers from abroad. The Knights also spread the idea of unionism and initiated a new type of union organization: the industrial union, an industrywide union of skilled and unskilled workers.

GOMPERS AND THE AFL   The craft unions (skilled workers) opposed the industrial unionism of the Knights. Leaders of the crafts unions feared that joining with unskilled laborers would mean a loss of their craft's identity and a loss of the skilled workers' greater bargaining power. Thus in the summer of 1886, delegates from craft unions met at Columbus, Ohio, and organized the American Federation of Labor (AFL). In structure it differed from that of the Knights in that it was a federation of national craft organizations, each of which retained a large degree of autonomy and exercised greater leverage against management.

Samuel Gompers served as president of the AFL from its start until his death, in 1924, with only one year's interruption. Born in England of Dutch Jewish ancestry, Gompers came to the United States as a teenager, joined the Cigarmakers' Union in 1864, and became president of his New York local in 1877. Gompers and other leaders of the union focused on concrete economic gains—higher wages, shorter hours, better working conditions—and avoided involvement with utopian ideas or politics.

Gompers had a thick hide, liked to talk and drink with workers in the back room, and advocated the strike to achieve labor's objectives. His preference, though, was to achieve those objectives through agreements with management that included provisos for union recognition in the form of closed shops (which could hire only union members) or union-preference shops (which could hire others only if no union members were available).

The AFL at first grew slowly, but by 1890 it had already surpassed the Knights of Labor in membership. By the turn of the century, it claimed 500,000 members in affiliated unions; in 1914, on the eve of World War I, it had 2 million; and in 1920 it reached a peak of 4 million. But even then the AFL embraced less than 15 percent of the nation's nonagricultural workers. All unions, including the unaffiliated railroad brotherhoods, accounted for little more than 18 percent of those workers. Organized labor's strongholds were in transportation and the building trades. Most of the larger manufacturing industries—including textiles, tobacco, and packinghouses—remained almost untouched.

THE HOMESTEAD STRIKE   Two violent labor incidents in the 1890s scarred the emerging industrial-union movement and set it back for forty years: the Homestead steel strike of 1892 and the Pullman strike of 1894. Those dramatic labor conflicts in several respects represented the culminating events of the Gilded Age, a bewildering era during which huge corporations came to exercise overweening influence over American life. Both events pitted organized labor in a bitter contest against two of the nation's largest and most influential corporations. In both cases the stakes were enormous. The two strikes not only represented a test of strength for the organized labor movement but also served to reshape the political landscape at the end of the nineteenth century.

The Amalgamated Association of Iron and Steel Workers, founded in 1876, had by 1891 a membership of more than 24,000 and was probably the largest craft union at the time. But it excluded unskilled steelworkers and had failed to organize the larger steel plants. The massive Homestead Works near Pittsburgh was an important exception. There the union, which included a fourth of Homestead's 3,800 workers, had enjoyed friendly relations with Andrew Carnegie's company until Henry Clay Frick became its president in 1889. A showdown was delayed until 1892, however, when the union contract came up for renewal. Carnegie, who had expressed sympathy for unions in the past, had gone on a lengthy hunting trip to his native Scotland and left matters in Frick's hands. Yet Carnegie knew what was afoot: a cost-cutting reduction in the number of higher-paid skilled workers and a deliberate attempt to smash the union. "Am with you to the end," he wrote to Frick.

As negotiations dragged on, the company announced on June 25 that it would deal with workers as individuals unless an agreement with the union was reached by June 29. A strike—or, more properly, a lockout of unionists—began on that date. Even before the negotiations ended, Frick had begun barricading the plant and had hired as plant guards 300 Pinkerton detectives whose specialty was union busting. On July 6, 1892, a fourteen-hour battle erupted, in which seven workers and three Pinkertons died. In the end the Pinkertons surrendered and marched away, taunted and beaten by crowds in the street. Six days later 8,500 state militiamen appeared at the plant to protect the strikebreakers hired to restore production. The strike dragged on until

November, but by then the union was dead, its leaders charged with murder and treason. Its cause was not helped when an anarchist, a Lithuanian immigrant, tried to assassinate Frick, shooting him twice and stabbing him four times. Much of the local sympathy for the strikers evaporated.

Penniless and demoralized, the defeated workers ended their walkout on November 20 and accepted the company's terms. Only a fifth of the strikers were hired back. Carnegie and Frick, with the support of local, state, and national government officials, had eliminated the union. Across the nation in 1892, state militias intervened to quash twenty-three labor disputes. In the ongoing struggles between workers and owners, big business held sway—in the workplace and in state governments. The Homestead strike was symptomatic of the overweening power of industrial capitalism. By 1899, Andrew Carnegie could report to a friend: "Ashamed to tell you [of my] profits these days. Prodigious!"

THE PULLMAN STRIKE Even more than Homestead, the Pullman strike of 1894 was a notable walkout in American history. It paralyzed the economies of the twenty-seven states and territories making up the western half of the nation. It grew out of a dispute at Pullman, Illinois, a model corporate town built on 4,000 acres outside Chicago, where workers of the Pullman Palace Car Company were housed in neat brick homes nestled on grassy lots along shaded streets. The town's idyllic appearance was deceptive, however. Employees were required to live there, pay rents and utility costs that were higher than those in nearby towns, and buy their goods from company stores. With the onset of the depression of 1893, George Pullman laid off 3,000 of his 5,800 employees and cut wages 25 to 40 percent, but not his rents and other charges. After Pullman fired three members of a workers' grievance committee, a strike began on May 11, 1894.

During this tense period, Pullman workers had been joining the new American Railway Union, founded the previous year by Eugene V. Debs. A charismatic man who led by example and the electric force of his convictions, Debs was a tireless spokesman for labor radicalism who strove to organize *all* railway workers—skilled and unskilled—into the American Railway Union. His earnest appeal generated a tremendous response, and soon he was in charge of a powerful new labor organization. He quickly turned his attention to the controversy in Pullman, Illinois.

In June 1894, after George Pullman refused Debs's plea for arbitration, the union workers stopped handling Pullman railcars. By the end of July they had tied up most of the railroads in the Midwest. The rail owners hired strikebreakers ("scabs") to connect mail cars to Pullman cars so that interference

Eugene V. Debs

Founder of the American Railway Union and later candidate for president as head of the Socialist Party of America.

with Pullman cars would entail interference with the federal mail. U.S. Attorney General Richard Olney, a former railroad attorney, swore in 3,400 special deputies to keep the trains running. When clashes occurred between the deputies and some of the strikers, lawless elements ignored Debs's plea for an orderly boycott and repeated some of the violent scenes of the 1877 strike.

Finally, on July 3, 1894, President Grover Cleveland answered an appeal from the railroads to send federal troops into the Chicago area, where the strike was centered. Illinois governor John Peter Altgeld issued a vigorous protest, insisting that the state could keep order, but Cleveland claimed authority and a duty to ensure delivery of the mail. "If it takes every dollar in the Treasury and every soldier in the United States to deliver a postal card in Chicago," he vowed, "that postal card should be delivered."

As strikers clashed with troops and burned hundreds of railcars, the federal district court granted an injunction forbidding any interference with the mail or any effort to restrain interstate commerce. On July 13 the union called off the strike, and a few days later the district court cited Debs for violating the injunction, and he served six months in jail. The Supreme Court upheld the decree in the case of *In re Debs* (1895) on broad grounds of national sovereignty. Debs served his term, during which he read deeply in socialist literature, and he emerged to devote the rest of his life to socialism.

SOCIALISM AND THE UNIONS   The major American unions for the most part never allied themselves with socialists, as many European labor movements did. Although socialist ideas had been circulating in the United States at least since the 1820s, the movement gained little notice before the rise of Daniel De Leon in the 1890s as the dominant figure in the Socialist Labor party. De Leon proposed to organize industrial unions with a socialist purpose and to build a political party that would abolish the state once it gained power. His ideas seem to have influenced Vladimir Lenin, leader of Russia's Bolshevik revolution of 1917, but De Leon preached revolution at the ballot box, not by violence.

To many, De Leon seemed doctrinaire and inflexible. Eugene Debs was therefore more successful at building a socialist movement in America. In 1897, Debs announced that he was a socialist and organized the Social Democratic party from the remnants of the American Railway Union; he received over 96,000 votes as its candidate for president in 1900. In 1901 his followers joined a number of secessionists from De Leon's party, led by Morris Hillquit of New York, to set up the Socialist Party of America. Debs polled over 400,000 votes as the party's candidate for president in 1904 and more than doubled that, to more than 900,000 votes, or 6 percent of the popular vote, in 1912.

By 1912 the Socialist party seemed well on the way to becoming a permanent fixture in American politics. Thirty-three cities had Socialist mayors. The party sponsored five English-language daily newspapers, eight foreign-language dailies, and a number of weeklies and monthlies. In the Southwest the party built a sizable grassroots following among farmers and tenants. But it reached its peak in 1912. It would be racked by disagreements over America's participation in World War I and was split thereafter.

THE WOBBLIES   During the years of Socialist party growth, a parallel effort to revive industrial unionism emerged, led by the Industrial Workers of the World (IWW), nicknamed the Wobblies. The chief base for this group was the Western Federation of Miners, organized at Butte, Montana, in 1893. Like the Knights of Labor, it was designed to include all workers, skilled or unskilled. Its roots were in the mining and lumber camps of the West, where unstable conditions of employment created a large number of nomadic workers, to whom neither the AFL's pragmatic approach nor the socialists' political appeal held much attraction. The revolutionary goal of the Wobblies was an idea labeled syndicalism by its French supporters: the ultimate destruction of the state and its replacement by one big union. How that union would govern remained vague.

The Wobblies reached out to the fringe elements with the least power and influence, chiefly the migratory workers of the West and the ethnic groups of the East. Always ambivalent about diluting their revolutionary principles, Wobblies scorned the usual labor agreements even when they participated in them. They engaged in spectacular battles with employers but scored few victories. The largest was a textile strike at Lawrence, Massachusetts, in 1912; the strikers won wage raises, overtime pay, and other benefits. But the next year a strike of silk workers at Paterson, New Jersey, ended in disaster, and the IWW entered a rapid decline.

The fading of the movement was accelerated by the hysterical opposition the Wobblies aroused. Its members branded as anarchists, bums, and criminals, the IWW was effectively destroyed during World War I, when most of its leaders were jailed for their militant opposition to the war. Nonetheless, the Wobblies left behind a rich folklore of nomadic working folk and a gallery of heroic agitators.

A NATION TRANSFORMED

By the end of the nineteenth century, the accelerating Industrial Revolution had transformed the nature of work and social life, generated a new urban consciousness and culture, and unleashed rising class tensions. With each passing year, more and more people jettisoned traditional rural folkways in favor of urban environs and enticing economic and social opportunities. As centers of production and consumption, the new industrial cities controlled the pace of national life.

The Industrial Revolution occurred at different rates and produced different effects across the expanding nation. Despite the energetic efforts of New South boosters, the states of the former Confederacy, burdened by a chronic shortage of capital and a poorly educated populace, lagged well behind the rest of the nation in industrial development, urban expansion, and per capita income.

The recurring theme of American life after the Civil War was an acute sense of accelerated social and intellectual change. The velocity and scope of change at midcentury and after was bewildering. Some believed that the United States had lost much of its stability and cohesion as a result of urban-industrial development and western expansion. It had become a loose aggregate of competing individuals, separated from one another by economic differences and ethnic, racial, and class prejudices. How to restore a sense of community and cohesion would become the collective challenge of all Americans.

End of Chapter Review

CHAPTER SUMMARY

- **Second Industrial Revolution** The postwar economy was characterized by large-scale industrial development and a burgeoning agriculture sector. The Second Industrial Revolution was fueled by the creation of national transportation and communications systems, the use of electric power, and the application of scientific research to industrial processes. The federal government encouraged growth by imposing high tariffs and granting the railroad companies public land.

- **Rising Big Business** The leading entrepreneurs were extraordinarily skilled at organizing and controlling industry. John D. Rockefeller eventually controlled nearly every facet of the oil industry, consolidating that control through trusts and holding companies. Andrew Carnegie, who believed that competition benefited both society and business, came to dominate the steel industry by buying struggling companies. J. Pierpont Morgan, an investment banker, not only controlled most of the nation's railroads but also bought Carnegie's steel interests in 1901, thereby creating the nation's first billion-dollar company.

- **Labor Conditions and Organizations** The labor force was largely composed of unskilled workers, including recent immigrants and growing numbers of women and children. Some children as young as eight years of age worked twelve hours a day in coal mines and southern mills. In hard times, business owners cut wages without discounting the rents they charged for company housing or the prices they charged in company stores.

- **Rising Labor Unions** It was difficult for unskilled workers to organize effectively. Strikebreakers were plentiful because new immigrants were desperate for work. Business owners often had recourse to state and local militias, which would be mobilized against strikers in the face of perceived anarchy. Craft unions became more successful at organizing as the American Federation of Labor focused on concrete economic gains and better working conditions and avoided involvement in politics.

CHRONOLOGY

1855	Bessemer converter process allows steel to be made quickly and inexpensively
1859	First oil well is struck, in Titusville, Pennsylvania
1869	First transcontinental railroad is completed, at Promontory, Utah
1876	Alexander Graham Bell patents his telephone
1876	Thomas A. Edison makes the first successful incandescent lightbulb
1877	Great Railroad Strike
1882	John D. Rockefeller organizes the Standard Oil Trust
1886	In the Haymarket incident, a bomb set off at a Chicago labor rally kills and wounds police officers
1886	American Federation of Labor is organized
1892	Homestead Strike
1894	Pullman Strike
1901	J. Pierpont Morgan creates the U.S. Steel Corporation

KEY TERMS & NAMES

21

THE EMERGENCE OF URBAN AMERICA

FOCUS QUESTIONS wwnorton.com/studyspace

- What accounted for the rise of cities in America?
- How did the "new immigration" change America at the end of the nineteenth century?
- What new forms of mass entertainment had emerged by 1900?
- What was the impact of Darwinian thought on social sciences?
- What were some of the literary and philosophical trends of the late nineteenth century?

Cities are humanity's greatest creation. And in America during the second half of the nineteenth century, cities grew at a rate unparalleled in world history. The late nineteenth century, declared an economist in 1899, was "not only the age of cities, but the age of great cities." Between 1860 and 1910 the urban population of the United States mushroomed from 6 million to 44 million. By 1920 more than half the nation's population lived in urban areas. The rise of big cities created a distinctive urban culture. People from different ethnic and religious backgrounds and every walk of life poured into the high-rise apartment buildings and congested tenements springing up in every major city. They came in search of jobs, wealth, and excitement.

Not surprisingly, the rise of metropolitan America created an array of social problems. Rapid urban development produced widespread poverty and political corruption. It also produced dirt and disease, crowded housing, and unsafe working conditions in factories, mines, mills, and slaughterhouses.

People needed basic services, such as education, transportation, sewers, fresh water, inoculations against disease, and factory inspections to prevent unsafe working conditions. Broadened access to public education and to public health services would eventually improve literacy and lower infant mortality rates. Breakthroughs in medical science would bring cures for tuberculosis, typhoid, and diphtheria—although those infectious diseases would remain the century's leading killers. But in the meantime, the question of how to feed, clothe, shelter, and educate the new arrivals taxed the imagination and patience of many urban leaders.

AMERICA'S MOVE TO TOWN

The prospect of good jobs and social excitement lured people to the cities from the countryside and overseas. City people became recognizably urban in demeanor and outlook. The contrasts between farm and city life grew more vivid with each passing year.

EXPLOSIVE URBAN GROWTH   The frontier was a safety valve for urban unrest, the historian Frederick Jackson Turner said in his influential thesis on American development. Its cheap lands afforded a release for the population pressures mounting in the cities. If there were such a thing as a safety valve in his own time, however, he had it exactly backward. The flow of population toward cities was greater than the flow toward the West. Much of the westward migration in fact was itself an urban movement, spawning new towns near the mining digs or at the railheads. On the Pacific coast a greater proportion of the population was urbanized than anywhere else; its major concentrations were first around San Francisco Bay and then in Los Angeles, which became a boomtown after the arrival of the Southern Pacific and Santa Fe Railroads in the 1880s. In the Northwest, Seattle also grew quickly, first as the terminus of three transcontinental railroad lines and, by the end of the century, as the staging area for the Yukon gold rush. Minneapolis, St. Paul, Omaha, Kansas City, and Denver were no longer the mere villages they had been in 1860. The South, too, produced new cities: Durham, North Carolina, and Birmingham, Alabama, which were centers of tobacco and iron production, and Houston, Texas, which handled cotton and cattle and, later, oil. The industrial explosion powered the growth of new cities during this period.

Several technological innovations enabled cities to expand vertically to accommodate their surging populations. In the 1870s, innovations in heating,

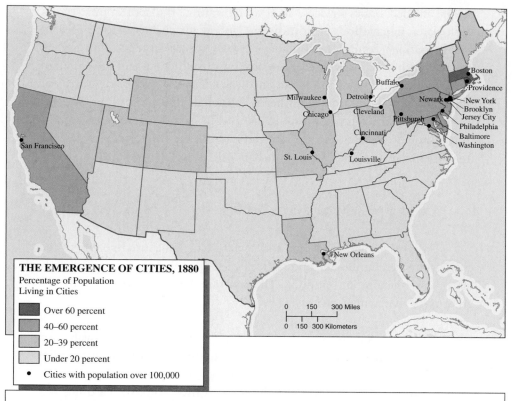

THE EMERGENCE OF CITIES, 1880
Percentage of Population
Living in Cities

- Over 60 percent
- 40–60 percent
- 20–39 percent
- Under 20 percent
- • Cities with population over 100,000

Which states had the largest urban population in 1880? What drove the growth of western cities? How were western cities different from eastern cities?

such as steam circulating through pipes and radiators, contributed to the building of multiple-apartment dwellings, since fireplaces were no longer needed. In 1889 the Otis Elevator Company installed the first electric elevator, which made possible the erection of taller buildings—before the Civil War few structures had risen higher than three or four stories. During the 1880s, engineers developed cast-iron and steel-frame structures, which were stronger than brick and thereby enabled the construction of "skyscrapers," which depend on steel frames and girders.

Cities also expanded horizontally after the introduction of important transportation innovations. Before the 1890s the chief power sources of urban transport were either animals or steam. Horse- and mule-drawn streetcars had appeared in antebellum cities, but they were slow and cumbersome, and cleaning up manure from the streets added to their cost. In 1873, San

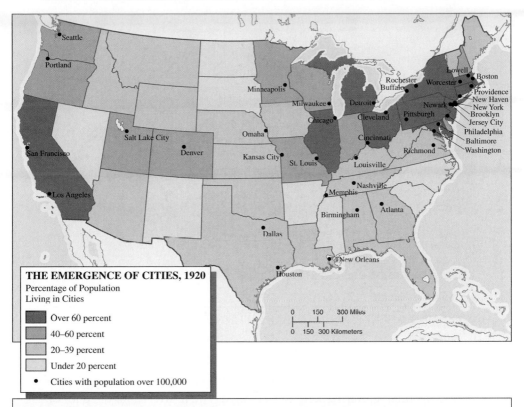

THE EMERGENCE OF CITIES, 1920
Percentage of Population
Living in Cities

Over 60 percent
40–60 percent
20–39 percent
Under 20 percent
• Cities with population over 100,000

How did technology change urban life in the early twentieth century? What was the role of mass transit in expanding the urban population? How did the demographics of the new cities change between 1880 and 1920?

Francisco became the first city to use cars pulled by steam-driven cables. Some cities used steam-powered commuter trains on elevated tracks, but by the 1890s electric trolleys were preferred. Mass transportation received an added boost around the turn of the century, when subway systems began to operate in Boston, New York, and Philadelphia.

The spread of mass transit allowed large numbers of people to become commuters, and a growing middle class retreated from downtown to live in quieter tree-lined "streetcar suburbs," whence they could travel into the central city for business or entertainment (though laborers generally stayed put, unable to afford even the nickel fare). Urban growth often became a sprawl, since it usually took place without plan, in the interest of a fast buck, and without thought to the need for parks and public services.

Urban mass transit

A horse-drawn streetcar moving along rails in New York City.

THE ALLURE AND PROBLEMS OF THE CITIES The wonders of the cities—their glittering new electric lights, their streetcars, telephones, department stores, vaudeville shows and other amusements, newspapers and magazines, and a thousand other attractions—cast a magnetic lure on rural youth. The new cities threw into stark contrast the frustration of unending toil and the isolation of country life. In times of rural depression, thousands left farms for the cities in search of opportunity and personal freedom. Yet those who moved to the city often traded one set of problems for another. Workers in the big cities often had no choice but to live in crowded apartments, most of which were poorly designed. In 1900, Manhattan's 42,700 tenements housed almost 1.6 million people. Such unregulated urban growth created immense problems of health and morale.

During the last quarter of the nineteenth century, cities became so cramped and land so scarce that architects were forced to build upward. In New York City this resulted in tenement houses. These structures, usually six to eight stories tall and jammed tightly against one another, housed twenty-four to thirty-two families. Some city blocks housed almost 4,000 people. The early tenements were poorly heated and had communal toilets outside in a yard or alley. Shoehorned into their quarters, families had no privacy,

Urbanization and the environment

A garbage cart retrieves trash in New York City, ca. 1890

free space, or sunshine; children had few places to play except in the streets; infectious diseases and noxious odors were rampant. Not surprisingly, the mortality rate among the urban poor was much higher than that of the general population. In one poor Chicago district at the end of the century, three out of five babies died before their first birthday.

CITY POLITICS   The sheer size of the cities helped create a new form of politics to coordinate citywide services such as public transportation, sanitation, and utilities. Urban political machines thus developed, consisting of local committeemen, district captains, and ultimately a political boss. While the bosses granted patronage favors (awarding city jobs to supporters) and engaged in graft, buying votes and taking kickbacks, they also provided needed services. They distributed food, coal, and money to the poor; found jobs for those who were out of work; sponsored English-language classes for immigrants; organized sports teams, social clubs, and neighborhood gatherings; fixed problems at city hall; and generally helped newcomers adjust to their new life. In return the political professionals felt entitled to some reward for having done the grubby work of the local organization.

CITIES AND THE ENVIRONMENT   Nineteenth-century cities were filthy and disease ridden, noisy and smelly. They overflowed with garbage, contaminated water, horse manure, roaming pigs, and untreated sewage. Providing clean water was a chronic problem, and raw sewage was dumped into streets and waterways. Epidemics of water-related diseases such as cholera, typhoid fever, and yellow fever ravaged populations. Animal waste was pervasive. In 1900, for example, there were over 3.5 million horses in American cities, each of which generated 20 pounds of manure and several gallons of urine daily. In Chicago alone, 82,000 horses produced 300,000 tons of manure each year. The life expectancy of urban draft horses was only two years, which meant that thousands of horse carcasses had to be disposed of each year. In New York City, 15,000 dead horses were removed annually.

During the late nineteenth century, municipal reformers organized to clean up the cities. The "sanitary reformers"—public health officials and municipal engineers—persuaded city governments to banish hogs and cattle, mount cleanup campaigns, establish water and sewage systems, institute trash collection, and replace horses with electric streetcars. By 1900, 94 percent of American cities had developed regular trash-collection services.

Yet such improvements in public health involved important social and ecological trade-offs and caused unanticipated problems. Waste that once had been put into the land was now dumped into waterways. Similarly, solving the horse-manure problem involved trade-offs. The manure dropped on city streets caused stench and bred countless flies, many of which carried diseases such as typhoid fever. But urban horse manure also had benefits. Farmers living on the outskirts of cities used it to fertilize hay and vegetable crops. City-generated manure was the agricultural lifeblood of the vegetable farms outside New York, Baltimore, Philadelphia, and Boston.

Ultimately, however, the development of public water and sewer systems and flush toilets separated urban dwellers and their waste from the agricultural cycle at the same time that the emergence of refrigerated railcars and massive meatpacking plants separated most people from their sources of food. While the advances provided great benefits, a flush-and-forget-it mentality emerged. Well into the twentieth century, people presumed that running water purified itself, so they dumped massive amounts of untreated waste into rivers and bays. The high phosphorous content of bodily waste dumped into streams led to algae blooms that sucked the oxygen out of the water and unleashed a string of environmental reactions that suffocated fish and affected marine ecology.

THE NEW IMMIGRATION

The Industrial Revolution during the second half of the nineteenth century brought to American shores waves of immigrants from every part of the globe. By 1900 nearly 30 percent of the residents of major cities were foreign-born. These newcomers provided much-needed labor, but their arrival also generated ugly racial and ethnic tensions.

AMERICA'S PULL   The migration of foreigners to the United States has been one of the most powerful forces shaping American history, and this was especially true after the Civil War. The tide of immigration rose from just under 3 million in the 1870s to more than 5 million in the 1880s, then fell to a little over 3.5 million in the depression decade of the 1890s and rose to its high-water mark of 8.8 million in the first decade of the new century. Immigrants moved from the agricultural areas of eastern and southern Europe directly to the cities of America. Once in the United States, they wanted to live with others of like language, customs, and religion, and they lacked the means to go west and settle on farms.

This nation of immigrants continued to draw new inhabitants for much the same reasons as before and from much the same segments of society. Immigrants took flight from famine, cholera, or the lack of economic opportunity in their native lands. They fled racial, religious, and political persecution and compulsory military service.

Yet more immigrants were probably pulled by America's opportunities than were pushed out by conditions at home. American industries, seeking cheap labor, sent recruiters abroad. Railroads, eager to sell land and build up the traffic on their lines, distributed tempting propaganda in a medley of languages. Under the Contract Labor Act of 1864, the federal government itself encouraged immigration: it allowed companies to recruit foreign workers by paying for their passage and then recouping the money from the immigrants' wages. The law was repealed in 1868, but not until 1885 did the government forbid companies to import contract labor, a practice that put immigrants under the control of their employers.

A NEW WAVE   Before 1880 immigrants were mainly from northern and western Europe. By the 1870s, however, that pattern had begun to change. The proportion of immigrants from southern and eastern Europe rose sharply. After 1890 they made up a majority of the newcomers, and by the first decade of the new century they formed 70 percent of the immigrants to the United

States. Among these new immigrants were Italians, Hungarians, Czechs, Slovaks, Poles, Serbs, Croats, Russians, Romanians, and Greeks—all people whose culture and language were markedly different from those of western Europe and whose religion for the most part was Judaism or Catholicism.

ELLIS ISLAND   Most immigrants arriving in America passed through a reception center on a tiny island off the New Jersey coast, a mile south of Manhattan, near the Statue of Liberty. In 1892, Ellis Island opened its doors to the "huddled masses" of the world. In 1907, the reception center's busiest year, more than 1 million new arrivals passed through the receiving center, an average of about 5,000 per day; in one day alone, immigration officials processed some 11,750.

MAKING THEIR WAY   Once on American soil, immigrants felt exhilaration, exhaustion, and usually a desperate need for work. Many were greeted by family and friends who had arrived earlier, others by representatives of the many immigrant-aid societies or by agents offering the men jobs

Steerage deck of the S.S. *Pennland*, 1893

These immigrants are about to arrive at Ellis Island in New York Harbor. Many newcomers to America settled in cities because they lacked the means to take up farming.

in mines, mills, or sweatshops. Since most immigrants knew little if any English and nothing about American employment practices, they were easy subjects for exploitation. In exchange for some whiskey and a job, obliging recruiters claimed a healthy percentage of their wages. Among Italians and Greeks these agents were known as padrones, and they came to dominate the labor market in New York. Other contractors provided train tickets to cities such as Buffalo, Pittsburgh, Cleveland, Chicago, Milwaukee, Cincinnati, and St. Louis.

Strangers in a new land, most of the immigrants gravitated to neighborhoods populated by their own kind. The immigrant enclaves—nicknamed Little Italy, Little Hungary, Chinatown, and so on—served as crucial transitional communities between the newcomers' Old World past and their New World future. In such kinship communities, immigrants practiced their religion, clung to their native customs, and conversed in their native tongue. But they paid a price for such community solidarity. When the "new immigrants" moved into an area, older residents typically moved out, taking with them whatever social prestige and political influence they had achieved. The

The Registry Room at Ellis Island

Inspectors asked arriving passengers twenty-nine probing questions, including "Are you a polygamist?"

quality of life quickly deteriorated as housing and sanitation codes then went unenforced.

THE NATIVIST RESPONSE   Then, as now, many native-born Americans saw the wave of new immigration as a threat, and the undercurrent of nativism so often present in American culture surfaced during the late nineteenth century, mainly expressed in anti-Catholic and anti-Semitic sentiments. But more than religious prejudice underlay hostility toward the latest newcomers. Cultural differences confirmed in the minds of nativists the assumption that the Nordic peoples of the old immigration were superior to the Slavic, Italian, Greek, and Jewish peoples of the new immigration. Many of the new immigrants were illiterate, and more appeared so because they could not speak English. Some resorted to crime, and political and social radicals turned up in sufficient numbers to encourage nativists to blame labor disputes on alien elements.

Nativism led to a movement to restrict immigration, but it had mixed success beyond the exclusion of certain individuals deemed undesirable. In 1891, Congressman Henry Cabot Lodge of Massachusetts took up the cause of excluding illiterates, a measure that would have affected much of the new wave of immigrants even though literacy in English was not required. Bills embodying the restriction passed Congress several times during the next twenty-five years but were vetoed by Presidents Grover Cleveland, William H. Taft, and Woodrow Wilson. In 1917, however, Congress overrode Wilson's veto.

Advocates of immigration restriction during the late nineteenth century did succeed in excluding the Chinese, who were victims of every act of discrimination that the new European immigrants suffered and more. They were not white; they were not Christian; many were not literate. By 1880 there were some 75,000 Chinese in California, about a ninth of the state's population. Railroad owners found them hardworking. Many white workers, however, resented them for accepting lower wages, but their greater sin, a New York newspaper editor stressed, was perpetuating "those disgusting habits of thrift, industry, and self-denial."

Exclusion of the Chinese began in 1880, when the urgent need for railway labor had ebbed. A new treaty with China permitted the United States to "regulate, limit, and suspend" Chinese immigration, and in 1882 Congress passed a bill authorizing a ten-year suspension of Chinese immigration. The legislation closing the doors to Chinese immigrants received overwhelming support. The Chinese Exclusion Act was periodically renewed before being extended indefinitely in 1902. Not until 1943 were barriers to Chinese immigration finally removed.

Although the Chinese Exclusion Act sharply reduced the flow of Chinese immigrants, it did not stop the influx completely. In 1910 the West Coast counterpart to Ellis Island opened on rugged Angel Island, six miles offshore from San Francisco, to process tens of thousands of Asian immigrants, most of them Chinese. Those arrivals from China, who could claim a Chinese-American parent were allowed to enter, as were certain officials, teachers, merchants, and students. The powerful prejudice the Chinese immigrants encountered helps explain why over 30 percent of the arrivals at Angel Island were denied entry.

POPULAR CULTURE

The sprawling new cities created new patterns of recreation and leisure. Popular culture took on new or greatly expanded dimensions that endowed life with a more cosmopolitan quality. For example, traveling circuses brought entertainment to small towns as well as large cities. Creative promoters such as Phineas T. Barnum and James A. Bailey made the circus the most eclectic form of entertainment. In the congested metropolitan areas, politics became as much a form of public entertainment as it was a means of providing civic representation and public services. People flocked to hear visiting candidates give speeches in cavernous halls, on outdoor plazas, or from railway cars. In cities such as New York, Philadelphia, Boston, and Chicago, membership in a political party was akin to belonging to a social club. In addition, labor unions provided activities that were more social than economic in nature, and members often visited the union hall as much to socialize as to discuss working conditions. The sheer number of people congregated in cities also helped generate a market for new forms of mass entertainment, such as traveling Wild West shows, vaudeville shows, and spectator sports.

VAUDEVILLE   Growing family incomes and innovations in urban transportation—cable cars, subways, electric streetcars and streetlights—enabled more people to take advantage of urban cultural life. By far the most popular—and most diverse—form of theatrical entertainment in the late nineteenth century was vaudeville. The term derives from a French word for a play accompanied by music. It emerged in the United States in seedy beer halls whose owners sought to attract more customers by offering a free show.

Early "variety" shows featured comedians, singers, musicians, blackface minstrels, farcical plays, animal acts, jugglers, gymnasts, dancers, mimes, and magicians. Vaudeville houses became popular gathering places for all social

Vaudeville

For as little as one cent, Vaudeville offered entertainment to customers.

classes and types—men, women, and children—all of whom were expected to behave according to middle-class standards of gentility and decorum.

SALOON CULTURE The most popular destinations for working-class Americans with free time were saloons and dance halls. The saloon was the poor-man's social club during the late nineteenth century. By 1900 there were more saloons in the United States than there were grocery stores and meat markets. New York City alone had 10,000, or one for every 500 residents. Chicago had one saloon for every 335 people; Houston, one for every 300; San Francisco, one for every 215. Often sponsored by beer brewers and frequented by local politicians, saloons offered a free lunch to encourage patrons to visit and buy 5¢ beer or 15¢ whiskey.

Saloons provided much more than food and drink, however; they were in effect public homes, offering haven and fellowship to people who often worked ten hours a day, six days a week. Saloons were especially popular among male immigrants seeking friends and companionship in a new land. Saloons served as busy social hubs and were often aligned with local political machines. In New York City in the 1880s, most of the primary elections and local political caucuses were conducted in saloons. Saloons were defiantly male enclaves. Although women and children occasionally entered a saloon—through a side door—in order to carry home a pail of beer (called "rushing the growler") or to drink at a backroom party, the main bar at the front was for men only. Some saloons provided "snugs," small separate rooms for female patrons.

Saloons aroused intense criticism. Anti-liquor societies such as the Women's Christian Temperance Union and the Anti-Saloon League charged that saloons contributed to alcoholism, divorce, crime, and absenteeism from work. The reformers demanded that saloons be closed down. Yet drunkenness in saloons was the exception rather than the rule. Most patrons of working-class saloons had little money to waste, and recent studies have revealed that the average amount of money spent on liquor was no more than 5 percent of a man's annual income. Saloons were the primary locus of the workingman's leisure time and political activity. As a journalist observed, "The saloon is, in short, the social and intellectual center of the neighborhood."

OUTDOOR RECREATION   The congestion and disease associated with city life led many people to participate in forms of outdoor recreation intended to restore their vitality and improve their health. People sought places within the city to escape the tenements and the factories and offices. New York City in the 1850s set up a park commission, which hired Frederick Law Olmsted to design and plan Central Park. Olmsted went on to design parks for Boston, Brooklyn, Chicago, Philadelphia, and San Francisco. Although originally intended as places where people could walk and commune with nature, parks soon offered more vigorous forms of exercise and recreation. Croquet lawns and tennis courts were among the first additions because they took up little space and required little maintenance.

Even more popular than croquet or tennis was cycling, or "wheeling." In the 1870s, bicycles began to be manufactured in the United States, and by the end of the century a bicycle craze had swept the country. Bicycles were especially popular with women who chafed at the restricting conventions of the Victorian era. The new vehicles offered exercise, freedom, and access to the countryside.

The urban working poor could not afford to acquire a bicycle or join a croquet club, however. Nor did they have as much free time as the affluent. They toiled long hours six days a week, and at the end of their long days and on Sundays they sought recreation and fellowship on street corners or on the front stoops of their apartment buildings. Organ grinders and other musicians would perform on the sidewalks among the food vendors. Many ethnic groups, especially the Germans and the Irish, formed male singing,

Tandem tricycle

In spite of the danger and discomfort of early bicycles, "wheeling" became a popular form of recreation and mode of transportation.

drinking, or gymnastic clubs. Working folk also attended bare-knuckle boxing matches or baseball games and on Sundays would gather for picnics. By
the end of the century, large-scale amusement parks such as the one at
Brooklyn's Coney Island provided entertainment for the entire family. Yet
many inner-city youth could not afford the trolley fare, so the crowded
streets and dangerous alleys remained their playgrounds.

WORKINGWOMEN AND LEISURE   In contrast to the male public
culture centered in saloons, the leisure activities of working-class women,
many of them immigrants, were more limited at the end of the nineteenth
century. Married women were so encumbered by housework and maternal
responsibilities that they had little free time. Married working-class women
often used the streets as their public space. Washing clothes, supervising
children, or shopping at the local market provided opportunities for fellowship with other women.

Steeplechase Park, Coney Island, Brooklyn, New York

Members of the working class could afford the inexpensive rides at this popular amusement park.

Single women had more opportunities for leisure and recreation than did working mothers. They flocked to dance halls, theaters, amusement parks, and picnic grounds. On hot summer days many working-class folk went to public beaches. With the advent of movie theaters during the second decade of the twentieth century, the cinema became the most popular form of entertainment for women.

Young single women participated in urban amusements for a variety of reasons: escape, pleasure, companionship, and autonomy. As a promotional flyer for a movie theater promised, "If you are tired of life, go to the movies. If you are sick of troubles rife, go to the picture show. You will forget your unpaid bills, rheumatism and other ills, if you stow your pills and go to the picture show." Although some parents and social reformers tried to restrict young single women's freedom to engage in urban recreation and entertainment, many young women followed their own wishes and in so doing helped carve out their own social sphere.

SPECTATOR SPORTS   In the last quarter of the nineteenth century, new spectator sports such as college football and basketball and professional baseball gained mass appeal, reflecting the growing urbanization of life. People could gather easily for sporting events in the large cities. And news of the games could be conveyed quickly by newspapers and specialized sports magazines that relied upon telegraph reports. Saloons also posted the scores. Athletic rivalries between distant cities were made possible by the network of railroads spanning the continent. Spectator sports became urban extravaganzas, unifying the diverse ethnic groups in the large cities and attracting people with the leisure time and ready cash to spend on watching others perform—or bet on the outcome.

Football emerged as a modified form of soccer and rugby. The College of New Jersey (Princeton) and Rutgers played the first college football game in 1869. Some 200 students and other spectators saw Rutgers win, 6 to 4. By the end of the century, dozens of colleges and high schools had football teams, and some college games attracted more than 50,000 spectators.

Baseball card, 1887

The excitement of rooting for the home team united all classes.

Basketball was invented in 1891, when Dr. James Naismith, a physical education instructor, nailed two peach baskets to the walls of the Young Men's Christian Association training school in Springfield, Massachusetts. Naismith wanted to create an indoor winter game that could be played between the fall football and spring baseball seasons. Basketball quickly grew in popularity among boys and girls. All-female Vassar and Smith Colleges added the sport in 1892. In 1893, Vanderbilt University in Tennessee became the first college to field a men's team.

Baseball laid claim to being America's national pastime at midcentury. Contrary to popular opinion, Abner Doubleday did not invent the game. Instead, Alexander Cartwright, a New York bank clerk and sportsman, is recognized as the father of organized baseball. In 1845 he gathered a group of merchants, stockbrokers, and physicians to form the Knickerbocker Base Ball Club of New York.

The first professional baseball team was the Cincinnati Red Stockings, which made its appearance in 1869. In 1900 the American League was organized, and two years later the first World Series was held. Baseball became the national pastime and the most democratic sport in America. People from all social classes (mostly men) attended the games, and ethnic immigrants were among the most faithful fans. Cheering for a city baseball team gave uprooted people a common loyalty and a sense of belonging. Only white players were allowed in the major leagues, however. African Americans played on "minor league" teams or in all-black Negro leagues.

By the end of the nineteenth century, sports of all kinds had become a major cultural phenomenon in the United States. A writer for *Harper's Weekly* announced in 1895 that "ball matches, football games, tennis tournaments, bicycle races, [and] regattas, have become part of our national life." They "are watched with eagerness and discussed with enthusiasm and understanding by all manner of people, from the day-laborer to the millionaire."

EDUCATION AND THE PROFESSIONS

THE SPREAD OF PUBLIC EDUCATION   The growth of public education, spurred partly by the determination to "Americanize" immigrant children, helped quicken the emergence of a new urban society after the Civil War. In 1870 there were 7 million pupils in public schools; by 1920 the number had more than tripled. Despite such progress, leaders in education struggled to overcome a pattern of political appointments, corruption, and incompetence in the public schools.

The spread of secondary schools accounted for much of the increased enrollment. In antebellum America private academies had prepared those who intended to enter college. At the beginning of the Civil War, there were only about 100 public high schools in the whole country, but their number grew to about 800 in 1880 and to 6,000 at the turn of the century.

HIGHER EDUCATION   Colleges at this time sought to instill discipline and morality, with a curriculum heavy on mathematics and the classics (and, in church-related schools, theology), along with ethics and rhetoric. History, modern languages and literature, and some science courses were tolerated, although laboratory work was usually limited to a professor's demonstration in class.

The college-student population rose from 52,000 in 1870 to 157,000 in 1890 and 600,000 in 1920. During those years the number of institutions

Women as students

An astronomy class at Vassar College, 1880.

rose from 563 to about 1,000. To accommodate the diverse needs of these growing numbers, colleges moved from rigidly prescribed courses toward an elective system. The new approach allowed students to favor their strong points and colleges to expand their scope. But as the prominent Massachusetts politician Henry Cabot Lodge complained, it also allowed students to "escape without learning anything at all by a judicious selection of unrelated subjects taken up only because they were easy or because the burden imposed by those who taught them was light."

Colleges remained largely male enclaves, but women's access to higher education did improve markedly in the late nineteenth century. Before the Civil War a few colleges had already become coeducational, and state universities in the West were commonly open to women from the start. But colleges in the South and the East fell in line very slowly. Vassar, opened in 1865, was the first women's college to teach by the same standards as the best of the men's colleges. In the 1870s two more excellent women's schools appeared in Massachusetts: Wellesley and Smith, the latter being the first to set the same admission requirements as men's colleges. Thereafter the older women's colleges rushed to upgrade their standards in the same way.

The dominant new trend in American higher education after the Civil War was the rise of the graduate school. Heretofore most professors had a knowledge more broad than deep. With some notable exceptions they engaged in little research, nor were they expected to advance the frontiers of knowledge. Gradually, however, more and more American scholars studied at German universities, where training was more systematic and focused. After the Civil War the German system became the basis for the modern American graduate university. By the 1890s the doctorate degree was fast becoming a requirement for a professorship.

REALISM IN THOUGHT, CULTURE, AND LITERATURE

Much as popular culture was transformed as a result of the urban-industrial revolution, intellectual life adapted to new social realities. Before the Civil War various forms of idealism dominated American thought. Although quite diverse in motive and method, idealists shared a basic conviction that fundamental truths rested in the unseen world of ideas and spirit or in the distant past rather than in the tangible world of fact and contemporary experience. The most prominent writers, artists, and philosophers were more concerned with Romantic or biblical themes than with common aspects of "real" life.

At midcentury and after, however, a more realistic sensibility began to challenge this idealistic tradition. This realistic movement matured into a full-fledged cultural force during the second half of the nineteenth century. More and more thinkers, writers, and artists focused on the emerging realities of scientific research and technology, factories and railroads, cities and immigrants, wage labor and social tensions.

The rise of realism resulted from a transformed social, intellectual, and moral landscape. The horrors of the Civil War led many people to adopt a more realistic outlook, as did the growing influence of a modern scientific belief that empirical evidence constituted the only admissible basis for knowledge.

The prestige of empirical science increased enormously during the second half of the nineteenth century as researchers explored electromagnetic induction, the conservation of matter, the laws of thermodynamics, and the relationship between heat and energy. Breakthroughs in chemistry led to new understandings about the formation of compounds and the nature of reactions. Discoveries of fossils opened up new horizons in geology and paleontology, and greatly improved microscopes enabled zoologists to decipher cell structures.

Charles Darwin

Darwin's theories influenced more than a century of political debate.

DARWINISM AND SOCIAL DARWINISM Every field of thought in the post–Civil War years felt the impact of Charles Darwin's *On the Origin of Species* (1859). In that seminal work, Darwin argued that existing species, including humanity itself, had evolved through a long process of "natural selection" from less complex forms of life: those species that adapted to survival by reason of quickness, shrewdness, or other advantages reproduced their kind, while others died away. This idea of evolution shocked people who held conventional religious views in that it contradicted a literal interpretation of the creation stories in the biblical book of Genesis. Heated arguments arose between scientists and clergymen. Some of the faithful rejected Darwin's doctrine while others found their faith severely shaken. Many people, however, eventually came to reconcile science and religion, viewing evolution as a natural process created by God.

The temptation to apply evolutionary theory to the social (human) world proved irresistible. Darwin's fellow Englishman Herbert Spencer became the first major prophet of what came to be called social Darwinism, and he exerted an important influence on American thought. Spencer argued that human society and institutions, like plant and animal species, passed through the process of natural selection, which resulted in what he called the "survival of the fittest."

If, as Spencer believed, society naturally evolved for the better, then individual freedom was inviolable, and any government interference with the competitive process of social evolution was a serious mistake. Social Darwinism thus endorsed a hands-off government policy, then known as laissez-faire; it decried the government regulation of business, the proposals for a graduated income tax, sanitation and housing regulations, and even protection of consumers against medical quacks. Such initiatives, no matter how well intended, would only help the "unfit" survive and thereby impede progress. The only acceptable charity for social Darwinists was voluntary, and even that was of dubious value. Spencer warned that "fostering the good-for-nothing at the expense of the good, is an extreme cruelty."

For Spencer and his many supporters, successful businessmen and corporations were the engines of social progress. If small businesses were crowded out by trusts and monopolies, that too was part of the evolutionary process. Corporate titan John D. Rockefeller told his Baptist Sunday-school class that the "growth of a large business is merely a survival of the fittest."

REFORM DARWINISM   Herbert Spencer's use of Darwin to promote "rugged individualism" did not go without challenge. Reform found its major philosopher in an obscure civil servant, Lester Frank Ward, who fought his way up from poverty and never lost his empathy for the underdog. Ward's book *Dynamic Sociology* (1883) singled out one product of evolution that Spencer and others had neglected: the human brain. Humans, unlike animals, had a mind that could plan for and shape the future. Far from being the helpless pawn of powerful evolutionary forces, Ward argued, humanity could actively shape the process of societal improvement. The competition extolled by Spencer and other social Darwinists was in fact highly wasteful, as was the natural competitive process: plant or cattle breeding, for instance, could actually improve upon the results of natural selection.

Ward's so-called reform Darwinism held that cooperation, not competition, would best promote progress. Government could become the agency of progress by striving first to ameliorate poverty, which impeded the development of the mind, and then to promote the education of the masses. "Intelligence, far more than necessity," Ward wrote, "is the mother of invention," and "the influence of knowledge as a social factor, like that of wealth, is proportional to the extent of its distribution." Intellect, rightly informed by science, could plan successfully. In the benevolent "sociocracy" of the future, Ward argued, legislatures would function mainly to sanction decisions worked out in the sociological laboratory.

PRAGMATISM   Around the turn of the century, the concept of evolutionary human and social development found expression in a philosophical principle set forth in mature form by the Harvard professor William James in his book *Pragmatism: A New Name for Some Old Ways of Thinking* (1907). James shared Lester Frank Ward's concern with the role of ideas in the process of evolution. Pragmatists, said James, believed that ideas gain their validity not from their inherent truth but from their social consequences and practical applications. Thus scientists could test the validity of their ideas in the laboratory and judge their import by their applications. Pragmatism reflected a quality often looked upon as genuinely American: the inventive, experimental spirit that recognized that science—and society—are characterized by change rather than fixity.

John Dewey, who would become the chief philosopher of pragmatism after James, preferred the term *instrumentalism,* by which he meant that ideas were instruments for action, especially for promoting social reform. Dewey, unlike James, threw himself into movements for the rights of labor and women, the promotion of peace, and the reform of education. He believed that education was the process through which society would gradually progress toward greater social equality and harmony.

Realism in Fiction and Nonfiction

Literature also felt the impact of new scientific ideas and the modern urban scene. A rebellious group of young writers discarded the Romanticism and sentimentalism of antebellum culture in favor of fiction and poetry that depicted contemporary reality without moralizing.

CLEMENS Samuel Langhorne Clemens (Mark Twain) was a transitional figure between Romanticism and realism. A native of Missouri, he was im-

A Tramp Abroad (1880)

Mark Twain in the frontispiece to his travel narrative.

pelled to work at age twelve, becoming first a printer and then a Mississippi riverboat pilot. When the Civil War shut down the river traffic, he briefly joined a Confederate militia company, then left with his brother for Nevada, where he wrote for a local newspaper. He moved on to California in 1864 and first gained widespread notice with his tall tale of the gold country, "The Celebrated Jumping Frog of Calaveras County" (1865). With the success of *Roughing It* (1872), an account of his western years, he moved to Hartford, Connecticut, and was able to set himself up as a full-time author and hilarious lecturer.

Clemens was the first significant writer born and raised west of the Appalachian Mountains. His early writings accentuate his western background, but for his greatest books he drew heavily upon his boyhood in the border slave state of Missouri and the tall-tale tradition of southwestern humor. In *The Adventures of Tom Sawyer* (1876), he evoked the prewar Hannibal, Missouri, where his own boyhood was cut so short. Clemens's masterpiece, *The Adventures of Huckleberry Finn* (1884), created unforgettable characters in Huck Finn, his shiftless father, the runaway slave Jim, the Widow Douglas, "the King," and "the Duke." Huck Finn embodied the instinct of every red-blooded boy to "light out for the territory" whenever polite society set out to civilize him. Huck's effort to help his friend Jim escape bondage expressed well the moral dilemmas imposed by slavery on everyone.

LITERARY NATURALISM   Realism grew into a powerful literary movement during the 1880s, but during the 1890s it took on a new character in the writings of the so-called naturalists. This group of young literary rebels imported scientific determinism into literature, viewing people as prey to natural forces and internal drives without control or full understanding of them. Frank Norris thus pictured in *McTeague* (1899) the descent into madness of a San Francisco dentist and his wife, driven by greed, violence, and lust. Stephen Crane in *Maggie: A Girl of the Streets* (1893) and *The Red Badge of Courage* (1895) portrayed people caught up in environments that were beyond their control. *Maggie* depicts a tenement girl driven to prostitution and death amid scenes so grim and controversial that Crane had to finance the book's publication himself. *The Red Badge of Courage,* his masterpiece, evokes fear, nobility, and courage amid the carnage of the Civil War.

Two naturalists, Jack London and Theodore Dreiser, achieved a degree of popular success. London was both a professed socialist and a believer in the German philosopher Friedrich Nietzsche's doctrine of the superman. In adventure stories such as *The Call of the Wild* (1903) and *The Sea Wolf* (1904), London celebrated the triumph of brute force and the will to survive.

Theodore Dreiser did not celebrate the overwhelming power of social and biological forces; he dissected them for the reader. The result was powerfully disturbing to readers accustomed to more genteel fare. Dreiser shocked the public probably more than the others with protagonists who sinned without remorse and without punishment. *Sister Carrie* (1900), for example, shows Carrie Meeber surviving illicit loves and going on to success on the stage.

SOCIAL CRITICISM   Behind their dogma of determinism, several of the naturalists harbored intense outrage at human misery and social injustice. Their indignation was shared by an increasing number of journalists and social critics who addressed themselves more directly to protest and re-form. One of the most influential of these reformers was Henry George, a journalist who vowed to seek out the cause of poverty in the midst of the industrial progress he saw around him. The basic social problem, George reasoned, was the "unearned increment" in wealth that came to those who owned land. He published the fruit of his thought in *Progress and Poverty* (1879), a thick, rambling, and difficult book whose earnest moralism and sympathetic tone helped it sell 2 million copies in several languages.

George held that everyone had a basic right to the use of the land, since it was provided by nature to all. Nobody had a right to the increasing value that accrued from it, however, since that was created by the community, not by its owner. He proposed simply to tax the "unearned" increment in the value of the land, or the rent. George's "single-tax" idea generated much dis-cussion, but his influence centered on the paradox he posed in his title, *Progress and Poverty,* and his plea for social cooperation and equality.

Another prominent social critic, Thorstein Veblen, brought to his work a background of formal training in economics and the purpose of making that subject into an evolutionary or historical science. In his best-known work, *The Theory of the Leisure Class* (1899), he examined the pecuniary values of the affluent and introduced phrases that have since become com-monplace in our language: *conspicuous consumption* and *conspicuous leisure.* With the advent of industrial society, Veblen argued, the showy display of money and property became the conventional basis of social status. For the upper classes, moreover, it became necessary to spend time nonproductively as evidence of the ability to afford a life of leisure.

The Social Gospel

While novelists, journalists, and commentators were writing about the rising social tensions and injustices of late-nineteenth-century America, more and more people were addressing these problems through social ac-tion. Some reformers focused on legislative solutions to social problems; others stressed philanthropy or organized charity. A few militants promoted socialism or anarchism. Whatever the method or approach, however, social reformers were on the march at the turn of the century, and their activities gave American life a new urgency and energy.

THE RISE OF THE INSTITUTIONAL CHURCH Churches re-sponded slowly to the mounting social concerns, for American Protestantism had become one of the main props of the established order. The Reverend Henry Ward Beecher, for instance, pastor of the fashionable Plymouth Congregational Church in Brooklyn, preached material success, social Darwinism, and the unworthiness of the poor.

As the middle classes moved out to the streetcar suburbs, their churches followed. From 1868 to 1888, for instance, seventeen Protestant churches abandoned the area south of Fourteenth Street in Manhattan. In the center of Chicago, 60,000 residents had no church, Protestant or Catholic. Where churches became prosperous, they fell under the spell of complacent respectability and do-nothing social Darwinism. Some prominent clergymen expressed open disdain for the lower classes. Not surprisingly, more and more working-class people felt out of place in churches where affluence was both worshipped and flaunted.

Gradually, however, some religious leaders realized that Protestantism was in danger of losing its working-class constituency unless it reached out to the urban poor. Two organizations were created expressly for that purpose: the Young Men's Christian Association (YMCA) entered the United States from England in the 1850s and grew rapidly after 1870, and the Salvation Army, founded in London in 1878, entered the United States a year later. Individual urban churches also began to develop institutional features that were more social than strictly religious in function. Church leaders

A Salvation Army group

Flint, Michigan, 1894.

acquired gymnasiums, libraries, lecture rooms, and other facilities in an effort to draw working-class people back to organized religion.

RELIGIOUS REFORMERS   Church reformers who feared that Christianity was becoming irrelevant to the needs and aspirations of the working poor began preaching what came to be called the social gospel. Washington Gladden of Columbus, Ohio, maintained that true Christianity resided not in rituals, dogmas, or even the mystical experience of God but in the principle that "thou shalt love thy neighbor as thyself." Christian law should therefore govern the workplace, with laborer and employer united in serving each other's interests. The "law of greed and strife," he insisted, "is not a natural law; it is unnatural; it is a crime against nature; the law of brotherhood is the only natural law." In attacking the premises of social Darwinism, Gladden thus argued for labor's right to organize, supported maximum-hours laws and factory inspections, and endorsed anti-trust legislation.

EARLY EFFORTS AT URBAN REFORM

THE SETTLEMENT HOUSE MOVEMENT   While preachers of the social gospel dispensed inspiration, other dedicated reformers attacked the problems of the slums from residential community centers called settlement houses. By 1900 perhaps 100 settlement houses existed in America, some of the best known being Jane Addams and Ellen Starr's Hull-House in Chicago and Lillian Wald's Henry Street Settlement in New York City.

Jane Addams

One of the heroic leaders of the settlement house movement.

The settlement houses were staffed mainly by young middle-class idealists, a majority of them college-trained women who had few other outlets for meaningful work. Settlement workers sought to broaden the horizons and improve the lives of slum dwellers in diverse ways. At Hull-House, for instance, staff members recruited the neighborhood children for clubs and kindergartens and set up a nursery for the infant children of working mothers. Settlement houses were also meant to provide workingmen with an alternative to the saloon as a place of recreation and an alternative to the neighborhood political boss as a source of social services. Their programs gradually expanded to include health clinics, lectures, music and art studios, employment bureaus, men's clubs, gymnasiums, and savings banks.

Settlement house leaders realized, however, that the spreading slums made their work as effective as bailing out the ocean with a teaspoon. They therefore organized political support for tenement laws, public playgrounds, juvenile courts, mothers' pensions, workers' compensation laws, and legislation prohibiting child labor.

WOMEN'S EMPLOYMENT AND ACTIVISM Settlement house workers, insofar as they were paid, made up but a fraction of all gainfully employed women. With the rapid population growth in the late nineteenth century, the number of employed women steadily increased, as did the percentage of women in the labor force. These changes in occupational status had little connection to the women's rights movement, however, which increasingly focused on the issue of suffrage. Immediately after the Civil War, Susan B. Anthony, a seasoned veteran of the movement, demanded that the Fifteenth Amendment guarantee the vote for women as well as black men. But she made little impression on those who insisted that women belonged solely in the home.

In 1869 the unity of the women's movement disintegrated in a manner reminiscent of the anti-slavery rift three decades before. The question once again was whether the movement should concentrate on one overriding issue or broaden its focus. Susan B. Anthony and Elizabeth Cady Stanton founded the National Woman Suffrage Association to promote a women's suffrage amendment to the Constitution, but they looked upon suffrage as but one among many feminist causes to be promoted. Later that same year, Lucy Stone, Julia Ward Howe, and other leaders formed the American Woman Suffrage Association, which focused single-mindedly on the vote as the first and most basic reform.

In 1890, after three years of negotiation, the rival groups united as the National American Woman Suffrage Association, with Elizabeth Cady Stanton as president for two years, followed by Susan B. Anthony until 1900. The work thereafter was carried on by a new generation of activists, led by Anna Howard Shaw and Carrie Chapman Catt. Over the years the movement achieved some local and partial victories as a few states granted women suffrage in school board or municipal elections. In 1869 the territory of

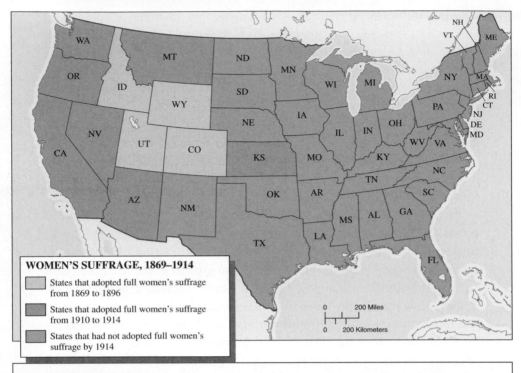

WOMEN'S SUFFRAGE, 1869–1914

States that adopted full women's suffrage from 1869 to 1896

States that adopted full women's suffrage from 1910 to 1914

States that had not adopted full women's suffrage by 1914

Which states first gave women the right to vote? Why did it take fifty-one years, from Wyoming's grant of full suffrage to women until ratification of the Nineteenth Amendment, for women to receive the right to vote? How was suffrage part of a larger women's reform movement?

Wyoming provided full suffrage to women and after 1890 retained women's suffrage when it became a state. Three other western states soon followed suit, but not until New York acted in 1917 did a state east of the Mississippi River adopt universal suffrage.

Despite the focus on the vote, women did not confine their public activism to that issue. In 1866 the Young Women's Christian Association, a parallel to the YMCA, appeared in Boston and spread elsewhere. The New England Women's Club, started in 1868 by Julia Ward Howe and others, was an early example of the women's clubs that proliferated to such an extent that a General Federation of Women's Clubs was established in 1890 to tie them together nationally. Many women's clubs confined themselves to "literary" and social activities, but others became deeply involved in charities and reform. The New York Consumers' League, formed in 1890, and the National

Consumers' League, established nine years later, sought to make the buying public, chiefly women, more aware of degrading labor conditions.

TOWARD A WELFARE STATE   Even without the support of voting women in most places, many states adopted rudimentary measures to regulate big business and labor conditions in the public interest. They passed laws to regulate railroads and working conditions, but the laws were generally poorly enforced or overturned by the courts. In the meantime, it was often the local political machines that stepped in to help those who were suffering. While local and federal governments lacked a bureaucracy to assist those who had fallen on hard times, the political machines in the cities supplied temporary jobs, food, or other necessities. The machines, then, were the precursor to the modern welfare state.

At the end of the nineteenth century, opinion in the country stood poised between conservative rigidities and a growing sense that new conditions imposed new personal and government responsibilities. The last two decades of the nineteenth century had already seen a slow erosion of free-market values, which had found their most secure home in the courts. There emerged instead a concept of the general-welfare state, which called upon the government to act on behalf of the whole society rather than allow rugged individualism to run rampant. The conflict between government intervention and laissez-faire values spilled over into the new century, but by the mid–twentieth century, after the Progressive movement and the New Deal, the nation would be firmly committed to the premises of the general-welfare state.

End of Chapter Review

CHAPTER SUMMARY

- **Rise of Cities** America's cities grew in all directions. Electric elevators and new steel-frame construction allowed architects to extend buildings upward. Mass transit allowed the middle class to retreat to suburbs. Crowded tenements bred disease and crime and created an opportunity for urban political bosses to accrue power, in part by distributing to the poor the only relief that existed.

- **New Immigration** By 1900, 30 percent of Americans were foreign-born, with many immigrants coming from eastern and southern Europe rather than western and northern Europe, like most immigrants of generations past. Thus their languages and culture were vastly different from those of native-born Americans. They tended to be Catholic or Jewish rather than Protestant. Beginning in the 1880s, nativists advocated immigration laws to exclude the Chinese and the poor and demanded that immigrants pass a literacy test. A federal immigration station on Ellis Island, in New York Harbor, opened in 1892 to process immigrants arriving by ship from across the Atlantic.

- **Mass Entertainment** Cities began to create urban parks, like New York's Central Park, as places for all citizens to stroll, ride bicycles, or play games such as tennis. Vaudeville shows emerged as a popular form of entertainment. Saloons served as local social and political clubs for men. It was in this era that football, baseball, and basketball emerged as spectator sports.

- **Social Darwinism** Charles Darwin's *On the Origin of Species* shocked people who believed in a literal interpretation of the Bible's account of creation. Darwin's scientific theory was applied to human society and social institutions by Herbert Spencer and William Graham Sumner, who equated economic and social success with "survival of the fittest" and advanced the idea that government should not interfere to promote equality.

- **Rise of Realism** American literature responded to the changes in society at this time. Samuel L. Clemens (Mark Twain) wrote humorously about his experiences and observations and later created masterpieces that playfully comment on social issues. The movement known as naturalism shocked many readers in the 1890s by depicting individuals as victims of a brutal world. Social critics such as Henry George were shocked by the vast disparities between rich and poor. The social gospel movement, in which the religious community reached out to the poor, was another response to America's poverty.

CHRONOLOGY

1858	Construction of New York's Central Park begins
1859	Darwin's *On the Origin of Species* is published
1882	Congress passes the Chinese Exclusion Act
1889	Hull-House, a settlement house, opens in Chicago
1889	Otis Elevator Company installs the first electric elevator
1890	National American Woman Suffrage Association is formed
1891	Basketball is invented
1892	Ellis Island, a federal center for processing immigrants, opens
1900	Baseball's National League is formed

KEY TERMS & NAMES

Ellis Island p. 626

Chinese Exclusion Act
p. 628

nativist p. 628

Frederick Law Olmsted
p. 631

social Darwinism p. 638

Herbert Spencer p. 638

William James p. 639

pragmatism p. 639

John Dewey p. 640

Mark Twain p. 640

social gospel p. 642

Jane Addams p. 644

settlement houses p. 644

22

GILDED AGE POLITICS AND AGRARIAN REVOLT

FOCUS QUESTIONS wwnorton.com/studyspace

- What were the major features of American politics during the Gilded Age?
- What were the major issues in politics during this period?
- What were the main problems facing farmers in the South and the Midwest after the Civil War?
- How and why did farmers become politicized?
- What was significant about the election of 1896?

In 1873 the writers Mark Twain and Charles Dudley Warner created an enduring label for the post–Civil War era when they collaborated on a novel titled *The Gilded Age*. The book depicts an age of widespread political corruption, corporate greed, and social vulgarity. Generations of political scientists and historians have since reinforced the two novelists' judgment. As a young college graduate in 1879, future president Woodrow Wilson described the state of the post–Civil War political system: "No leaders, no principles; no principles, no parties."

PARADOXICAL POLITICS

Political life in the Gilded Age, the thirty-five years between the end of the Civil War and the end of the nineteenth century, had several distinctive elements. Local politics, especially in cities crowded with waves of new immigrants, was usually controlled by "rings"—small groups of political insiders who managed the nomination and election of candidates, ran primaries, and influenced policy. Each ring typically had a powerful "boss" who ran things, using his "machine"—a network of neighborhood activists and officials—to govern the town or city. Bosses organized neighborhoods (precincts), mediated disputes, picked candidates, helped the needy, and distributed patronage (municipal jobs and contracts) to loyal followers and corporate contributors. The various city rings and bosses were usually corrupt and rarely efficient, but they did bring structure, stability, and services to rapidly growing and often chaotic inner-city communities. Colorful figures such as New York City's William "Boss" Tweed shamelessly ruled, plundered, and occasionally improved municipal government, often through dishonest means and frequent bribes. Until his arrest in 1871 and his conviction in 1873, Tweed used the Tammany Hall ring to dominate the nation's largest city.

National political parties during the Gilded Age were much more dominant forces than they are today. Party loyalty was powerful, often extending over many generations. Parties also were the nexus of political activity. They controlled access to political offices, dominated elections, and shaped policy making. Throughout the last third of the nineteenth century, a close balance between Republicans and Democrats in Congress created the sense of a stalemate. Neither party was willing to embrace controversial issues or take bold initiatives because neither had a commanding advantage with the electorate. Timidity prevailed. The Gilded Age has long been viewed as a time of political mediocrity, in which the parties refused to confront "real issues" such as the runaway growth of an unregulated economy and its attendant social injustices.

Voters of the time nonetheless thought politics was very important. Voter turnout during the Gilded Age was commonly about 70 to 80 percent, even in the South, where the disfranchisement of African Americans was not yet complete. (By contrast, the turnout for the 2008 presidential election was almost 57 percent.) The paradox of such a high rate of voter participation in the face of the inertia at the national political level raises an obvious question: how was it that leaders who failed to address

THE "BRAINS"

William "Boss" Tweed

Tweed is represented here as having a money-bag face and a $15,500 diamond stickpin.

the "real issues" of the day presided over the most highly organized and politically active electorate in U.S. history?

The answer is partly that the politicians and the voters believed that they
were dealing with crucial issues: tariff rates, the initial efforts to regulate corporations, monetary policy, Indian disputes, civil service reform, and immigration. But the answer also reflects the extreme partisanship of the times
and the essentially local nature of political culture during the Gilded Age.

PARTISAN POLITICS Most Americans after the Civil War were intensely loyal to the Democratic or Republican party. Political parties gave
people an anchor for their activity and their loyalty in an unstable world.
Local party officials took care of those who voted their way and distributed
appointive public offices and other favors to party loyalists. These "city machines" used patronage and favoritism to retain the loyalty of business
supporters while providing jobs, food, or fuel to working-class voters who
had fallen on hard times. The party faithful eagerly took part in rallies and
picnics, deriving from them a sense of camaraderie as well as an opportunity
for recreation that offered a welcome relief from their usual workday routine.

Party loyalties and voter turnout in the late nineteenth century reflected
religious and ethnic divisions as well as geographic differences. The Republi-
can party attracted mainly Protestants of British descent. Its base was New
England, and its other strongholds were New York and the Upper Midwest.
The Republicans, the party of Abraham Lincoln, could rely upon the votes of
African Americans and Union veterans of the Civil War.

The Democrats, by contrast, tended to be a heterogeneous, often unruly
coalition embracing southern whites, immigrants and Catholics of any origin in the northern states, Jews, freethinkers, skeptics, and all those repelled
by the "party of morality." As one Chicago Democrat explained, "A Republican is a man who wants you t' go t' church every Sunday. A Democrat says if
a man wants to have a glass of beer on Sunday he can have it."

Republicans pressed nativist policies, calling for restrictions on both
immigration and the employment of foreigners. They also promoted the
teaching of the "American" language in the schools. The cause of banning
alcoholic beverages revived along with nativism in the 1880s. Among the
immigrants who crowded into the growing cities were many Irish, Germans,
and Italians, who tended to enjoy alcoholic beverages. Republicans increasingly saw saloons as the central social evil around which all others revolved,
including vice, crime, political corruption, and neglect of families, and they
associated these problems with the ethnic groups that frequented saloons.

POLITICAL STALEMATE AT THE NATIONAL LEVEL   Between 1869 and 1913, from the presidency of Ulysses S. Grant through that of William Howard Taft, Republicans monopolized the White House except for the two nonconsecutive terms of the New York Democrat Grover Cleveland, but Republican domination was more apparent than real. Between 1872 and 1896 no president won a majority of the popular vote. In each of those presidential elections, sixteen states invariably voted Republican and fourteen voted Democratic, leaving a pivotal six states whose results might change. The important swing-vote role played by two of those states, New York and Ohio, helps explain the election of eight presidents from those states from 1872 to 1908.

Lackluster presidents also contributed to the political stalemate. No chief executive between Abraham Lincoln and Theodore Roosevelt exercised "strong" leadership. None challenged the prevailing view that Congress, not the White House, should formulate policy. Senator John Sherman of Ohio expressed the widely held notion that the legislative branch should predominate in a republic: "The President should merely obey and enforce the law."

Republicans controlled the Senate and Democrats controlled the House during the Gilded Age. Only during 1881 to 1883 and 1889 to 1891 did a Republican president coincide with a Republican Congress, and only between 1893 and 1895 did a Democratic president enjoy a Democratic majority in Congress. The counterbalancing strength of the parties in Congress and the fear in each party of alienating key factions deterred any vigorous initiatives in Congress. Because most bills required bipartisan support to pass both houses and because legislators tended to vote along party lines, the Democrats and the Republicans pursued a policy of evasion on the national issues of the day. Only the tariff provoked clear-cut divisions, between protectionist Republicans and low-tariff Democrats, but there were individual exceptions even on that. On the important questions of the money supply, regulation of big business, farm problems, civil service reform, and immigration, the parties differed very little. As a result, they primarily became vehicles for seeking office and dispensing patronage in the form of government jobs and contracts.

STATE AND LOCAL INITIATIVES   Unlike those of today, Americans during the Gilded Age expected little direct support from the federal government; most significant political activity occurred at the state and local levels. Residents of the western territories were largely forced to fend for themselves rather than rely upon federal authorities. They formed towns, practiced vigilante justice, and made laws on their own. Once incorporated into the Union, the former territories retained much of their autonomy.

Thus state governments after the Civil War were the primary centers of political activity and innovation. Over 60 percent of the nation's spending and taxing was exercised by state and local authorities. Then, unlike today, the large cities spent far more on local services than did the federal government. And three fourths of all public employees worked for state and local governments. Local issues such as prohibition, Sunday closing laws, and parochial-school funding often generated more excitement than complex debates over tariffs and monetary policies. It was the state and local governments that first sought to curb the power and restrain the abuses of corporate interests.

CORRUPTION AND REFORM: HAYES TO HARRISON

During the Gilded Age, states attempted to regulate big business; most of those efforts were overturned by the courts, however. A close alliance thus developed between business owners and political leaders at every level. Railroad passes, free entertainment, and a host of other favors were freely provided to politicians, newspaper editors, and other leaders in positions to influence public opinion or affect legislation.

Both Republican and Democratic leaders also squabbled over the "spoils" of office, the appointive offices at the local and national levels. After each election it was expected that the victorious party would throw out the defeated party's appointees and appoint its own men to office. The patronage system of awarding government jobs to supporters invited corruption. It also was so time-consuming that it distracted elected officials from more important issues. Yet George Washington Plunkitt, a Democratic boss in New York City, spoke for many Gilded Age politicians when he explained that "You can't keep an organization together without patronage. Men ain't in politics for nothin'. They want to get somethin' out of it." Each party had its share of corrupt officials willing to buy and sell government appointments or congressional votes, yet each also witnessed the emergence of factions promoting honesty in government. The struggle for "cleaner" government soon became one of the foremost issues of the day.

HAYES AND CIVIL SERVICE REFORM   In the aftermath of Reconstruction, President Rutherford B. Hayes embodied the "party of morality." Hayes brought to the White House in 1877 a new style of uprightness, in

"The Bosses of the Senate"

This 1875 cartoon bitingly portrays the period's alliance between big business and politics.

sharp contrast to the graft and corruption practiced by members of the Grant administration. The son of an Ohio farmer, Hayes had been wounded four times in the Civil War and had been promoted to the rank of major general. Elected governor of Ohio in 1867, he served three terms.

Hayes's presidency suffered from the supposedly secret deal that awarded him victory over the New York Democrat Samuel Tilden in the 1876 election. Snide references to Hayes as "His Fraudulence" denied him any chance at a second term, which he renounced from the beginning. Hayes's Republican party was split between so-called Stalwarts and Half-Breeds, led respectively by Senators Roscoe Conkling of New York and James G. Blaine of Maine. The difference between these Republican factions was even murkier than that between the two major parties. The Stalwarts had been stalwart in their support of President Grant during the furor over the misbehavior of his cabinet members. They also promoted Radical Reconstruction of the South and the "spoils system" of distributing federal political jobs to party loyalists. The Half-Breeds acquired their name because they were only half-loyal to Grant and half-committed to reform of the spoils system.

Hayes aligned himself with the growing public discontent over political corruption in the Grant administration. In promoting civil service reform, he issued an executive order in 1877 declaring that those already in office (for the most part Grant's appointees) would be dismissed only for the good of the government and not for political reasons. For all of Hayes's efforts to clean house, he retained a limited vision of government's role in society. On the economic issues of the day, he held to a conservative line that would guide his successors for the rest of the century. His solution to labor troubles, demonstrated during the Great Railroad Strike of 1877, was to send in federal troops and break the strike. His answer to the demands of farmers and debtors that he expand the currency was to veto the Bland-Allison Act, which provided for a limited expansion of silver currency through the government's purchase of $2 million to $4 million in silver coins per month. (The bill was passed when Congress overrode Hayes's veto.)

GARFIELD AND ARTHUR With Hayes out of the running for a second term, the Stalwarts, led by Conkling, brought Ulysses S. Grant forward for a third time, still a strong contender despite the tarnish of his administration's scandals. For two days the Republican Convention in Chicago was deadlocked, with Grant holding a slight lead over James G. Blaine and John Sherman. When Wisconsin's delegates suddenly switched their votes to former House Speaker (now Senator-elect) James A. Garfield, the convention stampeded to the dark-horse candidate from Ohio. As a sop to the Stalwarts, the convention tapped Chester A. Arthur, of customhouse notoriety, for vice president.

The Democrats named Winfield Scott Hancock, a Union general during the Civil War, to counterbalance the Republicans' "bloody-shirt" attacks on their party as the vehicle of secession. In the close election, Garfield eked out a plurality of only 39,000 votes, or 48.5 percent of the vote, but with a comfortable margin of 214 to 155 in the Electoral College.

On July 2, 1881, after only four months in office, President Garfield was walking through the Washington, D.C., railroad station when a deranged man, Charles Guiteau, shot him in the back. "I am a Stalwart," Guiteau shouted to the arresting officers. "Arthur is now President of the United States." Two months later, Garfield died of complications resulting from the shooting.

Chester Arthur, one of the chief henchmen of Stalwart leader Roscoe Conkling, was now president. Little in his past suggested that he would rise above spoils politics. But Arthur, a wealthy, handsome widower who loved fine wines and sported a lavish wardrobe and billowing sideburns, demonstrated surprising leadership qualities. He distanced himself from Conkling and the Stalwarts and established a genuine independence.

Most startling of all was Arthur's emergence as something of a civil service and tariff reformer. The assassin Guiteau had unwittingly galvanized public support of political reform. A civil service reform bill sponsored by "Gentleman George" Pendleton, a Democratic senator from Ohio, passed in 1883, setting up a three-member Civil Service Commission independent of the cabinet departments, the first such federal agency established on a permanent basis. About 14 percent of all government jobs would now be filled on the basis of competitive examinations rather than political connections. What was more, the president could enlarge the class of jobs based on merit at his discretion, as many presidents later did.

Meanwhile, the tariff continued to be the most controversial national political issue. The high tariff, a heritage of the Civil War, had by the early 1880s raised federal revenues to a point where the government was enjoying a surplus that drew money into the Treasury and out of circulation, thus impeding economic growth. Some argued that lower tariff rates would reduce consumer prices by enabling foreign competition and at the same time leave more money in circulation. In 1882, Arthur named a special tariff commission, which recommended a 20 to 25 percent rate reduction, but Congress's effort to enact the proposal was marred by logrolling (the trading of votes to benefit different legislators' local interests). The result was the "mongrel tariff" of 1883, so called because of its different rates for different commodities. Overall, the new tariff provided for a slight rate reduction, but it also raised the duty on some products.

THE SCURRILOUS CAMPAIGN   As the 1884 presidential election neared, Chester Arthur's record as an unexpected reformer might have attracted voters, but it did not please the leaders of his party. The Republicans dumped Arthur and turned to the majestic senator James G. Blaine of Maine, leader of the Half-Breed Republicans. Blaine was the consummate politician. He inspired the party faithful with his oratory, and at the same time he knew how to wheel and deal in the backrooms.

During the campaign, however, letters surfaced that linked Blaine to efforts to exchange his influence for selfish gain. For the reform element of the Republican party, this was too much, and many bolted the ticket. Party regulars scorned the idealists as "goo-goos"—the good-government crowd who ignored partisan realities—and one newspaper editor jokingly tagged them Mugwumps, after an Algonquian word for a self-important chieftain.

Senator James G. Blaine of Maine

The Republican candidate in 1884.

The rise of the Mugwumps influenced the Democrats to nominate the New Yorker Stephen Grover Cleveland as a reform candidate. Elected mayor of Buffalo in 1881, Cleveland first attracted national attention for battling corruption in that city. In 1882 he was elected governor of New York, and he continued to build a reform record by fighting New York City's corrupt Tammany Hall ring. As mayor and as governor, he repeatedly vetoed what he considered special-privilege bills serving selfish interests. Cleveland possessed little charisma but impressed the public with his stubborn integrity. He was a crusader against corruption, and as such he drew many of those making up the growing chorus of political reformers.

But a scandal erupted when the *Buffalo Evening Telegraph* revealed that as a bachelor, Cleveland had had an affair with an attractive Buffalo widow, Maria Halpin. Mrs. Halpin had named Cleveland as the father of a boy born to her in 1874. Cleveland had responded by providing financial support when the child was placed in an orphanage. The respective personal escapades of Blaine and Cleveland provided the 1884 campaign with some of the most colorful battle cries in political history: "Blaine, Blaine, James G. Blaine, the continental liar from the state of Maine," Democrats chanted; Republicans countered with "Ma, ma, where's my pa? Gone to the White House, ha, ha, ha!"

Near the end of the mudslinging campaign, Blaine and his supporters committed two fateful blunders. The first occurred at New York's fashionable Delmonico's restaurant, where Blaine attended a lavish fund-raising dinner with a clutch of millionaire bigwigs. Cartoons and accounts of this "Belshazzar's feast" festooned the opposition press for days.

The second fiasco occurred when a Protestant minister visiting the Republican headquarters in New York City insolently referred to the Democrats as the party of "rum, Romanism, and rebellion." Blaine let pass the implied insult to Irish Catholics—a fatal oversight, since he had always cultivated Irish American support with his anti-English talk and public reminders that his mother was Catholic. Democrats spread the word that Blaine was anti-Irish and anti-Catholic. The two incidents may have tipped the election. The electoral vote, in Cleveland's favor, stood at 219 to 182, although the popular vote ran far closer: Cleveland's plurality nationwide was fewer than 30,000 votes.

CLEVELAND AND THE SPECIAL INTERESTS For all of Cleveland's hostility to the spoils system and politics as usual, he represented no sharp break with the conservative public policies of his Republican predecessors, except in opposing government favors to business. He held to a strictly limited view of government's role in both economic and social matters, a rigid philosophy illustrated by his 1887 veto of a bill to aid drought-stricken farmers. Back to Congress it went, with a lecture on the need to limit the powers and functions of government. "Though the people support the government, the government should not support the people," Cleveland asserted.

Cleveland also incurred the wrath of many Union war veterans with his firm stand against expanded pensions. Congress had passed the first Civil War pension law in 1862 to provide for Union veterans disabled in service and for the widows, orphans, and dependents of veterans. By 1882 the Grand Army of the Republic, an organization of Union veterans and a powerful pressure group, was trying to get pensions paid for any disability, no matter how it was incurred. Meanwhile, many veterans succeeded in getting legislators to pass private pension bills. Insofar as time permitted, Cleveland examined the bills critically and vetoed the dubious ones. The issue reached a climax in 1887 when Cleveland vetoed a new dependents pension bill containing more liberal benefits for veterans and their families. Cleveland argued that it would become a refuge for frauds rather than a "roll of honor."

In about the middle of his term, Cleveland advocated an important new policy: railroad regulation. Since the late 1860s, states had adopted laws regulating railroads, and from the early 1870s Congress had debated federal legislation. In 1886 a Supreme Court decision spurred action. Reacting to the case of *Wabash, St. Louis, and Pacific Railroad Company v. Illinois*, in which the Court had ruled that a state could not regulate rates on interstate traffic, Cleveland urged that since this "important field of control and regulation [has] thus been left entirely unoccupied," Congress should act.

It did, and in 1887 Cleveland signed into law an act creating the Interstate Commerce Commission (ICC), the first independent federal regulatory commission. The law required that all freight and passenger railroad rates be "reasonable and just," and it empowered the ICC to investigate railroads and prosecute violators of its regulations. Railroads were also forbidden to grant secret rebates to preferred shippers or enter into pools (agreements among

Grover Cleveland

As president, Cleveland made the issue of tariff reform central to the politics of the late 1880s.

competing companies to fix rates). The commission's actual powers proved to be weak, however, when first tested in the courts.

THE TARIFF Cleveland's most dramatic challenge to the power of special interests focused on tariff reform. Why was the tariff such an important and controversial issue? During the late nineteenth century, Republican party officials and business leaders assumed that national prosperity and high tariffs were closely linked. Others disagreed. Many observers concluded that the formation of huge corporate "trusts" was not a natural development of a maturing capitalist system. Instead, critics charged that government tariff policies had fostered big business at the expense of small producers and retailers by effectively shutting out foreign imports, thereby enabling American corporations to dominate their markets and charge higher prices for their products. By shielding manufacturers from foreign competition, critics argued, the tariff made it easier for them to combine and form ever-larger entities.

Cleveland agreed. Having decided that the rates were too high and too often inequitable, he devoted his entire annual message to Congress in 1887 to the subject. Cleveland noted that tariff revenues had bolstered the federal surplus, making the Treasury "a hoarding place for money needlessly withdrawn from trade and the people's use." The high tariff, he added, pushed up prices for everybody and benefited only a few politically powerful manufacturing interests. The wise solution was to spur Congress to look at the items on the tariff list, more than 4,000 of them, with an eye to eliminating as many as possible and lowering all the remaining duties. Cleveland's tariff proposal accomplished his purpose of drawing party lines more firmly. For the first time in years, the upcoming presidential election would provide a sharp difference between the major parties on an issue of substance—the tariff.

THE ELECTION OF 1888 Cleveland was the obvious nominee of his party for reelection in 1888. The Republicans, now calling themselves the GOP (Grand Old Party), turned to the obscure Benjamin Harrison. The grandson of a former president, Harrison boasted a good war record, and little in his political record would offend any voter. The Republican platform accepted Cleveland's challenge to make the tariff the chief issue. To ensure against tariff reduction, manufacturers obligingly filled up Harrison's campaign fund, which was used to denounce Cleveland's un-American "free-trade" stance and his vetoes of bills providing for veterans' pensions.

On the eve of the election, Cleveland suffered a devastating blow from a dirty campaign trick. Posing as an English immigrant and using the false name Charles F. Murchison, a California Republican had written the British ambassador, Sir Lionel Sackville-West, asking his advice on how to vote. Sackville-West hinted in reply that the man should vote for Cleveland. Published two weeks before the election, the "Murchison letter" aroused a storm of protest against foreign intervention and suggested a link between Cleveland and British free traders.

Still, the outcome in the election was very close. Cleveland won the popular vote by 5,538,000 to 5,447,000, but that was little comfort. The distribution of votes was such that Harrison, with the key states of Indiana and New York on his side, carried the Electoral College by 233 to 168.

REPUBLICAN REFORM UNDER HARRISON   As president, Benjamin Harrison was a competent figurehead overshadowed by his flamboyant secretary of state, James G. Blaine. Harrison's first step was to reward those responsible for his victory. He owed a heavy debt to the Union war veterans, which he discharged by naming the head of the veterans' group to the office of federal pension commissioner. The new commissioner proceeded to approve veterans' pensions with such abandon that the secretary of the interior removed him from office six months later. In 1890, Harrison signed the Dependent Pension Act, substantially the same measure that Cleveland had vetoed three years earlier. Any war veteran unable to make a living by manual labor for whatever reason was granted a monthly pension. The pension rolls would almost double by 1893.

During the first two years of Harrison's term, the Republicans controlled the presidency and both houses of Congress for the second time since 1875. They made the most of their clout. During 1890 several significant pieces of legislation made their way to the White House for Harrison's signature. In addition to the Dependent Pension Act, the president approved the Sherman Anti-Trust Act, the Sherman Silver Purchase Act, the McKinley Tariff Act, and the admission of Idaho and Wyoming as new states, following the admission of the Dakotas, Montana, and Washington in 1889.

"King of the World"

Republican reform targeted the growing power of monopolies, such as that of Rockefeller's Standard Oil.

Both parties had pledged during the campaign to address the growing power of trusts and monopolies. The Sherman Anti-Trust Act, named for Ohio senator John Sherman, chairman of the committee that drafted it, forbade contracts, combinations, or conspiracies in restraint of trade or in the effort to establish monopolies in interstate or foreign commerce. A broad consensus put the vague law through, but its passage turned out to be largely symbolic. During the next decade successive administrations rarely enforced the new law, in part because of confusion about what constituted "restraint of trade." From 1890 to 1901, the Justice Department instituted only eighteen anti-trust suits, and four of those were against labor unions.

Congress, meanwhile, debated currency legislation against the backdrop of growing distress in the farm regions of the West and the South. Hard-pressed farmers demanded increased coinage of silver to inflate the currency supply and raise commodity prices, making it easier for them to earn the money they needed to pay their debts. The silverite forces were also strengthened, especially in the Senate, by members from new western states with silver-mining interests. Congress thus passed the Sherman Silver Purchase Act, replacing the Bland-Allison Act of 1878. The new act required the Treasury to purchase 4.5 million ounces of silver each month and to issue in payment paper money redeemable in gold or silver. Although it doubled the amount of silver purchased, that was still too little to inflate the nation's overall money supply. The stage was thus set for the currency issue to eclipse all others during the financial panic that would sweep the country three years later.

Republicans viewed their victory over Cleveland in 1888 as a mandate not just to maintain the protective tariff but to raise it. Piloted through Congress by the prominent Ohio representative William McKinley, the McKinley Tariff of 1890 raised duties on manufactured goods to the highest level ever. The absence of a public consensus for higher tariffs became clearly visible in the 1890 midterm elections: voters repudiated the Republican-sponsored McKinley Tariff with a landslide of Democratic votes. In the new House, Democrats outnumbered Republicans by almost three to one; in the Senate the Republican majority was reduced to eight. One of the election casualties was Congressman McKinley himself. But there was more to the election than the tariff. Voters also reacted to the baldly partisan measures of the Harrison administration and to its extravagant expenditures on military pensions and other programs.

The large Democratic vote in 1890 may also have been a reaction to Republican efforts to legislate on a local level against government-supported Catholic (parochial) schools. In many districts with a high percentage of Catholic constituents, Democratic legislators had defied the principle of separation of church and state by allocating local tax revenues to help support those schools. In 1889, Wisconsin Republicans pushed through a law that struck at parochial schools and turned large numbers of outraged Catholic immigrants into Democratic activists. Protestant Republicans also sought to ban alcoholic beverages. Between 1880 and 1890 sixteen out of twenty-one states outside the South held referenda on a constitutional prohibition of alcohol, although only six states actually voted for prohibition. With this assault on drinking, Republicans were playing a losing game, arousing anti-prohibitionists on the Democratic side. In 1890 the Democrats swept state after state.

THE FARM PROBLEM AND AGRARIAN PROTEST MOVEMENTS

The 1890 election reflected more than a reaction against the Republican tariff, patronage politics, extravagant spending, and moralizing. The Democratic victory revealed a deep-seated unrest in the farming communities of the South and the western Midwest, as well as in the mining towns of the Rocky Mountains. As the congressional Democrats took power, the beginnings of an acute economic crisis appeared on the horizon: farmers' debts mounted as crop prices plummeted.

Frustrated by the unwillingness of Congress to meet their demands and ease their plight, disgruntled farmers focused on political efforts. Like so many of their counterparts laboring in urban factories, they realized that social change required demonstrations of power, and power lay in numbers—and organization. Unlike labor unions, however, the farm organizations faced a complex array of economic variables affecting their livelihood. They had to deal with more than just management. Bankers, food processors, railroad and grain-elevator operators, as well as the world commodities market, all affected the agricultural sector. So, too, did unpredictable forces of nature: droughts, blizzards, insects, and erosion.

There were also important obstacles to collective action by farmers. Farmers' rugged individualism and physical isolation made communication and organization especially difficult. Another hurdle was that agricultural interests had diverged after the Civil War and in some cases conflicted with one another. On the Great Plains, for example, the railroads were the largest landowners. In addition, there were large absentee landowners, some foreign, who leased out vast tracts of land. There were also huge "bonanza" farms that employed hundreds of seasonal workers. Yet the majority of farmers were simple rural folk in the South and West who were moderate-size landowners, small land speculators, tenant farmers, sharecroppers, and hourly wage workers. It was the middle-size landowners who were most affected by rapidly rising land values and rising indebtedness. Those farmers were concerned with land values and crop prices, while tenants, sharecroppers, and farmhands supported land-distribution schemes that would give them access to their own land.

Given such a diversity of interests within the agricultural sector, farm activists discovered that it was often difficult to develop and maintain a cohesive political organization. Yet for all the difficulties, they persevered, and the results were dramatic, if not completely successful. Thus, for example, the deep-seated unrest in the farming communities of the South and the West began to find voice in the Granger movement, the Farmers' Alliances, and the new People's party (also known as the Populist party), agrarian movements of considerable political and social significance.

ECONOMIC CONDITIONS   Since the end of the Civil War, many farmers in the South and Midwest suffered worsening economic and social conditions. The source of their problems was a long decline in commodity prices, from 1870 to 1898, the result of domestic increases in production and growing international competition for world markets. Considerations of abstract economic forces puzzled many farmers, however. How could one speak of overproduction when so many remained in need? Instead, many farmers assumed, there must be a screw loose somewhere in the system.

The railroads and the food processors who handled the farmers' products were seen as the villains. Farmers resented the high railroad freight rates that

"I Feed You All!"

This 1875 poster shows the farmer at the center of society.

prevailed in farm regions with no alternative forms of transportation. High tariffs also operated to the farmers' disadvantage, because they protected manufacturers from foreign competition, allowing them to raise the prices of factory goods upon which farmers depended. Farmers, however, had to sell their wheat, cotton, and other staples in foreign markets, where competition lowered prices. Tariffs inflicted a double blow on farmers because, insofar as they hampered imports, they indirectly hampered exports, by making it harder for foreign buyers to get the currency or exchange necessary to purchase American crops.

Debt, too, had been a perennial agricultural problem. After the Civil War, farmers had grown ever more enmeshed in debt: western farmers incurred mortgages to cover the costs of land and machinery, while southern farmers were forced to pledge their crops to the local merchant in exchange for food and supplies. As commodity prices dropped, the debt burden grew because farmers had to cultivate more wheat or cotton to raise the same amount of money. By growing more, they furthered the vicious cycle of surpluses and price declines.

THE GRANGER MOVEMENT   When the Department of Agriculture sent Oliver H. Kelley, a former Minnesota farmer and post-office clerk, on a tour of the South in 1866, it was the farmers' isolation that most impressed him. To address the problem, Kelley in 1867 founded the National Grange of the Patrons of Husbandry, better known as the Grange (an old word for granary). In the next few years the Grange mushroomed, reaching a membership as high as 1.5 million by 1874. While the Grange started out as a social and educational response to the isolation of farm folk, as it grew, it began to promote farmer-owned cooperatives for the buying and selling of crops. The Grangers' goal was to free farmers from the conventional "middlemen" to whom they were forced to pay high fees.

The Grange soon became indirectly involved in politics, through independent third parties, especially in the Midwest during the early 1870s. The Grangers' chief political goal was state regulation of the rates charged by railroads and crop warehouses. In five states they brought about the passage of "Granger laws," which were soon challenged in the courts. In a key case involving warehouse regulation, *Munn v. Illinois* (1877), the Supreme Court affirmed that the state, according to its "police powers," had the right to regulate property that was clothed in a public interest.

"Gift for the Grangers"

A promotional print for Grange members showing scenes of farming and farm life.

Although such legal victories bolstered the Granger cause, the movement gradually declined as members' energies were drawn off into cooperatives, whereby farmers would make collective agreements about the storage and sale of their crops. Other former Grange members focused on political action. In 1875, out of the independent political movements, grew the Greenback party, which favored expanding of the money supply by means of more paper money. In the 1878 midterm elections the

Greenbacks polled over 1 million votes and elected fifteen congressmen. But in 1880 the party's fortunes declined, and it disintegrated after 1884.

FARMERS' ALLIANCES   As the Grange lost energy, another consortium of farm organizations grew in size and significance: the Farmers' Alliances. Like the Grange, the Farmers' Alliances offered social and recreational activities for their members, but they also emphasized political action. Struggling farmers throughout the South and Midwest, where tenancy rates were highest, rushed to join the Alliance movement. They saw in collective action a way to seek relief from the hardships created by chronic indebtedness, declining crop prices, and devastating droughts. Yet unlike the Grange, which was a national organization that tended to attract larger and more prosperous farmers, the Alliance was a grassroots organization representing marginal farmers. It would become the largest and most dynamic farmers' movement in American history.

The Alliance movement swept across the southern cotton belt and established strong positions in Kansas and the Dakotas. In 1886 a white minister in Texas, which had one of the largest and most influential Alliance movements, responded to the appeals of African American farmers by organizing the Colored Farmers' National Alliance. The white leadership of the Alliance movement in Texas endorsed this development because the Colored Alliance stressed that its objective was economic justice, not social equality. By 1890 the Alliance movement had members from New York to California, numbering about 1.5 million, and the Colored Farmers' National Alliance claimed over 1 million members.

A powerful attraction for many isolated, struggling farmers and their families was the sense of community provided by the Alliance network. The Alliance movement welcomed rural women and men over sixteen years of age who displayed a "good moral character," believed in God, and demonstrated "industrious habits." Lawyers and blacks were excluded. Women embraced the opportunity to engage in economic and political issues. An Alliance publication made the point explicitly: "The Alliance has come to redeem woman from her enslaved condition, and place her in her proper sphere." The number of women in the movement grew rapidly, and many assumed key leadership roles in the "grand army of reform."

The Alliance movement sponsored some 1,000 rural newspapers to spread the word about the farm problem. It also recruited 40,000 lecturers, who fanned out across the countryside to help people understand the tyrannical forces arrayed against the farm sector: bankers and creditors, Wall Street, railroads, and corporate giants who controlled both the markets and the political process. Unlike the Grange, however, the Alliance proposed an elaborate economic program. In 1890, Alliance agencies and exchanges in some eighteen states claimed a business of $10 million, but they soon went the way of the Granger cooperatives, victims of both discrimination by wholesalers, manufacturers, railroads, and bankers and their own inexperienced management and overextended credit.

In 1887, Charles W. Macune, the new Alliance president, proposed that Texas farmers create their own Alliance Exchange in an effort to free themselves from their dependence upon grain processors and banks. Members of the exchange would sign joint notes (to be exchanged for cash), borrow money from banks, and purchase their goods and supplies from a new corporation created by the Alliance in Dallas. The exchange would also build its own warehouses to store and market members crops. While their crops were being stored, member farmers would be able to obtain credit from the warehouse cooperative so that they could buy household goods and supplies.

This grand cooperative scheme collapsed when Texas banks refused to accept the paper money from Alliance members. Macune and others then focused their energies on what Macune called a "subtreasury plan." Under this scheme, farmers would be able to store their crops in new government warehouses and obtain government loans for up to 80 percent of the value of their crops at 1 percent interest. Besides providing immediate credit, the plan would allow the farmer the leeway to hold a crop for a better price later, since he would not have to sell it immediately at harvesttime to pay off debts. The plan would also promote inflation because the loans to farmers would be made in new legal-tender notes.

The subtreasury plan went before Congress in 1890 but was never adopted. Its defeat, as well as setbacks to other Alliance proposals, convinced many farm leaders that they needed more political power in order to secure railroad regulation, currency inflation, state departments of agriculture, anti-trust laws, and farm credit.

FARM POLITICS   In the farm states west of the Mississippi River, where hard times had descended after the blizzards of 1887, farmers demanded third-party political action to address their concerns. In the South, however, white Alliance members hesitated to bolt the Democratic party, seeking instead to influence or control it. Both approaches gained startling success, with independent parties under various names upsetting the political balance in western states.

The farm protest movement produced colorful leaders, especially in Kansas, where Mary Elizabeth Lease emerged as a fiery speaker. Born in Pennsylvania, Lease migrated to Kansas, taught school, raised a family, and failed at farming in the mid-1880s. She then studied law and became one of the state's first female attorneys. At the same time, she took up public speaking on behalf of various causes, including freedom from English rule for her ancestral Ireland, prohibition of alcoholic beverages, and women's right to vote. By the end of the 1880s, Lease had joined the Alliance as well as the Knights of Labor, and she soon applied her oratorical gifts to the cause of free silver. A tall, proud, imposing woman, Lease drew attentive audiences. "The people are at bay," she warned in 1894; "let the bloodhounds of money beware." She urged angry farmers to obtain their goals "with the ballot if possible, but if not that way then with the bayonet." Like so many of the Populists, Lease viewed the urban-industrial East as the enemy of the working classes. "The great common people of this country," she shouted, "are slaves, and monopoly is the master. The West and South are bound and prostrate before the manufacturing East."

Mary Elizabeth Lease, 1890

A charismatic leader in the farm protest movement.

In the South the Alliance forced the Democrats to nominate candidates pledged to their program. In 1890 the southern states elected four pro-Alliance governors, seven pro-Alliance legislatures, forty-four pro-Alliance congressmen, and several senators. Among the most respected of the southern Alliance leaders was Thomas E. Watson of Georgia. The son of prosperous slaveholders who had lost everything after the Civil War, Watson became a successful lawyer and colorful orator on behalf of the Alliance cause. He took the lead in urging African American tenant farmers and sharecroppers to join with their white counterparts in ousting the white political elite. "You are kept apart," he told black and white farmers, "that you may be separately fleeced of your earnings."

THE POPULIST PARTY AND THE ELECTION OF 1892 As economic conditions worsened, agrarian activists decided to form a new

national political party. In 1891 delegates from farm, labor, and reform organizations met in Cincinnati to discuss the creation of the People's party. Few
southerners attended, but many delegates endorsed the third-party idea
after their failure to win over the Democratic party to the subtreasury plan.
In 1891, William Peffer of Kansas and Tom Watson of Georgia were the first
People's party candidates elected to the Senate. In 1892 a larger meeting in
St. Louis proposed a national convention of the People's party at Omaha to
adopt a platform and choose national candidates.

The 1892 Populist platform focused on issues of finance, transportation, and land. Its financial program demanded implementation of the
subtreasury plan, unlimited coinage of silver, an increase in the money supply, and a graduated income tax, whose rates would rise with personal levels
of income. As for transportation, the party called for the government to na-
tionalize the railroads, as well as the telephone and telegraph systems. It also
called for the government to reclaim from railroads and other corporations
lands "in excess of their actual needs" and to forbid land ownership by immigrants who were not citizens. Finally, the platform endorsed the eight-
hour workday and laws restricting immigration, taking these positions to
win support from urban workers, whom Populists looked upon as fellow
"producers." The party's platform turned out to be more exciting than its
candidate, Iowa's James B. Weaver. Though an able, prudent man, Weaver
carried the stigma of his defeat on the Greenback ticket twelve years before.
To attract southern voters who might be distracted by Weaver's service as
a Union general, the party named a former Confederate general for vice
president.

The Populist party was the startling new feature of the 1892 campaign.
The Democrats renominated Grover Cleveland, and Republicans turned
again to Benjamin Harrison. The tariff remained the chief issue between
them. The outcome, however, was different. Both major candidates polled
over 5 million votes, but Cleveland carried a plurality of the popular vote
and a majority of the Electoral College. Weaver gained over 1 million votes,
10 percent of the total, and carried Colorado, Kansas, Nevada, and Idaho, for
a total of twenty-two electoral votes. In Kansas the Populists won the governor's office, four congressional seats, and control of the state senate. In
neighboring Nebraska they won control of both statehouses.

POPULISM AND RELIGION   Religion played a crucial role in the rise
of Populism. At the new party's 1892 convention, one of the delegates said the
gathering was like "a religious revival, a crusade, a Pentecost of politics in

which a tongue of flame sat upon every man, and each spoke as the spirit gave him utterance." Populists believed that God was on their side in the fight to "save our republican institutions and common Christianity from decay and death." A Populist flyer promoting the new political party declared that "we are men that fear God and love his commands." Alliance meetings and Populist rallies often occurred in evangelical Protestant churches. They began with prayers and included the singing of hymns, the passing of an offering plate, and a period of instruction, or "exhortation." Speakers promoted the "conversion" of voters to the sacred cause. Evangelical ministers and lay leaders were in the vanguard of the agrarian social and political organizations. A leading evangelical Populist, the Reverend Thomas Dixon, argued that the farm revolt was "the result of divine inspiration." It constituted "a great social and moral revolution" that "would elevate mankind" and "purify politics."

THE ECONOMY AND THE SILVER SOLUTION

INADEQUATE CURRENCY   While agitated farmers were funneling their discontent into politics and businessmen were consolidating their holdings, a fundamental weakness in the economy was about to manifest itself in a major economic collapse. The nation's money supply in the late nineteenth century lacked the flexibility to grow along with the expanding economy. From 1865 to 1890, the amount of currency in circulation per capita decreased about 10 percent. Currency deflation raised the cost of borrowing money, as a tight money supply caused bankers to hike interest rates on loans.

Metallic currency dated from the Mint Act of 1792, which authorized free and unlimited coinage of silver and gold at a ratio of 15 to 1, meaning that the amount of precious metal in a silver dollar weighed fifteen times as much as that in a gold dollar, a reflection of the relative value of gold and silver at the time. "Free and unlimited coinage" simply meant that owners of precious metals could have any quantity of their gold or silver coined free, except for a nominal fee to cover costs.

A fixed ratio of the values of gold and silver did not reflect fluctuations in the market value of the metals, however. When gold rose to a market value higher than that reflected in the official ratio, owners ceased to present it for coinage. The country was actually on a silver standard until 1837, when Congress changed the ratio to 16 to 1, which soon reversed the situation. Silver became more valuable in the open market than in coinage, and the country drifted to a gold standard. This state of affairs prevailed until 1873, when Congress passed a general revision of the coinage laws and dropped the then-unused provision for the coinage of silver.

This occurred just when silver production in the western states began to increase, however, reducing its market value through the growth in supply. Soon advocates of currency inflation began to denounce the "crime of '73," which they had scarcely noticed at the time. Gradually suspicion grew that bankers and merchants had conspired in 1873 to ensure a scarcity of money. But the pro-silver forces had little more legislative success than the advocates of greenback inflation. The Bland-Allison Act of 1878 and the Sherman Silver Purchase Act of 1890 provided for some silver coinage, but too little in each case to offset the overall contraction of the nation's money supply.

THE DEPRESSION OF 1893 Just ten days before Grover Cleveland started his second presidential term in 1893 (the only nonconsecutive second term of a president in U.S. history), the Philadelphia and Reading Railroad declared bankruptcy, setting off a national financial panic. Not only was business affected, but entire farm regions were also devastated by the spreading depression. A quarter of the cities' unskilled workers lost their

National panic

The New York Stock Exchange on the morning of Friday, May 5, 1893.

jobs, and by the fall of 1893 over 600 banks had closed and 15,000 businesses had failed. Farm foreclosures soared. By 1894 the economy had reached bottom. The catastrophic depression lasted another four years, with unemployment hovering at 20 percent. In New York some 35 percent were unemployed, and 20,000 homeless people camped out at police stations and other makeshift shelters. Violent labor strikes at Pullman, Illinois, and at the Homestead Works steel-making plant outside Pittsburgh symbolized the fracturing of the social order. In 1894 some 750,000 workers went on strike, millions found themselves unemployed, and railroad construction workers, laid off in the West, began tramping east and talked of marching on Washington, D.C.

One protest group that reached Washington was "Coxey's Army," led by Jacob S. Coxey, a wealthy Ohio quarry owner turned Populist who demanded that the federal government provide the unemployed with meaningful work. Coxey, his wife, and their son, Legal Tender Coxey, rode in a carriage ahead of some 400 hardy protesters who finally straggled into Washington. There Coxey was arrested for walking on the grass. Although his ragtag army dispersed peacefully, the march on Washington, as well as the growing political strength of Populism, struck fear into the hearts of many Americans. Critics portrayed Populists as "hayseed socialists" whose election would endanger property rights and the entire capitalist system.

The 1894 congressional elections, taking place amid this climate of mushrooming anxiety, represented a severe setback for the Democrats, who paid politically for the economic downturn, and the Republicans were the chief beneficiaries. The third-party Populists emerged with six senators and seven representatives. They had polled 1.5 million votes for their congressional candidates and expected the festering discontent to carry them to national power in 1896.

SILVERITES VERSUS GOLDBUGS   The course of events would dash that hope, however. In the mid-1890s national attention focused on the currency issue. One of the causes of the 1893 depression was the failure of a major British bank, which had led many British investors to sell their American stocks and bonds in return for gold. Soon after Grover Cleveland's inauguration, the U.S. gold reserve had fallen below $100 million. To plug the drain on the Treasury, by stopping the issuance of silver notes redeemable in gold, the president sought repeal of the Sherman Silver Purchase Act. Cleveland won the repeal in 1893, but at the cost of an irreparable division in his own party. One embittered pro-silver Democrat labeled the president a traitor.

Western silver interests now escalated their demands for silver coinage, presenting a strategic dilemma for Populists: should the party promote the long list of varied reforms it had originally advocated, or should it try to ride the silver issue into power? The latter seemed the practical choice. As a consequence, the Populist leaders decided, over the protests of more radical members, to hold their 1896 nominating convention last, confident that the two major parties would at best straddle the silver issue and they would then reap a harvest of bolting silverite Republicans and Democrats.

THE ELECTION OF 1896   Contrary to those expectations, the major parties took opposing positions on the currency issue. The Republicans, as expected, chose Ohioan William McKinley on a gold-standard platform. On

William Jennings Bryan

His "cross of gold" speech at the 1896 Democratic Convention roused the delegates and secured him the party's presidential nomination.

the Democratic side the pro-silver forces gathered to wrest control of the party from Cleveland and the fiscal conservatives. In William Jennings Bryan the silver Democrats found a crusading, charismatic leader. A fervent Baptist and advocate of the free coinage of silver, Bryan was a two-term congressman from Nebraska who had been defeated in the senate race in 1894. At the 1896 convention the self-assured Bryan delivered a speech that had most of the 20,000 delegates on their feet and many in tears. Like a revivalist at a camp meeting, he galvanized the audience with the emotion of his appeal. Bryan spoke for silver and the New West, for the "hardy pioneers" and against the "financial magnates" of the urban East as well as Cleveland's "do-nothing" response to the depression. He directly challenged Republicans as well as Cleveland and the gold Democrats with a compelling Christian metaphor: "You shall not press down upon the brow of labor this crown of thorns. You shall not crucify mankind upon a cross of gold!"

The next day the theatrical Bryan was nominated on the fifth ballot, and in the process the Democratic party was fractured beyond repair—for the time being. Disappointed pro-gold Cleveland Democrats were so disgusted by Bryan's inflationary program and Populist rhetoric that they walked out of the convention and nominated their own candidate, who then announced, "Fellow Democrats, I will not consider it any great fault if you decide to cast your vote for [the Republican] William McKinley."

When the Populists met in St. Louis two weeks later, they faced an impossible choice. "If we fuse [with the Democrats]," one Populist admitted, "all the silver men we have will leave us for the more powerful Democrats." But if the Populists named their own candidate, they would divide the silver vote with Bryan and give the election to McKinley. In the end the delegates backed Bryan but chose their own vice-presidential candidate, Georgia's Thomas Watson, and invited the Democrats to drop their vice-presidential nominee, an action Bryan refused to countenance.

THE ELECTION OF 1896	Electoral Vote	Popular Vote
William McKinley (Republican)	**271**	**7,100,000**
William J. Bryan (Democrat/Populist)	176	6,500,000

How did Bryan's "cross of gold" speech divide the Democratic party? How was McKinley's strategy different from Bryan's? Why was Bryan able to carry the West and the South but unable to win in cities and the Northeast?

During the 1896 campaign the thirty-six-year-old Bryan crisscrossed the country, using his spellbinding eloquence to support "the struggling masses" of workers, farmers, and small-business owners and promising the panacea of the unlimited coinage of silver. By contrast, McKinley conducted a "front-porch campaign," receiving select delegations of supporters at his home in Canton, Ohio, and giving only prepared responses. His campaign manager, Mark Hanna, shrewdly portrayed Bryan as a radical whose "communistic spirit" would ruin the capitalist system. Many observers agreed with the portrait.

By preying upon such fears, the McKinley campaign raised vast sums of money to finance an army of 1,400 Republican speakers who stumped the country in his support. In the end the Democratic-Populist-silverite candidates were overwhelmed. McKinley won the popular vote by 7.1 million to 6.5 million and the Electoral College vote by 271 to 176.

Bryan carried most of the West and the South but garnered little support in the metropolitan centers east of the Mississippi and north of the Ohio and Potomac Rivers. Urban workers saw little to gain from the inflation promoted by Bryan and the silverites. Factory workers in the cities found it easier to identify with McKinley's "full dinner pail" campaign slogan than with Bryan's free silver. Moreover, in the critical midwestern battleground, from Minnesota and Iowa eastward to Ohio, Bryan carried not a single state. Many ethnic voters, normally drawn to the Democrats, were repelled by Bryan's evangelical Baptist style. Farmers in the East and the Midwest, moreover, were hurting less than those in the wheat and cotton belts. With less tenancy and a greater diversity of crops in those farm regions, prospering farmers saw little attraction in agrarian radicalism.

A NEW ERA

The election of 1896 was a climactic political struggle between rural and metropolitan America, and metropolitan America won. As its first important act, the McKinley administration called a special session of Congress to raise the tariff again. The Dingley Tariff of 1897 became the highest ever. By 1897, prosperity was returning, helped along by inflation of the currency, which bore out the arguments of the Greenbackers and silverites. But the inflation came, in one of history's many ironies, not from silver but from a new flood of gold onto the market and into the mints. During the 1880s and 1890s, discoveries of gold in South Africa, Canada, and Alaska led to spectacular new gold rushes, a return to the gold standard, and an end to the free-silver movement.

At the close of the nineteenth century, the old issues of tariff and currency policy, which had dominated national politics since the Civil War, gave way to global concerns: the outbreak of the War of 1898 and the acquisition of territories outside the Western Hemisphere. At the same time, the advent of a new century brought new social and political developments. Although the Populist movement faded with William Jennings Bryan's defeat, most of the progressive policies promoted by Bryan Democrats and Populists, dismissed as too radical and controversial in 1896, would be implemented over the next two decades. Bryan's impassioned candidacy helped transform the Democratic party into a vigorous instrument of "progressive" reform during the early twentieth century. Democrats began to promote anti-trust prosecutions, state laws to limit the working hours of women and children, the establishment of a minimum wage, and measures to support farmers and protect labor union organizers. As the United States looked ahead to a new century, it began to place more emphasis on the role of the national government in society and the economy.

End of Chapter Review

CHAPTER SUMMARY

- **Gilded Age Politics** Americans were intensely loyal to the two major parties, which operated on a local scale by distributing favors. "City machines" also provided working-class men with jobs and gave relief (money or necessities) to the poor, thereby winning votes. New York's Tammany Hall ring under the boss William Marcy Tweed best exemplifies the corruption resulting from this system. The major political parties shared power nearly equally during the Gilded Age, and neither party was willing to embrace bold initiatives.

- **National Politics** Politicians focused on tariff reform, the regulation of corporations, Indian wars and Indian policy, civil service reform, and immigration. In the 1884 presidential election, Republicans favoring reform, dubbed Mugwumps, bolted their party to support the Democrat, Grover Cleveland, a reformer.

- **Farm Problems** Farmers had serious grievances at the end of the nineteenth century. Commodity prices were falling because of domestic overproduction and international competition, and many farmers had gone into debt: they had bought new machinery on credit at high interest rates and were paying the railroads exorbitant rates to ship their goods to market without receiving the rebates that large corporations had the leverage to demand. In addition, high tariffs allowed manufacturers to raise the price of goods that farmers needed.

- **Farm Movements** Despite farmers' traditional reluctance to organize, many reacted to their difficulties by joining the Granger movement, which promoted farmer-owned cooperatives, and, subsequently, Farmers' Alliances, grassroots social organizations that also promoted political action. The Alliances became a major force in the Midwest and the South. Influenced by their success, delegates from farm, labor, and reform organizations in 1892 established the People's party, also known as the Populist party. Populists sought greater regulation of business by the federal government and the free coinage of silver (because they hoped that the ensuing inflation would make it easier for them to repay their debts). To appeal to urban voters, they endorsed the eight-hour workday and restrictions on immigration.

- **Rise of Populism** The Populists did well in 1892 and, with the depression of 1893, had high hopes for the next presidential election. But the Democrat, William Jennings Bryan stole the silver issue from the Populists. The Populists thus fused with the Democrats, but Bryan lost the election to the Republicans, who in a well-organized, well-financed campaign won the urban northeastern vote by portraying the Democratic candidate as a dangerous radical. The People's party did not recover from the blow.

Part Six

MODERN AMERICA

The United States entered the twentieth century on a wave of unrelenting change. In 1800 the nation was a rural, agrarian society largely detached from the concerns of international affairs. By 1900 the United States had become a highly industrialized urban culture with a growing involvement in world politics and commerce. In other words, the nation was on the threshold of modernity.

The prospect of modernity both excited and scared Americans. Old truths and beliefs clashed with unsettling scientific discoveries and social practices. People debated the legitimacy of Darwinism, the existence of God, the dangers of jazz, and the federal effort to prohibit the sale of alcoholic beverages. The automobile and airplane helped shrink distances, and communications innovations such as radio and film contributed to a national consciousness. In the process the United States began to emerge from its isolationist shell.

Noninvolvement in foreign wars and nonintervention in the internal affairs of foreign governments formed the pillars of foreign policy until the end of the century. During the 1890s, however, expanding commercial interests around the world led Americans to extend the horizons of their concerns. Imperialism was the order of the day among the great European powers, and a growing number of American expansionists demanded that the United States also adopt a global ambition and join in the hunt for new territories and markets. Such mixed motives helped spark the War of 1898 and helped justify the resulting acquisition of colonies outside the continental United States. Entangling alliances with European powers soon followed.

The outbreak of the Great War in Europe in 1914 posed an even greater challenge to the American tradition of isolation and nonintervention. The prospect of a German victory over the French and the British threatened the European balance of power, which had long ensured the security of the United States. By 1917 it appeared that Germany might emerge triumphant and begin to menace the Western Hemisphere. Woodrow Wilson's crusade to use American intervention in World War I to transform the world order in accordance with his idealistic principles severed U.S. foreign policy from its isolationist moorings. It also spawned a prolonged debate about the role of the United States in world affairs, a debate that World War II would resolve for a time on the side of internationalism.

While the United States was entering the world stage as a formidable military power, it was also settling into its role as a great industrial power.

Cities and factories sprouted across the landscape. An abundance of new jobs served as a magnet attracting millions of immigrants. They were not always welcomed, nor were they readily assimilated. Ethnic and racial strife, as well as labor agitation, increased after 1900. In the midst of such social turmoil and unparalleled economic development, reformers made their first sustained attempt to adapt their political and social institutions to the realities of the industrial age. The worst excesses and injustices of urban-industrial development—corporate monopolies, child labor, political corruption, hazardous working conditions, urban ghettos— were finally addressed in a comprehensive way. During the Progressive Era (1890–1917) local, state, and federal governments sought to rein in the excesses of industrial capitalism and develop a more efficient public policy.

A conservative Republican resurgence challenged the notion of the new regulatory state during the 1920s. Free enterprise and corporate capitalism witnessed a dramatic revival. But the stock market crash of 1929 helped propel the United States and the world into the worst economic downturn in history. The unprecedented severity of the Great Depression renewed public demands for federal programs to protect the general welfare. "This nation asks for action," declared President Franklin D. Roosevelt in his 1933 inaugural address. The many New Deal initiatives and agencies instituted by Roosevelt and his Democratic administration created the framework for a welfare state that has since served as the basis for American public policy.

The New Deal helped revive public confidence and put people back to work, but it did not end the Great Depression. It took a world war to restore full employment. The necessity of mobilizing the nation in support of the Second World War also accelerated the growth of the federal government. And the incredible scope of the war helped catapult the United States into a leadership role in world politics. The creation and use of nuclear bombs ush- ered in a new era of atomic diplomacy that held the fate of the world in the balance. For all of the new creature comforts associated with modern life, Americans in 1945 found themselves living amid an array of new anxieties, not the least of which was a global "cold war" against communism.

23

AN AMERICAN EMPIRE

FOCUS QUESTIONS wwnorton.com/studyspace

- What motivated America's "new imperialism"?
- What was the role of religion as a motive for American territorial expansion?
- What were the causes of the War of 1898?
- What did America gain from the War of 1898?
- What were the main achievements of Theodore Roosevelt's foreign policy?

Throughout the nineteenth century most Americans displayed what one senator called "only a languid interest" in foreign affairs. The overriding priorities of the time were industrial development, western settlement, and domestic politics. Foreign relations simply were not important to the vast majority of people. After the Civil War an isolationist mood swept across the United States as the country basked in its geographic advantages: wide oceans as buffers, the British navy situated between America and the powers of Europe, and militarily weak neighbors in the Western Hemisphere.

Yet the notion of America's having a Manifest Destiny ordained by God to expand its territory and its influence remained alive in the decades after the Civil War. Several prominent political and business leaders argued that the rapid industrial development of the United States required the acquisition—or conquest—of foreign territories in order to gain easier access to vital raw materials. In addition, as their exports grew, American companies and farmers became increasingly intertwined in the world economy. This involvement, in turn, required an expanded naval force to protect the global shipping lanes. And a modern steam-powered navy needed bases where its ships could replenish their supplies of coal and water. For these reasons and others the United States during the last quarter of the nineteenth century began to expand its military presence beyond the Western Hemisphere, often at the expense of other nations' sovereignty.

Toward the New Imperialism

By the late nineteenth century, European powers had already unleashed a new surge of imperialism in Africa and Asia, where they had seized territory, established colonies, and promoted economic exploitation, racial superiority, and Christian evangelism. Writing in 1902, the British economist J. A. Hobson declared that imperialism was "the most powerful factor in the current politics of the Western world."

IMPERIALISM IN A GLOBAL CONTEXT Western imperialism had economic roots; it was above all a quest for new markets and sources of raw materials. The Second Industrial Revolution generated such dramatic increases in production that business leaders felt compelled to find new markets for their burgeoning supply of goods and new sources of investment for their growing supply of capital. Manufacturers, on the other hand, were eager to find new sources of raw materials to supply their expanding needs. At the same time, the aggressive nationalism and bitter rivalries of the European powers made all of them compete with one another as they expanded their far-flung empires.

The result was a widespread process of imperial expansion into Africa and Asia. Beginning in the 1880s, the British, French, Belgians, Italians, Dutch, Spanish, and Germans used military force and political guile to conquer those continents. Each of the imperial nations, including the United States, dispatched Christian missionaries to convert native peoples. By 1900 some 18,000 Christian missionaries were scattered around the world. Often the conversion to Christianity was the first step in the loss of a culture's indigenous traditions. Western religious activities also influenced the colonial power structure. As a British nationalist explained such global ambitions, "Today, power and domination rather than freedom and independence are the ideas that appeal to the imagination of the masses—and the national ideal has given way to the imperial." This imperial outlook triggered clashes among the Western powers that would lead to unprecedented conflict in the twentieth century.

AMERICAN IMPERIALISM   As the European nations expanded their control over much of the rest of the world, the United States also began to acquire territories outside the North American continent. Most Americans became increasingly aware of world markets as developments in transportation and communication quickened the pace of commerce and diplomacy. From the first, agricultural exports had been the basis of economic growth. Now the conviction grew that American manufacturers had matured to the point where they could outsell foreign competitors in the world market. But should the expansion of markets lead to territorial expansion as well—or to intervention in the internal affairs of other countries? On such points, Americans disagreed, but a small yet influential group of public officials embraced the idea of acquiring overseas possessions, regardless of the implications. These expansionists included Senators Albert J. Beveridge of Indiana and Henry Cabot Lodge of Massachusetts, Theodore Roosevelt, and not least of all, naval captain Alfred Thayer Mahan.

During the 1880s, Captain Mahan had become a leading advocate of sea power and Western imperialism. In 1890 he published *The Influence of Sea Power upon History, 1660–1783*, in which he argued that national greatness and prosperity flowed from sea power. Modern economic development called for a powerful navy, a strong merchant marine, foreign commerce, colonies, and naval bases. Mahan championed America's "destiny" to control the Caribbean, build an isthmian canal, and spread Western civilization in the Pacific. His ideas were widely circulated in popular journals and within the U.S. government.

Yet even before Mahan's writings became influential, a gradual expansion of the navy had begun. In 1880 the nation had fewer than 100 seagoing vessels, many of them rusting or rotting at the docks. By 1896 eleven powerful new battleships had been built or authorized.

IMPERIALIST THEORY   Claims of racial superiority bolstered the new imperialist spirit. Spokesmen in each Western country, including the United States, used the arguments of social Darwinism to justify economic exploitation and territorial conquest. Among nations as among individuals, expansionists claimed, the fittest survive and prevail. John Fiske, a historian and popular lecturer on Darwinism, developed racial corollaries from Darwin's ideas. In *American Political Ideas Viewed from the Standpoint of*

Universal History (1885), he stressed the superior character of "Anglo-Saxon" institutions and peoples. The English-speaking "race," he argued, was destined to dominate the globe and transform the institutions, traditions, language—even the blood—of the world's peoples. Josiah Strong, a Congregationalist minister, added the sanction of religion to theories of racial and national superiority. In his book *Our Country: Its Possible Future and Its Present Crisis* (1885), Strong asserted that the "Anglo-Saxons" embodied two great ideas: civil liberty and "a pure spiritual Christianity." The Anglo-Saxon was "divinely commissioned to be, in a peculiar sense, his brother's keeper."

EXPANSION IN THE PACIFIC

For Josiah Strong and other expansionists, Asia offered an especially alluring target for American imperialism. President Andrew Johnson's secretary of state, William H. Seward, believed that the United States must inevitably exercise commercial domination "on the Pacific Ocean, and its islands and continents." Eager for American manufacturers to exploit Asian markets, Seward believed the United States first had to remove all foreign interests from the northern Pacific coast and gain access to that region's valuable ports. To that end, Seward cast covetous eyes on the British colony of British Columbia, sandwiched between Russia's possessions in Alaska and the Washington Territory.

Late in 1866, while encouraging British Columbians to consider making their colony a U.S. territory, Seward learned of Russia's desire to sell Alaska. He leaped at the opportunity, and in 1867 the United States bought Alaska for $7.2 million, less than 2¢ an acre. "Seward's folly" of buying the Alaskan "icebox" proved to be the biggest bargain since the Louisiana Purchase.

SAMOA AND HAWAII   Seward's successors at the State Department sustained his expansionist vision. During the post–Civil War years the United States sought coaling stations and trading posts in the Pacific Ocean, and it laid claim to various small islands and atolls. Two of those island groups were especially strategic: Samoa and Hawaii (also known as the Sandwich Islands). In 1878 the Samoans signed a treaty granting the United States a naval base on one of its islands. The following year the German and British governments worked out similar arrangements on other Samoan islands. In Hawaii the Americans had a clearer field to exploit. The islands, a united kingdom since 1795, hosted a sizable settlement of American missionaries and planters. The Hawaiian Islands were strategically more important to the United States than Samoa was, since their occupation by another major power might have posed a threat to American sugar interests and even to defense of the continent.

In 1875 the Hawaiians signed a reciprocal trade agreement, according to which their sugar entered the United States duty-free. Twelve years later they granted the United States a naval base at Pearl Harbor, near Honolulu. Those agreements prompted a boom in sugar growing, and American settlers in Hawaii came to dominate the economy. In 1887 the Americans forced Hawaii's king to create a constitutional government, which they controlled.

Queen Liliuokalani

The Hawaiian queen sought to preserve her nation's independence.

Hawaii's political climate changed sharply when the king's sister, Queen Liliuokalani, ascended the throne in 1891 and tried to reclaim power. Shortly before that, the McKinley Tariff had destroyed Hawaii's favored position in the sugar trade by putting the sugar of all countries on the duty free list and granting growers in the United States a 2¢ subsidy per pound of sugar. The resultant economic crisis and discontent in Hawaii led the white population to revolt early in 1893 and seize power. U.S. Marines supported the coup. Within a month the new American-dominated government sent a delegation to Washington and signed a treaty annexing Hawaii to the United States.

These events occurred just weeks before President Benjamin Harrison left office, however, and Democratic senators blocked the treaty's ratification. President Cleveland withdrew the treaty and sent a special commissioner to Hawaii to investigate. The commissioner ordered the marines home and reported that Americans on the islands had acted improperly. Most Hawaiians opposed annexation, said the commissioner, who thought the revolution had been engineered mainly by U.S. sugar planters hoping for annexation in order to be eligible for the new subsidy for sugar grown in the United States. Cleveland therefore proposed to restore the queen in return for amnesty to the revolutionists. The provisional government refused to step down, however, and on July 4, 1894, it proclaimed the islands the Republic of Hawaii, which included in its constitution a standing provision for annexation to the United States.

In 1897, when William McKinley became president, he was looking for an excuse to annex the Hawaiian Islands. This excuse was found when the Japanese, also hoping to take over the islands, sent warships to Hawaii. McKinley responded by sending U.S. warships and asking the Senate to annex the territory. When the Senate could not muster the two-thirds majority needed to approve the treaty, McKinley used a joint resolution of the House and the Senate to achieve his aims. The resolution passed by simple majorities in both houses, and the United States annexed Hawaii in the summer of 1898.

THE WAR OF 1898

Until the 1890s a nagging ambivalence about acquiring overseas territories had checked America's drive to expand. Suddenly, in 1898 and 1899, inhibitions collapsed, and the United States embarked on an aggressive program of global expansion.

"CUBA LIBRE"   Throughout the second half of the nineteenth century, Cubans had repeatedly revolted against Spanish rule, only to be ruthlessly put down. Cuba was one of Spain's oldest colonies and had become a major export market for the mother country. Yet American investments in Cuba, mainly in sugar and mining, were steadily increasing—the United States in fact traded more with Cuba than Spain did—and the growing economic interest in their island neighbor made Americans sympathetic to the idea of Cuban independence. So when Cubans revolted against Spanish rule on February 24, 1895, public feeling in the United States was with the rebels.

Events in Cuba supplied exciting copy for the press. William Randolph Hearst's *New York Journal* and Joseph Pulitzer's *New York World* were at the time locked in a monumental competition for readers. "It was a battle of gigantic proportions," one journalist wrote, "in which the sufferings of Cuba merely chanced to furnish some of the most convenient ammunition." The sensationalism in covering events in Cuba came to be called yellow journalism, and Hearst emerged as its undisputed champion.

PRESSURE FOR WAR   American neutrality in the Cuban struggle for independence changed sharply when William McKinley entered office in 1897. His platform had endorsed Cuban independence as well as U.S. control of

Hawaii and the construction of an isthmian canal. Knowing that the Cuban rebels enjoyed American support, Spain offered autonomy (self-government without formal independence) in return for peace. The Cubans rejected the offer. Spain was thus impaled on the horns of a dilemma, unable to end the rebellion and unready to give up Cuba.

Early in 1898, events moved rapidly to arouse American opinion against Spain. On February 9 Hearst's *New York Journal* released the text of a letter from a Spanish official, Depuy de Lôme, to a friend in Havana. In the letter, which had been stolen from the post office by a Cuban spy, de Lôme called President McKinley "weak and a bidder for the admiration of the crowd." The breach in diplomatic etiquette was such that de Lôme resigned to prevent further embarrassment to his government.

Six days later, during the night of February 15, 1898, the U.S. battleship *Maine* exploded and sank in Havana Harbor, with a terrible loss of 260 men. The ship's captain, one of only 84 survivors, scribbled a telegram to Washington: "*Maine* blown up in Havana Harbor at nine forty tonight and destroyed. Many wounded and doubtless more killed or drowned. . . . Public opinion should be suspended until further report." But those eager for a war with Spain saw no need to withhold judgment; they demanded an immediate declaration of war. Theodore Roosevelt, then serving as the assistant secretary of the navy, called the sinking "an act of dirty treachery on the part of the Spaniards." The United States, he declared, "needs a war."

A naval court of inquiry reported that an external mine had sunk the ship. Lacking hard evidence, the court made no effort to fix the blame, but the yellow press had no need of evidence. The *New York Journal* gleefully reported: "The Whole Country Thrills with War Fever." The outcry against Spain rose in a crescendo with the words "Remember the *Maine!* To Hell with Spain!" Few of those promoting war wrestled with the obvious fact that the Spanish government was determined to avoid a confrontation with the United States and therefore had nothing to gain from sinking the *Maine*. (A comprehensive study in 1976 concluded that the sinking of the *Maine* was an accident, the result of an internal explosion triggered by a fire in its coal bunker.)

The weight of outraged public opinion and the influence of militant Republicans such as Theodore Roosevelt and Henry Cabot Lodge eroded President McKinley's neutrality. On March 9, the president pushed through Congress a $50 million defense appropriation. The Spanish government, sensing the growing militancy in the United States, announced a unilateral cease-fire in early April. On April 10 the Spanish ambassador gave the U.S. State Department a message that amounted to a surrender. But the message came too late. The following day, McKinley sent Congress his war message.

The sinking of the *Maine* in Havana Harbor

The uproar created by the incident and its coverage in the "yellow press" helped to push President William McKinley to declare war.

He asked for the power to use armed forces in Cuba to protect U.S. property and trade. On April 20 a joint resolution of Congress declared Cuba independent and demanded withdrawal of Spanish forces. The Teller Amendment, added on the Senate floor, disclaimed any U.S. designs on Cuban territory. McKinley signed the resolution and sent a copy to the Spanish government. On April 22 the president announced a blockade of Cuba, an act of war under international law. Rather than give in to an ultimatum, the Spanish government declared war on April 24. Determined to be first, Congress declared war the next day, making the declaration retroactive to April 21, 1898.

Why such a rush to war after the message from Spain had indicated that it was ready for an armistice? No one knows for sure, but it seems apparent that too much momentum and popular pressure had built up for a confidential message to change the course of events. Also, leaders of the business

News announcements, 1898

A crowd watches men post news announcements outside the New York Tribune building, during the War of 1898.

community were demanding a quick resolution of the problem. Many of them lacked faith in the willingness or ability of the Spanish government to resolve the crisis. Still, it is fair to ask why McKinley did not take a stronger stand for peace. He might have defied Congress and public opinion, but in the end he deemed the political risk too high. The ultimate blame for war, if blame must be levied, belongs to the American people for letting themselves be whipped into such a hostile frenzy.

MANILA   The war itself lasted only 114 days. The American victory marked the end of Spain's once-great New World empire and the emergence of the United States as a world power. But if war with Spain saved many lives by ending the insurrection in Cuba, it also led to brutal U.S. efforts to suppress another insurrection, in the Philippines, and it created a host of commitments in the Caribbean and the Pacific that would haunt American policy makers throughout the twentieth century.

The War of 1898 was barely under way before the U.S. Navy produced a spectacular victory in an unexpected quarter: Manila Bay. While public attention centered on Cuba, young Theodore Roosevelt focused on the Spanish-controlled Philippines in the western Pacific Ocean: the assistant secretary of the navy had ordered Commodore George Dewey to engage Spain's ships in the Philippines in case of war. President McKinley had approved the orders. Arriving late on April 30, 1898, Dewey's squadron destroyed or captured all the Spanish warships in Manila Bay. While Dewey waited for reinforcements, Emilio Aguinaldo, whom he had brought out of exile to make trouble for the Spanish, declared the Philippines independent on June 12. Once Dewey's reinforcements arrived, the American forces, with the help of Filipino insurrectionists under Aguinaldo, liberated Manila from Spanish control on August 13.

THE CUBAN CAMPAIGN   While these events transpired halfway around the world, the fighting in Cuba reached a surprisingly quick climax. The U.S. Navy blockaded the Spanish fleet at Santiago while an invasion force of some 17,000 American troops was hastily assembled at Tampa, Florida. One significant unit was the First Volunteer Cavalry, better known as the Rough Riders and best remembered because Lieutenant Colonel Theodore Roosevelt was second in command. Eager to get "in on the fun" and "to act up to my preachings," Roosevelt had quit the Navy Department after war was declared. He ordered a custom-fitted blue uniform with yellow trim, grabbed a dozen pairs of spectacles, and rushed to help organize a colorful volunteer regiment of Ivy League athletes, leathery ex-convicts, Indians, and southwestern sharpshooters.

The major land action of the Cuban campaign occurred on July 1. While a much larger American force attacked Spanish positions at San Juan Hill, a smaller unit, including the dismounted Rough Riders—most of whose horses were still in Florida—and two African American regiments, seized the enemy position atop nearby Kettle Hill. Theodore Roosevelt later claimed that he "would rather have led that charge than [have] served three terms in the U.S. Senate." A friend wrote to Roosevelt's wife that her husband was "revelling in victory and gore."

On July 3, Spain's ships made a gallant run for it, but the aging vessels were little match for the newer American fleet. The casualties were one-sided: 474 Spanish were killed or wounded and 1,750 taken prisoner, while only one American was killed and one wounded. Spanish officials in Santiago surrendered on July 17. On July 25 an American force moved onto the Spanish-held island of Puerto Rico.

The next day the Spanish government in Madrid sued for peace. After discussions lasting two weeks, negotiators signed an armistice on August 12, 1898, less than four months after the war's start and the day before American troops entered Manila. The peace protocol specified that Spain should give up Cuba and that the United States should annex Puerto Rico and occupy the city, bay, and harbor of Manila pending the transfer of power in the Philippines.

And so the "splendid little war," as the future secretary of state John Hay called it in a letter to Roosevelt, officially ended. It was splendid only in the sense that its cost was relatively slight. Of the more than 274,000 Americans who served during the war and the ensuing demobilization, 5,462 died, but only 379 in battle. Most succumbed to malaria, typhoid, dysentery, or yellow fever. At such a cost the United States was launched onto the world stage as a great power, with all the benefits—and burdens—of that new status.

THE DEBATE OVER ANNEXATION   The United States and Spain signed the Treaty of Paris on December 10, 1898, but the status of the Philippines remained in limbo. President McKinley, who claimed at first that he could not locate the Philippines on a map, gave ambiguous signals to the peace commission, which itself was divided. There had been no demand for annexation of the Philippines or other Spanish possessions before the war, but Commodore Dewey's victory at Manila Bay quickly aroused expansionist fever. Business leaders began thinking of the commercial possibilities in the nearby continent of Asia, such as oil for the lamps of China and textiles for its millions of inhabitants. Missionary societies yearned to convert "the little brown brother" to Christianity. Although most of these Filipino candidates for conversion were already Catholic, the word went forth that the Philippines should be taken for the sake of their souls. Spanish negotiators raised the delicate point that U.S. forces had no claim by right of conquest and had even taken Manila after the armistice. American negotiators finally offered the Spanish $20 million as compensation for possession of the Philippines, as well as Puerto Rico in the Caribbean and Guam in the Pacific.

Meanwhile, Americans had taken other giant steps in the Pacific. Congress had annexed Hawaii in the midst of the war. In 1899, after another outbreak of fighting over the royal succession in Samoa, Germany and the United States agreed to partition the Samoa Islands. The United States annexed the easternmost islands; Germany took the rest.

The Treaty of Paris was opposed by most Democrats and Populists and some Republicans. Anti-imperialists argued that the unprecedented acquisition of the Philippines would undermine democracy. They appealed to

"Well, I Hardly Know Which to Take First!"

At the end of the nineteenth century, it seemed that Uncle Sam had developed a considerable appetite for foreign territory.

traditional isolationism, American principles of self-government, the inconsistency of liberating Cuba and annexing the Philippines, involvement in foreign entanglements that would undermine the logic of the Monroe Doctrine, and the danger that the Philippines would be expensive if not impossible to defend. The prospect of incorporating into the United States so many alien peoples was also troubling. Some critics insisted that the former Spanish colonies were not capable of establishing self-sustaining democracies. "Bananas and self-government cannot grow on the same piece of land," one senator claimed.

The opposition might have been strong enough to kill the treaty had not William Jennings Bryan influenced the vote for approval. A formal end to the war, he argued, would open the way for the future independence of Cuba and the Philippines. Ratification finally came on February 6, 1899. But President McKinley had no intention of granting the Philippines their independence. He insisted that the United States take control of the islands as an act of "benevolent assimilation." In February 1899 an American soldier outside Manila fired on Filipino nationalists, and the United States found itself in a new war.

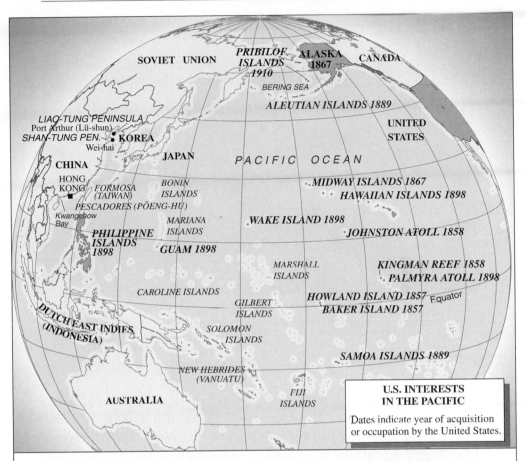

SOVIET UNION
PRIBILOF ISLANDS 1910
ALASKA 1867
CANADA
BERING SEA
ALEUTIAN ISLANDS 1889
LIAO-TUNG PENINSULA
Port Arthur (Lü-shun)
SHAN-TUNG PEN.
Wei-hai
KOREA
JAPAN
UNITED STATES
PACIFIC OCEAN
CHINA
HONG KONG
FORMOSA (TAIWAN)
PESCADORES (PŌENG-HÚ)
Kwangchow Bay
BONIN ISLANDS
MIDWAY ISLANDS 1867
HAWAIIAN ISLANDS 1898
PHILIPPINE ISLANDS 1898
MARIANA ISLANDS
GUAM 1898
WAKE ISLAND 1898
JOHNSTON ATOLL 1858
KINGMAN REEF 1858
PALMYRA ATOLL 1898
MARSHALL ISLANDS
CAROLINE ISLANDS
GILBERT ISLANDS
HOWLAND ISLAND 1857
BAKER ISLAND 1857
Equator
DUTCH EAST INDIES (INDONESIA)
SOLOMON ISLANDS
SAMOA ISLANDS 1889
NEW HEBRIDES (VANUATU)
AUSTRALIA
FIJI ISLANDS

U.S. INTERESTS IN THE PACIFIC

Dates indicate year of acquisition or occupation by the United States.

Why was President McKinley eager to acquire territory in the Pacific and the Caribbean? What kind of political system did the U.S. government create in Hawaii and in the Philippines? How did Filipinos and Hawaiians resist the Americans?

Since Aguinaldo's forces were more or less in control of the islands outside Manila, what followed over the next two years was largely an American war of conquest.

THE PHILIPPINE-AMERICAN WAR   The American effort to suppress Filipino nationalism lasted three years, eventually involved some 126,000 U.S. troops, and took the lives of hundreds of thousands of Filipinos (most of them civilians) and 4,234 American soldiers. The nature of the war also cost the United States much of its professed benevolence. It was a sordid conflict, with massacres committed by both sides. Within the first year of the

The "water cure"

A prisoner of war being tortured during the Philippine-American War.

war in the Philippines, American newspapers had begun to report an array of atrocities committed by U.S. forces—villages burned, prisoners tortured and executed. A favorite means of torture was the "water cure," whereby a Filipino would be placed on his back on the ground. While American soldiers stood on his outstretched arms and feet, salted water would be poured into the captive's mouth and nose until his stomach was bloated, whereupon the soldiers would stomp on the prisoner's abdomen, forcing all of the water out. This process would be repeated until the captive told the soldiers what they wanted to know—or he died. A Senate investigation revealed the scope of such atrocities, but in the end the senators did nothing. Their attitude resembled that of President Theodore Roosevelt, who was convinced that "nobody was seriously damaged" by the "water cure," whereas "Filipinos had inflicted terrible tortures upon our own people." Still, he wrote, "torture is not a thing that we can tolerate." Yet he did tolerate such torture, in large part because he believed that the American army was bringing peace and order and freedom to the Philippines. The "dark abuses" were the price Americans paid for the "progress of humanity." Thus did the United States alienate and destroy a Filipino independence movement modeled after America's own struggle for independence from Great Britain. Organized Filipino

Turmoil in the Philippines

Emilio Aguinaldo (seated third from right) and other leaders of the Filipino insurgence.

resistance had collapsed by the end of 1899, but even after the American capture of Aguinaldo in 1901, sporadic guerrilla action lasted until mid-1902.

Against the backdrop of this nasty guerrilla war, the great debate over annexation continued in the United States. In 1899 several anti-imperialist groups united to form the American Anti-Imperialist League. The league attracted members representing many shades of opinion. The industrialist Andrew Carnegie footed the bills; on imperialism, at least, the union leader Samuel Gompers agreed with the steel king. The usually soft-spoken philosopher William James exploded in voicing his opposition to the expansionists: "God damn the United States for its vile conduct in the Philippine Isles!" The selfish proponents of imperialism, he declared, had caused the nation to "puke up its ancient soul."

RELIGION AND EMPIRE   Among those supporting the war against Spain and the imperial conquest of Spain's Caribbean and Pacific colonies were many religious leaders. In Boston, for example, the *Herald* reported that Protestant ministers were the most rabid supporters of America's new imperialism. The time was ripe for "evangelization of the world." Foreign missionary activity had soared after the Civil War as Protestants asserted that Christianity was the "highest and purest form of religion in the world" and evangelicals eagerly spread the blessings of Christianity around the globe.

Protestant missionaries and their supporting organizations unabashedly promoted the global superiority of the Anglo-Saxon "race" and the Christian religion, and they were often virulently anti-Catholic. The *California Christian Advocate*, for example, cheered the declaration of war with Catholic Spain: "The war is the Kingdom of God coming!" Another Protestant magazine, the *Pacific Advocate*, announced that "the cross will follow the flag" as "righteous" American soldiers prepared to liberate Cuba from Spanish control. Another evangelical declared that missionary activity was itself "a war of conquest." For Catholic Americans, however, the war against Spain, one of the oldest and most intensely Catholic nations in the world, was more problematic. They objected to Protestant plans to evangelize the Catholic Cubans. A Catholic official warned that efforts to convert the Catholics of Cuba, Puerto Rico, and the Philippines "would be the speediest and most effective way to make the inhabitants of those islands discontented and opposed to America."

In the debate over America's annexing the Spanish colonies, religious arguments held sway. Senator Albert Beveridge, an ardent imperialist, declared that "we are God's chosen people." The United States, he added, had a "sacred duty" to bring the blessings of American Christianity to the lands acquired from Spain. Others shared this notion of providential responsibility for the "backward" peoples of the world. Lyman Abbott, a prominent Protestant clergyman and editor, said that America was a divine instrument of Christian imperialism. It was, he said, "the function of the Anglo-Saxon race to confer these gifts of civilization, through law, commerce, and education, on the uncivilized people of the world." Abbott lambasted the anti-imperialists:

> It is said that we have no right to go to a land occupied by barbaric people and interfere with their life. It is said that if they prefer barbarism they have a right to be barbarians. I deny the right of a barbaric people to retain possession of any quarter of the globe. What I have already said I reaffirm: barbarism has no rights which civilization is bound to respect. Barbarians have rights which civilized people are bound to respect, but they have no right to their barbarism.

Abbott and others insisted that the United States could not shirk its providential duty to "save" the former Spanish colonies from barbarism.

ORGANIZING THE ACQUISITIONS   In the end the imperialists won the debate. President McKinley quickly moved to set up a civil government in the Philippines. On July 4, 1901, the U.S. military government came to an end, and under an act of Congress, Judge William Howard Taft became the civil governor. The Philippine Government Act, passed by Congress on July 1, 1902, declared the Philippine Islands an "unorganized territory." The Tydings-McDuffie Act, in 1934, offered independence after ten more years, and independence finally took effect on July 4, 1946.

Closer to home, Puerto Rico had been acquired in part to serve as a U.S. outpost guarding the approach to the Caribbean and any future isthmian canal. In 1900 the Foraker Act established a civil government on the island. Residents of the island were declared citizens of Puerto Rico; they were not made citizens of the United States until 1917. In 1952, Puerto Rico became a commonwealth with its own constitution and elected officials, a unique status. Like a state, Puerto Rico is free to change its constitution insofar as it does not conflict with the U.S. Constitution.

Liberated Cuba, American authorities soon learned, posed problems at least as irksome as those in the new possessions. After the American occupation forces had restored order, started schools, and improved sanitary conditions, they began handing the reins of power to the Cubans. The Platt Amendment, added to an army appropriations bill passed by Congress in 1901, sharply restricted the new government's independence, however. The amendment required that Cuba never impair its independence by signing a treaty with a third power, that it keep its debt within the government's power to repay it out of ordinary revenues, and that it acknowledge the right of the United States to intervene in Cuba for the preservation of Cuban independence and the maintenance of "a government adequate for the protection of life, property, and individual liberty." Finally, Cuba had to sell or lease to the United States lands to be used for coaling or naval stations, a proviso that led to a U.S. naval base at Guantánamo Bay.

IMPERIAL RIVALRIES IN EAST ASIA

THE "OPEN DOOR"   During the 1890s the United States was not the only nation to emerge as a world power. Another was Japan. Commodore Matthew Perry's voyage of 1853–1854 had opened Japan to Western ways, and the island nation had expanded in earnest after the 1860s. Flexing its new muscles, Japan defeated China's stagnant empire in the First Sino-Japanese War (1894–1895) and as a result acquired the island of Formosa (modern-day Taiwan). China's weakness, demonstrated in the war, led Russia, England, France, and Germany to renew their scramble for "spheres of influence" on that remaining frontier of imperialist expansion.

"The Open Door"

Cartoon depicting Uncle Sam propping open a door for China with a brick labeled "U.S. Army and Navy Prestige," as colonial powers look on.

The possibility that those competing powers would carve up China and erect tariff barriers in their own spheres of influence dimmed the bright prospect of American trade with China. Yet the British had much to lose in a tariff war, for they already enjoyed substantial trade with China, so in 1899 they suggested that the United States join them in preserving China's commercial and territorial integrity. The State Department agreed that something must be done, but Secretary of State John Hay preferred to act alone rather than in concert with the British.

What came to be known as the Open Door policy was outlined in Hay's Open Door Note, dispatched in 1899 to London, Berlin, and St. Petersburg and a little later to Tokyo, Rome, and Paris. It proposed to keep China open to trade with all countries on an equal basis. None except Britain accepted Hay's principles, but none rejected them either, so Hay simply announced that all powers had accepted the policy.

The Open Door policy was rooted in the self-interest of American businesses eager to exploit Chinese markets. Yet it also tapped the deep-seated sympathies of those who opposed imperialism, especially as it pledged to protect China's territorial integrity. But it had little legal standing. When the Japanese, concerned about Russian pressure in Manchuria, asked how the United States intended to enforce the Open Door policy, Hay replied that the United States was "not prepared" to do so. So it would remain for forty years, a hollow but dangerous commitment, until continued Japanese expansion would bring about war with America in 1941.

THE BOXER REBELLION   A new Asian crisis arose in 1900 when a group of Chinese nationalists known to the Western world as Boxers (Fists of Righteous Harmony) rebelled against foreign involvement in China, surrounding the foreign embassies in Peking. The British, Germans, Russians, Japanese, and Americans quickly mounted a military expedition to relieve the embassy compound. Hay, fearful that the intervention might become an excuse to dismember China, seized the chance to further refine his Open Door policy. The United States, he declared in a circular letter of July 3, 1900, sought a solution that would "preserve Chinese territorial and administrative integrity" as well as "equal and impartial trade with all parts of the Chinese Empire." Six weeks later the expedition reached Peking and broke the Boxer Rebellion.

BIG-STICK DIPLOMACY

More than any other American political leader of his time, Theodore Roosevelt transformed the role of the United States in world affairs. The nation had emerged from the War of 1898 a world power, and he insisted that this status entailed major new responsibilities. To ensure that the United States accepted its international obligations, Roosevelt stretched both the Constitution and executive power to the limit. In the process he pushed a reluctant nation onto the center stage of world affairs.

ROOSEVELT'S RISE   In the fall elections of 1898, Republicans benefited from the euphoria of military victory, increasing their majority in Congress. That hardly amounted to a mandate for imperialism, however, since the election preceded most of the debates on the issue. But in 1900 the Democrats turned once again to William Jennings Bryan, who sought to make imperialism the "paramount issue" of the campaign. The Democratic platform condemned the Philippine conflict as "an unnecessary war" that had "placed the United States, previously known . . . throughout the world as the champion of freedom, in the false and un-American position of crushing with military force the efforts of our former allies to achieve liberty and self-government." The Republicans welcomed the opportunity to disagree. They renominated William McKinley and named as his running mate Theodore Roosevelt, who had been elected governor of New York after his self-inflated role in the War of 1898.

The trouble with Bryan's idea of a solemn referendum on imperialism was the near impossibility of making any presidential contest so simple. Bryan himself complicated his message by insisting once again on the free coinage of silver, and the tariff became an issue again as well. The Republicans' biggest advantage was probably the return to national prosperity, which they were fully ready to take credit for. Those who opposed imperialism but also opposed free silver or tariff reduction faced a bewildering choice.

The outcome was a victory for McKinley greater than his last, 7.2 million to 6.4 million popular votes and 292 to 155 electoral votes. There had been no clear-cut referendum on annexations, but the question was settled nonetheless, although it would take another year and a half to subdue the Filipino rebels. The job would be finished under the direction of another president, however.

On September 6, 1901, at a reception at the Pan-American Exposition in Buffalo, an anarchist named Leon Czolgosz (pronounced chole-gosh) approached McKinley, a pistol concealed in his bandaged hand, and fired at point-blank range. McKinley died eight days later, thereby elevating Theodore Roosevelt to the White House. "Now look," erupted Republican senator Mark Hanna, "that damned cowboy is President of the United States!"

Six weeks short of his forty-third birthday, Roosevelt was the youngest man ever to take charge of the White House, but he had more experience in public affairs than most and more vitality than any. Born in 1858, the son of a wealthy New York merchant and a Georgia belle, Roosevelt had grown up in Manhattan in cultured comfort, had visited Europe as a child, spoke German fluently, and had graduated from Harvard Phi Beta Kappa in 1880. Roosevelt loved rigorous exercise and outdoor adventure. Boxer, wrestler, and outdoorsman, he was also a voracious reader, a renowned historian and essayist, and a zealous moralist.

Roosevelt studied law briefly and within two years of graduation from college won election to the New York legislature. That same year he published *The Naval War of 1812*, the first of numerous historical, biographical, and other works to flow from his pen. He seemingly had the world at his feet— and then disaster struck. In 1884 his beloved mother, only forty-eight years old, died. Eleven hours later, in the same house, his twenty-two-year-old wife struggled with kidney failure before dying in his arms, having recently given birth to their only child. Roosevelt was distraught and bewildered. "The light has gone out of my life," he wrote in his diary. The double funeral was so wrenching that the officiating minister wept throughout his prayer. In an attempt to recover from this "strange and terrible fate," Roosevelt turned his baby daughter over to his sister, quit his political career, sold the family house, and moved west to take up the cattle business in the Dakota Territory. The blue-blooded New Yorker relished hunting, leading roundups, capturing outlaws, fighting Indians—and reading novels by the campfire. Although his western career lasted only two years, he never got over being a cowboy.

Back in New York City, Roosevelt remarried and ran unsuccessfully for mayor; he later served six years as civil service commissioner in Washington, D.C., and two years as New York City's police commissioner. After President

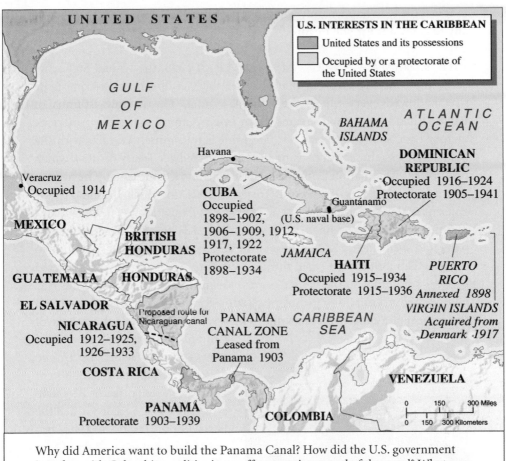

UNITED STATES

U.S. INTERESTS IN THE CARIBBEAN

☐ United States and its possessions

☐ Occupied by or a protectorate of the United States

GULF
OF
MEXICO

ATLANTIC
OCEAN

BAHAMA
ISLANDS

Havana

DOMINICAN
REPUBLIC
Occupied 1916–1924
Protectorate 1905–1941

Veracruz
Occupied 1914

MEXICO

CUBA
Occupied
1898–1902,
1906–1909, 1912,
1917, 1922
Protectorate
1898–1934

Guantánamo
(U.S. naval base)

BRITISH
HONDURAS

JAMAICA

HAITI
Occupied 1915–1934
Protectorate 1915–1936

PUERTO
RICO
Annexed 1898

GUATEMALA HONDURAS

EL SALVADOR

VIRGIN ISLANDS
Acquired from
Denmark 1917

NICARAGUA
Occupied 1912–1925,
1926–1933

Proposed route for
Nicaraguan canal

PANAMA
CANAL ZONE
Leased from
Panama 1903

CARIBBEAN
SEA

COSTA RICA

VENEZUELA

PANAMÁ
Protectorate 1903–1939

COLOMBIA

0   150   300 Miles
0   150   300 Kilometers

Why did America want to build the Panama Canal? How did the U.S. government interfere with Colombian politics in an effort to gain control of the canal? What was the Roosevelt Corollary?

McKinley appointed him assistant secretary of the navy in 1897, Roosevelt did all he could to promote the war with Spain over Cuba. "A just war," he insisted, "is in the long run far better for a man's soul than the most prosperous peace."

Roosevelt combined his boundless energy with an unshakable righteousness that led him to cast every issue in moral and patriotic terms. He saw the presidency as his "bully pulpit," and he was eager to preach fist-smacking sermons on the virtues of honesty, civic duty, and the strenuous life to his national flock. But appearances were deceiving. His energy left a false impression of impulsiveness, and the talk of morality cloaked a cautious pragmatism. Roosevelt could get carried away, but as he said of his foreign-policy actions, that was likely to happen only when "I am assured that I shall be able eventually to carry out my will by force."

THE PANAMA CANAL   After the War of 1898, the United States became more deeply involved than ever in the Caribbean, where one issue overshadowed every other: the Panama Canal. The narrow isthmus of Panama had long excited dreams of an interoceanic canal. After America's victory over Spain, Secretary of State John Hay commenced talks with the British ambassador about revising the Clayton-Bulwer Treaty of 1850, which prohibited either nation from constructing a transoceanic canal. The negotiations led to the Hay-Pauncefote Treaty of 1901, in which Britain gave its consent to the American plan for a canal across Panama.

Other obstacles remained, however. From 1881 to 1887, a French company had spent nearly $300 million and had sacrificed some 20,000 lives to dig less than a third of a canal through Panama. The company now offered to sell its holdings to the United States. Meanwhile, Secretary of State Hay had opened negotiations with Ambassador Tomás Herrán of Colombia on the subject of a canal across Panama, which was then a reluctant province of Colombia. In return for a canal zone six miles wide, the United States agreed to pay $10 million in cash and a rental fee of $250,000 a year. The U.S. Senate ratified the Hay-Herrán Treaty in 1903, but the Colombian senate held out for $25 million in cash.

Colombia's rejection of the treaty heightened the desire of Panamanian rebels for independence. An employee of the French canal company then hatched a plot in collusion with the company's representative, Philippe Bunau-Varilla. Bunau-Varilla visited Roosevelt and Hay and then, apparently with inside information, informed the Panamanian rebels that the U.S.S. *Nashville* would arrive at Colón, Panama, on November 2, 1903.

Digging the canal

President Theodore Roosevelt operating a steam shovel during his 1906 visit to the Panama Canal.

An army of some 500 Panamanians revolted against Colombian rule the next day. Colombian troops, who could not penetrate the overland jungle, found U.S. ships blocking the sea-lanes. On November 13 the Roosevelt administration made good on its collusion with the revolutionaries by recognizing Panama's independence, and on November 18 Roosevelt and the new Panamanian ambassador, who happened to be Bunau-Varilla, signed a treaty extending the Canal Zone from six to ten miles in width. For $10 million down and $250,000 a year, the United States received "in perpetuity the use, occupation and control" of the Canal Zone. Colombia eventually got its $25 million, in 1921, but only after America's interest in Colombian oil had lubricated the wheels of diplomacy. There was no apology, but the payment was made to remove "all misunderstandings growing out of the political events in Panama, November, 1903." The strategic canal opened on August 15, 1914, two weeks after the outbreak of World War I in Europe. It was a tribute to American engineering and a boon to American commerce and the Panamanian economy.

THE ROOSEVELT COROLLARY Even without the canal the United States would have been concerned with the stability of the Caribbean region, and particularly with the activities of any hostile power there. A prime excuse for intervention in those days was to force the collection of debts owed to foreigners. In 1904 a crisis over the Dominican Republic's debts prompted Roosevelt to formulate U.S. policy. In his annual address to Congress in 1904, he outlined what came to be known as the Roosevelt Corollary to the Monroe Doctrine: the principle, in short, that since the Monroe Doctrine prohibited European intervention in the region, the United States was justified in intervening first to forestall involvement by European nations. Roosevelt suggested that the United States could exercise an "international police power" in its own sphere of influence. As put into practice by mutual agreement with the

The world's constable

President Theodore Roosevelt wields "the big stick," symbolizing his aggressive diplomacy.

Dominican Republic in 1905, the Roosevelt Corollary called for the United States to appoint a collector of customs, who would apply a portion of the nation's revenues to debt payments owed American companies. The principle, applied peaceably in 1905, became the basis for military interventions later on.

THE RUSSO-JAPANESE WAR   In east Asia, meanwhile, the principle of equal trading rights embodied in the Open Door policy was tested when tensions between Russia and Japan flared into a fight over China and Korea. On February 8, 1904, war broke out when Japanese warships devastated the Russian fleet. The Japanese then occupied Korea and drove the Russians back across the Yalu River into Manchuria. But neither side could score a knockout blow, and neither relished a prolonged war. When the Japanese signaled President Roosevelt that they would welcome a negotiated settlement, he sponsored a peace conference, held in Portsmouth, New Hampshire. With the Treaty of Portsmouth (1905), the concessions all went to the Japanese. Russia acknowledged Japan's "predominant political, military, and economic interests in Korea" (Japan would annex the kingdom in 1910), and both powers agreed to evacuate Manchuria.

RELATIONS WITH JAPAN   Japan's show of strength in the war with Russia raised doubts about the security of the Philippines. During the Portsmouth talks, Roosevelt sent Secretary of War William Howard Taft to meet with the Japanese foreign minister in Tokyo. The two men arrived at the Taft-Katsura Agreement of July 29, 1905, in which the United States accepted Japanese control of Korea, and Japan disavowed any designs on the Philippines. Three years later the Root-Takahira Agreement, negotiated by Secretary of State Elihu Root and the Japanese ambassador, promised to respect each other's possessions and reinforced the Open Door policy by supporting "the independence and integrity of China" and "the principle of equal opportunity for commerce and industry in China."

Behind the diplomatic facade of goodwill, however, lay simmering mutual distrust. For many Americans the Russian threat in east Asia now gave way to distrust of Japan's "yellow peril" (a term apparently coined by Germany's kaiser Wilhelm II). Racial animosities on the West Coast helped sour relations with Japan. In 1906, San Francisco's school board ordered students of Chinese, Japanese, and Korean descent to attend a separate public school. The Japanese government sharply protested the show of ethnic prejudice, and President Roosevelt managed to talk the school board into changing its policy. For its part, Japan agreed to limit sharply its issuance of visas to the

United States. This "Gentleman's Agreement" of 1907, the precise terms of which have never been revealed, halted the influx of Japanese immigrants and brought some respite to racial agitation in California.

THE UNITED STATES AND EUROPE   At the same time that the United States was expanding into Asia and the Caribbean, events in Europe also required attention. While Roosevelt was mediating the Russo-Japanese War in 1905, another crisis was brewing in Morocco, where the Germans and French fought for control. Roosevelt felt that the United States had something at stake in preventing the outbreak of a major war. At the behest of Germany, he talked the French and the British into attending an international conference at Algeciras, Spain, with American delegates present. Roosevelt then maneuvered the Germans into accepting his compromise proposal. The Act of Algeciras, signed in 1906, affirmed the independence of Morocco and guaranteed an open door for trade there. Roosevelt received the Nobel Peace Prize in 1906 for his work at Portsmouth and Algeciras. Despite all his bellicosity on other occasions, he had earned it.

Before Roosevelt left the White House, in March 1909, he celebrated America's rise to the status of a world power with one great flourish. In late 1907 he sent the entire U.S. Navy, by then second in strength only to the British fleet, on a grand tour around the world. It was the first such display of American naval might in the Pacific, and many feared the reaction of the Japanese, for whose benefit Roosevelt had in fact staged the show. They need not have worried, for in Japan the flotilla received the greatest welcome of all. Thousands of schoolchildren turned out, waving tiny American flags and singing "The Star-Spangled Banner" in English. The triumphal procession continued home by way of the Mediterranean and steamed back into American waters in early 1909, just in time to close out Roosevelt's presidency on a note of success.

Yet it was a success that would have mixed consequences. Roosevelt's ability to deploy American power abroad was burdened by a racist ideology shared by many prominent political figures of the time. He once told the graduates of the Naval War College that all "the great masterful races have been fighting races, and the minute that a race loses the hard fighting virtues . . . it has lost the right to stand as equal to the best." On another occasion he called war the best way to promote "the clear instinct for race selfishness" and insisted that "the most ultimately righteous of all wars is a war with savages." Such a belligerent and bigoted attitude would come back to haunt the United States in world affairs—and at home.

CHAPTER SUMMARY

- **New Imperialism** By the beginning of the twentieth century, the idea of a manifest destiny and American industrialists' need for new markets for their goods fueled America's "new imperialism." The ideology of social Darwinism was used to justify the colonization of less industrially developed nations as white Americans held that their own industrial superiority proved their racial superiority and, therefore, the theory of the survival of the fittest. White Americans rationalized further that they had a duty to Christianize and uplift "backward" peoples.

- **Religion and Imperialism** Protestant missionaries felt impelled to take Christianity to native peoples throughout the world. The evangelical missionaries were anti-Catholic and in the Philippines refused to distinguish between Catholic Filipinos and non-Christians. An indigenous people's acceptance of Christianity was the first step toward the loss of their indigenous culture.

- **War of 1898** Spain still had an extensive empire, and Cuba was one of its oldest colonies. When Cubans revolted against Spain in 1895, many Americans were sympathetic to their demand for independence. The insurrection was harshly suppressed, and sensational coverage in certain New York newspapers further aroused Americans' sympathy. Early in 1898, the publication of a letter by Spain's minister to the United States, Depuy de Lôme, which criticized President McKinley, and then the explosion of the U.S. battleship *Maine* in Havana Harbor propelled America into a war with Spain despite the reluctance of President McKinley and many business interests.

- **Results of the War of 1898** Although the Teller Amendment declared that the United States had no intention of annexing Cuba, America curtailed Cuba's freedom and annexed other territories taken from Spain in the War of 1898. Insurrection followed in the Philippines when insurgents saw that the islands would be administered by the United States. In the treaty that ended the war, America gained Puerto Rico as well as Guam and other islands in the Pacific. Meanwhile, Hawaii had been annexed during the war.

- **Big-Stick Diplomacy** As president, Theodore Roosevelt actively pursued an imperialist foreign policy, confirming the United States' new role as a world power. He arbitrated the treaty that ended the Russo-Japanese War, proclaimed the Open Door policy with China; allowed his administration to engage in dealings that made possible American control over the Panama Canal, and sent the navy's entire fleet around the world as a symbol of American might. He articulated an extension of the Monroe Doctrine whereby the United States might intervene in disputes between North and South America and other world powers.

CHRONOLOGY

1894	Republic of Hawaii is proclaimed
1895	Cuban insurrection breaks out against Spanish rule
1898	U.S. battleship *Maine* explodes in Havana Harbor
1898	War of 1898
1898	United States annexes Hawaii
1899	U.S. Senate ratifies the Treaty of Paris, ending the War of 1898
1899–1902	Filipino insurgents resist U.S. domination
1900	International alliance quells the Boxer Rebellion
1903	Panamanians revolt against Colombia
1904	Russo-Japanese War
1907	Great White Fleet circumnavigates the globe in a demonstration of America's rise to world-power status
1914	Panama Canal opens

KEY TERMS & NAMES

Alfred Thayer Mahan's *The Influence of Sea Power upon History, 1660–1783* p. 687

Queen Liliuokalani p. 689

William Randolph Hearst's *New York Journal* p. 690

Joseph Pulitzer's *New York World* p. 690

de Lôme letter p. 691

Teller Amendment p. 692

Theodore Roosevelt p. 694

George Dewey p. 694

Emilio Aguinaldo p. 694

Rough Riders p. 694

Open Door policy p. 701

Roosevelt Corollary to the Monroe Doctrine p. 707

24

THE PROGRESSIVE ERA

FOCUS QUESTIONS   wwnorton.com/studyspace

- Who were the progressives, and what were some of their major causes?

- Who were the muckrakers, and what impact did they have?

- What were Theodore Roosevelt's and William Taft's progressive programs, and what were those programs' goals?

- Why was the election of 1912 significant?

- How was Woodrow Wilson's progressivism different from Roosevelt's?

Theodore Roosevelt's emergence as a national leader coincided with the onset of what historians have labeled the Progressive Era (1890–1917). Progressivism was very diverse in its motives and methods. It was less an organized movement than a multi-faceted response to the problems created by unregulated industrialization, unplanned urbanization, and unrelenting immigration. Progressives believed that American life was threatened by social instability, economic injustice, and political corruption. But progressives were not despondent. They were convinced that society could be improved through creative initiatives and concerted action. By working together in a spirit of community, individuals, organizations, and governments could ensure the "progress" of American society. And in fact they did so through an array of reforms and initiatives, some of which conflicted with one another. By the 1920s, progressives had implemented significant changes in all levels of government and across all levels of society.

The progressive impulse arose in response to many societal changes, the most powerful of which were the devastating depression of the 1890s and its attendant social unrest. The depression brought hard times to the cities, worsened already-dreadful factory conditions, deepened distress in rural areas, and provoked both the fears and the conscience of the rapidly growing middle and upper-middle classes. Although the United States boasted the highest per capita income in the world, it also harbored some of the poorest people. In 1900 an estimated 10 million of the 82 million Americans lived in desperate poverty. Most of the destitute were immigrants living in the major cities.

By the turn of the century, so many outraged activists were at work seeking to improve social conditions and political abuses that people began to speak of a Progressive Era, a time of fermenting idealism, moral and religious fervor, and constructive social, economic, and political change. The scope of the social crisis was so vast and complex that new remedies were needed. Old prejudices toward the poor and needy had to be changed. Reform needed to become more pragmatic and scientific. "The conditions of life forced by our civilization upon the poor in our great cities are undemocratic, unchristian, and unrighteous," said Vida Scudder, a settlement house leader. But the efforts to address widespread poverty had to be "wholly free from the spirit of social dogmatism and doctrinaire assertion. . . . As we become more practical, we also become better idealists."

ELEMENTS OF REFORM

Political progressives crusaded against the abuses of urban political bosses and corporate robber barons. Their goals were greater democracy, honest and efficient government, more effective regulation of big business and "special interests," and greater social justice for working people.

The progressive movement represented the animating spirit of the times rather than a single organized group or party. What reformers shared was a common assumption that the complex social ills and tensions generated by the urban-industrial revolution required expanding the scope of local, state, and federal government authority so as to elevate the public interest over private greed. Many progressives were motivated by religious beliefs that led some of them to concentrate on moral reforms such as the prohibition of alcoholic beverages and Sunday closing laws.

The "real heart of the movement," declared one reformer, was "to use the government as an agency of human welfare." Governments were now called upon to provide a broad range of direct public services: schools, good roads (a movement propelled first by cyclists and then by automobilists), conservation of natural resources, public health and welfare, care of the disabled, and farm loans and farm demonstration agents (county workers who visited farms to demonstrate new technology), among others. Such initiatives represented the first tentative steps toward what would become known during the 1930s and thereafter as the welfare state.

THE ANTECEDENTS OF PROGRESSIVISM   The progressive impulse began at the local level in the 1880s as a response to problems caused by industrialization and urbanization and only gradually emerged on the national level. Beginning in the large cities of the East and the Midwest, private citizens worked to improve basic public services such as sewerage, housing, and transportation. Reformers of local government believed in greater efficiency, less favoritism, and more expertise. They wanted to reorder government itself through detailed budgets, audits, and a more rationalized structure of government offices. Early efforts to improve public health, education, and factory conditions grew out of a desire to improve the administration and enforcement of local and state laws.

Another significant force in fostering the spirit of progressivism was the growing prominence of socialist critiques of living and working conditions. The Socialist party of the time, small but earnest and vocal, served as the left wing of progressivism. Most progressives found socialist remedies unacceptable, and the main progressive reform impulse grew in part from a desire to counter the growing appeal of socialist doctrines by promoting more mainstream reforms. More important in spurring progressive reform were social critics who dramatized the need for action through investigative journalism.

THE MUCKRAKERS   Chronic urban poverty, unsafe working conditions, infectious diseases, and child labor in unhealthy factories were complex social issues; remedying them would take more than an idealistic desire to effect change in government, public health, and working conditions. The public's consciousness needed to be raised, a process that required publicizing both scandals and festering social ills. A group of investigative journalists dubbed "muckrakers" rose to the challenge. These writers, who thrived on exposing corruption and social injustice, got their name when Theodore Roosevelt compared them to a character in John Bunyan's *Pilgrim's Progress:* "A man that could look no way but downwards with a muckrake in his hands." "Muckrakers are often indispensable to . . . society," Roosevelt said, "but only if they know when to stop raking the muck."

Henry Demarest Lloyd was one of the first muckrakers. His book *Wealth against Commonwealth* (1894) provided a critical examination of the Standard

Oil Company and other monopolies. Lloyd exposed the growth of corporate giants responsible to none but themselves, able to corrupt if not control governments. Lincoln Steffens, in a series of articles later collected into a book, *The Shame of the Cities* (1904), similarly revealed the prevalence of municipal corruption. Another early muckraker was Jacob Riis, a Danish immigrant who exposed slum conditions in *How the Other Half Lives* (1890). The chief outlets for these social critics were the popular middle-class magazines that began to flourish in the 1890s, such as the *Arena* and *McClure's*.

Without the muckrakers, progressivism would never have achieved widespread popular support. In feeding a growing public appetite for facts about modern social problems, the muckrakers demonstrated one

Cover of McClure's Magazine, 1902

This cover features Ida Tarbell's muckracking series on the Standard Oil Company.

of the salient features of the progressive movement, and one of its central failures. The progressives were stronger on diagnosis than on remedy. They harbored a naive faith in the power of democracy. Reveal the facts, expose corruption, arouse public indignation, and bring government closer to the people, they assumed, and the correction of evils would follow automatically. The cure for the ills of democracy was, to progressive reformers, a more enlightened and engaged democracy.

FEATURES OF PROGRESSIVISM

DEMOCRACY   The most important progressive reform intended to democratize government and foster greater grassroots political participation was the direct primary, in which candidates would be nominated by the vote of all party members rather than by a few political bosses who selected candidates for the parties. After South Carolina adopted the first statewide primary in 1896, the concept spread within two decades to nearly every other state.

The primary was but one expression of a broad progressive movement for greater public participation in the political process. In 1898, South Dakota became the first state to adopt the initiative and referendum, procedures that allow voters to enact laws directly. If a designated number of voters petitioned to have a measure put on the ballot (the initiative), the electorate could then vote it up or down (the referendum). Oregon also adopted a spectrum of reform measures, including a voter-registration law (1899), the initiative and referendum (1902), the direct primary (1904), a sweeping corrupt-practices act (1908), and the recall (1910), whereby public officials could be removed by a public petition and vote. By 1920 nearly twenty states had adopted the initiative and referendum, and nearly a dozen had adopted the recall. The direct election of U.S. senators by the people, rather than by the state legislatures, was another progressive political reform. The popular election of senators required a constitutional amendment, and by 1912 the Senate finally agreed to the Seventeenth Amendment, which was ratified by the states in 1913.

EFFICIENCY   A second major theme of progressivism was the "gospel of efficiency." In the business world during the early twentieth century, Frederick W. Taylor, the original "efficiency expert," developed an array of scientific industrial management techniques designed to cut manufacturing costs and enhance productivity. Taylorism, as scientific management came to be known, promised to reduce waste through the detailed analysis of labor processes. By meticulously studying the time it took each worker to perform a task, Taylor prescribed the optimal technique for the average worker and established detailed performance standards for each job classification. The promise of higher wages, he believed, would motivate workers to exceed "average" expectations.

Instead, many workers resented Taylor's innovations. They saw in scientific management a tool to make employees work faster than was healthy or fair. Yet Taylor's controversial efficiency system brought concrete improvements in productivity, especially among those industries whose production processes were highly standardized and whose jobs were precisely defined.

In government the efficiency movement called for nonpartisan "experts" to replace bureaucrats and demanded the reorganization of agencies to prevent redundancy, establish clear lines of authority, and assign accountability to specific officials. The most ardent disciple of the principle of "scientific" government by experts was Wisconsin governor Robert M. La Follette, "Fighting Bob," who established a Legislative Reference Bureau staffed by professors and specialists to provide research, advice, and help in the drafting of legislation designed to curb the power of special interests and promote social justice. This "Wisconsin idea" of efficient government was widely publicized and copied by other states.

Two progressive ideas for making municipal government more efficient gained headway in the first decade of the new century. One, the commission system, was first adopted by Galveston, Texas, in 1901, when local government collapsed in the aftermath of a devastating hurricane that killed 6,000 people and destroyed half the town. The system placed ultimate authority

Robert M. La Follette

A progressive proponent of expertise in government.

in a board composed of elected administrative heads of city departments—commissioners of sanitation, police, utilities, and so on. By 1914 more than 400 towns and small cities across the country had adopted the commission system. The more durable idea, however, was the city-manager plan, under which a professional administrator ran the municipal government in accordance with policies set by the elected council and mayor. Staunton, Virginia, first adopted the plan in 1908. By 1914 the National Association of City Managers had heralded the arrival of a new profession.

REGULATION   Of all the problems facing American society at the turn of the century, one engaged a greater diversity of reformers and elicited more solutions than any other: the regulation of giant corporations, which became a third major theme of progressivism. Beginning in the 1870s, states had tried to regulate the freight rates of railroads and the working conditions in other businesses, only to be thwarted by Supreme Court rulings. The judges declared that only the federal government could regulate companies involved in interstate commerce. By the 1890s the growth of monopolistic corporations had spurred reformers to act on a national level. Some progressives believed that the problems of concentrated economic power and its abuses should be left to business to work out for itself, a policy known as laissez-faire. Others advocated an active government policy of trust-busting in the belief that restoring old-fashioned competition was the best way to prevent economic abuses.

Efforts to restore the competitiveness of small firms proved unworkable, however, in part because breaking up large corporations was a very complicated endeavor. As a consequence, the main thrust of progressive reform over the years was toward regulation, rather than dissolution, of big businesses. To some extent, regulation and "stabilization" won acceptance among business leaders because whatever respect they paid to competition in principle, they preferred not to face it in practice. As time passed, however, regulatory agencies often came under the influence or control of those they were supposed to regulate.

SOCIAL JUSTICE   A fourth important feature of the progressive spirit was the impulse toward social justice, which manifested itself in an array of activities: the promotion of private charities; efforts by sanitation reformers to clean up cities through personal hygiene, municipal sewers, and public-awareness campaigns; and campaigns aimed at regulating child labor and the consumption of alcohol. Led by women, the settlement house movement of the late nineteenth century had spawned a corps of social workers and genteel reformers animated by religious ideals and devoted to the uplift of slum dwellers. By 1910 there were over 400 settlement houses in cities across the country.

Child labor

A young girl working as a spinner in a cotton mill in Vermont, 1910.

The settlement house movement, led by Jane Addams, Ellen Gates Starr, and Lillian Wald, manifested an important aspect of progressivism: women, mostly middle-class married women, were the driving force behind the grassroots progressive movement. In massive numbers they fanned out to address social ills. The Women's Christian Temperance Union (WCTU), founded in 1874, was the largest women's group in the nation at the end of the nineteenth century, boasting 300,000 members. Frances Willard, the dynamic president of the WCTU between 1879 and 1898, adopted the motto "do everything" to emphasize that all social problems were interconnected. Members of the WCTU strove to close saloons, improve prison conditions, shelter prostitutes and abused women and children, support female labor unions, and champion women's suffrage. The WCTU also lobbied for the eight-hour workday, the regulation of child labor, better nutrition, the federal inspection of food processors and drug manufacturers, free kinder-gartens and public playgrounds, and uniform marriage and divorce laws across the states.

But with time it became apparent that social evils extended beyond the reach of private charities and demanded government intervention. Labor legislation was perhaps the most significant reform to emerge from the drive for social justice. It emerged first at the state level. The

Frances Elizabeth Willard

Willard founded the WCTU and lobbied for women's suffrage.

National Child Labor Committee, organized in 1904, led a movement for state laws banning the still-widespread employment of young children. Within ten years the committee helped foster in most states new laws banning the labor of underage children (the minimum age varying from twelve to sixteen) and limiting the hours older children might work.

Closely linked to the child-labor reform movement was a concerted effort to regulate the hours of work for women. Spearheaded by Florence Kelley, the head of the National Consumers' League, this progressive crusade promoted the passage of state laws addressing the long working hours imposed on women who were wives and mothers.

The Supreme Court pursued a curiously erratic course in ruling on new state labor laws. In *Lochner v. New York* (1905), the Court voided a ten-hour-workday law because it violated workers' "liberty of contract" to accept any terms they chose. Then in *Muller v. Oregon* (1908), the high court upheld a ten-hour-workday law for women. The justices relied largely on sociological data that attorney Louis D. Brandeis presented regarding the adverse effects of long hours on the health and morals of women. In

Bunting v. Oregon (1917), the Court accepted a ten-hour workday for both men and women but for twenty more years held out against state minimum-wage laws.

Legislation to protect workers against avoidable accidents gained momentum from disasters such as the 1911 fire at the Triangle Shirtwaist Company in New York City, in which 146 workers died, mostly Jewish and Italian immigrants, most of them women and many of them in their teens, because the owner kept the stairway doors locked to prevent theft. Workers trapped on the three upper floors of the ten-story building died in the fire or leaped to their death. Stricter building codes and factory-inspection acts followed.

PROGRESSIVISM AND RELIGION   Religion was a crucial source of energy for progressive reformers. Christians and Jews embraced the social gospel, seeking to express their faith through aid to the less fortunate. Jane Addams called the impulse to found settlement houses for the waves of immigrants arriving in American cities "Christian humanitarianism." She and others often used the phrase "social righteousness" to explain the connection between social activism and religious belief. Protestants, Catholics, and Jews worked closely together to promote state laws providing for minimum-wage levels and shorter workdays. Some of the reformers applied their crusade for social justice to organized religion itself. Frances Willard, who spent time as a traveling evangelist, lobbied church organizations to allow women to become ministers. As she said, "If women can organize missionary societies, temperance societies, and every kind of charitable organization . . . why not permit them to be ordained to preach the Gospel and administer the sacraments of the Church?"

PROHIBITION   For many progressive activists with strong religious convictions, the cause of liquor prohibition was the foremost societal concern. The WCTU had been battling the sale of alcoholic beverages since 1874, but the most successful political action followed the formation in 1893 of the Anti-Saloon League, an organization that pioneered the strategy of the single-issue pressure group. In 1913 the league endorsed an amendment to the Constitution prohibiting the sale of all alcoholic beverages, which was adopted by Congress in 1917. By the time it was ratified, two years later, state and local action had already dried up areas occupied by nearly three fourths of the nation's population.

ROOSEVELT'S PROGRESSIVISM

While most progressive initiatives originated at the state and local levels, national reform efforts began to appear around 1900. Theodore Roosevelt brought to the White House in 1901 an expansive vision of the presidency that well suited the cause of progressive reform. In one of his first addresses to Congress, he stressed the need for a new political approach. When the Constitution was first drafted in 1787, he explained, the nation's social and economic conditions were quite unlike those at the dawn of the twentieth century. Modern urban-industrial society required more active government involvement.

More than any other president since Abraham Lincoln, Roosevelt possessed an activist bent. Still, his initial approach to reform was cautious. He sought to avoid the extremes of socialism on the one hand and laissez-faire individualism on the other. A skilled political maneuverer, he broke the tradition of the Gilded Age presidents by serving as a very active chief executive. Roosevelt greatly expanded the role and visibility of the presidency, as well as the authority and scope of the federal government. He cultivated party leaders in Congress and steered away from such divisive issues as the tariff and regulation of the banks. And when he did approach the explosive issue of the trusts, he took care to reassure the business community. For him politics was the art of the possible. Unlike the more radical progressives and the doctrinaire "lunatic fringe," as he called it, he would take half a loaf rather than none at all.

THE TRUSTS On the issue of huge business trusts, Roosevelt endorsed the "sincere conviction that combination and concentration should be, not prohibited, but supervised and within reasonable limits controlled." In 1902 he proposed a "Square Deal" for all, calling for enforcement of existing anti-trust laws and stricter controls on big business. Effective regulation, he insisted, was better than a futile effort to restore small business by breaking up all giant corporations, which might be achieved only at a cost to the efficiencies of scale gained in larger operations.

Because Congress balked at regulatory legislation, Roosevelt forced the issue by a more vigorous federal prosecution of the Sherman Anti-Trust Act of 1890. He chose his target carefully. In the case against the sugar trust (*United States v. E. C. Knight and Company*, 1895), the Supreme Court had declared manufacturing strictly an *intrastate* activity. Most railroads, however, were beyond question engaged in *interstate* commerce and thus subject to federal

Roosevelt's duality

Theodore Roosevelt as an "apostle of prosperity" (top) and as a Roman tyrant (bottom). Roosevelt's energy, spirit, self-righteousness, and impulsiveness elicited sharp reactions.

authority. Consequently, in 1902, Roosevelt moved against the Northern Securities Company, a holding company merging the competing Great Northern and Northern Pacific Railroads. Roosevelt attacked the trust for essentially forming a monopoly, and in 1904, in *United States v. Northern Securities Company,* the Supreme Court ordered the combination dissolved. Roosevelt continued to use his executive powers to enforce the Sherman Anti-Trust Act, but he avoided conflict in Congress by proposing no further anti-trust legislation. Altogether, his administration brought about twenty-five anti-trust suits.

THE 1902 COAL STRIKE   Roosevelt also used the "big stick" against corporations in the coal strike of 1902. On May 12 some 150,000 members of the United Mine Workers (UMW) walked off the job in West Virginia and Pennsylvania. They demanded a 20 percent wage increase, a reduction in daily working hours from ten to nine, and formal recognition of their union by management. The operators dug in their heels and shut down the mines in an effort to starve out the miners, many of whom were immigrants from eastern Europe. One mine owner revealed the social prejudices of the era when he asserted, "The miners don't suffer—why, they can't even speak English."

Previous presidents such as Rutherford Hayes and Grover Cleveland had responded to labor unrest by dispatching federal troops. But the coal strike had not become violent when Roosevelt aggressively intervened. He was concerned about the approach of winter amid a nationwide coal shortage and the effects of the strike on the fall congressional elections—he told a friend that the public would blame the Republicans if coal were in short supply. By October 1902 the strike had caused the price of coal to soar, and hospitals and schools reported empty coal bins. Roosevelt thus decided upon a bold move: he invited leaders of both sides to a conference in Washington, where he appealed to their "patriotism, to the spirit that sinks personal considerations and makes individual sacrifices for the public good." The mine owners attended the conference but refused even to speak to the UMW leaders. The "extraordinary stupidity and temper" of the "wooden-headed" owners infuriated Roosevelt. With the conference deadlocked, the president threatened to take over the mines and send in the army to run them. Militarizing the mines would have been an act of dubious legality, but the owners feared that Roosevelt might do it and that public opinion would support him.

The coal strike ended on October 23 with an agreement to submit the issues to an arbitration commission named by the president. The agreement enhanced the prestige of both Roosevelt and the union's leader, although it produced only a partial victory for the miners. By the arbitrators' decision in 1903, the miners won a nine-hour workday but only a 10 percent wage increase and no union recognition by the owners.

AN EXPANDING GOVERNMENT   In 1903, Congress strengthened both anti-trust enforcement and government regulation by creating a new federal agency, the Department of Commerce and Labor, and passing the Elkins Act, which made it illegal for corporations to take, as well as to give, secret rebates to their preferred customers. The newly established Bureau of Corporations had no direct regulatory powers, but it did have a mandate to report on the activities of interstate corporations. Its findings could lead to anti-trust suits, but its purpose was rather to help corporations correct malpractices and avoid the need for lawsuits. Many companies cooperated, but others held back. When Standard Oil refused to turn over its records, the government brought an anti-trust suit that resulted in the company's dissolution in 1911. The Supreme Court ordered the American Tobacco Company broken up at the same time.

ROOSEVELT'S SECOND TERM

Roosevelt's energy and policies built a coalition of progressive- and conservative-minded voters who assured his election in his own right in 1904. The Democrats, having twice lost with William Jennings Bryan, turned to Alton B. Parker, who as chief justice of New York's supreme court, had upheld labor's right to the closed shop (requiring that all employees be union members) and the state's right to limit hours of work. Despite Parker's liberal record, party leaders presented him as a safe conservative. Yet the effort to portray their Democratic candidate as more conservative than Roosevelt proved a futile gesture for the party that had twice nominated Bryan. Despite Roosevelt's trust-busting, most business leaders, according to the *New York Sun,* preferred the "impulsive candidate of the party of conservatism to the conservative candidate of the party which the business interests regard as permanently and dangerously impulsive."

Roosevelt's invincible popularity and the sheer force of his personality swept him to an impressive victory of 7.6 million votes to Parker's 5.1 million, with 336 electoral votes for Roosevelt and 140 for Parker. The Democratic nominee Parker carried only the Solid South of the former Confederacy and two border states, Kentucky and Maryland. On election night, Roosevelt announced that he would not run again, a statement he later would regret.

LEGISLATIVE LEADERSHIP   Elected in his own right, Roosevelt approached his second term with heightened confidence and a stronger commitment to progressive reform. In 1905 he devoted most of his annual message to the need for greater regulation and control of big business. The independent Roosevelt took aim at the railroads first.

Roosevelt asked Congress to extend the authority of the Interstate Commerce Commission to give it more effective control over railroad freight rates. He had to mobilize all the pressure and influence at his disposal to push through the bill introduced by Representative Peter Hepburn of Iowa. Enacted in 1906, the Hepburn Act gave the ICC the power to set maximum freight rates. The commission no longer had to go to court to enforce its decisions. The Hepburn Act also extended the ICC's regulatory reach beyond railroads, to pipelines, freight companies, sleeping-car companies, bridges, and ferries.

On the very day after passage of the Hepburn Act, a growing movement for the regulation of meat packers, food processors, and makers of drugs and patent medicines reached fruition. Discontent with abuses in the processing of food and drugs had grown rapidly as a result of muckrakers' disclosures. The chief chemist of the Agriculture Department, for example, supplied telling evidence of harmful additives used in the preparation of "embalmed meat" and other food products. Others reported on dangerous ingredients in some patent medicines.

Perhaps the most telling blow against such abuses was struck by Upton Sinclair's novel *The Jungle* (1906), which graphically portrays the filthy conditions in Chicago's meatpacking industry. Roosevelt read *The Jungle*—and reacted quickly. He sent two federal agents to Chicago to investigate, and their report confirmed all that Sinclair had said. Soon Roosevelt and Congress were hammering out a bill to address the problems.

The meat industry

Pigs strung up along the hog-scraping rail at Armour's packing plant in Chicago, ca. 1909.

The Meat Inspection Act of 1906 required federal inspection of meats destined for interstate commerce and empowered officials in the Agriculture Department to impose sanitary standards. The Pure Food and Drug Act, enacted the same day, placed restrictions on the makers of prepared foods and patent medicines and forbade the manufacture, sale, or transportation of adulterated, misbranded, or harmful foods, drugs, and liquors.

With the achievements of 1903 and 1906, Theodore Roosevelt's campaign for regulatory legislation reached its chief goals and in the process moved the federal government a great distance from the laissez-faire policies that had prevailed before the turn of the century.

CONSERVATION   One of the most enduring legacies of Roosevelt's leadership was his energetic support for the emerging environmental conservation movement. Roosevelt was the first president to challenge the long-standing myth of America's having inexhaustible natural resources. In fact, Roosevelt declared that conservation of natural resources was the "great material question of the day." He and other early conservationists were convinced that the tradition of freewheeling individual and corporate exploitation of the environment must be supplanted by the scientific management of the nation's natural resources for the long-term public benefit. "The things that will destroy America," he said, "are prosperity at any price, peace at any price, safety first instead of duty first, the love of soft living and the get-rich-quick theory of life."

After the Civil War a growing number of conservation organizations and individual activists had begun to oppose the unregulated exploitation of natural resources and sought to preserve wilderness areas. Just as reformers promoted the regulation of business and industry for the public welfare, conservationists championed efforts to manage and preserve the natural environment for future generations. Among the first promoters of resource conservation were ardent sportsmen among the social elite (including Theodore Roosevelt), who worried that rapacious commercial hunters and trappers were killing game animals to the point of extermination. In 1886, for example, the sportsman-naturalist George Bird Grinnell, editor of *Forest and Stream*, founded the Audubon Society to protect wild birds from being decimated for their plumage. Two years later Grinnell, Roosevelt, and a dozen other recreational hunters formed the Boone and Crockett Club, named in honor of Daniel Boone and Davy Crockett, the legendary frontiersmen. The club's goal was to ensure that big-game animals and fish were protected for posterity, a goal shared by national monthly newspapers such as *American Sportsman, Forest and Stream,* and *Field and Stream.* By 1900 most states had enacted laws regulating game hunting and had created game refuges and wardens to enforce the new rules, much to the chagrin of local hunters, including Indians, who now were forced to abide by state laws designed to protect the interests of wealthy recreational hunters.

Along with industrialists concerned about water quality, Roosevelt and the sportsmen conservationists formed a powerful coalition promoting the rational government management of natural resources: rivers and streams, forests, minerals, and natural wonders. Those concerns, as well as the desire of railroad companies to transport tourists to destinations featuring majestic scenery, led the federal government to displace Native Americans in order to establish the 2-million-acre Yellowstone National Park in 1872 at the junction of the Montana, Wyoming, and Idaho Territories (the National Park Service would be created in 1916 after other parks had been established). In 1881, Congress created a Division of Forestry (now the U.S. Forest Service) within the Department of the Interior. At the same time, New York State officials established a Forest Commission in 1885 to manage timber in the vast state-owned acreage of the Adirondack Mountains. Seven years later the legislature created the 5-million-acre Adirondack Park. The legislature also imposed restrictions on hunting in state forests and created a "forest police" to enforce the new regulations. As president, Theodore Roosevelt created fifty federal wildlife refuges, approved five new national parks, and designated as national monuments unfit for economic use such natural treasures as the Grand Canyon.

In 1898, while serving as vice president, Roosevelt had endorsed the appointment of Gifford Pinchot, a close friend and the nation's first professional forester, as the head of the Division of Forestry. Pinchot and Roosevelt believed that conservation entailed the scientific management of natural resources to serve the public interest. Pinchot explained that the conservation movement sought to promote the "greatest good for the greatest number for the longest time."

Roosevelt and Pinchot championed the progressive notion of efficiency and government regulation. They were not romantics about nature, nor were they ecologists; they did not understand the complex interdependence of trees, plants, insects, and animals, nor did they appreciate the environmental benefits of natural fires. Instead, they were utilitarian progressives determined to ensure that entrepreneurs and industrialists exploited nature in appropriate ways. As Pinchot insisted, "The first principle of conservation is development." He sought to ensure the wisest "use of the natural resources now existing on this continent for the benefit of the people who live here now."

The president and Pinchot were especially concerned about the millions of acres of public land still owned by the government. Over the years vast

Roosevelt's western tour

Roosevelt visited Yellowstone National Park in 1903.

tracts of federal land had been given away or sold at discount prices to large business enterprises. Roosevelt and Pinchot were determined to end such carelessness. They championed the systematic management of natural resources by government experts trained to promote the most efficient public use of the environment. "Forestry," Pinchot explained, "is handling trees so that one crop follows another." He and Roosevelt opposed the mindless clear-cutting of entire forests for short-term profit and sought to restrict particular forests from any economic development. In fact, Roosevelt as president used the Forest Reserve Act (1891) to exclude from settlement or harvest some 172 million acres of federal timberland. Lumber companies were furious, but Roosevelt held firm. As he bristled, "I hate a man who skins the land."

FROM ROOSEVELT TO TAFT

Toward the end of his second term, Roosevelt crowed: "I have had a great time as president." But he was ready to move on, and he held to his 1904 decision not to run again. Instead, he sought to have his secretary of war, William Howard Taft, replace him, and the Republican Convention ratified the choice on its first ballot in 1908. The Democrats, whose conservative strategy had backfired in 1904, decided to give William Jennings Bryan one more chance. Still vigorous at forty-eight, Bryan retained a faithful following, but once again it was not enough. In the end, voters opted for Roosevelt's chosen successor, leaving Bryan only the southern states plus Nebraska, Colorado, and Nevada. The real surprise of the election was the strong showing of the Socialist party candidate, labor hero Eugene V. Debs, who attracted 421,000 votes, illustrating the mounting intensity of working-class unrest.

Born to a prominent Cincinnati family, Taft boasted more experience in public service than any other president since Martin Van Buren. After graduating second in his class at Yale, he had progressed through appointive

William Howard Taft

Speaking at Manassas, Virginia, in 1911.

offices, from assistant prosecutor, tax collector, and judge in Ohio to solicitor in the Justice Department, federal judge, governor general in the Philippines, and secretary of war. The presidency was the only elective office he ever held. Later he would be appointed chief justice of the Supreme Court (1921–1930), a job more suited to his temperament.

Taft never felt comfortable in the White House. He once observed that whenever someone said "Mr. President," he looked around for Roosevelt. The political dynamo in the family was his wife, Helen, who had wanted the presidency more than he. One of the major tragedies of Taft's presidency was that Helen Taft suffered a debilitating stroke soon after they entered the White House, and for most of his term she remained unable to serve as his political adviser.

TARIFF REFORM   A former student of the social Darwinist William Graham Sumner, Taft had absorbed the laissez-faire views of his mentor and therefore differed with orthodox Republican protectionism. Against Roosevelt's advice he had promised a tariff reduction during the campaign, and true to his word he called a special session of Congress to consider his proposal eleven days after his inauguration. But if Taft seemed bolder in pressing an issue that Roosevelt had skirted, he proved less adroit in shepherding legislation through Congress.

A reduced tariff passed the House with surprising ease. Before the Senate passed the bill, however, it made more than 800 changes, most of which raised tariff rates. Outraged by the obvious catering to special state and local interests, a group of ten progressive Republicans joined the Democrats in an unsuccessful effort to defeat the bill. Taft at first agreed with them but then, fearful of a party split, backed the Republican majority and agreed to an imperfect bill. Temperamentally conservative, inhibited by scruples about interfering too much with the legislative process, Taft drifted into the orbit of the Republican Old Guard and quickly alienated the progressive wing of his party, whom he tagged "assistant Democrats."

BALLINGER AND PINCHOT In 1910, President Taft's policies drove the wedge deeper between the conservative and progressive Republican factions. What came to be known as the Ballinger-Pinchot controversy made Taft appear to be a less reliable custodian of Roosevelt's conservation policies than he actually was. The controversy arose after Taft's secretary of the interior, Richard A. Ballinger, turned over coal-rich federal lands in Alaska to a group of investor friends. Apparently without Ballinger's knowledge, this group had already agreed to sell part of the land to a mining syndicate. When Gifford Pinchot, chief of forestry, revealed the scam, Taft fired Pinchot for insubordination. A joint congressional investigation later exonerated Ballinger of all charges of fraud or corruption, but conservationist suspicions created such pressure that he resigned in 1911.

In firing Pinchot, Taft had acted according to the strictly legal view that his training had taught him to value. But the unsavory circumstances surrounding the incident tarnished Taft's public image. Events had conspired to cast the president in a conservative role at a time when progressive sentiment was riding high. The result was a sharp setback in the congressional elections of 1910, first by the widespread defeat of pro-Taft candidates in the Republican primaries and then by the

Joseph Cannon

Caricature of Cannon enjoying too much decision-making power as House Speaker.

election of a Democratic majority in the House and enough Democrats in the Senate to allow progressive Republicans to wield the balance of power.

TAFT AND ROOSEVELT   In 1910, Theodore Roosevelt returned from extended travels abroad. With news accounts highlighting Taft's "betrayal" of Roosevelt's programs, the former president's followers urged him to take action. After hesitating for several months, Roosevelt again entered the political arena. At a speech in Kansas, he issued a stirring call for an array of new federal regulatory laws, a federal social-welfare program, and new measures of direct democracy, including the old Populist demands for the initiative, recall, and referendum on a nationwide basis. Thereafter, Roosevelt intensified his criticism of the Taft administration.

Equally critical of Taft was Senator Robert La Follette of Wisconsin, who in 1911 helped organize the National Progressive Republican League and soon became its leading candidate for the Republican party nomination. A militant reformer fiercely committed to greater government regulation of business and civil rights for all Americans, La Follette was more of a crusader than a politician. Complicating matters for the Republicans, Roosevelt officially threw his hat into the ring in 1912. Even though many of La Follette's supporters rushed to embrace the ex-president, the Wisconsin idealist stubbornly refused to give way. He felt that Roosevelt was not genuinely committed to the sweeping reforms necessary for a truly progressive America.

The rebuke implicit in Roosevelt's decision to run against Taft, his chosen successor, was in many ways undeserved. During Taft's first year in office, one political tempest after another had left his image irreparably damaged. The three years of solid achievement that followed could not restore its luster or reunite his divided party. Taft had at least attempted tariff reform, which Roosevelt had never dared. And in the end his administration set aside more public land for conservation in four years than

The Bull Moose candidate in 1912

A skeptical view of Theodore Roosevelt.

Roosevelt's had in nearly eight, and it brought more anti-trust suits, by a score of eighty to twenty-five. Taft also established the Bureau of Mines and the federal Children's Bureau (1912). He supported both the Sixteenth Amendment (1913), which authorized a federal income tax, and the Seventeenth (1913), which provided for the popular election of senators instead of their appointment by state legislatures.

Despite Taft's progressive record, Roosevelt turned against his former friend and lieutenant. Brusquely pushing aside La Follette's claim to the progressive Republican mantle, Roosevelt won most of the Republican primaries in 1912, even in Taft's Ohio. But such popular support was no match for Taft's advantages as president and party leader. The Taft forces nominated their man at the national convention by the same steamroller tactics that had nominated Roosevelt in 1904. Outraged at such "naked theft," the Roosevelt delegates issued a call for a Progressive party convention, which assembled in Chicago on August 5. The new third-party supporters were a curious mixture of social gospel clergymen and laymen, college presidents, professors, journalists, businessmen, and social workers. Roosevelt told the group he felt "fit as a bull moose" in accepting their nomination. Now it was the Democrats' turn.

WILSON'S PROGRESSIVISM

WILSON'S RISE   The emergence of Thomas Woodrow Wilson as the Democratic nominee in 1912 climaxed a political rise even more rapid than that of Grover Cleveland. In 1910, before his entering the race for election as governor of New Jersey, Wilson had been president of Princeton University but had never run for public office. Born in Staunton, Virginia, in 1856, the son of a stern Presbyterian minister, he had grown up in Georgia and the Carolinas during the Civil War and Reconstruction.

Driven by a sense of destiny and duty, Wilson was resolute, humane, rigid, and self-exacting to a fault. He nurtured a righteous commitment to principle, and his fits of tenacious inflexibility would prove to be his greatest weakness. Running as a reform candidate, Wilson was elected governor of New Jersey. After his election he pressured New Jersey lawmakers to enact a workers' compensation law, a corrupt-practices law, measures to regulate public utilities, and ballot reforms. Such strong leadership in a state known as the home of the trusts because of its lenient incorporation laws brought Wilson to national attention.

In the spring of 1911, a group of southern Democrats in New York opened a Wilson presidential campaign headquarters, and Wilson set forth on strenuous tours to all regions of the country, denouncing special privilege and political bossism. Wilson believed that the president of the country should be as active in directing legislation as in steering the administration and guiding the enforcement of laws. In calling for a stronger presidency, Wilson expressed views closer to Roosevelt's than to Taft's. He likewise shared Roosevelt's belief that politicians should promote the general welfare rather than narrow special interests. And like Roosevelt he was critical of big business, organized labor, socialism, and agrarian radicalism.

Despite a fast start the Wilson campaign seemed headed for defeat by convention time, and House Speaker Champ Clark of Missouri seemed destined to win the nomination. On the fourteenth ballot, however, William Jennings Bryan, having decided that party conservatives were behind Clark, went over to Wilson; others followed, and Wilson captured the nomination.

THE ELECTION OF 1912 The 1912 presidential election involved four candidates: Wilson and Taft represented the two major parties, while Eugene Debs ran as a Socialist, and Roosevelt headed the Progressive party ticket. They all shared a basic progessive assumption that the old notion of do-nothing government was bankrupt; modern conditions required active intervention to promote the general welfare of American society.

No sooner did the campaign open than Roosevelt's candidacy almost ended. While stepping into a car in Milwaukee, he was shot by a crazed man. The bullet went through his overcoat, spectacles case, and fifty page speech, then fractured a rib before lodging just below his right lung. Roosevelt demanded that he be driven to the auditorium to deliver his speech. In a dramatic gesture he showed the audience his bloodstained shirt and punctured text and vowed, "It takes more than this to kill a bull moose."

With Taft and Debs trailing, the campaign settled down to a debate over the competing ideologies of the two front-runners: Roosevelt's New Nationalism and Wilson's New Freedom. The fuzzy ideas that Roosevelt fashioned into his New Nationalism had first been presented systematically in *The Promise of American Life* (1909), a widely influential book by Herbert Croly, a New York journalist. Its central point was that progressives must give up Jeffersonian prejudices against big government and use the power of government to achieve democratic ends in the public interest.

Roosevelt's New Nationalism would enable government to promote social justice and enact such reforms as graduated income and inheritance taxes, workers' compensation for disabling injuries or illnesses, regulations to improve the working conditions of women and children, and a stronger Bureau of Corporations. These ideas and more went into the platform of his

Progressive party, which called for a federal trade commission with sweeping authority over business and a tariff commission to set rates on a "scientific basis."

Before the end of his administration, Wilson would be swept into the current of such New Nationalism, too, but initially he adhered to the decentralizing anti-trust traditions of his party. Wilson relied heavily for his political stances on Louis D. Brandeis, the progressive lawyer from Boston, who focused Wilson's thought much as Croly had focused Roosevelt's. Brandeis's design for Wilson's New Freedom program differed from Roosevelt's New Nationalism in its belief that the federal government should restore competition rather than regulate monopolies. It required eliminating all trusts, lowering tariffs, and breaking up the concentration of financial power on Wall Street. Brandeis and Wilson also dreamed of turning over most federal social programs to the states and cities. In this sense they saw the vigorous expansion of federal power as a temporary necessity, not a permanent condition. Having restored competition and diffused power and programs, the national government would revert to its aloof heritage. Roosevelt, who was convinced that both corporate concentration and an expanding federal government were permanent developments, dismissed the New Freedom as mere nostalgia.

The Republican schism between Taft and Roosevelt opened the way for Woodrow Wilson to win by 435 electoral votes to 88 for Roosevelt and 8 for Taft. The 1912 election was significant in a number of respects. First, it was a high-water mark for progressivism. The candidates debated the basic issues in a campaign unique in its focus on vital alternatives and its highly philosophical tone. And the Socialist party, the left wing of progressivism, polled over 900,000 votes for Eugene V. Debs, about 6 percent of the total vote, its highest proportion ever.

Second, the election gave the Democrats effective national power for the first time since the Civil War. For two years during the second administration of Grover Cleveland, from 1893 to 1895, they had held the White House and majorities in both houses of Congress, but they had quickly fallen out of power during the severe economic depression of the 1890s. Now, under

Wilson's reforms

Woodrow Wilson campaigning from a railroad car.

Wilson, the Democrats again held the presidency and enjoyed majorities in the House and Senate.

Third, Wilson's election brought southerners back into the orbit of national and international affairs in a significant way for the first time since the Civil War. Five of Wilson's ten cabinet members were born in the South, and pious William Jennings Bryan, the secretary of state, was an idol of the southern masses. At the president's right hand, and one of the most influential members of the Wilson circle, was "Colonel" Edward M. House of Texas. Wilson described House as "my second personality." Southern legislators, by virtue of their seniority, held most committee chairmanships. As a result,

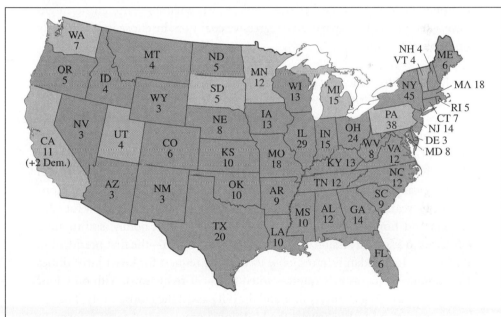

THE ELECTION OF 1912	Electoral Vote	Popular Vote
Woodrow Wilson (Democrat)	435	6,300,000
Theodore Roosevelt (Progressive)	88	4,100,000
William H. Taft (Republican)	8	3,500,000

Why was Taft so unpopular? How did the division between Roosevelt and Taft give Wilson the victory? Why was Wilson's victory in 1912 significant?

much of the progressive legislation of the Wilson era would bear the names of the southern Democrats who guided the bills through Congress.

WILSONIAN REFORM   Wilson's 1913 inaugural address vividly expressed the ideals of economic reform that inspired many progressives. "We have been proud of our industrial achievements," he observed, "but we have not hitherto stopped thoughtfully enough to count the human cost." He promised a lower tariff and a new nationally regulated banking system. Whereas Roosevelt had been a strong president by force of personality, Wilson became a strong president by force of conviction. The president, he argued, must become the dynamic voice in national affairs. Wilson courted popular support, but he also courted members of Congress through personal contacts, invitations to the White House, and speeches to Congress. He used patronage power to reward friends and punish enemies. Though he might have acted through a bipartisan progressive coalition, he chose instead to rely upon party loyalty.

THE TARIFF   The new president's leadership met its first test on the issue of tariff reform. Tariffs were originally needed to protect infant American industries from foreign competition. Now, however, Wilson believed, tariffs were being abused by corporations to suppress foreign competition and keep consumer prices high. He often claimed that the "tariff made the trusts," believing that tariffs had encouraged the growth of industrial monopolies and degraded the political process by spawning armies of paid lobbyists who invaded Congress each year. In attacking high tariffs, Wilson sought to strike a blow for consumers and honest government. He acted quickly and boldly, summoning Congress to a special session and addressing it in person—the first president to do so since John Adams. In response to Wilson's request for lower tariff duties to promote competition, Congress voted for tariff reductions, with only four Democrats crossing the party line, and the bill passed the House easily. The opposition centered in the Senate, the traditional graveyard of tariff reform. In the end, Louisiana's two "sugar senators" were the only Democrats to vote against the bill. The Underwood-Simmons Tariff of 1913 reduced the overall average duty from about 37 percent to about 29 percent. Although the Wilson administration lowered tariff rates, it raised revenues with the first federal income tax levied under the newly ratified Sixteenth Amendment.

THE FEDERAL RESERVE ACT   Before the new tariff had cleared the Senate, the administration proposed the first major banking and currency reform since the Civil War. Ever since Andrew Jackson had killed the second

Bank of the United States in the 1830s, the nation had been without a central bank. Instead, the country's money supply was administered by hundreds of private banks. Such a decentralized system fostered instability and inefficiency. It also gave disproportionate influence to banks centered in New York City. By 1913 virtually everyone had agreed that the banking system needed restructuring. Wilson told Congress that a federal banking system was needed to ensure that "the banks may be the instruments, not the masters, of business and of individual enterprise and initiative."

The Federal Reserve Act of 1913 created a new national banking system with twelve regional Federal Reserve banks, each owned by member banks in its district. All national banks became members of the new Federal Reserve System; state banks could join if they wished. Each member bank had to subscribe 6 percent of its capital to the Federal Reserve bank and deposit a portion of its reserve there.

This arrangement made it possible to expand both the money supply and bank credit in times of high business activity or as the level of borrowing increased. A Federal Reserve Board exercised general supervision over the activities of the member banks and adjusted interest rates to fight inflation or stimulate business. It is hard to exaggerate the significance of the passage of the Federal Reserve Act. Through Wilson's skillful leadership, Congress took a major step in providing the nation with a sound yet flexible currency system and at the same time helped decentralize the money supply.

ANTI-TRUST LAWS Wilson made trust-busting the central focus of the New Freedom because the concentration of economic power had continued to grow despite the Sherman Anti-Trust Act and the federal watchdog agency, the Bureau of Corporations. During the summer of 1914, Wilson decided to make a strong Federal Trade Commission (FTC) the cornerstone of his anti-trust program. Created in 1914, the

"Reading the Death Warrant"

Woodrow Wilson's plan for banking and currency reform spells the death of the "money trust," according to this cartoon.

five-member commission replaced Roosevelt's Bureau of Corporations and assumed new powers to define "unfair trade practices" and issue "cease-and-desist" orders when it found evidence of unfair competition.

Henry D. Clayton, an Alabama Democrat, drafted an anti-trust bill, passed in 1914, that outlawed practices such as price discrimination (charging different customers different prices for the same goods); "tying" agreements, which limited the right of dealers to handle the products of competing manufacturers; and corporations' acquisition of stock in competing corporations. In every case, however, conservative forces in the Senate qualified these provisions by tacking on the weakening phrase "where the effect may be to substantially lessen competition" or words of similar effect. And conservative southern Democrats and northern Republicans amended the Clayton Anti-Trust Act to allow for broad judicial review of the FTC's decisions, further weakening its freedom of action. In accordance with the president's recommendation, however, corporate officials were made personally responsible for any violations.

Agrarian reformers allied with organized labor won a stipulation in the Clayton Act declaring that farm and labor organizations were not per se unlawful combinations in restraint of trade. Injunctions in labor disputes, moreover, were not to be handed down by federal courts unless "necessary to prevent irreparable injury to property." President Wilson himself admitted that the act did little more than affirm the right of unions to exist by forbidding their dissolution for being in restraint of trade.

Administration of the anti-trust laws generally proved disappointing to the more vehement progressives under Wilson. The Justice Department offered advice to business owners interested in arranging matters so as to avoid anti-trust prosecutions. The appointment of conservatives to the Interstate Commerce Commission and the Federal Reserve Board won plaudits from the business world and profoundly disappointed progressives.

SOCIAL JUSTICE   Wilson's political agenda focused on restoring economic opportunity and competition. He had in fact never been a strong progressive of the social-justice persuasion. He carried out his promises to lower the tariff, reorganize the banking system, and strengthen the anti-trust laws, but he was not inclined to go much further. The New Freedom was now complete, he wrote late in 1914; the future would be "a time of healing because [it would be] a time of just dealing."

The sweep of events and the pressures of more far-reaching progressives pushed Wilson beyond where he intended to go on some points. Yet Wilson retained several social blind spots. Although he endorsed state action for women's suffrage, he declined to support a federal suffrage amendment because his party platform had not done so. He withheld support from federal child-labor legislation because he regarded it as a state matter, and he opposed a bill providing federal loans for strapped farmers on the grounds that it was "unwise and unjustifiable to extend the credit of the government to a single class of the community."

PROGRESSIVISM FOR WHITES ONLY Like many other progressives, Woodrow Wilson showed little interest in the plight of African Americans. In fact, he shared many of the racist attitudes prevalent at the time. Although Wilson never joined the Ku Klux Klan and he denounced its "reign of terror," he sympathized with its motives of restoring white rule in the postwar South and relieving whites of the "ignorant and hostile" power of the black vote. As a student at Princeton, Wilson had detested the enfranchisement of blacks, arguing that Americans of Anglo-Saxon origin would always resist domination by "an ignorant and inferior race."

Later, as a politician, Wilson courted black voters, but he rarely consulted African American leaders and repeatedly avoided opportunities to associate with them in public. Many of the southerners he appointed to his cabinet

The privileged elite

President Wilson and the First Lady ride in a carriage.

were uncompromising racists who systematically segregated the employees in their agencies. When black leaders protested these actions, Wilson replied that such racial segregation was intended to eliminate "the possibility of friction" in the federal workplace.

PROGRESSIVE RESURGENCE   The need to weld a winning political coalition in 1916 pushed Wilson back on the road of reform. Progressive Democrats were restless, and after war broke out in Europe in 1914, further divisions in the party arose over defense preparedness and foreign policy. At the same time the Republicans were repairing their own rift. The Progressive party showed little staying power in the 1914 midterm election, and Roosevelt showed little will to preserve it. Most observers recognized that Wilson could gain reelection only by courting progressives of all parties. In 1916 the president scored points with them when he nominated Louis D. Brandeis to the Supreme Court. Conservatives waged a vigorous battle against Brandeis, but Senate progressives rallied to win confirmation of the social-justice champion as the first Jewish member of the Supreme Court.

Wilson, meanwhile, began to embrace the broad program of farm and labor reforms he had earlier spurned. The agricultural sector continued to suffer from a shortage of capital. To address the problem, Wilson supported a proposal to set up special rural banks to sponsor farm loans. With this boost the Federal Farm Loan Act became law in 1916. It created twelve Federal Land banks, which paralleled the Federal Reserve banks and offered low-interest loans to farmers.

Farmers with the newfangled automobiles had more than a passing interest as well in the Federal Highways Act of 1916, which provided dollar-matching contributions to states with highway departments that met certain federal standards. The measure authorized the distribution of $75 million over five years and marked a sharp departure from Jacksonian opposition to internal improvements at federal expense, just as the Federal Reserve System departed from Jacksonian banking principles. Although the argument that highways were one of the nation's defense needs had weakened constitutional scruples against the act, the Highways Act still restricted support to "post roads" used for the delivery of mail. A renewal act in 1921 would mark the beginning of a systematic network of numbered U.S. highways.

The progressive resurgence of 1916 broke the logjam on workplace reforms as well. Advocates of child-labor legislation persuaded Wilson to overcome doubts about its constitutionality and sign the Keating-Owen Act, which excluded from interstate commerce goods manufactured by children under the age of fourteen. But the Supreme Court soon ruled it unconstitutional on the grounds that regulation of interstate commerce could not extend to the conditions of labor. On the other hand, the Supreme Court upheld the Adamson Act of 1916, which mandated the eight-hour workday for railroad workers.

In Wilson's first term, progressive government reached its zenith. Progressivism had conquered the old premise that the government is best that governs least. Progressivism, a loose amalgam of agrarian, business, government, and social reform, amounted in the end to a movement for active government on behalf of the public interest.

LIMITS OF PROGRESSIVISM

Like all great historic movements, progressivism contained elements of paradox and irony. Despite all the talk of greater democracy at the turn of the century, it was also the age of disenfranchisement of African Americans in the South and xenophobic reactions to "new" immigrants. The initiative and referendum, supposedly democratic reforms, proved subject to manipulation by well-financed publicity campaigns. And much of the public policy of the time came to be formulated by experts and members of appointed boards, not by broad segments of the population. There is a fine irony in the fact that the drive to increase the political role of ordinary people paralleled efforts to strengthen executive leadership and exalt professional expertise. This much-ballyhooed Progressive Era of efficiency and expertise, in business as well as government, generated a situation in which more and more key decisions were made by unelected policy makers.

Progressivism was largely a middle-class movement in which the poor and unorganized had little influence. It is surprising that a movement so dedicated to democratic rhetoric should experience so steady a decline in voter participation. In 1912, the year of Roosevelt's Bull Moose campaign, voting dropped off by between 6 and 7 percent. The new politics of issues and charismatic leaders proved to be less effective in turning out voters than traditional party organizations and bosses had been. And by 1916 the optimism of an age that looked to infinite progress was already confronted by a vast slaughter. Europe had stumbled into a horrific war, and America would soon be drawn in. The twentieth century, which had dawned with such bright hopes, held in store episodes of unparalleled carnage.

End of Chapter Review

CHAPTER SUMMARY

- **Progressivism** Progressives believed that industrialization and urbanization were negatively affecting American life. They were middle-class idealists in both political parties who sought reform and regulation in order to ensure social justice. Many progressives wished to curb the powers of local political machines and establish honest and efficient government. They also called for an end to child labor, laws promoting safety in the workplace; a ban on the sale of alcoholic beverages, legislation curbing trusts, and women's suffrage.

- **Muckrakers** Theodore Roosevelt named the journalists whose works exposed social ills "muckrakers." New inexpensive popular magazines, such as *McClure's*, published articles about municipal corruption, horrendous conditions in meat-packing plants and urban slums, and predatory business practices. By raising public awareness of these issues, muckrakers contributed to major changes in the workplace and in governance.

- **Square Deal Program** President Roosevelt used his executive position to endorse his Square Deal program, which included regulating trusts, arbitrating the 1902 coal strike, regulating the railroads, and cleaning up the meat and drug industries. Taft continued to bust trusts and reform the tariff, but Republican party bosses, reflecting their big business interests, ensured that the tariff reductions were too few to satisfy the progressives in the party. Roosevelt decided to seek the Republican presidential nomination in 1912 because of progressives' disillusionment with Taft.

- **Presidential Election of 1912** In 1912, after the Republicans renominated Taft, Roosevelt's supporters bolted the convention, formed the Progressive party, and nominated Roosevelt. Although some Democratic progressives supported Roosevelt, the split in the Republican party led to Woodrow Wilson's success. Having won a majority in both houses of Congress as well as the presidential election, the Democrats effectively held national power for the first time since the Civil War.

- **Wilsonian Progressivism** Although Wilson was a progressive, his approach was different from Roosevelt's. His New Freedom program promised less federal intervention in business and a return to such traditional Democratic policies as a low tariff. Wilson began a rigorous anti-trust program and oversaw the establishment of the Federal Reserve System. He opposed federal programs promoting social justice and initially withheld support for federal regulation of child labor and a constitutional amendment guaranteeing women's suffrage. A southerner, he believed blacks were inferior and supported segregation.

CHRONOLOGY

1902	Theodore Roosevelt attempts to arbitrate the coal strike
1902	Justice Department breaks up Northern Securities Company
1903	Congress passes the Elkins Act
1906	Upton Sinclair's *The Jungle* is published
1906	Congress passes the Meat Inspection Act and the Pure Food and Drug Act
1908	Supreme Court issues *Muller v. Oregon* decision
1909	William Taft is inaugurated president
1911	Triangle Shirtwaist Company fire
1913	Congress passes the Federal Reserve Act
1914	Congress passes the Clayton Anti-Trust Act
1916	Louis Brandeis is nominated to fill a seat on the Supreme Court

KEY TERMS & NAMES

25

AMERICA AND
THE GREAT WAR

FOCUS QUESTIONS wwnorton.com/studyspace

- Why did Woodrow Wilson involve the United States in Mexico's affairs?
- What were the causes of World War I in Europe?
- Why did the United States enter the Great War in Europe?
- How did Wilson promote his peace plan?
- Why did the United States fail to ratify the Treaty of Versailles?
- What were the consequences of the war at home and abroad?

Throughout the nineteenth century the United States reaped the benefits of its geographic distance from the wars that plagued Europe. The Atlantic Ocean provided a welcome buffer. During the early twentieth century, however, the nation's comfortable isolation ended. Expanding world trade entwined American interests with the fate of Europe. In addition, the development of steam-powered ships and submarines meant that foreign navies could threaten American security. At the same time, the election of Woodrow Wilson in 1912 brought to the White House a stern and often self-righteous moralist determined to impose his standards for right conduct on renegade nations. This combination of circumstances made the outbreak of war in Europe in 1914 a profound crisis for the United States, a crisis that would transform the nation's role in international affairs.

WILSON AND FOREIGN AFFAIRS

President Woodrow Wilson had no experience or expertise in foreign relations. The former college professor admitted before taking office, "It would be an irony of fate if my administration had to deal chiefly with foreign affairs." But events in Latin America and Europe were to make the irony all too real. From the summer of 1914, when a catastrophic world war erupted in Europe, foreign relations increasingly preoccupied Wilson's attention.

Although lacking in international experience, Wilson did not lack ideas or convictions about global issues. He saw himself as a man of destiny who would help create a new world order governed by morality and idealism rather than crass national interests. Both he and Secretary of State William Jennings Bryan believed that America had a religious duty to promote democracy around the world. How to foster such democratic idealism and self-determination abroad, however, remained a thorny issue, as Wilson soon discovered in responding to rapidly changing events on his own continent.

INTERVENTION IN MEXICO Wilson's first challenge emerged within American's southern neighbor, Mexico. Between 1876 and 1910, Porfirio Díaz had dominated Mexico. As military dictator he had suppressed opposition and showered favors upon wealthy allies and foreign investors. Eventually, however, the dictator's grip slipped, and in 1910 popular resentment boiled over in revolt. Revolutionary armies occupied Mexico City, and in 1911 Díaz fled.

The leader of the rebellion, Francisco Madero, proved unable to manage the tough customers attracted to the revolt by the scramble for power. In 1913, Madero's chief of staff, General Victoriano Huerta, assumed power, and Madero was murdered soon afterward. President Wilson challenged the legitimacy of Huerta's violent coup but expressed sympathy with a revolutionary faction led by Venustiano Carranza and began to put diplomatic pressure on Huerta. "I am going to teach the South American republics to elect good men," he vowed to a British diplomat.

Early in 1914, Wilson removed an arms embargo against Mexico in order to help Carranza's forces, and he stationed U.S. warships off Veracruz to halt foreign arms shipments to Huerta. On April 9, 1914, several American sailors gathering supplies in Tampico strayed into a restricted area and were arrested. The Mexican officials quickly released them and apologized to the U.S. naval commander. There the incident might have ended, but the naval officer demanded that the Mexicans salute the American flag. Wilson backed him up and won from Congress authority to use force to bring Huerta to

Pancho Villa

Villa (center) and his followers rebelled against the president of Mexico and
antagonized the United States with violent attacks against "gringos."

terms. Before the Tampico incident could be resolved, Wilson sent a naval force
to Veracruz. U.S. marines and sailors went ashore on April 21, 1914, occupying
the city at a cost of 19 American lives; at least 200 Mexicans were killed.

In Mexico the U.S. occupation aroused the opposition of all factions, and
Huerta rallied support against a foreign invasion. At this juncture, Wilson
accepted a mediation offer by the ABC (Argentina, Brazil, and Chile) powers,
which proposed the withdrawal of U.S. forces, the removal of Huerta, and the
installation of a provisional government. Huerta refused to step down, but
the moral effect of the proposal, his isolation abroad, and the growing
strength of his foes soon forced him to leave office. The Carranzistas entered
Mexico City, and the Americans left Veracruz. Wilson's "missionary diplomacy" seemed to have worked. In 1915 the United States and several Latin
American governments recognized Carranza as president of Mexico.

But no sooner had the Carranzistas taken power than they began to
squabble among themselves for the spoils of office. The most incendiary confrontation occurred between Carranza and his foremost general, the popular
Pancho Villa, a charismatic former bandit who shrewdly claimed to represent
"the people" behind the revolution. Enraged by America's recognition of
Carranza as the de facto leader of Mexico, Villa, in early 1916, led an attack

that murdered sixteen American mining engineers. It was a deliberate attempt to provoke U.S. intervention, discredit Carranza, and build up Villa as an opponent of the "gringos." Two months later Villa's band of renegades entered Columbus, New Mexico, burned the town, and killed seventeen Americans.

A furious Woodrow Wilson sent General John J. Pershing and a force of 11,000 soldiers deep inside Mexico. For nearly a year, Pershing's troops chased Villa through northern Mexico, but missing their quarry, they returned home in 1917. Carranza then pressed his own war against the bandits and in 1917 put through a new liberal constitution. Mexico was establishing a more orderly government, almost in spite of Wilson's actions rather than because of them.

PROBLEMS IN LATIN AMERICA   In the Caribbean, Wilson found it as hard to act on his democratic ideals as it was in Mexico. During President Taft's term, from 1909 to 1913, the United States had practiced "dollar diplomacy." The policy had its origin in 1909, when Taft had personally cabled the Chinese government on behalf of American investors interested in forming an international consortium to finance railroad lines in China. In Latin America, dollar diplomacy worked differently and with somewhat more success. The idea was to encourage American bankers to help prop up the finances of shaky Caribbean governments.

One of the first applications of Wilsonian idealism to foreign policy came when the president renounced dollar diplomacy. The government, he declared, was not supporting any "special groups or interests." Despite Wilson's public stand against using military force to back up American investments, however, he kept U.S. marines in Nicaragua, where they had been sent by President Taft in 1912 to prevent renewed civil war. There they would stay almost continuously until 1933. In 1915, Wilson dispatched more marines, this time to Haiti, after the country experienced two successive revolutions and subsequent government disarray. The U.S. forces stayed until 1934. Turmoil in the Dominican Republic brought U.S. marines to that country in 1916, where they remained until 1924. The presence of U.S. military force in the region only worsened the already prevalent irritation at "Yankee imperialism."

AN UNEASY NEUTRALITY

During the summer of 1914, problems in Mexico and Central America loomed larger in Wilson's thinking than the gathering storm in Europe. When the thunderbolt of war struck Europe in August 1914, Americans were

How did the European system of alliances spread conflict across all of Europe? How was World War I different from previous wars? How did the war in Europe lead to ethnic tensions in the United States?

stunned. Whatever the troubles in Mexico, whatever disorders and interventions agitated other countries, it seemed unreal that civilized Europe could descend into such an orgy of destruction. At the beginning of the twentieth century, Europe had been peaceful and prosperous. The great powers had worked out what seemed to be a balance of power among themselves. No one imagined a new—and unnecessary—industrialized form of war erupting that would assume such horrible proportions and involve such unprecedented ruthlessness. Between 1914 and 1921 the war was directly responsible for the deaths of over 9 million combatants and the horrible wounding of 15 million more; it would produce at least 3 million widows and 6 million orphans. The war's horror and destructiveness, its obscene butchery and ravaged landscapes, defied belief.

World War I erupted when the Austrian archduke Franz Ferdinand was assassinated by a Serbian nationalist. Austria-Hungary's determination to punish Serbia, and Russia's military mobilization in sympathy with Slavic Serbia, triggered a conflict between the two major European systems of alliances: the Triple Alliance, or Central Powers (Germany, Austria-Hungary, and Italy), and the Triple Entente, or Allied Powers (France, Great Britain, and Russia). The sequence of decisions leading to World War I had unfolded with little thought to their consequences. When Russia refused to stop its army's mobilization, Germany, which backed Austria-Hungary, declared war on Russia on August 1, 1914, and on Russia's ally France two days later. Germany then invaded Belgium to get at France, an action that brought Great Britain into the war on August 4. Japan, eager to seize German holdings in the Pacific, declared war on August 23, and Turkey entered on the side of the

Verdun

A landscape image from Verdun, taken immediately after the battle, shows how the firepower ravaged the land.

Central Powers on October 29. Although allied with the Central Powers, Italy initially stayed out of the war and in 1915 struck a bargain by which it joined the Allied Powers.

The First World War proved to be unlike any previous conflict in its scope and carnage. Machine guns, high-velocity rifles, aerial bombing, poison gas, flame throwers, land mines, long-range artillery, and armored tanks changed the nature of warfare and produced massive casualties and widespread destruction. Over 65 million men served in the armed forces on both sides, and over 9 million combatants were killed in action. Another 19 million were wounded. During the Battle of Verdun, in France, which lasted from February to December 1916, some 32 million artillery shells were fired—1,500 shells for every square meter of the battlefield. Such devastating firepower ravaged the landscape, turning farmland and forests into wasteland.

Trench warfare gave the First World War its lasting character. Most of the great battles involved hundreds of thousands of men crawling out of their muddy, rat-infested trenches and crossing a no-man's-land to attack enemy positions, only to be pushed back a day or a week later. In addition to the dangers of enemy fire, soldiers were forced to deal with flooded trenches and

Fighting on the western front

A gun crew firing on entrenched German positions, 1918.

terrible diseases such as trench fever and trench foot, which could lead to amputation. Lice and rats were constant companions. The stench was unbearable. Soldiers on both sides ate, slept, and fought among the dead and amid the reek of death.

INITIAL REACTIONS As the trench war along the western front in Belgium and France stalemated, casualties soared and pressure for U.S. intervention increased. On July 1, 1916, the first day of the Battle of the Somme, 20,000 British soldiers were killed and 40,000 others were wounded—in less than twenty-four hours. Shock in the United States over the sudden outbreak of war in Europe gave way to gratitude that an ocean stood between America and the killing fields. President Wilson repeatedly urged Americans to remain "neutral in thought as well as in action."

That was more easily said than done. More than a third of Americans were first- or second-generation immigrants who retained strong ties to their old country. Among the 13 million immigrants from the countries at war, the 8 million German Americans were by far the largest group, and the 4 million Irish Americans harbored a deep-rooted enmity toward England. These groups instinctively leaned toward the Central Powers.

Old-line Americans, largely of British origin, supported the Allied Powers. Those Americans also identified with France, which had contributed to American culture and ideas and to independence itself. Britain and France, if not their ally Russia, seemed the custodians of democracy, while Germany seemed the embodiment of autocracy and militarism. If not a direct threat to the United States, Germany would pose at least a potential threat if it destroyed the balance of power in Europe. High officers of the U.S. government were pro-British in thought from the outset of the war.

A STRAINED NEUTRALITY At first the war in Europe brought a slump in American exports and the threat of a depression, but by the spring of 1915 the Allies' demand for food and military supplies generated an economic boom. France and Britain bought so much from the United States that they soon needed loans to continue making purchases. Early in the war, Secretary of State William Jennings Bryan, a strict pacifist, declared that loans to any warring nation were "inconsistent with the true spirit of neutrality." Technically he was correct, but Wilson, for all his public professions of neutrality, was in fact determined to aid Great Britain. He quietly began approving credit to sustain trade with the Allies. American investors would advance over $2 billion to the Allies, mostly Britain and France, before the United States entered the war, and only $27 million to Germany.

The administration nevertheless clung to its official stance of neutrality through two and a half years of warfare in Europe and tried to uphold the traditions of "freedom of the seas," which had guided American policy since the Napoleonic Wars of the early nineteenth century. Transatlantic trade assumed a new importance as the German army's advance through Belgium toward Paris bogged down into the stalemate of trench warfare. In a war of attrition, survival depended upon access to supplies, and in such a war British naval power counted for a great deal. In November 1914 the British declared the whole North Sea a war zone and sowed it with mines. Four months later they announced that they would seize ships carrying goods produced by or intended for their enemies.

NEUTRAL RIGHTS AND SUBMARINES British actions, including the blacklisting of companies that traded with the enemy and censoring the mail, raised old issues of neutral rights, but the German reaction introduced an entirely new question. In the face of the British blockade, whereby only submarines could venture out to harass the enemy, the German government proclaimed a war zone around the British Isles. Enemy ships in those waters would be sunk by submarines, the Germans declared. As the chief advantage of U-boat (*Unterseeboot*) warfare was in surprise, the German decision violated the established international procedure of stopping an enemy vessel and providing for the safety of passengers and crew before sinking it. Since the British sometimes flew neutral flags as a ruse, neutral ships in this war zone would also be in danger.

The United States pronounced the new German submarine policy "an indefensible violation of neutral rights" and warned that Germany would be held to "strict accountability" for any destruction of American lives and property. Then, on May 7, 1915, a German U-boat torpedoed the passenger liner *Lusitania*, which exploded and sank within eighteen minutes. Before the ship's departure from New York, bound for Liverpool, the German embassy had published warnings in American newspapers against travel to the war zone, but 128 Americans were nonetheless among the 1,198 persons lost.

Americans were outraged. To quiet the uproar over the *Lusitania*, Wilson urged patience: "There is such a thing as a man being too proud to fight. There is such a thing as a nation being so right that it does not need to convince others by force that it is right." But his previous demand for "strict accountability" forced him to make a stronger response. On May 13, Secretary of State Bryan reluctantly demanded that the Germans abandon unrestricted submarine warfare, disavow the sinking of the *Lusitania*, and pay reparations to the victims' families. The Germans responded that the passenger ship was armed

"All the News That's Fit to Print."

The New York Times.

THE WEATHER
Fair today and Sunday; fresh to strong southwest to west winds

VOL. LXIV...NO. 20,923.   NEW YORK, SATURDAY, MAY 8, 1915.—TWENTY-FOUR PAGES.   ONE CENT In Greater New York | TWO CENTS

LUSITANIA SUNK BY A SUBMARINE, PROBABLY 1,000 DEAD; TWICE TORPEDOED OFF IRISH COAST; SINKS IN 15 MINUTES; AMERICANS ABOARD INCLUDED VANDERBILT AND FROHMAN; WASHINGTON BELIEVES THAT A GRAVE CRISIS IS AT HAND

THE LOST CUNARD STEAMSHIP LUSITANIA

The *Lusitania*

Americans were outraged when a German torpedo sank the *Lusitania* on May 7, 1915.

(which it was not) and carried a secret cargo of small arms and ammunition (which it did). A second State Department message, on June 9, repeated American demands in stronger terms. Bryan, unwilling to risk war over the issue, resigned in protest. His successor, Robert Lansing, signed the note.

In response to the uproar over the *Lusitania,* the German government had secretly ordered U-boat captains to avoid sinking large passenger vessels. When, despite the order, two American lives were lost in the sinking of the New York–bound British liner *Arabic,* the German government declared on September 1, 1915, "Liners will not be sunk by our submarines without warning and without safety of the lives of noncombatants, provided that the liners do not try to escape or offer resistance." With this so-called Arabic Pledge, Wilson's resolute stand seemed to have won a victory for his policy.

THE DEBATE OVER PREPAREDNESS   The *Lusitania* incident and, more generally, the quarrels over protecting neutral commerce during wartime contributed to a growing demand in the United States for a stronger army and navy. After the *Lusitania* sinking the outcry from preparedness advocates grew into a clamor. In his annual message in 1915, Wilson alerted Congress to his plans for war preparedness. The response was far from unanimous. Progressives and pacifists, especially in the rural South and the West, opposed military expansion.

Wilson eventually accepted a compromise between advocates of an expanded force under federal control and advocates of a traditional citizen army. The National Defense Act of 1916 expanded the regular army from 90,000 to 175,000 and permitted a gradual enlargement to 223,000. It also increased the National Guard to 440,000. The Naval Construction Act of 1916 authorized between $500 million and $600 million for a three-year shipbuilding program.

Forced to relent on military preparedness, progressive opponents of a buildup insisted that the financial burden should rest upon the wealthy executives of companies trading with Great Britain they held responsible for pushing the nation toward war. The income tax became their weapon. Supported by a groundswell of popular support, legislators wrote into the Revenue Act of 1916 changes that doubled the basic income tax rate from 1 to 2 percent, lifted the surtax on income over $2 million to 13 percent, added an estate tax graduated up to a maximum of 10 percent, levied a 12.5 percent tax on gross receipts of munitions makers, and added a new tax on corporations. The new taxes amounted to the most clear-cut victory for radical progressives in the entire Wilson period, a victory that Wilson supported in preparation for the upcoming presidential election.

THE ELECTION OF 1916   As the 1916 election approached, Republicans hoped to regain their normal electoral majority, and Theodore Roosevelt hoped to be their leader again. But in 1912 he had committed the deadly sin of bolting his party. His eagerness for the United States to enter the war also scared many voters. Needing somebody who would draw Bull Moose Progressives back into the fold, the Republican regulars turned to Justice Charles Evans Hughes, a progressive governor of New York from 1907 to 1910. On the Supreme Court since 1910, he had neither endorsed a candidate in 1912 nor spoken out on foreign policy.

The Democrats, as expected, chose Woodrow Wilson once again. Their platform endorsed a program of social-welfare legislation and a reasonable degree of military preparedness. The party further endorsed women's suffrage and pledged support for a postwar league of nations to enforce peace with collective-security measures against aggressors. The Democrats' most popular issue was a pledge to keep the nation out of the war in Europe. The peace theme, refined in the slogan "He kept us out of war," became the rallying cry of the Wilson campaign.

The candidates in the 1916 presidential election were remarkably similar. Both Wilson and Hughes were the sons of preachers; both were attorneys and former professors; both had been progressive governors; both were

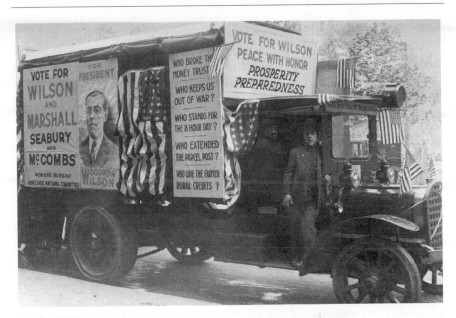

Peace with honor

Woodrow Wilson's policies of neutrality proved popular in the 1916 campaign.

known for their pristine integrity. Theodore Roosevelt highlighted the similarities between them when he called the bearded Hughes a "whiskered Wilson." Wilson, however, proved to be the better campaigner. In the end, Wilson's twin pledges of peace and progressivism, brought victory. The final vote showed a Democratic sweep of the Far West and the South, enough for narrow victories in the Electoral College, by 277 to 254, and in the popular vote, by 9 million to 8.5 million. Wilson also carried many social-justice progressives who in 1912 had supported Roosevelt's Bull Moose campaign.

LAST EFFORTS FOR PEACE Immediately after the election, Wilson offered to mediate an end to the European war, but neither side was willing to abandon its major war aims. Wilson then made one more appeal, in the hope that public opinion would force the hands of the warring governments. Speaking before the Senate, he asserted that this would have to be a "peace without victory," for only a "peace among equals" could endure.

Although Wilson did not know it, he was already too late. Exactly two weeks before he spoke, German military leaders had decided to wage unrestricted submarine warfare on all shipping in the Atlantic. Faced with weakening resources in a war of attrition, the Germans took the calculated risk of provoking American anger in the hope of scoring a quick knockout.

On January 31, 1917, Germany announced the new policy, effective the next day: all vessels would be sunk without warning.

On February 3, 1917, Wilson informed a joint session of Congress that the United States had broken diplomatic relations with the German government. He added that he still did not believe the Germans would do what they said they felt at liberty to do—only overt acts would persuade him that they intended to sink neutral ships. In case of such acts, he would take measures to protect American seamen and citizens.

Then, on March 1, Wilson learned that the British had intercepted an important message from the German foreign minister Arthur Zimmermann to his ambassador in Mexico. The note offered an alliance and financial aid to Mexico in case of war between the United States and Germany. In return for attacking the United States, Mexico would recover "the lost territory in Texas, New Mexico, and Arizona." All this was contingent on war with the United States, but an electrified public read in it an aggressive intent. Later in March, on the other side of the world, another bombshell burst when a revolution overthrew Russia's czarist government and established the provisional government of a Russian republic. The fall of the czarist autocracy gave Americans the illusion that all the major Allied powers were now fighting for constitutional democracy—an illusion that was shattered in November 1917, when the Bolsheviks, led by Vladimir Lenin, seized power in Russia and established a Communist dictatorship.

America's Entry into the War

In March 1917, German submarines did the unthinkable: they sank five American merchant vessels. On April 2, Wilson asked Congress to recognize that imperial Germany and the United States were at war. As he insisted, "The world must be made safe for democracy." The war resolution passed the Senate by a vote of 82 to 6 on April 4. The House concurred, 373 to 50, and Wilson signed the measure on April 6, 1917.

How had matters come to this, less than three years after Wilson's proclamation of neutrality? Prominent among the various explanations of America's entrance into the war were the effects of British propaganda and America's substantial trade with the Allies, which some observers credited to self-interested munitions makers. Some Americans thought German domination of Europe would be a threat to U.S. security, especially if it meant the destruction or capture of the British navy. Such factors, however, would not have been decisive without the issue of submarine warfare. That issue need not have become decisive either, since such neutrals as Norway, Sweden, and Denmark took relatively heavier losses yet stayed out of the war. But once Wilson had taken a stand for the traditional rights of neutral nations and noncombatants, he was to some extent at the mercy of decisions by the German high command.

AMERICA'S EARLY ROLE   The scope of America's role in the European war remained unclear for a time. Few on either side of the Atlantic expected more than a token U.S. military effort. Despite Congress's preparedness measures, the army remained small and untested. The navy also was largely undeveloped. But the U.S. Navy made a major contribution when it persuaded the Allies to adopt a system of escorting merchant ships in group convoys, which resulted in an impressive decrease in Allied shipping losses to German submarines.

Within a month of America's declaration of war, the British and French requested money for more supplies, a request Congress had anticipated in the Liberty Loan Act, which added $5 billion to the national debt in "liberty bonds." Of this amount, $3 billion could be lent to the Allied Powers. The United States was also willing to furnish naval support, financial credits, supplies, and munitions. But to train a large army, equip it, and send it across a submarine-infested ocean seemed out of the question.

The United States agreed to send a token military force to bolster Anglo-French morale, and on June 26, 1917, the first American contingent, about 14,500 men commanded by General John J. Pershing, began to disembark on the French coast. After reaching Paris, Pershing decided that the war-weary Allies would be unable to mount an offensive by themselves. He therefore requested that

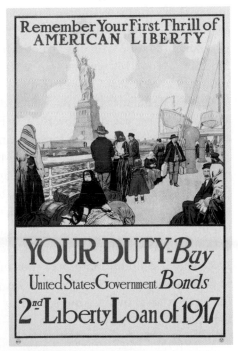

The thrill of American liberty

This Liberty Loan poster urges immigrants to do their duty for their new country by buying government bonds.

Wilson send 1 million American troops by the following spring, and the president obliged.

When the United States entered the war, the combined strength of the regular army and National Guard was only 379,000; at the end it would be 3.7 million. The need for such large numbers of troops forced Wilson to authorize conscription. Under the Selective Service Act of May 18, 1917, all men aged twenty-one to thirty (later, eighteen to forty-five) had to register for the draft and could be drafted for military service. In the course of the war, about 2 million American men crossed the Atlantic, and about 1.4 million of them saw combat.

MOBILIZING A NATION   One of the most obvious effects of American entry into the war was a dramatic increase in the size and power of the federal government. Complete economic mobilization on the home front was necessary to conduct the war efficiently. In 1916, Congress had created a Council of National Defense, which in turn set up other wartime agencies. The U.S. Shipping Board, organized in 1917, within two years was constructing more than forty steel and ninety wooden ships monthly. In 1917, Congress created a Food Administration, headed by Herbert Hoover, a future president, who sought to raise crop production while reducing civilian consumption of foodstuffs. "Food will win the war" was the slogan. Hoover directed a conservation campaign that "Hooverized" the country with "meatless Tuesdays," "wheatless Wednesdays," "porkless Saturdays," the planting of victory gardens, and the creative use of leftovers. The Fuel Administration introduced the country to daylight saving time and "heatless Mondays" to save fuel.

The War Industries Board (WIB), established in 1917, soon became the most important of all the mobilization agencies. Wilson summoned Bernard Baruch, a brilliant Wall Street investor, to head the board, giving him a virtual dictatorship over the economy. The WIB could allocate raw materials, tell manufacturers what to produce, order construction of new plants, and with presidential approval, fix prices. Despite such efforts, however, the unprecedented mobilization process was often chaotic. Men were drafted only to discover there were no uniforms, weapons, or housing for them. Most of the artillery used by the American army in France had to be acquired from the Allies.

A NEW LABOR FORCE   The closing off of immigration from Europe during the war and the movement of almost 4 million men into the armed services created a labor shortage. To meet it, women, African Americans, and other ethnic minorities were encouraged to enter industries and engage in agricultural activities heretofore dominated by white men. Northern businesses sent recruiting agents into the Deep South to find workers for their factories and mills, and over 400,000 southern blacks began the Great Migration northward during the war years, a mass movement that continued unabated through the 1920s and changed the political dynamics of northern cities. Mexican Americans followed the same migratory pattern. Recruiting agents and newspaper editors portrayed the North as the "land of promise" for southern blacks suffering from their region's depressed agricultural economy and rising racial intimidation and violence. By 1930 the number of African Americans living in the North was triple that of 1910.

But the newcomers were not always welcomed above the Mason-Dixon line. Many white workers resented the new arrivals, and racial tensions sparked clashes across the country. In 1917 over forty African Americans and nine whites were killed during a riot over employment in a defense plant in East St. Louis, Illinois. Two years later the toll of a Chicago race riot was nearly as high, with twenty-three African Americans and fifteen whites left dead. In these and other incidents of racial violence, the pattern was the same: whites angered by the influx of southern blacks into their communities would seize upon an incident as an excuse to rampage through black neighborhoods, killing, burning, and looting while white policemen looked the other way or encouraged the mobs.

For women, American intervention in World War I had more positive effects. Initially women supported the war effort in traditional ways. They helped organize war-bond and war-relief drives, conserved foodstuffs and war-related materials, supported the Red Cross, and joined the army nurse corps. But as the scope of the war widened, both government and industry sought to mobilize women workers for service on farms, loading docks, and railway crews, as well as in the armaments industry, machine shops, steel and lumber mills, and chemical plants. Many women leaders saw such opportunities as a breakthrough. "At last, after centuries of disabilities and discrimination," said a speaker at a Women's Trade Union League meeting in 1917, "women are coming into the labor [force] and festival of life on equal terms with men."

In fact, however, war-generated changes in female employment were limited and brief. About 1 million women participated in "war work," but they usually were young, single, and already working outside the home. Most returned to their previous jobs once the war ended. In fact, male-dominated unions encouraged women to revert to their stereotypical domestic roles after the war. The Central Federated Union of New York baldly insisted that "the same patriotism which induced women to enter industry during the war should induce them to vacate their positions after the war." The anticipated gains of women in the workforce failed to materialize. In 1920 the 8.5 million working women made up a smaller percentage of the labor force than had working women in 1910. Still, one tangible result of women's contributions to the war effort was Woodrow Wilson's decision to endorse women's suffrage. In the fall of 1918, he told the Senate that giving women the vote was "vital to the winning of the war."

WAR PROPAGANDA   War needs also led the government to mobilize public opinion. On April 14, 1917, eight days after the declaration of war, President Wilson established the Committee on Public Information. Its executive director, George Creel, a Denver journalist, sold Wilson on the idea that the best approach to influencing public opinion was "expression, not repression"—propaganda instead of censorship. Creel organized a propaganda machine to convey the Allies' war aims to the people and, above all, to the enemy, where it might encourage public pressure to end the fighting.

The Beast of Berlin

A scene from the movie *The Beast of Berlin*, which gave audiences a propagandistic view of World War I.

CIVIL LIBERTIES   By arousing public opinion to a frenzy, the war effort spawned grotesque campaigns of "Americanism" and witch-hunting. Wilson had foreseen these consequences. "Once lead this people into war," he told a newspaper editor, "and they'll forget there ever was such a thing as tolerance." Popular prejudice equated anything German with disloyalty. Schools even dropped German-language courses.

While mobs hunted spies and chased rumors, the federal government stalked bigger game, with often absurd results. The Espionage and Sedition Acts of 1917 and 1918 suppressed criticism of government leaders and war policies. These laws led to more than 1,500 prosecutions and 1,000 convictions. Such repression disillusioned many progressives. Senator Robert La Follette declared that those engaged in such a "witch-hunt" were trying "to throw the country into a state of terror, to coerce public opinion, stifle criticism, suppress discussion of the issues of the war, and put a quietus on all opposition. It is time for the American people to assert and maintain their rights."

These acts targeted radicals. Eugene V. Debs, who had polled over 900,000 votes as the Socialist candidate for president in 1912, was arrested and sentenced to ten years in prison for encouraging draft resistance. In 1920, still in jail, he polled nearly 1 million votes for president.

In an important decision just after the war, the Supreme Court upheld the Espionage and Sedition Acts. *Schenck v. United States* (1919) sustained the conviction of a man for circulating anti-draft leaflets among members of the armed forces. In this case, Justice Oliver Wendell Holmes observed, "Free speech would not protect a man in falsely shouting fire in a theater, and causing a panic." The Sedition Act applied where there was "a clear and present danger" that free speech in wartime might create evils Congress had a right to prevent.

AMERICA AT WAR

American troops played little more than a token role in the European fighting until early 1918, by which time the Allied position had turned desperate. In October the Italian lines collapsed in the face of the Austrian offensive. In November, having suffered millions of casualties and widespread food and ammunition shortages, the provisional government of the Russian republic succumbed to a revolution led by Vladimir Lenin and his Bolshevik party, which promised the Russian people "peace, land, and bread." With German troops deep in Russian territory and armies of "White" Russians organizing to resist the Bolsheviks, Lenin concluded a separate peace with the Germans, the Treaty of Brest-Litovsk, on March 3, 1918. The Central Powers were then free to concentrate their forces on the western front, and the American war effort thus became a "race for France," to restore the balance of strength in that arena. The French premier Georges Clemenceau appealed to the Americans to accelerate their mobilization. "A terrible blow is imminent," he predicted to an American journalist. "Tell your Americans to come quickly."

THE WESTERN FRONT   On March 21, 1918, Clemenceau's prediction came true when the Germans began the first of several offensives in France and Belgium to try to end the war before the Americans arrived in force. By May 1918 there were 1 million fresh U.S. troops in Europe, and for the first time they made a difference. During early June a marine brigade blocked the Germans at Belleau Wood, and army troops took Vaux and opposed the Germans at Château-Thierry. Though these relatively modest actions had limited military significance, their effect on Allied morale was immense.

The turning point in France, the Second Battle of the Marne, erupted on July 15, 1918. The Germans assaulted the French lines, but within three days they had stalled, and the Allies began to roll the German front back into

The Meuse-Argonne offensive

U.S. soldiers fire an artillery gun in Argonne, France.

ENGLAND

NORTH SEA

NETHERLANDS

Rotterdam

Antwerp

Oostende

Dieppe

Ghent

Schelde River

Brussels

Calais

Ypres

Boulogne

Armentières

Lille

Mons

BELGIUM

Meuse River

Cologne

GERMANY

Koblenz

Arras

Cambrai

Amiens

Cantigny

Somme River

Oise River

Sedan

LUXEMBOURG

Compiègne

Soissons

BELLEAU WOOD

Château-Thierry

Aisne River

ARGONNE FOREST

Étain

Verdun

Metz

Reims

Vesle R.

Seine River

Paris

Marne River

Epernay

Versailles

FRANCE

St.-Mihiel

Nancy

Moselle River

Strasbourg

SWITZERLAND

Rhine River

Strait of Dover

**WORLD WAR I,
THE WESTERN FRONT, 1918**

--- Western front, March 1918

— German offensive, spring 1918

→ Allied counteroffensive

— Western front, November 1918

0   50 Miles

0   50 Kilometers

Why was the war on the western front a stalemate for most of World War I? What was the effect of the arrival of the American troops? Why was the Second Battle of the Marne the turning point of the war?

Belgium. On September 12 an army of more than 500,000 staged the first strictly American offensive of the war, aimed at German forces at St.-Mihiel. Within three days the Germans had pulled back. Two weeks later the massive Meuse-Argonne offensive employed U.S. divisions in a drive toward the rail center at Sedan, which supplied the entire German front. The largest U.S. action of the war resulted in 117,000 American casualties, including 26,000 dead. All along the front from Sedan to Flanders, the Germans were in retreat. "America," wrote a German commander, "thus became the decisive power in the war."

Meanwhile, in an effort to prevent Allied supplies stockpiled in Russia from falling into German hands and to encourage the counter-revolutionary Russian "Whites" in their civil war against the "Reds," fourteen Allied nations sent troops into eastern Russia. On August 2, 1918, some 8,000 Americans joined the expedition and remained on Russian soil until April 1920. But the Allied intervention in Russia was a colossal failure. The Bolsheviks were able to consolidate their power and defeat the Whites. Lenin and the Soviets never forgave the West for attempting to thwart their revolution.

THE FOURTEEN POINTS   As the conflict in Europe was ending, neither the Allies nor the Central Powers, despite Wilson's prodding, had stated openly what they hoped to gain from the bloodletting. Wilson insisted that the Americans had no selfish war aims. "We desire no conquest, no dominion," he stressed in his war message. Unfortunately for his idealistic purpose, the Bolsheviks later published copies of secret treaties in which the British and French had promised territorial gains in order to win Italy, Romania, and Greece to their side. When an Interallied Conference in Paris late in 1917 failed to agree on a statement of aims, Wilson formulated his own.

With advice from a panel of experts, Wilson drew up a peace plan that would be labeled the Fourteen Points. These he presented to a joint session of Congress on January 8, 1918, "as the only possible program" for peace. The first five points called for open diplomacy, freedom of the seas, removal of trade barriers, armaments reduction, and an impartial adjustment of colonial claims based upon the interests of the populations involved. Most of the remaining points called upon the Central Powers to evacuate occupied lands and allow political self-determination for various nationalities, a crucial principle for Wilson. Point 14, the capstone in Wilson's thinking, called for the formation of a "league" of nations to protect global peace. When the Fourteen Points were made public, African American leaders asked the president to add a fifteenth point: an end to racial discrimination. Wilson did not respond.

Wilson sincerely believed in the Fourteen Points, but they also served important political purposes. One of their aims was to keep Russia in the war by stating a more progressive purpose—a vain hope, as it turned out. Another was to reassure the citizens of the Allied Powers that they were involved in a noble cause. A third was to drive a wedge between the governments of the Central Powers and their people by offering a reasonable peace. But the chaos into which Central Europe descended in 1918 as Germany and Austria-Hungary verged on starvation and experienced socialist uprisings took matters out of Wilson's hands.

THE END OF THE WAR   On October 3 a new German chancellor made the overtures for peace on the basis of the Fourteen Points. The Allies accepted the Fourteen Points as a basis of a peace treaty but with two significant reservations: the right to discuss freedom of the seas further and the demand for reparations (financial compensation to the victors) for war damages.

Meanwhile, German morale plummeted, culminating in a naval mutiny. Germany's allies, Bulgaria, Turkey, and Austria-Hungary, dropped out of the war during the early fall of 1918. On November 9 the kaiser, head of the German Empire, abdicated, and a German republic was proclaimed. Two days later, on November 11, 1918, an armistice was signed, ceasing the hostilities. Under the armistice the Germans agreed to evacuate occupied territories, pull their troops back behind the Rhine River, and surrender their navy, railroad equipment, and other matériel. The Germans were assured that Wilson's Fourteen Points would be the basis of the peace conference.

During its nineteen months of participation in the war, the United States saw 126,000 of its servicemen killed. Germany's war dead totaled over 2 million, including civilians; France lost nearly 1.4 million combatants, the United Kingdom lost 703,000 soldiers, and Russia lost 1.7 million. The new Europe emerging from the conflagration would be much different: more violent, more polarized, more cynical, less sure of itself, and less capable of decisive action. The United States, for good or ill, would be sucked into the vacuum of power created by the destructiveness of the Great War.

THE FIGHT FOR PEACE

DOMESTIC UNREST   Woodrow Wilson made a fateful decision to attend the Paris Peace Conference, which convened on January 18, 1919, and would last almost six months. No U.S. president had ever left the country while in office, and doing so dramatized all the more Wilson's messianic vision and his goal of a lasting peace. From one viewpoint it was a shrewd move, for his prestige and determination made a difference at the Paris peace talks. But during his prolonged trip abroad, he lost touch with political developments at home, where his political coalition was already unraveling under the pressures of wartime discontent. Western farmers complained about the government's control of wheat prices while eastern business leaders chafed at federal revenue policies designed, according to the *New York Sun,* "to pay for the war out of taxes raised north of the Mason and Dixon Line." Organized labor, despite real gains during the war, groused about inflation and the problems of reconversion to a peacetime economy.

In the midterm elections of 1918, Wilson defied his advisers and urged voters to elect a Democratic Congress to support his foreign policies. Republicans, who for the most part had supported Wilson's war measures, took affront. So, too, did many voters. In elections held a week before the armistice, the Democrats lost control of both houses of Congress. With an opposition majority in the new Congress, Wilson further weakened his standing by failing to appoint a prominent Republican to the American delegation headed for Paris and the treaty negotiations. Former President Taft suggested that Wilson's real intention in going to Paris was "to hog the whole show."

When Wilson reached Paris in December 1918, enthusiastic demonstrations greeted him. At the conference table, however, he had to deal with some tough-minded statesmen who did not share his utopian zeal. The Paris Peace Conference lasted from January to June 1919. It included delegates from all countries that had declared war or broken diplomatic relations with Germany. But it was dominated by the Big Four: the prime ministers of Britain, France, and Italy and the president of the United States. The British prime minister David Lloyd George was a gifted politician fresh from electoral

The Paris Peace Conference

Woodrow Wilson (second from left) with Georges Clemenceau of France (center) and Arthur Balfour of Great Britain (second from right) during the Paris Peace Conference.

victory following a campaign whose slogan declared, "Hang the kaiser." Italy's prime minister, Vittorio Orlando, was there to pick up the spoils promised his country in the secret 1915 Treaty of London. The French premier Georges Clemenceau, a stern realist, demanded severe measures to weaken Germany and guarantee French security.

THE LEAGUE OF NATIONS   Woodrow Wilson insisted that his cherished League of Nations come first at the conference and in the treaty. Whatever compromises he might have to make regarding territorial boundaries and financial claims, whatever mistakes might result, Wilson believed that a league of nations committed to collective security would maintain international stability. Wilson presided over the commission to draft a league charter. Article X of the charter, which he called "the heart of the League," pledged member nations to consult on military and economic sanctions against aggressors. The use of armed force would be a last resort. The League structure would allow each member an equal voice in the Assembly; the Big Five (Britain, France, Italy, Japan, and the United States) and four rotating members would make up the Council; the administrative staff, in Geneva, Switzerland, would make up the Secretariat; and a Permanent Court of International Justice (set up in 1921 and usually called the World Court) could "hear and determine any dispute of an international character."

On February 14, 1919, Wilson delivered the finished draft of the League charter to the Allies and departed the next day for a visit home. Already he faced opposition. The Republican Henry Cabot Lodge, the powerful chairman of the Senate Foreign Relations Committee, claimed that the League's covenant was unacceptable. His statement of March 4 bore the signatures of thirty-nine Republican senators or senators-elect, more than enough to block ratification.

TERRITORY AND REPARATIONS   Back in Paris in the spring of 1919, Wilson grudgingly acceded to French demands for territorial concessions and reparations payments by Germany. The Allied statesmen also agreed that the Allies would occupy a demilitarized German Rhineland for fifteen years and that the League of Nations would administer Germany's coal-rich Saar Basin. France could use the Saar mines for fifteen years, after which the region's voters would determine whether to join Germany or France.

In other territorial matters, Wilson had to compromise his unrealistic principle of national self-determination. As a result of the Great War, four long-standing multinational empires had disintegrated: the Russian, Austro-Hungarian, German, and Ottoman (Turkish). Hundreds of millions of people

EUROPE AFTER THE TREATY OF VERSAILLES, 1918

········· 1914 boundaries

☐ New nations

☐ Plebiscite areas

☐ Occupied area

Why was self-determination difficult for states in Central Europe? How did territorial concessions weaken Germany?

had to be reorganized into new nations. There was in fact no way to make Europe's boundaries correspond to its tangled ethnic groupings because mixed populations were scattered throughout Central Europe. In some areas, moreover, national self-determination yielded to other interests, such as trade and defense. The result was a reorganized map of Central Europe in which portions of the former Austro-Hungarian Empire became independent, most notably Czechoslovakia and Yugoslavia, and portions were attached to Poland, Romania, and Italy. Ethnic and nationalist tensions continued and would contribute to the crisis that culminated in World War II.

The discussion of reparations was among the longest and most bitter at the conference. Despite a pre-armistice agreement that Germany would be liable only for civilian damages, Clemenceau and Lloyd George proposed that Germany pay reparations for the entire cost of the war. On this point, Wilson made perhaps his most fateful concessions. He agreed to a clause in the treaty in which Germany accepted responsibility for starting the war and thus for its entire financial cost. The "war guilt" clause offended Germans and provided a source of persistent bitterness upon which Adolf Hitler would later capitalize.

On May 7, 1919, the victorious powers presented the treaty to the German delegates, who returned three weeks later with 443 pages of criticism. A few small changes were made, but when the Germans still refused to sign, the French prepared to move their army across the Rhine River. Finally, on June 28, 1919, the Germans gave up and signed the treaty at Versailles.

WILSON'S LOSS AT HOME   On July 8, 1919, Woodrow Wilson returned home with the Versailles Treaty amid a great clamor of popular support. A third of the state legislatures had endorsed the League of Nations, as had thirty-three of the nation's forty-eight governors. Wilson called upon the Senate to accept the "great duty" of ratifying the treaty. Senator Henry Cabot Lodge, however, doubted that the Paris negotiators could make "mankind suddenly virtuous by a statute or a written constitution." Lodge relished a fight. He knew the undercurrents already stirring up opposition to the treaty: the resentment felt by German, Italian, and Irish groups, the disappointment of many progressives with Wilson's compromises on reparations and boundaries, the distractions of demobilization and resulting domestic problems, and the revival of isolationism.

Others agreed. In the Senate a group of "irreconcilables," fourteen Republicans and two Democrats, opposed U.S. participation in the League on any terms. They

"The League of Nations Argument in a Nutshell"

Jay N. "Ding" Darling's summation of the League controversy.

were mainly western and midwestern progressives who feared that new foreign commitments would threaten domestic programs and reforms. The irreconcilables would be useful to Lodge's purpose, but he belonged to a larger group, "reservationists," who insisted upon limiting U.S. involvement in the League. Wilson said that he had already amended the covenant to these ends, pointing out that with a veto in the League Council, the United States could not be obligated by the League to do anything against its will.

Lodge, who set more store by the old balance of power than by Wilson's idea of collective security, offered a set of amendments—his reservations. Wilson responded by agreeing to interpretive reservations but to nothing that would reopen the negotiations with Germany and the Allies. He especially opposed the amendments weakening Article X of the League of Nations covenant, which provided for collective action by the signatory governments against aggression.

By September 1919, with momentum for the treaty slackening, Wilson decided to go directly to the people. Against the advice of doctors and friends, he set forth on a grueling railroad tour through the Midwest to the West Coast, pounding out speeches on his typewriter between stops. In all he traveled 8,000 miles in twenty-two days, giving thirty-two major addresses, which included dire warnings of the consequences the nation and the world would face if the treaty were not approved.

For a while, Wilson seemed to be regaining the initiative, but on October 2, 1919, he suffered a severe stroke that left him paralyzed on his left side and an invalid for the rest of his life. For seventeen months his protective wife, Edith, kept him isolated from all but the most essential business. The illness intensified Wilson's stubbornness. He might have done better to have secured the best compromise possible, but he refused to yield and continued to be needlessly confrontational. As he scoffed to an aide, "Let Lodge compromise."

Lodge resolved to amend the treaty before it was ratified. Between November 7 and 19, the Senate adopted fourteen of Lodge's reservations to the Versailles Treaty, most having to do with the League of Nations. Wilson refused to make any compromises or concessions. As a result, his supporters found themselves thrown into an unlikely combination with the irreconcilables, who opposed the treaty under any circumstances. The Senate vote on the treaty with Lodge's reservations was 39 for and 55 against. On the question of taking the original treaty without reservations, irreconcilables and reservationists combined to defeat ratification again, with 38 for and 53 against.

In the face of strong public criticism, however, the Senate voted to reconsider. On March 19, 1920, twenty-one intransigent Democrats deserted Wilson and joined the reservationists, but the treaty once again fell short of the required two-thirds majority. The real winners were the smallest of the three groups in the Senate, neither the Wilsonians nor the reservationists but the irreconcilables.

When Congress declared the war at an end by a joint congressional resolution on May 20, 1920, Wilson vetoed the action; it was not until after he left office that a joint congressional resolution officially ended the state of war with Germany and Austria-Hungary, on July 2, 1921. Peace treaties with Germany, Austria, and Hungary were ratified on October 18, 1921, but by then Warren Gamaliel Harding was president of the United States.

LURCHING FROM WAR TO PEACE

The Versailles Treaty, for all the time it spent in the Senate before being defeated, was but one issue clamoring for public attention in the turbulent period after the war. The year 1919 began with ecstatic victory parades that soon gave way to widespread labor unrest, race riots, domestic terror, and government tyranny. Demobilization of the armed forces and the government's war effort proceeded in haphazard fashion. The War Industries Board closed shop on January 1, 1919, and the sudden cancellation of war-related contracts left workers and business leaders to cope with reconversion to a peacetime economy on their own. Wilson's leadership was missing. He had been preoccupied by the war and the League, and once bedridden by his illness, he became grim and peevish. His rudderless administration floundered through rough waters during its last two years.

THE SPANISH FLU   Amid the initial confusion of postwar life, many Americans confronted a virulent menace that produced far more casualties than the war itself. It became known as the Spanish flu, and its contagion spread around the globe. Erupting in the spring of 1918 and lasting a year, the pandemic killed more than 22 million people worldwide, twice as many as died in World War I. In the United States alone it accounted for over 675,000 deaths, nearly seven times the number of combat deaths in France.

American servicemen returning from France brought the flu with them, and it raced through the congested army camps and naval bases. By September 1918 the epidemic had spread to the civilian population. In that month 10,000 Americans died from the disease. Municipal health officers fined people for spitting on the sidewalks or sneezing without a handkerchief. Millions of people wore surgical masks to work. Still the death toll rose. From September 1918 to June 1919, a quarter of the population contracted the illness.

By the spring of 1919, the pandemic had finally run its course. It ended as suddenly—and as inexplicably—as it had begun. Although another outbreak occurred in the winter of 1920, the population had grown more resistant to its assaults. No plague, war, famine, or natural catastrophe in world history had killed so many people in such a short time.

THE ECONOMIC TRANSITION   Disease was only one of many challenges confronting postwar America. Consumer prices continued to rise steeply after the war, and discontented workers, released from wartime constraints, were more willing to strike for their demands. In 1919 more than 4 million workers walked out in thousands of disputes with management. After a general strike in Seattle, public opinion of militant workers began to turn hostile.

The most celebrated postwar labor confrontation was the Boston police strike, which inadvertently launched a presidential career. On September 9, 1919, most of Boston's police force went out on strike, demanding recognition of their union. Massachusetts governor Calvin Coolidge was furious; he mobilized the National Guard to arrest looters and restore order. After four days the strikers were ready to return, but the police commissioner fired them all. When labor leader Samuel Gompers appealed for their reinstatement, Coolidge responded in words that suddenly turned him into a national figure: "There is no right to strike against the public safety by anybody, anywhere, anytime."

RACIAL FRICTION   The summer of 1919 also sparked a season of deadly race riots across the nation. Whites invaded the black section of Longview, Texas, in search of a teacher who had allegedly accused a white woman of a liaison with a black man. They burned shops and houses and ran several African Americans out of town. A week later in Washington, D.C., reports of black assaults on white women aroused white mobs, and for four days gangs of white and black rioters waged a race war in the streets until soldiers and driving rains ended the fighting.

These were but preliminaries to the Chicago riot of late July, in which 38 people were killed, 537 injured, and 1,000 left homeless. It all started on the shores of Lake Michigan when a black youth's raft drifted into the whites' beach area and whites started stoning him. The climactic disorders of the summer occurred in the rural area around Elaine, Arkansas, where African American tenant farmers tried to organize a union. According to official reports, 5 whites and 25 blacks were killed in the violence, but whites told one reporter that in fact more than 100 blacks had died. Altogether, twenty-five race riots erupted in 1919, and there were eighty racial lynchings.

THE RED SCARE   Public reaction to the wave of labor strikes and race riots reflected the impact of Russia's Bolshevik Revolution. Some radicals thought America's domestic turbulence, like that in Russia, was the first scene in a drama of world revolution. Many Americans decided that they might be right. After all, Lenin's tiny Bolshevik faction in Russia had exploited confusion to impose its will on the entire nation. Wartime hysteria against all things German was thus readily transformed into a postwar Red Scare.

Fears of revolution in America were fueled by the actions of militants. In April 1919 the postal service intercepted nearly forty homemade mail bombs addressed to prominent citizens. One slipped through and blew off the hands of a Georgia senator's maid. In June another bomb destroyed the front of Attorney General A. Mitchell Palmer's house in Washington.

In June 1919 the Justice Department decided to deport radical aliens, and Attorney General Palmer set up as the head of the department's new General Intelligence Division the young J. Edgar Hoover, who began to collect files on radicals. Raids began on November 7, 1919, when federal agents swooped down on offices of the Union of Russian Workers in twelve cities. Many of those arrested were deported without a court hearing. On January 2, 1920, police raids in dozens of cities swept up some 5,000 suspects, many taken from their homes without search warrants. That same month the New York State legislature expelled five duly elected Socialist members.

Basking in popular approval, Palmer continued to warn of the Red menace, but like other fads and alarms, the ugly mood of intolerance passed. By the summer of 1920, the Red Scare had begun to evaporate. Communist revolutions in Europe died out, leaving Bolshevism isolated in Russia. Bombings in the United States tapered off; the wave of strikes and race riots receded. The reactionary attorney general began to seem more threatening to civil liberties than the handful of radicals he uncovered. By September 1920, when a bomb explosion at the corner of Broad and Wall Streets in New York City killed thirty-eight people, Americans were ready to take it for what it was: the work of a crazed mind and not the start of a revolution.

The Red Scare nonetheless left a lasting mark on American life. Part of its legacy was the continuing crusade for "100 percent Americanism" and restrictions on immigration. It also left a stigma on labor unions (already weakened by their internal ethnic and racial tensions) and contributed to the anti-union open-shop campaign—the American plan, its sponsors called it. But for many thoughtful Americans the chief residue of the Great War, President Wilson's physical collapse, and its chaotic aftermath was a profound disillusionment.

End of Chapter Review

CHAPTER SUMMARY

- **Wilson and Mexico** Woodrow Wilson wanted to foster democratic governments in Latin America; he got the United States involved in Mexican politics after Mexico experienced several military coups. The popular Pancho Villa tried to gain power in Mexico by promoting an anti-American program, even making raids across the border into New Mexico.

- **Causes of WWI** Europe had developed a system of alliances that divided the continent in two. Democratic Britain and France, along with the Russian Empire, had formed the Triple Entente. Central Powers were comprised of the new German empire, Austria-Hungary, and Italy. The assassination of the heir to the Austro-Hungarian throne by a Serbian nationalist triggered the world war.

- **U.S. Enters WWI** Most Americans supported the Triple Entente, or Allied Powers, at the outbreak of World War I. The Wilson administration declared the nation neutral but allowed businesses to extend credit to the Allies to purchase food and military supplies. Americans were outraged by the Germans' use of unlimited submarine warfare, especially the 1915 sinking of the British liner *Lusitania*. In 1917 unrestricted submarine activity and the revelation of the Zimmermann telegram, in which the Germans sought to incite the Mexicans to wage war against the United States, led the United States to enter the Great War.

- **Wilson's Peace Plan** Wilson insisted that the United States wanted no selfish gains from the war, only a new, democratic Europe to emerge from the old empires. His famous Fourteen Points speech outlined his ideas for the establishment of continent-wide democratic nation-states and a league of nations.

- **Treaty of Versailles** The United States did not ratify the Treaty of Versailles because Wilson had alienated the Republican senators whose support he needed for ratification. A coalition of "irreconcilables" formed in the Senate: midwestern and western progressives who feared that involvement in a league of nations would stifle domestic reforms and that ratification would necessitate involvement in future wars. The irreconcilables were joined by "reservationists," who would accept the treaty with certain limitations on America's involvement in the League of Nations. Wilson's illness and his refusal to compromise ensured failure of ratification.

- **Consequences of WWI** As a result of the war, four European empires were dismantled, replaced by small nation-states. The reparations imposed on Germany and the "war guilt" clause laid the foundations for German bitterness and led to the rise of Adolf Hitler and the Nazi party. The presence of a Communist regime in the old Russian Empire had major consequences in America. Fear of communism at home, which first manifested itself in the Red Scare of 1919, became a major theme in the twentieth century.

CHRONOLOGY

1914	United States intervenes in Mexico
1914	World War I begins in Europe
1915	British liner *Lusitania,* with Americans aboard, is torpedoed without warning by a German submarine
1916	Congress passes the National Defense Act
March 1917	Zimmermann telegram reveals that Germany is attempting to incite Mexico to enter the war against the United States
April 1917	United States enters the Great War
January 1918	Woodrow Wilson delivers his Fourteen Points speech
November 11, 1918	Representatives of warring nations sign armistice
1919	Supreme Court issues *Schenck v. United States* decision
May 1919	Treaty of Versailles is presented to the Germans
1919	Race riots break out in Chicago
1919	U.S. attorney general launches Red Scare
July 1921	Joint resolution of Congress officially ends the war among the United States, Germany, and Austro-Hungary

KEY TERMS & NAMES

Francisco "Pancho" Villa p. 746

John J. Pershing p. 747

dollar diplomacy p. 747

Unterseeboot p. 752

Bolsheviks p. 756

Food Administration p. 758

George Creel p. 760

Committee on Public Information p. 760

western front p. 762

Fourteen Points p. 764

League of Nations p. 767

Henry Cabot Lodge p. 767

reparations p. 767

A. Mitchell Palmer p. 773

2 6
THE MODERN TEMPER

FOCUS QUESTIONS wwnorton.com/studyspace

- What accounted for the nativism of the 1920s?
- What was meant by the Jazz Age?
- How did the new social trends of the 1920s challenge traditional attitudes?
- What was modernism, and how did it influence American culture?

The horrors of World War I dealt a shattering blow to the widespread belief that Western civilization was steadily progressing, an assumption that had been a powerful stimulus of progressivism. The editors of *Presbyterian* magazine announced in 1919 that the "world has been convulsed" by the terrible war, and "every field of thought and action has been disturbed."

The war's colossal carnage disillusioned young intellectuals and spurred a new "modernist" sensibility among artists and writers. At once a mood and a movement, as well as a label for a historical era and a cultural style, modernism appeared first in Europe at the end of the nineteenth century and had become a pervasive international force by 1920. It arose out of a widespread recognition that Western civilization had entered an era of bewildering change. New technologies, new modes of transportation and communication, and new scientific discoveries such as quantum mechanics, relativity theory, and Freudian psychology, combined to rupture traditional perceptions of reality and generate new forms of artistic expression. Modernism manifested itself in a cluster of diverse intellectual and artistic movements: impressionism, futurism, dadaism, surrealism, Freudianism. As the French painter Paul Gauguin acknowledged, the upheavals of modernism produced "an epoch of confusion."

At the same time that the war provided an accelerant for modernism, it stimulated volatile social tensions and political radicalism. The postwar wave of strikes, bombings, anti-Communist hysteria, and race riots convinced many Americans that the country had entered a frightening new era of turmoil and turbulence. Conflict abounded. Defenders of tradition located the germs of radicalism in the polyglot cities teeming with immigrants and foreign ideas. The reactionary mood of the 1920s fed on a growing tendency to connect American nationalism with nativism, Anglo-Saxon racism, and militant Protestantism. In sum, postwar America was a fractured society animated by violent contrasts and seething social tensions.

REACTION IN THE TWENTIES

NATIVISM   That so many political radicals in the United States were immigrants strengthened the suspicion that the seeds of sedition were foreign-born. In the early 1920s over half the white men and a third of the white women working in industry were foreign-born, most of them from central or eastern Europe. That socialism and anarchism were prevalent in those regions made such immigrant workers especially suspicious in the eyes of "old stock" Americans.

The most celebrated case of nativist prejudice involved two Italian immigrant anarchists: shoemaker Nicola Sacco and fish peddler Bartolomeo Vanzetti. They were arrested on May 5, 1920, for stealing $16,000 and killing a paymaster and his guard. Both were armed when arrested, both lied to police about their activities, and both were identified by eyewitnesses. The Sacco and Vanzetti case occurred at the height of Italian immigration to the United States and against the backdrop of numerous terror attacks by anarchists, including the 1920 bombing that killed thirty-eight people on Wall Street in New York City. At the trial of Sacco and Vanzetti the judge was openly prejudicial. He privately referred to the defendants as "anarchist bastards." Sacco and Vanzetti were convicted and ordered executed, but appeals of the verdict lasted seven years. People then and since have insisted that Sacco and Vanzetti were sentenced more for their political beliefs and their ethnic origin than for any crime they had committed. The case became a great radical and liberal cause of the 1920s, but despite pleas for mercy and worldwide demonstrations on behalf of the two men, Sacco and Vanzetti were executed in 1927. Recent investigations have pointed to their likely guilt.

The surging postwar nativism generated new efforts to restrict immigration. Congress, alarmed at the influx of foreigners after 1919, passed the Emergency Immigration Act of 1921, which restricted European arrivals each year to 3 percent of the foreign-born of any nationality as shown in the 1910 census. The Immigration Act of 1924 reduced the number to 2 percent based on the 1890 census, which included fewer of the "new" immigrants from southern and eastern Europe. This law set a permanent limitation, which became effective in 1929, of slightly over 150,000 immigrants per year based on the "national origins" of the U.S. population as of 1920. In signing the law, President Calvin Coolidge pledged, "America must be kept American."

However inexact the quotas, their purpose was clear: to tilt the balance in favor of the old immigration from northern and western Europe, which was assigned about 85 percent of the total. The law completely excluded people from east Asia. Yet it left the gate open to immigrants from Western Hemisphere countries, so that an ironic consequence was a substantial increase in the Hispanic Catholic population. People of Latin American descent (chiefly Mexicans, Puerto Ricans, and Cubans) became the fastest-growing ethnic minority in the country.

Klan rally

In 1925, 40,000 Klan members paraded down Pennsylvania Avenue in Washington, D.C.

THE KLAN   During the postwar years the tradition of nativist prejudice against "foreigners" took on a new form: a revived Ku Klux Klan modeled on the vigilante group founded in the South after the Civil War. The new Klan was devoted to "100 percent Americanism" rather than to the old Confederacy, and it restricted its membership to native-born white Protestants. It was determined to protect its warped notion of the American way of life not only from blacks but also from Roman Catholics, Jews, and immigrants. In going nativist, the new Klan spread far outside the South. It thrived in small towns and cities in the North and especially in the Midwest. And it was preoccupied with the defense of white ("native") women and Christian morals.

The Klan represented a vicious reflex against the modern and the alien, against shifting moral standards, the declining influence of churches, and the social permissiveness of cities and colleges. In the Southwest the Klan became more than anything else a moral crusade. "It is going to drive the bootleggers forever out of this land," declared a Texan. "It is going to bring clean moving pictures . . . clean literature . . . break up roadside parking . . . enforce the laws . . . protect homes." Instead, the Klan terrorized and assaulted blacks and immigrants. Although the Klan was very successful at raising money and electing Klan-backed local politicians, it rarely succeeded in its goal of coercing African Americans and immigrants to leave its members' communities. In the mid-1920s the Klan's peak membership may have been as high as 4 million, but its influence diminished as quickly as its numbers grew. Nativist excitement declined after passage of the 1924 immigration law. The Klan also suffered from recurrent factional quarrels and schisms. And its willing use of violence tarnished its moral pretensions.

FUNDAMENTALISM   While the Klan saw a threat mainly in the "alien menace," many adherents of the old-time religion saw threats from modernism in the churches: new ideas that the Bible should be studied in the light of modern scholarship (the "higher criticism") or that it could be reconciled with scientific theories of evolution. When such modernist notions surfaced in schools and even pulpits, fundamentalism, grounded in a literal interpretation of the Bible, took on a new militancy.

Among the rural fundamentalist leaders only William Jennings Bryan, the former presidential candidate and secretary of state, had the following, prestige, and eloquence to make the movement a popular crusade. By 1920, Bryan was showing signs of age, but he remained as silver-tongued as ever in his espousal of a unique blend of progressive populism and religious fundamentalism. In 1921 he promoted laws prohibiting the teaching of Darwinian evolution in the public schools. Anti-evolution bills emerged in legislatures, but the only victories came in the South—and there were few of those.

The climax of the crusade came in Tennessee, where in 1925 the state legislature outlawed the teaching of evolution in public schools and colleges. A young science teacher at a high school in Dayton, Tennessee, John T. Scopes,

Courtroom scene during the Scopes trial

The media, food vendors, and others flocked to Dayton, Tennessee, for the case against John Scopes, the teacher who taught evolution.

accepted an offer from the American Civil Liberties Union to defend a test case. It soon was a case heard round the world. Before the opening of the twelve-day "monkey trial" in July 1925, the streets of Dayton swarmed with publicity hounds, curiosity seekers, evangelists and atheists, hucksters, and a mob of reporters.

The two stars of the show were Bryan, who led the prosecution of Scopes for teaching evolution in violation of Tennessee law, and Clarence Darrow, a renowned Chicago trial lawyer and articulate agnostic, who defended Scopes by challenging the anti-evolution law. The trial quickly became a debate between fundamentalism and modernism. When the judge (a practicing evangelist) damaged Darrow's case by ruling out scientific testimony on evolution, most observers assumed the trial was over.

But the defense rebounded by calling Bryan as an expert witness on biblical interpretation. Darrow, who had once supported Bryan as a presidential candidate, now relentlessly entrapped the statesman in literal-minded inter-pretations and exposed his ignorance of biblical history and scholarship. Bryan insisted that a "great fish" had swallowed Jonah and that Joshua had made the sun stand still—both, according to Darrow, "fool ideas that no intelligent Christian on earth believes." It was a bitter scene. At one point the two men, their patience exhausted in the broiling summer heat, lunged at each other, shaking their fists, leading the judge to adjourn the court.

The next day the testimony ended. The only issue before the court, the judge ruled, was whether Scopes had in fact taught evolution. He was found guilty, but the Tennessee Supreme Court, while upholding the law, overruled the $100 fine on a legal technicality. The chief prosecutor accepted the higher court's advice against "prolonging the life of this bizarre case" and dropped the issue. With more prescience than he knew, Bryan had described the trial as a "duel to the death." Five days after it closed, he died of a heart condition aggravated by heat and fatigue.

PROHIBITION   The reaction against modern social attitudes took many forms. Prohibition of alcoholic beverages offered another example of re-forming zeal channeled into a drive for moral righteousness and conformity. Moralists had been campaigning against excessive drink since the eighteenth century. Around 1900, however, the leading temperance organizations, the Women's Christian Temperance Union and the Anti-Saloon League, shifted their efforts from reforming individuals to campaigning for a national pro-hibition law. The Anti-Saloon League became one of the most effective pressure groups in history, mobilizing Protestant churches behind its single-minded battle to elect "dry" candidates. Proponents of prohibition often displayed blatant ethnic and social prejudices. The head of the Anti-Saloon League castigated German Americans because they "eat like gluttons and drink like swine." For many anti-alcohol crusaders, the primary goal of eliminating alcoholic beverages seemed to be policing the behavior of the poor, the foreign-born, and the working class. One prohibitionist referred to Italian immigrants as "Dagos, who drink excessively [and] live in a state of filth."

The 1916 elections produced in both houses of Congress two-thirds ma-jorities supporting an amendment to the Constitution prohibiting alcoholic beverages. Soon the wartime spirit of sacrifice, the need to use grain for food rather than booze, and wartime hostility to German American brewers transformed the cause into a virtual test of patriotism. On December 18, 1917, Congress sent to the states the Eighteenth Amendment, which one

Prohibition

A 1926 police raid on a speakeasy, where illegal "bootleg" liquor was sold.

year after ratification, on January 16, 1919, banned the manufacture, sale, and transportation of intoxicating liquors nationwide.

The new amendment did not keep people from drinking, however. Congress never supplied adequate enforcement, if such were even possible given the public thirst, the spotty support of local officials, and the profits to be made in bootlegging. In Detroit, across the river from Ontario, Canada, where booze was legal, the liquor industry during Prohibition was second in size only to the auto industry. Speakeasies, hip flasks, and cocktail parties were among the social innovations of the era, along with increased drinking by women. As the popular humorist Will Rogers quipped, "Prohibition is better than no liquor at all."

It would be too much to say that Prohibition gave rise to organized crime, for systematic vice, gambling, and extortion had long been practiced and were often tied in with saloons. But Prohibition supplied ruthless, flamboyant criminals, such as "Scarface" Al Capone, with an enormous source of income, while the automobile and the submachine gun provided criminals with greater mobility and greater firepower. Organized crime bosses showed remarkable gifts for exploiting loopholes in the law when they did not simply bribe policemen and politicians.

Capone was by far the most celebrated criminal of the 1920s. In 1927 he pocketed $60 million from his bootlegging, prostitution, and gambling empire, and he flaunted his wealth as well as his open disregard for legal authorities. He bludgeoned to death several police lieutenants and ordered the execution of dozens of his criminal competitors. Law-enforcement officials began to smash his bootlegging operations in 1929, but they were unable to pin anything on him until a Treasury agent infiltrated his gang and uncovered evidence that was used to convict him later that year of tax evasion. He was sentenced to eleven years in prison.

In the light of the illegal activities of Capone and other members of organized-crime syndicates, it came as opposing no great surprise when a national commission in 1931 reported that enforcement of Prohibition had broken down. Still, the commission voted to extend Prohibition, and President Herbert Hoover chose to stand by what he called the "experiment, noble in motive and far-reaching in purpose."

THE ROARING TWENTIES

In many ways the reactionary temper of the 1920s and the repressive movements to which it gave rise seemed the dominant trends of the decade. But they arose in part as opposing reactions to disruptive social and intellectual currents. During those years a new cosmopolitan, urban America confronted provincial small-town and rural America, and cultural conflict reached new levels of tension.

Young urban intellectuals dismissed the old-fashioned values of the hinterlands. Sinclair Lewis's novel *Main Street* (1920) caricatured the stifling life of a prairie town, depicting a "savorless people, gulping tasteless food, and sitting afterward, coatless and thoughtless, in rocking chairs prickly with inane decorations, listening to mechanical music, saying mechanical things about the excellence of Ford automobiles, and viewing themselves as the greatest race in the world." The banality of small-town life became a pervasive theme in much of the literature of the time, and the heartland responded to such criticisms of rural folkways with counterimages of cities infested with vice, crime, corruption, and foreigners.

THE JAZZ AGE   The writer F. Scott Fitzgerald dubbed the postwar era the Jazz Age because young people were willing to experiment with new forms of recreation and sexuality. The new jazz music bubbling up in New Orleans, Kansas City, Memphis, New York City, and Chicago blended African

Frankie "Half Pint" Jackson and his band at the Sunset Cafe, Chicago, in the 1920s

Jazz emerged in the 1920s as an especially American expression of the modernist spirit. African American artists bent musical conventions to give fuller rein to improvisation and sensuality.

and European traditions to form a distinctive sound. The syncopated rhythms of jazz were immensely popular among rebellious young adults and helped spawn carefree new dance steps such as the Charleston and the black bottom, whose gyrations shocked guardians of morality.

If people were not listening to ragtime or jazz or to the family radio shows that became the rage in the 1920s, they were frequenting movie theaters. By 1930 there were more than 23,000 theaters around the country, and they drew more than 95 million customers each week. In Muncie, Indiana, a small city of 35,000, nine movie theaters were operating seven days a week. Films became even more popular after the introduction of sound in 1927.

THE NEW MORALITY Much of the shock to traditionalists during the Jazz Age came from the changes in manners and morals evidenced first among young people and especially on college campuses. In *This Side* *of Paradise* (1920), a novel of student life at Princeton, F. Scott Fitzgerald wrote of "the great current American phenomenon, the 'petting party.'" None of the Victorian mothers, he said, "had any idea how casually their daughters were accustomed to be kissed." From such novels and from magazines and movies, many Americans learned about the cities' wild parties, illegal drinking, promiscuity, and speakeasies.

Sex came to be discussed with surprising frankness during the 1920s. Much of the talk derived from a spreading awareness of Dr. Sigmund Freud, the Viennese father of psychoanalysis. By the 1920s his ideas had begun to infiltrate popular culture. Books and magazines now included discussions of of libido, Oedipus complexes, sublimation, and repression.

Fashion also reflected the rebellion against prudishness and a loosening of inhibitions. In 1919 women's skirts were typically six inches above the ground; by 1927 they were at the knee, and the "flapper," with her bobbed hair, rolled stockings, cigarettes, lipstick, and sensuous dancing, was providing a shocking model of the new feminism. The name *flapper* derived from the way young female rebels allowed their galoshes to flap around their ankles. Conservative moralists saw the flappers as just another sign of a degenerating society. Others saw in the "new woman" an expression of American individualism.

By 1930, however, the thrill of rebellion was waning; the revolution against Victorian morality had run its course—for a while. Its extreme expressions in time aroused doubts that the indulgence of lust equaled liberation. And the much-discussed revolution in morals was also greatly exaggerated. The twenties roared for only a small proportion of the population. F. Scott Fitzgerald reminded Americans in 1931 that the Jazz Age was jazzy for only the "upper tenth" of the population. Still, some new folkways had come to stay. In the late

The "new woman" of the 1920s

Two flappers dance atop the Hotel Sherman in Chicago, 1926.

1930s a survey disclosed that among college women almost half had had sexual relations before marriage.

THE WOMEN'S MOVEMENT At the same time that many women were embracing new sexual mores, all women were being liberated politically. The suffrage movement, which had been in the doldrums since 1896, sprang back to life in the second decade of the new century. In 1912, Alice Paul, a Quaker social worker, returned from an apprenticeship with the militant suffragists of England to chair the Congressional Committee of the National American Woman Suffrage Association (NAWSA). Paul instructed female activists to be more aggressive and confrontational: to picket state legislatures, target and "punish" politicians who failed to endorse suffrage, chain themselves to public buildings, provoke police to arrest them, and

Votes for women

Suffragettes march in New York City in 1912, their children by their side.

undertake hunger strikes. By 1917, Paul and her followers were picketing the White House and deliberately inviting arrest, after which they went on hunger strikes in prison.

In 1915 the more moderate but equally persistent Carrie Chapman Catt had once again become head of NAWSA. For several years, President Woodrow Wilson had evaded the issue of a suffrage amendment, but he supported a plank in the 1916 Democratic platform encouraging states to embrace women's suffrage. He addressed NAWSA that year and thereafter worked closely with its leaders. For several years, President Woodrow Wilson had evaded the issue of a suffrage amendment, but he supported a plank in the 1916 Democratic platform encouraging states to embrace women's suffrage. In 1916 he also addressed NAWSA, which by then was once again headed by Carrie Chapman Catt, a more moderate feminist than Paul but equally persistent. Thereafter Wilson worked closely with NAWSA's leaders.

The courageous proponents of women's suffrage put forth several arguments in favor of voting rights. Many assumed that the right to vote and hold office was a matter of simple justice: women were just as capable as men in exercising the rights and responsibilities of citizenship. Others insisted that women were morally superior to men and therefore would raise the quality of the political process by their participation in it. They also would be less prone to use warfare as a solution to international disputes and national differences. Women voters, advocates argued, would also promote the welfare of society rather than partisan or selfish gains. Allowing women to vote would create a great engine for progressive social change. One activist explicitly linked women's suffrage with the social gospel, declaring that women embraced Christ more readily than men and if they were elected to public office, they would "far more effectively guard the morals of society and the sanitary conditions of cities."

Yet the women's suffrage movement was not immune from the prevailing social, ethnic, and racial prejudices of the day. Carrie Chapman Catt echoed the fears of many middle- and upper-class urban dwellers when she warned of the danger that "lies in the votes possessed by the males in the slums of the cities, and the ignorant foreign [immigrant] vote." She added that the nation, with "ill-advised haste" had enfranchised "the foreigner, the Negro and the Indian" but still balked at women voting. In the South, suffragists catered to generations of deeply embedded racism. One of them declared in 1903 that giving white women the vote "would insure immediate and durable white supremacy."

Whatever the motives, President Wilson finally endorsed the "Susan B. Anthony amendment" in speeches to the House and Senate in 1918. In a speech on September 18, he said, "We have made partners of the women in this war. Shall we admit them only to a partnership of suffering and sacrifice and toil and not to a partnership of right?" After six months of delay, debate, and failed votes, the Congress passed the Nineteenth Amendment in the spring of 1919 and sent it to the states for ratification. Tennessee's legislature was the last of thirty-six state assemblies to approve the amendment, and it did so in dramatic fashion. The initial vote was deadlocked 48–48. Then a twenty-four-year-old legislator named Harry Burn changed his vote to yes at the insistence of his mother. The Nineteenth Amendment was ratified on August 18, 1920. It was the climactic achievement of the Progressive Era.

Women thereafter entered politics in growing numbers, but they did not have the transformative effect that boosters had predicted. As it turned out, women tended to vote like men on most issues. One group, however, wanted something more. Alice Paul set a new goal: an equal rights amendment that would eliminate any remaining legal distinctions between the sexes, including the special legislation for the protection of working women that had been put on the books during the previous fifty or so years. Alice Paul saw the equal rights amendment introduced in Congress in 1923; forty-nine years later she would see her amendment adopted. After her death, however, it would fall short of ratification.

Although the sharp increase in the number of women in the workforce during World War I proved short-lived, in the longer view a steady increase in the number of employed women occurred in the 1920s and 1930s. Still, women remained concentrated in traditional occupations, finding employment primarily as domestics, office workers, teachers, clerks, salespeople, dressmakers, milliners, and seamstresses. On the eve of World War II, women's work was little more diversified than it had been at the beginning of the century, but by 1940 it would be on the brink of a major transformation.

THE "NEW NEGRO" The discrimination experienced by both African Americans and women displayed many parallels, and their struggles for equality have frequently coincided. The most significant development in African American life during the early twentieth century was the Great Migration northward from the South. A massive movement of blacks from the South to the North began in 1915–1916, when rapidly expanding war industries were experiencing a labor shortage, leaving openings in the

North that were filled by African Americans. Altogether between 1910 and 1920 the Southeast lost some 323,000 blacks, or 5 percent of the 1920 native black population, and by 1930 it had lost another 615,000, or 8 percent of the 1920 African American population. The migration led to a slow but steady growth in black political influence in northern cities. African Americans were freer to speak and act in a northern setting, and they gained political leverage by settling in large cities in states with many electoral votes.

Along with political activity came a bristling spirit of protest, a spirit that received cultural expression in a literary and artistic movement labeled the Harlem Renaissance. Claude McKay, a Jamaican immigrant, was the first significant writer of the movement, which sought to rediscover black folk culture. Poems collected in McKay's *Harlem Shadows* (1922) expressed defiance in such titles as "If We Must Die" and "To the White Fiends." Other emergent black writers included Langston Hughes, Zora Neale Hurston, Countee Cullen, Alain Locke, Jean Toomer, and James Weldon Johnson.

The spirit of the "new Negro" also found an outlet in what came to be called Negro nationalism, which exalted blackness, black cultural expression, and at its most extreme, black exclusiveness. The leading spokesman for such views was the flamboyant Marcus Garvey. Racial bias, Garvey said, was so ingrained in whites that it was futile to appeal to their sense of justice. He advised blacks to liberate themselves from the surrounding white culture. "We have outgrown slavery," he declared, "but our minds are still enslaved to the thinking of the Master Race."

Garvey endorsed the "social and political separation of all peoples to the extent that they promote their own ideals and civilization." Such a separatist message appalled other African American leaders. W. E. B. Du Bois, for example, labeled Garvey "the most dangerous enemy of the Negro race. . . . He is either a lunatic or a traitor." Garvey and his aides created

Marcus Garvey

Garvey was the founder of the Universal Negro Improvement Association and a leading spokesman for "Negro nationalism" in the 1920s.

their own black version of Christianity, organized their own fraternal lodges and community cultural centers, started their own businesses, and published their own newspaper. Garvey's message of racial pride and self-reliance appealed to many blacks who had arrived in the northern cities during the Great Migration and had grown embittered with the hypocrisy of American democracy during the postwar economic slump. Garvey declared that the only lasting hope for blacks was for them to flee America and build their own republic in Africa.

In 1916, Garvey brought to New York City the Universal Negro Improvement Association, which he had started in his native Jamaica two years before. He quickly enlisted 500,000 members, and claimed as many as 6 million by 1923. At the peak of his popularity, however, Garvey was convicted of mail fraud. He was imprisoned from 1925 until 1927, when he was pardoned and deported to Jamaica by President Calvin Coolidge. Garvey died in obscurity in London in 1940, but the memory of his movement kept alive an undercurrent of racial pride that would reemerge later under the slogan of black power.

Even more influential in promoting black rights was the National Association for the Advancement of Colored People (NAACP). Founded in 1910, it was led by northern white liberals and black leaders such as Du Bois. Its main strategy was getting the federal government to enforce the Fourteenth and Fifteenth Amendments. In 1919 the NAACP launched a campaign against lynching, still a common atrocity in many parts of the country and most of whose victims were black. An anti-lynching bill making mob murder a federal offense passed the House in 1922 but lost to a filibuster by southern senators. Nonetheless, the bill stayed before the House until 1925, and continuing agitation on the issue helped to reduce lynchings, which declined to a third of what they had been the previous decade. But one lynching was too many for a so-called progressive society.

THE CULTURE OF MODERNISM

After 1920 changes in the realms of science and social thought were perhaps even more dramatic than those affecting women and African Americans. As the twentieth century advanced, the faith in progress and reform expressed by progressives fell victim to a series of frustrations and disasters, including the Great War, the failure of the League of Nations to win approval in the United States, Woodrow Wilson's physical and political collapse, and the failure of Prohibition. On a grander scale, startling new findings in physics further shook prevailing assumptions.

SCIENCE AND SOCIAL THOUGHT   Physicists of the early twentieth century altered the image of the cosmos in bewildering ways. Since Isaac Newton's research in the late seventeenth century, conventional wisdom had held that the universe was governed by laws that the scientific method could ultimately uncover. A world of such certain order and rationality had bolstered hopes of infinite progress in human knowledge.

This rational world of order and certainty disintegrated at the beginning of the new century when Albert Einstein, a young German physicist, announced his theory of relativity, which maintained that space, time, and mass were not absolutes but instead were relative to the location and motion of the observer. Newton's eighteenth-century mechanics, according to Einstein's relativity theory, worked well enough at relatively slow speeds, but the more nearly one approached the velocity of light (about 186,000 miles per second), the more all measuring devices would change accordingly, so that yardsticks would become shorter, clocks and heartbeats would slow down, even the aging process would ebb.

Relativity was not the only disconcerting concept that Einstein discovered. The farther one reached out into the universe and the farther one reached down into the minute world of the atom, the more certainty dissolved. The discovery of radioactivity in the 1890s showed that atoms were not irreducible units of matter and that some of them emitted particles of energy. This meant, Einstein noted, that mass and energy were not separate phenomena but interchangeable. By 1921, when Einstein was awarded the Nobel Prize, his abstract concept of relativity had become internationally recognized—and popularized. Hundreds of books about relativity had been published. His theories also had consequences that Einstein had not foreseen. Younger physicists built upon them to further transform notions of reality and the universe.

The pace of theoretical physics quickened as the twentieth century unfolded. The German physicist Max Planck discovered that electromagnetic emissions of energy, whether as electricity or light, came in little bundles that he called quanta. The development of quantum theory suggested that atoms were far more complex than once believed. In 1927 the pioneering German physicist Werner Heisenberg announced that the activities within an atom were ultimately indescribable. One could never know both the position and the velocity of an electron, Heisenberg concluded, because the very process of observation would affect the behavior of the particle, altering its position or its velocity.

Heisenberg's simple, yet startling "uncertainty principle" meant that human knowledge had limits. Just as Enlightenment thinkers had drawn on Isaac Newton's principles of gravitation two centuries before to formulate their views on the laws governing society, the ideas of relativity and uncertainty in the twentieth century persuaded some people to deny the relevance of absolute values in any sphere of society, thus undermining the concepts of personal responsibility and absolute standards. Anthropologists aided the process by transforming the word *culture,* which had before meant "refinement," into a term for the whole system of ideas, folkways, and institutions within which any group lives. Even the most primitive societies had a culture, and all things being relative, one culture should not impose its value judgments upon another. Two anthropologists, Ruth Benedict and Margaret Mead, were especially effective in spreading this viewpoint.

MODERNIST ART AND LITERATURE   The cluster of scientific ideas associated with Charles Darwin, Sigmund Freud, and Albert Einstein helped inspire a modernist revolution in the minds of many intellectuals and creative artists during the early twentieth century. The modernist world was one in which, as Karl Marx said, "all that is solid melts into air." Modernism arose out of a widespread recognition that Western civilization was entering an era of bewildering change. New technologies, new modes of transportation and communication, and new scientific discoveries combined to transform the nature of everyday life and to generate dramatic new forms of artistic expression and architectural design.

Whereas nineteenth-century writers and artists took for granted an accessible world that could be readily observed and accurately represented, self-willed modernists viewed reality as something to be created rather than copied, expressed rather than reproduced. As a consequence, they concluded that the subconscious regions of the psyche were more interesting and more potent than reason, common sense, and logic.

In the various arts such concerns spawned abstract painting, atonal music, free verse, stream-of-consciousness narrative, and interior monologues in stories and novels. Writers showed an intense concern with new forms of expression in an effort to violate expectations and shock their audiences.

The chief American prophets of modernism were living in Europe: Ezra Pound and T. S. Eliot in London and Gertrude Stein in Paris. All were deeply concerned with creating new and often difficult styles of modernist expression. Pound, as foreign editor of *Poetry,* served as the conduit through which many American poets achieved publication in the leading journals and magazines promoting experimentalism. At the same time he became the leader of the imagist movement, a revolt against the ornamental verbosity of Victorian poetry in favor of the concrete image.

Ezra Pound's brilliant protégé was the St. Louis–born Harvard graduate T. S. Eliot, who in 1915 contributed to *Poetry* his first major poem, "The Love Song of J. Alfred Prufrock," the musings of an ineffectual man who "after tea and cakes and ices" could never find "the strength to force the moment to its crisis." Eliot went to Oxford in 1913 and soon decided to make England his home and poetry his career. He rejected the nineteenth century's "cheerfulness, optimism, and hopefulness," as well as the traditional notion of poetry as the literal representation of a beautiful world. The modern poet, he insisted, must "be able to see beneath both beauty and ugliness; to see the boredom, and the horror and the glory." Eliot's *The Waste Land* (1922) made few concessions to readers in its obscure allusions, its juxtaposition of unexpected metaphors, its deep sense of postwar disillusionment and melancholy, and its suggestion of a burned-out civilization. The poem became for an alienated younger generation almost the touchstone of the modern temper.

Gertrude Stein, another voluntary exile, settled in Paris in 1903 and became an early champion of experimentalism and a collector of modern art. Long regarded as no more than the literary eccentric who wrote, "Rose is a rose is a rose is a rose," she would later be recognized as one of the chief promoters of the modernist prose style. At the time she was known chiefly through her influence on such literary expatriates of the 1920s as Sherwood Anderson and Ernest Hemingway, whom she told, "All of you young people who served in the war, you are the lost generation."

The earliest chronicler of that "lost" generation, F. Scott Fitzgerald, blazed up brilliantly and then quickly flickered out like the tinseled, carefree, sad young characters in his novels. Successful and famous at age twenty-four, having published *This Side of Paradise* in 1920, he, along with his wife, Zelda, experienced and depicted the "greatest, gaudiest spree in history." What gave depth to the best of Fitzgerald's work was what a character in *The Great Gatsby* (1925), his finest novel, called "a sense of the fundamental decencies" amid all the surface gaiety—and almost always a sense of impending doom.

Ernest Hemingway suffered even more from a psychic wound inflicted by an uncaring world. For him literature was a means of defense, a way to strike back, and in the process find a meaning for himself rather than accept one imposed by society. Hemingway's novels *The Sun Also Rises* (1926) and *A Farewell to Arms* (1929) depict a desperate search for "real" life and the doomed, war-tainted love affairs of Americans of the "lost" generation. Hundreds of writers tried to imitate Hemingway's terse style, but few had his gift, which lay less in what he had to say than in the way he said it.

THE SOUTHERN RENAISSANCE   As modernist literature arose in response to the changes taking place in the United States and Europe, so southern literature of the 1920s reflected a regional world in the midst of rebirth. A southern renaissance in writing emerged from the conflict between the dying world of tradition and the modern commercial world struggling to come to life in the aftermath of the Great War. While in the South the conflict of values aroused the Ku Klux Klan and fundamentalist furies that tried desperately to bring back the world of tradition, it also inspired the creativity of the South's young writers.

Two of the most notable of the new southern writers were Thomas Wolfe and William Faulkner. Fame rushed in first on Wolfe and his native Asheville, North Carolina, which he wrote about in his first novel, *Look Homeward, Angel.* "Against the Victorian morality and the Bourbon aristocracy of the South," Wolfe had "turned in all his fury," wrote newspaper editor Jonathan Daniels, a former classmate. Despite his lust for experience and knowledge, his demonic drive to escape the encircling hills for the "fabled" world outside, and his agonized search for some "lost lane-end into heaven," Wolfe never completely severed his roots in the South.

William Faulkner's achievement, more than Wolfe's, was rooted in the coarsely textured social world that produced him. Born near Oxford, Mississippi, he grew up there and transmuted his hometown into the fictional Jefferson, in Yoknapatawpha County. In writing *Sartoris* (1929), he began to discover that his "own little postage stamp of native soil was worth writing about" and that he "would never live long enough to exhaust it." With *Sartoris* and the creation of his mythical land of Yoknapatawpha, Faulkner kindled a blaze of creative energy. Next, as he put it, he wrote his gut into *The Sound and the Fury* (1929). It was one of the triumphs of the modernist style, but most early readers, taking their cue from the title instead of the critics, believed that its complex prose and themes signified nothing.

Modernism and the southern literary renaissance, both of which emerged from the crucible of the Great War and its aftermath, were products of the

1920s. But the widespread alienation felt by the writers and artists of the 1920s did not survive the decade. The onset of the Great Depression in 1929 sparked a renewed sense of commitment and affirmation in the arts, as if people could no longer afford the art-for-art's-sake emphasis of the 1920s. Alienation would give way to social engagement in the decade to come.

CHAPTER SUMMARY

- **Nativism** With the end of the Great War, race riots and the fear of communism ushered in a wave of virulent nativism. With many "old stock" Americans fearing that many immigrants were socialists, Communists, or anarchists, Congress passed laws to restrict immigration. The revived Ku Klux Klan was devoted to "100 percent Americanism" and regarded Catholics, Jews, immigrants, and African Americans as threats to America.

- **Jazz Age** The fads and attitudes of the 1920s, perhaps best represented by the frantic rhythms of jazz music and the fast-paced, sexy movies from Hollywood, led F. Scott Fitzgerald to dub the decade the Jazz Age. The hemlines of women's dresses rose, and sex was openly discussed. The Harlem Renaissance gave voice to black literature and music, and African Americans in northern cities felt freer to speak out against racial injustice and express pride in their race.

- **Reactionary Mood** Many white Americans felt that their religion and way of life were under attack by modern trends. They feared that women's newly earned right to vote might destabilize the family and that scientific scholarship would undermine biblical truth. These modern and traditional forces openly clashed at the Scopes trial in Dayton, Tennessee, in 1925, where the right to teach evolution in public schools was tested in court.

- **Modernism** The carnage of the Great War shattered Americans' belief in the progress of Western civilization. In the movement known as modernism, young artists and intellectuals reflected this disillusionment. For modernists, no longer could the world be easily observed through reason, common sense, and logic; instead, reality was something to be created and expressed through new artistic and literary forms, like abstract painting, atonal music, free verse in poetry, and stream-of-conscious narrative and interior monologues in stories and novels.

CHRONOLOGY

1910	National Association for the Advancement of Colored People is founded
1916	Marcus Garvey brings to New York the Universal Negro Improvement Association
1920	Prohibition begins
1920	Nineteenth Amendment, guaranteeing women's suffrage, is ratified
1920	F. Scott Fitzgerald's *This Side of Paradise* is published
1921	Albert Einstein receives the Nobel Prize in physics
1921	Congress passes the Emergency Immigration Act
1922	T. S. Eliot's *The Waste Land* is published
1923	Alice Paul's equal rights amendment is introduced in Congress
1924	Congress passes the Immigration Act
1925	Scopes "monkey trial" tests the teaching of evolution in Tennessee public schools

KEY TERMS & NAMES

27
REPUBLICAN
RESURGENCE
AND DECLINE

FOCUS QUESTIONS   wwnorton.com/studyspace

- To what extent were the policies of the 1920s a rejection of progressivism?
- Why were the 1920s an era of conservatism?
- What drove the growth of the American economy in the 1920s?
- What were the causes of the stock market crash and the Great Depression?

The progressive political coalition that elected Theodore Roosevelt in 1904 and reelected Woodrow Wilson in 1916 had fragmented by 1920. It began to show signs of fissure during the war, when radicals and other reformers were disaffected by America's involvement. After the war, in 1919, Roosevelt died at age sixty, just as he was beginning a campaign for the 1920 Republican presidential nomination. On the Democratic side, Wilson's support continued to erode as his health problems incapacitated him. Beyond Washington, organized labor resented the administration's unsympathetic attitude toward the strikes of 1919–1920, and western farmers complained that wartime price controls on commodities had discriminated against them. While prominent intellectuals grew disillusioned with the popular support for Prohibition, the Ku Klux Klan, and religious fundamentalism, many among the middle class lost interest in political activism. They instead channeled their energies into building a new business civilization based upon mass production and mass consumption, greater leisure, and the introduction of labor-saving electrical appliances in the home. Moreover, progressivism's final triumphs at the national level crystallized before the war's end: the Eighteenth Amendment, which outlawed alcoholic beverages, was ratified in 1919, and the Nineteenth Amendment, which extended women's suffrage to the entire country, became law a year later.

Progressivism did not completely disappear in the 1920s, however. Although smaller in number, reformers remained active in Congress during much of the decade even while the White House was in conservative Republican hands. The progressive impulse for "good government" and extended public services remained strong, especially at the state and local levels, where movements for better roads, education, public health, and social welfare gained momentum during the decade. At the same time, however, the reactionary temper of the times gave rise to the grassroots drive for moral righteousness and conformity animating the Ku Klux Klan and the fundamentalist and prohibitionist movements.

"NORMALCY"

THE ELECTION OF 1920   After World War I most Americans grew weary of Wilson's crusading idealism and suspicious of leaders promoting reform. Wilson himself recognized the shifting public mood. "It is only once in a generation," he remarked, "that a people can be lifted above material things. That is why conservative government is in the saddle two-thirds of the time."

At the Republican Convention in 1920, the three strongest presidential contenders canceled each other out in the balloting. The party leaders then turned to a stunning mediocrity, the affable Ohio senator Warren G. Harding, who set the tone of his campaign when he told a Boston audience; "America's present need is not heroics, but healing; not nostrums, but normalcy; not revolution, but restoration; not agitation, but adjustment; not surgery, but serenity; not the dramatic, but the dispassionate; not experiment, but equipoise; not submergence in internationality, but sustainment in triumphant nationality." Harding caught the mood of the times—a longing for "normalcy" and contentment with the status quo.

Harding's promise of a "return to normalcy" reflected his own conservative values and folksy personality. The son of an Ohio farmer, he described himself not as an intellectual or a crusader but "just a plain fellow" who was "old-fashioned and even reactionary in matters of faith and morals." Such a description, however, suggests a certain puritan regimen that Harding never practiced. Far from being an old-fashioned moralist in his personal life, he drank bootleg liquor in the midst of Prohibition, smoked and chewed tobacco, relished weekly poker games, and had numerous liaisons and several children with women other than his austere wife, whom he called "the Duchess." The general public, however, remained unaware of Harding's escapades. Instead, voters saw him as a handsome, charming, gregarious, and lovable politician. A man of self-confessed limitations in vision, leadership, and intellectual power, he once admitted that "I cannot hope to be one of the great presidents, but perhaps I may be remembered as one of the best loved." He got his wish.

The Democrats in 1920 hoped that Harding would not be president at all. James Cox, a former newsman and former governor of Ohio, won the presidential nomination of a fragmented Democratic party on the forty-fourth ballot. For vice president the convention named New Yorker Franklin D. Roosevelt, who as assistant secretary of the navy occupied the same position his Republican cousin Theodore Roosevelt had once held.

The Democrats suffered from the breakup of the Wilsonian coalition and the conservative postwar mood. In the words of the progressive journalist William Allen White, Americans in 1920 were "tired of issues, sick at heart of ideals, and weary of being noble." The country voted overwhelmingly for Harding's promised "return to normalcy." Harding polled 16 million votes to 9 million for Cox, who carried no state outside the Democratic Solid South.

EARLY APPOINTMENTS AND POLICY Harding in office had much in common with Ulysses Grant. His cabinet, like Grant's, mixed some of the best men in the party with some of the worst. Charles Evans Hughes became a distinguished secretary of state. Herbert Hoover in the Commerce Department, Andrew W. Mellon in the Treasury Department, and Henry C. Wallace in the Agriculture Department were also efficient, forceful figures. Of the others, Secretary of the Interior Albert B. Fall landed in prison and Attorney General Harry M. Daugherty only narrowly escaped prosecution. Many lesser offices went to members of the soon notorious "Ohio gang," a group of Harding's Ohio friends, headed

MR. MELLON GETS THE PAN
—Fitzpatrick in the St. Louis *Post-Dispatch*

Andrew Mellon

Mellon was accused of allowing his Aluminium Company of America to become a monopoly.

by Daugherty, with whom the president met regularly for poker games lubricated with illegal liquor.

Harding and his friends set about dismantling or neutralizing as many components of progressivism as they could. Harding's four appointments to the Supreme Court were all conservatives, including Chief Justice William Howard Taft, who announced that he had been "appointed to reverse a few decisions." During the 1920s the Taft court struck down a federal child-labor law and a minimum-wage law for women, issued numerous injunctions against striking unions, and made rulings limiting the powers of federal regulatory agencies.

The Harding administration established a pro-business tone reminiscent of the McKinley White House of the 1890s. To sustain economic growth, Secretary of the Treasury Mellon promoted government spending cuts and federal tax reductions. As Ronald Reagan would argue sixty years later, Mellon insisted that tax cuts should go mainly to the rich, on the assumption that wealth in the hands of the few would spur economic growth through increased capital investment.

At Mellon's behest, Congress first repealed the wartime excess-profits tax and lowered the maximum rate on personal income from 65 percent to 50 percent. Subsequent revenue acts eventually lowered the maximum tax rate to 20 percent. The Revenue Act of 1926 extended further benefits to high-income individuals by lowering estate taxes and repealing the gift tax. Much of the tax money released to the wealthy by these acts seems to have fueled the speculative excess of the late 1920s as much as it boosted consumer spending and entrepreneurial activity. Mellon, however, did balance the federal budget for a time. Government expenditures fell, as did the national debt.

In addition to tax cuts, Mellon favored the time-honored Republican policy of high tariffs on imported goods. So, too, did spokesmen for several emerging industries. Wartime innovations in chemical and metal processing revived the argument for protection of infant American industries from foreign competition. The Fordney-McCumber Tariff of 1922 dramatically increased rates on chemical and metal products as a safeguard against the revival of German industries that had previously commanded the field. To please the farmers, the new act further extended the duties on imported farm products.

Higher tariffs had unexpected consequences, however. During the war the United States had been transformed from a debtor nation to a creditor nation. Foreign capital had long flowed into the United States, playing an important role in fueling economic expansion. But the private and public

credits given the Allies to purchase American supplies during the war had reversed the pattern. Mellon now insisted that the European powers repay all
that they had borrowed during the war, but the American tariff walls erected
against imports made it all the harder for other nations to sell their products
in the United States and thereby acquire dollars with which to repay their
war debts. For nearly a decade further extensions of U.S. loans and investments sent more dollars abroad, postponing the settling of accounts.

Rounding out the Republican economic program was a more lenient attitude toward government regulation of corporations. Neither Harding nor
his successor, Calvin Coolidge, could dissolve the regulatory agencies created
by progressivism, but they named commissioners who promoted "friendly"
government regulation. Harding appointed conservatives to the Interstate
Commerce Commission, the Federal Reserve Board, and the Federal Trade
Commission. One senator characterized the new appointments as "the nullification of federal law by a process of boring from within." Republican senator Henry Cabot Lodge agreed, noting, "We have torn up Wilsonism by the
roots."

ADMINISTRATIVE CORRUPTION   Republican conservatives such
as Lodge, Mellon, Coolidge, and Hoover were operating out of a sincere
philosophical conviction intended to benefit the nation. By contrast, the
crass members of Harding's Ohio gang used their White House connections
to line their own pockets. In 1923, Harding learned that the head of the
Veterans Bureau was systematically looting the government's medical and
hospital supplies. The corrupt administrator resigned and fled to Europe,
and Harding's general counsel committed suicide.

Not long afterward a close crony of Attorney General Harry Daugherty's
also shot himself. The man held no federal appointment, but he had set up
an office in the Justice Department from which he peddled influence for a fee.
Daugherty himself was implicated in the fraudulent handling of German
assets seized after the war. When investigated, he refused to testify on the
grounds that he might incriminate himself. Twice brought to court, he was
never indicted; possibly the lack of evidence was a result of his destruction
of pertinent records. These were but the most visible of the many scandals
that touched the Justice Department, the Prohibition Bureau, and other federal agencies under Harding.

But one major scandal rose above all others. Teapot Dome, like the Watergate break-in fifty years later, became the catchword for an era of government
corruption. A government-owned oil deposit on federal land in Wyoming,

Teapot Dome had been set aside to be administered by the Interior Department under Albert Fall. Fall let private companies exploit the oil deposits, arguing that such contracts were in the government's interest. Yet he acted in secret, without allowing competitive bids.

Suspicion grew when Fall's personal standard of living suddenly skyrocketed. It turned out that he had taken "loans" of about $400,000 (which came in "a little black bag") from oil executives. For the rest of his life, Fall insisted that the loans were unrelated to the oil leases and that he had contrived a good deal for the government, but at best the questionable circumstances revealed his fatal blindness to propriety.

Harding himself avoided public disgrace. How much he knew of the scandals swirling around him remains unclear, but he knew enough to give the appearance of being troubled. "My God, this is a hell of a job!" he confided to a journalist. "I have no trouble with my enemies, I can take care of my enemies all right. But my damn friends, my God-damn friends. . . . They're the ones that keep me walking the floor nights!" In 1923, Harding left on what

"Juggernaut" of corruption

This 1924 cartoon alludes to the dimensions of the Teapot Dome scandal.

would be his last journey, a speaking tour to the West Coast and a trip to the Alaska Territory. In Seattle he suffered an attack of food poisoning, recovered briefly, then died in a San Francisco hotel.

Not since the death of Lincoln had there been such an outpouring of grief for a "beloved president," for the kindly, ordinary man who found it in his heart (as Wilson had not) to pardon Eugene Debs, the former Socialist candidate who had been jailed for opposing U.S. intervention in World War I. As Harding's funeral train moved toward Washington, D.C., then back to Ohio, millions stood by the tracks to honor their lost leader.

Eventually, however, grief yielded to scorn and contempt. For nearly a decade after Harding's death, scandalous revelations concerning his administrative officials were paraded before congressional committees and then the courts. Harding's extramarital affairs also came to light. As a result of the amorous detours and corrupt associates, Harding's foreshortened administration came to be viewed as one of the worst in history. More recently, however, scholars have credited Harding with leading the nation out of the turmoil of the postwar years and creating the foundation for the decade's remarkable economic boom. They also stress that he was a hardworking president who played a far more forceful role in shaping economic and foreign policies than was previously believed. Harding also promoted diversity and civil rights. He appointed Jews to key federal positions. No previous president had promoted women's rights as forcefully as Harding did. Still, even Harding's foremost scholarly defender admits that he lacked good judgment and "probably should never have been president."

"SILENT CAL" The news of Harding's death came when Vice President Calvin Coolidge was visiting his father in the mountain village of Plymouth, Vermont, his birthplace. There, at 2:47 A.M. on August 3, 1923, by the light of a kerosene lamp, Colonel John Coolidge administered the oath of office to his son. The rustic simplicity of Plymouth, the very name itself, evoked just the image of traditional values and solid integrity that the country would long for amid the wake of the Harding scandals.

Coolidge brought to the White House a clear conviction that the presidency should revert to its passive stance of the Gilded Age and defer to the leadership of Congress. Americans embraced the unflappability and unstained integrity of Silent Cal and his conservatism. Even more than Harding, Coolidge identified the nation's welfare with the success of big business. "The chief business of the American people is business," he intoned. "The man who works there worships there." Where Harding had sought to balance the interests of labor, agriculture, and industry, Coolidge focused on

Conservatives in the White House

Warren Harding (left) and Calvin Coolidge (right).

industrial development at the expense of the other two areas. He sought to unleash the free-enterprise system, and even more than Harding, he strove to end government regulation and reduce taxes.

THE ELECTION OF 1924 In filling out Harding's unexpired term, Calvin Coolidge distanced himself from the scandals and put two lawyers of undoubted integrity in charge of the prosecutions. A man of honesty and ability, a good administrator who delegated well and managed Republican factions adroitly, Coolidge quietly took control of the Republican party machinery and seized the initiative in the campaign for the 1924 nomination, which he won with only token opposition.

The Coolidge luck held as the Democrats again fell victim to internal dissension, prompting humorist Will Rogers's classic statement that "I am a member of no organized political party. I am a Democrat." The party's divisions reflected the deep rift between the new urban culture of the twenties and the more traditional hinterland, a gap that the party could not bridge. It took 103 ballots to bestow a tarnished nomination on John W. Davis, a prominent New York City lawyer from West Virginia who could nearly outdo Coolidge in conservatism.

While the Democrats bickered, a new farm-labor coalition was mobilizing a third-party effort. Meeting in Cleveland, Ohio, on July 4, 1924, farm and labor groups reorganized the Progressive party and nominated Wisconsin senator Robert M. La Follette for president. La Follette also won the support of the Socialist party and the American Federation of Labor.

In the campaign, Coolidge focused on La Follette, whom he called a dangerous radical who would turn America into a "communistic and socialistic state." The country preferred to "keep cool with Coolidge," who swept both the popular and the electoral votes by decisive majorities. Davis took only the solidly Democratic South, and La Follette carried only his native Wisconsin.

THE NEW ERA

Business executives interpreted the 1924 Republican victory as a vindication of their leadership, and Coolidge saw in the decade's surging prosperity a confirmation of his pro-business philosophy. In fact, the prosperity and technological achievements of the time had much to do with Coolidge's victory over the Democrats and Progressives. Many middle-class voters who had formed an important part of the Progressive coalition were now absorbed instead into the new corporate and consumer world created by advances in communications, transportation, and business organization. As more and more commentators stressed, the United States was entering a "new era" of advanced capitalism. The 1920s were years of extraordinary innovation and inventiveness.

THE CONSUMER CULTURE   The economy was changing markedly during the 1920s. Dramatic increases in efficiency meant that the marketplace was flooded with new consumer delights. Goods once available only to the wealthy were now accessible to the general public. Middle-class consumers could own cameras, wristwatches, cigarette lighters, vacuum cleaners, and washing machines. But the production of those enticing new goods would produce economic havoc if people did not abandon their traditional notions of frugality and go on a buying spree. Hence, business leaders, salespersons, and public relations experts began a concerted effort to eradicate what was left of the original Protestant ethic's emphasis on plain living.

The public had to be taught the joys of carefree consumerism, and the new industry of mass advertising obliged. By portraying impulse buying as a therapeutic measure to bolster self-esteem, advertisers shrewdly helped undermine notions of frugality. In his popular novel *Babbitt,* Sinclair Lewis

The rise of radio

The radio brought this farm family together and connected them to the outside world. By the end of the 1930s, millions would tune in to newscasts, soap operas, sports events, and church services.

recognized advertising's impact upon middle-class life: "These standard advertised wares—toothpastes, socks, tires, cameras, instantaneous hot water heaters—were the symbols and proofs of excellence."

Inventions in communications, such as motion pictures, radio, and telephones, were transforming social life and creating a more homogeneous national culture. In 1905 the first movie house opened, in Philadelphia, and within three years there were nearly 10,000 movie theaters nationwide. During the next decade, Hollywood, California, became the center of movie production, spinning out Westerns and the timeless comedies of Mack Sennett's Keystone Company, where slapstick comedians, most notably Charlie Chaplin, perfected their art, transforming it into a powerful form of social criticism. By the mid-1930s every large city and most small towns had movie theaters, and films replaced oratory as the chief mass entertainment, growing into a multimillion-dollar industry that catered to the working poor as well as to the affluent. In the mid-1920s motion pictures were attracting 50 million people weekly, or half the national population.

Radio broadcasting had an even more spectacular growth. The first radio commercial aired in 1922. By the end of that year, there were over 500 stations and some 3 million receivers in action. In 1927, Congress established a Federal Radio Commission to regulate the industry; in 1934 it became the Federal Communications Commission, with authority over other forms of communication as well. Calvin Coolidge was the first president to address the nation by radio, and he did so each month, paving the way for Franklin Roosevelt's popular and influential "fireside chats."

A nationwide mass culture replaced the local and regional economies of the nineteenth century. The leading advertising agency explained in 1926 that the advent of nationally circulated magazines, chain stores, syndicated news features, motion pictures, national brand names, and radio programs was creating "a nation which lives to [the same] pattern everywhere." Nonetheless, even though working-class folk could buy brand goods, phonographs, and radios, as well as movie tickets, the new consumer culture did not erase social distinctions. "Participating in mass culture," as one historian stressed, "made them feel no more mainstream or middle class, no less ethnic, religious, or working class than they already felt."

AIRPLANES, AUTOMOBILES, AND THE ECONOMY Advances in transportation were equally startling. Wilbur and Orville Wright, owners of a Dayton, Ohio, bicycle shop, built the first airplane, which they flew on a beach near Kitty Hawk, North Carolina, in 1903. The use of planes advanced slowly until the outbreak of war in Europe in 1914. An American aircraft industry developed during the war but foundered in the postwar demobilization. In 1925 the government began to subsidize the industry through airmail contracts, and the following year it started a program of federal aid to air transport and navigation, making available funds for the construction of airports.

Aviation received a psychological boost in 1927 when Charles A. Lindbergh Jr. flew the first transatlantic solo flight, traveling from New York to Paris in thirty-three and a half hours. The scope of the New York City parade honoring Lindbergh surpassed even the celebration of victory in World War I. The accomplishments of Lindbergh and other aviators helped catapult the aviation industry into prominence. By 1930 there were forty-three airline companies in operation in the United States.

Nonetheless, by far the most significant transportation development of the twentieth century was the automobile. The first motor car had been manufactured for sale in 1895, but the founding of the Ford Motor Company in 1903 revolutionized the industry. Ford's reliable Model T appeared in 1908 at a price of $850 (in 1924 it would sell for $290). Henry Ford aimed "to democratize the

Ford Motor Company's Highland Park plant, 1913

Gravity slides and chain conveyors contributed to the mass production of automobiles.

automobile. When I'm through everybody will be able to afford one, and about everyone will have one." He was right. In 1916 the number of cars manufactured passed 1 million; by 1920 more than 8 million were registered, and in 1929 there were more than 23 million. The production of automobiles stimulated the whole economy by consuming large amounts of steel, rubber, glass, and textiles. It gave rise to a gigantic market for oil products just as the Spindletop gusher in Texas heralded the opening of vast southwestern oil fields. The automotive revolution also quickened the movement for good roads, introduced efficient mass-production assembly-line techniques to other industries, speeded transportation and tourism, encouraged the sprawl of suburbs, and sparked real estate booms in California and Florida.

STABILIZING THE ECONOMY   During the 1920s the efficiency craze, which had been a prominent feature of the progressive impulse, powered the wheels of mass production and consumption and became a cardinal belief of Republican leaders. As Harding's and Coolidge's dynamic secretary of commerce, Herbert Hoover transformed the trifling Commerce Department into the most active agency of those two Republican administrations. During a period of government retrenchment, Hoover promoted expansion. He sought out new markets for business and sponsored more than 1,000 conferences on product design, production, and distribution. He also extended the wartime emphasis on standardization to include, for example, automobile tires and paving bricks, bedsprings and toilet paper.

Most of all, Hoover endorsed the burgeoning trade-association movement. The organization of business trade associations became his favorite instrument for "stabilization," to avoid the waste inherent in competition. Through such associations, executives in a given field shared information on sales, purchases, shipments, production, and prices. That information allowed them to plan with more confidence and thereby more accurately predict costs, set prices, and assess markets while maintaining a more stable workforce and paying steadier wages. Sometimes abuses crept in as the associations skirted the edge of legality by engaging in price-fixing and other monopolistic practices, but the Supreme Court in 1925 held the practice of sharing information as such to be within the law.

THE BUSINESS OF FARMING   During the Harding and Coolidge administrations, agriculture remained the weakest sector in the economy, in many ways as weak as it had been during the 1890s, when cities flourished and much of rural America languished. For a brief time after World War I, farmers' hopes soared on wings of prosperity. The wartime boom lasted into 1920, and then commodity prices collapsed as European farmers resumed high levels of production. Low prices persisted into 1923, especially in the wheat and corn belts. A bumper cotton crop in 1926 resulted in a price collapse and an early taste of depression in much of the South, where foreclosures and bankruptcies spread.

In some ways, farmers shared the business outlook of the so-called New Era. Many commercial farms, like many corporations, were getting larger, more efficient, and more mechanized. By 1930 about 13 percent of all farmers had tractors, and the proportion was even higher on the western plains. Better plows and other new machines were part of the mechanization process that accompanied improved crop yields, fertilizers, and methods of animal breeding.

Farm organizations of the 1920s moved from the attempted alliance with urban labor that had marked the Populist era toward a new view of farmers as profit-conscious business owners. During the postwar farm depression, farm groups formed regional commodity-marketing associations, which enabled them to negotiate ironclad contracts with producers for the delivery of their crops over a period of years. These associations also brought order to the marketing of farm products, requiring uniform standards and grades, efficient handling and advertising, and a business-like organization with professional technicians and executives.

But if concern with marketing co-ops and other business-like approaches drew farmers further from populist traditions, nagging problems still invited political solutions. The most effective political response to the collapse of farm prices in the early 1920s was the formation of the farm bloc, a congressional coalition of western Republicans and southern Democrats that put through a program of agricultural legislation from 1921 to 1923. During that period the farm bloc passed bills exempting farm cooperatives from anti-trust laws and creating new credit banks that could lend to cooperative producing and marketing associations.

In the spring of 1924, Senator Charles L. McNary of Oregon and Representative Gilbert N. Haugen of Iowa introduced a bill to secure "equality for agriculture in the benefits of the protective tariff." Their plan sought to dump American farm surpluses on the world market in order to raise commodity prices in the home market. The goal was to achieve "parity"—that is, to raise domestic farm prices to a point where farmers would have the same purchasing power relative to other commodity prices that they had enjoyed between 1909 and 1914, a time viewed in retrospect as a golden age of American agriculture. A McNary-Haugen bill finally passed both houses of Congress in 1927 and again a year later, only to be vetoed both times by President Coolidge, who criticized the measure as an unsound effort at price-fixing and un-American and unconstitutional to boot. Nonetheless, the bill catapulted the farm problem into the arena of national debate, defined it as a problem of crop surpluses, and revived the political alliance between the South and the West.

SETBACKS FOR UNIONS   Urban workers more than farmers shared in the affluence of the 1920s. "A workman is far better paid in America than anywhere else in the world," a French visitor wrote in 1927, "and his standard of living is enormously higher." Nonfarm workers gained about 20 percent in real wages between 1921 and 1928, while farm income rose only 10 percent. The benefits of this rise were distributed unevenly, however. Miners and textile workers suffered a decline in real wages. In these and other trades, technological unemployment followed the introduction of new production methods and more efficient machines, because technology eliminated some jobs at the same time that it created others.

Organized labor did no better than organized agriculture in the 1920s. Even though President Harding had supported the practice of collective bargaining and tried to reduce the twelve-hour workday and the six-day workweek so that laborers "may have time for leisure and family life," he ran into stiff opposition in Congress. Overall, unions suffered a setback after the growth years of the war as the Red Scare and the strikes of 1919 created concerns that unions practiced political subversion. The brief postwar depression of 1921 further weakened the unions, as did the popularity of open-shop

The Gastonia strike

These female textile workers pit their strength against that of a national guardsman during the strike at the Loray Mill in Gastonia, North Carolina, in 1929.

associations. While the open shop in theory implied only the employer's right to hire anyone, in practice it often meant discrimination against unionists and the refusal to recognize unions even in shops where most of the workers belonged to one. Prosperity, propaganda, welfare capitalism, and active hostility combined to cause union membership to drop from about 5 million in 1920 to 3.5 million in 1929.

PRESIDENT HOOVER, ENGINEER

HOOVER VERSUS SMITH   On August 2, 1927, while on vacation in the Black Hills of South Dakota, President Coolidge passed to reporters slips of paper with the curious statement "I do not choose to run for President in 1928." Exactly what he meant puzzled observers and has since perplexed historians. Apparently he at least half hoped to be drafted at the convention, but his statement cleared the way for Herbert Hoover to mount an active campaign for the Republican nomination. Well before the 1928 Republican Convention in Kansas City, Hoover was too far in the lead to be stopped. The party platform took credit for postwar prosperity, debt and tax reduction, and the high protective tariff that had been in operation since 1922 ("as vital to American agriculture as it is to manufacturing"). It rejected the McNary-Haugen program but promised to create a farm board to manage crop surpluses more efficiently.

The Democratic nomination went to Governor Alfred E. Smith of New York. The Democratic party had had its fill of factionalism in 1924, and all remained fairly harmonious until Smith revealed in his acceptance speech a desire to liberalize Prohibition. Hoover, by contrast, had pronounced the outlawing of alcoholic beverages "a great social and economic experiment, noble in motive and far-reaching in purpose," and he called for improved enforcement.

The two candidates projected sharply different images. Hoover was the Quaker son of middle America, the successful engineer and businessman from rural Iowa, the brilliant architect of Republican prosperity, a simple man who dressed plainly, spoke tersely, and followed his strong conscience. Smith was the prototype of those things that rural and small-town America distrusted: the son of Irish immigrants, Catholic, and a critic of Prohibition.

Campaign sheet music

The sheet music for the Democratic nominee, Alfred Smith (left) and the Republican nominee, Herbert Hoover (right) drew on popular tunes and motifs of the time.

Outside the large cities such qualities were handicaps that Smith could scarcely surmount, for all his affability and wit. Protestant fundamentalists launched a furious attack on him. The Klan mailed out thousands of post-cards proclaiming that the Catholic New Yorker was the Antichrist.

In the third consecutive Republican landslide, Hoover won 21 million popular votes to Smith's 15 million and an even more top-heavy electoral majority of 444 to 87. Hoover even cracked the Solid South, leaving Smith only six Deep South states plus Massachusetts and Rhode Island. The election was above all a vindication of Republican prosperity, but the shattering defeat of the Democrats concealed a major political realignment in the making. Smith had nearly doubled the vote for the Democratic candidate of four years before. Smith's image, though a handicap in the hinterlands, swung big northern cities back into the Democratic column. In the agricultural states of the West, there were signs that some disgruntled farmers had switched over to the Democrats. A coalition of urban workers and unhappy farmers was in the making, and the Great Depression of the 1930s would solidify it.

HOOVER IN CONTROL   The milestone year of 1929 dawned with high hopes. The economy seemed solid, income was rising, and the chief architect of Republican prosperity was about to enter the White House. "I have no fears for the future of our country," Hoover told his inauguration audience. "It is bright with hope."

Forgotten in the rush of later events would be Hoover's credentials as a progressive, humanitarian president. Over the objection of Treasury Secretary Mellon, he announced a plan for tax reductions in the low-income brackets. He shunned corrupt patronage practices, and he refused to countenance "Red hunts" or interference with peaceful picketing of the White House. He also defended his wife's right to invite prominent African Americans to the White House, and he sought more money for all-black Howard University.

Hoover showed greater sympathy than Coolidge for the struggling

Herbert Hoover

"I have no fears for the future of our country," Hoover told the nation at his inauguration in 1929.

agricultural sector. In 1929 he pushed through Congress the Agricultural Marketing Act, which established both a Federal Farm Board with a revolving loan fund of $500 million to help farm cooperatives market commodities and a program enabling the Farm Board to set up "stabilization corporations" empowered to buy surpluses. To open up glutted markets, he also proposed higher tariffs on imported farm products. After a fourteen-month struggle with competing interests, however, Hoover settled for a generally upward revision of tariffs on manufactures as well as farm goods. The Hawley-Smoot Tariff of 1930 carried duties to a new high. Average rates went from about 32 to 40 percent. More than 1,000 economists petitioned Hoover to veto the bill because, they predicted, it would raise prices paid by consumers, damage the export trade and thus hurt farmers, promote inefficiency, and provoke foreign reprisals. Events proved them right, but Hoover felt that he had to go along with his party in an election year. That proved to be a disastrous mistake, for it only exacerbated the growing economic depression.

THE ECONOMY OUT OF CONTROL   Depression? Most Americans during the 1920s had come to assume that there would never be another depression. Their misguided optimism proved to be an important factor in generating the economic free fall after 1929. After 1921 the idea that American business had entered a new era of *permanent* growth had taken hold. Such naive talk helped promote an array of get-rich-quick schemes.

Until 1927 stock values had risen with profits, but then they began to soar on wings of fanciful speculation. Treasury secretary Mellon's tax reductions had released money that, with the help of aggressive brokerage houses, found its way to Wall Street. One could now buy stock on margin—that is, make a small down payment (usually 10 percent) and borrow the rest from a broker, who held the stock as security against a down market. If the stock price fell and the buyer failed to provide more cash, the broker could sell the stock to cover his loan.

Gamblers in the market ignored warning signs. By 1927 residential construction and automobile sales were catching up to demand, business inventories had risen, and the rate of consumer spending had slowed. By mid-1929, production, employment, and other gauges of economic activity were declining. Still the stock market rose, driven by excessive confidence and perennial greed. By 1929 the stock market had become a fantasy world. Conservative financiers and brokers who counseled caution went unheeded. Hoover worried, too, and he sought to discourage speculation, but to no avail. On September 4 stock prices wavered, and the next day they dropped. The great bull market staggered on into October, trending downward but with enough good days to keep hope alive. On October 22 a leading bank president told reporters, "I know of nothing fundamentally wrong with the stock market or with the underlying business and credit structure."

THE CRASH AND ITS CAUSES The next day, stock values tumbled, and the day after that a wild scramble to unload stocks lasted until word arrived that leading bankers had formed a pool to buy stocks and halt the slide. For the rest of the week, stock prices steadied, but after a weekend to think the situation over, people began to sell their stocks. On Tuesday, October 29, the most devastating single day in the market's history to that point, the index dropped almost 13 percent. The plunge in prices fed on itself as brokers sold the shares they held for buyers who failed to come up with more cash. During October the value of stocks on the New York Stock Exchange fell by an average of 37 percent.

Business and government leaders initially expressed hope. According to President Hoover, "the fundamental business of the country" was sound. Some speculators who got out of the market went back in for bargains but found themselves caught in a slow erosion of values. By 1933 the value of stocks on the New York Stock Exchange was less than 20 percent of the value at the market's 1929 peak.

Caution was now the watchword for consumers and business leaders. Buyers held out for lower prices, orders fell off, wages fell or ceased altogether, and the decline in purchasing power brought further cutbacks in business activity. From 1929 to 1932, personal income declined by more than half. Unemployment continued to rise dramatically, from 1.6 million in 1929 to 12.8 million in 1933, from 3 percent to 25 percent of the labor force. Farmers, already in trouble, faced catastrophe as commodity prices were cut in half. More than 9,000 banks closed during this period, hundreds of factories and mines shut down, entire towns were abandoned, and thousands of farms were sold to pay debts. A cloud of gloom spread across the nation.

The stock market crash alone did not cause the Great Depression, but it did reveal major structural flaws in the economy and in government policies. Too many businesses during the 1920s had maintained prices and taken profits while holding down wages. As a result, about a third of the nation's personal income went to only 5 percent of the population. By plowing profits back into expansion rather than raising wages, business brought on a growing imbalance between rising productivity and declining purchasing power. As the demand for goods declined, the rate of investment in new plants and equipment also began to decline. For a time the softness of purchasing power was concealed by an increase in installment buying, and the deflationary effects of high tariffs were concealed by the volume of foreign loans and investments, which supported foreign demand for American goods. But the flow of American capital abroad began to dry up when the stock market became a more attractive investment. Swollen profits and dividends enticed the rich into market speculation. When trouble came, the bloated corporate structure collapsed.

Government policies also contributed to the debacle. The domineering secretary of the Treasury in the 1920s, Andrew Mellon, displayed a supreme confidence in market capitalism. He himself was one of the wealthiest men in the world. To him the appropriate role of government was to promote free enterprise by cutting taxes, reducing regulation, and balancing the budget. Mellon's tax reductions led to oversaving by the consuming public, which helped diminish the demand for consumer goods. The growing money supply fed the fever of speculation by lowering interest rates. Hostility toward unions discouraged collective bargaining and may have worsened the prevalent imbalances in income. High tariffs discouraged foreign trade. Lax enforcement of anti-trust laws encouraged concentration, monopolies, and high prices.

Another culprit was the gold standard. The world monetary system remained fragile throughout the 1920s. When economic output, prices, and savings began dropping in 1929, policy makers—certain that they had to keep their currencies tied to gold at all costs—either did nothing or tightened money supplies, thus exacerbating the downward spiral. The only way to restore economic stability within the constraints of the gold standard was to let prices and wages continue to fall. The best policy, Andrew Mellon advised, would be to "liquidate labor, liquidate stocks, liquidate the farmers, liquidate real estate," allowing the downturn to "purge the rottenness out of the system." Such passivity helped turn a recession into the world's worst depression.

THE HUMAN TOLL OF THE DEPRESSION The devastating collapse of the economy caused immense social hardships across the nation. By 1933, 13 million people were out of work, and many more found themselves working fewer hours. African Americans and Mexicans were usually the first laid off. Factories shut down, banks closed, and farms went bankrupt; millions of people found themselves not only jobless but also homeless and penniless. Hungry people lined up at soup kitchens; others rummaged through trash cans behind restaurants. Local welfare agencies were swamped with appeals for charity and quickly ran out of funds. Many of the destitute slept on park benches or in alleys. Others congregated in makeshift shelters in vacant lots. Thousands of desperate men in search of jobs rode the rails. These hobos, or tramps, as they were derisively called, sneaked onto empty railway cars and rode from town to town looking for work. During the winter homeless people wrapped themselves in newspapers to keep warm, sarcastically referring to their coverings as Hoover blankets. Some grew weary of their grim fate and ended their lives. Suicide rates soared during the 1930s. America had never before experienced social distress on such a scale.

HOOVER'S EFFORTS AT RECOVERY Although the policies of public officials helped bring on economic collapse, few political or economic leaders acknowledged the severity of the crisis: all that was needed, they thought, was a slight correction of the market. Those who held to the theory of limited government, such as Andrew Mellon, thought the economy would cure itself. Government should do nothing; the depression should be allowed to run its course until the economy had purged itself of its excesses. Hoover, however, was unwilling to sit by and let events take their course. In fact, he did more than any previous president had done in such dire economic circumstances. Still, his own philosophy, now hardened into dogma, set strict limits on action by the federal government, and he refused to set his philosophy aside even to meet the unprecedented emergency.

Hoover believed that the country's main need was confidence. In speech after speech, he exhorted the public to keep up hope. He asked business and labor leaders to keep the mills and shops open, maintain wage levels, and spread out the work to avoid layoffs—in short, to let the shock fall on corporate profits rather than on purchasing power. In return, union leaders, who had little choice, agreed to refrain from making wage demands and staging strikes.

While reassuring the public, however, Hoover also accelerated the start of government construction projects in order to provide jobs, but state and local cutbacks more than offset the new federal spending. At Hoover's demand, the Federal Reserve returned to an easier credit policy, and Congress passed a modest tax reduction to put more purchasing power into people's pockets. The high Hawley-Smoot Tariff, proposed at first to help farmers, brought reprisals abroad, devastating foreign trade.

As always, depression hurt the political party and president in power. Near the city dumps and along railroad tracks, the dispossessed huddled in shacks of tar paper and galvanized iron, in old packing boxes and abandoned cars. These squalid settlements were labeled Hoovervilles; a Hoover flag was an empty pocket turned inside out. Such scornful labels reflected the quick erosion of Hoover's political support. In 1930 the Democrats gained their first national victory since 1916, winning a majority in the House and enough gains in the Senate to control it in coalition with farm-state Republicans in the West.

CONGRESSIONAL INITIATIVES With a new Congress in session, demands for federal action impelled Hoover to stretch his philosophy of government to its limits. He was ready now to use government resources to at least shore up the financial institutions. In early 1932 the new Congress responded to pleas from the desperate banking sector by setting up the Reconstruction Finance Corporation (RFC) to provide emergency loans to banks, life-insurance companies, building-and-loan societies, farm-mortgage associations, and railroads. The RFC staved off some bankruptcies, but Hoover's critics charged that it favored business at the expense of workers. The RFC nonetheless remained a key federal agency throughout the decade and during World War II.

Further help to the financial structure came with the Glass-Steagall Act of 1932, which increased the availability of commercial loans. It also released about $750 million in gold formerly used to back Federal Reserve notes, countering the effect of foreign withdrawals and domestic hoarding of gold at the same time that it enlarged the supply of credit. For homeowners the Federal Home Loan Bank Act of 1932 created with Hoover's blessing a series of discount banks for home mortgages. They provided to savings-and-loan

Impact of the Depression

Two children set up shop in a Hooverville in Washington, D.C.

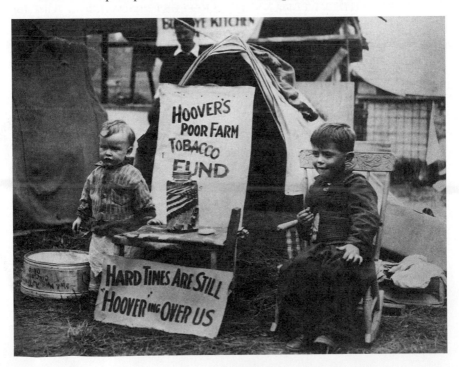

associations a service much like the one that the Federal Reserve System provided to commercial banks.

Hoover's critics argued that all these measures reflected a dubious "trickle-down" theory. If government could help banks and railroads, asked New York senator Robert F. Wagner, "is there any reason why we should not likewise extend a helping hand to that forlorn American, in every village and every city of the United States, who has been without wages since 1929?" The contraction of credit devastated such debtors as farmers and those who made purchases on the installment plan or held balloon mortgages, whose monthly payments increased over time.

By 1932, members of Congress were filling the hoppers with bills to provide federal relief directly to distressed people. At that point, Hoover might have pleaded "dire necessity," taken the leadership of the relief movement, and salvaged his political fortunes. Instead, he held back and only grudgingly edged toward federal humanitarian relief. On July 21, 1932, he signed the Emergency Relief Act, which avoided a federal dole (direct cash payments to individuals) but gave the RFC $300 million for relief loans to the states, authorized loans of up to $1.5 billion for state and local construction projects, and appropriated $322 million for federal construction.

FARMERS AND VETERANS IN PROTEST   Government relief for farmers had long since been abandoned. Faced with total loss, some farmers defied the law. Angry mobs stopped foreclosures and threatened to lynch bankers and judges. In Nebraska, farmers burned corn to keep warm; dairy farmers dumped milk into roadside ditches in an effort to raise prices. Like voluntary efforts to reduce the number of acres cultivated, these strikes generally failed, but they vividly dramatized the farmers' frustration and anger.

Fears of organized revolt arose when unemployed World War I veterans converged on Washington, D.C., in the spring of 1932. The "Bonus Expeditionary Force" grew quickly to more than 20,000. Their purpose was to get immediate payment of the cash bonus to 4 million war veterans that Congress had voted in 1924 in the form of life insurance payable in 1945 (earlier to heirs of deceased veterans). The House approved a bonus bill, but when the Senate voted it down, most of the veterans went home. The rest, along with their wives and children, having no place to go, camped in vacant government buildings and in a shantytown within sight of the Capitol. The chief of the Washington police gave the squatters a friendly welcome and won their trust, but a fearful White House fretted. Eager to disperse the destitute veterans, Hoover persuaded Congress to vote funds to buy their tickets home. More left, but others stayed even after Congress adjourned, hoping at least to meet with the embattled president.

Anger and frustration

Unemployed veterans, members of the Bonus Expeditionary Force, clash with Washington, D.C. police at Anacostia Flats in July 1932.

Late in July the administration ordered the shantytown razed. In the ensuing melee a policeman panicked, fired into the crowd, and killed two veterans. The secretary of war then dispatched about 700 soldiers under General Douglas MacArthur, who was aided by junior officers Dwight D. Eisenhower and George S. Patton. The soldiers easily drove out the unarmed veterans and their families and burned the shacks. General MacArthur self-righteously explained in his report that when dealing with "riotous elements," a show of "obvious strength gains a moral ascendancy." MacArthur hysterically claimed that the "mob," spurred by "the essence of revolution," was about to seize control of the government. To most Americans the Bonus Army was more pathetic than threatening. The spectacle of army troops using tanks to dislodge unarmed veterans did not help Hoover's eroding image.

The stress took its toll on Hoover's health and morale. "I am so tired," he sometimes sighed, "that every bone in my body aches." As the months passed, presidential news conferences grew more strained and less frequent. When friends urged Hoover to seize the reins of leadership, he replied, "I can't be a Theodore Roosevelt" or "I have no Wilsonian qualities." His gloom and growing sense of futility were apparent to the country. In a mood more despairing than rebellious, Americans waited impatiently to see what the next presidential campaign would bring.

End of Chapter Review

- **"Return to Normalcy"** Although progressivism lost its appeal after the Great War, the Eighteenth Amendment (paving the way for Prohibition) and the Nineteenth Amendment (guaranteeing women's suffrage) marked the culmination of that movement at the national level. Reformers still actively worked for good and efficient government at the local level, but overall the drive was for a "return to normalcy"—conformity and moral righteousness.

- **Era of Conservatism** Many Americans, particularly people in rural areas and members of the middle class, wanted a return to a quieter, more conservative way of life after World War I, and Warren Harding's landslide Republican victory allowed just that. The policies of Harding's pro-business cabinet were reminiscent of those of the McKinley White House more than two decades earlier. Union membership declined in the 1920s as workers' rights were rolled back by a conservative Supreme Court and in response to fears of Communist subversion. Workers, however, shared in the affluence of the 1920s, thereby contributing to the rise of a mass culture.

- **Growth of Economy** The budget was balanced through reductions in spending and taxes, while tariffs were raised to protect domestic industries, setting the tone for a prosperous decade. Harding's successor, Calvin Coolidge, actively promoted the interests of big business. The public responded enthusiastically to the mass marketing of new consumer goods such as radios and affordable automobiles. Agriculture, however, lagged after the wartime boom evaporated.

- **The Great Depression** The stock market crash revealed the structural flaws in the economy, but it did not cause the Great Depression. Government policies throughout the twenties—high tariffs, lax enforcement of anti-trust laws, an absence of checks on speculation, and adherence to the gold standard—contributed to the onset of the Depression. Hoover's attempts to remedy the problems were too few and too late. Banks failed, businesses closed, homes and jobs were lost.

CHRONOLOGY

1903	Wright Brothers fly the first airplane
1903	Ford Motor Company is founded
1922	First radio commercial is aired
1923	President Warren Harding dies in office
1927	Charles Lindbergh Jr. makes first solo transatlantic flight
1928	Herbert Hoover is elected president
October 29, 1929	Stock market crashes
1930	Congress passes Hawley-Smoot Tariff
1932	Congress sets up the Reconstruction Finance Corporation
1932	Congress passes the Glass-Steagall Act
1933	Bonus Expeditionary Force converges on Washington to demand payment of bonuses promised to war veterans

KEY TERMS & NAMES

"return to normalcy" p. 799

Warren Harding p. 799

Andrew Mellon p. 800

Ohio gang p. 800

Teapot Dome p. 802

"Silent Cal" p. 804

Model T Ford p. 808

Herbert Hoover p. 809

McNary-Haugen bills p. 811

Alfred E. Smith p. 813

Great Depression p. 814

buying (stock) on margin p. 815

Reconstruction Finance Corporation p. 819

Bonus Expeditionary Force p. 820

28

NEW DEAL AMERICA

FOCUS QUESTIONS

wwnorton.com/studyspace

- What were the immediate challenges facing Franklin Roosevelt in March 1933?
- What were the lasting social effects of the New Deal legislation?
- Why did the New Deal draw criticism from conservatives and liberals?
- How did the New Deal expand the federal government's authority?
- What were the major cultural changes of the 1930s?

U pon arriving in the White House in March 1933, Franklin Delano Roosevelt (FDR) inherited a nation mired in the third year of an unprecedented depression. No other business slump had been so deep, so long, so baffling, or so painful. One out of every four Americans was unemployed, and in many large cities nearly half the adults were out of work. Some 500,000 Americans had lost homes or farms because they could not make their mortgage payments. Thousands of banks had failed; millions of depositors had lost their life savings. The global depression had also helped accelerate the rise of fascism and communism. Totalitarianism was on the march in Europe and Asia—and democratic capitalism was on the defensive. President Roosevelt and a supportive Congress immediately adopted bold measures to relieve the human suffering, restore confidence, and promote economic recovery. Such initiatives provided the foundation for what came to be called welfare capitalism.

FROM HOOVERISM TO THE NEW DEAL

On June 14, 1932, while the ragtag Bonus Army was still encamped in Washington, D.C., Republicans gathered in Chicago to renominate Herbert Hoover. The delegates went through the motions in a mood of defeat. The Democrats, in contrast, converged on Chicago later in the month confident that they would nominate the next president. New York governor Franklin D. Roosevelt had already lined up most of the delegates, and he won the nomination on the fourth ballot.

In a dramatic gesture, Roosevelt appeared in person to accept the nomination instead of awaiting formal notification. He told the expectant delegates, "I pledge you, I pledge myself to a new deal for the American people." What the New Deal would be in practice Roosevelt had little idea as yet, but he was much more flexible and willing to experiment than Hoover. What was more, his upbeat personality communicated joy and hope, as did his campaign song, "Happy Days Are Here Again."

FRANKLIN ROOSEVELT   Born in 1882 into a wealthy family, educated by governesses and tutors at his father's Hudson River estate, Franklin Roosevelt led the cosmopolitan life of a young patrician. After attending an elite Massachusetts boarding school, he earned degrees from Harvard College and Columbia University Law School. While a law student, he married Anna Eleanor Roosevelt, a niece of President Theodore Roosevelt, his own distant cousin.

In 1910, Franklin Roosevelt won a Democratic seat in the New York State Senate. As a freshman legislator he displayed the contradictory qualities that would characterize his political career: he was an aristocrat who empathized with common folk, a traditionalist with a penchant for experimentation, an affable charmer with an infectious smile and upturned chin who harbored profound convictions, and a skilled political tactician with a shrewd sense of timing and a distinctive willingness to listen to and learn from others.

In 1912, Roosevelt had backed Woodrow Wilson, and for both of Wilson's terms he served as his assistant secretary of the navy. Then, in 1920, largely on the strength of his name, he gained the Democratic vice-presidential nomination. Political defeat was followed by personal crisis when in 1921, at the age of thirty-nine, Roosevelt contracted polio, which left him permanently crippled, unable to stand or walk without braces. But his prolonged struggle with this disability transformed the snobbish young aristocrat. A friend recalled that Roosevelt emerged from his struggle with polio "completely warm-hearted, with a new humility of spirit" that led him to identify with the poor and the suffering. For seven years, aided by his talented wife, Roosevelt strengthened his body, and in 1928 he ran for governor of New York and won. Reelected by a whopping majority of 700,000 in 1930, he became the Democratic front-runner for the presidency in 1932.

Behind the public facade of a cheery and self-confident politician, Roosevelt was at times a crass manipulator of people and power. Obsessed with gaining the highest office in the land, he was willing to sacrifice all else in his life—marriage, health, staff, friends—to that end. Roosevelt occasionally inflated his own accomplishments and took credit for those of others, but his own strengths and achievements were considerable. A born leader, he had a talent for surrounding himself with capable people and getting the most out of them. Most important, however, was his bulldog determination to succeed, to overcome all obstacles, to triumph over despair and adversity, and in the process to achieve greatness.

THE 1932 CAMPAIGN   Partly to dispel doubts about his health, Roosevelt set forth on a grueling campaign tour in 1932. He blamed the Depression on Hoover and the Republicans, and he began to define what he meant by the New Deal. Like Hoover, Roosevelt pledged to balance the budget, but he left open the loophole that he would incur short-term deficits to prevent starvation. He was evasive on the tariff, and on farm policy he offered several options pleasing to farmers but ambiguous enough not to alarm city dwellers. He came out unequivocally for strict regulation of electric companies, and he consistently stood by his party's pledge to repeal the Prohibition amendment. Perhaps most important, he recognized that a mature economy would require imaginative national planning: "The country needs, and, unless I mistake its temper, the country demands bold, persistent experimentation." What came across to voters, however, was less the content of his speeches than his irrepressible confidence.

The dour Hoover, by contrast, had no confidence. Democrats, he argued, ignored the international causes of the Depression. Roosevelt's reckless proposals, Hoover warned, "would destroy the very foundations of our American system." But few were listening. Frustrated by the persistent Depression, the country wanted a new course, a new leadership, a new deal.

Some voters took a dim view of both major candidates. Those who believed that only a radical departure would suffice supported the Socialist party candidate, Norman Thomas, who polled 882,000 votes, and a few went on to support the Communist party candidate, who won 103,000 votes. The wonder is that a desperate people did not turn in greater numbers to such radical alternatives. Instead, they swept Roosevelt into office by a whopping margin.

The "New Deal" Candidate

Governor Franklin D. Roosevelt, the Democratic nominee for president in 1932, campaigning in Topeka, Kansas. Roosevelt's confidence inspired voters.

THE INAUGURATION   For the last time the country waited four months, until March 4, for a new president and Congress to take office. The Twentieth Amendment, ratified on January 23, 1933, provided that the president would thereafter take office on January 20 and the newly elected Congress on January 3.

Amid spreading destitution and misery, unemployment continued to rise during the bleak winter of 1932–1933, and panic struck the banking system. As bank after bank collapsed, frantic people rushed to their own banks to remove their savings. The run on the banks exacerbated the crisis and paralyzed the economy. When the Hoover administration left office, four fifths of the nation's banks were closed, and the country was on the brink of economic paralysis.

The profound crisis of confidence that greeted Roosevelt when he took office on March 4, 1933, gave way to a mood of expectancy. The new president promised vigorous action. He asserted "that the only thing we have to fear is fear itself." He would not merely exhort, he promised: "This nation asks for action, and action now!" He called for "broad executive power to

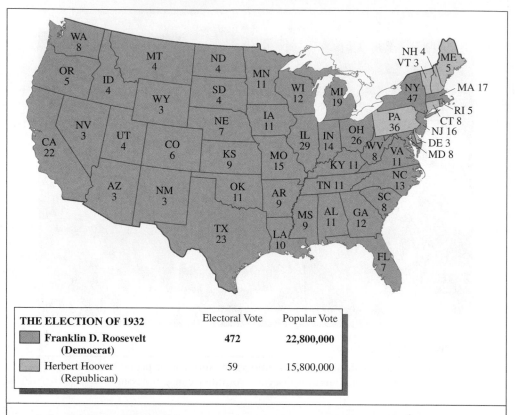

THE ELECTION OF 1932	Electoral Vote	Popular Vote
Franklin D. Roosevelt (Democrat)	472	22,800,000
Herbert Hoover (Republican)	59	15,800,000

Why did Roosevelt appeal to voters struggling during the Depression? What were Hoover's criticisms of Roosevelt's "New Deal"? What policies defined Roosevelt's New Deal during the presidential campaign?

wage a war" against the economic crisis. It was exactly what a distraught nation wanted to hear. One citizen wrote Roosevelt that the speech was "the finest thing this side of heaven. It seemed to give the people, as well as myself, a new hold on life."

COMPETING SOLUTIONS When Roosevelt and the New Dealers arrived in Washington, they were confronted by three major challenges: reviving the devastated economy, relieving the human misery brought on by the Great Depression, and alleviating the desperate plight of farmers and their families. Roosevelt's "brain trust" of advisers developed conflicting opinions about how best to turn the economy around. Some promoted vigorous enforcement of the anti-trust laws as a means of restoring business competition; others argued for the opposite, saying that anti-trust laws should be suspended so as to enable large corporations to collaborate with the federal government in "managing" the economy. Still others called for a massive expansion of welfare programs and a prolonged infusion of government spending to address the profound human crisis and revive the economy.

For his part, Roosevelt vacillated among these three schools of thought. In part his approach reflected the political reality that conservative southern Democrats controlled the Congress and the president could not risk alienating these powerful proponents of balanced budgets and limited government. Roosevelt's inconsistencies also reflected his own outlook. He was a pragmatist rather than an ideologue. As he once explained, "Take a method and try it. If it fails admit it frankly and try another." Roosevelt's New Deal would therefore take the form of a series of trial-and-error actions, several of which were misguided failures.

Roosevelt and his advisers initially settled on a three-pronged strategy. First, they sought to remedy the financial crisis and provide short-term emergency relief for the jobless. Second, they tried to promote industrial recovery by dramatically increasing federal spending and by facilitating cooperative agreements between management and organized labor. Third, they attempted to raise commodity prices (and thereby farm income) by paying farmers to reduce the size of their crops and herds. By reducing the overall supply of farm products, prices for grain and meat would eventually rise. None of these initiatives worked perfectly, but their combined effect was to restore hope and energy to a nation paralyzed by fear and uncertainty.

STRENGTHENING THE MONETARY SYSTEM   On his second day in office, Roosevelt followed through on his pledge to act decisively: he called a special session of Congress and declared a four-day bank holiday to halt hysteria and restore confidence in the financial system. It took the Democratic-controlled Congress only seven hours to pass the Emergency Banking Relief Act, which permitted sound banks to reopen and provided managers for those still in trouble. On March 12, 1933, in the first of his radio-broadcast "fireside chats," the president insisted that it was safer to "keep your money in a reopened bank than under the mattress." The following day, deposits in reopened banks exceeded withdrawals. Having ended the bank panic, Roosevelt slashed military pensions and government payrolls and then urged Congress to pass the Twenty-first Amendment, which ended Prohibition.

Those measures were but the beginning of an avalanche of executive and legislative action. Between March 9 and June 16, 1933, the so-called Hundred Days, Congress passed more than a dozen of Roosevelt's major proposals, a body of legislation whose scope was unprecedented in American history.

The galloping snail

A vigorous Roosevelt drives Congress to action in this *Detroit News* cartoon from March 1933.

With the banking crisis over, an acute debt problem continued to paralyze farmers and homeowners, along with a lingering distrust of the banks. By early 1933, banks were foreclosing on farm mortgages at the rate of 20,000 per month. By executive decree, Roosevelt reorganized all farm credit agencies into the Farm Credit Administration. Congress then authorized the extensive refinancing of farm mortgages at lower interest rates to stem the tide of foreclosures. The Home Owners' Loan Act provided a similar service to city dwellers through the Home Owners' Loan Corporation, which refinanced mortgage loans at lower monthly payments for strapped homeowners. The Banking Act further shored up confidence in the banking system, by creating the Federal Deposit Insurance Corporation to insure personal bank deposits up to $5,000. It also required commercial banks to separate themselves from investment-brokerage operations.

Roosevelt and Congress also tightened the regulation of Wall Street. The Federal Securities Act required that new stock and bond issues register with the Federal Trade Commission and, later, with the Securities and Exchange Commission, a new agency that regulated the chaotic stock and bond markets.

RELIEF MEASURES Another urgent priority in 1933 was relieving the widespread personal distress caused by the Depression. Hoover had steadfastly resisted using federal funds to provide direct assistance to the unemployed. Roosevelt had fewer qualms.

Congress took a first step toward relief with the creation of the Civilian Conservation Corps (CCC), which provided useful jobs to working-class men aged eighteen to twenty-five. Nearly 3 million CCC workers thereafter performed a variety of jobs in forests, parks, and recreational areas and on soil-conservation projects. They built roads, bridges, campgrounds, and fish hatcheries; planted trees; taught farmers how to control soil erosion; and fought fires. Directed by army officers and foresters, they worked under military discipline and were perhaps the most direct analogue of an army at war in the whole New Deal. Like the military at the time, CCC camps were racially segregated.

The Federal Emergency Relief Administration (FERA) addressed the broader problems of human distress. Designed as a shared undertaking of the federal government and state and city governments, it was in fact shaped and directed by the Roosevelt administration. Harry L. Hopkins, a tireless social worker from Iowa who had directed Roosevelt's relief program in New York State, headed the new effort and became the second most powerful figure in the administration. He pushed the FERA with a boundless energy, spending $5 million within two hours of taking office. FERA funds created jobs by financing state construction of over 5,000 public buildings and 7,000 bridges, organized adult literacy programs, financed college education for poor students, and set up day-care centers for low-income families. The FERA also helped local agencies dispense food and clothing to the needy.

The first large-scale experiment with *federal* work relief, which put people directly on the government payroll at competitive wages, came with the formation of the Civil Works Administration (CWA). Created in November 1933, when it had become apparent that the state-sponsored programs funded by the FERA were inadequate, the CWA provided federal jobs and wages to those unable to find work that winter. It was hastily conceived and implemented but during its four-month existence put to work over 4 million people. The agency organized a variety of useful projects: making highway repairs and laying sewer lines, constructing or improving more than 1,000 airports and 40,000 schools, and providing 50,000 teaching jobs that helped keep rural schools open. As the number of people employed by the CWA soared, the program's costs skyrocketed to over $1 billion. Roosevelt balked at the expenditures and worried that people would become dependent upon federal jobs. So in the spring of 1934, he ordered the CWA dissolved. By April some 1 million workers were again unemployed.

Roosevelt nevertheless continued to favor providing jobs over doling out cash to the unemployed. In 1935, therefore, he asked, for an array of new federal job programs, and Congress responded by passing a $4.8-billion bill providing work relief for the jobless. To manage these programs, Roosevelt created the Works Progress Administration (WPA), headed by Harry Hopkins. Hopkins was told to provide millions of jobs quickly, and as a result some of the new jobs appeared to be make-work or mere "leaning on shovels." But by the time the WPA died, during World War II, it had left permanent monuments on the landscape in the form of buildings, bridges, hard-surfaced roads, airports, and schools.

The WPA also employed a wide range of talented Americans in the Federal Theatre Project, the Federal Art Project, the Federal Music Project, and the Federal Writers' Project. Talented writers such as Ralph Ellison, John Cheever, and Saul Bellow found work writing travel guides to the United States, and Orson Welles directed Federal Theatre Project productions. Critics charged that these programs were frivolous, but Hopkins replied that writers and artists needed "to eat just like other people." The National Youth Administration (NYA), also under the WPA, provided part-time employment to students, set up technical training programs, and aided jobless youths. Twenty-seven-year-old Lyndon Johnson was director of an NYA program in Texas, and Richard Nixon, a penniless Duke University law student, found work through the NYA at 35¢ an hour. Although the WPA took care of only about 3 million out of some 10 million jobless at any one time, in all it helped some 9 million Americans weather desperate times before it expired in 1943.

RECOVERY THROUGH REGULATION

In addition to rescuing the banks and providing immediate relief for the unemployed, Roosevelt and his advisers promoted the recovery of the agricultural and industrial sectors. Roosevelt's brain trust of university-trained experts, lawyers, and professors initially believed that the trend toward economic concentration was inevitable: big businesses were not going to disappear. The brain trust also believed that the mistakes of the 1920s showed that the only way to operate an integrated economy at full capacity and in the public interest was through stringent federal regulation and organized central planning in cooperation with big business, not by breaking up huge corporations. The success of government-led economic planning during World War I reinforced such ideas. New recovery programs sprang from those beliefs.

AGRICULTURAL RECOVERY   The sharp decline in crop prices after 1929 meant that many farmers could not afford to plant or harvest their crops. The Agricultural Adjustment Act of 1933 created the Agricultural Adjustment Administration (AAA), which sought to help raise commodity prices by paying farmers to cut back production. The money for the benefit payments made to farmers would be raised from a "processing tax" levied on the businesses that processed farm products (such as cotton gins, flour mills, and meatpacking plants).

As a complement to the AAA, Roosevelt created the Commodity Credit Corporation. This CCC extended loans to farmers above the market price of their crops, which were kept off the market in federal warehouses. If crop prices rose over time, a farmer could repay the loan, retrieve the crops, and sell them. If prices did not rise, the government kept the crops in storage, and the farmer kept the loaned money.

By the time Congress acted on the farm bills in 1933, the growing season was already under way, and the prospect of another bumper cotton crop created an urgent problem. The AAA reluctantly sponsored a plow-under program. To destroy a growing crop was a "shocking commentary on our civilization," Agriculture Secretary Henry A. Wallace lamented. "I could tolerate it only as a cleaning up of the wreckage from the old days of unbalanced production." In addition to plowing under ripening crops, the AAA encouraged farmers to destroy young livestock in order to reduce their supply and thereby raise prices.

For a while these farm measures worked. By the end of 1934, Wallace could report significant declines in wheat, cotton, and corn production and a simultaneous increase in commodity prices. Farm income increased by 58 percent between 1932 and 1935. The AAA was only partially responsible for the gains, however. The devastating drought that settled over the Great Plains between 1932 and 1935 played a major role in reducing production and creating the epic "dust bowl" migrations so poignantly evoked in John Steinbeck's novel *The Grapes of Wrath*. Many migrant families had actually been driven off the land by AAA benefit programs that encouraged large farmers to take land worked by tenants and sharecroppers out of cultivation.

Although it created unexpected problems, the AAA achieved successes in boosting the overall farm economy. Many conservatives, however, opposed its sweeping powers, and on January 6, 1936, the Supreme Court, in *United States v. Butler,* ruled the AAA's tax on food processors unconstitutional. The administration hastily devised a new plan to achieve crop reduction indirectly, with the Soil Conservation and Domestic Allotment Act (1936), which it pushed through Congress in six weeks. The new act omitted processing taxes and acreage quotas but provided benefit payments to farmers who engaged in soil-conservation practices and cut back on soil-depleting staple crops. Since the money to pay benefits came out of general funds and not from taxes, the approach was not vulnerable to lawsuits.

The act was an almost unqualified success as an engineering and educational project because it helped heal the scars of erosion and the plague of dust storms. But soil conservation nevertheless failed as a device for limiting production. With their worst lands taken out of production, farmers cultivated their fertile acres more intensively. In response, Congress passed the Agricultural Adjustment Act of 1938, which reestablished the earlier programs but left out the processing taxes. Benefit payments to farmers would come from general federal funds. Increasingly, federal farm programs came to dominate the nation's agricultural economy.

INDUSTRIAL RECOVERY   The industrial counterpart to the AAA was the National Industrial Recovery Act (NIRA), passed in 1933. The NIRA had two major components. One created the Public Works Administration (PWA), granting $3.3 billion for public buildings, highway programs, flood control, bridges, tunnels, and aircraft carriers. Under the direction of Interior Secretary Harold L. Ickes, the PWA indirectly served the purpose of work relief. Ickes focused on well-planned permanent improvements, and he used private contractors rather than workers on the government payroll. PWA workers built Virginia's Skyline Drive, New York's Triborough Bridge, the Overseas Highway from Miami to Key West, and Chicago's subway system.

The more controversial and ambitious part of the NIRA created the National Recovery Administration (NRA), headed by the colorful former army general Hugh S. Johnson. Modeled on the War Industries Board of 1917–1918, its purpose was twofold: to stabilize the business sector by reducing chaotic competition through the implementation of codes that set wages and prices and to generate more purchasing power for consumers by providing jobs, defining labor standards, and raising wages. The NRA raised trade union hopes for the protection of basic hour and wage standards and liberal hopes for comprehensive government planning for the economy.

In each industry, committees representing management, labor, and government drew up fair-practice codes. The labor standards were quite progressive. Every code set a forty-hour workweek and minimum weekly wages of $13 ($12 in the South, where living costs were considered lower), which more than doubled earnings in some cases. Labor by children under the age of sixteen was prohibited.

Labor unions, already hard-pressed by the economic downturn and a loss of members, were understandably concerned about the NRA's efforts to reduce competition by allowing businesses to cooperate in fixing wages and prices as well as production levels. To gain their support, the NRA included a provision that guaranteed the right of workers to organize unions. While prohibiting employers from interfering with union-organizing efforts, however, the NRA did not create adequate enforcement measures, nor did it require employers to bargain in good faith with labor representatives.

For a time the NRA worked, and an air of confidence began to replace the depression blues as the downward spiral of wages and prices subsided. But as soon as economic recovery began, critics charged that the larger companies were dominating the code negotiations, that they were using the codes to stifle competition by dividing up markets and entrenching their own positions, and that price-fixing among industry giants was robbing small producers of the chance to compete. The NRA wage codes also excluded agricultural and domestic workers—three out of every four employed African Americans.

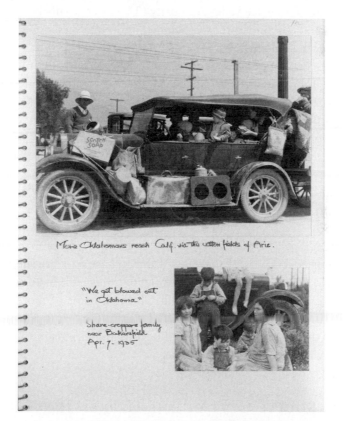

A sharecropper's family affected by the Oklahoma dust bowl

When the drought and dust storms showed no signs of relenting, many people headed west toward California.

The effort to develop detailed codes for every industry in the nation proved an administrative nightmare, and the daily annoyances of code enforcement inspired growing hostility among business executives.

By 1935 the NRA had developed more critics than friends, and a full economic recovery was nowhere in sight. In 1935, when the Supreme Court declared the NRA unconstitutional, few mourned. Yet the NRA experiment left an enduring mark. With dramatic suddenness the industry codes had set important new workplace standards, such as the forty-hour workweek and the abolition of child labor. The NRA's endorsement of collective bargaining also spurred union growth.

REGIONAL PLANNING   The wide-ranging scope of the New Deal embraced more than the centralized planning approaches of the NRA. The creation of the Tennessee Valley Authority (TVA) was a truly bold venture to revitalize one of the most underdeveloped and poverty-stricken regions of the country, where disease and illiteracy were rampant.

In May 1933, Congress created the TVA as a multipurpose public corporation. The TVA sought to bring cheap electricity to the Tennessee Valley, build fertilizer plants, provide jobs and recreation, and educate rural folk in the ways of modern life. By 1936 the TVA had six dams completed or under way, and the agency had developed a plan to build nine high dams on the Tennessee River, which would create the "Great Lakes of the South." The TVA, moreover, opened the rivers to boat and barge traffic, fostered soil conservation and forestry, experimented with fertilizers, and drew new industry to the region.

The TVA's success at generating greater power consumption and lower electricity rates awakened private utilities to the mass consumer markets. It also transported farmers of the valley from the age of kerosene to the age of electricity. Although 90 percent of urban dwellers had electricity by 1930, only 10 percent of rural Americans did. Through loans of more than $321 million to rural cooperatives, the Rural Electrification Administration paved the way for the electrification of 288,000 rural households in the Tennessee Valley and across the nation.

THE SOCIAL COST OF THE DEPRESSION

Although New Deal programs helped ease the devastation wrought by the Depression, they did not restore prosperity or end the widespread human suffering. Throughout the 1930s the Depression continued to take a toll on ordinary Americans who remained in the throes of a shattered economy that was only slowly working its way back to health during the 1930s.

CONTINUING HARDSHIPS   As late as 1939, some 9.5 million workers (17 percent of the labor force) remained unemployed. Prolonged economic hardship continued to create personal tragedies and tremendous social strains. Poverty led desperate people to do desperate things. Petty theft soared during the 1930s, as did street-corner begging, homelessness, and prostitution. Although the divorce rate dropped, in part because couples could not afford to live separately or pay the legal fees to obtain a divorce, all too often husbands down on their luck simply deserted their wives and children. A 1940 survey revealed that 1.5 million husbands had left home.

With their future uncertain, married couples often decided not to have children; the birthrate plummeted. Couples with children sometimes could not support them. In 1933 the Children's Bureau reported that one out of every five children was not getting enough to eat. Struggling parents often sent children to live with relatives or friends. Some 900,000 children left home and joined the army of homeless "tramps."

DUST BOWL MIGRANTS   In the southern plains of the Midwest and the Mississippi Valley, a decade-long drought spawned an environmental and human catastrophe known as the dust bowl. Colorado, New Mexico, Kansas, Nebraska, Texas, and Oklahoma were the hardest hit. As crops withered, income plummeted. Unrelenting winds swept across the treeless plains, scooping up millions of tons of parched topsoil into billowing dark clouds that floated east across entire states, engulfing farms and towns in what were called black blizzards. A massive dust storm in May 1934 darkened skies from Colorado to the Atlantic seaboard, depositing silt on porches and rooftops as well as on ships in the Atlantic Ocean. In 1937 there were seventy-two major dust storms. The worst of them killed livestock and people and caused railroads to derail and automobiles to careen off roads. By 1938 over 23 million acres of prairie land had lost most of its topsoil.

What made these dust storms worse than normal was the transition during the early twentieth century from scattered subsistence farming to widespread industrial agriculture. Huge "factory farms" used dry-farming techniques to plant vast acres of wheat, corn, and cotton. The advent of powerful tractors, deep-furrow plows, and mechanical harvesters greatly increased the scale and intensity of farming—and the indebtedness of farmers. The mercurial cycle of falling crop prices and rising indebtedness led farmers to plant as much and as often as they could. Overfarming and overgrazing

Dust storm approaching, 1930s
When a dust storm blew in, it brought utter darkness, as well as the sand and grit that soon covered every surface, both indoors and out.

disrupted the fragile ecology of the plains by decimating the native prairie grasses that stabilized the nutrient-rich topsoil. Constant plowing loosened vast amounts of dirt, which were easily swept up by powerful winds during the devastating drought of the 1930s. Hordes of grasshoppers followed the gigantic dust storms and devoured what meager crops were left standing. Human misery paralleled the environmental devastation. Parched farmers could not pay mortgages, and banks foreclosed on their property. Suicides and divorces soared in the dust bowl states. With each year, millions of people abandoned their farms.

Uprooted farmers and their families formed a migratory stream flowing from the blighted South and Midwest toward California, buoyed by currents of hope and desperation. The West Coast was rumored to have plenty of jobs. So off they went on a cross-country trek in search of new opportunities. Although frequently lumped together as "Okies," most of the dust bowl refugees were from cotton belt communities in Arkansas, Texas, and Missouri, as well as Oklahoma. During the 1930s and 1940s, some 800,000 people left those four states and headed to the Far West. Not all were farmers; many were white-collar workers and retailers whose jobs had been tied to the health of the agriculture sector. Most of the dust bowl migrants were white, and most were adults in their twenties and thirties who relocated with spouses and children. Some traveled on trains or buses; others hopped a freight train or hitched a ride; most rode in their own cars, the trip taking four to five days on average.

The dust bowl migrants who had come from cities gravitated to California's urban areas—Los Angeles, San Diego, or San Francisco. Many of the newcomers, however, moved into the San Joaquin Valley, the agricultural heartland of the state. There they discovered that California was no paradise. Only a few of the migrants could afford to buy land. Most found themselves competing with local Latinos and Asians for seasonal work as pickers in the cotton fields or orchards of large corporate farms. Living in tents or crude cabins and frequently on the move, they suffered from exposure and poor sanitation.

They also felt the sting of social prejudice. The writer John Steinbeck explained that "Okie us'ta mean you was from Oklahoma. Now it means you're a dirty son-of-a-bitch. Okie means you're scum. Don't mean nothing in itself, it's the way they say it." Such hostility toward the migrants drove a third of them to return to their home states. Most of the farmworkers who stayed tended to fall back upon their old folkways rather than assimilate into their new surroundings. These gritty "plain folk" had brought with them their own prejudices against blacks and ethnic minorities, as well as a potent tradition of evangelical Protestantism and a distinctive style of music variously labeled country, hillbilly, or cowboy. This "Okie" subculture remains a vivid part of California society.

MINORITIES AND THE NEW DEAL   The Great Depression was especially traumatic for the most disadvantaged groups. However progressive Franklin Roosevelt was on social issues, he failed to assault long-standing patterns of racism and segregation for fear of alienating conservative southern Democrats in Congress. As a result, many of the New Deal programs were for whites only. The Federal Housing Administration, for example, refused to guarantee mortgages on houses purchased by blacks in white neighborhoods. In addition, both the CCC and the TVA practiced racial segregation.

The efforts of the Roosevelt administration to raise crop prices by reducing production proved especially devastating for African Americans and Mexican Americans. To earn the federal payments for reducing crops as provided by the AAA and other New Deal agriculture programs, many farm owners would first take out of cultivation the marginal lands worked by tenants and sharecroppers, many of whom were blacks or Latinos. The effect

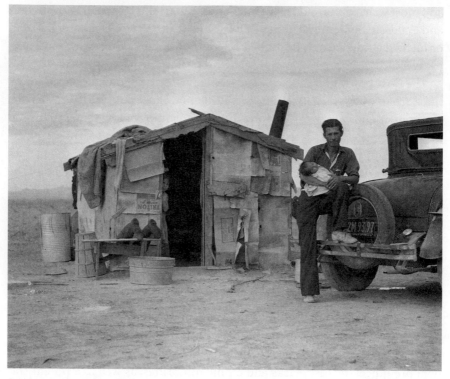

Migratory Mexican field worker at home

On the edge of a frozen pea field in Imperial Valley, California, this home
to a migratory Mexican family reflects both poverty and impermanence.

was to drive the landless off farms and eliminate the jobs of many migrant
workers. Over 200,000 African American tenant farmers nationwide were
displaced by the AAA.

Mexican Americans suffered as well. Thousands of Mexicans had migrated
to the United States during the 1920s, most of them settling in California,
New Mexico, Arizona, Colorado, Texas, and the midwestern states. But
because many of them Americans were unable to prove their citizenship,
either because they were ignorant of the regulations or because their migratory work hampered their ability to meet residency requirements, they were
denied access to the new federal relief programs under the New Deal. As economic conditions worsened, government officials called for the deportation
of Mexican-born Americans to avoid the cost of providing them with public

services. By 1935 over 500,000 Mexican Americans and their American-born children had returned to Mexico. The state of Texas alone returned over 250,000 people.

Native Americans were also devastated by the Great Depression. They initially were encouraged by Roosevelt's appointment of John Collier as the commissioner of the Bureau of Indian Affairs (BIA). Collier steadily increased the number of Native Americans employed by the BIA and strove to ensure that Indians gained access to the various New Deal relief programs. Collier's primary objective, however, was passage of the Indian Reorganization Act. He wanted the new legislation to replace the provisions of the 1887 Dawes Act, which had sought to "Americanize" Indians by breaking up their tribal land and allocating it to individuals. Collier insisted that the Dawes Act had produced only widespread poverty and demoralization. He hoped to reinvigorate Indian cultural traditions by restoring land to tribes, granting Indians the right to charter business enterprises and establish self-governing constitutions, and providing federal funds for vocational training and economic development. The act that Congress finally passed was a much-diluted version of Collier's original proposal, however.

CULTURE IN THE THIRTIES

In view of the celebrated—if exaggerated—alienation of writers, artists, and intellectuals rebelling against the materialism of the 1920s, one might have expected the onset of the Great Depression to have deepened their despair. Instead, it brought a renewed sense of militancy and affirmation, as if society could no longer afford the art-for-art's-sake outlook of the 1920s. By the summer of 1932, even the "golden boy" of the lost generation, the writer F. Scott Fitzgerald, had declared that "to bring on the revolution, it may be necessary to work within the Communist party." But few Americans remained Communists for long. Being a notoriously independent lot, most left-wing writers rebelled at demands to hew to a shifting party line. And many abandoned communism upon learning that the Soviet leader Joseph Stalin practiced a tyranny more horrible than anything under the czars.

LITERATURE AND THE DEPRESSION   Among the Depression-era writers who addressed themes of immediate social significance, two novelists deserve special notice: John Steinbeck and Richard Wright. The single piece of fiction that best captured the ordeal of the Depression, Steinbeck's

The Grapes of Wrath (1939), treats workers as people rather than ideological tools. Steinbeck had traveled with displaced "Okies" fleeing the Oklahoma dust bowl to pursue jobs in the fields of California's Central Valley. This firsthand experience allowed him to create a vivid tale of the Joad family's painful journey west from Oklahoma.

Among the most talented of the young novelists emerging in the 1930s was Richard Wright, an African American born near Natchez, Mississippi. The grandson of former slaves and the son of a sharecropper who deserted his family, Wright ended his formal schooling in the ninth grade (as valedictorian of his class). He then worked in Memphis and greedily devoured books he borrowed on a white friend's library card, all the while saving up to go north to escape the racism of the segregated South. In Chicago the Federal Writers' Project gave him a chance to develop his talent. His period as a Communist, from 1934 to 1944, gave him an intellectual framework that did not overpower his fierce independence. *Native Son* (1940), Wright's masterpiece tells the story of Bigger Thomas, a product of the ghetto, a man hemmed in, and finally impelled to murder, by forces beyond his control.

POPULAR CULTURE   While many writers and artists dealt directly with the human suffering and social tensions spawned by the Great Depression, the more popular cultural outlets, such as radio programs and movies, provided patrons with a welcome escape from the decade's grim realities.

By the 1930s, radio had become a major source of family entertainment. More than 10 million families owned a radio, and by the end of the decade the number had tripled. Millions of housewives listened to radio "soap operas," ongoing dramas that were broadcast daily in fifteen-minute episodes and derived their name from their sponsors, soap manufacturers.

Late-afternoon radio programs were directed at children home from school. In the evening after supper, families would gather around the radio to listen to newscasts; comedies such as *Amos 'n' Andy* and the husband-and-wife team of George Burns and Gracie Allen; adventure dramas such as *Jack Armstrong, The Lone Ranger, Dick Tracy*, and *The Green Hornet;* and big-band musical programs, all interspersed with commercials. On Sundays most radio stations broadcast church services. Fans could also listen to baseball and football games or boxing matches. Franklin Roosevelt was the first president to take full advantage of the popularity of radio broadcasting. He hosted sixteen "fireside chats" to generate public support for his New Deal initiatives.

Movies were even more popular than radio shows. In the late 1920s what had been silent films were transformed by the introduction of sound. The "talkies" made movies the most popular form of entertainment during

The Marx Brothers

In addition to their vaudeville antics, the Marx Brothers satirized social issues such as Prohibition.

the 1930s—much more popular than they are today. The introduction of double features in 1931 and the construction of outdoor drive-in theaters in 1933 also boosted interest and attendance. More than 60 percent of the population—70 million people—saw at least one movie each week.

The movies of the 1930s rarely dealt directly with hard times. Exceptions were the film versions of *Gone with the Wind* (1939) and *The Grapes of Wrath* (1940). Much more common were movies intended for pure entertainment; they transported viewers into the realm of adventure, spectacle, humor, and fantasy. People relished shoot 'em up gangster films, animated cartoons, spectacular musicals, "screwball" comedies, and horror films such as *Dracula* (1931), *Frankenstein* (1931), *The Mummy* (1932), and *Werewolf of London* (1935).

The best way to escape the daily troubles of the Depression was to watch one of the zany comedies of the Marx Brothers, former vaudeville performers. As one Hollywood insider explained, the movies of the 1930s were intended to "laugh the big bad wolf of the depression out of the public mind." *The Cocoanuts* (1929), *Animal Crackers* (1930), and *Monkey Business* (1931) introduced Americans to the anarchic antics of Chico, Groucho, Harpo, and Zeppo

Marx, who combined slapstick humor with verbal wit to create plotless masterpieces of irreverent satire.

THE SECOND NEW DEAL

During Roosevelt's first year in office, his programs and his personal charms generated massive support. The president's travels and speeches, his twice-weekly press conferences, and his radio-broadcast fireside chats brought vitality and warmth in contrast to Hoover's aloof coldness. In the congressional elections of 1934, the Democrats increased their strength in both the House and the Senate, an almost unprecedented midterm victory for a party in power. Only seven Republican governors remained in office throughout the country.

ELEANOR ROOSEVELT   One of the reasons for Roosevelt's popularity was his wife, Eleanor, who became an enormous political asset and would prove to be one of the most influential and revered leaders of the time. From an early age, Eleanor Roosevelt had embraced social service. Her compassion resulted in part from the loneliness she experienced as she was growing up and in part from the sense of betrayal she felt upon learning in 1918 that her husband was engaged in an extramarital affair with Lucy Mercer, her secretary. In the face of personal troubles, Eleanor Roosevelt "lived to be kind." Compassionate without being maudlin, more stoic than sentimental, she exuded warmth and sincerity, and she challenged the complacency of the comfortable and the affluent.

The First Lady

An intelligent, principled, and candid woman, Eleanor Roosevelt became a political figure in her own right. Here she is serving as guest host for a radio program, ca. 1935.

Eleanor Roosevelt redefined the role of the presidential spouse. She was the first woman to address a national political convention, to write a nationally syndicated column, and to hold regular press conferences.

A tireless advocate and agitator, Eleanor crisscrossed the nation, representing the president and the New Deal, defying local segregation ordinances to meet with African American leaders, supporting women's causes and organized labor, highlighting the plight of unemployed youth, and imploring Americans to live up to their egalitarian and humanitarian ideals.

CRITICISM Public criticism of the New Deal during Franklin Roosevelt's first year in office was muted. But not for long. The Depression's downward slide had been halted, but unemployment remained high (10 million were out of work in 1935, more than 20 percent of the workforce), and prosperity remained elusive. "We have been patient and long suffering," said a farm leader in October 1933. "We were promised a New Deal. . . . Instead we have the same old stacked deck." Even more unsettling to some was the dramatic growth of executive power and the emergence of welfare capitalism, whereby workers developed a sense of entitlement to federal support programs. In 1934 a group of conservative businessmen and politicians, including Alfred E. Smith and John W. Davis, two former Democratic presidential candidates, formed the American Liberty League to oppose New Deal measures as violations of personal and property rights.

More potent threats to Roosevelt came from the hucksters of social panaceas. The most flamboyant of the group was Louisiana's "Kingfish," Senator Huey P. Long. A short, strutting man, Long sported pink suits and pastel shirts, red ties, and two-toned shoes. He was a brilliant but unscrupulous reformer driven by a relentless urge for power and attention. First as Louisiana's governor, then as political boss of the state, Long had delivered tax favors, roads, schools, free textbooks, charity hospitals, and better public services. That he had become a sort of state dictator in the process, using bribery, physical intimidation, and blackmail to achieve his ends, seemed irrelevant to many of his ardent supporters.

In 1933, Long joined Roosevelt in Washington as a Democratic senator. He initially supported the New Deal but quickly grew suspicious of the

"The Kingfish"

Huey Long, governor of Louisiana. Although he often led people to believe he was a country bumpkin, Long was a shrewd lawyer and consummate politician.

NRA's collusion with big business. He had also grown jealous of Roosevelt's mushrooming popularity, having developed his own aspirations for the Oval Office. Promoting himself as a true if self-indulgent friend of the people, Long devised his own plan for dealing with the Great Depression.

Long's Share-the-Wealth program proposed to confiscate large personal fortunes, guarantee every family a cash grant of $5,000 and every worker an annual income of $2,500, provide pensions to the aged, reduce working hours, pay veterans' bonuses, and ensure a college education for every qualified student. It did not matter to him that his projected budgets failed to add up or that his program offered little to promote an economic recovery. Whether he had a workable plan or not, by early 1935 the charismatic Long was claiming 7.5 million supporters across the country.

Another popular social scheme was hatched by a gray-haired California doctor, Francis E. Townsend. Outraged by the sight of three elderly women

Promoters of welfare capitalism

Dr. Francis E. Townsend, Rev. Gerald L. K. Smith, and Rev. Charles E. Coughlin (left to right) attended the Townsend Recovery Plan convention in Cleveland, Ohio.

raking through garbage cans in Long Beach, Townsend called for government pensions for the aged. In 1934 he began promoting the Townsend Recovery Plan, which would pay $200 a month to every citizen over sixty who retired from employment and promised to spend the money within each month. The plan had the lure of providing financial security for the aged and stimulating economic growth. Critics noted that the cost of his program, which would benefit 9 percent of the population, would be more than half the national income. Yet Townsend was indifferent to details. "I'm not in the least interested in the cost of the plan," he blandly told a House committee.

A third huckster of panaceas, Father Charles E. Coughlin, the Roman Catholic "radio priest," founded the National Union for Social Justice in 1935. In broadcasts over the CBS radio network, he promoted schemes for the coinage of silver and made attacks on bankers that increasingly hinted at anti-Semitism.

Coughlin, Townsend, and Long drew support largely from desperate lower-middle-class Americans. Of the three, Long had the widest following. A 1935 survey showed that he could draw over 5 million votes as a third-party candidate for president in 1936, perhaps enough to undermine Roosevelt's chances of reelection. Beset by pressures from both ends of the political spectrum, Roosevelt hesitated for months before deciding to "steal the thunder" from the left by instituting an array of new programs. "I'm fighting Communism, Huey Longism, Coughlinism, Townsendism," Roosevelt told a reporter in early 1935. He needed "to save our system, the capitalist system," from such "crackpot ideas." Political pressures impelled Roosevelt to move to the left, but so did the growing influence within the administration from Supreme Court justices Louis Brandeis and Felix Frankfurter. These powerful advisers urged Roosevelt to be less cozy with big business and to push for restored competition and heavy taxes on large corporations.

OPPOSITION FROM THE COURT   A series of Supreme Court decisions finally spurred the president to act. On May 27, 1935, the Court killed the National Industrial Recovery Act by a unanimous vote. The defendants in *Schechter Poultry Corporation v. United States,* quickly tagged the "sick-chicken" case, had been convicted of selling an "unfit chicken" and violating other NRA code provisions. The high court ruled that Congress had delegated too much power to the executive branch when it granted the code-making authority to the NRA. Congress had also exceeded its power under the commerce clause by regulating intrastate commerce. The poultry in question, the Court decided, had "come to permanent rest within the state," although earlier it had been moved across state lines. In a press conference soon afterward, Roosevelt fumed: "We have been relegated to the horse-and-buggy definition of interstate commerce." The same line of conservative judicial reasoning, he warned, might endanger other New Deal programs.

LEGISLATIVE ACHIEVEMENTS OF THE SECOND NEW DEAL

To rescue his legislative program from such judicial and political challenges, Roosevelt in 1935 ended the stalemate in Congress and launched the second phase of the New Deal. He demanded several pieces of "must" legislation, most of which Congress passed within a few months.

The National Labor Relations Act, often called the Wagner Act for its sponsor, New York senator Robert Wagner, gave workers the right to bargain with employers through unions of their own choice and prohibited employers from interfering with union activities. The Wagner Act also created a National Labor Relations Board to supervise plant elections and certify unions as bargaining agents where a majority of the workers approved. The board could also investigate the actions of employers and issue "cease-and-desist" orders against specified unfair practices.

Social Security

A poster distributed by the government to educate the public about the new Social Security Act.

The Social Security Act of 1935, Roosevelt announced, was the New Deal's "cornerstone" and "supreme achievement." Indeed, it has proved to be the most significant and far-reaching of all the New Deal initiatives. The concept was by no means new. Progressives during the early 1900s had proposed a federal system of social security for the aged, indigent, disabled, and unemployed. Other nations had already enacted such programs, but the United States remained steadfast in its tradition of individual self-reliance. The Great Depression revived the idea, however, and Roosevelt masterfully guided the legislation through Congress.

The Social Security Act included three major provisions. Its centerpiece was a federally administered pension fund for retired people over the age of sixty-five and their survivors. Beginning in 1937, workers and employers contributed payroll taxes to establish the fund. Benefit payments started in 1940 and averaged $22 per month, a modest sum even for those depressed times. Roosevelt stressed that the pension program was not intended to guarantee a comfortable retirement; it was designed to supplement other sources of income and protect the elderly from some of the "hazards and vicissitudes of life." Only later did Americans come to perceive of Social Security as the *primary* source of retirement income for most of the aged.

The Social Security Act also set up a shared federal-state unemployment-insurance program, financed by a payroll tax on employers. In addition, the new legislation committed the national government to a broad range of social-welfare activities based upon the assumption that "unemployables"—people who were unable to work—would remain a state responsibility while the national government would provide work relief for the able-bodied. To that end the law inaugurated federal grants-in-aid for three state-administered public-assistance programs—old-age assistance, aid to dependent children, and aid to the blind—and further aid for maternal, child-welfare, and public health services.

When compared with similar programs in Europe, the Social Security system was quite conservative. It was the only government pension program in the world financed by taxes on the earnings of workers: most other countries funded such programs out of general revenues. The Social Security payroll tax was also a regressive tax: it entailed a single fixed rate for all, regardless of income level. It thus hurt the poor more than the rich, and it also impeded Roosevelt's efforts to revive the economy because it removed from circulation a significant amount of money: the new Social Security tax took money out of workers' pockets and placed it in a pension trust fund, exacerbating the shrinking money supply that was one of the main causes of the Depression. By taking discretionary income away from workers, the government blunted the sharp increase in public consumption needed to restore the health of the economy. In addition, the Social Security system initially excluded 9.5 million workers who most needed the new program: farm laborers, domestic workers, and the self-employed, a disproportionate percentage of whom were African Americans.

Roosevelt regretted the limitations of the Social Security Act, but he knew that they were necessary compromises in order to see it through Congress and enable it to withstand court challenges. As he replied to an aide who criticized funding the pension program through employee contributions:

> I guess you're right on the economics, but those taxes were never a problem of economics. They are politics all the way through. We put those payroll contributions there so as to give the contributors a moral, legal, and political right to collect their pensions and their unemployment benefits. With those taxes in there, no damn politician can ever scrap my Social Security program.

The last of the major bills making up the second phase of the New Deal was the Revenue Act of 1935, sometimes called the Wealth-Tax Act but popularly known as the soak-the-rich tax. The Revenue Act raised tax rates on income above $50,000. Estate and gift taxes also rose, as did the corporate tax on all but small corporations (those with an annual income below $50,000).

Business leaders fumed over Roosevelt's tax and spending policies. The wealthy resented their loss of status and the growing power of government and labor. They railed against the New Deal and Roosevelt, whom they called a traitor to his own class. Visitors at the home of J. P. Morgan Jr. were cautioned not to mention Roosevelt's name lest it raise Morgan's blood pressure. By "soaking" the rich, Roosevelt stole much of the thunder from the political left, although the results of his tax policy fell short of the promise. The new soak-the-rich tax failed to increase federal revenue significantly, nor did it result in a significant redistribution of income. Still, the prevailing view was that the president had moved in a dangerously radical direction. Roosevelt countered by stressing his basic conservatism and asserting that he had no love for socialism: "I am fighting communism. . . . I want to save our system, the capitalistic system." Yet he added that to save it from revolutionary turmoil required a more equal "distribution of wealth."

ROOSEVELT'S SECOND TERM

On June 27, 1936, Roosevelt accepted the Democratic party's nomination for a second term. He promised to continue to promote a government motivated by a "spirit of charity" rather than a government "frozen in the ice of its own indifference."

THE ELECTION OF 1936 The popularity of Roosevelt and the New Deal impelled the Republican Convention in 1936 to avoid candidates too closely identified with the "hate-Roosevelt" contingent. The party chose

Governor Alfred M. Landon of Kansas, a former Bull Moose Progressive who had endorsed many New Deal programs. He was probably more liberal than most of his backers and clearly more so than the party's platform, which lambasted the New Deal for usurping power.

The Republicans hoped that the followers of Huey Long, Charles Coughlin, Francis Townsend, and other dissidents would combine to draw enough votes away from Roosevelt to throw the election to them. But that possibility faded when an assassin, the son-in-law of a Louisiana judge whom Long had sought to remove, gunned down the Kingfish in 1935. Coughlin, Townsend, and a remnant of the Long movement supported Representative William Lemke of North Dakota on a Union party ticket, but it was a forlorn effort, polling only 882,000 votes.

In 1936, Roosevelt forged a new electoral coalition that would affect national politics for years to come. While holding the support of most traditional Democrats in the North and the South, the president made strong gains among beneficiaries of New Deal farm programs in the West. In the

Campaigning for a second term

Roosevelt campaigning with labor leader John L. Lewis (to the right of Roosevelt) and Martin McIntyre (far right) in Wilkes-Barre, Pennsylvania.

northern cities he held on to the ethnic groups helped by New Deal welfare measures. Many middle-class voters whose property had been saved by New Deal initiatives flocked to support him, as did intellectuals stirred by the ferment of new ideas coming from the government. The revived labor union movement threw its support to Roosevelt, and in the most profound departure of all African American voters for the first time cast the majority of their ballots for a Democratic president. "My friends, go home and turn Lincoln's picture to the wall," a Pittsburgh journalist told black Republicans. "That debt has been paid in full." The final tally revealed that 81 percent of those with an income under $1,000 a year opted for Roosevelt, as did 79 percent of those earning between $1,000 and $2,000. By contrast, only 46 percent of those earning over $5,000 voted for FDR.

In his acceptance speech to the Democratic Convention, Roosevelt abandoned efforts to reassure corporate leaders. As the Americans of 1776 had sought freedom from political autocracy, he noted, the Americans of 1936 sought freedom from the "economic royalists." He later claimed that never before had business leaders been "so united against one candidate." They were "unanimous in their hate for me—and I welcome their hatred." Roosevelt campaigned with tremendous buoyancy, and he wound up carrying every state except Maine and Vermont, with a popular vote of 27.7 million to Landon's 16.7 million. Democrats would also dominate Republicans in the new Congress, by 77 to 19 in the Senate and 328 to 107 in the House. After the lopsided victory, Roosevelt rode a wave of popularity into his second term.

THE COURT-PACKING PLAN   Soon after his landslide reelection, however, Roosevelt found himself deluged in a sea of troubles. His second inaugural address, delivered on January 20, 1937, promised even greater reforms. The challenge to American democracy, he maintained, was that millions of citizens "at this very moment are denied the greater part of what the very lowest standards of today call the necessities of life. . . . I see one-third of a nation ill-housed, ill-clad, ill-nourished." He viewed the election of 1936 as a mandate for even more extensive government action, and the overwhelming Democratic majorities in Congress ensured the passage of new legislation to buttress the Second New Deal. But one major roadblock stood in the way: the Supreme Court.

By the end of its 1936 term, the Court had ruled against New Deal programs in seven of the nine major cases it reviewed. Suits against the Social Security and Wagner Acts were pending. Given the conservative bent of the

Court, the Second New Deal seemed in danger of being nullified, just as much of the original New Deal had been.

For that reason, Roosevelt resolved to change the Court's conservative stance by enlarging the Court, a move for which there was ample precedent and power. Congress, not the Constitution, determines the size of the Court, which at different times has numbered six, seven, eight, nine, and ten justices and in 1937 numbered nine. On February 5, 1937, Roosevelt sent his plan to enlarge the Court to Congress, without having consulted congressional leaders He wanted to create up to fifty new federal judges, including six new Supreme Court justices, and diminish the power of the judges who had served ten or more years or had reached the age of seventy.

But the "Court-packing" maneuver, as opponents quickly tagged the president's scheme, backfired. It was a shade too contrived, much too brazen, and far too political. By implying that some judges were impaired by senility, Roosevelt affronted the elder statesmen of Congress and the Court, especially Justice Louis D. Brandeis, who was both the oldest and the most liberal of the Supreme Court judges. Roosevelt's scheme also ran headlong into a deep-rooted public veneration of the courts and aroused fears that a future president might use the precedent for quite different purposes.

As it turned out, unforeseen events derailed Roosevelt's drive to change the Court. A sequence of Court decisions during the spring of 1937 reversed previous judgments in order to uphold the Wagner and Social Security Acts. In addition, a conservative justice resigned, and Roosevelt named to the vacancy one of the most consistent New Dealers, Senator Hugo Black of Alabama.

Roosevelt later claimed he had lost the battle but won the war. The Court had reversed itself on important New Deal legislation, and the president was able to appoint justices in harmony with the New Deal. But the episode fractured the Democratic party and blighted Roosevelt's prestige. For the first time, Democrats in large numbers deserted the president, and the Republican opposition found a powerful issue to use against the administration. During the first eight months of 1937, the momentum of Roosevelt's 1936 landslide victory ebbed. As Secretary of Agriculture Henry Wallace later remarked, "The whole New Deal really went up in smoke as a result of the Supreme Court fight."

A NEW DIRECTION FOR UNIONS   Rebellions meanwhile erupted on other fronts while the Court-packing bill pended. Under the impetus of the New Deal, the labor union movement stirred anew. John L. Lewis, head of the United Mine Workers, increased membership in the UMW from 150,000 to

500,000 within a year. Spurred by Lewis's example, Sidney Hillman of the Amalgamated Clothing Workers and David Dubinsky of the International Ladies Garment Workers joined him in promoting a campaign to organize workers in the mass-production industries. As leaders of industrial unions (composed of all types of workers in a particular industry), which were in the minority by far, they found the smaller, more restrictive craft unions (composed of skilled male workers only, with each union serving just one trade) to be obstacles to organizing the country's basic industries.

In 1935, with the passage of the Wagner Act, the industrial unionists formed a Committee for Industrial Organization (CIO), and craft unionists (in the AFL) began to fear submergence by the mass unions of mostly unskilled workers. Jurisdictional disputes spread among the unions, and in 1936 the AFL expelled the CIO unions, which then formed a permanent structure, called after 1938 the Congress of Industrial Organizations (also known by the initials CIO). The rivalry spurred both groups to greater unionizing efforts.

The CIO's major organizing drives in the automobile and steel industries began in 1936, but they were thwarted by management's use of blacklisting, private detectives, labor spies, vigilante groups, and other forms of intimidation to suppress the unions. Early in 1937 automobile workers spontaneously adopted a new technique, the "sit-down strike," in which workers refused to leave a plant until employers had granted collective-bargaining rights to their union.

Led by the fiery young autoworker and union organizer Walter Reuther, thousands of employees at the General Motors assembly plants in Flint, Michigan, occupied the factories and stopped all production. Yet management refused to recognize the union efforts, and the standoff lasted over a month before the company finally relented and signed a contract recognizing the United Automobile Workers. Other automobile manufacturers soon followed suit. And the following month, U.S. Steel capitulated to the Steel Workers Organizing Committee (later the United Steelworkers of America), granting the union recognition and its members a 10 percent wage hike and a forty-hour workweek.

Having captured two giants of heavy industry, the CIO went on in the next few years to organize much of industrial America: the rubber, oil, and electronics industries and a good part of the textile industry, in which unionists had to fight protracted struggles to organize scattered plants. The slow pace of labor organizing in textiles denied the CIO a major victory in the South comparable to its swift conquest of automobiles and steel in the North, but even down South a labor movement gained a foothold. Union membership in the United States grew from under 3 million in 1933 to 8.5 million in 1940. Wages rose and working conditions improved because of their efforts. Whether by design or accident, union members became solidly Democratic.

A SLUMPING ECONOMY   During the years 1935 and 1936 the economy finally showed signs of recovery. By the spring of 1937, economic output had moved above the 1929 level. But worried about deficits and rising inflation, Roosevelt ordered sharp cuts in federal spending. At the same time the Treasury began to reduce disposable income by collecting $2 billion in Social Security from employee paychecks. Private spending could not fill the gap left by reductions in government spending, and big business still lacked the faith to risk large capital investments. The result was the slump of 1937, which was sharper than that of 1929 but was called by the press a recession, to distinguish it from a depression. By the end of 1937, an additional 4 million people had been thrown out of work; grim scenes of the earlier depression reappeared. The 1937 recession ignited a fierce debate within the administration. One group, led by Treasury Secretary Henry Morgenthau, favored less federal spending and a balanced budget. The other group, which included Harry Hopkins and Harold Ickes, argued for renewed government spending and stricter enforcement of anti-trust laws.

ECONOMIC POLICY AND LATER REFORMS   Roosevelt seemed bewildered by the recession, but he eventually endorsed the ideas of the spenders. In the spring of 1938, he asked Congress to adopt a large-scale spending program intended to increase mass purchasing power, and Congress voted almost $3.3 billion, mainly for public-works projects. In a short time the increase in spending reversed the economy's decline, but the recession and Roosevelt's reluctance to adopt massive, sustained government spending forestalled the achievement of full recovery. Only the massive crisis of World War II would return the U.S. economy to full production and full employment.

The 1937 recession further eroded Roosevelt's prestige and dissipated the mandate of the 1936 elections. The only major reforms enacted in Roosevelt's second term were the Wagner-Steagall National Housing Act, the Bankhead-Jones Farm Tenant Act, and the Fair Labor Standards Act. The Housing Act of 1937 set up the U.S. Housing Authority in the Department of the Interior, which extended long-term loans to local agencies willing to assume part of the cost of slum clearance and public housing. The agency also subsidized rents for low-income residents.

"A Prop against Human Erosion"

Editorial cartoonist Daniel Fitzpatrick
comments on the passing of the
Minimum Wage and Hour Law.

The Farm Tenant Act, passed in 1937, was to be administered by a new agency, the Farm Security Administration (FSA). The program offered loans to prevent marginally profitable farm owners from sinking into tenancy. It also offered loans to help tenants purchase their own farms. But by the late 1930s the idea of small homesteads was doomed to failure. American mythology still exalted the family farm, but in reality the ever-larger agricultural unit predominated. In the end the FSA proved to be little more than another relief operation that tided a few farmers over during difficult times. Sadly, a more effective answer to the problem awaited national mobilization for war, which moved many tenants into military service or the defense industry, broadened their horizons, and taught them skills that enabled them to leave the farm altogether.

The Fair Labor Standards Act of 1938 applied only to employees in enterprises that operated in or affected interstate commerce. It set a minimum wage of 40¢ an hour and a maximum workweek of forty hours, to be put into effect over several years. The act also prohibited the employment of children under the age of sixteen. Southern congressmen howled in opposition to the bill because it raised wages in their region and thus increased employers' expenses.

THE LEGACY OF THE NEW DEAL

SETBACKS FOR THE PRESIDENT   Although critics were unable to defeat the Fair Labor Standards Act, their stiff resistance revealed that an effective opposition to the New Deal was emerging within the president's own party, especially in the conservative southern wing. Southern Democrats were at best uneasy bedfellows of organized labor and African Americans, and more and more of them began cooperating with conservative Republicans. By the end of 1937, a formidable anti–New Deal bloc had developed in Congress.

Meeting of the anti–New Dealers

Senator Ellison D. "Cotton Ed" Smith of South Carolina cringes at the thought of a fourth term for Roosevelt, while meeting with fellow anti–New Dealers at the Mayflower Hotel in Washington.

As the political season of 1938 advanced, Roosevelt unfolded a new idea as momentous as his Court-packing plan: a proposal to reshape the Democratic party in the image of the New Deal. He announced his plan to campaign in Democratic primaries as the party leader with the goal of seeing his own supporters nominated. Instead of succeeding, however, the effort to shape the state elections backfired and broke the spell of presidential invincibility, or what was left of it. As in the Court-packing fight, Roosevelt had risked his prestige while handing his adversaries a combustible issue to use against him. His opponents tagged his intervention in the primaries an attempt to "purge" the Democratic party of its southern conservatives; the word evoked visions of Adolf Hitler and Joseph Stalin, tyrants who had purged their Nazi and Communist parties with blood.

The elections of November 1938 resulted in another setback for the administration, caused in part by the friction among the Democrats. FDR had failed in his efforts to liberalize the party by ousting southern conservatives. The Democratic dominance in the House fell from 229 to 93, in the Senate from 56 to 42. The margins remained large, but the president now headed an increasingly divided party. In his State of the Union message in 1939, Roosevelt for the first time proposed no new reforms. He did manage, however, to put through his plan to streamline the executive branch. Under the Administrative Reorganization Act of 1939, the president could "reduce, coordinate, consolidate, and reorganize" the agencies of government. With that, Roosevelt's domestic innovations feebly ended.

A HALFWAY REVOLUTION   The New Deal had petered out as war was erupting in Asia and Europe, but it had wrought several enduring changes. By the end of the 1930s, the power of the national government was vastly larger than it had been in 1932, and hope had been restored to people who had grown disconsolate. But the New Deal entailed more than just bigger government and revived public confidence. It also constituted a significant change from the older liberalism embodied in the progressivism of Theodore Roosevelt and Woodrow Wilson. Those reformers, despite their sharp differences, had assumed that the function of progressive government was to use aggressive regulation to ensure that the people had an equal opportunity to pursue their notions of happiness.

Franklin Roosevelt and the New Dealers went beyond the concept of regulated capitalism by insisting that the government not simply *respond* to social crises but also take positive steps to *avoid* them. To this end, the New Deal's various benefit programs sought to ensure a minimum level of well-being for all Americans. The New Deal had established minimum qualitative standards for labor conditions and public welfare and helped middle-class Americans hold on to their savings, their homes, and their farms. The protection afforded by bank-deposit insurance, unemployment pay, and Social Security pensions would come to be universally accepted as a safeguard against future depressions.

In implementing his domestic program, Roosevelt steered a zigzag course between the extremes of laissez-faire capitalism and socialism. The first New Deal experimented for a time with a managed economy under the NRA but abandoned that experiment for a turn toward enforcing competition through regulation and increased government spending. This tactic finally produced full employment during World War II.

Roosevelt himself, impatient with political theory, was flexible in developing policy: he kept what worked and discarded what did not. The result was, paradoxically, both profoundly revolutionary and profoundly conservative. Roosevelt sharply increased the regulatory functions of the federal government and laid the foundation for what would become an expanding welfare system. Despite what his critics charged, however, his initiatives fell far short of socialism; they left the basic capitalist structure in place. In the process of such bold experimentation and dynamic preservation, the New Deal represented a "halfway revolution" that permanently altered the nation's social and political landscape.

CHAPTER SUMMARY

- **Stabilizing the Economy** In March 1933 the economy, including the farm sector, was shattered; millions of Americans were without jobs and the most basic necessities of life. FDR and his "brain trust" of advisers set out to restore confidence in the economy by supporting the banking industry and providing short-term emergency relief for the unemployed, promoting industrial recovery, and reducing the size of crops by raising commodity prices.

- **The New Deal** Initially most of the New Deal programs were conceived as temporary relief and recovery efforts. They eased hardships but did not restore prosperity. It was during the Second New Deal that reform measures, such as Social Security and the Wagner Act, reshaped the nation's social structure.

- **New Deal Criticisms** Some conservatives criticized the New Deal for violating personal and property rights and steering the nation toward socialism. Some liberals believed that the measures did not tax the wealthy enough to provide the aged and disadvantaged with adequate financial security.

- **Federal Expansion** The New Deal expanded the powers of the national government by establishing regulatory bodies and laying the foundation of a social welfare system. The federal government would in the future regulate business to some extent to avoid social and economic problems.

- **Culture of the 1930s** The literature of the 1930s turned away from the alienation from materialism that characterized the literary works of the previous decade's "lost generation." John Steinbeck and Richard Wright, for example, realistically depicted ordinary people living in, and suffering through, extraordinary times. Radio comedies and the new "talking" movies allowed people to escape their daily troubles.

CHRONOLOGY

March 1933	Congress passes the Emergency Banking Relief Act
March 1933	Congress passes the Beer-Wine Revenue Act
March 1933	Congress establishes the Civilian Conservation Corps
May 1933	Congress creates the Tennessee Valley Authority
June 1933	Congress establishes the Federal Deposit Insurance Corporation
November 1933	Congress creates the Civil Works Administration
1935	President Roosevelt creates the Works Progress Administration
1935	Congress passes the Wagner Act
1935	Social Security goes into effect
1939	Steinbeck's *Grapes of Wrath* is published
1940	Richard Wright's *Native Son* is published

KEY TERMS & NAMES

New Deal p. 825

Franklin D. Roosevelt p. 825

Twenty-first Amendment
p. 829

Federal Writers' Project
p. 832

Agricultural Adjustment Act
p. 832

dust bowl p. 833

National Industrial Recovery
Act p. 834

National Recovery
Administration p. 834

Indian Reorganization
Act p. 841

Eleanor Roosevelt p. 844

Second New Deal p. 844

Huey Long p. 845

Share-the-Wealth program
p. 846

Court-packing plan
p. 857

2 9

FROM ISOLATION
TO GLOBAL WAR

> FOCUS QUESTIONS wwnorton.com/studyspace
>
> - What was the effect of isolationism and the peace movement on American politics between the two world wars?
> - What events in Europe seemed to herald another international conflict in the 1930s?
> - How did the United States respond to German aggression in Europe in the late 1930s?
> - How did events in Asia lead to Japan's attack on Pearl Harbor?

In the late 1930s the winds of war swept across Asia and Europe, abruptly shifting the focus of American politics from domestic to foreign affairs. Roosevelt, like Woodrow Wilson before him, had to turn his attention from social and economic reform to military preparedness and war. And the public again had to wrestle with a painful choice: involve the country in volatile world affairs or remain aloof and officially neutral.

POSTWAR ISOLATIONISM

THE LEAGUE AND THE UNITED STATES   Between Woodrow Wilson and Franklin Roosevelt lay two decades of relative isolation from foreign entanglements. The post–World War I mood of indifference to global affairs set the pattern. The voters in 1920 expressed their resistance to international commitments, and President-elect Harding lost little time in disposing of American membership in the League of Nations. The spirit of isolation found other expressions as well: higher tariffs, the Red Scare, and the restrictive immigration laws with which the nation all but shut the door to newcomers.

The United States may have felt the urge to insulate itself from a wicked world, but it could hardly ignore its substantial global interests. American business had expanding worldwide connections. Investments and loans abroad put in circulation the dollars that enabled foreigners to purchase American exports. America's overseas possessions, moreover, directly involved the country in world affairs, especially in the Pacific. Even the League of Nations was too great an organization to ignore. After 1924 the United States gradually entered into joint efforts with the League in such tasks as policing the international trade in drugs and arms, and American diplomats took part in a variety of economic, cultural, and technical conferences.

WAR DEBTS AND REPARATIONS   Probably nothing did more to heighten American isolationism during the 1920s and 1930s—or anti-American feeling in Europe—than the war-debt tangle. When in 1917 the Allies had begun to exhaust their sources of private credit in the United States, the U.S. government advanced them millions of dollars, first for the war effort and then for postwar reconstruction.

To Americans the repayment of the war debts seemed a simple matter of obligation, but Europeans commonly had a different perception. The French and the British had insisted that they could repay their war-related debts to the United States only as they collected reparations from defeated Germany. Twice during the 1920s the resulting strain on Germany brought the structure of international payments to the verge of collapse, and both times the Reparations Commission called in American bankers to work out rescue plans.

The whole structure finally did collapse during the Great Depression. In 1931, President Hoover negotiated a moratorium on both German reparations and Allied payment of war debts. At the end of 1932, after Hoover's debt moratorium ended, most European countries defaulted on their war debts to the United States. In retaliation, Congress passed the Johnson Debt Default Act of 1934, which prohibited private loans to any defaulting government.

ATTEMPTS AT DISARMAMENT   After World War I many Americans decided that the armaments race had caused the war and that arms limitations treaties would bring lasting peace. The United States had no intention of maintaining a large army, but under the shipbuilding program begun in

1916, it had constructed a fleet second only to that of Britain. Neither the British nor the Americans relished a naval armaments race, but both were alarmed by the growth of Japanese military power.

Since 1914, Japanese-American relations had grown increasingly strained. During World War I, Japan had taken China's Shan-tung Peninsula and the islands of Micronesia from Germany. In 1917, after the United States entered the war, Viscount Kikujiro Ishii visited Washington to secure American recognition of Japan's expanded position in Asia, dropping hints that Germany had several times tried to get Japan to quit the war. To forestall the loss of an ally in the war, Secretary of State Robert Lansing had signed an ambiguous agreement saying that "Japan has special interests in China." Americans were unhappy with the Lansing-Ishii Agreement, but it was viewed as the only way to keep Japan in the war.

After the war ended, Japanese-American relations deteriorated. To address the problem, President Warren Harding invited eight key countries to the Washington Naval Conference of 1921. It opened with a surprise announcement by the U.S. secretary of state, Charles Evans Hughes, who laid out a plan to destroy most of the world's navies. Delegates from the United States, Britain, Japan, France, and Italy signed the Five-Power Treaty (1922), incorporating

The Washington Conference, 1921

The Big Five at the conference were (from left) Iyesato Tokugawa (Japan), Arthur Balfour (Great Britain), Charles Evans Hughes (United States), Aristide Briand (France), and Carlo Schanzer (Italy).

Hughes's plan for tonnage limits on their navies and a moratorium of ten years during which no battleships would be built. The five powers also agreed to refrain from further fortification of their Pacific possessions. The agreement in effect partitioned the world: U.S. naval power became supreme in the Western Hemisphere, Japanese power in the western Pacific, and British power from the North Sea to Singapore.

Two other major agreements emerged from the Washington Conference. With the Four-Power Treaty, the United States, Britain, Japan, and France agreed to respect one another's possessions in the Pacific. The Nine-Power Treaty for the first time pledged the signers to support the principle of the Open Door enunciated by Secretary of State John Hay in 1899. The Open Door enabled all nations to compete for trade and investment opportunities in China on an equal footing rather than allow individual nations to create economic monopolies in particular regions of that country. The signers of the Nine-Power Treaty also promised to respect the territorial integrity of China. The powers, in addition to those signing the Five-Power Treaty, were China, Belgium, Portugal, and the Netherlands.

With these agreements in hand, President Harding could boast of a brilliant diplomatic stroke that relieved citizens of the need to pay for an enlarged navy and defused potential conflicts in the Pacific. Yet the agreements were without obligation and without teeth. The signers of the Four-Power Treaty agreed only to consult, not to help one another. The formal endorsement of the Open Door in the Nine-Power Treaty was just as ineffective, for the United States remained unwilling to use force to uphold the principle. Moreover, the naval-disarmament treaty set tonnage limits only on battleships and aircraft carriers; the race to build cruisers, destroyers, submarines, and other smaller craft continued.

THE KELLOGG-BRIAND PACT   During and after World War I the fanciful ideal of simply abolishing war seized the American imagination. Peace societies thrived, and the glorious vision of ending war by the stroke of a pen culminated in the Kellogg-Briand Pact of 1928. This unique treaty originated when the French foreign minister Aristide Briand proposed to President Calvin Coolidge's secretary of state, Frank B. Kellogg, an agreement whereby the two countries would never go to war with each other. Kellogg countered with a scheme to have all nations sign the pact, an idea all the more acceptable to the many peace organizations of the day.

The Pact of Paris (its official name), signed on August 27, 1928, declared that the signatories "condemn recourse to war . . . and renounce it as an instrument of national policy." Eventually sixty-two nations joined the pact, but all reserved "self-defense" as an escape hatch. The U.S. Senate included a reservation declaring the Monroe Doctrine necessary to America's self-defense and then ratified the agreement by a vote of 85 to 1. A Virginia senator who voted for "this worthless, but perfectly harmless peace treaty" wrote a friend that he feared it would "confuse the minds of many good people who think that peace may be secured by polite professions of neighborly and brotherly love."

THE "GOOD NEIGHBOR" POLICY   In Latin America the spirit of peace and noninvolvement helped allay long-festering resentments against the United States, which had freely intervened in the Caribbean during the first two decades of the century. In 1924, American marines left the Dominican Republic after an eight-year occupation. U.S. troops left Nicaragua a year later but returned in 1926 with the outbreak of disorder and civil war. In 1927 the Coolidge administration negotiated an agreement for U.S.-supervised elections, but one rebel leader, César Augusto Sandino, held out, and the marines stayed until 1933.

In 1930, President Hoover improved America's image in Latin America by permitting publication of a memorandum that denied that the Monroe Doctrine justified U.S. intervention in Latin America. It stopped short of repudiating intervention on any grounds, but that fine point hardly blunted the celebration in Latin America. Although Hoover never endorsed this so-called Clark Memorandum, named for American diplomat Reuben Clark, he never ordered military intervention in the region. Before he left office, steps had been taken to withdraw American forces from Nicaragua and Haiti.

Franklin D. Roosevelt likewise embraced the policy of the "good neighbor" and soon advanced it in practice. In 1933, at the Seventh Pan-American Conference, the United States supported a resolution declaring that no nation "has the right to intervene in the internal or external affairs of another." Under President Roosevelt the marines completed their withdrawal from Nicaragua and Haiti, and in 1934 the president negotiated with Cuba a treaty that abrogated the Platt Amendment of 1901, which had given the United States a formal right to intervene in Cuba.

WAR CLOUDS

JAPANESE INCURSIONS INTO CHINA   Improving U.S. relations in the Western Hemisphere during the 1930s proved an exception in an otherwise dismal world scene as war clouds darkened over Europe and Asia. Actual conflict erupted in Asia first, where unsettled social and political conditions in China had attracted foreign encroachments since before the beginning of the century. Chinese nationalist aspirations in 1929 and China's subsequent clashes with Russia convinced the Japanese that their own extensive investments in Manchuria, including the South Manchurian Railway, were in danger.

Japanese military occupation of Manchuria began with the Mukden incident of 1931, when an explosion destroyed a section of railroad track near that city. The Japanese army based in Manchuria to guard the railway blamed the incident on the Chinese and used it as a pretext to occupy all of Manchuria. In 1932 the Japanese converted Manchuria into the puppet empire of Manchukuo.

The Manchuria incident, as the Japanese called their undeclared war, flagrantly violated the Nine-Power Treaty, the Kellogg-Briand Pact, and Japan's pledges as a member of the League of Nations. But when China asked the League and the United States for help, neither obliged. President Herbert Hoover refused to invoke military or economic sanctions.

In early 1932, Japan's indiscriminate bombing of civilians in Shanghai, China's great port city, aroused Western indignation but no action. When the League of Nations condemned Japanese aggression in 1933, Japan withdrew from the League. Thereafter, hostilities in Manchuria gradually subsided and ended with a truce. An uneasy peace settled upon east Asia for four years, during which time Japan's military leaders extended their political sway in Tokyo.

ITALY AND GERMANY   The rise of the Japanese militarists paralleled the rise of totalitarian dictators in Italy and Germany. In 1922, Benito Mussolini had seized power in Italy after organizing the Fascist movement, a composite of superheated nationalism and socialism. The party's program, and above all Mussolini's promise to restore order and pride in a country fragmented by dissension and self-doubts, enjoyed a wide appeal. Once in power, Mussolini largely abandoned the socialist part of his platform and gradually suppressed all opposition. By 1925 he was wielding dictatorial power as Il Duce (the Leader).

There was always something ludicrous about the strutting, bombastic Mussolini. Italy, after all, was a minor European power. But Germany was another matter, and most Americans were not amused, even at the beginning, by Il Duce's German counterpart, Adolf Hitler. Hitler's National Socialist German Workers' (Nazi) party duplicated the major features of Italian fascism, including the ancient Roman salute. Hitler capitalized on the weakness of Germany's postwar government, the poverty and despair caused by a severe economic depression, and festering German resentment toward the Versailles Treaty.

Named chancellor on January 30, 1933, Hitler swiftly won dictatorial powers and in 1934 assumed the title Führer (national leader). The Nazi police state cranked up the engines of tyranny, persecuting Jews, whom Hitler blamed for Germany's troubles, and re-arming in defiance of the Versailles Treaty. Hitler flouted international agreements, pulled Germany out of the League of Nations in 1933, and threatened to extend control over all German-speaking peoples. Despite Hitler's provocations, the European democracies lacked the will to resist.

RUSSIAN RECOGNITION Isolationist sentiment in the United States grew even more potent during the early 1930s, but one significant exception to American insularity was Roosevelt's decision to favor official recognition

Axis leaders

Mussolini and Hitler in Munich, June 1940.

of Soviet Russia. By 1933 the reasons for America's refusal to recognize the Bolshevik regime had grown stale. Seen as an expansive market for U.S. goods, the Soviet Union stirred fantasies of an American trade boom, much as China had at the beginning of the century. Japanese expansionism in Asia, moreover, gave the Soviet Union and the United States a common foreign-policy concern. Given an opening by the shift of opinion, Roosevelt invited the Soviet commissar for foreign affairs to visit Washington, D.C. After nine days of talks, a formal exchange of notes on November 16, 1933, signaled the renewal of diplomatic relations. The Soviet commissar promised that his country would abstain from promoting Communist propaganda in the United States, extend religious freedom to Americans in the Soviet Union, and reopen the question of unpaid Russian debts to the United States.

THE MARCH OF AGGRESSION   After 1932 a catastrophic chain of events in Asia and Europe sent the world hurtling toward disaster. In 1934, Japan renounced the Five-Power Treaty. The next year, Mussolini commenced Italy's conquest of Ethiopia. That same year a referendum in Germany's Saar Basin, held in accordance with the Versailles Treaty, delivered the coal-rich region into the hands of Hitler. In 1936, Hitler's armed forces reoccupied the Rhineland, a direct violation of the Versailles Treaty. The French did nothing to oust the German force, however.

The year 1936 also brought the Spanish Civil War, which began with an uprising of the Spanish armed forces in Morocco, led by General Francisco Franco, against the democratically elected Spanish republic. Over the next three years, Franco established a fascist dictatorship with help from Hitler and Mussolini while the European democracies left the Spanish republic to its fate.

On July 7, 1937, Japanese and Chinese troops clashed at the Marco Polo Bridge, west of Peking, and the incident quickly developed into a full scale war. World War II had begun in Asia two years before it would erupt in Europe. That same year, Japan and Italy joined Germany in establishing an alliance known as the Rome-Berlin-Tokyo "Axis."

By 1938 the peace of Europe trembled in the balance. Having rebuilt German military power, Hitler forced the *Anschluss* (union) of Austria with Germany in March 1938. Six months later British and French leaders, recognizing the situation's severity but failing to comprehend Hitler's ruthlessness, sought to appease the German leader by agreeing to abandon the Sudetenland

AGGRESSION IN EUROPE, 1935–1939
← Aggressive moves
Axis powers

Keeping in mind the terms of the Treaty of Versailles, explain why Hitler began his campaign of expansion by invading the Rhineland and the Sudetenland. Why would Hitler have wanted to retake the Polish Corridor? Why did the attack on Poland begin World War II, whereas Hitler's previous invasions of his European neighbors did not?

in Czechoslovakia, a country that probably had the second-strongest army in central Europe. Germany promptly took the mountainous Sudetenland, largely German in population, which had been given to Czechoslovakia at the Paris Peace Conference in 1919 because of its strategic importance to that new nation's defense.

After promising that the Sudetenland would be his last territorial demand, Hitler brazenly broke his pledge in 1939: he occupied the remainder of Czechoslovakia and seized former German territory from Lithuania. In quick succession the Spanish republic collapsed on March 28, and Mussolini seized the kingdom of Albania on April 7. On September 1, 1939, Hitler launched his conquest of Poland. A few days before, he had signed a non-aggression pact with Soviet Russia. Having deserted Czechoslovakia, Britain and France now honored their commitment to go to war if Poland was invaded.

DEGREES OF NEUTRALITY   During these years of deepening crisis, the Western democracies seemed paralyzed, hoping in vain that each concession would appease the appetites of fascist dictators. Americans retreated more deeply into isolation. The neutrality laws of the 1930s sought to keep the United States insulated from the quarrels of Europe. But while Americans wanted to steer clear of war altogether, their sympathies were more strongly than ever with the Western democracies, and the triumph of fascist aggression in Europe aroused fears for national security. The Neutrality Act of 1935 forbade the sale of arms and munitions to all belligerents (warring nations) whenever the president proclaimed that a state of war existed. It also declared that Americans who traveled on belligerents' ships did so at their own risk. Roosevelt would have preferred discretionary authority to levy an embargo only against aggressors, but he reluctantly accepted the act because it was to be effective for only six months.

Yet on October 3, 1935, just weeks after Roosevelt signed it, Italy invaded Ethiopia, and Roosevelt invoked the Neutrality Act. When Congress reconvened in 1936, it extended the arms embargo and added a provision forbidding loans to belligerents. It was in July 1936, while Italian troops were mopping up the last resistance in Ethiopia, that the Spanish Civil War broke out. Roosevelt then became more isolationist than some of the most extreme isolationists. Although the Spanish Civil War involved a fascist uprising against a recognized democratic government, Roosevelt accepted the French and British position that only their nonintervention would keep the fight from spreading to the rest of Europe.

The conflict in Spain led Roosevelt to seek a "moral embargo" on the arms trade, and he encouraged Congress to extend the neutrality laws to instances of civil war. Congress did so in 1937 with only one dissenting vote. The Western democracies then stood by as German and Italian soldiers, planes, and armaments supported Franco's overthrow of Spanish democracy.

In the spring of 1937, Congress passed another neutrality law, which continued restraints on arms sales and loans, forbade Americans to travel on the ships of nations at war, and prohibited the arming of American merchant ships trading with warring nations. The new law also empowered the president to require that goods other than arms or munitions exported to belligerents be sold on a cash-and-carry basis (that is, the nation purchasing the goods would have to pay cash and transport the cargo in its own ships). This was an ingenious scheme to preserve a profitable trade without running the risk of war.

The new law had its first test in July 1937, when Japanese and Chinese forces clashed at the Marco Polo Bridge. Since neither side declared war, Roosevelt was able to avoid invoking the neutrality law, which would have favored the Japanese, since China had greater need of American arms but few means to get supplies past the Japanese navy. A flourishing international trade in munitions evolved as ships carried American military equipment across the Atlantic to England, where it was reloaded onto British ships bound for Hong Kong. Roosevelt, by his refusal to invoke the neutrality laws, had challenged strict isolationism.

Neutrality

A 1938 cartoon shows U.S. foreign policy entangled by the serpent of isolationism.

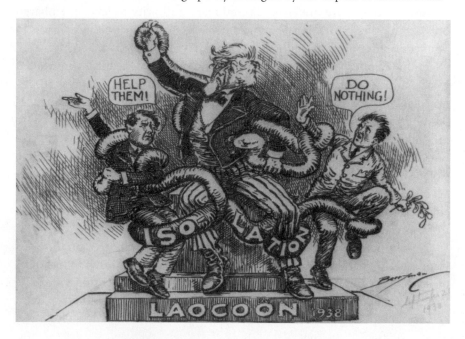

Roosevelt soon ventured a step further. In Chicago on October 5, 1937, he denounced the "reign of terror and international lawlessness" whereby 10 percent of the world's population threatened the peace of the other 90 percent. He called for a "quarantine" against those nations "creating a state of international anarchy and instability from which there is no escape through mere isolation or neutrality." Public reaction to the speech was mixed, but the president nevertheless quickly backed off from its implications and refused to spell out any program for dealing with aggression.

After the German occupation of Czechoslovakia in 1939, Roosevelt began to abandon his neutral stance. He could no longer pretend impartiality in the deepening European struggle. He began to educate the public about the menace of unchecked fascism. He urged Congress to repeal the munitions embargo and permit the United States to sell arms on a cash-and-carry basis to Britain and France, but to no avail. "You haven't got the votes," Vice President John Nance Garner told him, "and that's all there is to it." When the Germans attacked Poland on September 1, Roosevelt proclaimed official neutrality but in a radio talk stressed that he would not, like Woodrow Wilson in 1914, ask Americans to remain neutral in thought because "even a neutral has a right to take account of the facts."

Roosevelt summoned Congress into special session and asked again for amendments to the Neutrality Act. "I regret the Congress passed the Act," he confessed. "I regret equally that I signed the Act." Under the Neutrality Act of 1939, Britain and France could buy supplies with cash and in their own ships take away weapons or anything else they wanted. American ships, on the other hand, were excluded from the ports of warring nations and from specified war zones. Roosevelt then designated as a war zone the Baltic Sea, the waters around Great Britain and Ireland, and the waters from Norway south to the coast of Spain. One unexpected effect of this move was to relieve Hitler of any inhibitions about using unrestricted submarine warfare to blockade Britain.

Once the great democracies of western Europe faced war, American public opinion, appalled at Hitler's expansive tyranny, rallied to aid its allies without being drawn into the war itself. For a time it seemed that the Western Hemisphere could remain insulated. After the Nazis overran Poland in less than a month, the war settled into a stalemate in early 1940 that began to be called the phony war. What lay ahead, it seemed, was a long war of attrition—much like World War I—in which Britain and France would have the resources to outlast Hitler. That illusion lasted from October 1939 until the spring of 1940.

THE STORM IN EUROPE

BLITZKRIEG   In the spring of 1940, the long winter lull in the European fighting suddenly erupted into *blitzkrieg* (lightning war). At dawn on April 9, without warning, Nazi troops occupied Denmark and landed along the Norwegian coast. Denmark fell in a day, Norway within a few weeks. On May 10, Hitler unleashed dive bombers and tank divisions on neutral Belgium and the Netherlands. On May 21, German troops moving down the valley of the Somme River reached the English Channel, cutting off a British force sent to help the Belgians and the French. A desperate evacuation from the French beaches at Dunkirk enlisted every available boat, from warship to tug. Amid the chaos some 338,000 soldiers, about a third of them French, escaped to England.

Having outflanked France's heavily fortified defense perimeter, the Maginot Line, the German forces rushed ahead, cutting the French armies to pieces and spreading panic by strafing refugees. On June 14 the Nazi swastika flew over Paris.

The Blitz

In London, St. Paul's Cathedral looms above the destruction wrought by German bombs during the Blitz. Churchill's response: "We shall never surrender."

AMERICA'S GROWING INVOLVEMENT   Britain now stood alone, but its new prime minister, Winston Churchill, breathed defiance. "We shall go on to the end," he pledged; "we shall never surrender." Nevertheless, America seemed suddenly vulnerable as Hitler unleashed his air force against Britain. President Roosevelt called for a military buildup and the production of 50,000 combat planes a year. In 1940, Congress voted more than $17 billion for defense. In response to Churchill's appeal for military supplies, the War and Navy Departments began releasing stocks of arms, planes, and munitions to the British.

The world crisis transformed Roosevelt. Having been stalemated for much of his second term by congressional opposition to his domestic program, he was revitalized by the war in Europe. Nervous cabinet officers, military leaders, and diplomats now encountered a decisive president willing to exert executive authority on behalf of Britain, which in the summer of 1940, in the desperate Battle of Britain, finally forced the Germans to give up plans to invade the British Isles. Submarine warfare, meanwhile, strained the resources of the battered Royal Navy. Churchill urgently requested the transfer of American destroyers to help protect convoys from submarines.

"The Only Way We Can Save Her [Democracy]"

Political cartoon suggesting the U.S. not intervene in European wars.

Secret negotiations led to an executive agreement under which fifty "overaged" U.S. destroyers went to the British in return for ninety-nine-year American leases on naval and air bases in Newfoundland, Bermuda, and islands in the Caribbean. Roosevelt disguised the action as necessary for defense of the hemisphere. Two weeks later, on September 14, 1940, Congress adopted the first peacetime conscription in American history. All 16 million men aged twenty-one to thirty-five were required to register, those chosen in a lottery and found fit were required to fulfill a year's military service within the United States.

The new state of affairs prompted vigorous debate between "internationalists," who believed national security demanded aid to Britain, and isolationists, who charged that Roosevelt was drawing the United States into an unnecessary war. In 1940, internationalists organized the nonpartisan Committee to Defend America by Aiding the Allies, drawing its strongest support from the East and West Coasts and the South. Two months later isolationists formed the America First Committee. The isolationists argued that a Nazi victory over Great Britain, while distasteful, would pose no threat to American national security.

FDR'S THIRD TERM   In the midst of these profound global crises, the quadrennial presidential campaign came due. Isolationist sentiment was strongest in the Republican party, yet its nominee took a different stance.

Wendell L. Willkie was a former Democrat who had voted for Roosevelt in 1932. An Indiana farm boy whose disheveled charm inspired strong loyalty, he openly supported aid to the Allies.

The Nazi victory in France ensured that Roosevelt would decide to run for an unprecedented third term. The president cultivated party unity with his foreign policy and kept a sphinxlike silence about his intentions. The world crisis reconciled southern conservatives to the man whose foreign policy, at least, they supported. At the convention in Chicago, Roosevelt won the nomination for a third term with only token opposition. For his new running mate, he tapped his secretary of agriculture, Henry A. Wallace, a devoted supporter who would appeal to farm voters.

Throughout the summer, Roosevelt assumed the role of a man above the political fray, busy rather with urgent matters of defense and diplomacy. Because Willkie's foreign-policy ideas mirrored Roosevelt's, the Republican nominee was reduced to attacking New Deal red tape and promising to run the programs better. Roosevelt won the election by a comfortable margin of 27 million votes to Willkie's 22 million and by a wider margin, 449 to 82, in the Electoral College. Though the popular vote was closer than it had been in any presidential election since 1916, the dangerous world situation had persuaded a majority of voters to back the Democrats' slogan: "Don't switch horses in the middle of the stream."

THE "ARSENAL OF DEMOCRACY" Bolstered by the mandate for a third term, Roosevelt moved quickly to provide greater aid to besieged Britain, whose cash was running out. Since direct government loans would arouse memories of earlier war-debt defaults—the Johnson Debt Default Act of 1934 forbade such loans anyway—the president created an ingenious device to bypass that issue and yet supply British needs: the "lend-lease" program. In a fireside chat, Roosevelt told the nation that America must become "the great arsenal of democracy" to help prevent Britain's fall, and to do so it must make new efforts to help the British purchase American supplies. The lend-lease bill, introduced in Congress on January 10, 1941, authorized the president to sell, lend, or lease arms and other equipment and supplies to "any country whose defense the President deems vital to the defense of the United States."

For two months a bitter debate over the lend-lease bill raged in Congress and around the country. Isolationists saw it as the point of no return. Administration supporters denied that lend-lease would lead to American involvement in the war, but they knew that it did increase the risk. Lend-lease became law in early 1941, and Britain and China were the first beneficiaries.

While the nation debated, the war intensified. Italy had officially entered the European war as Hitler's ally in June 1940. In late 1940, as the American presidential campaign approached its climax, Mussolini launched attacks on Greece and, from Italian-controlled Libya, assaulted the British in Egypt. But his troops had to fall back in both cases, and in the spring of 1941 German forces under General Erwin Rommel joined the Italians in Libya, forcing the British to withdraw to Egypt, their resources having been drained to help Greece. In April 1941, Nazi armored divisions overwhelmed Yugoslavia and Greece, and by the end of May airborne forces had subdued the Greek island of Crete, putting Hitler in a position to menace the entire Middle East.

With Hungary, Romania, and Bulgaria forced into the Axis fold, Hitler controlled nearly all of Europe, but his ambition was unbounded. On June 22, 1941, Nazi troops suddenly fell upon the Soviet Union, their ally, hoping to use another lightning stroke to eliminate the potential threat on Germany's eastern front. The Nazis massed 3.6 million soldiers on a 2,000-mile front from the Arctic Ocean to the Black Sea. After retreating for four months, however, Russian soldiers and civilians rallied to defend Leningrad, Moscow, and Sevastopol. During the winter of 1941–1942, a ferocious Soviet counterattack proved to be the most important development of the war in Europe. Still, in the summer of 1941 the Nazi juggernaut appeared unstoppable.

Winston Churchill had already decided to provide British support to the Soviet Union in case of such an attack. Roosevelt adopted the same policy, offering American aid to Russia two days after the German invasion in late June 1941. Stalinist Russia, so long as it held out against the Germans, ensured Britain's survival. American aid was now indispensable to Europe's defense, and the logic of lend-lease led to deeper American involvement. To deliver aid to Britain, supply ships had to maneuver through the German submarine "wolf packs" in the North Atlantic. So in April 1941, Roosevelt informed Churchill that the U.S. Navy would extend its patrol areas in the North Atlantic nearly to Iceland.

In August 1941, Roosevelt and Churchill held a secret meeting off the coast of Newfoundland. There they drew up a statement of international principles known as the Atlantic Charter. Their joint statement called for the self-determination of all peoples, economic cooperation, freedom of the seas, and a new international system of collective security. The Soviet Union later endorsed the charter.

Having entered into a joint statement of war aims with the anti-Axis powers, the United States soon became involved in shooting incidents in the North Atlantic. After a German submarine attacked a U.S. battleship, the president ordered American ships to "shoot on sight" any German or Italian raiders ("rattlesnakes of the Atlantic") that ventured into American waters. Five days later the U.S. Navy announced that it would convoy British-bound merchant ships all the way to Iceland.

Further attacks prompted Congress to make more changes in the 1939 Neutrality Act requested by the president. On November 17, Congress removed the bans on arming merchant vessels and allowed them to enter combat zones and belligerent ports. Step-by-step the United States was giving up neutrality and embarking on naval warfare against Germany. Still, Americans hoped to avoid the final step of all-out war. The decision to go to war would be made in response to aggression in an unexpected quarter—Hawaii.

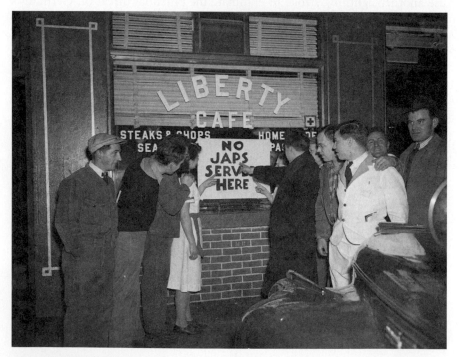

Repercussions of rising tension between the U.S. and Japan

A sign reading "No Japs served here" appeared on a cafe window near the Boston fish pier, December 1941.

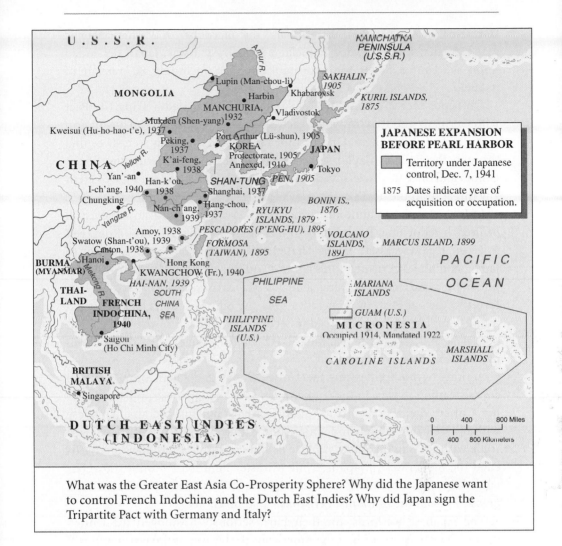

JAPANESE EXPANSION BEFORE PEARL HARBOR

Territory under Japanese control, Dec. 7, 1941

1875 Dates indicate year of acquisition or occupation.

What was the Greater East Asia Co-Prosperity Sphere? Why did the Japanese want to control French Indochina and the Dutch East Indies? Why did Japan sign the Tripartite Pact with Germany and Italy?

THE STORM IN THE PACIFIC

JAPANESE AGGRESSION   After the Nazi victories in Europe during the spring of 1940, America's relations with Japan took a turn for the worse. Japanese militarists, bogged down in the vastness of China, now eyed new temptations in Southeast Asia. They wanted to incorporate into their

"Greater East Asia Co-Prosperity Sphere" the oil, rubber, and other strategic materials that their crowded homeland lacked. As it was, Japan depended upon the United States for important supplies, including 80 percent of its fuel.

On September 27, 1940, the Tokyo government signed a Tripartite Pact with Germany and Italy, by which each pledged to declare war on any nation that attacked any of them. On April 13, 1941, while the Nazis were sweeping through the Balkans, Japan signed a nonaggression pact with the Soviet Union, and once the Nazis invaded Russia in June, the Japanese were freed of any threat from the north.

In July 1941, Japan announced that it was creating a protectorate over all of French Indochina. Responding to this latest act of aggression, Roosevelt froze all Japanese assets in the United States, restricted exports of oil to Japan, and took the armed forces of the Philippines into the U.S. Army and put their commander, General Douglas MacArthur, in charge of all U.S. forces in the Far East. By September 1941 the oil restrictions had tightened into a complete embargo. Forced to secure oil supplies elsewhere, the Japanese army and navy began planning attacks on the Dutch and British colonies in Southeast Asia.

Actions by both sides put the United States and Japan on a collision course leading to war. In his regular talks with the Japanese ambassador to the United States, Secretary of State Cordell Hull insisted that Japanese withdrawal from French Indochina and China was the price of renewed trade with the United States. A more flexible position might have strengthened the moderates in Japan. Prime Minister Fumimaro Konoe, however, while known as a man of liberal principles who preferred peace, caved in to pressures from the militants. Perhaps he had no choice.

The Japanese warlords, for their part, seriously misjudged the United States. The desperate wish of the Americans to stay out of the war might still have enabled the Japanese to conquer the British and Dutch colonies in the Pacific. But the warlords decided that they dared not leave the U.S. Navy intact and the Philippines untouched on the flank of their new lifeline to the south.

TRAGEDY AT PEARL HARBOR   Thus a tragedy began to unfold with a fatal certainty, mostly out of sight of the American people, whose attention was focused on the Nazi submarine threat in the Atlantic. Late in August 1941, Prime Minister Konoe proposed a meeting with President Roosevelt.

Secretary of State Hull urged the president not to meet unless agreement on fundamental issues could be reached in advance. On September 6 the Japanese government approved a surprise attack on Hawaii and gave Konoe six more weeks in which to reach a settlement.

The Japanese emperor's concern about the risk of an attack afforded the prime minister one last chance to pursue a compromise, but the presence of Japanese troops in China remained a stumbling block to any American agreement. In October, Konoe urged War Minister Hideki Tōjō to consider withdrawing Japanese forces while saving face by keeping some troops in north China. Instead, the inflexible Tōjō forced Konoe to resign in October. Tōjō himself became prime minister the next day. The war party was now in complete control of the Japanese government.

By late November, Washington officials knew that war was imminent. Reports of Japanese troop transports moving south from Formosa prompted U.S. officials to send warnings to Pearl Harbor and Manila and to the British government. The massive Japanese movements southward clearly signaled attacks on the British and the Dutch. American leaders had every reason to expect war in the southwest Pacific, but none expected that Japan would commit most of its aircraft carriers to another attack 5,000 miles away, at Pearl Harbor, the major American base in the Pacific.

On the morning of December 7, 1941, American servicemen decoded the last part of a secret Japanese message breaking off the diplomatic negotiations in Washington. Tōjō instructed Japan's ambassador to deliver the message at 1 P.M. (7:30 A.M. in Honolulu), about a half hour before the attack was to begin, but delays held up delivery by more than an hour. The War Department sent out an alert at noon that something was about to happen, but the message, which went by commercial wire because radio contacts were broken, arrived in Hawaii eight and a half hours later. Even so, the decoded Japanese message did not mention Pearl Harbor specifically, and U.S. military leaders there would probably have assumed the attack was to come in Southeast Asia.

It was still a sleepy Sunday morning in Hawaii when the first Japanese planes roared down the west coast and the central valley of Oahu to begin their assault. For nearly two hours the Japanese planes kept up their fierce attack. Of the eight U.S. battleships in Pearl Harbor, three were sunk, and the others were badly battered. Altogether, nineteen ships were sunk or disabled. At the airfields on the island, the Japanese destroyed about 180 planes. Before it was over, the raid had killed more than 2,400 American military personnel and civilians.

The attack on Pearl Harbor

This view from an army airfield shows the destruction brought on by the surprise attack.

The surprise attack fulfilled the dreams of its planners, but it fell short of total success in two ways. The Japanese ignored oil-storage tanks in Hawaii, without which the surviving U.S. ships might have been forced back to the West Coast, and they missed the American aircraft carriers that had fortuitously left port a few days earlier. In the naval war to come, those aircraft carriers would be decisive.

Later that day (December 8 in the western Pacific), Japanese forces invaded the Philippines, Guam, Midway, Hong Kong, and the Malay Peninsula. With one stroke the Japanese had silenced America's debate on neutrality—a suddenly unified and vengeful nation resolutely prepared for the struggle.

The day after the attack on Pearl Harbor, President Roosevelt told Congress that December 7 was "a date which will live in infamy," and he asked for a declaration of war. It was approved with only one dissenting vote, by

Representative Jeanette Rankin of Montana, a pacifist who was unable in good conscience to vote for war in 1917 or 1941. On December 11, Germany and Italy impetuously declared war on the United States. The separate wars in Asia and Europe had become one global conflict—and American isolationism was cast aside.

End of Chapter Review

CHAPTER SUMMARY

- **Isolationism** America distanced itself from global affairs—a stance reflected in the Red Scare, laws limiting immigration, and high tariffs. Yet America could not ignore the international events because its business interests became increasingly global. Although the United States never joined the League of Nations, it sent unofficial observers to Geneva. The widespread belief that arms limitations would reduce the chance of future wars led America to participate in the Washington Naval Conference of 1921 and the Kellogg-Briand Pact of 1928.

- **Totalitarianism** Totalitarian dictators came to power in Europe in the 1920s and 1930s. In Italy, Benito Mussolini assumed control by promising law and order. Adolf Hitler's National Socialist German Workers' party succeeded in part by responding to the humiliation that many Germans felt after Germany's defeat in the Great War. Hitler rearmed Germany in defiance of the Treaty of Versailles and aimed to unite all German speakers in a new German empire. Civil war in Spain and the growth of the Soviet Union under Joseph Stalin contributed to a precarious balance of power in Europe between the major nations.

- **American Neutrality** By 1938, Hitler had annexed Austria and seized the German-dominated areas of Czechoslovakia. By March 1939, Hitler seized the rest of Czechoslovakia. He faced no opposition until he sent troops to invade Poland in September of 1939, after signing a nonaggression pact with the Soviet Union. At last, the British and French governments believed that they had no option but to declare war. The United States issued declarations of neutrality, but with the fall of France, President Roosevelt's administration accelerated American aid to France and Britain.

- **Japanese Threat** The bombing of an American gunboat in China by Japanese planes in 1937 alienated Americans. Further Japanese aggression in Asia contributed to the deterioration of U.S.-Japanese relations. After Japan allied itself with Germany and Italy and announced its intention to take control of French Indochina, President Roosevelt froze Japanese assets in the United States and restricted oil exports to Japan. The Japanese leadership, fearing that the U.S. Navy might challenge its conquests, decided to bomb the Pacific Fleet at Pearl Harbor, Hawaii. The attack was a surprise, carried out without a declaration of war.

CHRONOLOGY

1921	Representatives of the United States, Great Britain, France, Italy, and Japan attend the Washington Naval Conference
1922	United States begins sending observers to the League of Nations
1922	Benito Mussolini comes to power in Italy
1928	More than sixty nations sign the Kellogg-Briand Pact pledging not to go to war with one another, except in matters of self-defense
1933	Adolf Hitler becomes chancellor of Germany
1939	Soviet Union agrees to a nonaggression pact with Germany
September 1939	German troops invade Poland
1940	Battle of Britain
September 1940	Germany, Italy, and Japan sign the Tripartite Pact
December 7, 1941	Japanese launch surprise attack on U.S. military base at Pearl Harbor, Hawaii

KEY TERMS & NAMES

"good neighbor" policy p. 866

Mukden incident p. 867

Benito Mussolini, "Il Duce" p. 867

Adolf Hitler, "Führer" p. 867

National Socialist German Workers' (Nazi) party p. 867

Axis Powers p. 869

blitzkreig p. 874

"internationalists" p. 875

Wendell L. Willkie p. 876

lend-lease bill p. 876

30

THE SECOND
WORLD WAR

FOCUS QUESTIONS

 wwnorton.com/studyspace

- What effect did World War II have on American society?
- How did the Allied forces win the war in Europe?
- How did the United States gain the upper hand in the Pacific sphere?
- What efforts did the Allies make to shape the postwar world?

The Japanese attack on Pearl Harbor ended a period of uneasy neutrality for the United States, and it plunged the nation into a global conflict that would cost the lives of over 400,000 Americans. The war would also transform social and economic life, as well as international affairs. The Second World War would become the most destructive and far-reaching conflict in history. It was so terrible in its intensity and obscene in its cruelties that it altered the image of war itself. Devilish new instruments of destruction were invented—plastic explosives, proximity fuses, rockets, jet airplanes, and atomic weapons—and systematic genocide emerged as an explicit war aim of the Nazis. The scorching passions of such a total war blanched many moral scruples. Racist propaganda flourished on both sides, and intense hatred of the enemy caused many military and civilian prisoners to be executed. Over 50 million deaths resulted from the war, two thirds of them civilians. The physical destruction was incalculable. Whole cities were leveled, nations dismembered, and societies transformed. The world is still coping with the consequences.

AMERICA'S EARLY BATTLES

At the end of 1941, the United States was woefully unprepared to wage a world war on multiple fronts. The army and navy were understaffed and underequipped. And it would take months for the economy make the transition to full-scale military production. Yet time was of the essence. Japanese and German forces had seized the initiative and were on the move. Momentum was on their side.

SETBACKS IN THE PACIFIC   For months after Pearl Harbor, the news from the Pacific was "all bad," as President Roosevelt confessed. The well-armed and well-led Japanese captured a string of Allied outposts in the three months before the end of December 1941: Guam, Wake Island, the Gilbert Islands, Hong Kong, Singapore, and Java. Other British and American territories toppled like dominoes. The Japanese capture of Rangoon, in Burma (Yangon in present-day Myanmar), in March 1942 cut off the Burma Road, the main supply route to China. By May the Japanese had ousted U.S. forces from the Philippines, and they controlled a new empire that stretched from Burma eastward through the Dutch East Indies and extended to Wake Island and the Gilbert Islands.

The Japanese might have consolidated an almost impregnable empire with the resources they had seized. But leaders of the Japanese navy succumbed to what one of its admirals later called victory disease: intoxicated with easy victories, they decided to push farther into the South Pacific, isolate Australia, and strike again at Hawaii. Japanese planners hoped to destroy the American navy before the productive power of the United States could be brought to bear on the war effort.

CORAL SEA AND MIDWAY   During the spring of 1942, American forces finally halted the Japanese advance toward Australia in two key naval clashes. The Battle of the Coral Sea (May 7–8, 1942) stopped a fleet convoying Japanese troop transports toward New Guinea. Planes from the *Lexington* and the *Yorktown* sank one Japanese aircraft carrier, damaged another, and destroyed smaller ships. American losses were greater, but the Japanese designs on Australia were thwarted.

Less than a month after the Coral Sea conflict, Admiral Isoroku Yamamoto, the Japanese naval commander, led his fleet toward Midway, the westernmost of Hawaii's inhabited islands, from which he hoped to render Pearl Harbor helpless. This time it was the Japanese who were the victims of surprise. American cryptanalysts had by then broken the Japanese

Early defeats

U.S. prisoners of war, captured by the Japanese in the Philippines, 1942.

naval code, and Admiral Chester Nimitz, commander of the central Pacific, knew their plan of attack. He reinforced Midway with planes and the aircraft carriers *Enterprise, Hornet,* and *Yorktown.*

The first Japanese foray against Midway, on June 4, 1942, severely damaged the American installations on the island, but at the cost of about a third of the Japanese planes. Meanwhile, American dive bombers caught three of the four Japanese carriers in the process of servicing their planes. The decks of the Japanese ships were cluttered with bombs, gasoline, and planes. Dive bombers sank three of them during the first assault. Later the Japanese lost another carrier, but not before its planes had disabled the *Yorktown.* The only other major American loss was a destroyer. The Japanese defeat at Midway was the turning point of the Pacific war. It demonstrated that aircraft carriers, not battleships, would decide the naval conflict.

SETBACKS IN THE ATLANTIC   Early Allied setbacks in the Pacific were matched by losses in the Atlantic. Since the blitzkrieg of 1940, German submarine "wolf packs" had wreaked havoc in the North Atlantic. In 1942, German U-boats appeared off American shores and began to attack coastal ships, most of them tankers. Nearly 400 ships were lost in American waters before effective countermeasures brought the problem under control. The naval command hastened the building of small escort vessels, meanwhile pressing into patrol service all kinds of surface craft and planes, some of them civilian. During the second half of 1942, these efforts sharply reduced American losses.

MOBILIZATION AT HOME

Roosevelt's declaration of war ended not only the long public debate on isolation and intervention but also the long economic depression that had ravaged the country during the 1930s. The war effort required all of America's immense productive capacity and full employment of the workforce. For 1942 alone the government ordered 60,000 planes, 45,000 tanks, and 8 million tons of merchant shipping. The next year's goals were even higher. Mobilization was in fact already further along than preparedness had been in 1916–1917. The draft had been in effect for more than a year, and the army had grown to more than 1.4 million men by July 1941. Congress quickly extended the term of military service to six months after the war's end. Men between the ages of eighteen and forty-five were now drafted. Altogether, more than 15 million American men and women would serve in the armed forces during the war. The average soldier or sailor was twenty-six years old, stood five feet eight inches, and weighed 144 pounds, an inch taller and eight pounds heavier than the average recruit in World War I. Less than half the servicemen had finished high school.

ECONOMIC CONVERSION   The economy, too, was already partially mobilized for war, by lend-lease and the defense buildup. Congress had authorized the president to reshuffle government agencies and to allot materials and facilities as needed for defense, with penalties for any agency that failed to comply. The War Production Board, created in 1942, directed the conversion of manufacturing to war production. The Office of Scientific Research and Development mobilized thousands of scientists to design the many technologies and devices that contributed to the war effort, which would include radar, sonar, the proximity fuse, and the bazooka.

The pressure of wartime needs and the stimulus of government spending more than doubled the gross national product between 1940 and 1945. Government expenditures during the war years soared. The total was about 10 times what America spent in World War I and 100 times the expenditures during the Civil War. The massive infusion of government capital into the economy also encouraged greater centralization and consolidation in private industry. Larger companies tended to win the most government contracts, and the more they won, the larger they became. Conversely, those without government contracts withered and died. In 1942 alone, 300,000 businesses shut down.

USE IT UP – WEAR IT OUT – MAKE IT DO!

OUR LABOR AND OUR GOODS ARE FIGHTING

War-effort advertisement

The Office of War Information created the ad's slogan in 1943.

America's basic economic problem during the war years was no longer creating jobs but finding workers for the booming shipyards, aircraft factories, and munitions plants. Millions of people who had lived on the margins of the economic system, especially women, were now brought fully into the workforce. Pockets of stubborn poverty did not disappear, but for most civilians the war spelled neither severe hardship nor suffering but a better life than ever before, despite shortages and the rationing of consumer goods. Labor unions benefited directly from the dramatic growth of the civilian workforce. Union membership increased significantly during the war years, from about 11 million to 15 million.

ECONOMIC CONTROLS   Increased family income and government spending during the war raised fears of inflation. Some of the available money went into taxes and war bonds, but even so, more purchasing power was sent chasing scarce consumer goods just as industrial production was converting to war needs. Consumer durables such as cars, washing machines, and nondefense housing in fact ceased to be produced at all. In the face of such wartime shortages, only strict restraints would keep prices from soaring out of sight. In 1941, Roosevelt created the Office of Price Administration, and the following year Congress authorized it to set price ceilings. With prices frozen, basic consumer goods had to be allocated through rationing, which began with tires and was gradually extended to other scarce items such as sugar, coffee, meat, and gasoline.

At first, however, wages and farm prices were not tightened, and this complicated matters. War prosperity offered farmers a chance to recover from two decades of distress, and farm-state legislators raised both floors and ceilings on farm prices. Higher food prices reinforced workers' demands for higher wages. To relieve this inflationary pressure, the president won new authority to control wages and farm prices. Businesses and workers chafed at the new controls, and on occasion the government was forced to seize industries threatened by strikes. The coal mines and railroads were nationalized for a short time in 1943. Despite these problems the government's program to stabilize the war economy succeeded. By the end of the war, consumer prices had risen only about 31 percent, a far better record than the World War I rise of 62 percent.

To make the economic controls work, the government launched a program to encourage the conservation of resources. As one popular slogan had it, "Use it up, wear it out, make it do or do without." People collected scrap metal and grew their own food in backyard "victory gardens." In 1942, when the war plants faced a rubber shortage, President Roosevelt asked citizens to turn in "old tires, old rubber raincoats, old garden hoses, rubber shoes, bathing caps, gloves—whatever you have that is made of rubber."

DOMESTIC CONSERVATISM   Despite the government's efforts to encourage sacrifices for the war effort, Americans expressed their discontent with price controls, labor shortages, rationing, and a hundred other petty vexations. They manifested those concerns against Roosevelt liberalism at the polls in a reaction that indicated a growing political conservatism. In 1942 the congressional elections registered a national swing away from the New Deal. Republicans gained forty-six seats in the House and nine in the Senate, chiefly in the farm areas of the midwestern states. Democratic losses outside the South strengthened the southern delegation's position within the party, and the delegation itself reflected conservative victories in southern primaries. A coalition of conservatives dismantled "nonessential" New Deal agencies, including the National Youth Adminstration, the Civilian Conservation Corps, and the Farm Security Administration.

Organized labor, despite substantial gains during the war, felt the impact of the conservative trend. In the spring of 1943, when John L. Lewis led the coal miners out on strike, Congress passed the Smith-Connally War Labor Disputes Act, which authorized the government to seize plants useful to the war effort. In 1943 a dozen states adopted laws restricting picketing and other union activities, and in 1944 Arkansas and Florida set in motion a wave of "right-to-work" legislation that outlawed the closed shop (requiring that all employees be union members).

SOCIAL EFFECTS OF THE WAR

MOBILIZATION AND THE DEVELOPMENT OF THE WEST   The dramatic expansion of defense production after 1940 and the mobilization of millions of people in the armed forces accelerated economic development and a population boom in the western states. Nearly 8 million people moved into the states west of the Mississippi River between 1940 and 1950. The Far West experienced the fastest rate of urban growth in the country. Small cities such as Phoenix and Albuquerque mushroomed while Seattle, San Francisco, Los Angeles, and San Diego witnessed dizzying growth. San Diego's population, for example, increased by 147 percent between 1941 and 1945. The migration of workers to new defense jobs in the West had significant demographic effects. Lured by news of job openings and higher wages, African Americans from Texas, Oklahoma, Arkansas, and Louisiana headed west. During the war years, Seattle's African American population jumped from 4,000 to 40,000, Portland's from 2,000 to 15,000.

CHANGING ROLES FOR WOMEN   The war marked an important watershed in the status of women. With millions of men going into military service, the demand for labor shook up old prejudices about sex roles in the workplace—and in the military. Nearly 200,000 women served in the Women's Army Corps (WAC) and the navy's equivalent, Women Accepted for Volunteer Emergency Service (WAVES). Lesser numbers joined the Marine Corps, the Coast Guard, and the Army Air Force.

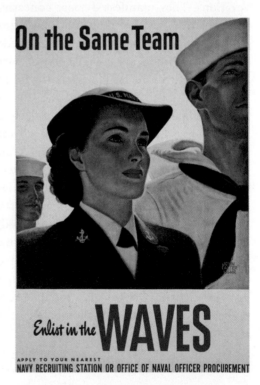

Over 6 million women entered the workforce during the war, an increase of more than 50 percent and in manufacturing alone an increase of some 110 percent. By 1944 over a third of all American women were in the labor force. Old barriers fell overnight as women became toolmakers machinists, riveters, crane operators, lumberjacks, stevedores, blacksmiths, and railroad workers. Desperate for laborers, the government launched an intense publicity campaign to draw women into traditional

Women in the military

This navy recruiting poster urged women to join the WAVES (Women Accepted for Volunteer Emergency Service).

male jobs. "Rosie the Riveter," an attractive woman depicted in overalls, served as the cover girl for the recruiting campaign.

One striking feature of the wartime economy was the proportion of older, married women in the workforce. In 1940 about 15 percent of married women were employed outside the home; by 1945, 24 percent were. In the workforce as a whole, married women for the first time outnumbered single women. Many women were eager to get away from the grinding routine of domestic life. One female welder remembered that her wartime job "was the first time I had a chance to get out of the kitchen and work in industry and make a few bucks. This was something I had never dreamed would happen." And it was something that many women did not want to relinquish after the war.

AFRICAN AMERICANS IN WORLD WAR II The most volatile social issue ignited by the war was African American participation in the defense effort. From the start, black leaders demanded equality in the armed forces and defense industries. Eventually about 1 million African Americans served in the armed forces, but most were assigned to segregated units. The most important departure from this pattern came with a 1940 decision to integrate officer-candidate schools, except those for air force cadets. A separate military flight school at Tuskegee, Alabama, trained about 600 African American pilots, many of whom distinguished themselves in combat.

Tuskegee Airmen, 1942

One of the last segregated military training schools, the flight school at Tuskegee trained African American men for combat during World War II.

War industries were even less hospitable to integration. "We will not employ Negroes," said the president of North American Aviation. In 1941, A. Philip Randolph, the brilliant head of the Brotherhood of Sleeping Car Porters, organized a march on Washington to demand an end to racial discrimination in defense industries. The Roosevelt administration, alarmed at the prospect of a mass descent on the capital, struck a bargain. Randolph called off the march in return for an executive order prohibiting racial discrimination in companies that received federal defense contracts.

African American leaders quickly challenged all kinds of discrimination, including racial segregation itself. Membership in the NAACP soared during the war, from 50,000 to 450,000. African Americans could look forward to greater political participation after the Supreme Court, in *Smith v. Allwright* (1944), struck down Texas's whites-only primary on the grounds that political primaries were part of the election process and thus subject to the Fifteenth Amendment's guarantee of the right to vote.

LATINOS IN THE LABOR FORCE   As rural folk moved to the western cities, many farm counties across the nation experienced a labor shortage. In an ironic about-face, local and federal government authorities who before the war had forced undocumented Mexican laborers back across the border now recruited them to harvest crops. Before it would assist in providing the needed workers, the Mexican government insisted that the United States ensure minimum working and living conditions. The result was the creation of the bracero program in 1942, whereby Mexico agreed to provide seasonal farmworkers in exchange for a promise by the U.S. government not to draft them into military service. The workers were hired on year long contracts, and American officials provided transportation from the border to their job sites. Under the bracero program some 200,000 Mexican farmworkers entered the western United States. At least that many more crossed the border as undocumented workers.

The rising tide of Mexican Americans in Los Angeles provoked a growing stream of anti-Latino editorials and incidents. Even though Mexican Americans fought in the war with great valor, earning seventeen Congressional Medals of Honor, there was constant conflict between servicemen and Mexican American gang members and teenage "zoot-suiters" in southern California. In 1943 several thousand off-duty sailors and soldiers, joined by hundreds of local white civilians, rampaged through downtown Los Angeles streets, assaulting Latinos, African Americans, and Filipinos. The weeklong violence came to be labeled the zoot-suit riots. (Zoot suits were the flamboyant suits popular in the 1940s and worn by some young Mexican American men.)

NATIVE AMERICANS AND THE WAR EFFORT   Indians supported the war effort more fully than any other group in American society. Almost a third of eligible Native American men, over 25,000 people, served in the armed forces. Another one fourth worked in defense-related industries. Thousands of Indian women volunteered as nurses or joined the WAVES. As was the case with African Americans, Indians benefited from the experiences afforded by the war. Those who left reservations to work in defense plants or to join the military gained new vocational skills as well as a greater awareness of opportunities available in the larger American society.

Marine Navajo "code talkers"

The Japanese were never able to break the Native Americans' codes used by signalmen, such as those shown here during the Battle of Bougainville in 1943.

Why did so many Native Americans fight in such high numbers for a nation that had stripped them of their land and decimated their heritage? Some felt that they had no choice. Mobilization for the war effort ended many New Deal programs that had provided Indians with jobs. Reservation Indians thus faced the necessity of finding new jobs elsewhere. Others viewed the Nazis and the Japanese warlords as threats to their own homeland. The most common sentiment animating Indian involvement in the war effort, however, seems to have been a genuine sense of patriotism.

Whatever the reasons, Indians distinguished themselves in the military. Unlike their African American counterparts, Indian servicemen were integrated into regular units. Perhaps the most distinctive activity performed by Indians was their service as "code talkers": every military branch used Indians to encode and decipher messages using their native languages.

INTERNMENT OF JAPANESE AMERICANS The record on civil liberties during World War II was on the whole better than that during World War I, if only because there was virtually no domestic opposition to the war effort after the attack on Pearl Harbor. Neither German Americans nor Italian Americans faced the harassments meted out to their counterparts in the previous war; few had much sympathy for Hitler or Mussolini. The shameful exception to an otherwise improved record was the treatment accorded to Americans of Japanese descent in the months following the attack on Pearl Harbor. One California barbershop offered "free shaves for Japs" but noted that it was "not responsible for accidents." Others were even blunter. Idaho's governor declared: "A good solution to the Jap problem would be to send them all back to Japan, then sink the island. They live like rats, breed like rats, and act like rats." Such attitudes were widespread, and the government finally succumbed to demands that it force all Japanese, citizens or not, into "war relocation camps" in the interior of the country.

Caught up in the war hysteria and racial prejudice unleashed by the attack on Pearl Harbor, President Roosevelt initiated the removal and confinement of Japanese Americans when he issued Executive Order 9066 on February 19, 1942. More than 60 percent of the internees were U.S. citizens; a third were under the age of nineteen. More than 100,000 people were eventually removed from their homes and businesses. Forced to sell their farms and businesses at great losses, the internees lost both their liberty and their property. Not until 1983 did the government acknowledge the injustice of the internment policy. Five years later Congress voted to give $20,000 and an apology to each of the 60,000 former internees who were still living.

THE ALLIED DRIVE TOWARD BERLIN

By mid-1942 the "home front" had begun to get news from the war fronts that some of the lines were holding at last. By midyear a fleet of American air and sea subchasers was suppressing German U-boats off the Atlantic coast. This event was all the more important because Allied war plans called for the defeat of Germany first.

WAR AIMS AND STRATEGY   There were good reasons for giving top priority to defeating Hitler: Nazi forces in western Europe and the Atlantic posed a more direct threat to the Western Hemisphere than did Japan, and Germany's war potential exceeded Japan's. Yet Japanese attacks involved Americans directly in the Pacific war from the start, and as a consequence more Americans went to the Pacific than crossed the Atlantic during the first year of fighting.

The Pearl Harbor attack brought British prime minister Winston Churchill to Washington, D.C., for talks about a joint war plan. Thus began a successful but not always harmonious wartime alliance between the United States and Great Britain. The meetings in Washington in 1942 affirmed the priority of winning the war against Germany. Agreement on war aims did not bring agreement on strategy, however. When Roosevelt and Churchill met at the White House a second time in 1942, they could not agree on the location of the first attack against the Nazis. American strategists wanted to strike German-held France directly across the English Channel before the end of 1942. With vivid memories of the last war, the British feared a mass blood-letting in trench warfare if they struck prematurely. In eastern Europe two totalitarian regimes—the Germans and the Soviets—waged a colossal war while managing mass death camps. Stalin's henchmen killed more captive peoples than Hitler's. The Soviets, while quietly victimizing their own, were also bearing the brunt of the German attack in the east. Thus they insisted that the Western Allies do something to relieve the pressure along the Russian front. Finally, the Americans accepted Churchill's proposal to invade French North Africa, now allied with Germany.

THE NORTH AFRICAN CAMPAIGN   On November 8, 1942, British and American units commanded by General Dwight D. Eisenhower landed in Morocco and Algeria. Completely surprised, French forces under the Vichy government (which collaborated with the Germans) had little will to resist. Farther east, British forces were pushing German armies back across

Libya. Before spring the Germans were caught in a gigantic pair of pincers. By April the British had linked up with American forces. Hammered from all sides and unable to retreat across the Mediterranean, an army of more than 200,000 Germans surrendered on May 12, 1943, leaving all of North Africa in Allied hands.

While the Battle of Tunisia was still unfolding, Roosevelt and Churchill met at Casablanca, Morocco. It was a historic occasion. No U.S. president had ever flown while in office, and none had ever visited Africa. But the absence of precedent did not deter Roosevelt. Stalin declined to leave the beleaguered Soviet Union for the meeting, but he continued to press for the opening of a second front in western Europe. Since the German invasion of Russia in 1941, over 90 percent of German military casualties had occurred on the eastern front. The British and American engagements with German forces in North Africa were minuscule in comparison with the scope and fury of the fighting in Russia.

Churchill and Roosevelt spent eight days at Casablanca hammering out key strategic decisions. The Americans wanted to launch a massive Allied invasion of German-occupied France as soon as possible, but the British still insisted that such a major assault was premature. They convinced the Americans that they should follow up a victory in North Africa with an assault on Sicily and Italy. Roosevelt and Churchill also decided to step up the bombing of Germany and to increase shipments of military supplies to the Soviet Union and the Nationalist Chinese forces fighting the Japanese.

Before leaving Casablanca, Roosevelt announced, with Churchill's endorsement, that the war would end only with the "unconditional surrender" of all enemies. This demand was designed to reassure Stalin that the Western Allies would not negotiate separately with the Germans. The West desperately needed Soviet cooperation in defeating Germany, and Roosevelt and Churchill were eager to reassure Stalin of their good intentions.

THE BATTLE OF THE ATLANTIC   While fighting raged in North Africa, the more crucial Battle of the Atlantic reached its climax on the high seas. Several factors contributed to the success of the Allied effort. Scientists had perfected a variety of detection devices: radar, which the British had already used to advantage in the Battle of Britain, bounced radio waves off objects and registered their position on a screen; sonar detected sound waves from submerged U-boats; sonobuoys, dropped from planes, radioed back their findings; and advanced magnetic equipment enabled aircraft to detect objects underwater.

By early 1943 in the western portion of the North Atlantic, there were at any given time an average of 31 convoys with 145 escorts and 673 merchant ships, as well as a number of heavily escorted troopships. None of the troopships going to Britain or the Mediterranean was lost. The U-boats kept up the Battle of the Atlantic until the war's end, but their commander later admitted that the battle had been lost by the end of May 1943. He credited the difference largely to radar. What he did not know then was that the Allies had a secret weapon: by early 1943 their cryptanalysts were routinely decoding German messages and telling their subchasers where to look for German U-boats.

SICILY AND ITALY On July 10, 1943, after the Allied victory in the North African campaign, about 250,000 British and American troops landed on the Italian island of Sicily, scoring a complete surprise. The German-Italian collapse in Sicily ended Mussolini's twenty years of Fascist rule. On July 25, 1943, Italy's king notified the dictator of his dismissal as prime minister. A new Italian government startled the Allies when it offered not only to surrender but also to switch sides in the war. Unfortunately, mutual suspicions prolonged talks until September 3, while the Germans poured reinforcements into Italy. Mussolini, plucked from imprisonment by a daring German airborne raid, became head of a puppet Fascist government in northern Italy.

Therefore the Allied assault on the Italian mainland did not turn into an easy victory. The main landing at Salerno on September 9 encountered heavy German resistance, as the steep terrain favored the defenders. The Americans, joined by British troops, nevertheless secured beachheads within a week and captured Naples. After a five-month siege of Rome, the Americans finally took the fabled city on June 4, 1944. Yet they enjoyed only a brief moment of glory, for the long-awaited cross-Channel landing in France, begun two days later, quickly became the focus of attention.

THE STRATEGIC BOMBING OF EUROPE Behind the long-postponed landings on the Normandy beaches lay months of preparation. While waiting, the U.S. Army Air Force and the Royal Air Force (RAF) had attacked the installations and troops making up what Hitler called "Fortress Europe." By 1943, American strategic bombers were full-fledged partners of the RAF in the effort to pound Germany into submission. Yet despite the widespread damage it caused, the strategic air offensive ultimately failed to dismantle German production or, as later studies found, break civilian

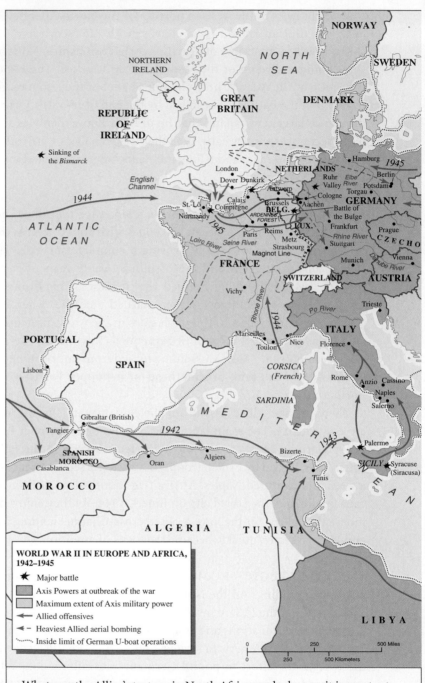

WORLD WAR II IN EUROPE AND AFRICA,
1942–1945

★   Major battle

▓   Axis Powers at outbreak of the war

▒   Maximum extent of Axis military power

→   Allied offensives

◄ -   Heaviest Allied aerial bombing

⋯   Inside limit of German U-boat operations

What was the Allies' strategy in North Africa, and why was it important for the invasion of Italy? Why did Eisenhower's plan on D-day succeed? What was the Battle of the Bulge? What was the role of strategic bombing in the war? Was it effective?

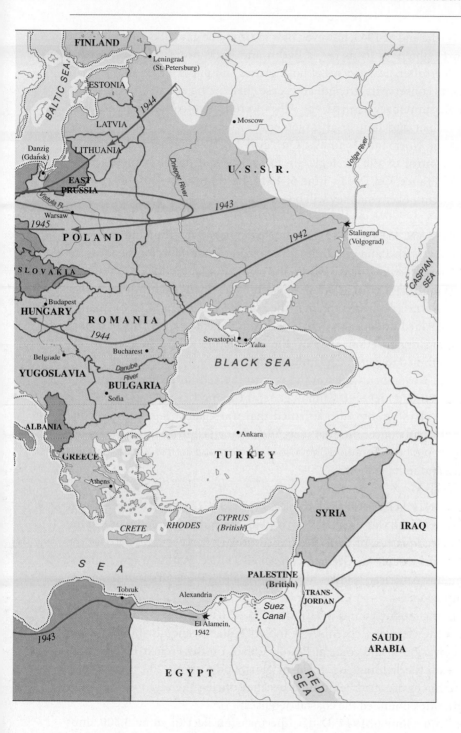

FINLAND

BALTIC SEA

Leningrad
(St. Petersburg)

ESTONIA

1944

LATVIA

Danzig
(Gdańsk)

LITHUANIA

Moscow

Dnieper River

U.S.S.R.

Volga River

EAST
PRUSSIA

Vistula R.

1943

Warsaw

1945

POLAND

1942

Stalingrad
(Volgograd)

CASPIAN SEA

SLOVAKIA

Budapest

HUNGARY

ROMANIA

1944

Sevastopol

Yalta

BLACK SEA

Belgrade

Bucharest

Danube River

YUGOSLAVIA

BULGARIA

Sofia

ALBANIA

Ankara

GREECE

TURKEY

Athens

CRETE

RHODES

CYPRUS
(British)

SYRIA

IRAQ

SEA

PALESTINE
(British)

TRANS-
JORDAN

Tobruk

Alexandria

Suez
Canal

El Alamein,
1942

1943

SAUDI
ARABIA

EGYPT

RED SEA

morale. By the end of 1943, however, new jettisonable gas tanks permitted Allied escort fighters to fly as far as Berlin and back, protecting the bomber groups. Thereafter, heavy losses of both planes and pilots forced the German Luftwaffe to conserve its strength and cease challenging every Allied mission.

With air supremacy assured, the Allies were free to concentrate on their primary urban and industrial targets and, when the time came, provide cover for the Normandy landings. On April 14, 1944, General Eisenhower assumed control of the strategic air forces for the invasion of German-controlled France. On D-day, June 6, 1944, he told the troops, "If you see fighting aircraft over you, they will be ours."

THE TEHRAN MEETING   Late in November 1943, Churchill and Roosevelt had met with Stalin in Tehran, Iran, to coordinate plans for the invasion of France and a Soviet offensive from the east. After Churchill and Roosevelt assured Stalin that a cross-Channel invasion was finally coming, the Soviet premier in return promised to enter the war against Japan after Germany's defeat. The Allied leaders also agreed to begin plans for a new international peacekeeping organization and for the occupation of postwar Germany. Politics continued to complicate military strategy.

Earlier in November, while on the way to the Tehran meeting, Churchill and Roosevelt had met with China's general Chiang Kai-shek in Cairo. The resulting Declaration of Cairo affirmed that war against Japan would continue until Japan's unconditional surrender, that all Chinese territories taken by Japan would be restored to China, and that "in due course Korea shall become free and independent."

D-DAY AND AFTER   In early 1944, General Dwight D. Eisenhower, smart, efficient, and well organized, arrived in London to take command at the Supreme Headquarters of the Allied Expeditionary Force and prepare for the cross-Channel assault on German-controlled France. Within a few months, over 1 million American soldiers were training along England's southern coast for the invasion.

The daring cross-Channel invasion of France, called Operation Overlord, surprised the Germans. Eisenhower fooled Hitler's generals into believing that the invasion would come at Pas-de-Calais, on the French-Belgian border. Instead, the landings occurred in Normandy, about 200 miles south. Airborne forces dropped behind the beaches during the night while planes and battleships pounded the coastal defenses.

At dawn on June 6, 1944, D-day, the invasion fleet of some 5,300 ships carrying 370,000 soldiers and sailors filled the horizon off the Normandy

Operation Overlord

General Dwight D. Eisenhower instructing paratroopers before they board their airplanes to launch the D-day assault.

coast. Overhead, thousands of Allied planes supported the invasion force. Sleepy German soldiers awoke to see the vast armada arrayed before them. Despite Eisenhower's meticulous planning and the imposing array of Allied troops and firepower, the D-day invasion almost failed. Cloud cover and German anti-aircraft fire caused many of the paratroopers and glider pilots to miss their landing zones. Oceangoing landing craft delivered their troops to the wrong locations. Low clouds led the Allied planes to drop their bombs too far inland. The naval bombardment was equally ineffective. In addition, rough seas made many soldiers seasick and capsized dozens of landing craft. Over 1,000 men drowned. Waterlogged radios failed to work, and the deafening noise of the artillery and gunfire made oral communication impossible.

On Utah Beach the American troops made it in against relatively light opposition, but farther east, on a four-mile segment designated Omaha Beach, bombardment failed to take out the German defenders, and the Americans were caught in heavily mined water. In just ten minutes, 197 of the 205 men in one rifle company were killed or wounded. By nightfall the bodies of some 5,000 killed or wounded Allied soldiers were strewn across Normandy's

The landing at Normandy

D-day, June 6, 1944. Before they could huddle under a seawall and begin to root out the region's Nazi defenders, soldiers on Omaha Beach had to cross a fifty-yard stretch that exposed them to bullets fired from machine guns housed in concrete bunkers.

beaches. German losses were even heavier; entire units were decimated or captured. Operation Overlord was the greatest amphibious invasion in the annals of warfare. It was also a climactic battle of World War II, but it was small when compared with the offensive launched by the Russians a few weeks after D-day. Between June and August 1944 the Red Army killed, wounded, or captured more German soldiers than were stationed in all of western Europe. Still, the Normandy invasion was a turning point in the war—and a pivotal point in America's rise to global power. With the beachhead secured, the Allied leaders knew that victory was now in their grasp.

Within two weeks after D-day, the Allies had landed 1 million troops, 556,000 tons of supplies, and 170,000 vehicles. They had seized a beachhead sixty miles wide and five to fifteen miles deep. They continued to pour men and supplies onto the beaches and to edge inland through the marshes and hedgerows. A stubborn Hitler issued disastrous orders to contest every inch of land. Field Marshal Erwin Rommel, convinced that all was lost, began to intrigue for a separate peace. Other like-minded German officers, sure that the war was hopeless, tried to kill Hitler at his headquarters on July 20, 1944, but the Führer survived the bomb blast, and hundreds of conspirators and suspects were tortured to death. Rommel was granted the option of suicide, which he took.

Meanwhile, Hitler's tactics brought calamity to the German forces in western France. On July 25, American units broke out westward into Brittany and eastward toward Paris. On August 15 a joint American-French invasion force landed on the French Mediterranean coast and raced up the Rhone Valley. German resistance in France collapsed. A division of the Free French Resistance, aided by American forces, had the honor of liberating Paris on August 25. Hitler's forces retreated toward the German border, and by mid-September most of France and Belgium had been cleared of enemy troops.

LEAPFROGGING TO TOKYO

Even in the Pacific, relegated to a lower priority, Allied forces had brought the war within reach of the enemy's homeland by the end of 1944. The war's first American offensive, in fact, had been in the southwest Pacific. There the Japanese, stopped at the Battles of Coral Sea and Midway, had thrust into the southern Solomon Islands and were building an airstrip on Guadalcanal, from which they would be able to attack Allied transportation routes to Australia. On August 7, 1942, two months before the North Africa landings, the First Marine Division landed on Guadalcanal and seized the airstrip.

MACARTHUR IN NEW GUINEA   Meanwhile, American and Australian forces under General Douglas MacArthur had begun to push the Japanese out of their positions on New Guinea's northern coast. These costly battles, fought through some of the hottest, most humid, and most mosquito-infested swamps in the world, secured the eastern tip of New Guinea by the end of January 1943.

At this stage, American war planners were confronted with two propositions by the leaders of rival branches of the armed service, the army and the navy. The vainglorious MacArthur, sometimes accused of being a legend in his own mind, proposed to move his forces westward along the northern coast of New Guinea toward the Philippines and ultimately to Tokyo. Naval admiral Chester Nimitz argued for a sweep through the islands of the central

SOVIET UNION

SEA OF OKHOTSK

Russians 1944–1945

SAKHALIN

MONGOLIA

MANCHURIA

KURIL ISLANDS

Peking

KOREA

SEA OF JAPAN

JAPAN

C H I N A

YELLOW SEA

Hiroshima

Tokyo

Nanking

Nagasaki

Shanghai

EAST CHINA SEA

BONIN ISLANDS

HIMALAYAS

Chungking

Stilwell Road

Ledo

1943

K'un-ming

Burma Road

Lashio

BURMA (MYANMAR)

INDIA

THAILAND

Rangoon (Yangon)

FRENCH INDOCHINA

FORMOSA (TAIWAN)

HONG KONG

OKINAWA

Iwo Jima

1945

PHILIPPINE SEA

1945

MARIANA ISLANDS

Saipan

Guam

Corregidor 1942

BATAAN PENINSULA

SOUTH CHINA SEA

Luzon

Manila

PHILIPPINES

Leyte

Mindanao

PALAU

CAROLINE

BRITISH MALAYA

BRUNEI

SARAWAK

BRITISH NORTH BORNEO

ADMIRALTY ISLANDS

1944–1945

Singapore

SUMATRA

Equator

BORNEO

CELEBES (SULAWESI)

MOLUCCAS

1943

BISMARCK SEA

DUTCH EAST INDIES

Java Sea

JAVA

TIMOR

NEW GUINEA

Port Moresby

INDIAN

OCEAN

1942

0   400   800   1,200 Miles
0   400   800   1,200 Kilometers

AUSTRALIA

What was "leapfrogging"? Why were the battles in the Marianas a major turning point in the war? What was the significance of the Battle of Leyte Gulf? How did the battle at Okinawa affect the way both sides proceeded in the war? Why did President Truman decide to drop atomic bombs on Hiroshima and Nagasaki?

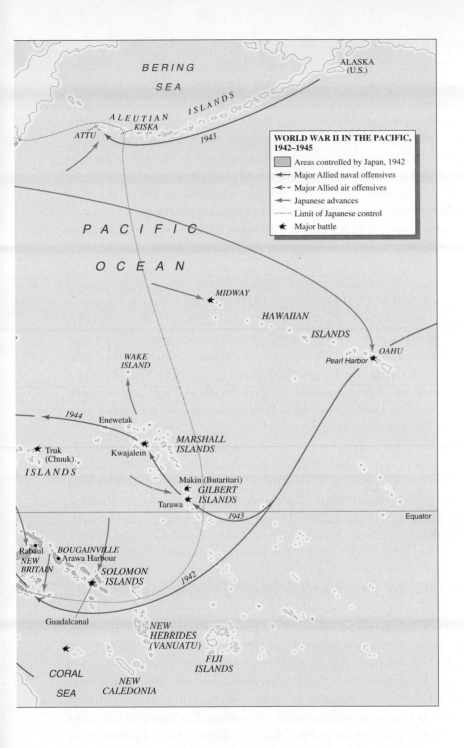

BERING SEA

ALASKA (U.S.)

ALEUTIAN ISLANDS
KISKA
ATTU
1943

PACIFIC

OCEAN

WORLD WAR II IN THE PACIFIC, 1942–1945

Areas controlled by Japan, 1942
Major Allied naval offensives
Major Allied air offensives
Japanese advances
Limit of Japanese control
★ Major battle

MIDWAY

HAWAIIAN

ISLANDS

WAKE ISLAND

OAHU
Pearl Harbor

1944 Enewetak

★ Truk (Chuuk)

Kwajalein

MARSHALL ISLANDS

ISLANDS

Makin (Butaritari)
★ GILBERT ISLANDS
Tarawa
1943
Equator

Rabaul
NEW BRITAIN
BOUGAINVILLE
Arawa Harbour
SOLOMON ISLANDS
1942

Guadalcanal

NEW HEBRIDES (VANUATU)

FIJI ISLANDS

CORAL

SEA

NEW CALEDONIA

Pacific to Formosa and China. The Combined Chiefs of Staff agreed to pursue both plans.

During the Battle of the Bismarck Sea (March 2–3, 1943), American bombers sank eight Japanese troopships and ten warships carrying reinforcements. Thereafter the Japanese dared not risk sending transports to reinforce points under siege, making it possible for the Allies to use the tactic of neutralizing Japanese strongholds with airpower and sea power and moving on, leaving them to die on the vine. Some called it leapfrogging or island-hopping, and it was a major factor contributing to the Allied victory. By the end of 1943, MacArthur's forces controlled the northern coast of New Guinea.

NIMITZ IN THE CENTRAL PACIFIC Admiral Nimitz's advance through the central Pacific had as its first target Tarawa in the Gilbert Islands. Tarawa was one of the most heavily protected islands in the Pacific. In a pitched battle nearly 1,000 U.S. soldiers, sailors, and marines lost their lives rooting out 4,000 Japanese soldiers who refused to surrender. The Gilbert Islands provided airfields from which the Seventh Air Force began softening up strong points in the Marshall Islands to the northwest. Japanese planes completely abandoned the region.

In the Battle of the Philippine Sea, fought mostly in the air on June 19–20, 1944, the Japanese lost 3 more carriers, 2 submarines, and over 300 planes, at a cost of only 17 U.S. planes. The battle secured the Mariana Islands, and soon large B-29 bombers were winging their way to the first systematic bombing of the Japanese homeland. Defeat in the Marianas convinced General Tōjō that the war was lost. On July 18, 1944, he and his entire cabinet resigned.

THE BATTLE OF LEYTE GULF With New Guinea and the Mariana Islands all but conquered, MacArthur and Nimitz focused on liberating the Philippines. MacArthur's forces assaulted the islands on October 20, 1944, landing first on Leyte. The Japanese, knowing that loss of the Philippines would cut them off from the essential resources of the Dutch East Indies (Indonesia), brought in fleets from three directions. The three encounters that resulted on October 25 came to be known collectively as the Battle of Leyte Gulf, the largest naval engagement in history. The Japanese lost most of their remaining sea power and the ability to defend the Philippines. Also remarkable was the first use of suicide attacks as Japanese pilots crash-dived into American ships, killing themselves in the process. Called kamikazes (a reference to the "divine wind" that centuries before was believed to have saved Japan from a Mongol invasion) by the Allies and *tokkotai* (meaning "special attack force") by the Japanese, most of the pilots were not fanatical volunteers. The majority of the thousand or so who died were very young student draftees (between the ages of seventeen and twenty-four) who had been ordered to steer their planes into Allied ships. Whatever their motives, the *tokkotai* caused substantial damage.

A NEW AGE IS BORN

ROOSEVELT'S FOURTH TERM   In 1944, war or no war, the calendar dictated another presidential election. This time the Republicans turned to a former crime fighter and New York governor, Thomas E. Dewey, as their candidate. No Democrat challenged Roosevelt, but a fight did develop over the second spot on the ticket. Vice President Henry Wallace had aggravated southern conservatives and northern city bosses, who feared his ties with labor unions, so Roosevelt finally chose the relatively unknown Missouri senator Harry S. Truman.

Dewey ran under the same handicap as Alf Landon and Wendell Willkie had before him. He did not propose to dismantle Roosevelt's programs; rather, he argued that it was time for younger men to replace the "tired" old leaders of the New Deal. The problem was that even though he was considerably younger than Roosevelt, Dewey showed few signs of vitality. Although blessed with a silky voice and a stylish wardrobe, he was ill at ease in public, stiff, formal, seemingly arrogant, and worst of all—dull. Roosevelt showed signs of illness and exhaustion, but nevertheless, on November 7, 1944, he was once again elected, this time by a popular vote of 25.6 million to 22 million and an electoral vote of 432 to 99.

CONVERGING MILITARY FRONTS   Meanwhile, Allied forces were mired in war in Europe; complete victory remained elusive. After the quick sweep across France, the Allies lost momentum in the fall of 1944 and settled down to slugging it out along the border of Germany. The armies would fight along this line all winter, but first, on December 16, 1944, the Germans sprang a surprise in the rugged Ardennes Forest, where the Allied line was thinnest. The Nazis advanced along a fifty-mile bulge in the Allied lines in Belgium and Luxembourg (hence the name the Battle of the Bulge) before they stalled at Bastogne. Reinforced by the Allies just before it was surrounded,

Bastogne held out for six days against relentless attacks. The American situation remained desperate until December 23, when the weather improved, allowing Allied airpower to drop supplies and attack the Germans. On December 26, the besieged American army at Bastogne was relieved.

Germany's sudden counterattack upset Eisenhower's timetable and made continued coordination with the Soviet army even more crucial. Having poured resources into the battle at Bastogne, the Nazis were unable to hold the eastern front when the Soviets began their final offensive in January 1945. The destruction of Hitler's last reserve units at the Battle of the Bulge also left open the door to Germany's heartland. The western offensives began in February, and by early March Allied forces were crossing the Rhine River into Germany. By that time the Soviet offensive on the eastern front had also reached the German border.

YALTA AND THE POSTWAR WORLD   As the final offensives against Germany got under way, the Big Three leaders met again, in early February 1945 at Yalta, a resort in southern Russia. While the focus at Tehran in 1943

The Yalta Conference

Churchill, Roosevelt, and Stalin confer on the shape of the postwar world in February 1945.

had been on wartime strategy, the leaders now discussed the shape of the postwar world. Stalin was self-confident, demanding, and sarcastic. He knew that the Soviet forces' control of key areas ensured that his demands would be met. Two aims loomed large in Roosevelt's thinking. One was the need to ensure that the Soviet Union would join the war against Japan. The other was based upon the lessons he had drawn from the previous world war. Chief among the mistakes to be remedied were the failures of the United States to join the League of Nations and of the Allies to maintain a united front in negotiations with the German aggressors after the war.

The Yalta meeting thus began by calling for a conference to create a new world organization, called the United Nations. The conferees also decided that substantive decisions in the new organization's Security Council would require the agreement of its five permanent members: the United States, Britain, the Soviet Union, France, and China.

GERMANY AND EASTERN EUROPE   With Hitler's Third Reich empire stumbling to its doom, the leaders at Yalta had to make arrangements for the postwar governance of Germany. The war map dictated the basic pattern of occupation zones: the Soviet Union would control eastern Germany, and the Western Allies would control the rich industrial areas of the west. The national capital of Berlin, isolated within the Soviet zone, would be jointly occupied. Churchill and Roosevelt insisted that liberated France receive a zone along its border with Germany and one in Berlin. Austria was similarly divided, with Vienna, like Berlin, under joint occupation within the Soviet zone. Russian demands for reparations of $20 billion to the Allies, half of which would go to the Soviet Union, were referred to a reparations commission. That commission never reached agreement, although the Soviets took untold amounts of German machinery and equipment from their occupation zone.

With respect to Eastern Europe, where Soviet forces were advancing on a broad front, there was little the Western Allies could do to influence events. Poland became the main focus of Western concern. Britain and France had gone to war in 1939 to defend it, and now, six years later, the course of the war had ironically left Poland's fate in the hands of the Soviets. Events had long foreshadowed the outcome. When they entered Poland in 1944, the Soviets allowed a puppet regime in Lublin to take control of civil administration. The Soviets refused to recognize the legitimacy of Poland's government-in-exile in London, formed by officials who had fled the country following Hitler's invasion in 1939. With Soviet troops at the gates of Warsaw, the underground resistance in the city rose up against the Nazi occupiers. But because the Polish underground supported the Polish government-in-exile, the Soviet armies idled for two months while the Nazis killed thousands of Poles in Warsaw, potential rivals of the Soviets' Lublin puppet government.

At Yalta the Big Three promised to sponsor free elections, democratic governments, and constitutional safeguards of freedom throughout Europe. The Yalta Declaration of Liberated Europe reaffirmed faith in the principles of the Atlantic Charter and the Declaration of the United Nations, but in the end it made little difference. It may have postponed Communist takeovers in Eastern Europe for a few years, but before long Communist members of coalition governments had purged the opposition. Russia, twice invaded by Germany in the twentieth century, was determined to create compliant buffer states between it and the German state.

YALTA'S LEGACY Critics later attacked the Yalta agreements for "giving" Eastern Europe over to Soviet domination. Some argued that Roosevelt's declining health allowed him to buckle under Stalin's insistent demands. Yet the course of the war, not personal diplomacy, shaped the actions at Yalta. The Soviets had the upper hand in Eastern Europe. Perhaps the most bitterly criticized of the Yalta accords was a secret agreement on the Far East, made public after the war. The Combined Chiefs of Staff estimated that Japan could hold out for eighteen months after the defeat of Germany. Costly campaigns thus lay ahead, and the atomic bomb was still an expensive and untested gamble.

Roosevelt thus believed he had no choice but to accept Stalin's demands on postwar arrangements in the Far East, subject technically to agreement later by China's general Chiang Kai-shek. Stalin wanted continued Soviet control of Outer Mongolia through its puppet People's Republic, acquisition of the Kuril Islands from Japan, and recovery of rights and territory lost after the Russo-Japanese War of 1905. Stalin in return promised to enter the war against Japan two or three months after the German defeat, recognize Chinese sovereignty over Manchuria, and conclude a treaty of friendship and alliance with the Chinese Nationalists. Roosevelt's concessions would later appear in a different light, but given their geographic advantages in Asia, as in Eastern Europe, the Soviets were in a position to get what they wanted in any case.

THE COLLAPSE OF THE THIRD REICH By 1945 the collapse of Nazi resistance was imminent, but President Roosevelt did not live to join the celebrations. Throughout 1944 his health had been declining, and on April 12, 1945, while drafting a speech, he died from a cerebral hemorrhage.

Hitler's Germany collapsed less than a month later. The Allied armies rolled up almost unopposed to the Elbe River, where they met advance detachments of Soviets on April 25. Three days later Italian partisans killed Mussolini as he tried to flee. In Berlin, which was under siege by the Soviets, Hitler married his mistress, Eva Braun, in an underground bunker on April 30, just before killing her and himself. On May 2, Berlin fell to the Soviets. That day, German forces in Italy surrendered. On May 7, the Germans signed an unconditional surrender treaty in the Allied headquarters at Reims, France.

Massive victory celebrations on V-E day, May 8, 1945, were tempered by the tragedies that had engulfed the world: mourning for the lost president and the death and mutilation of untold millions. Most shocking was the Allied armies' confirmation of the existence of the death camps in which Nazis had sought to apply their "final solution" to the "Jewish problem": the wholesale extermination of some 6 million Jews, along with more than 1 million others from occupied countries.

May 8, 1945

The celebration in New York City's Times Square on V-E day.

During the war, reports from Red Cross and underground sources had amassed growing evidence of Germany's systematic genocide of European Jews. Stories appeared in major American newspapers as early as 1942, but they were nearly always buried on inside pages. Reports of such horror seemed beyond belief. In addition, American government officials, even some Jewish leaders, dragged their feet on the question for fear that relief efforts for Jewish refugees might stir latent anti-Semitism at home. Finally Roosevelt had set up a War Refugee Board in 1944. It managed to rescue about 200,000 European Jews and some 20,000 others. But more might have been done. The Allies rejected a plan to bomb the rail lines leading to Auschwitz the largest death camp in Poland, although American planes hit industries five miles away. Moreover, few refugees were accepted by the United States. The Allied handling of the Holocaust was inept at best and disgraceful at worst.

A GRINDING WAR AGAINST JAPAN   The sobering thought that Japan must still be defeated cast a further pall over the victory celebrations. American forces continued to assault the Japanese Empire in the early months of 1945, but at a heavy cost. On February 19, 1945, U.S. marines invaded Iwo Jima, a volcanic island 760 miles from Tokyo that was needed in order to provide a fighter escort for bombers over Japan and a landing strip for disabled B-29 bombers. It took nearly six weeks to secure the site from Japanese defenders hiding in caves, and the cost was high: more than 20,000 American casualties, including nearly 7,000 deaths.

The fight for Okinawa, beginning on Easter Sunday, April 1, was even bloodier. The island was large enough to afford a staging area for the planned invasion of the Japanese islands, and its capture required the largest amphibious operation of the Pacific war, involving some 300,000 troops. The fight raged until late June, incurring nearly 50,000 American casualties. The Japanese lost an estimated 140,000, including about 42,000 Okinawans. When resistance on Okinawa collapsed, the Japanese emperor instructed his new prime minister to seek peace, but he included conditions unacceptable to the Allies.

THE ATOMIC BOMB   In 1939 the physicist Albert Einstein had alerted President Roosevelt to German research on nuclear fission. In response the president in 1940 had launched the $2-billion top-secret Manhattan Project, involving over 120,000 scientists and technicians in several locations. In a laboratory in Los Alamos, New Mexico, under the direction of J. Robert

The American Chemical Society exhibit on atomic energy

J. R. Oppenheimer points to a photograph of the huge column of smoke and flame caused by the bomb upon Hiroshima.

Oppenheimer, a group of physicists worked out the scientific and technical problems of the bomb's construction. On July 16, 1945, the first atomic fireball rose from the desert. Oppenheimer said later that in the bunker where observers watched the test blast, "a few people laughed, a few people cried, most people were silent." President Harry S. Truman, thrust into the presidency upon Roosevelt's death in April, wrote in his diary, "We have discovered the most terrible bomb in the history of the world."

Word of the new weapon changed all strategic calculations. How to use this awful weapon posed profound problems. Some scientists favored a demonstration explosion for the Japanese in a remote area, but that idea was vetoed because only two bombs were available, and even those might misfire.

The choice of targets received more consideration. After deciding against Kyōto, Japan's ancient capital and repository of national and religious treasures, priority went to Hiroshima, a port city of 400,000 people in southern Japan, which was a center of war industries, headquarters of the Japanese Second General Army, and command center for the homeland's defenses.

On July 25, 1945, President Truman ordered the atomic bomb dropped if Japan did not surrender before August 3. Although an intense scholarly debate has emerged over the decision to drop the bomb, it is clear that Truman believed that the atomic bomb would save lives by avoiding an American invasion against defenders who would fight like "savages, ruthless, merciless, and fanatic."

The ferocious Japanese defense of Okinawa had convinced military planners that an amphibious invasion of Japan itself, scheduled to begin on November 1, 1945, could cost as many as 250,000 Allied casualties and even more Japanese losses. Moreover, some 100,000 Allied prisoners of war being held in Japan would most likely be executed when an invasion began. It is important to remember as well that the bombing of cities and the consequent killing of civilians had become accepted military practice during 1945. Once the Japanese navy was destroyed, American ships had roamed the Japanese coastline, shelling targets onshore. American planes had bombed at will and mined the waters of the Inland Sea. Tokyo, Nagoya, and other major cities had been devastated by firestorms created by incendiary bombs. The firebomb raids on Tokyo on a single night in March 1945 killed 100,000 civilians and left over 1 million people homeless. The use of atomic bombs on Japanese cities was thus seen as a logical next step to end the war without an invasion of Japan. As it turned out, American scientists greatly underestimated the physical effects of the atomic bomb. They predicted that 20,000 people would be killed. The number would be much higher.

On July 26, the heads of the American, British, and Chinese governments issued the Potsdam Declaration, demanding that Japan surrender or face "prompt and utter destruction." The deadline passed, and at 8:15 A.M. on August 6, flying at 31,600 feet, a B-29 bomber named *Enola Gay* released the five-ton uranium bomb nicknamed Little Boy. Forty-three seconds later, as the *Enola Gay* turned sharply to avoid the blast, the bomb tumbled to an altitude of 1,900 feet, where it exploded as planned with the force of 20,000 tons of TNT. A blinding flash of light was followed by a fireball towering to 40,000 feet. The tail gunner on the *Enola Gay* described the scene: "It's like bubbling molasses down there . . . the mushroom is spreading out . . . fires are springing up everywhere . . . it's like a peep into hell."

The aftermath of "Little Boy"

This image shows the wasteland that remained after the atomic bomb "Little Boy" decimated Hiroshima in 1945.

The shock wave, firestorm, cyclonic winds, and radioactive rain killed some 80,000 people. By the end of the year, the death toll had reached 140,000 as the effects of radiation burns and infection took their toll. In addition, 70,000 buildings were destroyed, and four square miles of the city turned to rubble.

Two days after the Hiroshima bombing an opportunistic Soviet Union, eager to share the spoils of victory, hastened to enter the war in Asia. The Allies had long been urging Stalin to join their fight against the Japanese, but the Soviet dictator had delayed as long as possible so as to conserve economic and human resources. Now, however, with the Japanese on the verge of capitulation, he rushed to engage the Japanese in order to share in the spoils of victory. Truman and his aides, frustrated by the stubborn refusal of Japanese military and political leaders to surrender and fearful that the Soviet Union's entry into the war would complicate negotiations, ordered the second atomic bomb dropped. On August 9, a B-29 aircraft named *Bockscar*, carrying a bomb dubbed Fat Man, flew over its primary target, Kokura. The city was so shrouded in haze and smoke from an earlier air raid, however, that *Bockscar* turned to its secondary target, Nagasaki, where at 11:02 A.M. it dropped its terrifying bomb, killing 36,000 people. That night the Japanese emperor urged his cabinet to surrender on the sole condition that he remain as sovereign. The next day the U.S. government announced its willingness to let the emperor keep his throne, but under the authority of an Allied supreme commander. Frantic exchanges ended with Japanese acceptance of the terms on August 14, 1945, when the emperor himself delivered a radio message announcing the surrender to his people. On September 2, 1945, General MacArthur and other Allied representatives accepted Japan's formal surrender on board the battleship *Missouri*.

THE FINAL LEDGER

Thus ended the most deadly conflict in human history. One estimate has it that 70 million fought in the war, at a cost of some 50 million military and civilian dead, including those murdered in Nazi concentration camps. The Soviet Union suffered the greatest losses of all: over 13 million military deaths, more than 7 million civilian deaths, and at least 25 million left homeless. World War II was more costly for the United States than any other foreign war: 292,000 battle deaths and 114,000 other deaths. But in proportion to its population, the United States suffered a loss far smaller than that of any of the other major Allies or their enemies, and American territory escaped the devastation inflicted on so many other parts of the world.

World War II transformed American life. Mobilization for the war stimulated a phenomenal increase in productivity and brought full employment, thus ending the Great Depression and laying the foundation for an era of unprecedented prosperity. New technologies and products developed for military purposes—radar, computers, electronics, plastics and synthetics, jet engines, rockets, atomic energy—began to transform the private sector as well. And new opportunities for African Americans and other minorities as well as for women set in motion changes that would culminate in the civil rights movement of the 1960s and the feminist movement of the 1970s.

The Democratic party benefited from the war effort by solidifying its control of both the White House and Congress. The dramatic expansion of the federal government occasioned by the war continued after 1945. Presidential authority and prestige increased enormously at the expense of congressional and state power. The isolationist sentiment in foreign relations that had been so powerful in the 1920s and 1930s disintegrated as the United States emerged from the war with far-flung global responsibilities and interests. Thus the war's end opened a new era for the United States in the world arena. It accelerated the growth of American power while devastating all other world powers, leaving the United States economically and militarily the strongest nation on earth.

CHAPTER SUMMARY

- **WWII and American Society** White and black Americans migrated to states West of the Mississippi, and especially to the Far West, to take jobs in factories; unemployment was soon a thing of the past. Farmers, too, recovered from hard times. Many women took nontraditional jobs, some in the military. About 1 million African Americans served in the military, in segregated units. Among the most famous were some 600 pilots trained in Tuskegee, Alabama. Japanese Americans, however, lost their civil rights; they were interned in "war relocation camps" in the interior, far from the West Coast, where most of them had lived and worked.

- **Road to Allied Victory** The immediate war aim was to defeat Adolf Hitler in Europe. In 1942, British and American troops were engaging German and Italian troops in North Africa; and by 1943, all of North Africa was controlled by the Allies. From there they launched attacks on Sicily and then Italy. Joseph Stalin, meanwhile, demanded a full-scale Allied attack on the Atlantic coast to ease pressure on the eastern front, but D-day was delayed until June 6, 1944. Meanwhile, areas under Axis control were heavily bombed in an unsuccessful attempt to pound Germany into submission.

- **The Pacific War** The Japanese advance was halted as early as June 1942 with the Battle of Midway. Then began the process of regaining territory island by island. The American army fought slow, costly battles in New Guinea, then, in 1943, headed toward the Philippines. Fierce resistance at Iwo Jima and Okinawa and Japan's refusal to surrender after the firebombing of Tokyo led the new president, Harry Truman, to order the use of the newly developed atomic bomb.

- **Postwar World** In January 1942, twenty-six nations at was with the Axis Powers, seeing the need for a permanent peacekeeping force, signed the Declaration of the United Nations. The Big Three—Franklin Roosevelt, Winston Churchill, and Joseph Stalin—meeting in Yalta, on the Crimean Sea, in February 1945, decided that Europe would be divided into occupation zones, in which the Allies would sponsor free elections and democratic governments. It soon became clear, however, that Stalin would not honor that agreement.

CHRONOLOGY

May 1942	Battle of the Coral Sea
June 1942	Battle of Midway
January 1943	Roosevelt, Churchill, and the Combined Chiefs of Staff meet at Casablanca
July 1943	Allied forces land on Sicily
November–December 1943	Roosevelt and Churchill meet Stalin for the first time, in Tehran
June 6, 1944	D-day
February 1945	At the Yalta Conference, Roosevelt, Churchill, and Stalin plan the shape of the postwar world
February 1945	U.S. Marines capture Iwo Jima
April 12, 1945	Franklin Roosevelt dies
April 30, 1945	Hitler commits suicide
May 8, 1945	V-E day
August 6, 1945	Atomic bomb is dropped on Hiroshima
August 9, 1945	Atomic bomb is dropped on Nagasaki
September 2, 1945	Japanese surrender

KEY TERMS & NAMES

Part Seven

THE

AMERICAN

AGE

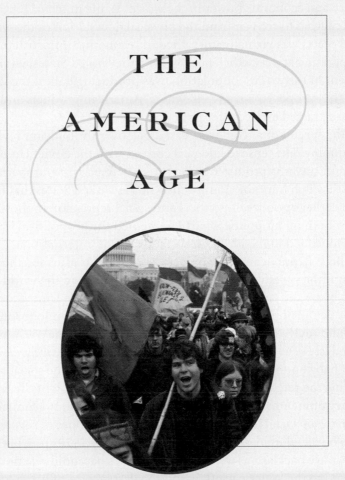

T he United States emerged from World War II the preeminent military and economic power in the world. While much of Europe and Asia struggled to recover from the physical devastation of the war, the United States was virtually unscathed, its economic infrastructure intact and operating at peak efficiency. By 1955 the United States, with only 6 percent of the world's population, was producing half of the world's goods. In Europe, Japan, and elsewhere, American products and popular culture attracted excited attention.

Yet the specter of a "cold war" cast a pall over the buoyant revival of the economy. The tense ideological contest with the Soviet Union and Communist China produced numerous foreign crises and sparked a domestic witch hunt for Communists in the United States that far surpassed earlier episodes of political and social repression in the nation's history. Both major political parties accepted the geopolitical assumptions embedded in the ideological cold war with international communism. Both Republican and Democratic presidents affirmed the need to "contain" the spread of Communist influence around the world.

This bedrock assumption eventually embroiled the United States in a costly war in Southeast Asia, which destroyed Lyndon Johnson's presidency and revived isolationist sentiments. The Vietnam War was also the catalyst for a countercultural movement in which young idealists of the "baby boom" generation promoted many overdue social reforms, including the reforms that were the focus of the civil rights, feminist, and environmental movements. But the youth revolt also contributed to an array of social ills, from street riots to drug abuse to sexual promiscuity. The social upheavals of the 1960s and early 1970s provoked a conservative backlash as well. Richard Nixon's paranoid reaction to his critics led to the Watergate affair and the destruction of his presidency.

Through all of this turmoil, however, the basic premises of welfare-state capitalism that Franklin Roosevelt had instituted with his New Deal programs remained essentially intact. With only a few exceptions, both Republicans and Democrats after 1945 came to accept the notion that the federal government must assume greater responsibility for the welfare of individuals than had heretofore been the case. Even Ronald Reagan, a sharp critic of liberal social-welfare programs, recognized the need for the federal government to provide a "safety net" for those who could not help themselves.

This fragile consensus on public policy began to disintegrate in the late 1980s amid stunning international events and less visible domestic changes. The internal collapse of the Soviet Union and the disintegration of European communism surprised observers and sent policy makers scurrying to respond to a post–cold war world in which the United States remained the only legitimate superpower. After forty-five years, American foreign policy was no longer centered on a single adversary, and world politics lost its bipolar quality. During the early 1990s the two Germanys reunited, apartheid in South Africa ended, and Israel and the Palestinians signed a treaty providing peace—for a while.

At the same time, U.S. foreign policy began to focus less on military power and more on economic competition and technological development. In those arenas, Japan and a reunited Germany challenged the United States for preeminence. By reducing the public's fear of nuclear annihilation, the end of the cold war also reduced American interest in foreign affairs. The presidential election of 1992 was the first since 1936 in which foreign-policy issues played virtually no role. This was an unfortunate development, for post–cold war world affairs remained volatile and dangerous. The implosion of Soviet communism after 1989 unleashed a series of ethnic, nationalist, and separatist conflicts. Responding to pleas for assistance, the United States found itself drawn into crises in faraway locations, such as Bosnia, Somalia, Kosovo, Afghanistan, and Iraq.

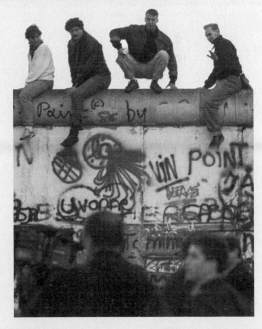

As the new multipolar world careened toward the end of a century and the start of a new millennium, fault lines began to appear in the American social and economic landscape. A gargantuan federal debt and rising annual deficits threatened to bankrupt a nation that was becoming top-heavy with retirees. Without fully realizing it, much less appreciating its cascading consequences, the American population was becoming disproportionately old. The number of people aged ninety-five to ninety-nine doubled between 1980 and 1990, and the number of centenarians increased 77 percent. The proportion of the population aged sixty-five and older rose steadily during the 1990s. By the year 2010, over half of the elderly population was over seventy-five. This demographic fact harbored profound social and political implications. It exerted increasing stress on health-care costs, nursing-home facilities, and the very survival of the Social Security system.

At the same time that the gap between young and old was increasing, so, too, was the disparity between rich and poor. This trend threatened to stratify a society already experiencing rising levels of racial and ethnic tension. Between 1960 and 1990 the gap between the richest 20 percent of the population and the poorest 20 percent doubled. Over 20 percent of all American children in 1990 lived in poverty, and the infant-mortality rate rose. The infant-death rate in Japan was less than half that in the United States. Despite the much-ballyhooed "war-on-poverty" programs initiated by Lyndon Johnson and continued in one form or another by all of his successors, the chronically poor at the start of the twenty-first century were more numerous and more bereft of hope than in 1964.

31

THE FAIR DEAL AND CONTAINMENT

FOCUS QUESTIONS wwnorton.com/studyspace

- How did the cold war emerge?
- How did Harry Truman respond to the Soviet occupation of Eastern Europe?
- What was Truman's Fair Deal?
- What was the background of the Korean War, and how did the United States become involved?
- What were the roots of McCarthyism?

No sooner did the Second World War end than a "cold war" began. The uneasy wartime alliance between the United States and the Soviet Union had collapsed by the fall of 1945. The two strongest nations to emerge from the carnage of World War II could not bridge their ideological differences over such basic issues as human rights, individual liberties, economic freedom, and religious beliefs. Mutual suspicion and a race to gain influence and control over the so-called third world countries further polarized the two nations. The defeat of Japan and Germany had created power vacuums that sucked the United States and the Soviet Union into an unrelenting war of words fed by clashing geopolitical interests. At the same time, the devastation wrought by the war in western Europe and the exhaustion of its peoples led to anti-colonial uprisings in Asia and Africa that threatened to strip Britain and France of their empires. The postwar world was thus an unstable one in which international tensions shaped the contours of domestic politics and culture as well as foreign relations.

Demobilization under Truman

TRUMAN'S UNEASY START   "Who the hell is Harry Truman?" Roosevelt's chief of staff asked the president in the summer of 1944. The question was on more lips when, after less than twelve weeks as vice president, Harry Truman took the presidential oath on April 12, 1945. Clearly he was not as charismatic or as magisterial as Franklin Roosevelt, and that was one of the burdens he would bear. Roosevelt and Truman came from quite different backgrounds. For Truman there had been no inherited wealth, no early contact with the great and near great, no European travel, no Harvard—indeed, no college at all. Born in 1884 in western Missouri, Truman grew up in Independence, outside Kansas City. Too nearsighted to join in the activities of other boys, Truman became bookish and introverted. After high school, however, he spent a few years working in Kansas City banks and grew into an outgoing young man.

During World War I, Truman served in France as captain of an artillery battery. Afterward he opened a clothing business, but it failed during the recession of 1922, and Truman then entered politics. In 1934, Missouri sent him to the U.S. Senate, where he remained fairly obscure until he chaired a committee investigating corruption in defense industries during World War II.

Harry Truman was a plain, decent man who evoked the spirit of Andrew Jackson: his decisiveness, his feistiness, his family loyalty. But that was a side of the man the people came to know only as he settled into the presidency. On his first full day as president, as the war in Asia ground on, he remained awestruck. "Boys, if you ever pray, pray for me now," he told a group of reporters. "I don't know whether you fellows ever had a load of hay fall on you, but when they told me yesterday what had happened, I felt like the moon, the stars and all the planets had fallen on me."

Truman favored much of the New Deal and was even prepared to extend its scope, but he was uneasy with many of the most ardent New Deal reformers. Within ninety days of taking office, he had replaced much of the Roosevelt cabinet with his own choices. On the whole his cabinet was more conservative in outlook and included several mediocrities. Truman suffered the further handicap of seeming to be a caretaker for the remainder of Roosevelt's term. Few expected him to run on his own in 1948.

The new president gave a significant clue to his domestic policies on September 6, 1945, when he sent Congress a comprehensive peacetime program

The Eldridge General Store, Fayette County, Illinois

Postwar America quickly demobilized, turning its attention to the pursuit of abundance.

that proposed to enlarge the New Deal. Its twenty-one points included expansion of unemployment insurance to cover more workers, a higher minimum wage, a permanent Fair Employment Practices Committee, slum clearance and low-rent housing, regional development of the nation's river valleys, and a public-works program. "Not even President Roosevelt asked for so much at one sitting," charged the House Republican leader. "It's just a plain case of out-dealing the New Deal." But Truman did not have the same success as Roosevelt in getting his legislation through Congress. Beset by other problems, Truman soon saw his new domestic proposals mired in disputes over the transition to a peacetime economy.

CONVERTING TO PEACE   The raucous celebrations that greeted Japan's surrender signaled a rapid demobilization of the armed forces and a return to domestic pursuits. The public demanded that the president and Congress bring the troops home as soon as possible. By 1947 the total armed forces had shrunk to 1.5 million from a wartime high of 12 million. By early 1950 the army had been reduced to 600,000 troops.

The military veterans returned to colleges, jobs, wives, and babies. Population growth, which had dropped off sharply in the Depression decade, now soared. Americans born during this postwar period composed what came to be known as the baby boom generation, an oversize population cohort that would become a dominant force shaping the nation's social and economic life.

The end of the war, with its sudden demobilization and conversion to a peacetime economy, generated labor unrest and strikes but not the postwar depression that many had feared. Several shock absorbers cushioned the economic impact of demobilization: unemployment insurance and other Social Security benefits; the Servicemen's Readjustment Act of 1944, known as the GI Bill of Rights, under which the federal government spent $13 billion on military veterans for education, vocational training, medical treatment, unemployment insurance, and loans for building houses and going into business; and most important, the pent-up demand for consumer goods that was fueled by wartime shortages. Instead of sinking into depression after the war, the economy enjoyed a spurt of private investment in new production facilities and equipment.

CONTROLLING INFLATION   The most acute economic problem facing postwar America was not depression but inflation. During the war, America was essentially fully employed. The government also froze wages and prices—and prohibited labor strikes. When wartime controls were removed, prices shot up. Prices of farm commodities soared 14 percent in one month and by the end of 1945 were 30 percent higher than they had been in August. As prices rose, so, too, did corporate profits. Labor unions increasingly demanded that they receive their share of the postwar bounty.

Within six weeks of the war's end, corporations confronted union demands for higher wages and better benefits. A series of strikes followed. By January 1946 more workers were on strike than ever before in U.S. history. In response to a threatened rail strike, President Truman, miffed at what he considered to be excessive union demands, threatened to draft striking railroad workers into the armed forces. The strike ended a few weeks later.

The wartime Office of Price Administration maintained some restraint on price increases while gradually ending the rationing of most goods. After the 1946 congressional elections, Truman gave up the battle to control consumer prices.

PARTISAN CONFLICT   Before the 1946 congressional elections, public discontent ran high, with most of it directed against the administration. Labor union supporters tagged Truman "the No. 1 strikebreaker," while much of the public, angry at striking unions, blamed the White House for the strikes. Critics of the administration had a field day coining campaign slogans. The most effective was the simple "Had enough?" attributed to a

Boston ad agency: the message was that the Democrats had simply been in power too long. In the end, Republicans won majorities in both houses of Congress for the first time since 1928.

The rising public criticism of organized labor spurred the new Republican Congress to pass the Taft-Hartley Labor Act of 1947 to curb the power of the unions. It banned the closed shop (in which nonunion workers could not be hired) but permitted a union shop (in which workers newly hired were required to join the union) except where banned by state law. The anti-union legislation included provi-

Taft-Hartley Act cartoon

Taft and Hartley look for John Lewis, the head of the Mine Workers Union.

sions forbidding "unfair" union practices such as "featherbedding" (paying for work not done), refusing to bargain in good faith, and contributing to political campaigns. Furthermore, union leaders had to take oaths declaring that they were not members of the Communist party. The act also forbade strikes by federal employees and imposed a "cooling-off" period of eighty days on any strike that the president found to be dangerous to the national health or safety.

Truman's veto of the "shocking" Taft-Hartley bill, which unions called "the slave-labor act," restored his credit with labor and brought many unionists who had voted Republican in 1946 back to the Democratic fold. But the bill passed over the president's veto. Its most severe impact was probably on the CIO's Operation Dixie, a drive to win unions a more secure foothold in the South. By 1954 fifteen states, mainly in the South, had used the Taft-Hartley Act's authority to pass "right-to-work" laws forbidding union shops. Those laws also eroded union strength in the North as many firms began to migrate to right-to-work southern states.

Yet the conflicts between Truman and Congress obscured the high degree of bipartisan cooperation in matters of government reorganization and foreign policy. In 1947 a bipartisan majority in Congress passed the National Security Act, which created a National Military Establishment, headed by the secretary of defense with subcabinet Departments of the Army, the Navy, and the Air Force, and the National Security Council, which included the president, the secretary of defense and the heads of the new subcabinet departments, and the secretary of state, among others. The act made permanent the Joint Chiefs of Staff, a wartime innovation, and established the Central Intelligence Agency (CIA) to coordinate global intelligence gathering.

THE COLD WAR

BUILDING THE UNITED NATIONS   The wartime military alliance against Nazism disintegrated after 1945, and the United States entered into a "cold war" with the Soviet Union. The pragmatic Roosevelt had expected that the great powers in the postwar world would have separate geographic spheres of influence but believed he had to temper such realpolitik with an organization "which would satisfy widespread demand in the United States for new idealistic or universalist arrangements for assuring the peace."

On April 25, 1945, two weeks after Roosevelt's death and two weeks before the German surrender, delegates from fifty nations at war with the Axis met in San Francisco to draw up the Charter of the United Nations. Additional members would be admitted by a two-thirds vote of the General Assembly. This body, one of the two major agencies set up by the charter, included delegates from all member nations and was to meet annually in regular session to approve the budget, receive annual reports from UN agencies, and choose members of the Security Council and other bodies.

The Security Council, the other major charter agency, would remain in permanent session and would have "primary responsibility for the maintenance of international peace and security." Its eleven members (fifteen after 1965) included six (later ten) members elected for two-year terms and five permanent members: the United States, the Soviet Union, Britain, France, and China. Each permanent member could veto any question of substance. The Security Council might investigate any dispute, recommend settlement or reference to another UN body—the International Court of Justice at The Hague, in the Netherlands—and take measures, including the use of military force. The U.S. Senate, in sharp contrast to the reception it gave the League of Nations, ratified the UN charter by a vote of 89 to 2.

DIFFERENCES WITH THE SOVIETS   There were signs of trouble in the wartime alliance linking Britain, the Soviet Union, and the United States as early as the spring of 1945 as the Soviet Union set up compliant governments in the nations of Eastern Europe, violating the Yalta promises of democratic elections. Protests against such actions led to Soviet counterprotests that the British and the Americans were negotiating a German surrender in Italy "behind the back of the Soviet Union."

Such was the atmosphere when Truman entered the White House. A few days before the San Francisco conference to organize the United Nations, the president gave Soviet foreign minister Vyacheslav Molotov a tongue-lashing in Washington on the Polish situation. "I have never been talked to like that in my life," Molotov protested. "Carry out your agreements," Truman snapped, "and you won't get talked to like that."

On May 12, 1945, four days after victory in Europe, Winston Churchill sent Truman a telegram: "What is to happen about Europe? An iron curtain is drawn down upon [the Russian] front. We do not know what is going on behind [it]. . . . Surely it is vital now to come to an understanding with Russia, or see where we are with her, before we weaken our armies mortally." Nevertheless, as a gesture of goodwill, and over Churchill's protest, the U.S. forces withdrew from the occupation zone in Germany that had been assigned to the Soviet Union at Yalta. Americans still hoped that the Yalta agreements would be carried out, and they were even more eager to have Soviet help in defeating Japan.

Although the Soviets admitted British and American observers to their sectors of Eastern Europe, there was little the Western powers could have done to prevent Soviet control of the region even if they had kept up their military strength. The presence of Soviet armed forces frustrated the efforts of non-Communists to gain political influence in Eastern European countries. Opposition leaders were exiled, silenced, executed, or imprisoned.

Secretary of State James F. Byrnes, who took office in 1945, struggled through 1946 with the problems of postwar treaties. In early 1947 the Council of Foreign Ministers finally produced treaties for Italy, Hungary, Romania, Bulgaria, and Finland that confirmed Soviet control over Eastern Europe, which in Russian eyes seemed but a parallel to American control over Japan and Western control over most of Germany and all of Italy. The Yalta Conference's guarantees of democracy in Eastern Europe had turned out much like the Open Door policy in China, little more than pious rhetoric sugarcoating the realities of power and national interest. The Soviet Union controlled Eastern Europe and refused to budge.

CONTAINMENT   By the beginning of 1947, relations with the Soviet Union had become even more troubled. The year before, Stalin had pronounced international peace impossible "under the present capitalist development of the world economy." His statement impelled George F. Kennan, counselor of the U.S. embassy in Moscow, to send an 8,000-word dispatch to the State Department, in which he sketched the roots of Soviet policy.

More than a year later, Kennan, back at the State Department in Washington, spelled out his ideas for a proper response to the Soviets. In a 1947 article published anonymously in *Foreign Affairs*, he provided a brilliant historical and psychological analysis of Soviet insecurity and postwar intentions. He predicted that the Soviets would try to fill "every nook and cranny available . . . in the basin of world power." Therefore, he insisted, the United States must pursue "a long-term, patient but firm and vigilant *containment* of Russian expansive tendencies."

Kennan's "containment" concept dovetailed with the outlook of Truman and his advisers. They all harbored a growing fear that the Soviet lust for power reached beyond Eastern Europe, posing dangers in the eastern Mediterranean, the Middle East, and western Europe itself. The Soviet Union especially sought access to the Mediterranean region, long important to Russia for purposes of trade and defense. After the war the Soviet Union pressed Turkey for territorial concessions and the right to build naval bases on the Bosporus, an important gateway between the Black Sea and the Mediterranean. In 1946, civil war broke out in neighboring Greece between a British-backed government and a Communist-led faction that held the northern part of the country. In 1947 the British ambassador informed the U.S. government that the British could no longer bear the economic and military burden of aiding Greece and suggested that the United States assume the responsibility.

THE TRUMAN DOCTRINE AND THE MARSHALL PLAN   On March 12, 1947, Truman asked Congress for $400 million in economic and military aid to Greece and Turkey. In his speech to Congress, the president announced what quickly became known as the Truman Doctrine. Although intended as a response to a specific crisis, its rhetoric was universal. "I believe," Truman declared, "that it must be the policy of the United States to support free peoples who are resisting attempted subjugation by armed minorities or by outside pressures." In 1947, Congress passed the Greek-Turkish aid bill and by 1950 had spent $659 million on the program. Turkey achieved economic stability, and Greece defeated a Communist insurrection in 1949.

Such immediate gains created long-term problems, however. The Truman Doctrine marked the beginning of a contest that people began to call a cold war. Greece and Turkey were but the front lines in an ideological struggle between East and West for world power and influence. That struggle quickly focused on western Europe, where wartime damage had devastated factory production and a severe drought in 1947, followed by a harsh winter, had destroyed crops. Coal shortages in London left only enough fuel to heat and light homes for a few hours each day. In Berlin, people were freezing or starving to death. The transportation system in Europe was in shambles: bridges were out, canals clogged, and rail networks destroyed. Amid the chaos the Communist parties of France and Italy were flourishing.

In the spring of 1947, former general George C. Marshall, who had replaced James Byrnes as secretary of state, called for massive aid to rescue western Europe from disaster and possible Communist subversion. "Our policy," he pledged, "is directed not against country or doctrine, but against hunger, poverty, desperation, and chaos." Marshall offered aid to all European countries, including the Soviet Union, but Moscow refused to participate in the "imperialist" scheme.

In late 1947, Truman submitted his proposal for the European Recovery Program to Congress. Soon thereafter a Communist coup d'état in Czechoslovakia

"It's the Same Thing"

The Marshall Plan, which distributed aid throughout Europe, is represented in this 1949 cartoon as a modern tractor driven by a prosperous farmer. In the foreground a poor, overworked man is yoked to an old-fashioned "Soviet" plow, forced to go over the ground of the "Marshal Stalin Plan," while Stalin himself tries to persuade others that "it's the same thing without mechanical problems."

ended the last remaining coalition government in Eastern Europe. The Communist seizure of power in Prague assured congressional passage of the Marshall Plan, which from 1948 until 1951 provided $13 billion to promote European economic recovery.

DIVIDING GERMANY   The Marshall Plan drew the nations of western Europe closer together, but the breakdown of the wartime alliance with the Soviet Union left the problem of postwar Germany unsettled. The German economy had stagnated, requiring the U.S. Army to carry a staggering burden of relief to prevent civilians from starving. Slowly occupation zones evolved into functioning governments. In 1948 the British, French, and Americans merged their zones, and the "West Germans" elected delegates to a federal constitutional convention.

THE OCCUPATION OF GERMANY AND AUSTRIA

French zone   U.S. zone
British zone   Soviet zone

How did the Allies divide Germany and Austria at the Yalta Conference? What was the "iron curtain"? Why did Truman airlift supplies to Berlin?

Soviet resentment of the Marshall Plan and the political unification of West Germany led the Soviets, in April 1948, to restrict road and rail traffic into West Berlin; on June 23 they stopped all traffic. The next day the Soviets cut off electricity to the western sector of the divided city. The Soviets hoped the blockade would force the Allies to give up either Berlin or the plan to unify Germany. It was war by starvation and intimidation, but Truman stood firm. After considering the use of armed convoys to supply West Berlin, he opted for a massive airlift. At the time it seemed like an impossible task. But the Allied air forces quickly brought in planes from around the world, and soon they were flying in up to 13,000 tons of food, coal, and other supplies a day.

The massive airlift went on for months. Finally, on May 12, 1949, after extended talks, the Soviets lifted the blockade. Before the end of the year, the Federal Republic of Germany had a functioning government. At the end of May 1949, an independent German Democratic Republic arose in the Soviet-dominated eastern zone, thus dividing Germany into two independent states.

ALLIANCES As relations between the Soviets and western Europe chilled, transatlantic unity ripened into a formal military alliance. On April 4, 1949, diplomats signed the North Atlantic Treaty. Twelve nations were represented: the United States, Britain, France, Belgium, the Netherlands, Luxembourg, Canada, Denmark, Iceland, Italy, Norway, and Portugal. Greece and Turkey joined the alliance in 1952, West Germany in 1955, and Spain in 1982. The treaty pledged that an attack against any one of the members would be considered an attack against all. A council of the North Atlantic Treaty Organization (NATO) would govern the alliance. In 1950 the council voted to create an integrated defense force for western Europe. Five years later the Warsaw Treaty Organization appeared as the Eastern European counterpoint to NATO.

The eventful year of 1948 produced another foreign-policy decision with long-term consequences. Late in 1947 the UN General Assembly voted to partition Palestine into Jewish and Arab states. Despite fierce Arab opposition, Jewish leaders proclaimed the independence of the new State of Israel on May 14, 1948. President Truman, who had been in close touch with Jewish leaders at home and abroad, ordered immediate recognition of the new state; the United States was the first nation to do so.

The neighboring Arab states thereupon attacked Israel, which held its own. UN mediators gradually worked out truce agreements with Israel's Arab neighbors, restoring an uneasy peace by May 11, 1949, when Israel joined the United Nations. But the mutual hatred and intermittent warfare between Israel and the Arab states have festered ever since, complicating

NATO

NATO is depicted as a symbol of renewed strength for a battered Europe.

U.S. foreign policy, which has aimed to maintain friendship with both sides while insisting on the legitimacy of the Israeli nation.

CIVIL RIGHTS DURING THE 1940S

The social tremors triggered by World War II and the onset of the cold war transformed America's racial landscape. The government-sponsored racism of the German Nazis, the Italian Fascists, and the Japanese imperialists focused attention on the need for the United States to improve its own race relations and to provide for equal rights under the law.

For most of his political career, Harry Truman had shown little concern for the plight of African Americans. He had grown up in western Missouri assuming that blacks and whites preferred to be segregated from one another. As president, however, he began to reassess his convictions. In the fall of 1946, Truman hosted a delegation of civil rights activists who urged him to condemn the resurgence of the Ku Klux Klan and the lynching of African Americans. Truman soon appointed a Committee on Civil Rights to investigate racist violence and recommend preventive measures. In its report the committee urged the renewal of the Fair Employment Practices Committee and the creation of a permanent civil rights commission to investigate abuses. It also argued that federal aid be denied to any state that mandated segregated schools and public facilities.

On July 26, 1948, Truman banned racial discrimination in the hiring of federal employees. Four days later he issued an executive order ending racial segregation in the armed forces. The air force and navy quickly complied, but the army dragged its feet until the early 1950s. By 1960 the armed forces were the most racially integrated of all national organizations.

JACKIE ROBINSON   Meanwhile, racial segregation was being confronted in a much more public field of endeavor: professional baseball. In April 1947, as the baseball season opened, the National League's Brooklyn Dodgers included the first black player to cross the color line in major league baseball: Jackie Robinson. Born in Georgia and raised in California, Robinson was an army veteran and baseball player in the Negro leagues. Branch Rickey, president of the Dodgers, selected Robinson to integrate professional baseball not only because of his athletic potential but also because of his willingness to control his temper in the face of virulent racism. During his first season with the Dodgers, teammates and opposing players viciously baited Robinson, pitchers threw at him, base runners spiked him, and spectators booed and taunted him in every city. Hotels refused him rooms, and restaurants denied him service. Hate mail arrived by the bucket load. On the other hand, black spectators were electrified by Robinson's courageous example; they turned out in droves to see him play.

As time passed, Robinson won over many racist fans and players with his quiet courage, self-deprecating wit, and determined performance. Soon other teams signed black players. Baseball's pathbreaking efforts stimulated the integration of football and basketball teams. Jackie Robinson vividly demonstrated that racism, not inferiority, impeded African American advancement in the postwar era and that segregation need not be a permanent condition of American life.

Jackie Robinson

Racial discrimination remained widespread throughout the postwar period. In 1947, Jackie Robinson of the Brooklyn Dodgers became the first black player in major league baseball.

SHAPING THE FAIR DEAL   As the 1948 election approached, the issue of civil rights presented daunting political challenges. While some Americans applauded Truman's efforts to desegregate the federal workforce, others were appalled. Liberals thought that his efforts were not bold enough. Southern conservative Democrats found him too radical. Truman's chances for winning the election of 1948 seemed bleak.

The president had a game plan for 1948, however. His advisers knew that to win another presidential term, he needed the midwestern and western farm belts. In metropolitan areas he needed to carry the union and African American vote, which Truman wooed by working closely with unions and pressing the cause of civil rights. Truman's advisers counted on the Solid South to stay in the Democratic column. With the South and the West, Truman could afford to lose some New Deal strongholds in the East and still win. This strategy erred chiefly in underrating the rebellion that would take four Deep South states out of Truman's camp because of his support for civil rights.

Truman used his State of the Union message to set the agenda for an election year. The 1948 speech offered something to nearly every group the

Democrats hoped to win over. The first goal, Truman remarked, was "to secure fully the essential human rights of our citizens," and he promised a special message later on civil rights. "To protect human resources," he proposed federal aid to education, increased and extended unemployment and retirement benefits, a comprehensive system of health insurance, more federal support for public housing, and the extension of rent controls. As one senator put it, the speech "raised all the ghosts of the old New Deal."

THE ELECTION OF 1948   The Republican majority in Congress for the most part spurned the Truman program, an action it would later regret. Scenting victory in November, Republican delegates again nominated Thomas Dewey, the former New York governor. The platform endorsed most of the New Deal reforms as an accomplished fact and approved the administration's bipartisan foreign policy; Dewey promised to run things more efficiently, however.

In July a glum Democratic Convention gathered in Philadelphia expecting to do little more than go through the motions but found itself surprised by a fierce debate over civil rights. To keep from stirring southern hostility, the administration sought a platform plank that opposed racial discrimination only in general terms. Activists, however, sponsored a plank that called on Congress to take action. Thirty-seven-year-old Minneapolis mayor Hubert H. Humphrey electrified the delegates and set off a ten-minute demonstration when he declared, "The time has arrived for the Democratic party to get out of the shadow of states' rights and walk forthrightly into the bright sunshine of human rights." Segregationist delegates from Alabama and Mississippi instead walked out of the convention.

A group of rebellious southern Democrats, miffed by Truman's progressive civil rights plank, met later in Birmingham, Alabama. There, while

"I Stand Pat!"

Truman's support of civil rights for African Americans had its political costs, as this 1948 cartoon suggests.

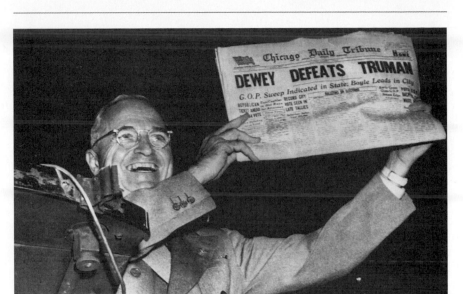

"Dewey Defeats Truman"

Truman's victory in 1948 was a huge upset, so much so that even the early edition of the *Chicago Daily Tribune* was caught off guard, running this premature headline.

waving Confederate flags and singing "Dixie," they nominated South Carolina governor Strom Thurmond on a States' Rights ticket, which was quickly dubbed the Dixiecrat party. The Dixiecrats denounced Truman's civil rights initiatives and defended states' rights against federal actions. They sought to draw enough electoral votes to preclude a majority for either major party, throwing the election into the House of Representatives, where they might strike a sectional bargain. A few days later the left wing of the Democratic party gathered in Philadelphia to name Henry A. Wallace on a Progressive party ticket. These splits in the Democratic ranks seemed to spell the final blow to Truman.

But Truman, undaunted, set out on a 31,000-mile "whistle-stop" train tour, during which he castigated the "do-nothing" Eightieth Congress, provoking cries from his audiences to "pour it on, Harry!" and "give 'em hell, Harry." Truman responded, "I don't give 'em hell. I just tell the truth and they think it's hell." Dewey, in contrast, ran a restrained campaign designed to avoid controversy. By so doing, he may have snatched defeat from the jaws of victory.

The polls and the pundits predicted a sure win for Dewey, but on election day Truman chalked up the biggest upset in history, taking 24.2 million votes (49.5 percent) to Dewey's 22 million (45.1 percent) and winning by a

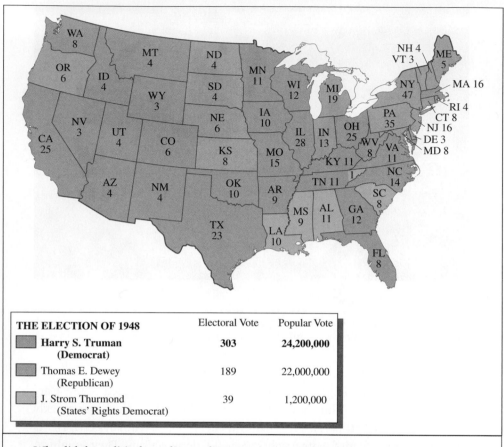

THE ELECTION OF 1948	Electoral Vote	Popular Vote
▓ Harry S. Truman (Democrat)	303	24,200,000
▓ Thomas E. Dewey (Republican)	189	22,000,000
▓ J. Strom Thurmond (States' Rights Democrat)	39	1,200,000

Why did the political pundits predict a Dewey victory? Why was civil rights a divisive issue at the Democratic Convention? How did the candidacies of Thurmond and Wallace help Truman?

thumping margin of 303 to 189 in the Electoral College. Thurmond and Wallace each got more than 1 million votes, but the revolt of right and left had worked to Truman's advantage. The Dixiecrat rebellion backfired by angering black voters, while the Progressive party's radicalism made it hard to tag Truman soft on communism. Thurmond carried four Deep South states, and his success hastened a momentous disruption of the Democratic Solid South. But Truman's victory carried Democratic majorities into Congress.

Truman viewed his upset victory as a vindication for the New Deal and a mandate for moderate liberalism. His 1949 State of the Union message repeated the agenda he had set forth the year before. "Every segment of our population and every individual," he stressed, "has a right to expect from his government a fair deal." Whether deliberately or not, he had invented a tag, the Fair Deal, to distinguish his program from the New Deal.

Some of Truman's Fair Deal proposals became law, but most of them were extensions or enlargements of New Deal programs already in place: a higher minimum wage, expansion of Social Security coverage, extension of rent controls, increased farm subsidies, and a sizable slum-clearance and public-housing program. Despite Democratic majorities in Congress, however, the conservative coalition of southern Democrats and Republicans disdained any drastic departures in domestic policy. Congress balked at civil rights bills, national health insurance, federal aid to education, and a plan to provide subsidies that would support farm income rather than farm prices. Congress also turned down Truman's demand for repeal of the Taft-Hartley Act.

THE COLD WAR HEATS UP

Global concerns, never far from center stage in the postwar world, plagued Truman's second term, as they had his first. Now some Americans began to fear that Communists were infiltrating their society. In his inaugural address, Truman called for an anti-Communist foreign policy resting on four pillars: the United Nations, the Marshall Plan, NATO, and a "bold new plan" for technical assistance to underdeveloped parts of the world, a program that came to be known as Point Four. This program to aid the postwar world never accomplished its goals, in part because other international problems soon diverted Truman's attention.

"LOSING" CHINA   One of the most intractable problems, the China tangle, was fast unraveling in 1949. The Chinese Nationalists, led by Chiang Kai-shek, had been fighting Mao Tse-tung (Mao Zedong)* and the Communists since the 1920s. The outbreak of war with Japan in 1937 halted the civil war, and both Roosevelt and Stalin believed that the Nationalists would control China after the war.

The commanders of U.S. forces in China during World War II, however, concluded that Chiang's government had become hopelessly corrupt, tyrannical, and inefficient. U.S. policy during and immediately after the war promoted peace between the factions in China. But when the civil war resumed

*The traditional (Wade-Giles) transliteration of Chinese, with pinyin transliterations in parentheses, is used in this text up to 1976. After Mao's death the Chinese government adopted the pinyin translations that are widely used today: Mao Tse-tung became Mao Zedong; Peking became Beijing.

in 1945, American forces ferried Nationalist armies back into the eastern and northern provinces as the Japanese withdrew.

It soon became a losing fight for the Nationalists as the Communists won over the land-hungry peasantry. By late 1949 the Nationalist government had fled to the island of Formosa, which it renamed Taiwan. Truman's critics asked bitterly, "Who lost China?" and a State Department report blamed Chiang for his failure to hold on to the support of the Chinese people. In fact it is hard to imagine how the U.S. government could have prevented a Communist victory short of undertaking a massive military intervention, which would have been risky, costly, and unpopular. After 1949 the United States continued to recognize the Nationalist government on Taiwan as the rightful government of China, delaying formal relations with Communist China for thirty years. In an effort to shore up friendly governments in Asia, the United States in 1950 recognized the French-supported government of Emperor Bao Dai in Vietnam and shortly afterward extended aid to the French in their battle against Ho Chi Minh's Vietnamese guerrillas.

As the Communists were securing control in China, U.S. intelligence discovered that the Soviets had set off an atomic explosion. News of the Soviet bomb in 1949 provoked an intense reappraisal of the strategic balance of power in the world, causing Truman in 1950 to order the construction of a hydrogen bomb, a weapon far more powerful than the atomic bomb, lest the Soviets make one first. In addition, the National Security Council recommended rebuilding conventional military forces to provide options other than nuclear war. Such a plan represented a major departure from America's time-honored aversion to keeping large standing armies in peacetime. It was also an expensive proposition. But the American public was growing more receptive to the nation's role as world leader, and an invasion of South Korea by Communist forces from the north clinched the issue for most Americans.

WAR IN KOREA   The Japanese had occupied Korea since 1910, and after their defeat and withdrawal in 1945 the victorious Allies faced the difficult task of creating a new Korean nation. Complicating that task was the fact that Soviet troops had advanced into northern Korea and accepted the surrender of Japanese forces above the 38th parallel, while U.S. forces had done the same south of that line. The Soviets quickly organized a Korean government along Stalinist lines, while the Americans set up a Western-style regime in the south.

Like the postwar division of Germany, the victors' decision to divide Korea began as a temporary expedient and ended as a permanent fact. With the onset of the cold war, it became clear that Soviet-American agreement on unification was no more likely in Korea than in Germany. By the end of 1948, separate Korean regimes had appeared in the two sectors, and occupation forces had withdrawn. The weakened state of the demobilizing American military contributed to the impression that South Korea was vulnerable to a Communist assault. Evidence in Soviet archives reveals that Stalin encouraged the North Koreans to use force to unify their country and oust the Americans from the peninsula. The Soviets helped design a war plan that called for North Korean forces to seize Seoul within three days and all of South Korea within a week. Stalin apparently assumed the United States would not intervene.

On June 25, 1950, over 80,000 North Korean soldiers crossed the boundary and swept down the peninsula. President Truman responded decisively. He and his advisers assumed that the North Korean attack was directed by Moscow and was a brazen indication of the aggressive designs of Soviet communism. Truman made two critical decisions. First, he decided to wage war under the auspices of the United Nations rather than unilaterally. Second, he decided to send troops without asking Congress for a formal declaration of war.

An emergency meeting of the UN Security Council quickly censured the North Korean "breach of peace." The Soviet delegate, who held veto power, was at the time boycotting the council because it would not seat Communist China in place of Nationalist China. On June 27, its first resolution having been ignored, the Security Council called on UN members to "furnish such assistance to the Republic of Korea as may be necessary to repel the armed attack and to restore international peace and security in the area."

Truman ordered American air, naval, and ground forces into action. Eventually, U.S. units numbered over 350,000, while the South Koreans contributed 500,000. In all, some fourteen other nations sent another 50,000 men. Later the UN authorized a unified command and put General Douglas MacArthur in charge. The defense of South Korea remained chiefly an American affair and one that set a precedent of profound consequence: war by order of a president rather than by vote of Congress. Yet it had the sanction of the UN Security Council and could technically be considered a "police action," not a war. Other presidents had ordered U.S. troops into action without a declaration of war, but never on such a scale.

Truman's conviction that the invasion of South Korea was orchestrated by Stalin led to two other decisions that had far-reaching consequences. First, Truman decided that the Korean conflict was actually a diversion for a Soviet invasion of western Europe, so he began a major expansion of American forces in NATO. Second, while dispatching U.S. military units to Korea and Europe, Truman increased assistance to the French troops in Indochina, creating the Military Assistance Advisory Group for Indochina—the start of America's deepening military involvement in Vietnam.

How did the surrender of the Japanese in Korea set up the conflict between Soviet-influenced North Korea and U.S.-influenced South Korea? What was General MacArthur's strategy for retaking Korea? Why did President Truman remove MacArthur from command?

For three months the fighting went badly for the South Korean and UN forces. By September they were barely hanging on to the Pusan perimeter in the southeast corner of Korea. Then, in a brilliant maneuver on September 15, 1950, General MacArthur landed a new force to the North Korean rear at Inch'ŏn. Synchronized with a breakout from Pusan, the sudden blow stampeded the enemy back across the border.

At that point, MacArthur persuaded Truman to allow him to push north and seek to reunify Korea. The Soviet delegate was now back in the Security Council, wielding his veto, so on October 7 the United States got approval for this course from the UN General Assembly, where the veto did not apply.

U.S. forces had crossed the North Korean boundary by October 1 and continued northward. President Truman, concerned about broad hints of Communist Chinese intervention, flew 7,000 miles to Wake Island for a conference with General MacArthur on October 15. There the general discounted chances that the Chinese Red Army would act, but if it did, he confidently predicted, "there would be the greatest slaughter."

That same day, Peking announced that Communist China "cannot stand idly by." On October 26, UN units reached the Yalu River, Korea's border with China. MacArthur predicted total victory by Christmas, but on the night of November 25, several hundred thousand Chinese "volunteers" counterattacked. Massive "human-wave" attacks, with the support of tanks and planes, turned the tables on the UN forces, sending them into a desperate retreat just at the onset of winter. It had become "an entirely new war," MacArthur concluded. Soon he was reporting that the war was dragging on because the administration refused to let him blockade the Chinese mainland.

Truman opposed leading the United States into the "gigantic booby trap" of a ground war with China, and the UN forces soon rallied. By January 1951 over 900,000 UN troops under General Matthew Ridgway finally secured their lines below Seoul and then launched a counterattack that in some places carried them back across the 38th parallel in March. When Truman seized the chance and offered negotiations to restore the boundary and end the war, General MacArthur undermined the move by issuing an ultimatum for China to make peace or suffer an attack. Truman decided then that he had no choice but to accept MacArthur's aggressive policy or fire him. Civilian control of the military was at stake, Truman later asserted. On April 11, 1951, the president removed MacArthur, whom he called Mr. Prima Donna, from all his commands and replaced him with Ridgway.

Truman's action set off an uproar across the country, and a tumultuous reception greeted MacArthur upon his first return home since 1937. MacArthur's dramatic speech to a joint session of Congress provided the climactic event. A Senate investigation showcased the administration's arguments, best summarized by General Omar Bradley, chairman of the Joint Chiefs of Staff. The MacArthur strategy, he said, "would involve us in the wrong war at the wrong place at the wrong time and with the wrong enemy." Most Americans found Bradley's logic persuasive.

On June 24, 1951, the Soviet representative at the United Nations proposed a cease-fire in Korea along the 38th parallel, which Secretary of State Dean Acheson accepted in principle a few days later. China and North Korea responded favorably—at the time, General Ridgway's "meat-grinder" offensive was inflicting severe losses. Truce talks started in July, only to drag on for

September 1950

American soldiers engaged in the recapture of Seoul from the North Koreans.

two years while the fighting continued. The chief snags were exchanges of prisoners and the South Korean president's insistence on unification.

By the time a truce was reached, on July 27, 1953, Truman had relinquished the White House to Dwight D. Eisenhower. The truce line followed the front at that time, mostly a little north of the 38th parallel, with a demilitarized zone separating the forces; repatriation of prisoners would be voluntary, supervised by a neutral commission. No peace conference ever took place, and Korea, like Germany, remained divided. The war had cost the United States more than 33,000 battle deaths and 103,000 wounded or missing. South Korean casualties, all told, were about 1 million, and North Korean and Chinese casualties an estimated 1.5 million.

ANOTHER RED SCARE   The costs of the Korean War included the far-reaching consequences of a second Red Scare, which had grown since 1945 as the domestic counterpart to the cold war abroad and reached a climax during the Korean conflict. Since 1938 the House Un-American Activities Committee (HUAC) had kept up a barrage of accusations about supposed subversives in the federal government.

In 1947 the HUAC subpoenaed nineteen prominent Hollywood writers, producers, and actors, intending to prove that Communist party members dominated the Screen Writers Guild, that they injected subversive propaganda into motion pictures, and that President Roosevelt had brought improper pressure to bear upon the industry to produce pro-Soviet films during the war. Ten of the witnesses, the so-called Hollywood Ten, jointly decided to use the First Amendment as a defense, and each of them refused to answer the question "Are you now or have you ever been a member of the Communist party?" All ten had been members of the party, but they would not answer the question as a matter of principle, claiming that party identification was their business, especially since membership in the Communist party at that time was not illegal in the United States. They were all judged to be in contempt and were sentenced to up to a year in prison. But greater punishment awaited them. The movie industry blacklisted the Hollywood Ten, denying them further work.

In the highly charged atmosphere of the postwar years, Truman decided that he, too, must become more vigilant in rooting out Communists from the government. On March 21, 1947, therefore, just nine days after he announced the Truman Doctrine, the president signed an executive order setting up procedures for an employee loyalty program in the federal government. Designed partly to protect the president's political flank, it failed to do so mainly because of disclosures of earlier Communist penetrations of the government that were few in number but sensational in character.

The case most embarrassing to the administration involved Alger Hiss, president of the Carnegie Endowment for International Peace, who had served in several government departments, including the State Department. Whittaker Chambers, a former Soviet agent and later an editor of *Time* magazine, told the HUAC in 1948 that Hiss had given him secret documents ten years earlier, when Chambers was spying for the Soviets. Hiss sued for libel, and Chambers produced microfilms of the State Department documents that he claimed Hiss had passed to him. Hiss denied the accusation, whereupon he was indicted and, after one mistrial, convicted in 1950. The charge was perjury, but he was convicted of lying about espionage, for which he could not be tried because the statute of limitations on that crime had expired.

President Truman, taking at face value the many testimonials to Hiss's integrity, had called the charges against him a "red herring." Secretary of State Dean Acheson compounded the damage when, meaning to express compassion, he pledged not "to turn my back on Alger Hiss." The Hiss affair had another political consequence: it raised to national prominence a young California congressman, Richard M. Nixon, who doggedly insisted on pursuing the case and then exploited an anti-Communist stance to win election to the Senate in 1950.

More cases of Communist infiltration surfaced. In 1950 the government disclosed the existence of a British-American spy network that had fed information about the development of the atomic bomb to the Soviet Union. These disclosures led to the arrest of, among others, Julius and Ethel Rosenberg.

JOSEPH McCARTHY'S WITCH HUNT   Revelations of Soviet spying encouraged politicians in both parties to exploit the public's fears. If a man of such respectability as Hiss was guilty, many wondered, who could be trusted? Early in 1950 a little-known Republican senator from Wisconsin, Joseph R. McCarthy, surfaced as the shrewdest and most ruthless exploiter of the nation's anxieties. He took up the cause of anti-communism with a vengeance, claiming that the State Department was infested with Communists and that he had a list of their names. Later there was confusion as to whether he had said there were 205, 81, 57, or "a lot" of names on the list and even whether the sheet of paper he brandished contained any such list. Confusion would typically surround McCarthy's charges.

McCarthy never uncovered a single Communist agent in the government. But with the United States at war with Korean Communists in mid-1950, he continued to arouse public fears. Republicans encouraged him to keep up

Joseph McCarthy

Senator McCarthy (left) and his aide Roy Cohn (right) exchange comments during testimony.

the game. In 1951 he listed Generals George Marshall and Dwight Eisenhower among the disloyal. He kept up his outrageous campaign without successful challenge until the end of the Korean War.

Fears of Communist espionage led Congress in 1950 to pass the McCarran Internal Security Act over President Truman's veto, requiring Communist and Communist-front organizations to register with the attorney general. Aliens who had belonged to totalitarian parties were barred from admission to the United States. Documents recently uncovered in Russian archives and U.S. security agencies reveal that the Soviets did indeed operate an extensive espionage ring in the United States after World War II. Russian agents recruited several hundred American spies to ferret out secrets regarding atomic weapons, defense systems, and military intelligence.

ASSESSING THE COLD WAR   In retrospect the onset of the cold war takes on an appearance of terrible inevitability. America's preference for international principles such as self-determination, free trade, and democracy conflicted with the Soviet Union's preference for international spheres of influence and totalitarian control. Russia, after all, had suffered two German invasions in the first half of the twentieth century, and Soviet leaders wanted tame buffer states on their borders for protection.

The people of Eastern Europe were again caught in the middle. But the Communists themselves held to a universal principle: world revolution. And since the time of President James Monroe, Americans had bristled at the thought of foreign intervention in their sphere of influence, the Western Hemisphere. Thus, to create a defensive shield against the spread of communism, the United States signed mutual defense treaties. Under a 1947 treaty signed at Rio de Janeiro, the nations of the Western Hemisphere agreed to aid any country in the region that was attacked. In 1951 the United States and Japan signed a treaty that permitted the United States to maintain military forces in Japan. That same year, American negotiators signed other mutual defense treaties with the Philippines, Australia, and New Zealand.

The policy initiatives of the Truman years led the country to abandon its long-standing aversion to peacetime alliances. It was a far cry from the world of 1796, when George Washington in his farewell address warned against "those overgrown military establishments which . . . are inauspicious to liberty" and advised his country "to steer clear of permanent alliances with any portion of the foreign world." But then Washington had warned only against participation in the "ordinary" combinations and collusions of Europe, and surely the postwar years had seen extraordinary events and unprecedented new alliances.

End of Chapter Review

CHAPTER SUMMARY

- **The Cold War** The cold war was an ideological contest between the democracies of the Western Hemisphere (especially the United States) and the Communist countries of the Eastern Hemisphere (especially the Soviet Union and China) that emerged after World War II. Immediately after the war, the Soviet Union established puppet governments in Eastern Europe, violating promises made at the Yalta Conference. The United States and the Soviet Union, former allies, differed on issues of human rights, individual liberties, and self-determination.

- **Containment** President Truman responded to the Soviet occupation of Eastern Europe with the policy of containment, the aim of which was to halt the spread of communism. Truman proposed giving economic aid to countries in danger of Communist control, such as Greece and Turkey; and with the Marshall Plan, he offered such aid to all European nations. In a defensive move, the United States in 1949 became a founding member of the North Atlantic Treaty Organization (NATO), a military alliance of Western democracies.

- **Truman's Fair Deal** Truman proposed not only to preserve the New Deal but also to expand it. He vetoed a Republican attempt to curb unions. He oversaw the expansion of Social Security and through executive orders ended segregation in the military and banned racial discrimination in the hiring of federal employees.

- **The Korean War** After a Communist government came to power in China in 1949, Korea became a "hot spot." The peninsula had been divided at the 38th parallel after World War II, with a Communist regime in the north and a Western-style regime in the south. After North Koreans crossed the dividing line in June 1950, Truman decided to go to war under the auspices of the United Nations and without asking Congress to declare war. The war was thus waged by the United States with the participation of more than a dozen member nations of the United Nations. A truce, concluded in July 1953, established a demilitarized zone on either side of the 38th parallel.

- **McCarthyism** The onset of the cold war inflamed another Red Scare. During the Korean War, investigations by the House Committee on Un-American Affairs (known as HUAC) sought to find "subversives" within the federal government. Senator Joseph R. McCarthy of Wisconsin exploited Americans' fears of Soviet spies' infiltrating the highest levels of the U.S. government. McCarthy was successful in the short term because, with most Eastern European nations being held as buffer states by the Soviet Union and the war in Korea being indirectly fought against Communist China, the threat of a world dominated by Communist governments seemed real to many Americans.

CHRONOLOGY

1944	Congress passes the Servicemen's Readjustment Act (GI Bill of Rights)
April 1945	Fifty nations at war with the Axis Powers sign the United Nations Charter
1947	Congress passes the Taft-Hartley Labor Act
1947	National Security Council is established
May 1948	Israel is proclaimed an independent nation
July 1948	Truman issues an executive order ending segregation in the U.S. armed forces
October 1948	Allied forces begin airlifting supplies to West Berlin
November 1948	Truman defeats Dewey in the presidential election
1949	North Atlantic Treaty Organization is created
1949	China "falls" to communism
1950	United States and other UN members go to war in Korea

KEY TERMS & NAMES

32

THROUGH THE PICTURE WINDOW: SOCIETY AND CULTURE, 1945–1960

FOCUS QUESTIONS wwnorton.com/studyspace

- Why did the U.S. economy grow rapidly in the postwar period?
- To what extent was conformity the main characteristic of society in the 1950s?
- What was the image of the family in this period, and what was the reality?
- What were the characteristics of the Beat generation?

Americans emerged from World War II elated, proud of their military strength and industrial might, and eager to enjoy peacetime prosperity. As the editors of *Fortune* magazine proclaimed in 1946, "This is a dream era, this is what everyone was waiting through the blackouts for. The Great American Boom is on." So it was. An American public that had known deprivation and sacrifice for a decade and a half began to enjoy unprecedented economic growth, access to a cornucopia of new consumer products, and social contentment—at least on the surface. By 1957 the editors of *U.S. News and World Report* had proclaimed that "never have so many people, anywhere, been so well off."

Amid the rising affluence and optimism, however, many social critics, writers, and artists expressed a growing sense of unease with what they deemed the vulgarity and superficiality of middle-class culture. Was postwar society becoming too complacent, too conformist, too materialistic? These questions reflected the perennial tension in American life between idealism and materialism, a tension that arrived with the first settlers and remains with us today. Americans have always struggled to accumulate goods and cultivate goodness. During the postwar era the nation tried to do both. For a while, at least, it appeared to succeed.

PEOPLE OF PLENTY

The dominant feature of post–World War II society was its remarkable prosperity. After a surprisingly brief postwar recession, businesses shifted from wartime production the peacetime manufacture of an array of consumer goods. The economy soared to record heights. The gross national product nearly doubled between 1945 and 1960, and the 1960s witnessed an even more spectacular expansion of the economy. By 1970 the gap between the living standard in the United States and that in the rest of the world had become a chasm: with 6 percent of the world's population, Americans produced and consumed nearly two thirds of its goods. Poverty remained a chronic condition for many among the rural poor and for the minorities living in urban ghettos, but their plight was largely ignored amid the wave of boosterism and consumerism.

Several factors contributed to this sustained economic surge. The massive federal expenditures to meet military needs during the war had catapulted the economy out of the Depression. High government spending continued to drive the postwar economy, thanks to the tensions generated by the cold war. Military-related research also helped spawn the new glamour industries of the postwar era: chemicals, electronics, and aviation.

Most of the other major industrial nations of the world—England, France, Germany, Japan, the Soviet Union—had been physically devastated during the war, leaving American manufacturers with a virtual monopoly on international trade. In addition, the widespread use of new and more efficient machinery and computers led to a 35 percent jump in the productivity of American workers between 1945 and 1955.

The major catalyst in promoting economic expansion after 1945, however, was the unleashing of pent-up consumer demand. During the war, civilians had postponed purchases of major items such as cars and houses and in the process had saved over $150 billion. Now they were eager to buy. The United States after World War II experienced a purchasing frenzy.

THE GI BILL OF RIGHTS   Part of that frenzy was indirectly financed by the federal government. People feared that a sharp postwar drop in military

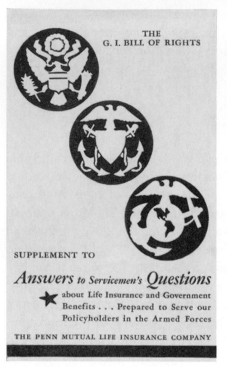

THE
G. I. BILL OF RIGHTS

SUPPLEMENT TO

Answers to Servicemen's Questions

★ about Life Insurance and Government
Benefits . . . Prepared to Serve our
Policyholders in the Armed Forces

THE PENN MUTUAL LIFE INSURANCE COMPANY

GI Bill of Rights supplement

This booklet informed servicemen about the new legislation.

spending and the sudden influx of veterans into the civilian workforce would send the economy into a downward spiral and produce widespread unemployment. Those concerns led Congress to pass the Servicemen's Readjustment Act of 1944. Popularly known as the GI Bill of Rights (*GI* meaning "government issue," a phrase that was stamped on military uniforms and was slang for "serviceman"), it led to the creation of a new government agency, the Veterans Administration. The GI Bill also provided unemployment pay for veterans for one year, preference for veterans seeking government jobs, loans for home construction, access to government hospitals, and generous subsidies for postsecondary education. Between 1944 and 1956 almost 8 million veterans took advantage of $14.5 billion in GI Bill subsidies to attend college or enroll in job-training programs. Some 5 million veterans bought new homes using GI Bill benefits. These two provisions of the GI Bill combined to produce a social revolution.

Before World War II approximately 160,000 Americans graduated from college each year. By 1950 the figure had more than tripled. In 1949, veterans accounted for 40 percent of all college enrollments. For the first time in the nation's history, a significant number of working-class men had the opportunity to earn a college degree. In turn a college education or vocational training served as a lever into the middle class and fostered economic security. The United States could boast the world's best-educated workforce.

But while the GI Bill helped erode class barriers, it was less successful in dismantling racial barriers. Many African American veterans could not take equal advantage of the education benefits. Most colleges and universities after the war remained racially segregated, by regulation or by practice. In 1946 only a fifth of the 100,000 African Americans who had applied for education benefits had enrolled in a program.

THE BABY BOOM   The return of some 12 million veterans to private life also helped generate the postwar baby boom, which peaked in 1957. Between 1946 and 1964, 76 million Americans were born, reversing a century-long decline in the nation's birthrate and creating a massive demographic upheaval whose repercussions are still being felt. Such a dramatic growth rate had a host of reverberating effects. Indeed, much of America's social history since the 1940s has been the story of the unusually large baby boom generation and its progress through the stages of life. The postwar surge in births created a massive demand for diapers, baby food, toys, medicine, schools, books, teachers, furniture, and housing. The baby boomers were raised during the 1950s and 1960s, a period of unprecedented prosperity and American omnipotence abroad, but they entered adulthood during the 1970s, a period of energy crises, inflationary pressures, and diminished national prestige. They inherited a nation flush with affluence and will bequeath a nation mired in debt. During their childhood the baby boomers lived amid a child-obsessed culture; in their youth the nation was youth obsessed. The iconoclastic Columbia University historian Richard Hofstadter worried that America was being overrun by the "overvalued child." The baby boomer novelist Benjamin Cheever confessed that "we were spoiled. No denying that. And we have spoiled our children."

AN EXPANDING CONSUMER CULTURE   The baby boom was accompanied by a postwar construction boom. The proportion of homeowners in the population increased by 50 percent between 1945 and 1960. And those new homes featured the latest electrical appliances: refrigerators, washing machines, sewing machines, vacuum cleaners, freezers, electric mixers, and television sets. By far the most popular new household product was the TV set. In 1946 there were 7,000 primitive black-and-white TV sets in the country; by 1960 there were 50 million high-quality sets. Nine out of ten homes had one, and by 1970, 38 percent of homes had the new color sets. What differentiated the affluence of the post–World War II era from earlier periods of prosperity was its ever-widening dispersion. In 1955, union leader George Meany proclaimed that "American labor never had it so good."

On the surface many African Americans were also beneficiaries of the wave of prosperity that swept over postwar society. By 1950, blacks were earning on average more than four times their 1940 wages. While gains had been made, however, African Americans and other minority groups lagged behind whites in their rate of improvement. Indeed, the gap between the average yearly income of whites and blacks widened during the 1950s. Yet the

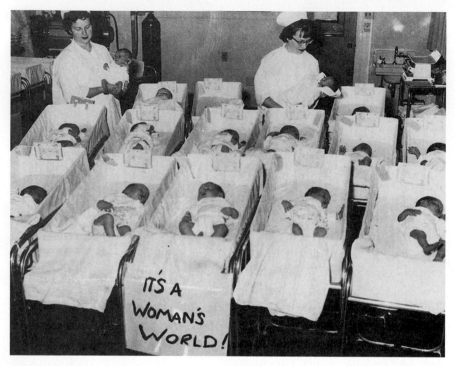

The baby boom

Much of America's social history since the 1940s has been the story of the baby boom generation.

desire to present a united front against communism led commentators to ignore issues of racial and economic injustice. Such corrosive neglect would fester and explode during the 1960s, but for now the emphasis was on consensus, conformity, and economic growth.

To perpetuate the postwar prosperity, economists repeated the basic marketing strategy of the 1920s: the public must be taught to consume more and expect more. Economists knew that Americans had more money than ever before. The average adult had twice as much *real* income in 1955 as in the rosy days of the late 1920s before the crash. Still, many people who had undergone the severities of the Depression and the rationing required for the war effort had to be weaned from a decade and a half of imposed frugality in order to nourish the growing consumer culture.

Advertising became a more crucial component of the consumer culture than ever before. Expenditures for TV ads increased 1,000 percent during the 1950s. Such startling growth rates led the president of NBC to claim in 1956 that the primary reason for the postwar economic boom was that "advertising has created an American frame of mind that makes people want more things, better things and newer things." Paying for such "things" was no problem. Between 1945 and 1957 consumer credit soared 800 percent. Whereas families in other industrialized nations were typically saving 10 to 20 percent of their income, American families by the 1960s were saving only 5 percent.

Young Americans in particular participated in the consumer culture. By the late 1950s the baby boom generation was entering its teens, and the disproportionate number of affluent adolescents generated a vast new specialized market for youth-oriented goods ranging from transistor radios,

Black cotillion dance

Presentation of the debutantes of 1954.

Hula-hoops, and rock-and-roll records to cameras, surfboards, *Seventeen* magazine, and Pat Boone movies. Most teenagers had far more discretionary income and free time than those of previous generations had had. Teens in the postwar era knew nothing of depressions or rationing; they were immersed in abundance from an early age and took for granted the notion of carefree consumption.

THE SUBURBAN FRONTIER   The population increase of the 1950s and 1960s was an urban as well as a suburban phenomenon. Dramatic new technological advances in agricultural production reduced the need for manual laborers. Almost 20 million Americans left the land for the city between 1940 and 1970. Much of the urban population growth occurred in the South, the Southwest, and the West, in an arc that stretched from the Carolinas to California, regions that by the 1970s were being lumped together and called the sunbelt. The dispersion of air-conditioning throughout these warm regions dramatically enhanced their attractiveness to northerners. But the Northeast remained the most densely populated area; by the early 1960s, 20 percent of the nation's population lived in the corridor that stretched south from Boston to Norfolk, Virginia.

While more people concentrated in cities, Americans after World War II were spreading out within the metropolitan areas. During the 1950s, suburbs grew six times faster than cities. By 1970 more people lived in suburbs

Suburban life

A woman vacuums her living room in Queens, New York, 1953, illustrating the 1950s ideal of domestic contentment facilitated by electrical appliances.

(76 million) than in central cities (64 million). Suburban development required cars, highways, and government-backed home mortgages. It also required bold entrepreneurs.

William Levitt, a brassy New York developer, led the suburban revolution. In 1947, on 1,200 acres of Long Island farmland, he built 10,600 houses that were inhabited by more than 40,000 people, mostly adults under thirty-five and their children. Other developers soon mimicked Levitt's suburbs around the country. Expanded automobile production and highway construction facilitated the rush to the suburbs as people were able to commute longer distances to work. Car production soared, and a car-dependent culture soon emerged. Widespread car ownership necessitated an improved road network. Local and state governments built many new roads, but the guiding force was the federal government. In 1947, Congress authorized the construction of 37,000 miles of federal highways, and nine years later it funded 42,000 additional miles of interstate expressways.

The federal government also fostered the suburban revolution through loans to developers and consumers. By insuring loans for up to 95 percent of the value of a house, the Federal Housing Administration made it easy for a builder to borrow money to construct low-cost homes. In addition, military veterans were given substantial assistance with home ownership. A veteran could buy a Levitt house with no down payment and monthly installments of $56. African Americans and other racial minorities, however, were often discriminated against. Contracts for homes in Levittown, Long Island, for example, specifically excluded "members of other than the Caucasian race." Such discrimination, whether explicit or implicit, was widespread; the nation's suburban population in 1970 was 95 percent white.

THE GREAT BLACK MIGRATION   World War II, like World War I, spurred a mass migration of rural southern blacks to the cities of other regions. This second migration was much larger in scope than the first, and its social consequences were much more dramatic. After 1945 more than 5 million southern blacks, mostly farm folk, left their native regions in search of better jobs, higher wages, decent housing, and greater social equality. During the 1950s, for example, the African American population of Chicago more than doubled. The South Side of Chicago soon became known as the capital of black America. It remains the neighborhood with the largest concentration of African Americans in the nation.

Many southern blacks streamed northward in search of a new promised land only to see their dreams dashed. In northern cities such as Chicago, Philadelphia, Newark, Detroit, New York, Boston, and Washington, D.C., African Americans from the rural South confronted harsh new realities.

Family on relief

Black families who migrated from the South became a part of a marginalized population in Chicago, dependent on public housing.

Slumlords often gouged them for rent, employers refused to hire them, and some union bosses denied them membership. Soon the promised land had become an ugly nightmare of slum housing, joblessness, illiteracy, dysfunctional families, welfare dependency, street gangs, pervasive crime, and racism.

The unexpected tidal wave of African American migrants severely taxed the resources of urban governments and the tolerance of white racists. Throughout the North angry whites attacked blacks who dared move into their neighborhoods. Northern cities sought to deal with the migrants and alleviate racial stress by constructing massive public-housing projects to accommodate the newcomers. These overcrowded all-black enclaves were essentially segregated prisons. To be sure, many African American migrants and their children did manage through extraordinary determination and ingenuity to "clear"—to climb out of the teeming ghettos and into the middle class. But most did not. As a consequence the great black migration produced a web of complex social problems in northern cities that in the 1960s would erupt into a crisis.

A CONFORMING CULTURE

In the 1950s, social commentators mostly ignored people and cultures outside the mainstream. As evidenced in many of the new look-alike suburbs sprouting up across the land, much of white middle-class social life during the two decades after World War II exhibited an increasingly homogenized character. Suburban life encouraged uniformity. People felt a need for companionship and a sense of belonging as they moved into communities of strangers. "Conformity," predicted a journalist in 1954, "may very well become the central social problem of this age."

CORPORATE LIFE   During World War II, big business had grown bigger. The government had relaxed its anti-trust activity, and huge defense contracts promoted corporate concentration and consolidation. In 1940, for example, the 100 largest companies were responsible for 30 percent of all manufacturing output; three years later they were producing 70 percent. After the war fewer and fewer people were self-employed; many now worked for large corporations, with manual labor giving way to mental labor for a large part of the workforce. In the huge companies as well as in similarly large government agencies and universities, the working atmosphere promoted conformity and regimentation rather than individualism.

WOMEN'S "PLACE"   Increasing conformity in middle-class business and corporate life was mirrored in the middle-class home. A special issue of *Life* magazine in 1956 featured the "ideal" middle-class woman, a thirty-two-year-old "pretty and popular" white suburban housewife, mother of four, who had married at age sixteen. Described as an excellent wife, mother, volunteer, and "home manager," she hosted dozens of dinner parties each year, sang in her church choir, worked with the PTA and the Campfire Girls, and was devoted to her husband. "In her daily round," *Life* reported, "she attends club or charity meetings, drives the children to school, does the weekly grocery shopping, makes ceramics, and is planning to study French." *Life*'s ideal of the middle-class woman reflected a veritable cult of feminine domesticity that witnessed a dramatic revival in the postwar era. The soaring birthrate reinforced the deeply embedded notion that a woman's place was in the home. "Of all the accomplishments of the American woman," the *Life* cover story proclaimed, "the one she brings off with the most spectacular success is having babies."

Even though millions of women had responded to wartime appeals and joined the traditionally male workforce, afterward they were encouraged—and

The new household

A Tupperware party in a middle-class suburban home.

even forced—to turn their jobs over to the returning veterans and resume their full-time commitment to home and family. Throughout the postwar era, educators, politicians, ministers, advertisers, and other commentators exalted the cult of domesticity and castigated the few feminists who were encouraging women to broaden their horizons beyond crib and kitchen. Women were to dismiss any thoughts of continuing their own career in the workplace and were to return to their traditional domestic roles. Nonetheless, despite the ideal of women remaining in the home and the stigma associated with violating this norm, the percentage of women working outside the home increased overall during the 1950s.

THE SEARCH FOR COMMUNITY   Americans were on the move after World War II. Some 20 percent of the population changed their place of residence each year. One cause of the mobility was the largest corporations' standard policy of relocating their sales and managerial employees. As they moved from central city to suburb, from suburb to suburb, from farm to city, from state to state, people searched for a sense of community and rootedness.

Billy Graham preaches to thousands, 1955

The Baptist evangelist used radio and television to promote his huge crusades, as droves of Americans, encouraged by the president, Congress, and billboard advertising, joined churches and attended revival meetings.

Hence Americans, even more than usual, became joiners: they joined civic clubs, garden clubs, car pools, and babysitting groups.

RELIGIOUS REVIVAL   Americans also joined churches and synagogues in record numbers. The postwar era witnessed a massive renewal of religious participation. In 1940 less than half the adult population belonged to a church; by 1960 over 65 percent were official communicants. Bible sales soared, and books, movies, and songs with religious themes were stunning commercial successes. Conservative Protestants found willing allies among Republican leaders in their effort to reaffirm America's Christian commitment. President Eisenhower repeatedly promoted a patriotic crusade to bring Americans back to God. "Recognition of the Supreme Being," he declared, "is the first, the most basic, expression of Americanism. Without God, there could be no form of American government, nor an American way of life." The president had himself joined a church for the first time only in 1953, but he characterized himself as the "most intensely religious man I know." Not to be outdone, Congress in 1954 added the phrase "under God" to the Pledge of Allegiance and in 1956 made the statement "In God We Trust" mandatory on all coins and currency. In 1956, Congress also made "In God We Trust" the national motto.

The prevailing tone of the popular religious revival of the 1950s was upbeat and soothing. Most ministers assumed that people were not interested in "fire-and-brimstone" harangues from the pulpit; congregants did not want their conscience overburdened with a sense of personal sin or social guilt about issues such as segregation and inner-city poverty. Instead, they wanted to be reassured that their own comfortable way of life was indeed God's will.

CRACKS IN THE PICTURE WINDOW

Yet despite widespread prosperity, all was not well in postwar America. The widely publicized affluence masked festering poverty in rural areas and urban ghettos. People were also profoundly anxious about the meaning of their lives and of life in general in the nuclear age. That tranquilizers were the fastest-growing medication suggested that considerable anxiety accompanied the nation's much-trumpeted affluence. Thus one of the most striking aspects of postwar American life was the sharp contrast between the prevailing sentiment that everything was fine and for the best as long as people believed in God, the "American way," and themselves and the increasingly bitter criticism of social life coming from artists, intellectuals, and other commentators.

THE LONELY CROWD   The criticism of postwar life and values began in the early 1950s and quickly gathered momentum. In *The Affluent Society* (1958), for example, the economist John Kenneth Galbraith warned that sustained economic growth would not necessarily solve chronic social problems. He reminded readers that for all of America's vaunted postwar prosperity, the nation had yet to confront, much less eradicate, the chronic poverty plaguing the nation's inner cities and rural hamlets. Postwar cultural critics also questioned the supposed bliss offered by middle-class suburban life. John Keats, in *The Crack in the Picture Window* (1956), launched a savage assault on life in the huge new suburban developments. Suburbanites, he concluded, were locked into a deadly routine, hounded by financial insecurity, engulfed by mass mediocrity, and living, in short, in a "homogeneous, postwar Hell."

Social critics in the 1950s repeatedly cited the huge modern corporation as an important source of regimentation in American life. The most provocative analysis of the docile new corporate character was David Riesman's *The Lonely Crowd* (1950). Riesman, a social psychologist, detected a fundamental

Suburban pastimes

A suburban family enjoys playing with Hula-hoops in their backyard.

shift in the dominant American personality from what he called the "inner-directed" type to the "other-directed" type. Inner-directed people, Riesman argued, possess a deeply internalized set of basic values implanted by strong-minded parents or other elders. Such an assured, self-reliant personality, Riesman claimed, had prevailed in nineteenth-century life. But during the mid–twentieth century a new, other-directed personality had displaced it. In the huge hierarchical corporations that abounded in postwar America, employees who could win friends and influence people thrived; rugged individualists indifferent to personal popularity did not. The other-directed people who adapted to the corporate culture had few internal convictions and standards; they did not follow their conscience so much as adapt to the prevailing standards of the moment. They were concerned more with being well liked than with being independent.

Riesman amassed considerable evidence to show that the other-directed personality was not just an aspect of the business world; its characteristics were widely dispersed throughout middle-class life. One of its sources, Riesman suggested, may have been Dr. Benjamin Spock's influential advice on raising children. Spock's popular manual, *The Common Sense Book of Baby and Child Care,* sold 1 million copies a year between its first appearance in 1946 and 1960. Spock stressed that parents should foster in their children qualities and skills that would enhance their chances in what Riesman called the "popularity market."

YOUTH CULTURE AND DELINQUENCY Heeding Dr. Spock's advice, most parents of the 1950s tended to be permissive with their children, who occupied a distinctive place in postwar life. One commentator described the American family in 1957 as a "child-centered anarchy." As the baby boomers were reaching adolescence during the 1950s, a distinctive teen subculture began to emerge. And as most adults in postwar society were striving to get along and to conform to the values of the club or civic group or corporation, so, too, were most young people embracing the values of their parents and the capitalist system.

Yet such conformity and striving for popularity masked a great deal of turbulence. During the 1950s a wave of juvenile delinquency swept across middle-class society. By 1956 over 1 million teens a year were being arrested. Car theft was the leading offense, but larceny, rape, and murder were not uncommon. A Boston judge announced that the entire city was being "terrorized" by juvenile gangs. What was causing the delinquency? J. Edgar Hoover, head of the Federal Bureau of Investigation, insisted that the root of

Youth culture

A drugstore soda fountain, a popular outlet for teenagers' consumerism in the 1950s.

the problem was a lack of religious training in more and more households. Others pointed to the growing number of urban slums, whose "brutish" environment could lead to criminality. Yet those factors failed to explain why so many middle-class kids from God-fearing families were becoming delinquents. One explanation may have been the unprecedented mobility of young people. Access to automobiles enabled teens to escape parental control, and in the words of one journalist, cars provided "a private lounge for drinking and for petting or sex episodes."

ROCK AND ROLL   Many concerned observers blamed the delinquency on a new form of music that emerged during the postwar era: rock and roll. In 1955, *Life* magazine published a long article about a mysterious new "frenzied teenage music craze" that was creating "a big fuss." Alan Freed, a Cleveland disc jockey, had coined the term *rock and roll* in 1951. At a record store he had noticed white teenagers buying rhythm and blues (R&B) records that had heretofore been purchased only by African Americans and Hispanic Americans. Freed began playing R&B records on the air but labeled the music rock and roll (a phrase used in African American communities to refer to dancing and sex) to surmount the racial barrier.

Freed's radio program was an immediate success, and its popularity helped bridge the gap between "white" and "black" music. African American singers such as Chuck Berry, Little Richard, and Ray Charles and Hispanic American performers such as Ritchie Valens (Richard Valenzuela) were suddenly the rage among young white middle-class audiences eager to claim their own cultural style and message.

At the same time, Elvis Presley, a young white truck driver and aspiring singer from Memphis, Tennessee, began experimenting with "rockabilly" music, his unique blend of gospel, country-and-western, and R&B rhythms and lyrics. In 1956 the twenty-one-year-old Presley released "Heartbreak Hotel," and over the next two years the sensual baritone won fourteen gold records and emerged as the most popular entertainer in history. His sexually suggestive stage performances, featuring twisting hips and a gyrating pelvis, drove teenagers wild.

Such hysterics prompted cultural conservatives to urge parents to confiscate and destroy Presley's records because they promoted "a pagan concept of life." A Catholic cardinal denounced Presley as a vile symptom of a new teen "creed of dishonesty, violence, lust and degeneration." Patriotic groups claimed that rock-and-roll music was a tool of Communist insurgents designed to corrupt American youth.

Yet rock and roll survived the assaults and in the process gave adolescents a self-conscious sense of belonging to a unique social

Elvis Presley, 1956

The teenage children of middle-class America made rock and roll a thriving industry in the 1950s and Elvis its first star. The strong beat of the music combined with the electric guitar, its signature instrument, produced a distinctive new sound.

group with distinctive characteristics and tastes. It also represented an unprecedented intermingling of racial, ethnic, and class identities.

ALIENATION IN THE ARTS   Dissatisfaction with the conventions and conformity of American society surfaced not only in rock and roll; it was manifested also in literature as well as in some of the artwork of the times. Many of the best novels and plays of the postwar period reinforced David Riesman's image of modern American society as a "lonely crowd" of individuals, hollow at the core, groping for a sense of belonging and affection. Arthur Miller's much-celebrated play *Death of a Salesman* (1949) explored this theme powerfully. Willy Loman, an aging, confused traveling salesman in decline, centers his life and that of his family on the notion of material success through personal popularity, only to be abruptly told by his boss that he is in fact a failure. Willy, for all his puffery about being well liked, admits that he is "terribly lonely." He has no real friends; even his relations with his family are neither honest nor intimate. When Willy finally realizes that he has been leading a counterfeit existence, he yearns for a life in which "a man is not a piece of fruit," but eventually he is so dumbfounded by his predicament that he decides he can endow his life with meaning only by ending it.

Nor are there many happy endings in the best novels of the postwar period. A brooding sense of resigned alienation dominated literary fiction in the two decades after 1945. The characters in novels such as James Jones's *From Here to Eternity* (1951), Ralph Ellison's *Invisible Man* (1952), Saul Bellow's *Dangling Man* (1944) and *Seize the Day* (1956), William Styron's *Lie Down in Darkness* (1951), and John Updike's *Rabbit, Run* (1961), among many others, tend to be like Willy Loman: restless, tormented, impotent individuals who are unable to fasten on a satisfying self-image and therefore can find neither contentment nor respect in an overpowering or impersonal world.

Many visual artists also explored the theme of desolate loneliness in urban-industrial American life. Virtually all of Edward Hopper's paintings, for example, depict isolated individuals, melancholy, anonymous, and motionless. The silence of his scenes is deafening, the monotony striking, the alienation absorbing.

A group of younger painters in New York City felt that postwar society was so chaotic that it denied any attempt at literal representation. Their anarchic technique came to be called abstract expressionism, and during the late 1940s and 1950s it dominated not only the American art scene but the international field as well. Abstract expressionists included Jackson Pollock, Robert Motherwell, Willem de Kooning, Arshile Gorky, Clyfford Still, Adolph Gottlieb, and Mark Rothko. "Abstract art," Motherwell declared, "is an effort to close the void that modern men feel."

In practice this meant that the *act* of painting was as important as the result and that art no longer had to represent one's visual surroundings. Instead, it could unapologetically represent the painter's personal thoughts and actions. Wyoming-born Pollock, for example, placed his huge canvases flat on the floor and then walked around each side, pouring and dripping his paint in an effort to "literally be *in* the painting." Such action paintings, with their commanding size, bold form, powerful color contrasts, and rough texture, were vibrant, frenzied, meditative, disorienting, and provocative.

THE BEATS The desire to liberate self-expression and reject middle-class conventions also animated a small but highly visible and controversial group of young writers, poets, painters, and musicians known as the Beats. These young men—Jack Kerouac, Allen Ginsberg, Gary Snyder, William Burroughs, and Gregory Corso, among others—rebelled against the mundane horrors

Allen Ginsberg

Ginsberg, considered the poet laureate of the Beat generation, reads his uncensored poetry to a crowd in Washington Square Park in New York City.

of middle-class life. The Beats were not lost in despair, however; they strenuously embraced life. But it was life on their own terms, and their terms were shocking to most observers.

The self-described Beats grew out of the bohemian underground in New York's Greenwich Village. Essentially apolitical throughout the 1950s, the Beats sought personal rather than social solutions to their hopes and anxieties. As Jack Kerouac insisted, his friends were not beat in the sense of beaten; they were "mad to live, mad to talk, mad to be saved." Their road to salvation lay in hallucinogenic drugs and alcohol, sex, a penchant for jazz and the street life of urban ghettos, an affinity for Buddhism, and a restless, vagabond spirit that took them speeding back and forth across the country between San Francisco and New York.

This existential mania for intense experience and frantic motion provided the subject matter for the Beats' writing. Ginsberg's long prose poem *Howl*, published in 1956, features an explicit sensuality as well as an impressionistic attempt to catch the color, movement, and dynamism of modern life. Kerouac published his autobiographical novel *On the Road* a year later. In frenzied prose it portrays the Beats' life of "bursting ecstasies" and maniacal traveling. *Howl* and *On the Road* elicited angry sarcasm from many reviewers, but the books enjoyed brisk sales, especially among young people. *On the Road* made the best-seller list, and soon the term *Beat generation* or *beatnik* referred to almost any young rebel who openly dissented from middle-class life.

A PARADOXICAL ERA

For all their eccentricities and vitality the Beats had little impact on the prevailing patterns of postwar social and cultural life. The same held true for most of the critics who attacked the smug conformity and excessive materialism they saw pervading their society. The public had become weary of larger social or political concerns in the aftermath of the Depression and the war. Instead, Americans eagerly focused on personal and family goals and material achievements.

Yet those achievements, considerable as they were, eventually created a new set of problems. The benefits of abundance were by no means equally distributed during the 1950s, and millions of people still lived in poverty. For those more fortunate, unprecedented affluence and security fostered greater leisure and independence, which in turn provided opportunities for pursuing more diverse notions of what the good life entailed. Yet the conformist mentality of the cold war era discouraged experimentation. By the mid-1960s, tensions between innovation and convention would erupt into open conflict. Many members of the baby boom generation would become the leaders of the 1960s rebellion against corporate conformity and consumerism. Ironically, the person who would warn Americans of the 1960s of the mounting dangers of the burgeoning "military-industrial complex" was the president who had long symbolized its growth: Dwight D. Eisenhower.

CHAPTER SUMMARY

- **Growth of U.S. Economy** High levels of government spending, begun before the war, continued during the postwar period. The GI Bill of Rights gave a boost to home buying and helped many veterans attend college and thereby enter the middle class. Unemployment was virtually nonexistent, and consumer demand for homes, cars, and the household goods that had been unavailable during the war fueled the economy, as did buying on credit.

- **Conformity in American Society** After World War II, with the growth of suburbs, corporations, and advertising, society appeared highly uniform, yet pockets of poverty persisted, and minorities did not prosper to the extent that white Americans did. Most white mothers did not work outside the home and were expected to find pleasure in housework. Attendance at worship services soared. The semblance of uniformity was perhaps a reaction to the feeling that society was threatened by an atheistic communism. Although popular culture reflected the affluence of the white middle class, the art and literature of the period hinted at an underlying alienation.

- **The American Family** Conformity extended to the image of the family as depicted on television and in magazines. Typically a family consisted of a father who worked in a city and a mother who stayed at home in the suburbs, devoting herself to home, husband, and children. This image did not reflect everyone's reality, however. A wave of juvenile delinquency swept middle-class society, and millions of Americans, especially minorities, lived in poverty during this era of affluence. The great black migration allowed some black families to climb into the middle class, but left many stuck in the teeming ghettos in northern cities.

- **The Beat Generation** Dissatisfaction with conformity was reflected in the literature and art of the Beat generation. Artists such as Edward Hopper dwelled on the desolate loneliness of urban settings, and a group of younger painters turned from realism to abstract expressionism in the belief that modern society was too chaotic to be represented in a literal manner. The Beats were a small yet highly visible group of writers and artists who rebelled against the regimented horrors of war and the mundane horrors of middle-class life. They sought their salvation through the use of hallucinogenic drugs, alcohol, sex, and music in their attempts to capture the vitality of modern life.

CHRONOLOGY

1944	Congress passes the Servicemen's Readjustment Act (GI Bill of Rights)
1949	Arthur Miller's *Death of a Salesman* is produced
1950	David Riesman's *The Lonely Crowd* is published
1952	Ralph Ellison's *Invisible Man* is published
1956	Elvis Presley's "Heartbreak Hotel" is released
1956	Allen Ginsberg's *Howl* is published
1957	Jack Kerouac's *On the Road* is published
1957	Baby boom peaks
1958	John Kenneth Galbraith's *The Affluent Society* is published

KEY TERMS & NAMES

consumer culture p. 957

suburbia p. 959

sunbelt p. 959

great black migration
p. 961

Levittown p. 961

baby boom p. 967

youth culture p. 967

rock and roll p. 968

Beats p. 971

beatnik p. 972

33

CONFLICT AND DEADLOCK: THE EISENHOWER YEARS

FOCUS QUESTIONS wwnorton.com/studyspace

- What were the main characteristics of Eisenhower's "dynamic conservatism"?
- What shaped American foreign policy in the 1950s?
- What events in Southeast Asia led to America's involvement in Vietnam?
- Why did the civil rights movement emerge in the 1950s?

The New Deal political coalition established by Franklin Roosevelt and sustained by Harry Truman posed a formidable challenge to Republicans after World War II. To counter the potent combination of Solid South white Democrats, African Americans, members of other minority groups, and organized labor, the Grand Old Party turned in 1952 to General Dwight David Eisenhower, a military hero capable of attracting independent voters as well as some Democrats. Eisenhower's commitment to a "moderate Republicanism" promised to slow the rate of government expansion while retaining many of the cherished social programs established by Roosevelt and Truman. Eisenhower promised to restore the authority of state and local governments and restrain the executive branch from political and social "engineering." In the process, the former general sought to reinforce traditional virtues and inspire Americans with a vision of a brighter future amid a continuing "cold war."

"TIME FOR A CHANGE"

By 1952 the Truman administration had piled up a heavy burden of political liabilities: a bloody stalemate in Korea, renewed wage and price controls at home, reckless charges of subversion and disloyalty among federal employees, and the exposure of corrupt lobbyists and influence peddlers who rigged favors in Washington. The disclosure of government corruption led Truman to fire nearly 250 employees of the Internal Revenue Service. Doubts lingered that he would ever finish the housecleaning.

THE POLITICAL RISE OF EISENHOWER   It was, in a slogan of the day, "time for a change," and Republicans saw public sentiment turning their way as the 1952 election approached. Republican leaders recruited General Dwight D. Eisenhower to be their candidate. Despite his roots in Kansas Republican conservatism, Eisenhower had initially supported Roosevelt and the New Deal, and he admired Roosevelt's wartime leadership. During the Truman years, however, Eisenhower reverted to the political party of his youth. In early 1952 he affirmed that he was a Republican and permitted his name to be entered in party primaries. He won the nomination on the first ballot, then balanced the ticket by selecting as his running mate a youthful Californian, the thirty-nine-year-old senator Richard M. Nixon, who had built a career on strenuous opposition to domestic "subversives."

THE ELECTION OF 1952   The Twenty-second Amendment, ratified in 1951, forbade any president from serving more than two terms. The amendment exempted the current incumbent, Harry Truman. But he had no desire to run again. Weary of the war in Korea and harassed by charges of subversion and corruption in his administration, Truman withdrew and gave his support to Illinois governor Adlai E. Stevenson, who roused the delegates to the Democratic Convention with an eloquent speech welcoming them to Chicago.

The 1952 campaign matched two contrasting personalities. Eisenhower, though a political novice, was a world military hero who had been in the public eye for a decade. Stevenson was hardly known outside Illinois. The genial Eisenhower, who disliked politics and politicians, pledged to clean up "the mess in Washington." To this he added a promise, late in the campaign, that as president-elect he would secure "an early and honorable" peace in Korea.

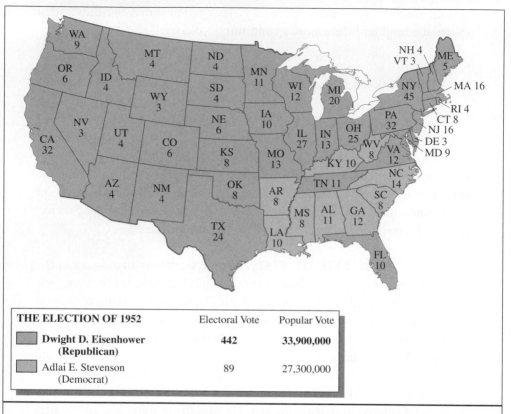

THE ELECTION OF 1952	Electoral Vote	Popular Vote
▨ Dwight D. Eisenhower (Republican)	442	33,900,000
▨ Adlai E. Stevenson (Democrat)	89	27,300,000

Why was the contest between Adlai Stevenson and Dwight Eisenhower so lopsided? Why was Eisenhower's victory in the South remarkable? Did Eisenhower's broad appeal help congressional Republicans win more seats?

Stevenson offered a keen intellect spiced with a quick wit, but his resolve to "talk sense" and "tell the truth to the American people" came across as too aloof, a shade too intellectual. The Republicans labeled him an egghead in contrast to Eisenhower, the folksy man of the people, the man of decisive action.

In the end, Stevenson's humor and intellect were no match for Eisenhower's popularity. The war hero triumphed in a landslide of nearly 34 million votes to a little over 27 million for Stevenson. The election marked a turning point in Republican fortunes in the South: for the first time since the 1850s, the South was moving toward a two-party system. Stevenson carried only eight southern states plus West Virginia; Eisenhower picked up five states on the periphery of the Deep South: Florida, Oklahoma, Tennessee, Texas, and Virginia. The "nonpolitical" Eisenhower had made it respectable, even fashionable, to vote Republican in the South. Elsewhere, too, the general made inroads into the Democrats' New Deal coalition, attracting supporters among the ethnic and religious minorities in the major cities who had long identified with the Democratic party.

The voters, it turned out, liked Eisenhower better than they liked his party. In the 1952 election, Democrats retained most of the governorships, lost control of the House by only eight seats, and broke even in the Senate. The congressional elections two years later would weaken the Republican grip on Congress, and Eisenhower would have to work with a Democratic Congress throughout his term in office.

EISENHOWER'S "HIDDEN-HAND" PRESIDENCY

IKE   Born in Denison, Texas, in 1890, Dwight David Eisenhower grew up in Abilene, Kansas, and attended the U.S. Military Academy at West Point, New York. As a general during World War II, he took command of American forces in the European theater and directed the invasion of North Africa in 1942. In 1944 he assumed command of Allied forces in preparation for the invasion of German-controlled Europe. After the war, by then the five-star general of the army, Eisenhower became chief of staff and supreme commander of NATO forces, with a brief interlude as president of Columbia University.

Far from being a "do-nothing" president, as some have charged, Eisenhower was an effective leader. The art of leadership, he once explained, required "persuasion—and conciliation—and education—and patience. That's the only kind of leadership I know—or believe in—or will practice." The public image of Ike was warm, sincere, and unpretentious, a man who rose above partisan politics. Those who were close to him have presented another side, however. When provoked, the genial general could unleash a fiery temper and release a stream of scalding profanity. One student of Eisenhower's leadership techniques has spoken of a "hidden-hand" presidency, in which Ike deliberately cultivated a public image of passivity to cloak his active involvement in policy decisions.

"DYNAMIC CONSERVATISM" AT HOME   Eisenhower called his domestic program dynamic conservatism, which meant being "conservative when it comes to money and liberal when it comes to human beings." Budget cutting was a high priority. Eisenhower warned repeatedly against the dangers of "creeping socialism," "huge bureaucracies," and budget deficits. His administration ended wage and price controls and reduced federal farm-price subsidies.

But although Eisenhower chipped away at New Deal programs, his presidency in the end served rather to legitimate the New Deal by keeping its basic structure and premises intact during an era of prosperity. In some ways the administration expanded the New Deal, especially after 1954, when it had the help of Democratic Congresses. Amendments to the Social Security Act in 1954 and 1956 brought coverage to millions in categories formerly excluded: professional people, domestic and clerical workers, farmworkers, and members of the armed forces. The federal minimum wage rose in 1955 from 75¢ to $1 an hour. Federal expenditures for public health rose steadily in the Eisenhower years, and low-income housing continued to be built, although on a much-reduced scale. Some farm-related aid programs were actually expanded.

Despite Eisenhower's disapproval of federal electric-power programs, he continued to support government public-works projects that served the national interest. Two such programs left major monuments to his presidency: the St. Lawrence Seaway and the interstate highways. The St. Lawrence Seaway, opened in 1959 as a joint venture with Canada, allowed oceangoing ships to reach the Great Lakes. The Federal-Aid Highway Act of 1956 authorized the federal government to contribute 90 percent of the cost of building 42,500 miles of limited-access interstate highways to serve the needs of commerce and defense, as well as the convenience of private citizens. The states provided the remaining 10 percent.

CONCLUDING AN ARMISTICE   America's new global responsibilities absorbed much of Eisenhower's attention. The most pressing problem when he entered office was the painful deadlock in the Korean peace talks. To break the stalemate, Eisenhower took a bold stand. In mid-May 1953 he stepped up aerial bombardment of Communist North Korea, then had Secretary of State John Foster Dulles warn the Chinese of his willingness to use atomic bombs. Whether for that reason or others, negotiations moved quickly toward an armistice along the established border just above the 38th parallel and toward a complicated arrangement for an exchange of prisoners that allowed captives to decide whether to accept or refuse repatriation.

On July 26, 1953, Eisenhower announced the conclusion of the Korean armistice agreement. No one knows if he actually would have forced the issue with atomic weapons. Perhaps the more decisive factors in bringing about a settlement were the mounting Chinese losses and the spirit of uncertainty and caution felt by the Russian Communists after the death of Joseph Stalin on March 5, 1953, six weeks after Ike's inauguration.

The Army-McCarthy hearings, June 1954

The attorney Joseph Welch (hand on head) listening incredulously to Senator McCarthy's claims of Communist infiltration of the U.S. Army.

CONCLUDING A WITCH HUNT   The Korean armistice helped to end the meteoric career of Senator Joseph McCarthy. The Wisconsin senator had launched a one-man crusade to root out Communists and spies. Eventually the logic of McCarthy's unscrupulous tactics led to his self-destruction, but not before he had left many careers and reputations in ruins. The Eisenhower Republicans thought their victory in 1952 would curb McCarthy's recklessness, but the senator grew more outlandish in both his charges and his investigative methods.

McCarthy finally overreached himself in the spring of 1954, when as chairman of the Senate's Government Operations Committee he made the absurd charge that the U.S. Army itself was "soft" on communism. The televised Army-McCarthy hearings displayed McCarthy at his worst, scowling at critics, bullying witnesses, repeatedly calling "point of order." He became the perfect foil for the army's gentle but unflappable legal counsel, Joseph Welch, whose rapier wit repeatedly drew blood. On December 2, 1954, the Senate voted 67 to 22 to "condemn" McCarthy for contempt of the Senate. McCarthy's political career collapsed. For all his attacks and inquiries he had never uncovered one Communist in the government. McCarthyism, Eisenhower joked, had become McCarthywasm. To the end, Eisenhower refused to "get down in the gutter with that guy" and sully the dignity of the presidency. He did work resolutely against McCarthy behind the scenes, but some scholars consider his "hidden-hand" approach to have been ineffective at best and cowardly at worst.

Chief Justice Earl Warren

One of the most influential Supreme
Court justices of the twentieth century.

Eisenhower believed that espionage posed a real danger to national security. He denied clemency to Julius and Ethel Rosenberg, who had been convicted of passing atomic secrets to the Russians, on the grounds that they "may have condemned to death tens of millions of innocent people." The Rosenbergs were electrocuted in 1953.

INTERNAL SECURITY The anti-Communist crusade survived McCarthy's downfall. Even before 1954, Eisenhower stiffened the government security program that Truman had set up in 1947. In 1953 he issued an executive order broadening the basis for firing subversive government workers, replacing Truman's criterion of "disloyalty" with the new category of "security risk." Under the new edict, federal workers could lose their jobs because of dubious political associations or personal behavior that might make them careless or vulnerable to blackmail. The Supreme Court, however, modified some of the more extreme expressions of this continuation of the Red Scare.

In 1953, Eisenhower appointed as chief justice of the Supreme Court former Republican governor Earl Warren of California, a decision he later pronounced the "biggest damnfool mistake I ever made." Warren, who had seemed safely conservative while in electoral politics, led an active Court on issues of civil rights and liberties. The Warren Court (1953–1969), under the chief justice's influence, became an important force for social and political change in the 1960s. In connection with security programs and loyalty requirements, the Court veered back in the direction of individual rights.

FOREIGN INTERVENTION

DULLES AND FOREIGN POLICY The Eisenhower administration promised new foreign-policy departures under the direction of Secretary of State John Foster Dulles. Grandson of one secretary of state and nephew of another, Dulles pursued a lifetime career as an international lawyer and sometime diplomat. Son of a minister and himself an earnest Presbyterian, Dulles, in the words of the British ambassador, resembled those old zealots of the wars of religion who "saw the world as an arena in which the forces of good and evil were continuously at war." But he was also a man of immense energy, intelligence, and experience.

The foreign-policy planks of the 1952 Republican platform, which Dulles wrote, showed both the moralist and the tactician at work. Truman's policy of "containing" communism was needlessly defensive, Dulles thought. Americans instead should promote the "liberation" of sovereign nations from Soviet domination. Eisenhower was quick to explain, however, that liberating Eastern Europe from Soviet control would not involve military force. He would promote independence "by every peaceful means, but only by peaceful means."

Yet for all his talk of liberating Eastern Europe, Dulles made no significant departure from the containment strategy created under Truman. Instead, he institutionalized containment in the rigid mold of his cold war rhetoric and extended it to the military strategy of deterrence. Dulles's endorsement of "massive retaliation" was an effort to get, in the slogan soon current, "more bang for the buck." By this time both the United States and the Soviet Union had exploded hydrogen bombs. With the new policy of deterrence, what Winston Churchill called a "balance of terror" had replaced the old balance of power. The threat of nuclear holocaust was terrifying, but the notion that the United States would risk such a disaster in response to local wars had little credibility.

Dulles's policy of "brinkmanship" depended for its strategic effect upon those very fears of nuclear disaster. Dulles argued in 1956 that in following a tough policy of confronting communism, a nation sometimes had to "go to the brink" of nuclear war. Such a firm stand had halted aggression in Korea in 1953 when America threatened to use

"Don't Be Afraid—I Can Always Pull You Back."

Secretary of State John Foster Dulles pushes a reluctant America to the brink of war.

atomic weapons. Dulles also employed brinkmanship in Indochina in 1954, when U.S. aircraft carriers moved into the South China Sea "both to deter any Red Chinese attack against Indochina and to provide weapons for instant retaliation."

INDOCHINA: THE BACKGROUND TO WAR   Like the rest of the old colonial world of Asia and Africa, French Indochina experienced a wave of nationalism after World War II, damaging both the power and the prestige of France. By the early 1950s most of British Asia was independent or on its way to independence: India, Pakistan, Ceylon (now Sri Lanka), Burma (now Myanmar), and the Malay States (now Malaysia). The Dutch and the French, however, were less willing to give up their colonies, a situation that created a dilemma for U.S. policy makers. Americans sympathized with the colonial nationalists but wanted Dutch and French help fending off the spread of communism. The Dutch and the French concentrated on maintaining control of their colonial empires, which meant that they had to reconquer areas that had passed from Japanese occupation into the hands of local patriots. The Truman administration had felt obliged to comply with Dutch and French pleas for aid.

French Indochina, created in the nineteenth century out of the old kingdoms of Cambodia, Laos, and Vietnam, offered a variation on colonial nationalism. During World War II, opposition to the Japanese occupation of Indochina was led by the Viet Minh (League for the Independence of Vietnam), whose members were nationalists who had fallen under the influence of Communists led by the magnetic rebel Ho Chi Minh. At the end of the war, the Viet Minh controlled part of northern Vietnam, and on September 2, 1945, Ho Chi Minh proclaimed a Democratic Republic of Vietnam, with its capital in Hanoi. Ho had secretly received American help against the Japanese during the war, but his bids for further aid after the war went unanswered. Vietnam was a

Ho Chi Minh

A seasoned revolutionary, Ho Chi Minh cultivated a humble, proletarian image of himself as Uncle Ho, a man of the people.

low priority in U.S. diplomatic concerns, which at the time were focused on restoring western Europe and containing the spread of communism there.

In 1946 the French government recognized Ho's new government as a "free state" within the French-Indochinese union. Before the year was out, however, Ho had opposed French efforts to establish another regime in the southern provinces, and his clash with the French soon expanded into the First Indochina War. This was a troubling development for the U.S. government. On the one hand, the United States resented France's determination to restore colonial rule. On the other hand, Truman was determined to see France become a bulwark against communism in Europe. As a result, the U.S. government acquiesced in France's efforts to crush Vietnamese nationalism.

The Viet Minh movement thereafter became more dependent upon the Soviet Union and Communist China for help. In 1950, with the outbreak of fighting in Korea, the struggle in Vietnam took on the appearance of a battleground in the cold war. When the Korean War ended, American aid to the French in Vietnam, begun by the Truman administration, escalated dramatically. By the end of 1953, the Eisenhower administration was paying about two thirds of the cost of the French war effort in Indochina.

Dien Bien Phu

Captured French soldiers march through the battlefield after their surrender.

But even with lavish U.S. aid the French were unable to suppress the well-organized and tenacious Viet Minh. In 1954 a major French force had been sent to Dien Bien Phu, in the northwest corner of Vietnam, near the Laotian border, in the hope of luring Viet Minh guerrillas into the open and overwhelming them with superior firepower. The French instead found themselves surrounded by a superior force that laid siege to their stronghold.

In March 1954 the French government requested an American air strike to relieve the pressure on Dien Bien Phu. Eisenhower seemed to endorse forceful action when he advanced his "domino theory" at a news conference on April 7. He implied that if Indochina fell to the Communists, the rest of Asia would be next. Eisenhower, however, opposed direct U.S. military action unless the British lent support. When they refused, the president backed away from unilateral action, explaining that it would be a "tragic error to go in alone as a partner of France."

America's decision not to intervene sealed the fate of the besieged French garrison at Dien Bien Phu. On May 7, 1954, the Viet Minh overwhelmed the courageous but vastly outnumbered French resistance. It was the very eve of the day on which an international conference at Geneva took up the question of Indochina. Six weeks later, as French forces continued to suffer defeats in Vietnam, a new French government promised an early settlement. On July 20, representatives of France, Britain, the Soviet Union, the People's Republic of China, and the Viet Minh signed the Geneva Accords and the next day produced their Final Declaration, which proposed to make Laos and Cambodia independent and divide Vietnam at the 17th parallel. The Viet Minh would take power in the north, and the French would remain south of the line until elections in 1956 would reunify Vietnam. American and South Vietnamese representatives refused to join in the accords or sign the Final Declaration.

Eisenhower announced that although the United States "had not itself been party to or bound by the decision taken at the Conference," any renewal of Communist aggression in Vietnam "would be viewed by us as a matter of grave concern." (He failed to note that the United States had agreed at Geneva to "refrain from the threat or use of force to disturb" the agreements that the U.S. refused to sign.) Ho Chi Minh and his government in Hanoi quickly sought to consolidate control throughout the north. In the hinterlands local Communists held kangaroo courts, trying and then executing landowners and confiscating their land. Residents of the north who wished to leave for the south did so with American aid. Over 900,000 refugees, most of them Catholics, relocated in the south, causing staggering logistical problems for the struggling new government there.

Power in the south gravitated to a new premier, Ngo Dinh Diem, a Catholic nationalist who had opposed both the French and the Viet Minh. Diem took office during the Geneva talks, after returning from exile in a New Jersey seminary. In 1954, Eisenhower offered to assist Diem if he would enact democratic reforms and distribute land to the peasants. U.S. aid took the form of training Diem's armed forces and police. Eisenhower remained opposed to the use of U.S. combat troops. He was convinced that such military intervention would bog down into a costly stalemate—as it eventually did.

Instead of instituting comprehensive reforms, however, Diem suppressed his political opponents on both the right and the left, offering little or no land distribution and permitting widespread corruption. In 1956 he refused to join in the elections to reunify Vietnam, and the United States endorsed his decision. But Diem's efforts to eliminate all opposition only played into the hands of the Communists, who found more and more recruits among the discontented peasantry. By 1957 guerrilla forces in the south, known as the Viet Cong, had begun attacks on the Diem government, and in 1960 the resistance formed its own political arm, the National Liberation Front. As guerrilla warfare gradually disrupted South Vietnam, Eisenhower was helpless to do anything but "sink or swim with Ngo Dinh Diem."

REELECTION AND FOREIGN CRISES

As the United States continued to forge postwar alliances and bring pressure to bear on foreign governments by practicing brinkmanship, a new presidential campaign unfolded. Despite having suffered a coronary seizure in the fall of 1955 and undergoing an operation for ilcitis (an intestinal inflammation) in early 1956, Eisenhower decided to run for reelection. He retained widespread public support although the Democrats controlled Congress. Meanwhile, new crises required him to take decisive action.

A LANDSLIDE FOR IKE   In 1956 the Republican Convention renominated Eisenhower by acclamation and again named Nixon the vice-presidential candidate. The party platform endorsed Eisenhower's "modern Republicanism." The Democrats turned again to Adlai Stevenson, with a platform that revived party issues: less "favoritism" to big business, repeal of the Taft-Hartley Act, increased aid to farmers, and tax relief for those in low-income brackets.

Neither candidate generated much excitement. The Democrats focused their fire on the heir apparent, Richard Nixon, a "man of many masks." Stevenson roused little enthusiasm for two controversial proposals: to replace military conscription with an all-volunteer army and to ban hydrogen-bomb tests by international agreement. Both involved military questions that put Stevenson at a disadvantage by pitting his judgment against that of a successful former general. Voters handed Eisenhower a landslide victory. In carrying Louisiana, Eisenhower became the first Republican to win a Deep South state since Reconstruction; nationally, he carried all but seven states.

CRISIS IN THE MIDDLE EAST   To forestall Soviet penetration in the Middle East, the Eisenhower-Dulles foreign policy cultivated Arab friendship, and in 1955 Dulles had completed his line of alliances across the northern tier of the Middle East. Under American sponsorship, Britain had joined Turkey, Iraq, Iran, and Pakistan in the Middle East Treaty Organization (METO), or the Baghdad Pact Organization, as the treaty was commonly called. But after Iraq, the only Arab member, withdrew in 1959, the alliance lost its cohesion and credibility. The Arab states remained aloof from the organization. These were the states of the Arab League (Egypt, Jordan, Lebanon, Syria, Iraq, Saudi Arabia, and Yemen), which had warred on Israel in 1948–1949 and remained committed to its destruction.

The most fateful developments in the Middle East turned on the rise of the Egyptian general Gamal Abdel Nasser, who overthrew King Farouk in 1952. Nasser's nationalist regime soon pressed for the withdrawal of British forces guarding the Suez Canal, the crucial link between the Mediterranean Sea and the Indian Ocean. Eisenhower and Dulles supported Nasser's demand, and in 1954 an Anglo-Egyptian treaty provided for British withdrawal within twenty months. Ownership of the canal remained with the Anglo-French Suez Canal Company, however.

Nasser, like other leaders of the third world, remained unaligned in the cold war and sought to play both sides off against each other. The United States in turn courted Egyptian support by offering a loan to build a huge hydroelectric plant at Aswān on the Nile River. From the outset the administration's proposal was opposed by Jewish constituencies concerned with Egyptian threats to Israel and by southern congressmen who feared the competition from Egyptian cotton. In 1956, when Nasser increased trade with the Soviet bloc and recognized Communist China, Dulles abruptly canceled the loan offer.

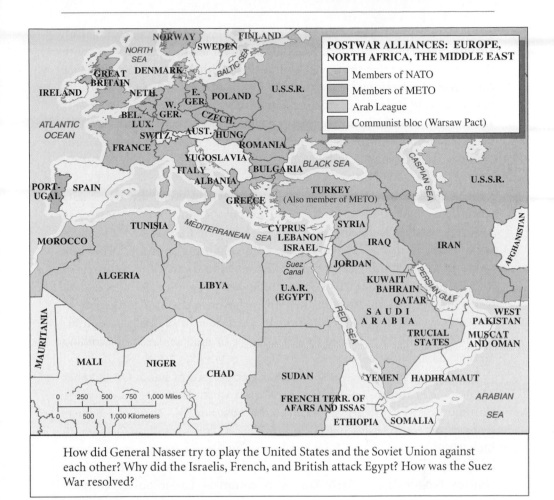

POSTWAR ALLIANCES: EUROPE, NORTH AFRICA, THE MIDDLE EAST

Members of NATO
Members of METO
Arab League
Communist bloc (Warsaw Pact)

How did General Nasser try to play the United States and the Soviet Union against each other? Why did the Israelis, French, and British attack Egypt? How was the Suez War resolved?

The outcome was far from a triumph of American diplomacy. The chief victims, it turned out, were Anglo-French interests in the Suez. Unable to retaliate against the United States, Nasser took control of the Suez Canal Company. The British and the French were furious. While negotiations dragged on, Israeli forces invaded the Gaza Strip and the Sinai Peninsula. Ostensibly their aim was to root out Arab guerrillas, but actually it was to synchronize with the British and the French, who began bombing Egyptian air bases and occupied Port Said, at the northern end of the canal.

The Suez War put the United States in a quandary. Either the administration could support its Western allies and see the troublesome Nasser crushed, or it could defend the UN Charter and champion Arab nationalism against imperialist aggression. Eisenhower opted for the latter course, with the unusual result that the Soviet Union sided with the United States. Once the threat of American embargoes had forced the Anglo-French-Israeli alliance to halt its advance against Egypt, the Soviets capitalized on the situation by threatening to use missiles against the Western aggressors. This belated bravado won for the Soviet Union in the Arab world some of the credit actually owed the United States.

REPRESSION IN HUNGARY   In the Soviet Union, Premier Nikita Khrushchev had come out on top in the post-Stalin power struggles. In 1956, Khrushchev had delivered a "secret" speech on the crimes of the Stalin era and had hinted at relaxed policies in neighboring countries. This new policy of "de-Stalinization" put Stalinist leaders in the satellite countries of Eastern Europe on the defensive and emboldened the more independent leaders to take action. Riots in the Polish city of Poznań led to the rise of Władysław Gomułka, a Polish nationalist, as leader of the Polish Communist party. Gomułka managed to win a degree of independence by avoiding an open break with the Soviets.

In Hungary, however, a similar movement got out of hand. On October 23, 1956, fighting broke out in Budapest, after which Imre Nagy, a moderate Communist, was installed as head of the government. Again the Soviets seemed content to let de-Stalinization follow its course, and on October 28 they withdrew their forces from Budapest. But Nagy's announcement three days later that Hungary would withdraw from the Warsaw Pact (a military alliance linking the Eastern European countries under Soviet control) brought Soviet tanks back into Budapest. Although Khrushchev was willing to relax relations with the Eastern European satellites, he refused to allow them to break with the Soviet Union or abandon their mutual defense obligations. The Soviets installed a more compliant leader in Hungary, János Kádár, and hauled Nagy off to Moscow, where a firing squad executed him in 1958. It was a tragic ending to an independence movement that at the outset promised the sort of moderation that might have vindicated George Kennan's policy of containment, if not Dulles's notion of liberation.

REACTIONS TO SPUTNIK   On October 4, 1957, the Soviets launched the first satellite, called *Sputnik 1*. Americans, until then complacent about their technical superiority, suddenly discovered an apparent "missile gap." If the Soviets were so advanced in rocketry, then perhaps they could hit American cities with missiles. All along, Eisenhower had known that the "missile gap" was more illusory than real, but he could not reveal the fact that high-altitude American U-2 spy planes were gathering that information.

Soviet success with its Sputnik program prompted the United States to increase defense spending, offer NATO allies intermediate-range ballistic missiles pending development of long-range intercontinental ballistic missiles (ICBMs), set up a new agency to coordinate space efforts, and establish a crash program in science education and military research. In 1958, Congress created the National Aeronautics and Space Administration (NASA) to coordinate research and development in the space program. Before the end of the year, NASA had unveiled a program to put people in orbit, but the first manned U.S. flight, by Commander Alan B. Shepard Jr., did not take place until May 5, 1961. Finally, in 1958, Congress enacted the National Defense Education Act, which authorized federal grants for training, especially in mathematics, science, and modern languages, as well as for student loans and fellowships.

FESTERING PROBLEMS ABROAD

Once the Suez and Hungary crises had faded from the front pages, Eisenhower enjoyed eighteen months of smooth sailing in foreign affairs. Nonetheless, a brief flurry of media attention occurred in 1958 when hostile demonstrations were held in Peru and Venezuela against Vice President Richard Nixon, who was on a goodwill tour of eight Latin American countries. Meanwhile, problems in the Middle East and Europe continued to fester, only to reemerge with new force in 1958. The cold war would again be played out in the Middle East and in Eastern Europe, as well as at America's back door, in Cuba.

THE MIDDLE EAST   By 1958, Congress had approved what came to be called the Eisenhower Doctrine, a resolution that promised to extend economic and military aid to Middle East nations and to use armed force if necessary to assist any such nation against military aggression by any Communist country.

Egypt's president Nasser, meanwhile, had emerged from the Suez crisis with heightened prestige, and in 1958 he created the United Arab Republic by a (short-lived) merger with Syria. Then a leftist coup in Iraq, supposedly inspired by Nasser and the Soviets, threw out the pro-Western government there. Lebanon, already unsettled by internal conflict, appealed to the United States for support to fend off a similar fate. Eisenhower immediately ordered 5,000 marines into Lebanon, limiting them to the capital, Beirut, and its airfield. He proposed to go no farther because, he said later, if the government was not strong enough to hold out with such protection, then "we probably should not be there." In October 1958, once the situation had stabilized and the Lebanese factions had reached a compromise, the U.S. forces withdrew.

BERLIN The problem of Berlin, an urban island of Western capitalism deep in Soviet-controlled East Germany, continued to fester with little chance of a resolution. Soviet premier Nikita Khrushchev called it a "bone in his throat." West Berlin served as a "showplace" of Western democracy and prosperity in the middle of Communist East Germany, a listening post for Western intelligence gathering, and a funnel through which news and propaganda from the West penetrated what the British leader Winston Churchill had called the iron curtain. Although East Germany had sealed its western frontiers, refugees could still pass from East to West Berlin. On November 10, 1958, however, Khrushchev threatened to give East Germany control of East Berlin and the air lanes into West Berlin. After the deadline he set, May 27, 1959, Western occupation authorities would have to deal with the East German government, in effect recognizing it, or face the possibility of another blockade.

Eisenhower refused to budge from his position on Berlin. At the same time, he refused to engage in saber rattling or even to cancel existing plans to reduce the overall size of the army. Khrushchev, it turned out, was no more eager for confrontation than Eisenhower. Khrushchev's deadline passed almost unnoticed. In September 1959 the Soviet premier visited the United States, stopping in New York, Washington, D.C., Los Angeles, San Francisco, and Iowa. In talks with Eisenhower, he endorsed "peaceful coexistence," and Eisenhower admitted that the Berlin situation was "abnormal." They agreed to discuss the problem at a summit meeting in the spring.

THE U-2 SUMMIT The planned summit meeting blew up in Eisenhower's face, however. On May 1, 1960, a Soviet rocket brought down an American U-2 spy plane over the Soviet Union. After a period of international jousting with Khrushchev, Eisenhower took personal responsibility for the incident—an unprecedented action for a head of state—and justified it on grounds of national security. At a summit meeting in Paris five days later, Khrushchev called upon the president to repudiate the U-2 flights, which had been going on for more than three years, and "pass severe judgment on those responsible." When Eisenhower refused, Khrushchev left the meeting.

Fidel Castro

Castro (center) became Cuba's Communist premier in 1959, following years of guerrilla warfare against the regime of Fulgencio Batista. He planned a social and agrarian revolution and opposed foreign control of the Cuban economy.

CASTRO'S CUBA Among all of Eisenhower's foreign troubles, the greatest thorn in his side was the Communist regime of Fidel Castro, which took power in Cuba on January 1, 1959, after two years of guerrilla warfare against a right-wing dictator. Castro's forces had the support of many Americans who hoped for a new day of democratic government in Cuba. But those hopes were dashed when American television reported unfair trials and summary executions conducted by the victorious leader. When Castro instituted programs of land reform and nationalization of foreign-owned property, relations with the United States worsened. Some observers believed, however, that by rejecting Castro's requests for loans and other help, the U.S. government lost a chance to influence the direction of the Cuban revolution. Some thought, too, that by acting upon the assumption that Communists had the upper hand in his movement, the administration may have ensured that fact.

Castro, on the other hand, eagerly accepted Soviet support. In 1960 he entered a trade agreement to swap Cuban sugar for Soviet oil and machinery. One of Eisenhower's last acts as president, on January 3, 1961, was to suspend diplomatic relations with Cuba. The president also secretly authorized the CIA to begin training a force of Cuban refugees for a new revolution. The final decision on the use of that force would rest with the next president, John F. Kennedy.

THE EARLY YEARS OF THE CIVIL RIGHTS MOVEMENT

While the cold war had produced a tense stalemate by the mid-1950s, race relations in the United States threatened to destroy the domestic tranquility masking years of injustice. Eisenhower entered office committed to civil rights in principle. During his first three years, public facilities in Washington, D.C., were desegregated. Beyond that, however, two aspects of the president's philosophy inhibited vigorous action in enforcing the principle of civil rights: his preference for state or local action over federal involvement and his doubt that laws could change deeply embedded racial attitudes. "I don't believe you can change the hearts of men with laws or decisions," he said. Eisenhower's passive stance meant that government leadership in the civil rights field came from the judiciary more than the executive or legislative branch of the government.

In the mid-1930s the NAACP had resolved to test the separate-but-equal doctrine that had upheld racial segregation since the *Plessy* decision in 1896. Charles H. Houston, vice dean of the Howard University Law School, laid the plans, and his former student Thurgood Marshall served as chief NAACP lawyer. They decided to begin their efforts to integrate society by focusing on higher education. But it took almost fifteen years to convince the courts that segregated schooling must end. In *Sweatt v. Painter* (1950), the Supreme Court ruled that a separate black law school in Texas was not equal in quality to the state's whites-only schools. The Court ordered the state to remedy the situation.

THE *BROWN* DECISION   By the early 1950s, challenges to state laws mandating segregation in the public schools were rising through the appellate courts. Five such cases, from Kansas, Delaware, South Carolina, Virgina, and the District of Columbia—usually cited by reference to the first, *Brown v. Board of Education of Topeka, Kansas*—came to the Supreme Court for joint argument by NAACP attorneys in 1952. Chief Justice Earl Warren wrote the opinion, handed down on May 17, 1954, in which a unanimous Court declared that "in the field of public education the doctrine of 'separate but

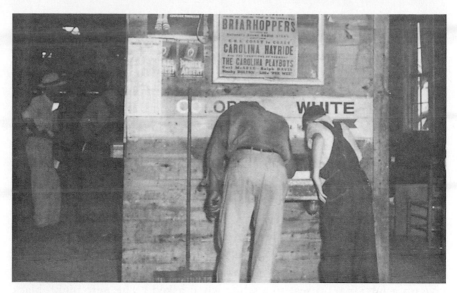

Civil rights stirrings

In the late 1930s the NAACP began to test the constitutionality of racial segregation.

equal' has no place." In support of its opinion, the Court cited sociological and psychological findings demonstrating that even if separate facilities were equal in quality, the mere fact of separating people by race engendered feelings of inferiority. A year later, after further argument, the Court directed that the process of racial integration should move "with all deliberate speed."

But Eisenhower refused to force states to comply with the Court's decisions. Privately he maintained "that the Supreme Court decision *set back* progress in the South *at least fifteen years.* The fellow who tries to tell me you can do these things by *force* is just plain *nuts.*" While token integration began as early as 1954 in the border states, hostility mounted in the Deep South and Virginia, led by the newly formed Citizens' Councils. The Citizens' Councils were middle- and upper-class versions of the Ku Klux Klan that spread quickly across the region and eventually included 250,000 members. Instead of physical violence and intimidation, the Councils used economic coercion against blacks who crossed racial boundaries. African Americans who defied white supremacy would lose their jobs, have their insurance policies canceled, or be denied personal loans or home mortgages. The Citizens' Councils grew so powerful in many communities that membership became almost a prerequisite for an aspiring white politician.

Before the end of 1955, opponents of court-ordered integration grew dangerously belligerent. Virginia senator Harry F. Byrd supplied a rallying cry: "Massive Resistance." In 1956, 101 members of Congress signed a "Southern Manifesto" denouncing the Supreme Court's decision in the *Brown* case as "a clear abuse of judicial power." In six southern states at the end of 1956, not a single black child attended school with whites.

THE MONTGOMERY BUS BOYCOTT   The essential role played by the NAACP and the courts in providing a legal lever for the civil rights movement often overshadows the courageous contributions of individual African Americans who took great personal risks to challenge segregation. In Montgomery, Alabama, for example, on December 1, 1955, Rosa Parks, a black seamstress committed to gaining equal rights, was arrested for refusing to give up her seat on a city bus to a white man. (As was the case in many southern communities, Montgomery had a local ordinance that required blacks to give up a bus or train seat to a white when asked.) The next night, black community leaders met in the Dexter Avenue Baptist Church to organize a massive bus boycott.

In Dexter Avenue's twenty-six-year-old pastor, Martin Luther King Jr., the movement found a charismatic leader. Born in Atlanta, the grandson of a slave and the son of a minister, King possessed intelligence, courage, and eloquence. After graduating from Morehouse College in Atlanta, he attended divinity school and earned a doctorate in philosophy from Boston University before accepting a call to preach in Montgomery. He inspired the civil rights movement with a compelling plea for nonviolent disobedience based upon the Gospels, the writings of Henry David Thoreau, and the example of Mahatma Gandhi in India. To his antagonists he said, "We will soon wear you down by our capacity to suffer, and in winning our freedom we will so appeal to your heart and conscience that we will win you in the process."

The Montgomery bus boycott achieved a remarkable solidarity. For more than a year, blacks used car pools, hitchhiked, or simply walked. But the white civic leaders held out against the boycott and against the pleas of a bus company tired of losing money. The boycotters finally won a federal case they had initiated against bus segregation, and in 1956 the Supreme Court affirmed that "the separate but equal doctrine can no longer be safely followed as a correct statement of the law." The next day, King and other African Americans boarded the buses.

To keep alive the spirit of the boycott, King and a group of associates in 1957 organized the Southern Christian Leadership Conference. Several days

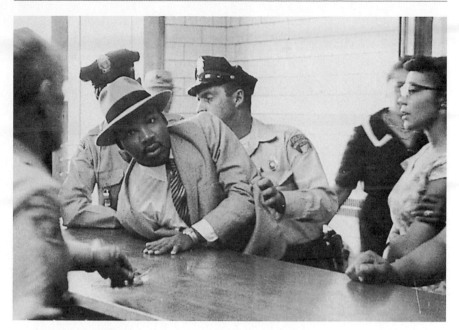

Montgomery, Alabama

Martin Luther King Jr., here facing arrest for leading a civil rights march, advocated nonviolent resistance to racial segregation.

later King found an unexploded dynamite bomb on his front porch. Two hours afterward he addressed his congregation:

> I'm not afraid of anybody this morning. Tell Montgomery they can keep shooting and I'm going to stand up to them; tell Montgomery they can keep bombing and I'm going to stand up to them. If I had to die tomorrow morning I would die happy because I've been to the mountain top and I've seen the promised land and it's going to be here in Montgomery.

THE ROLE OF RELIGION   The African American leaders of the civil rights movement were animated by powerful religious beliefs. Ministers were in the vanguard of the movement for racial equality and social justice. As the Reverend Andrew Young, one of King's lieutenants, said, "Ours was an evangelical freedom movement that identified salvation with not just one's personal relationship with God, but a new relationship between people black and white." African American congregations were the seedbed for civil rights

"Freedom" songs

Church congregation singing during the early civil rights movement.

protesters and volunteers. A deep religious faith bolstered those who risked life and freedom by marching, picketing, and protesting racial injustice. Numerous black churches were bombed by white racists who viewed them as the primary source of African American activism. The evangelical tradition in the African American community also provided many of the gospel "freedom" songs that enlivened civil rights marches and protests and gave solace and encouragement to those arrested. "We Shall Overcome," derived from an old gospel hymn, became the anthem of the civil rights movement.

An Atlanta newspaper reporter highlighted the courageous role of black churches in the movement when he asked, "Have they not provided the meeting-places, theme-song, and leaders for the center of non-violent protest?" The contrast with the indifferent attitude of southern white churches was vivid. White churches were "doing nothing at all," said the editor of the *Atlanta Constitution*. He explained that it was "strikingly clear that Christianity and the [black] churches have never been more relevant (taken as a whole)—or less on the sidelines."

THE CIVIL RIGHTS ACT   Despite President Eisenhower's reluctance to take the lead in desegregating schools, he supported the right of African Americans to vote. In 1956, hoping to exploit divisions between northern and southern Democrats and to reclaim some of the black vote for the Republicans, Eisenhower proposed legislation that became the Civil Rights Act of 1957, the first civil rights law passed since Reconstruction. It finally got through the Senate, after a year's delay, with the help of majority leader Lyndon B. Johnson, a Texas Democrat who won southern acceptance by watering it down. The Civil Rights Act established the Civil Rights Commission and a new Civil Rights Division in the Justice Department, which could seek injunctions to prevent interference with the right to vote. Yet by 1959 the Civil Rights Act had not added a single southern black to the voting rolls. Neither did the Civil Rights Act of 1960, which provided for federal court referees to register African Americans where a court found a "pattern and practice" of discrimination. This act, too, lacked teeth and depended upon vigorous presidential enforcement to achieve any real results.

DESEGREGATION IN LITTLE ROCK   A few weeks after passage of the Civil Rights Act of 1957, Arkansas governor Orval Faubus called out the National Guard to prevent nine African American students from entering Little Rock's Central High School under a federal court order. A conference between the president and the governor proved fruitless, but on court order Governor Faubus withdrew the National Guard. When the students tried to enter the school, a hysterical white mob forced local authorities to remove them. At that point, Eisenhower, who had said two months before that he could not "imagine any set of circumstances that would ever induce me to send federal troops," ordered 1,000 U.S. paratroopers to Little Rock to protect the black students, and he placed the Arkansas National Guard on federal service. The soldiers stayed through the school year.

In the summer of 1958, Faubus decided to close the high schools of Little Rock rather than allow integration, and court proceedings dragged on into 1959 before the schools could be reopened. In that year, massive resistance to integration in Virginia collapsed when both state and federal courts struck down state laws that had cut off funds to integrated schools. Thereafter, massive resistance for the most part was confined to the Deep South, where five states—from South Carolina west through Louisiana—still opposed even token integration.

ASSESSING THE EISENHOWER PRESIDENCY

Dwight Eisenhower entered office in 1953 after being elected in a landslide and held high approval ratings for ending the Korean War and handling foreign crises. He won a second landslide election in 1956. Yet support for the president did not translate into support for his party. Eisenhower's decisive win failed to swing a congressional majority for Republicans in either house, leaving the country in the hands of a Republican president and a Democratic Congress. Eisenhower was thus the first president to face three successive Congresses controlled by the opposition party. This meant that he could manage few initiatives in domestic policy, although he did oversee the admission of the first states that are not contiguous to the continental forty-eight: Alaska became the forty-ninth state on January 3, 1959, and Hawaii became the fiftieth on August 21, 1959.

During Eisenhower's second term the country experienced an economic slump, a drop in tax revenues, and a large federal deficit. The country also suffered the embarrassments of the U-2 spy-plane incident and Cuba's falling into the Communist orbit. Emotional issues such as civil rights, defense policy, and corrupt aides compounded Eisenhower's troubles. The president's reluctance to enforce civil rights rulings and his unwillingness to speak out on behalf of racial equality undermined his efforts to promote the general welfare. One observer called the Eisenhower years "the time of the great postponement," during which the president left domestic and foreign policies "about where he found them in 1953."

Yet opinion of Eisenhower's presidency has improved with time. Even critics now grant that Eisenhower succeeded in ending the war in Korea and settling the dust raised by Senator Joseph McCarthy. Although Eisenhower failed to end the cold war and in fact institutionalized global confrontation, he did sense the limits of American power and kept its application to low-risk situations. He also tried to restrain the arms race. Although he took few initiatives in addressing social and racial issues, he did sustain the major innovations of the New Deal. Although he tolerated unemployment of as much as 7 percent, he saw to it that inflation remained minimal during his two terms.

Eisenhower's January 17, 1961, farewell address to the American people showed his remarkable foresight in his own area of expertise, the military. He highlighted, perhaps better than anyone else could have, the dangers of a huge military establishment in a time of peace: "In the councils of government we must guard against the acquisition of unwarranted influence, whether sought or unsought, by the military-industrial complex. The potential for the disastrous rise of misplaced power exists and will persist." Eisenhower confessed that his great disappointment was that he could affirm only that "war has been avoided," not that "a lasting peace is in sight."

CHAPTER SUMMARY

- **Eisenhower's Dynamic Conservatism** As president, Eisenhower accepted most of the New Deal's social legislation. He expanded Social Security coverage and launched ambitious public works programs, such as the construction of the interstate highway system and the St. Lawrence Seaway. He opposed massive government spending and large budget deficits, however, so he cut spending on an array of domestic programs and on national defense.

- **American Foreign Policy in the 1950s** Eisenhower continued the policy of containment to stem the spread of communism. His first major foreign-policy accomplishment in this respect was to end the fighting in Korea. To confront Soviet aggression, Eisenhower relied on nuclear deterrence, which allowed for reductions in conventional military forces and thus led to budgetary savings.

- **Communism in S.E. Asia** After World War II, Truman and then Eisenhower believed that the French should regain control of Indochina so that the country could serve as a barrier against the spread of communism in Southeast Asia. Ho Chi Minh, a nationalist and a Communist, led the Viet Minh movement, which in 1954 defeated the French at the Battle of Dien Bien Phu. The Geneva Accords, adopted in 1954, temporarily divided the country in half, with the Viet Minh ruling in the north and the dictator Ngo Dinh Diem ruling in the south. Communist guerrilla forces, known as the Viet Cong, found recruits among discontented South Vietnamese and attacked the Diem government. By 1957 the Eisenhower administration had no option but to "sink or swim with Ngo Dinh Diem."

- **Civil Rights Movement** In the 1930s the National Association for the Advancement of Colored People began laying the foundation for challenging the "separate but equal" doctrine, through a series of test cases in federal courts. By the early 1950s, the NAACP was targeting state-mandated segregation in public schools. In the most significant case, *Brown v. Board of Education*, the Court nullified the "separate but equal" doctrine. Whereas white southerners defended their old way of life, rallying to a call for "massive resistance," African Americans and other proponents of desegregation sought to achieve integration through nonviolent means. The Montgomery, Alabama, bus boycott was significant because it was the first large-scale—and ultimately successful—instance of nonviolent resistance and because it galvanized the civil rights movement under the leadership of Dr. Martin Luther King Jr. The desegregation of a public high school in Little Rock, Arkansas, marked another turning point when President Eisenhower reluctantly threw the support of the federal government behind the integrationists.

CHRONOLOGY

March 1953	Joseph Stalin dies
June 1953	Ethel and Julius Rosenberg are executed
July 1953	Armistice is reached in Korea
April–July 1954	Army-McCarthy hearings are televised
1954	Supreme Court issues ruling in *Brown v. Board of Education of Topeka, Kansas*
July 1954	Geneva Accords propose a settlement to the war in Indochina
December 1955	Montgomery, Alabama, bus boycott begins
1956	In Suez War, Israel, Britain, and France attack Egypt
1956	Hungarian revolt against the Warsaw Pact is quickly suppressed
1957	Federal troops are ordered to guarantee the safety of students attempting to integrate Central High School in Little Rock, Arkansas
1957	Soviet Union launches *Sputnik 1*
1960	U-2 incident reveals that the United States is flying spy planes over the Soviet Union

KEY TERMS & NAMES

34

NEW FRONTIERS: POLITICS AND SOCIAL CHANGE IN THE 1960s

FOCUS QUESTIONS wwnorton.com/studyspace

- What were the goals of John F. Kennedy's New Frontier program, and how successful was it?

- What was the aim of Lyndon Johnson's Great Society program, and how successful was it?

- What were the achievements of the civil rights movement by 1968?

- Why did the United States become increasingly involved in Vietnam?

- Why and how did Kennedy attempt to combat communism in Cuba?

For those pundits who considered the social and political climate of the 1950s dull, the following decade would provide a striking contrast. The 1960s were years of extraordinary turbulence and innovation in public affairs—as well as tragedy and trauma. Many social ills that had been simmering for decades suddenly forced their way onto the national agenda. At the same time, the deeply entrenched assumptions of the cold war ideology directed against communism led the country into the longest, most controversial, and least successful war in its history.

THE NEW FRONTIER

KENNEDY VERSUS NIXON In 1960 there was little sense of dramatic change on the horizon. The presidential election that year featured two candidates—Richard M. Nixon and John F. Kennedy—with very different personalities and backgrounds. Though better known than Kennedy because of his eight years as Eisenhower's vice president, Nixon had developed the reputation of a cunning chameleon, the "Tricky Dick" who concealed his duplicity behind a series of masks.

Nixon possessed great ability, however, as well as tenacious energy and a compulsive love for combative politics. Born in suburban Los Angeles in 1913, he grew up in a Quaker family that struggled to make ends meet. After law school and military service in the Pacific during World War II, Nixon jumped into the political arena in 1946 as a Republican and surprised observers by unseating a popular congressman in southern California. He arrived in Washington eager to reverse the tide of New Deal liberalism. Four years later he won election to the Senate. In his campaigns, Nixon unleashed scurrilous personal attacks on his opponents, shrewdly manipulating the growing anti-Communist hysteria. Yet Nixon became a respected, effective legislator, and by 1950 he was the most requested Republican speaker in the country. His rapid rise to political stardom led to his being offered the vice-presidential nomination in 1952 and 1956. He was an active, highly visible vice president.

Although Kennedy lacked such experience and exposure, he boasted an abundance of assets, including a widely publicized record of heroism in World War II, a glamorous wife, a Harvard education, and a large, wealthy, Roman Catholic family. Yet the handsome forty-three-year-old candidate lacked national prominence and political distinction. Kennedy's record in the Senate was mediocre.

During his campaign for the 1960 Democratic presidential nomination, however, Kennedy had shown that he had energy, grace, and ambition. As the first Catholic to run for the presidency since Al Smith in 1928, he strove to dispel the impression that his religion was a major political liability. In his acceptance speech at the Democratic Convention, Kennedy found the stirring rhetoric that would stamp the rest of his campaign and his presidency: "We stand today on the edge of a New Frontier—the frontier of unknown opportunities and perils—a frontier of unfulfilled hopes and threats."

The turning point in the presidential campaign came when Richard Nixon agreed to debate his less prominent opponent on television. During the first of four debates, some 70 million viewers saw Nixon, still weak from a recent illness, perspiring heavily and looking haggard, uneasy, and even sinister before the camera. Kennedy, on the other hand, projected a cool poise that made him seem equal, if not superior, in his fitness for the office. Kennedy's popularity immediately shot up in the polls.

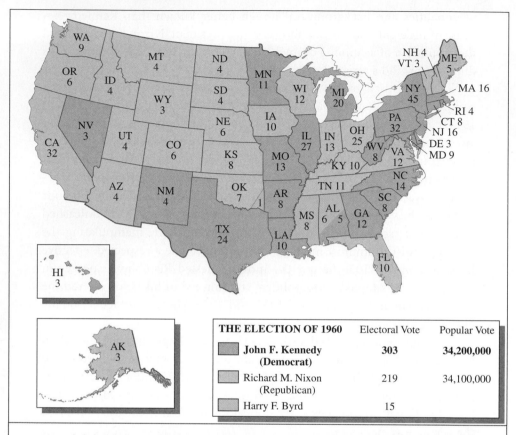

THE ELECTION OF 1960	Electoral Vote	Popular Vote
John F. Kennedy (Democrat)	**303**	**34,200,000**
Richard M. Nixon (Republican)	219	34,100,000
Harry F. Byrd	15	

How did the election of 1960 represent a sea change in American presidential politics? What event was the turning point in the campaign? How did John F. Kennedy win the election in spite of winning fewer states than Richard M. Nixon?

When the votes were counted, Kennedy and his running mate, Lyndon Johnson of Texas, had won the closest presidential election since 1888. The winning margin was only 118,574 votes out of more than 68 million cast. Kennedy's wide lead in the electoral vote, 303 to 219, belied the paper-thin margin in several key states.

THE NEW ADMINISTRATION   John F. Kennedy was the youngest person ever elected president, and he sought to attract to his cabinet the "best and the brightest" minds, men who would inject a tough, dispassionate, pragmatic, and vigorous outlook into government affairs. To that end he asked Robert McNamara, one of the whiz kids who had reorganized the Ford Motor Company, to bring his managerial magic to bear on the Department of Defense. Kennedy appointed Harvard professor McGeorge Bundy, whom he called "the second smartest man I know," as special assistant for national security affairs and chose as his secretary of state Dean Rusk, a career diplomat and former Rhodes scholar. When critics attacked the appointment of Kennedy's thirty-five-year-old brother Robert as attorney general, the president quipped, "I don't see what's wrong with giving Bobby a little experience before he goes into law practice."

The inaugural ceremonies set the tone of elegance and youthful vigor that would come to be called the Kennedy style. After the poet Robert Frost paid tribute to the administration in verse, Kennedy dazzled listeners with his uplifting rhetoric. "Let every nation know," he proclaimed, ". . . that we shall pay any price, bear any burden, meet any hardship, support any friend, oppose any foe, to assure the survival and success of liberty. And so, my fellow Americans: ask not what your country can do for you—ask what you can do for your country." Spines tingled; the glittering atmosphere and inspiring language of the inauguration seemed to herald an era of fresh promise and youthful energy.

THE KENNEDY RECORD   Despite his idealistic rhetoric, however, Kennedy had a difficult time launching his New Frontier domestic program. Elected by a razor-thin margin, he did not have a popular mandate. Nor did he show much skill in dealing with a Democratic majority in a Congress controlled by conservative southerners. Congress blocked his efforts to increase federal aid to education, provide health insurance for the aged, and create a department of urban affairs.

Administration proposals did nevertheless win some notable victories in Congress. They included a new Housing Act that appropriated nearly $5 billion for urban renewal over four years, an increase in the minimum wage, and enhanced Social Security benefits. Just two months into his administration, Kennedy launched the celebrated Peace Corps to supply volunteers for educational and technical service in underdeveloped countries. Kennedy also won support for an accelerated space program to land astronauts on the moon before the end of the decade. Congress readily approved a series of broad foreign-aid programs to help Latin American nations, dubbed the Alliance for Progress. Another important initiative was a bold tax-reduction bill intended to accelerate economic growth. Passed in 1964, after Kennedy's death, it provided a surprisingly potent boost to the economy. Perhaps Kennedy's most significant legislative accomplishment was the Trade Expansion Act of 1962, which eventually led to tariff cuts averaging 35 percent on goods traded between the United States and the European Economic Community (the Common Market).

Kennedy-Nixon debates

John Kennedy's poise and precision in the debates with Richard Nixon impressed viewers and voters.

THE WARREN COURT   Under Chief Justice Earl Warren the Supreme Court continued to be a decisive influence on domestic life during the 1960s. In *Gideon v. Wainwright* (1963), the Court required that every felony defendant be provided a lawyer regardless of the defendant's ability to pay. In 1964 the Court ruled in *Escobedo v. Illinois* that a person accused of a crime must also be allowed to consult a lawyer before being interrogated by police. Two years later, in *Miranda v. Arizona,* the Court issued perhaps its most bitterly criticized ruling when it ordered that an accused person in police custody be informed of certain basic rights: the right to remain silent; the right to know that anything said can be used against the individual in court; and the right to have a defense attorney present during interrogation. In addition, the Court established rules for police to follow in informing suspects of their legal rights before questioning could begin.

EXPANSION OF THE CIVIL RIGHTS MOVEMENT

The most important developments in domestic life during the 1960s occurred in civil rights. John F. Kennedy was initially reluctant to challenge conservative southern Democrats on the race issue. Nor was he as personally committed to civil rights as his younger brother Robert, the attorney general. Despite a few dramatic gestures of support for African American leaders, President Kennedy only belatedly grasped the moral and emotional significance of what would become the most widespread reform movement of the decade. Eventually, however, his conscience was pricked by the grassroots civil rights movement led by Martin Luther King Jr., a movement that would profoundly change the contours of American life.

SIT-INS AND FREEDOM RIDES   After the Montgomery bus boycott of 1955–1956, King's philosophy of "militant nonviolence" inspired thousands to challenge segregation and discrimination with direct action. At the same time, lawsuits to desegregate the schools activated thousands of parents and young people. The momentum generated a genuine mass movement when four black college students courageously sat down and demanded service at a "whites-only" Woolworth's lunch counter in Greensboro, North Carolina, on February 1, 1960. Within a week the "sit-in" movement had spread to six more towns in the state, and within two months demonstrations had occurred in fifty-four cities in nine states.

In 1960, student activists, black and white, formed the Student Nonviolent Coordinating Committee (SNCC), which worked with King's Southern Christian Leadership Conference (SCLC) to spread the civil rights movement. The sit-ins became "kneel-ins" at churches and "wade-ins" at segregated public swimming pools. During the year after the Greensboro sit-ins, over 3,600 black and white activists spent time in jail. In many communities they were struck with clubs, poked with cattle prods, pelted with rocks, burned with cigarettes, and subjected to unending verbal abuse. Nonetheless, the protesters refused to retaliate.

In May 1961 the Congress of Racial Equality (CORE) sent a group of black and white "freedom riders" on buses to test a federal ruling that had banned segregation on buses and trains and in their depots. In Alabama, mobs attacked the young travelers with fists and pipes, burned one of the buses, and assaulted Justice Department observers, but the demonstrators persisted, drawing national attention and generating new support for their cause. Yet President Kennedy was not inspired by the courageous freedom riders. Preoccupied with a crisis in Berlin, he ordered an aide to tell them to "call it off." Former president Harry Truman dismissed the bus activists northern "busybodies." It fell to Attorney General Robert Kennedy to use federal marshals to protect the freedom riders during the summer of 1961.

FEDERAL INTERVENTION   In 1962, the racist Governor Ross Barnett of Mississippi, a rabid racist who believed that God made "the Negro different to punish him," defied a court order by refusing to allow James Meredith, an African American student, to enroll at the University of Mississippi. Attorney General Robert Kennedy sent federal marshals to enforce the law. Federal troops then intervened, and Meredith was registered at Ole Miss, but only after two deaths and many injuries.

Everywhere, it seemed, African American activists and white supporters were challenging deeply entrenched patterns of segregation and prejudice. In 1963, Martin Luther King launched a series of demonstrations in Birmingham, Alabama, where Police Commissioner Eugene "Bull" Connor proved the perfect foil for King's tactic of nonviolent civil disobedience. Connor's policemen used dogs, tear gas, electric cattle prods, and fire hoses on the protesters while millions of Americans watched the confrontations on television.

King, who was arrested and jailed during the demonstrations, wrote his now-famous Letter from a Birmingham City Jail, a stirring defense of his nonviolent strategy that became a classic of the civil rights movement. "One who breaks an unjust law," he stressed, "must do so openly, lovingly, and

Birmingham, Alabama, May 1963

Eugene "Bull" Connor's police unleash dogs on civil rights demonstrators.

with a willingness to accept the penalty." In his letter, King signaled a shift in his strategy for social change. Heretofore he had emphasized the need to educate southern whites about the injustice of segregation and other patterns of discrimination. Now he focused more on gaining federal enforcement of the law and new legislation by provoking racists to display their violent hatred in public.

Southern traditionalists defied efforts to promote racial integration. In 1963, Alabama Governor George Wallace dramatically stood in the doorway of a building at the University of Alabama to block the enrollment of African American students, but he stepped aside in the face of insistent federal marshals. Later that night, NAACP official Medgar Evers was shot to death as he returned to his home in Jackson, Mississippi.

The high point of the integrationist phase of the civil rights movement occurred on August 28, 1963, when over 200,000 blacks and whites marched down the Mall in Washington, D.C., toward the Lincoln Memorial, singing "We Shall Overcome." The March on Washington for Jobs and Freedom was the largest civil rights demonstration in American history. Standing in front of Lincoln's statue, Martin Luther King delivered one of the century's memorable speeches: "Even though we face the difficulties of today and tomorrow, I still have a dream. It is a dream chiefly rooted in the American dream . . . one day . . . the sons of former slaves and the sons of former slaveowners will be able to sit together at the table of brotherhood." Such racial harmony had not yet arrived, however. Two weeks later a bomb exploded in a Birmingham church, killing four African American girls who had arrived early for Sunday school.

Yet King's dream—shared and promoted by thousands of other activists—survived. The intransigence and violence that civil rights workers encountered won converts to their cause across the country and forced whites nationwide to confront the myths of their own virtue and innocence with the brutal facts of racial hatred. Persuaded by his brother Robert, a man of greater conviction, compassion, and vision, and by the pressure of events, President Kennedy finally decided that enforcement of existing statutes was not enough; new legislation was needed to deal with the race question. In 1963 he told the nation that racial discrimination "has no place in American life or law," and he endorsed an ambitious civil rights bill intended to end discrimination in public facilities, desegregate public schools, and protect black voters. Southern conservatives, however, quickly blocked the bill in Congress. The backlash that had surfaced in the South in the 1930s in response to the expansion of Franklin Roosevelt's New Deal continued to shape Democratic politics in the region.

"I Have a Dream," August 28, 1963

Protesters in the March on Washington make their way to the Lincoln Memorial, where Martin Luther King Jr. delivered his now-famous speech.

Although Kennedy saw his support among southern voters plummet, he remained committed to the bill. As he told Martin Luther King: "This is a very serious fight. We're in this up to the neck. The worst trouble would be to lose the fight in Congress. . . . A good many programs I care about may go down the drain as a result of this [bill]—We may all go down the drain . . . so we are putting a lot on the line."

FOREIGN FRONTIERS

EARLY SETBACKS John F. Kennedy's record in foreign affairs was mixed, more spectacularly so than his domestic record. Upon taking office, he discovered that the CIA had in the works a secret operation designed to prepare 1,500 anti-Castro Cubans for an invasion of their homeland. The Joint Chiefs of Staff endorsed the plan; analysts reported that the invasion would inspire Cubans on the island to rebel against Castro. But the scheme, poorly conceived and poorly executed, had little chance of succeeding. When the invasion force landed at Cuba's Bay of Pigs on April 17, 1961, it was brutally subdued in two days, and over 1,100 men were captured.

Two months after the Bay of Pigs disaster, Kennedy met Soviet premier Nikita Khrushchev in Vienna. The volatile Khrushchev tried to bully the inexperienced Kennedy. He threatened to limit Western access to Berlin, the divided city located 100 miles within Communist East Germany. Kennedy was shaken by the aggressive Soviet stand. Upon his return home, he demonstrated his resolve by mobilizing Army Reserve and National Guard units. The Soviets responded by erecting the Berlin Wall, isolating West Berlin and preventing all movement between the two parts of the city.

THE CUBAN MISSILE CRISIS A year later, in the fall of 1962, Khrushchev and the Soviets posed another serious challenge, this time just ninety miles south of Florida. Khrushchev granted Fidel Castro's request for nuclear missiles in Cuba to protect the island from future American-sponsored invasions and to redress the strategic imbalance caused by the presence of U.S. missiles in Turkey aimed at the Soviet Union. While such missiles would hardly alter the worldwide military balance, they would be placed in areas not covered by American radar systems and, if launched, would go undetected, arriving without warning. More important to Kennedy was the psychological effect of American acquiescence to a Soviet presence on its doorstep. Khrushchev's apparent purpose was to demonstrate his toughness to Chinese and Soviet critics of his earlier advocacy of peaceful coexistence. But he misjudged the American response.

On October 14, 1962, U.S. intelligence flights discovered Soviet missile sites under construction in Cuba. Although the Soviet actions violated no law or treaty, the administration immediately decided that the missiles had to be removed; the only question was how. In a series of secret meetings, the Executive Committee of the National Security Council debated whether to launch a "surgical" air strike or a naval blockade of Cuba. President Kennedy wisely opted for a blockade, but since that would technically represent an act of war, it was called a quarantine. It offered the advantage of forcing the Soviets to shoot first, if matters came to that, and left open options of stronger action. Thus, Monday, October 22, began the most perilous week in world history. On that day the president announced the discovery of the missile sites in Cuba and the U.S. naval quarantine of the island nation.

Tensions grew as Khrushchev blustered that Kennedy had pushed humankind "toward the abyss of a world nuclear-missile war." Soviet ships, he declared, would ignore the quarantine. But on Wednesday, October 24, five

Soviet supply ships stopped short of the quarantine line. Two days later the Soviets offered to withdraw the missiles in return for a public pledge by the United States not to invade Cuba.

In the aftermath of the crisis, the United States took several symbolic steps to relax tensions: it agreed to sell surplus wheat to the Soviets; it installed a "hot-line" telephone between Washington and Moscow to provide instant contact between the heads of government; and it removed obsolete missiles from Turkey, Italy, and Britain. The United States also negotiated a treaty with Soviet and British representatives to end nuclear testing in the atmosphere. The treaty, ratified in September 1963, was an important move toward greater international cooperation on nuclear proliferation.

KENNEDY AND VIETNAM   As tensions with the Soviet Union were easing, a crisis was developing in Southeast Asia. Events there would lead to the greatest American foreign-policy debacle of the century. During John Kennedy's "Thousand Days" in office, the turmoil of Indochina never preoccupied public attention for any extended period, but it dominated international diplomatic debates from the time the administration entered office.

In South Vietnam, Premier Ngo Dinh Diem had failed to deliver promised social and economic reforms. His repressive tactics, directed not only against Communists but also against the Buddhist majority and other critics, played into the hands of his enemies. In 1961, White House assistant Walt Rostow and General Maxwell Taylor, the first in a long line of presidential emissaries to South Vietnam's capital, Saigon, proposed a major increase in the U.S. military presence, but Kennedy instead dispatched more military "advisers." When he took office, there had been 2,000 U.S. troops in South Vietnam; by the end of 1963, there were 16,000, none of whom had been officially committed to battle.

But the American-supported Diem regime continued to be its own worst enemy. By mid-1963 growing Buddhist demonstrations against Diem ignited the public discontent in South Vietnam and created consternation abroad. The spectacle of Buddhist monks setting themselves on fire on Saigon streets in protest of Diem's iron-fisted rule shocked Americans but brought from the Diem regime only a sarcastic comment by the premier's sister-in-law about "barbecued monks."

By the fall of 1963, the Kennedy administration had decided that Diem was a lost cause. When dissident Vietnamese generals proposed a coup d'état, the U.S. ambassador assured them that the Kennedy administration would not stand in the way. On November 1 the insurgent military leaders seized the government and murdered Diem. Yet the generals provided no more stability than had earlier regimes, and successive coups set South Vietnam's government spinning from one military leader to another.

KENNEDY'S ASSASSINATION   By the fall of 1963, President Kennedy had come to acknowledge the intractability of the situation in Vietnam. Some of his aides later argued that Kennedy would never have allowed a dramatic escalation of U.S. military involvement in Vietnam. Others strongly disagreed. The question is endless because it is unanswerable, and it is unanswerable because on November 22, 1963, while visiting Dallas, Texas, Kennedy was shot twice in the throat and head and died almost immediately. A few hours later Dallas police arrested Lee Harvey Oswald, a twenty-four-year-old ex-marine drifter who had worked in the Texas School Book Depository, from which the shots were fired at Kennedy. Yet before Oswald could be thoroughly interrogated, he, too, was killed. Two days after his arrest, as television cameras covered his transfer from one jail to another, Jack Ruby, a Dallas nightclub owner, stepped from the crowd of onlookers and fatally shot Oswald in the abdomen.

Oswald's death ignited a controversy over the assassination that still simmers. In December 1963, President Johnson appointed a commission to investigate Kennedy's murder. Headed by Chief Justice Earl Warren, it concluded that Oswald had acted alone. Yet many people were (and are) not convinced, and since 1963 dozens of conspiracy theories have been proposed. Some blame the CIA or the Mafia; others point to Fidel Castro, whom the CIA had once tried to assassinate. Still others insist that Cuban exiles in Miami, angered by Kennedy's failure to rescue their comrades during the Bay of Pigs fiasco, were behind the assassination. Whatever the actual story of the assassination, Kennedy's tragic death enshrined him in the public imagination as a martyred leader cut down in the prime of his life.

LYNDON JOHNSON AND THE GREAT SOCIETY

Lyndon Johnson took the presidential oath of office on board the plane that brought John F. Kennedy's body back to Washington from Dallas. Fifty-five years old, Johnson had spent twenty-six years on the Washington scene and had served nearly a decade as Senate Democratic leader, where he had displayed the greatest gift for compromise since Henry Clay. Johnson brought to the White House a marked change of style from his predecessor. A self-made and self-centered man, he had used gritty determination and shrewd manipulation to work his way out of a hardscrabble rural Texas homeland to become one of Washington's most powerful figures. He had none of Kennedy's elegance. He was a bundle of conflicting elements: earthy, idealistic, domineering, insecure, gregarious, ruthless, and compassionate. His ego was as huge as his ambition.

Those who viewed Johnson as a stereotypical southern conservative ignored his long-standing admiration for Franklin Roosevelt, the depth of his concern for the poor, and his heartfelt commitment to the cause of civil rights. Though a novice in foreign affairs, in the domestic arena during the 1950s Johnson had been unsurpassed in his ability to shepherd legislation through the gauntlet of special-interest lobbyists and Congress. He had once bragged that "Ike couldn't pass the Lord's Prayer in Congress without me." Johnson wanted to be the greatest president, the one who did the most good for the most people. And he would let nothing stand in the way of his grand ambition. He ended up promising far more than he could accomplish, raising false hopes and stoking fiery resentments.

POLITICS AND POVERTY Domestic policy was Johnson's first priority. He exploited the nation's grief after the assassination by declaring that Kennedy's legislative program, stymied in congressional committees,

The Johnson treatment

Lyndon Johnson used powerful body language to intimidate and manipulate anyone who dared disagree with him.

would be passed. Johnson loved the political infighting and legislative detail that Kennedy had loathed. The logjam in Congress that had blocked Kennedy's program broke under Johnson's forceful leadership, and a torrent of legislation poured through. At the top of Johnson's agenda were the stalled measures for a tax reduction and civil rights. In 1962, Kennedy had announced a then-unusual plan to jump-start the sluggish economy: a tax cut to stimulate consumer spending. Congressional Republicans opposed the idea because it would increase the federal budget deficit. And polls showed that public opinion was also skeptical. So

Kennedy had postponed the proposed tax cut for a year; it was still bogged down in Congress when the president was assassinated. Johnson broke the logjam, and the Revenue Act of 1964 provided a needed boost to the economy.

Likewise, the Civil Rights Act that Kennedy had presented to Congress in 1963 became law in 1964 through Johnson's forceful leadership. The bill prohibited racial segregation in public facilities such as bus terminals, restaurants, theaters, and hotels. And it outlawed long-standing racial discrimination in the registration of voters and the hiring of employees. President Johnson revived bipartisan efforts on its behalf, and the bill passed the House in February 1964. In the Senate, however, southern legislators launched a filibuster that lasted two months. Johnson finally prevailed, and the civil rights bill became law on July 2. But the new president knew that it had come at a political price. On the night after signing it, Johnson told an aide that "we have just delivered the South to the Republican Party for a long time to come."

The Civil Rights Act of 1964

President Johnson reaches to shake hands with Dr. Martin Luther King Jr. after presenting the civil rights leader with one of the pens used to sign the Civil Rights Act of 1964.

In addition to fulfilling Kennedy's major promises, Johnson launched an ambitious legislative program of his own. In his 1964 State of the Union address, he added to his must-do list a bold new idea that bore the Johnson brand: "This Administration today, here and now, declares unconditional war on poverty in America." The particulars of this "war on poverty" were to come later, the product of a task force at work before Johnson took office.

Americans had "rediscovered" poverty in 1962, when the social critic Michael Harrington published a powerful exposé titled *The Other America*. Harrington argued that more than 40 million people were mired in a "culture of poverty." Unlike the upwardly mobile immigrant poor at the beginning of the century, the modern poor were impervious to hope. President Kennedy had learned of *The Other America* in 1963 and asked his advisers to investigate the problem and suggest solutions. Upon taking office, Lyndon Johnson announced that he wanted an anti-poverty package that was "big and bold, that would hit the nation with real impact." Money for the program would come from the economic growth expected from the tax reduction of more than $10 billion that had passed in 1964.

The administration's war on poverty was embodied in an economic-opportunity bill that incorporated a wide range of programs: a Job Corps for inner-city youths, a Head Start program for disadvantaged preschoolers, work-study programs for college students, grants to farmers and rural businesses, loans to employers willing to hire the chronically unemployed, the Volunteers in Service to America (a domestic Peace Corps), and the Community Action Program, which would allow the poor "maximum feasible participation" in directing neighborhood programs designed for their benefit. Speaking at Ann Arbor, Michigan, Johnson called for a "Great Society" resting on "abundance and liberty for all. The Great Society demands an end to poverty and racial injustice, to which we are fully committed in our time." In theory it was liberalism triumphant; in practice its considerable achievements were accompanied by administrative bungling, corruption, and misguided idealism.

THE ELECTION OF 1964   As the 1964 election approached, Johnson was conceded the Democratic nomination from the start. He chose as his running mate Hubert H. Humphrey of Minnesota, the prominent liberal senator with the seemingly permanent smile and inexhaustible supply of optimism and energy.

The Republicans, meeting in San Francisco, were determined to offer an alternative to Johnson's liberalism. By 1960, Arizona senator Barry Goldwater, a millionaire department-store owner, had emerged as the leader of the party's conservative wing. A movement to nominate Goldwater had begun as early as 1961, mobilizing conservative activists to capture party caucuses and contest primaries. In 1964 they took an early lead, and Goldwater swept the all-important California primary. Thus his forces controlled the Republican Convention.

Goldwater displayed an unusual gift for frightening voters. Accusing the administration of waging a "no-win" war in Vietnam, he urged wholesale bombing of North Vietnam and left the impression of being trigger-happy. He also savaged Johnson's war on poverty and the New Deal tradition. At times he was foolishly candid. In Tennessee he proposed the sale of the Tennessee Valley Authority; in St. Petersburg, Florida, a major retirement community, he questioned the value of Social Security. He had voted against both the nuclear test ban and the 1964 Civil Rights Act. Republican campaign buttons claimed "In your heart, you know he's right." Democrats responded, "In your guts, you know he's nuts."

Johnson, on the other hand, appealed to the middle of the political spectrum. In contrast to Goldwater's bellicose rhetoric on Vietnam, he made a pledge that won great applause at the time and much comment later: "We are not about to send American boys nine or ten thousand miles from home to do what Asian boys ought to be doing for themselves."

The election was a landslide. Johnson polled 61 percent of the total vote; Goldwater carried only Arizona and five states in the Deep South. Johnson won the electoral vote by a whopping 486 to 52. In the Senate the Democrats increased their majority by two (68 to 32) and in the House by thirty-seven (295 to 140).

LANDMARK LEGISLATION   In 1965, Johnson took advantage of his electoral mandate to launch his ambitious Great Society program. It would, he promised, end poverty, renovate decaying central cities, provide every young American with the chance to attend college, protect the health of the elderly, enhance cultural life, clean up the air and water, and make the highways safer and prettier.

To accomplish those goals, the Johnson administration pushed legislation through Congress at a pace unseen since Franklin Roosevelt's Hundred Days. Priority went to health insurance and aid to education, proposals that had languished since President Truman had proposed them in 1945. The proposal for a comprehensive medical-insurance plan had long been stalled by the American Medical Association's ardent opposition. But now that Johnson had the votes, the AMA joined Republicans in supporting a bill serving those over age sixty-five. The act not only created the Medicare insurance program for the aged but also included another program, Medicaid, which provided states with federal grants to help cover medical payments for the indigent.

Five days after Johnson submitted his Medicare program, he sent to Congress his proposal for a massive increase in federal aid to elementary and secondary schools. Such proposals had been ignored since the 1940s, blocked alternately by issues of segregation and issues of separation of church and state. Now Johnson and congressional leaders devised a means of extending aid to "poverty-impacted" school districts regardless of their public or religious character.

The momentum generated by these measures had already begun to carry others along, and it continued through the following year. Altogether, the tide of Great Society legislation carried 435 bills through the Congress. Among them was the Appalachian Regional Development Act of 1966, which allocated federal funds for programs to enhance the standard of living in remote mountain areas that had long been pockets of desperate poverty. The Housing and Urban Development Act of 1965 provided for construction of 240,000 housing units. Rent supplements for low-income families followed in 1966, and in that year there began a new Department of Housing and Urban Development, headed by Robert C. Weaver, the first African American cabinet member.

THE IMMIGRATION ACT   Little noticed among the legislation flowing from Congress was a major new immigration bill that had originated in the Kennedy White House. President Johnson signed the Immigration and Nationality Services Act of 1965 in a ceremony held on Liberty Island in New York Harbor. In his speech, Johnson stressed that the new law would redress the wrong done to those "from southern and eastern Europe" and the "developing continents" of Asia, Africa, and Latin America. It would do so by abolishing the discriminatory quotas based upon national origins that had governed immigration policy since the 1920s.

The new law treated all nationalities and races equally. In place of national quotas, it created hemispheric ceilings on visas issued: 170,000 for persons from outside the Western Hemisphere, 120,000 for persons from within. It also stipulated that no more than 20,000 people could come from any one country each year. The new act allowed the entry of immediate family members of American residents without limit. During the 1960s, Asians and Latin Americans became the largest contingent of new Americans.

ASSESSING THE GREAT SOCIETY The Great Society programs included several successes. The Highway Safety Act and the National Traffic and Motor Vehicle Safety Act established safety standards for automobile manufacturers and highway design, and the scholarships provided for college students under the Higher Education Act were quite popular. Many Great Society initiatives aimed at improving the health, nutrition, and education of poor Americans, young and old, made headway. So, too, did efforts to clean up air and water pollution. Some of Johnson's programs were hastily designed or mismanaged, however, and others were vastly underfunded. Medicare, for example, removed incentives for hospitals to control costs, so medical bills skyrocketed. The Great Society helped reduce the number of people living in poverty, but it did so largely by providing federal welfare payments, not by finding people productive jobs. The war on poverty ended up being as disappointing as the war in Vietnam. Often funds appropriated

Great Society initiatives

President Johnson listens to Tom Fletcher, a father of eight children, describe some of the economic problems in his hometown.

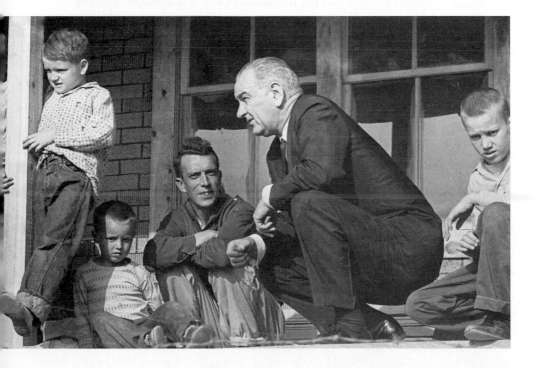

for a program never made it through the tangled bureaucracy to the needy. Widely publicized cases of welfare fraud placed a powerful weapon in the hands of those opposed to liberal social programs. By 1966 middle-class resentment over the cost and waste of the Great Society programs had generated a strong conservative backlash that fueled a Republican resurgence at the polls.

FROM CIVIL RIGHTS TO BLACK POWER

CIVIL RIGHTS LEGISLATION   Among the successes of the Great Society was a landmark piece of civil rights legislation: the Civil Rights Act of 1964, the most far-reaching civil rights measure ever enacted. It outlawed racial discrimination in hotels, restaurants, and other public accommodations. In addition, its provisions enabled the attorney general to bring suits to end school desegregation, relieving parents of that painful burden. Federally assisted programs and private employers alike were required to eliminate discrimination. An Equal Employment Opportunity Commission administered a ban on job discrimination by race, religion, national origin, or sex.

The Civil Rights Act increased the momentum of the movement. Early in 1965, Martin Luther King Jr. organized a voter-registration drive aimed at the 3 million unregistered African Americans in the South. On March 7 civil rights protesters began a march for voting rights from Selma, Alabama, to Montgomery, only to be violently dispersed by state troopers. A federal judge then agreed to allow the march, and President Johnson provided federal troops for protection. By March 25, when the demonstrators reached Montgomery, they numbered 35,000, and King delivered a rousing address from the steps of the state capitol.

Several days earlier, President Johnson had gone before Congress with a moving plea for voting-rights legislation. The resulting Voting Rights Act of 1965 ensured all citizens the right to vote. It authorized the attorney general to dispatch federal examiners to register voters. In states or counties where fewer than half the adults had voted in 1964, the act suspended literacy tests and other devices commonly used to defraud citizens of the vote. By the end of the year, some 250,000 African Americans were newly registered.

BLACK POWER   Amid this success, however, the civil rights movement began to fragment. On August 11, 1965, less than a week after the passage of the Voting Rights Act, Watts, a predominantly black and poor neighborhood in Los Angeles, exploded in a frenzy of rioting and looting. When the uprising ended, 34 were dead, almost 4,000 rioters were in jail, and property damage exceeded $35 million. The Watts upheaval marked the beginning of four long hot summers of racial conflagration. Riots in 1966 erupted in Chicago and Cleveland and in forty other American cities. The following summer, Newark and Detroit burst into flames. Detroit provided the most graphic instance of urban violence as tanks rolled through the streets to restore order.

In retrospect, it was understandable that the civil rights movement would shift its focus from the rural South to the plight of urban blacks. By the mid-1960s about 70 percent of African Americans lived in metropolitan areas, most of them in central-city ghettos that the postwar prosperity had bypassed. It also seems clear in retrospect that the nonviolent tactics that had worked in the South would not work in the large cities across the nation. In the North racial problems resulted from segregated residential patterns not amenable to changes in the law. Moreover, northern white ethnic groups did not have the cultural heritage that southern whites shared with blacks by virtue of their having lived together for so many generations. A special Commission on Civil Disorders noted that, unlike earlier race riots, which had been started by whites, the urban upheavals of the middle 1960s were initiated by African Americans themselves in an effort to destroy what they could not stomach and what civil rights legislation seemed unable to change.

In the midst of the violence, a new philosophy of racial separatism began to emerge. By 1966, "black power" had become the rallying cry of young activists. Radical members of SNCC had become estranged from Martin Luther King's theories of nonviolence. When Stokely Carmichael, a twenty-five-year-old graduate of Howard University, became head of SNCC in 1966, he adopted a separatist philosophy of black power and ousted whites from the organization. "We reject an American dream defined by white people and must work to construct an American reality defined by Afro-Americans," said a SNCC position paper. H. Rap Brown, who succeeded Carmichael as head of SNCC in 1967, even urged blacks to "get you some guns" and "kill the honkies." Meanwhile, Carmichael had moved on to the Black Panther party, founded in Oakland, California, in 1966. Headed by Huey P. Newton, Bobby Seale, and Eldridge Cleaver, the self-professed urban revolutionaries terrified the public. Eventually the Panthers fragmented in spasms of violence, much of which the FBI and local police officials helped to provoke.

The most articulate spokesman for black power was one of the earliest, Malcolm X (formerly Malcolm Little, the X denoting his lost African surname). Malcolm had risen from a ghetto childhood involving narcotics

Malcolm X

Malcolm X was the black power movement's most influential spokesman.

dealing and other crimes to become the chief disciple of Elijah Muhammad, a Black Muslim prophet who rejected Christianity as "the religion of white devils" and encouraged black culture and black pride. By 1964, Malcolm had broken with Elijah Muhammad and founded an organization committed to fostering alliances between African Americans and the nonwhite peoples of the world. He had also begun to abandon his earlier separatist agenda and violent tactics. But Malcolm was gunned down in Harlem by Black Muslim assassins in early 1965. With him went the most effective voice for urban black militancy. What made the assassination especially tragic was that Malcolm had just months before begun to abandon his strident anti-white rhetoric and preach a biracial message of social change.

Although widely publicized and highly visible, the black power movement never attracted more than a small minority of African Americans. Only about 15 percent of American blacks labeled themselves separatists. The preponderant majority continued to identify with the philosophy of nonviolent integration promoted by Martin Luther King and organizations such as the NAACP.

Despite its strident language and violence, the black power movement had two positive effects upon the civil rights movement. First, it prompted African Americans to take greater pride in their racial heritage. As Malcolm X often pointed out, prolonged slavery and institutionalized racism had eroded the self-esteem of many blacks in the United States. "The worst crime the white man has committed," he declared, "has been to teach us to hate ourselves." He and others helped blacks appreciate their African roots and their American accomplishments. It was Malcolm X who insisted that blacks call themselves African Americans as a symbol of pride in their roots and as a spur to learn more about their history as a people.

Second, the black power phenomenon forced King and other mainstream African American leaders and organizations to focus attention on the economic plight of poor inner-city blacks. Legal access to restaurants, schools, and other public accommodations, King pointed out, meant little to people mired in a culture of urban poverty. They needed jobs and decent housing as much as they needed legal rights. The time had come for radical measures "to provide jobs and income for the poor." Yet as King and others sought to escalate the war on poverty at home, the war in Vietnam was consuming more and more of America's resources and energies.

THE TRAGEDY OF VIETNAM

As domestic violence was escalating in America's inner cities, the war in Vietnam was reaching new levels of intensity and destruction. At the time of President Kennedy's death, there were 16,000 U.S. military advisers in Vietnam. Lyndon Johnson inherited from Kennedy and Eisenhower a long-standing commitment to prevent a Communist takeover in South Vietnam, along with a reluctance to assume the military burden for fighting the war. One president after another had done just enough to avoid being charged with having lost Vietnam. Johnson did the same, fearing that any other course would undermine his influence and endanger his Great Society programs in Congress. But this path took the United States deeper into an expanding military commitment in Southeast Asia. Early on, Johnson doubted that Vietnam was worth a deepening American military involvement. In May 1964 he told his national security adviser, McGeorge Bundy, that he had spent a sleepless night worrying about Vietnam: "It looks to me like we are getting into another Korea. . . . I don't think we can fight them 10,000 miles away from home. . . . I don't think it's worth fighting for. And I don't think we can get out. It's just the biggest damned mess that I ever saw."

ESCALATION   The official sanction for America's "escalation"—a Defense Department term favored in the Vietnam era—was the Tonkin Gulf resolution, approved by Congress on August 7, 1964. On that day, Johnson reported in a national television address that two American destroyers had been attacked by North Vietnamese vessels on August 2 and 4 in the Gulf of Tonkin, off the coast of North Vietnam. Johnson described the attacks, called the Gulf of Tonkin incident, as unprovoked. In truth the destroyers had been monitoring South Vietnamese raids against two North Vietnamese islands— raids planned by American advisers. The Tonkin Gulf resolution authorized the president to "take all necessary measures to repel any armed attack against the forces of the United States and to prevent further aggression."

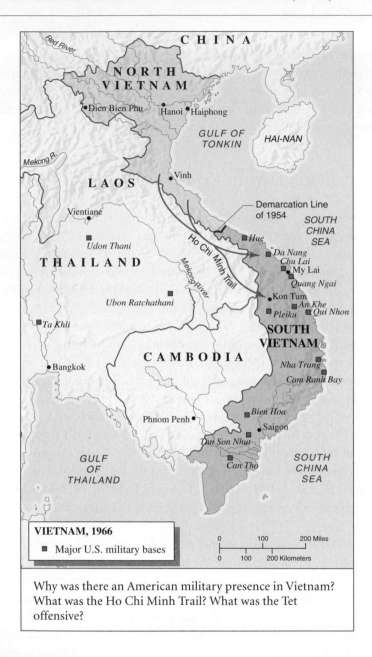

VIETNAM, 1966

■ Major U.S. military bases

0   100   200 Miles

0   100   200 Kilometers

Why was there an American military presence in Vietnam?
What was the Ho Chi Minh Trail? What was the Tet
offensive?

Three months after his landslide victory over Goldwater in November
1964, Johnson made the crucial decisions that would shape American policy
in Vietnam for the next four years. Viet Cong guerrilla attacks on American
forces in February 1965 led Johnson to launch Operation Rolling Thunder,
the first sustained bombing of North Vietnam, which was intended to stop

the flow of soldiers and supplies into the south. Six months later analysts concluded that the bombing had had little effect on the supplies pouring down the Ho Chi Minh Trail from North Vietnam through Laos and into South Vietnam. Still, the bombing continued.

In March 1965 the new U.S. army commander in Vietnam, General William C. Westmoreland, requested and got the first installment of combat troops, ostensibly to defend American airfields. By the end of 1965, there were 184,000 U.S. troops in Vietnam; in 1966 there were 385,000. As combat operations increased throughout South Vietnam, so did American casualties, announced on the nightly television news, along with the "body count" of alleged enemy dead.

THE CONTEXT FOR POLICY   Lyndon Johnson's decision to "Americanize" the Vietnam War, so ill-starred in retrospect, was entirely consistent with the foreign-policy principles pursued by all presidents after World War II.

The Tet offensive

Many Vietnamese were driven from their homes during the bloody street battles of the 1968 Tet offensive. Here, following a lull in the fighting, civilians carrying a white flag approach U.S. Marines.

The version of the theory to "contain" communism articulated in the Truman Doctrine, endorsed by Dwight Eisenhower and reaffirmed by John Kennedy, pledged opposition to the advance of communism anywhere in the world. Secretary of State Dean Rusk frequently warned that Thailand, Burma, and the rest of Southeast Asia would fall "like dominoes" to communism if American forces withdrew from Vietnam. Military intervention was thus a logical culmination of the assumptions widely shared by the foreign-policy establishment and leaders of both political parties since the early days of the cold war.

Nor did the United States blindly "stumble into a quagmire" in Vietnam, as some commentators maintained. Johnson insisted from the start that military involvement must not reach levels that would provoke the Chinese or Soviets to intervene with their own forces. He therefore exercised a tight rein over the bombing campaign, once boasting that "they can't even bomb an outhouse without my approval." Such a restrictive policy meant, in effect, that military victory was never possible. America's goal was not to win the war in a conventional sense by capturing enemy territory but to prevent the North Vietnamese and the Viet Cong from winning and, eventually, to force a negotiated settlement with the North Vietnamese. This meant that America would have to maintain a military presence as long as the enemy retained the will to fight.

"How Deep Do You Figure We'll Get Involved, Sir?"

Although U.S. soldiers were first sent to Vietnam as noncombatant advisers, they soon found themselves involved in a quagmire of fighting.

As it turned out, American public support for the war eroded faster than the will of the North Vietnamese leaders to tolerate devastating casualties and destruction. Systematic opposition to the war broke out on college campuses with the escalation of 1965. By 1967 antiwar demonstrations in New York City and at the Pentagon were attracting massive support. Nightly television accounts of the fighting—Vietnam was the first war to receive extended television coverage and hence was dubbed the living-room war—contradicted the official optimism.

In a war of political will, North Vietnam had the advantage. Johnson and his advisers grievously underestimated the tenacity of North Vietnam's commitment to unify Vietnam and expel the United States. While the United States fought a limited war for limited objectives, the Vietnamese Communists fought a total war for their survival. Just as General Westmoreland in early 1968 was assuring Johnson and the American public that his forces were on the verge of gaining the upper hand, the Communists were organizing widespread attacks that jolted American confidence and resolve.

THE TURNING POINT   On January 31, 1968, the first day of the Vietnamese New Year (Tet), the Viet Cong and the North Vietnamese defied a holiday truce to launch a wave of surprise assaults on American and South Vietnamese forces throughout South Vietnam. The old capital city of Hue fell to the Communists, and Viet Cong units temporarily occupied the grounds of the U.S. embassy in Saigon. Within a few days, however, American and South Vietnamese forces organized a devastating counterattack. General Westmoreland justifiably proclaimed the Tet offensive a major defeat for the Viet Cong. But while Viet Cong casualties were enormous, the psychological impact of the surprise attacks on the American public was more telling. The scope and intensity of the offensive contradicted upbeat claims by commanders that the war was going well. *Time* and *Newsweek* soon ran anti-war editorials urging American withdrawal. Polls showed that Johnson's popularity had declined to 35 percent. In 1968 the United States was spending $322,000 on every enemy soldier killed in Vietnam; the poverty programs at home received only $53 per person.

During 1968, Lyndon Johnson grew increasingly isolated. He suffered from depression and bouts of paranoia. The secretary of defense reported that a task force of prominent soldiers and civilians saw no prospect for a military victory; the stalemated war was undermining the Great Society programs. The Democratic party was also fragmenting. Robert Kennedy, now a senator from New York, was considering a run for the presidency in order to challenge Johnson's Vietnam policy. Senator Eugene McCarthy of Minnesota had already decided to oppose Johnson in the Democratic primaries. With anti-war students rallying to his candidacy, McCarthy polled a stunning 42 percent of the vote to Johnson's 48 percent in New Hampshire's March primary. It was a remarkable showing for a little-known senator. Each presidential primary now promised to become a referendum on Johnson's Vietnam policy.

On March 31, Johnson made a dramatic decision. He announced a limited halt to the bombing of North Vietnam and fresh initiatives for a negotiated cease-fire. Then he added a stunning postscript: "I shall not seek, and I will not accept, the nomination of my party for another term as your President." Although American combat troops would remain in Vietnam for five more years and the casualties would mount, the quest for military victory had ended. Now the question was how the most powerful nation in the world could extricate itself from Vietnam with a minimum of damage to its prestige and its South Vietnamese allies. It would not be easy. When direct negotiations with the North Vietnamese finally began in Paris in May 1968, they immediately bogged down over North Vietnam's demand for a halt to the bombing by the United States as a precondition for further discussion.

SIXTIES CRESCENDO

A TRAUMATIC YEAR Change moved at a fearful pace throughout the 1960s, but 1968 was the most turbulent and the most traumatic year of all. On April 4, only four days after Johnson's withdrawal from the presidential race, Martin Luther King Jr. was gunned down in Memphis, Tennessee. The assassin, James Earl Ray, had expressed hostility toward African Americans, but Americans continue to debate whether he was a pawn in an organized conspiracy. King's death set off an outpouring of grief among whites and blacks. It also set off riots in over sixty American cities.

Two months later, on June 5, Robert Kennedy was shot in the head by a young Palestinian who resented Kennedy's strong support of Israel. Kennedy died on the day after he had convincingly defeated Eugene McCarthy in the California Democratic primary, thereby momentarily assuming leadership of the anti-war forces in the race for the nomination for president.

CHICAGO AND MIAMI In August 1968, Democratic delegates gathered inside a Chicago convention hall to nominate Vice President Hubert Humphrey, while almost 20,000 police and national guardsmen and a small army of television reporters stood watch over several thousand diverse protesters herded together miles away in a public park. Chicago mayor Richard J. Daley, who had given "shoot-to-kill" orders to police during the April riots

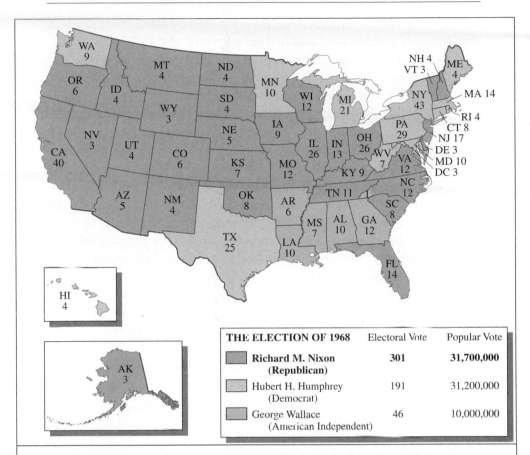

THE ELECTION OF 1968	Electoral Vote	Popular Vote
Richard M. Nixon (Republican)	301	31,700,000
Hubert H. Humphrey (Democrat)	191	31,200,000
George Wallace (American Independent)	46	10,000,000

How did the riots at the Chicago Democratic Convention affect the 1968 presidential campaign? What does the electoral map reveal about the support base for each of the three major candidates? How was Nixon able to win enough electoral votes in such a close, three-way presidential race? What was Wallace's appeal to over 10 million voters?

following King's assassination, warned that he would not tolerate disruptions. Nonetheless, riots broke out and were televised nationwide. As demonstrators chanted "The whole world is watching," police attacked the crowds with tear gas and billy clubs.

The Democratic party's liberal tradition was clearly in disarray, a fact that gave heart to the Republicans, who gathered in Miami Beach to nominate Richard Nixon and celebrate a remarkable political comeback. Nixon's narrow loss to Kennedy in 1960 had been followed by a disastrous defeat in the California gubernatorial race two years later. In what he labeled his "last press conference," he vowed never again to run for office. Yet Nixon displayed his remarkable resilience by returning to national politics in 1964, when he crisscrossed the nation in support of Goldwater's candidacy. For the next several years he remained active in politics, and in 1968 he was ready to take advantage of Johnson's crumbling popularity. He offered a vision of stability and order that appealed to a majority of Americans, soon to be called the silent majority.

But others were ready as well to challenge the Democratic party regulars. George Wallace, the Democratic governor of Alabama, ran on the American Independent party ticket. Wallace had made his political reputation as a brazen defender of segregation, but in his campaign for national office in 1968 he moderated his position on the race issue. And he appealed even more candidly than Nixon to the fears generated by rioting anti-war protesters, the welfare system, and the growth of the federal government. Wallace's platform was compelling in its simplicity: rioters would be shot, the war in Vietnam won, states' rights and law and order restored, open-housing laws repealed, and welfare cheats jailed.

Wallace's reactionary candidacy generated considerable appeal outside his native South, especially in white working-class communities, where resentment of Johnson's Great Society liberalism was rife. Although never a possible winner, Wallace had to be taken seriously: he could deny Humphrey or Nixon an electoral majority and thereby throw the choice into the House of Representatives, providing an appropriate climax to a chaotic year.

NIXON AGAIN   It did not happen that way. Richard Nixon enjoyed an enormous early lead in the polls, which narrowed as the 1968 election approached. George Wallace's campaign was hurt by his outspoken running mate, retired air force general Curtis LeMay, who suggested that nuclear weapons be used in Vietnam. In October 1968, Hubert Humphrey infuriated Johnson and the party bosses when he announced that, if elected, he would stop bombing North Vietnam "as an acceptable risk for peace."

In the end, Nixon and his running mate, Governor Spiro Agnew of Maryland, eked out a narrow victory of about 500,000 votes, a margin of about 1 percentage point. The electoral vote was more decisive, 301 to 191. Wallace won 10 million votes, 13.5 percent of the total, the best showing by a third-party candidate since Robert La Follette headed the Progressive ticket in 1924. All but one of Wallace's 46 electoral votes were from the Deep South.

Nixon swept all but four of the states west of the Mississippi, while Humphrey's support came almost exclusively from the Northeast.

So at the end of a turbulent year, near the end of a traumatic decade, a nation on the verge of violent chaos looked to Richard Nixon to provide what he had promised in the campaign: "peace with honor" in Vietnam and a middle ground on which a majority of Americans, silent or otherwise, could come together.

End of Chapter Review

- **Kennedy's New Frontier** President Kennedy promised "new frontiers" in domestic policy, but without a clear Democratic majority in Congress he was unable to increase federal aid to education, provide health insurance for the aged, create a cabinet-level department of urban affairs, or expand civil rights. He championed tariff cuts, however, and an expanded space program.

- **Johnson's Great Society** President Johnson was committed to social reform. He forced the Civil Rights Act through Congress in 1964 and declared "a war" on poverty. Under the Great Society, welfare was expanded, Medicare and Medicaid were created, more grants for college students were established, and racial quotas for immigration were abolished. These programs were expensive and, coupled with the soaring costs of the war in Vietnam, necessitated tax increases, which were unpopular.

- **Civil Rights' Achievements** By the 1960s significant numbers of African Americans and whites were staging non-violent sit-ins. In 1961, "freedom riders" attempted to integrate buses, trains, and bus and train stations in the South. The high point of the early phase of the civil rights movement was the 1963 March on Washington for Jobs and Freedom, at which Martin Luther King Jr. delivered his famous "I Have a Dream" speech. In 1964, President Johnson signed the far-reaching Civil Rights Act. In 1965, King set in motion a massive drive to enroll the 3 million southern African Americans who were not registered to vote. Later that year, Johnson persuaded Congress to pass the Voting Rights Act. The legislation did little to ameliorate the poverty of inner-city blacks or stem the violence that swept northern cities in the hot summers of the late 1960s. By 1968, nonviolent resistance had given way to the more militant black power movement.

- **Escalation in Vietnam** The United States supported the government of South Vietnam even though it failed to deliver promised reforms, win the support of its citizens, or defeat the Communist insurgents, the Viet Cong. Kennedy increased America's commitment by sending advisers, and Johnson went further, deploying combat troops. A turning point in the war was the Viet Cong's Tet offensive, which served to rally anti-war sentiment.

- **Communist Cuba** In early 1961, Kennedy inherited a CIA plot to topple the regime of Fidel Castro, the premier of Cuba. Kennedy naïvely agreed to the plot, whereby some 1,500 anti-Castro Cubans landed at Cuba's Bay of Pigs. The plotters failed to inspire a revolution, and most were quickly captured. Kennedy's seeming weakness in the face of Soviet aggression led the Russian premier, Nikita Khrushchev, to believe that the Soviets could install ballistic missiles in Cuba without American opposition. In October 1962 in a tense standoff, Kennedy ordered a blockage of Cuba and succeeded in forcing Khrushchev to withdraw the missiles.

CHRONOLOGY

1961	Bay of Pigs fiasco
1961	Soviets erect the Berlin Wall
October 1962	Cuban missile crisis
August 1963	March on Washington for Jobs and Freedom
November 1963	John F. Kennedy is assassinated in Dallas, Texas
1964	Congress passes the Civil Rights Act
August 1964	Congress passes the Tonkin Gulf resolution
1965	Malcolm X is assassinated by a rival group of black Muslims
1965	Riots break out in the African American community of Watts, California
January 1968	Viet Cong stage the Tet offensive
April 1968	Martin Luther King Jr. is assassinated
June 1968	Robert Kennedy is assassinated

KEY TERMS & NAMES

35

REBELLION AND REACTION IN THE 1960S AND 1970S

FOCUS QUESTIONS wwnorton.com/studyspace

- What characterized the social rebellion and struggles for civil rights in the 1960s and 1970s?

- How did the war in Vietnam end?

- What was Watergate, and why did it lead to Nixon's resignation?

- Why had the Middle East become an area of concern by the 1970s, and how did the Carter administration deal with crises in the area?

As Richard Nixon entered the White House in early 1969, he faced a nation whose social fabric was in tatters. Everywhere, it seemed, traditional institutions and notions of authority were under attack. The traumatic events of 1968 revealed how deeply divided American society had become and how difficult a task Nixon faced in carrying out his pledge to restore social harmony. The stability he promised proved elusive. His policies and his combative temperament heightened rather than reduced societal tensions. Those tensions reflected profound fissures in the post–World War II consensus promoted by Eisenhower and inherited by Kennedy and Johnson. Ironically, many of the same forces that had promoted the flush times of the Eisenhower years—the baby boom, the containment doctrine of anti-communism, and the superficial focus on the consumer culture—helped generate the social upheaval of the 1960s and 1970s.

THE ROOTS OF REBELLION

YOUTH REVOLT   By the early 1960s the postwar baby boomers were maturing. Now young adults, they differed from their elders in that they had experienced neither economic depression nor a major war. In record numbers they were attending colleges and universities: enrollment quadrupled between 1945 and 1970. Many universities had become sprawling institutions increasingly dependent upon research contracts from giant corporations and the federal government. As these "multiversities" grew more bureaucratic and hierarchical, they unwittingly invited resistance from students wary of involvement in what President Eisenhower had called the military-industrial complex.

The Greensboro student sit-ins in 1960 not only precipitated a decade of civil rights activism but also signaled an end to the supposed apathy that had enveloped college campuses and social life during the 1950s. Although primarily concerned with the rights and status of black people, the sit-ins, marches, protests, ideals, and sacrifices associated with the civil rights movement provided inspiring models and rhetoric for other groups demanding justice, freedom, and equality.

The free-speech movement

Mario Savio, a founder of the free-speech movement, speaks at a rally at the University of California at Berkeley.

During 1960–1961 a small but significant number of white students joined the sit-in movement. They and many others were also inspired by President Kennedy's direct appeals to their youthful idealism. Soon, however, it became clear that politics was mixed with principle in the president's position on civil rights. Later, as criticism of escalating American involvement in Vietnam mounted, more and more young people grew disillusioned with the government, corporations, and parental authority. Cynicism bred activism. By the mid-1960s a full-fledged youth revolt had erupted across the country, and rebels began to flow into two distinct yet frequently overlapping movements: the New Left and the counterculture.

THE NEW LEFT   The explicitly political strain of the youth revolt coalesced when Tom Hayden and Al Haber, two student radicals at the University of Michigan, formed Students for a Democratic Society (SDS) in 1960. Two years later Hayden drafted what became known as the Port Huron Statement. It begins: "We are the people of this generation, bred in at least moderate comfort, housed in universities, looking uncomfortably to the world we inherit."

Hayden's manifesto focused on the absence of individual freedom in modern life. The country, he insisted, was dominated by huge organizational structures—governments, corporations, universities—all of which conspired to oppress and alienate the individual. Inspired by the example of African American activism in the South, Hayden declared that students had the power to restore "participatory democracy" to American life by wresting "control of the educational process from the administrative bureaucracy" and then forging links with other dissident movements. He and others adopted the term New Left to distinguish their efforts at grassroots democracy from those of the Old Left of the 1930s, which had espoused an orthodox version of Marxism.

In the fall of 1964, students at the University of California at Berkeley took Hayden's program to heart. When the university's chancellor announced that sidewalk solicitations for political causes would no longer be allowed, several hundred students staged a sit-in. Over 2,000 more joined in, and after a tense standoff the administration relented.

The program and tactics of the SDS spread to universities across the country, but the focus changed as escalating involvement in Vietnam brought a dramatic expansion of the military draft and millions of young men faced the grim prospect of participating in an increasingly unpopular war. In fact, however, Vietnam, like virtually every other war, was a poor man's fight. In 1965–1966, thanks to deferments and exemptions, college students made up only 2 percent of all military inductees. Yet several thousand male collegians would flee to Canada or Sweden to escape the draft, while hundreds of thousands engaged in various protests against a war they considered immoral.

During the eventful spring of 1968—when Lyndon Johnson announced he would not run for reelection and Martin Luther King Jr. was assassinated—campus unrest reached a climax with the disruption of Columbia University in New York City. Mark Rudd, an SDS leader, and a small group of radicals protested the university's insensitive decision to disrupt a neighboring African American community in order to build a new gymnasium. The students occupied some campus buildings, and the protest quickly spread. During the following week more buildings were occupied, faculty and administrative offices were ransacked, and classes were canceled. University officials finally called in the New York City police. While arresting the protesters, officers injured innocent bystanders. Such excessive force angered many unaligned students, who then joined militants in staging a strike that shut down the university for the remainder of the semester. That spring similar clashes among students, administrators, and police occurred at Harvard, Cornell, and San Francisco State.

At the 1968 Democratic Convention in Chicago, the polarization of American society reached a bizarre climax. Inside the tightly guarded convention hall, Democrats were nominating Lyndon Johnson's faithful vice president, Hubert Humphrey, while Chicago's streets roiled with anti-war dissenters. The outlandish behavior of the anarchic protesters provoked an equally outlandish response from Chicago's Mayor Richard J. Daley and his army of police. As a national television audience watched, many police officers went berserk, clubbing and gassing demonstrators as well as bystanders caught up in the chaos. The televised spectacle lasted three days and generated a wave of anger among many middle-class Americans,

Upheaval in Chicago

The violence that accompanied the 1968 Democratic National Convention in Chicago seared the nation.

which Richard Nixon and the Republicans shrewdly exploited at their 1968 nominating convention in Miami Beach. At the same time, the Chicago riots fragmented the anti-war movement.

During 1968 the SDS fractured into rival factions, the most extreme of which called itself the Weathermen, a name derived from a lyric by Bob Dylan: "You don't need a weather man to know which way the wind blows." These hardened young activists launched a campaign of violence and disruption, firebombing university and government buildings and killing innocent people, as well as several of their own. Government forces arrested most of them, and the rest went into hiding. By 1971 the New Left was dead as a political movement. In large measure it had committed suicide by abandoning the pacifist principles that had inspired participants and given the movement its moral legitimacy. The larger anti-war movement also began to fade. There would be a wave of student protests against the Nixon administration in 1970–1971, but thereafter campus unrest virtually disappeared as American troops returned home from Vietnam and the draft ended.

If the social mood was changing during Richard Nixon's presidency, a large segment of the public persisted in the quest for social justice. A *New York Times* survey of college campuses in 1969 revealed that many students were refocusing their attention on the environment. This new ecological awareness would blossom in the 1970s into one of the most compelling items on the nation's social agenda.

THE COUNTERCULTURE   The numbing events of 1968 led other disaffected activists away from radical politics altogether, toward another manifestation of the sixties youth revolt: the counterculture. Long hair, blue jeans, tie-dyed shirts, sandals, mind-altering drugs, rock music, and group living arrangements were more important than revolutionary ideology or mass protest to the hippies, the direct descendants of the Beats of the 1950s. Advocates of the counterculture were, like their New Left peers, primarily young whites alienated by the Vietnam War, racism, political corruption and parental demands, runaway technology, and a crass corporate mentality that equated the good life with material goods. Disillusioned with organized political action, they embraced the credo announced by the zany Harvard professor Timothy Leary: "Tune in, turn on, drop out."

For some the counterculture entailed the embrace of Asian religions such as Buddhism. For others it centered on the frequent use of hallucinogenic drugs such as LSD. Collective living in urban enclaves such as San Francisco's Haight-Ashbury district and New York's East Village was the rage for a while, until conditions grew so crowded and violent that residents migrated elsewhere. Rural communes also attracted bourgeois rebels. During the 1960s and early 1970s, thousands of inexperienced romantics flocked to the countryside, eager to liberate themselves from parental and institutional restraints, live in harmony with nature, and coexist in an atmosphere of love and openness. Only a handful of their utopian homesteads survived more than a few months, however.

Huge outdoor rock concerts were a popular source of community for hippies. The largest of these was the Woodstock Music and Art Fair, held in 1969 on a 600-acre farm near the tiny rural town of Bethel, New York. For three days some 500,000 "flower children" reveled in good music and cheap marijuana. But the carefree spirit of the Woodstock festival was short-lived. When concert promoters tried to replicate the scene four months later, this time at a Rolling Stones concert at the Altamont Speedway near San Francisco, members of the Hells Angels motorcycle gang beat a man to death in front of the stage.

Woodstock

The Woodstock music festival drew nearly half a million people to a farm in Bethel, New York. The concert was billed as three days of "peace, music, . . . and love."

Just as the 1968 Democratic Convention in Chicago marked the end of the New Left as a vital political force, the violence at Altamont sharply diminished the appeal of the counterculture. Moreover, many of the flower children grew tired of their riches-to-rags existence and returned to college to become lawyers, doctors, politicians, or accountants. The search on the part of alienated youth for a better society and a good life was strewn with irony, hypocrisy, disillusionment, and tragedy.

FEMINISM   The ideal of liberation spawned during the 1960s helped accelerate a powerful women's rights crusade. Like the New Left, the new feminism drew much of its inspiration and many of its initial tactics from the civil rights movement. Its aim was to challenge the conventional cult of domesticity that had been touted as the ideal during the 1950s.

The mainstream women's movement was led by Betty Friedan. Her influential book, *The Feminine Mystique* (1963), launched a new phase of female protest on a national level. Women, Friedan wrote, had actually lost ground during the years after World War II, when many left wartime jobs and settled down in suburbia to care for their children. Advertisers and women's magazines promoted the "feminine mystique" of blissful domesticity. In Friedan's view the middle-class home had become "a comfortable concentration camp" where women saw their individual potential suffocated in an atmosphere of mindless materialism, daytime TV, and neighborhood gossip.

The Feminine Mystique inspired many women who felt trapped in their domestic doldrums. In 1966, Friedan and other activists founded the National Organization for Women (NOW), whose membership grew rapidly. NOW spearheaded

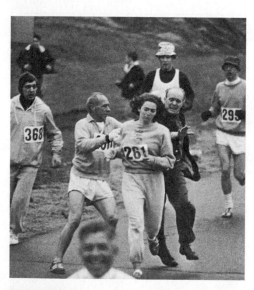

Feminist awakenings

In 1967, Syracuse University student Kathy Switzer challenged the Boston Marathon's tradition of excluding women. Officials tried to pull Switzer from the course, but with the aid of fellow runners she completed the race. Women did not become official entrants until 1971.

efforts to end job discrimination on the basis of sex, legalize abortion, and obtain federal and state support for child-care centers.

Pressured by NOW, Congress and the Supreme Court in the early 1970s advanced the cause of sexual equality. Under Title IX of the Education Amendments of 1972, colleges were required to institute "affirmative-action" programs to ensure equal opportunities for women in such areas as admissions, faculty and staff hiring, and athletics. Also in 1972, Congress overwhelmingly approved the equal-rights amendment to the Constitution. And in 1973 the Supreme Court, in *Roe v. Wade*, struck down state laws forbidding abortions during the first three months of pregnancy, a ruling based on the constitutional right to privacy. Meanwhile, many bastions of male education, including Yale and Princeton, led a new movement for coeducation that swept the nation.

By the end of the 1970s, however, sharp disputes between moderate and radical feminists had fragmented the women's movement. The movement's failure to broaden its appeal much beyond the confines of the white middle class caused reform efforts to stagnate. In 1982 the equal-rights amendment died, several states short of ratification. The very success of NOW's efforts to liberalize state abortion laws helped generate a powerful backlash, especially among Catholics and fundamentalist Protestants, who mounted a "right-to-life" crusade that helped ignite the conservative political insurgence in the 1970s and thereafter.

Yet the success of the women's movement endured despite setbacks. The growing political power of women and their expanding presence in the workforce combined to become one of the most significant developments of the era. By 1976 over half the married women in America and nine out of ten female college graduates were employed outside the home, a development that one economist called "the single most outstanding phenomenon of this century." Many career women, however, did not regard themselves as feminists; they took jobs because they and their families needed the money to achieve higher levels of material comfort. Whatever their motives, women were changing traditional sex roles and child-rearing practices to accommodate the two-career family, which had replaced the established pattern of male breadwinner and female housekeeper as the new American norm.

HISPANIC RIGHTS The activism that animated the crusade for women's rights also spread to various ethnic minority groups. The labor shortages during World War II had led defense industries to offer Hispanic Americans their first significant access to skilled-labor jobs. As was the case with African Americans, service in the military during the war years helped to heighten an American identity among Hispanic Americans and increase their desire for equal rights and opportunities.

But equality was elusive. After World War II, Hispanic Americans still faced widespread discrimination in hiring, housing, and education. Poverty was widespread. In 1960, for example, the median income of a Mexican American family was only 62 percent of that of a family in the general population. Hispanic American activists during the 1950s and 1960s mirrored the efforts of black civil rights leaders. They, too, denounced segregation, promoted efforts to improve the quality of public education, and struggled to increase Hispanic American political influence and economic opportunities.

One of the most popular initiatives was the use of the term *Chicano* as an inclusive label for all Mexican immigrants, Spanish Americans in New Mexico, old Californios (descendants of the inhabitants of California before it was seized by the United States, most of whom were Indians or of mixed ancestry), and Tejanos (descendants of the inhabitants of Texas before it became independent).* In southern California, members of Young Citizens for Community Action re-formed as Young Chicanos for Community Action, or the Brown Berets, a social-service group designed to promote self-reliance and local involvement within Mexican American neighborhoods. They protested the disproportionate number of Hispanics being killed in the Vietnam War and demanded improvements in their neighborhood schools.

Unlike their African American counterparts, however, Hispanic American leaders faced an awkward dilemma: what should they do about the continuing stream of undocumented Mexicans flowing across the border? Many Mexican Americans argued that their hopes for economic advancement and social equality were put at risk by the daily influx of Mexican laborers willing to accept low-paying jobs in the United States. Mexican American leaders thus helped end the bracero program in 1964 (which trucked in day laborers from Mexico) and in 1962 formed the United Farm Workers (UFW, originally the National Farm Workers Association) to represent Mexican American migrant workers.

The founder of the UFW was the charismatic Cesar Chavez. Born in 1927 in Yuma, Arizona, to Mexican immigrants, Chavez moved with his family to

---

*Hispanic, a term used in the United States to refer to people who are from, or trace their ancestry to, Spanish-speaking Latin America or Spain, came to be used increasingly after 1945 in conjunction with growing efforts to promote economic and social justice for those people. (Although frequently used as a synonym for *Hispanic*, the term *Latino* technically refers only to people of Latin American descent.)

California in 1939. There they joined thousands of other migrant farmworkers, moving from job to job, living in tents, cars, or ramshackle cabins. In 1944, at age seventeen, Chavez joined the navy. After the war he married and found work, first as a sharecropper raising strawberries and then as a migrant laborer in apricot orchards. In 1952, Chavez joined the Community Service Organization (CSO), a social-service group that sought to educate and organize the migrant poor so that they could become self-reliant. He founded new CSO chapters and was named general director in 1958.

Chavez left the organization in 1962 when it refused to back his proposal to establish a union for farmworkers. Other CSO leaders believed that it was impossible to organize migrant workers into an effective union. They thought the migrant workers were too mobile, too poor, too illiterate, too ethnically diverse, and too easily replaced by braceros. Moreover, farmworkers did not enjoy protected status under the National Labor Relations Act of 1935 (the Wagner Act). Unlike industrial laborers they were not guaranteed the right to organize or the right to receive a minimum wage. Nor did federal regulations govern the safety of their workplace.

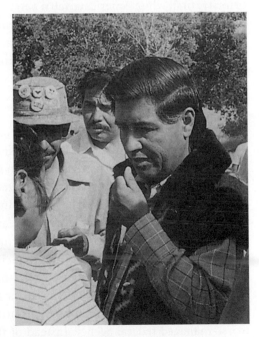

Despite such obstacles, Chavez resolved to organize migrant farmworkers. His fledgling National Farm Workers Association gained national attention in 1965 when it joined a strike by Filipino farmworkers against the corporate grape farmers in California's San Joaquin Valley. Chavez's courage and Catholic piety, his insistence upon nonviolent tactics, his reliance upon college-student volunteers, his skillful alliance with organized labor and religious groups—all combined to attract media interest and popular support.

United Farm Workers

Cesar Chavez (center) with organizers of the grape boycott. In 1968, Chavez ended a three-week fast by taking Communion and breaking bread with Senator Robert Kennedy.

Still, the grape strike itself brought no tangible gains. So Chavez organized a nationwide consumer boycott of grapes. In

1970 the grape strike and the consumer boycott finally succeeded in bringing twenty-six grape growers to the bargaining table. They signed formal contracts recognizing the UFW, and soon migrant workers throughout the West were benefiting from Chavez's strenuous efforts on their behalf. Wages increased, and working conditions improved. In 1975 the California state legislature passed a bill that required growers to bargain collectively with the elected representatives of the farmworkers.

The chief strength of the Hispanic movement lay less in the duplication of the civil rights strategies than in the rapid growth of the Hispanic population. In 1960, Hispanics in the United States numbered slightly more than 3 million; by 1970 their numbers had increased to 9 million; and by 2006 they numbered over 40 million, making them the largest minority in the country.

NATIVE AMERICAN RIGHTS   American Indians—many of whom had begun calling themselves Native Americans—also emerged as a political force in the late 1960s. Two conditions combined to make Indian rights a priority: first, white Americans felt a persistent sense of guilt for the destructive policies of their ancestors toward a people who had, after all, first settled the continent; second, the plight of the Native American minority was more desperate than that of any other group in the country. Indian unemployment was 10 times the national rate, life expectancy was 20 years lower than the national average, and the suicide rate was 100 times higher than that for whites.

Although President Lyndon Johnson recognized the poverty of the Native Americans and attempted to funnel federal anti-poverty-program funds into reservations, militants within the Indian community grew impatient with the pace of change. They organized protests and demonstrations against local, state, and federal agencies. In 1963 two Chippewas (Ojibwas) living in Minneapolis, George Mitchell and Dennis Banks, founded the American Indian Movement (AIM) to promote "red power." The leaders of AIM occupied Alcatraz Island in San Francisco Bay in 1969, claiming the site "by right of discovery." And in 1972 a sit-in at the Department of the Interior's Bureau of Indian Affairs (BIA) in Washington attracted national attention to their cause. The BIA was then—and still is—widely viewed as the worst-managed federal agency. Instead of finding creative ways to promote tribal autonomy and economic self-sufficiency, the BIA has served as a classic example of government paternalism gone awry.

Indian protesters subsequently discovered a more effective tactic than direct action and sit-ins: they went into federal courts armed with copies of old treaties and demanded that those documents become the basis for restitution.

In Alaska, Maine, South Carolina, and Massachusetts they won significant settlements that provided legal recognition of their tribal rights and financial compensation at levels that upgraded the standard of living on several reservations.

GAY RIGHTS The liberationist impulses of the 1960s also encouraged homosexuals to organize and assert their right to equal treatment. On June 27, 1969, New York City police raided the Stonewall Inn, a Greenwich Village bar popular with gay men. The patrons fought back, and the struggle spilled into the streets. Hundreds of other gays and their supporters joined the fracas against the police. Rioting lasted throughout the weekend. When it ended, homosexuals had forged a new sense of solidarity and a new organization, the Gay Liberation Front.

As news of the Stonewall riots spread across the country, the gay rights movement assumed national proportions. One of its main tactics was to encourage people to "come out," to make public their homosexuality. This was by no means an easy decision. By professing their homosexuality, gays faced social ostracism, physical assault, exclusion from the military and civil service, and discrimination in the workplace. Yet despite the risks, thousands of homosexuals did come out. By 1973 almost 800 gay organizations had been formed across the country, and every major city had a visible gay community and cultural life.

Like the civil rights crusade and the women's movement, however, the campaign for gay rights soon suffered from internal divisions and aroused a conservative backlash. Gay activists engaged in fractious disputes over tactics and objectives, and in a nationwide counterattack, conservative moralists and Christian fundamentalists succeeded in repealing new local laws banning discrimination against homosexuals. By the end of the 1970s, the gay movement had lost its initial momentum and was struggling to salvage many of its hard-won gains.

NIXON AND VIETNAM

The numerous liberation movements of the 1960s transformed the tone and texture of American social life. By the early 1970s, however, the national mood was swinging back toward conservatism. The election of Richard Nixon in 1968 and the rise of George Wallace as a national political force on the right reflected the emergence of the "silent majority," those white working-class and middle-class citizens who were determined to regain control of a society they feared was awash in permissiveness. Large as the gap was between the "silent majority" and the varied forces of dissent, the two sides agreed upon one thing: that the Vietnam War remained the dominant event of the time. Until the war ended and all American troops had returned home, the nation would find it difficult to achieve the equilibrium that the new president had promised.

GRADUAL WITHDRAWAL   Nixon and his special assistant for national security, Dr. Henry Kissinger, claimed to have a plan to achieve "peace with honor" in Vietnam. Peace, however, was long in coming and not very honorable when it arrived. The Nixon administration, even while withdrawing U.S. forces, held to a policy of refusing to let the North Vietnamese dominate Indochina. By the time a settlement was reached, in 1973, another 20,000 Americans had died, the morale of the American army had been shattered, millions of Asians had been killed or wounded, and fighting was continuing in Southeast Asia. In the end, Nixon's policy gained little that the president could not have accomplished in 1969.

The administration's new strategy in Vietnam moved along three fronts. The first front was the deadlocked Paris peace talks, where American negotiators demanded the withdrawal of North Vietnamese forces from South Vietnam and the preservation of the U.S.-supported regime of President Nguyen Van Thieu. The North Vietnamese and Viet Cong negotiators insisted on retaining a Communist military presence in the south, however, and on reunifying the Vietnamese people under a Communist-dominated government. There was no common ground on which to come together. Hidden from public awareness and from America's South Vietnamese allies were secret meetings between Henry Kissinger and the North Vietnamese.

On the second front, Nixon tried to defuse domestic unrest generated by the war. To this end he sought to "Vietnamize" the conflict by turning over most of the combat missions to Vietnamese units and sharply reducing the number of U.S. ground forces. To assuage the South Vietnamese, he provided more equipment and training for their army. From a peak of 560,000 in 1969, U.S. combat troops were withdrawn at a steady pace. By 1973 only 50,000 troops remained in Vietnam. In late 1969, Nixon also established a lottery system that clarified the likelihood of being drafted: only those with low lottery numbers would have to go. Nixon was more successful in reducing anti-war activity than in forcing concessions from the North Vietnamese negotiators in Paris.

On the third front, while reducing the number of troops in Vietnam, Nixon and Kissinger secretly expanded the air war to persuade the enemy to come to terms. On March 18, 1969, U.S. planes began Operation Menu, a fourteen-month-long bombing of Communist forces in Cambodia. Over 100,000 tons of bombs were dropped, four times the tonnage dropped on Japan during World War II. Congress did not learn of those raids until 1970, when Nixon announced what he called an "incursion" by U.S. troops into supposedly neutral Cambodia to "clean out" North Vietnamese staging areas.

DIVISIONS AT HOME   News of the Cambodia "incursion" came on the heels of another incident that rekindled public indignation against the war. Late in 1969 the story of the My Lai Massacre broke. During the next two years the public learned the gruesome tale of Lieutenant William Calley, who in 1968 had ordered the murder of over 300 Vietnamese civilians in the village of My Lai. Twenty-five officers were charged with complicity in the massacre and subsequent cover-up, but only Calley was convicted of murder. Nixon then granted him parole.

The loudest public outcry against Nixon's Indochina policy occurred in the wake of the Cambodian "incursion," in the spring of 1970. Campuses across the country witnessed a new wave of protests that closed hundreds of colleges and universities. At Kent State University, the Ohio National Guard was called in to quell rioting, during which the building housing the campus Reserve Officers' Training Corps (ROTC) was burned down by anti-war protesters. Pelted by rocks and verbal taunts, the poorly trained guardsmen panicked and opened fire on the demonstrators, killing four bystanders. Eleven days later, on May 15, Mississippi highway patrolmen riddled a dormitory at Jackson State College with bullets, killing two African American students. Although an official investigation of the Kent State episode condemned the "casual and indiscriminate shooting," polls indicated that the public supported the National Guard; students had "got what they were asking for."

The following year, 1971, the *New York Times* began publishing excerpts from a secret Defense Department study on the Vietnam War. The so-called Pentagon Papers, leaked to the press by a former Pentagon official, Daniel Ellsberg, confirmed what many critics of the war had long suspected: Congress and the public had not received the full story on the Gulf of Tonkin incident of 1964. Contingency plans for American entry into the war were being drawn up even while President Johnson was promising that combat troops would never be sent to Vietnam. The Nixon administration blocked publication of the Pentagon Papers, arguing that it would endanger national security and prolong the war. By a vote of 6 to 3, the Supreme Court ruled

Kent State University

National guardsmen shot and killed four bystanders during anti-war demonstrations on the campus of Kent State University in Ohio.

against the government. Newspapers throughout the country began publication the next day.

WAR WITHOUT END   Although Nixon's decision in the spring of 1970 to use American forces to root out Communist bases in Cambodia did bring a tactical victory, it also served to widen a war he had promised to end. Moreover, his hopes that the South Vietnamese units replacing U.S. forces could hold their own against the North Vietnamese were dashed when they suffered repeated defeats in 1971 and 1972. Disorganized, poorly led, and lacking tenacity, the South Vietnamese soldiers had to call upon U.S. air-power to fend off North Vietnamese offensives.

The deteriorating ground war along with mounting divisions at home and the approach of the 1972 presidential elections combined to produce a shift in the American negotiating position in Paris. In the summer of 1972, Henry Kissinger dropped his insistence upon the removal of all North Vietnamese troops from the south before the withdrawal of the remaining U.S. troops. On October 26, only a week before the presidential election, he announced, "Peace is at hand." But the Thieu regime in South Vietnam objected to the plan for a cease-fire, fearful that the continued presence of North Vietnamese troops in the south virtually guaranteed an eventual Communist victory. Hanoi then stiffened its position by demanding that Thieu resign.

The Paris peace talks broke off on December 16, 1972, and Nixon told his military advisers that only a massive show of American airpower would make the North Vietnamese more cooperative at the negotiating table. Two days later the newly reelected Nixon unleashed furious B-52 raids on Hanoi and Haiphong. The so-called Christmas bombings aroused worldwide protest, but Kissinger claimed Nixon's "jugular diplomacy" worked, for the talks in Paris soon resumed.

On January 27, 1973, the United States, North and South Vietnam, and the Viet Cong signed an "agreement on ending the war and restoring peace in Vietnam." The agreement showed that despite the Christmas bombings, the North Vietnamese never altered their basic stance: they kept 150,000 troops in the south and remained committed to the reunification of Vietnam under one government. What had changed since the previous fall was the willingness of the South Vietnamese, who were never allowed to participate in the negotiations, to accept these terms, albeit reluctantly, on the basis of Nixon's promise that the United States would respond "with full force" to any Communist violation of the agreement.

On March 29, 1973, the last U.S. combat troops left Vietnam. On that same day, almost 600 American prisoners of war, most of them downed pilots, were released from Hanoi. Within months, however, the war between north and south resumed, and the Communist forces gained the advantage. In Cambodia and Laos, where fighting had been more sporadic, a Communist victory also seemed inevitable.

In 1975 the North Vietnamese launched a full-scale armored invasion against the south. President Thieu appealed to Washington for assistance, but the Democratic majority in Congress refused, and on April 30, 1975, Americans watched on television as North Vietnamese tanks rolled into Saigon, soon to be renamed Ho Chi Minh City. The scene at the U.S. embassy in Saigon, where thousands of terrified Vietnamese fought to board the last departing helicopters, was a poignant, tragic ending to America's greatest foreign-policy disaster.

The longest war in U.S. history was finally over, leaving in its wake a bitter legacy. The Vietnam War, described as a noble crusade on behalf of democratic ideals, instead suggested that democracy was not easily transferable to third world regions lacking experience with civil liberties and representative government. The war eroded respect for the military so thoroughly that many young Americans came to regard military service as inherently corrupting and ignoble. The war, fought to show the world that the United States was united in its anti-Communist convictions, divided Americans more drastically than any event since the Civil War. The Vietnam War cost the nation some 58,000 deaths and $150 billion. Little wonder the dominant public reaction to the war's end was the urge to put Vietnam behind us and revert to a noninterventionist foreign policy.

NIXON AND MIDDLE AMERICA

Richard Nixon had been elected in 1968 as the representative of middle America, those middle-class citizens fed up with the liberal politics and radical culture of the 1960s. Nixon selected men for his cabinet and White House staff who would restore conservative values and carry out his orders with blind obedience. John Mitchell, the gruff attorney general who had been a senior partner in Nixon's New York law firm, was the new president's closest confidant. H. R. (Bob) Haldeman, an imperious former advertising executive, served as Nixon's chief of staff. As Haldeman explained, "Every President needs a son of a bitch, and I'm Nixon's. I'm his buffer, I'm his bastard." He was succeeded in 1973 by General Alexander Haig, whom Nixon described as "the meanest, toughest, most ambitious son of a bitch I ever knew." John Ehrlichman, a Seattle attorney and college schoolmate of Haldeman's, served as chief domestic-policy adviser. As secretary of state, Nixon tapped his old friend William Rogers, who had served as attorney general under Eisenhower. Rogers's control over foreign policy was quickly preempted by Henry Kissinger, a distinguished Harvard political scientist who served as national security adviser before becoming secretary of state in 1973. Kissinger came to dominate the Nixon administration's diplomatic planning and emerged as one of the most respected and internationally famous members of the staff. Nixon often had to mediate the tensions between Rogers and Kissinger, noting that the secretary of state considered the German-born Kissinger "Machiavellian, deceitful, egotistical, arrogant, and insulting," while Kissinger viewed Rogers as "vain, emotional, unable to keep a secret, and hopelessly dominated by the State Department bureaucracy."

DOMESTIC AFFAIRS   A major reason for Richard Nixon's election in 1968 was the effective "southern strategy" fashioned by his campaign staffers. To garner support among Republican delegates from the South and then win over southern voters in the election, Nixon had assured conservatives that he would slow federal enforcement of civil rights laws and appoint pro-southern justices to the Supreme Court. Once in office, Nixon followed through on his pledges. He appointed no African Americans to his cabinet and refused to meet with the Congressional Black Caucus. In 1970 he launched a concerted effort to block congressional renewal of the Voting Rights Act of 1965 and delay implementation of court orders requiring the desegregation of school districts in Mississippi. The Democratic-controlled Congress then extended the Voting Rights Act over Nixon's veto. The Supreme Court, in the first decision made under the new chief justice, Warren Burger— a Nixon appointee—ordered the integration of the Mississippi public schools. During Nixon's first term, and despite his wishes, affirmative action made major inroads, and more schools were desegregated than in all the Kennedy-Johnson years combined.

Nixon also failed in his attempts to block desegregation efforts in urban areas. The Burger Court ruled unanimously in *Swann v. Charlotte-Mecklenburg Board of Education* (1971) that school systems must bus students out of their neighborhood if necessary to achieve racial integration. Protests over desegregation now occurred more in the North and the West than in the South as white families in Boston, Denver, and other cities denounced the destruction of "the neighborhood school." Busing opponents won a limited victory when the Supreme Court ruled in 1974 that requiring the transfer of students from the inner city to the suburbs was unconstitutional. That ruling, along with the *Regents of the University of California v. Bakke* (1978) decision, which restricted the use of quotas to achieve racial balance in university classrooms, marked the transition of desegregation from an issue of simple justice to a more tangled thicket of conflicting group and individual rights.

It also reflected the growing conservatism of the Supreme Court, a trend encouraged by Nixon. The litany of liberal decisions during the 1960s had made the Warren Court a target for conservatives who resented what they regarded as the government's excessive protection of the "undeserving." Fate and the aging of the justices on the Warren Court gave Nixon the chance to make four new appointments. Only one, William Rehnquist, would consistently support Nixon's conservative interpretation of the Constitution, but overall the tenor of the Court did shift toward a more moderate stance.

Nixon also fervently desired to reverse the welfare-state policies of his Democratic predecessors. But the administration never succeeded in developing a comprehensive domestic agenda acceptable to Congress. Meanwhile, the Democratic Congress moved forward with new legislation: the right of eighteen-year-olds to vote in national elections (1970) and, under the Twenty-sixth Amendment (1971), in state and local elections as well; increases in Social Security benefits tied to the inflation rate; a rise in food-stamp funding; the Occupational Safety and Health Act (1970); and the Federal Election Campaign Act (1971). Moreover, in response to Nixon's proposal to decentralize responsibility for various programs, Congress passed a five-year revenue-sharing plan in 1972 that would distribute $30 billion of federal revenues to the states for use as they saw fit.

During Nixon's first term, Americans in large numbers began to lobby for government action to protect and improve the natural environment. In 1970, hundreds of thousands of activists rallied across the country in support of the first Earth Day. In response, Congress established new programs to control water pollution and passed the Clean Air Act (1970) over Nixon's veto. Congress also created the Environmental Protection Agency (EPA) to oversee federal guidelines for controlling air pollution, toxic wastes, and water quality. The EPA began requiring developers to perform environmental-impact studies before new construction could begin. The agency also set fuel-efficiency standards for automobiles and required manufacturers to reduce the level of carbon monoxide emissions from car engines.

ECONOMIC MALAISE The major domestic development during the Nixon years was a floundering economy. Exacerbated by the expense of the Vietnam War, the annual inflation rate began to rise in 1967, when it was at 3 percent. By 1973 it had reached 9 percent; a year later it was at 12 percent, and it remained in double digits for most of the 1970s. Unemployment, at a low of 3.3 percent when Nixon took office, climbed to 6 percent by the end of 1970 and threatened to keep rising. Somehow the American economy was undergoing a recession and an inflation at the same time. Economists coined the term *stagflation* to describe the syndrome that defied the orthodox laws of economics.

The economic malaise had at least three deep-rooted causes. First, the Johnson administration had attempted to pay for both the Great Society's social-welfare programs and the war in Vietnam without a major tax increase, thereby generating larger federal deficits, a major expansion of the money supply, and rapid price inflation. Second and more important, by the late 1960s American goods faced stiff competition in international markets from West Germany, Japan, and other emerging industrial powers. This development sharply reduced the export of American goods and generated a growing trade deficit. Third, the economy had grown heavily dependent upon cheap sources of energy.

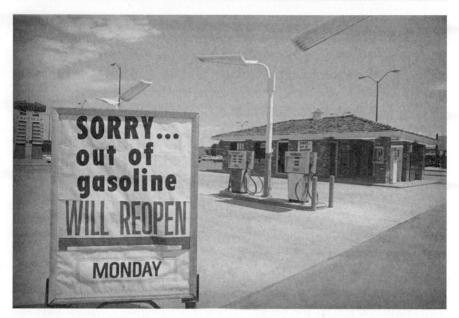

Oil crisis, 1973

The scarcity of oil was dealt with by the rationing of gasoline. Gas stations, such as this one in Colorado, closed on Sundays to conserve supplies.

Just as domestic petroleum reserves began to dwindle and dependence upon foreign sources increased, the nations in the Organization of Petroleum Exporting Countries (OPEC), centered in the Middle East, resolved to use their oil as a political and economic weapon. In 1973, after the United States sent massive aid to Israel during the Yom Kippur War, OPEC announced that it would not sell oil to nations supporting Israel and that it was raising its prices by 400 percent. American motorists thereafter faced long lines at gas stations, schools and offices closed temporarily, factories cut production, and the inflation rate soared.

Another condition leading to stagflation was the flood of new workers—mainly baby boomers and women—entering the labor market. From 1965 to 1980, the workforce grew by 40 percent, almost 30 million workers, a figure greater than the total labor force of France or West Germany. The number of new jobs created could not keep up, leaving many unemployed. At the same time, worker productivity declined, further increasing prices in the face of rising demand.

Stagflation posed a new set of economic problems, but the Nixon administration responded with old remedies. First it tried to reduce the federal deficit by raising taxes and cutting the budget. When the Democratic Congress refused to cooperate with that approach, the White House encouraged the Federal Reserve Board to reduce the money supply by raising interest rates. But that move backfired when the stock market quickly collapsed, plunging the economy into the "Nixon recession." A sense of desperation seized the White House. In 1969, when asked about government restrictions on wages and prices, Nixon had been adamant: "Controls. Oh, my God, no! . . . We'll never go to controls." On August 15, 1971, however, he reversed himself. He froze all wages and prices for ninety days, yet the economy still floundered. By 1973 the wage and price guidelines were made voluntary and were therefore almost entirely ineffective. Stagflation continued to plague the economy for the rest of the decade.

NIXON TRIUMPHANT

Confronting a Congress controlled by Democrats, Richard Nixon focused his energies on foreign policy, where presidential initiatives were less restricted. In tandem with Henry Kissinger, he achieved several major break-throughs. He also continued to support the efforts to beat the Soviets to the moon. In July 1969 the astronaut Neil Armstrong became the first person to walk on the moon. This extraordinary achievement buoyed American spirits at a time when troops were still mired in Vietnam, cities were boiling over

Race to the moon

In July 1969 a program begun by President Kennedy reached its goal: putting a man on the moon.

with racial unrest, and the economy was languishing. Similarly, Nixon's foreign-policy successes gave Americans new confidence in their government. His administration managed to improve U.S. relations with the major powers of the Communist world—China and the Soviet Union—and fundamentally shift the pattern of the cold war.

By 1969, Nixon had perceived that a new multipolar world order was emerging to replace the conventional cold war confrontation between the United States and the Soviet Union. Since 1945 the United States had lost its monopoly on nuclear weapons and its overwhelming economic dominance and

The United States and China

With President Richard Nixon's visit to China in 1972, the United States formally recognized China's Communist government. Here Nixon and Chinese premier Chou En-lai drink a toast.

geopolitical influence. The rapid rise of competing power centers in Europe, China, and Japan complicated international relations—China had replaced the United States as the Soviet Union's most threatening competitor—but also provided strategic opportunities, which Nixon and Kissinger seized.

In early 1970, Nixon announced a significant alteration in American foreign policy. The United States could no longer be the world's policeman against communism; the long-standing containment policy developed by President Truman must be revised: "America cannot—and will not—conceive *all* the plans, design *all* the programs, execute *all* the decisions, and undertake *all* the defense of the free nations of the world." In explaining what became known as the Nixon Doctrine, the president declared that "our interests must shape our commitments, rather than the other way around." The United States, he and Kissinger stressed, must become more strategic and more realistic in its commitments, and it would begin to establish selected partnerships with Communist countries in areas of mutual interest.

CHINA   In 1971, Henry Kissinger made a secret trip to Peking to explore the possibility of U.S. recognition of China. In 1972, Nixon himself arrived in Peking and made recognition an official and public fact. The irony of the

Henry Kissinger's "shuttle diplomacy"

President Sadat of Egypt and Secretary of State Henry Kissinger, during one of Kissinger's many visits to the Middle East, talk with reporters in an effort to bring peace.

event was overwhelming. Richard Nixon, the former anti-Communist crusader who had condemned the State Department for "losing" China in 1949, had accomplished a diplomatic feat that his Democratic predecessors could not. Yet it was because Nixon had been such an ardent anti-Communist that he could pull off the recognition of China: he could not be accused of going soft on communism.

DÉTENTE China sought the breakthrough in relations with the United States because its festering rivalry with the Soviet Union, with which it shares a long border, had become increasingly bitter. Soviet leaders, troubled by the Sino-American agreements, were also eager to ease tensions with the United States now that they had, as the result of a huge arms buildup following the Cuban missile crisis, achieved virtual parity with the United States in nuclear weapons. Once again Nixon surprised the world, announcing that he would visit Moscow in 1972 for discussions with Leonid Brezhnev, the Soviet premier.

What became known as détente with the Soviets offered the promise of a more orderly and restrained competition between the two superpowers. Nixon and Brezhnev signed the Strategic Arms Limitation Talks (SALT) agreement, which set ceilings on the number of long-range nuclear missiles each nation could possess and limited the construction of antiballistic missile systems. In effect the Soviets were allowed to retain a greater number of missiles with greater destructive power while the United States retained a lead in the total number of warheads. No limitations were placed on new weapons systems, though each side agreed to work toward a permanent freeze on all nuclear weapons.

SHUTTLE DIPLOMACY   The Nixon-Kissinger initiatives in the Middle East were less dramatic and less conclusive than the agreements with China and the Soviet Union, but they did show that the United States recognized Arab power in the region and its own dependence upon oil from Islamic states, which were fundamentally opposed to the existence of Israel. After Israel recovered from the initial shock of the Arab attacks that triggered the Yom Kippur War of 1973, it recaptured the Golan Heights and seized additional Syrian territory. Henry Kissinger, now secretary of state, initiated negotiations that led to a cease-fire and exerted pressure to prevent Israel from taking more Arab territory. American reliance upon Arab oil led to closer ties with Egypt and its president, Anwar el-Sadat, and more restrained support for Israel. Although Kissinger's "shuttle diplomacy," involving numerous visits to the capitals of the Middle East, won acclaim from all sides, it failed to find a comprehensive peace formula for the troubled region. It also ignored the problem of establishing a homeland for Palestinian refugees. But Kissinger's efforts did lay groundwork for the accord between Israel and Egypt in 1977.

THE ELECTION OF 1972   Nixon's foreign-policy achievements allowed him to stage the presidential campaign of 1972 as a triumphal procession. The first threat to his reelection came from the Democratic governor of Alabama, George Wallace, who had the potential to deprive the Republicans of conservative votes. But on May 15, 1972, Wallace was shot by a deranged man. Paralyzed below the waist, the governor was forced to withdraw from the campaign. Meanwhile, the Democrats were further ensuring Nixon's victory by nominating Senator George S. McGovern of South Dakota, a steadfast liberal who embodied anti-war principles and embraced progressive social-welfare policies. At the Democratic Convention, party reforms contributed to McGovern's nomination by increasing the representation of women, African Americans, and other minorities, but those reforms alienated the party regulars.

In 1972, Nixon won the greatest victory of any Republican presidential candidate in history, capturing 520 electoral votes to only 17 for McGovern. During the course of the campaign, McGovern had complained about the "dirty tricks" of the Nixon administration, most especially a curious incident during the summer of 1972 when burglars were caught breaking into the headquarters of the Democratic National Committee in the Watergate apartment complex in Washington, D.C. McGovern's accusations seemed shrill and biased at the time. Nixon and his staff made plans for "four more years" as the investigation of the fateful Watergate break-in unfolded.

WATERGATE

During the trial of the accused Watergate burglars in January 1973, the relentless prodding of Judge John J. Sirica led one of the accused to tell the full story of the Nixon administration's complicity in the episode. James McCord, security chief of the Committee to Re-elect the President (CREEP), was the first of many informers in a melodrama that unfolded over two years. It ended in the first resignation of a president in American history, the conviction and imprisonment of twenty-five officials of the Nixon administration, including four cabinet members, and the most serious constitutional crisis since the impeachment trial of President Andrew Johnson in 1868.

UNCOVERING THE COVER-UP   The trail of evidence pursued by Judge John Sirica, a grand jury, several special prosecutors, and a Senate committee headed by Democrat Samuel J. Ervin Jr. of North Carolina led directly to the White House. No evidence surfaced linking Nixon to the order to commit the break-in or suggesting that he had been aware of plans to burglarize the headquarters of the Democratic National Committee. From the start, however, Nixon participated in the cover-up, using his presidential powers to discredit and block the investigation. Perhaps most alarming was that the Watergate burglary proved to be just one small part of a larger pattern of corruption and criminality sanctioned by the Nixon White House. Having developed a compulsive view of his presidency as being above the law, Nixon had ordered intelligence agencies to spy on his most outspoken opponents, open their mail, and even burglarize their homes in an effort to uncover compromising information.

The Watergate cover-up began to unravel as various people, including John Dean, legal counsel to the president, began to cooperate with prosecuters. It unraveled further in 1973 when L. Patrick Gray, acting director of the FBI, resigned after confessing that he had destroyed several incriminating documents. On April 30 top Nixon aides John Ehrlichman and Bob Haldeman resigned, together with Attorney General Richard Kleindienst.

A few days later Nixon nervously assured the public in a television address, "I am not a crook." New evidence suggested otherwise. John Dean, whom Nixon had dismissed, testified before the Ervin committee and a rapt television audience that Nixon had approved the cover-up. In another bombshell disclosure, a White House aide told the committee that Nixon had installed a taping system in the White House and that many of the conversations about Watergate had been recorded.

A yearlong legal battle for the "Nixon tapes" began. Pleading "executive privilege," Nixon refused to release them. On July 24, 1974, in *United States v. Richard M. Nixon*, the Supreme Court ruled unanimously that the president must surrender all of the tapes. A few days later the House Judiciary Committee voted to recommend three articles of impeachment: obstruction of justice through the payment of "hush money" to witnesses and the withholding of evidence, abuse of power through the use of federal agencies to deprive citizens of their constitutional rights, and defiance of Congress by withholding the tapes. Before the House of Representatives could meet to vote on impeachment, however, Nixon handed over the complete set of White House tapes. On August 9, 1974, fully aware that the evidence on the tapes implicated him in the cover-up, Richard Nixon resigned from office, the only president ever to do so.

THE EFFECTS OF WATERGATE

Vice President Spiro Agnew did not succeed Nixon because Agnew himself had been forced to resign in October 1973 for accepting bribes from contractors before and during his term as vice president. The vice president at the time of Nixon's resignation was Gerald Ford, the former Michigan congressman and House minority leader, whom Nixon had appointed, with congressional approval, under the provisions of the Twenty-fifth Amendment (ratified in 1967). President Ford insisted that he had no intention of pardoning Nixon,

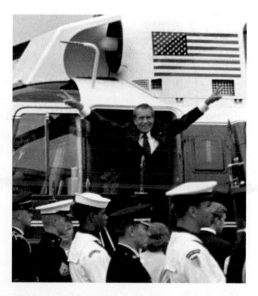

Nixon's resignation

Having resigned his office, Richard Nixon waves farewell outside the White House on August 9, 1974.

who was still liable for criminal prosecution. But a month after Nixon's resignation, on September 8, the new president issued the pardon, explaining that it was necessary to end the national obsession with the Watergate scandal. Many Americans suspected that Nixon and Ford had made a deal, though there was no evidence to confirm the speculation.

If there was a silver lining in Watergate's dark cloud, it was the vigor and resilience of the institutions that had brought a rogue president to justice: the press, Congress, the courts, and an aroused public opinion. The Watergate revelations led Congress to pass several pieces of legislation designed to curb executive power in the future. The War Powers Act (1973) requires a president to inform Congress within forty-eight hours if U.S. troops are deployed in combat abroad and to withdraw troops after sixty days unless Congress specifically approves their stay. In an effort to correct abuses of campaign funds, Congress enacted legislation in 1974 that set new ceilings on political contributions and expenditures. In reaction to the Nixon claim of "executive privilege" as a means of withholding evidence, Congress strengthened the 1966 Freedom of Information Act to require prompt responses to requests for information from government files and to place on government agencies the burden of proof for classifying information as confidential.

AN UNELECTED PRESIDENT

The Watergate crisis so dominated the Washington scene that major domestic and foreign problems received little executive attention. Stagflation, the perplexing combination of inflation and recession, worsened, as did the oil crisis. At the same time, Secretary of State Henry Kissinger, who assumed control over the management of foreign policy, watched helplessly as the South Vietnamese forces crumbled before North Vietnamese attacks, attempted with limited success to establish a framework for peace in the Middle East, and supported a CIA role in the overthrow of the popularly elected Marxist president of Chile.

THE FORD YEARS   Gerald Ford inherited those simmering problems, as well as the burden of being an unelected president. An amiable, honest man, Ford enjoyed widespread popular support for only a short time. "I am a Ford, not a Lincoln," he candidly recognized upon becoming vice president. His pardon of Nixon generated a storm of criticism. The *New York Times* called it "an unconscionable act."

Meeting at Vladivostok, in Siberia

President Gerald Ford shakes hands with Soviet Communist Party Chief Leonid Brezhnev.

As president, Ford adopted the posture he had developed as a conservative minority leader in the House: a nay-saying leader of the opposition who believed that the federal government exercised too much power over domestic affairs. In his fifteen months as president, Ford vetoed thirty-nine bills, outstripping Herbert Hoover's record in less than half the time. By resisting congressional pressure to reduce taxes and increase federal spending, he succeeded in plummeting the economy into the deepest recession since the Great Depression. Unemployment jumped to 9 percent in 1975, and the federal deficit hit a record the next year. Ford rejected wage and price controls to curb inflation, preferring voluntary restraints.

In foreign policy, Ford retained Henry Kissinger as secretary of state and pursued Nixon's goals of stability in the Middle East, rapprochement with China, and détente with the Soviet Union. Late in 1974, Ford met with Soviet leader Leonid Brezhnev and accepted the framework for another arms-control agreement that was to serve as the basis for SALT II. Meanwhile, Kissinger's tireless shuttling between Cairo and Tel Aviv produced an agreement: Israel promised to return to Egypt most of the Sinai territory captured in the 1967 War, and the two nations agreed to rely upon negotiations rather than force to settle future disagreements.

These limited but significant achievements should have enhanced Ford's image, but they were drowned in the sea of criticism and carping that followed the loss of South Vietnam to North Vietnam in the spring of 1975. Not only had a decade of American effort in Vietnam proved futile, but the Khmer Rouge, the Cambodian Communist movement, had also won a resounding victory, plunging Cambodia into a fanatic bloodbath. And the OPEC oil cartel was threatening another worldwide boycott while other third world nations denounced the United States as a depraved imperialistic power.

THE ELECTION OF 1976   Amid such turmoil, the Democrats could hardly wait for the 1976 election. At the Republican Convention, Ford thwarted a powerful challenge for the nomination from Ronald Reagan, a former California governor and Hollywood actor. The Democrats chose Jimmy Carter, a former naval officer and engineer turned peanut farmer who had served one term as governor of Georgia. Carter capitalized on the post-Watergate cynicism by promising never to "tell a lie to the American people" and by citing his independence from traditional Washington power politics.

To the surprise of many pundits, the little-known Carter revived the New Deal coalition of southern whites, blacks, urban labor, and ethnic groups to win the election, with 41 million votes to Ford's 39 million. Polls showed that the Carter victory benefited from a heavy turnout of African Americans in the South, where Carter swept every state but Virginia. Minnesota senator Walter F. Mondale, Carter's liberal running mate and a favorite among blue-collar workers and the urban poor, also gave the ticket a big boost. The real story of the election, however, was the low voter turnout. Almost half of America's eligible voters, apparently alienated by Watergate and the lackluster candidates, chose to sit out the election.

THE CARTER INTERREGNUM

EARLY SUCCESSES   During the first two years of his term, Jimmy Carter enjoyed several successes. His administration included more African Americans, Hispanics, and women than any before. He offered amnesty to the thousands of young men who had fled the country rather than serve in Vietnam, closing one of the remaining open wounds of that traumatic event. He reformed the civil service to provide rewards for meritorious performance, and he created new cabinet-level Departments of Energy and Education. Carter also pushed through Congress significant environmental initiatives, including a bill to regulate strip mining and a "superfund" to clean up chemical-waste sites.

His success was short-lived, however. In the summer of 1979, when renewed violence in the Middle East produced a second fuel shortage, motorists were again forced to wait in long lines for limited supplies of gasoline that they regarded as excessively expensive. Soon they directed their frustration at the White House. Opinion polls showed Carter with an approval rating of only 26 percent, lower than Nixon's during the worst moments of the Watergate crisis.

Several of Carter's early foreign-policy initiatives also got caught in political crossfires. Soon after his inauguration, Carter vowed that "the soul of our foreign policy" should be the defense of human rights abroad. But the human rights campaign aroused opposition from two sides: those who feared that it sacrificed a detached appraisal of national interest for high-level moralizing and those who believed that human rights were important but that the administration was applying the standard inconsistently.

THE CAMP DAVID ACCORDS Carter's crowning diplomatic achievement was brokering a peace agreement between Israel and Egypt. In 1978, Carter invited Egypt's president Anwar el-Sadat and Israel's prime minister Menachem Begin to Camp David, the presidential retreat in Maryland, for two weeks of difficult negotiations. The first part of the eventual agreement required Israel to return all land in the Sinai Peninsula in exchange for Egyptian recognition of Israel's sovereignty. This agreement was successfully implemented in 1982, when the last Israeli settler vacated the peninsula. But the second part of the agreement, calling for Israel to negotiate with Sadat to resolve the Palestinian refugee dilemma, began to unravel soon after the Camp David summit. Still, Carter and Secretary of State Cyrus Vance had orchestrated a dramatic display of high-level diplomacy that, whatever its limitations, made an all-out war between Israel and the Arab world less likely. It also represented a significant first step toward a comprehensive settlement of the region's volatile tensions.

MOUNTING TROUBLES Carter's crowning failure was his mismanagement of the economy. In effect he inherited a bad situation and let it worsen. Carter employed the same economic policies as Nixon and Ford to fight stagflation, but he reversed the order of the federal "cure," preferring to fight unemployment first with a tax cut and increased public spending. Unemployment declined slightly, from 8 to 7 percent in 1977, but inflation soared;

The Camp David Accords

Egyptian president Anwar el-Sadat (left), Jimmy Carter (center), and Israeli prime minister Menachem Begin (right) at the announcement of the Camp David Accords, September 1978.

at 5 percent when he took office, it reached 10 percent in 1978 and kept rising. During one month in 1980, it measured 18 percent. Like previous presidents, Carter then reversed himself to fight the other side of the economic malaise. By midterm he was delaying tax reductions and vetoing government spending programs that he had proposed in his first year. The result was the worst of all possible worlds—a deepened recession and inflation averaging between 12 and 13 percent per year.

IRAN   Then the Iranian crisis exploded, producing a yearlong barrage of unwelcome events that epitomized the inability of the United States to control world affairs. The crisis began in 1979 with the overthrow of the shah of Iran, long a staunch American ally and right-wing dictator. The revolutionaries who toppled the shah's government rallied around Ayatollah Ruhollah Khomeini, a fundamentalist Muslim leader who symbolized the militant Islamic values the shah had tried to replace with Western ways. Khomeini's hatred of the United States dated back to 1953, when the CIA had sponsored the overthrow of Iran's prime minister, Mohammed Mossadegh, an ardent nationalist who sought to rid his country of Western influence and interests. The 1953 coup had restored the shah's regime to power.

Late in 1979, Carter allowed the exiled shah to enter the United States to undergo cancer treatment. A few days later, on November 4, a frenzied Iranian mob stormed the U.S. embassy in Tehran and seized the staff. Khomeini applauded the mob action and demanded the shah's return, along with all his wealth, in exchange for the release of the fifty-two American hostages still held captive.

Carter was furious, but his options were limited. He appealed to the United Nations, but Khomeini scoffed at UN requests for the release of the hostages. Carter then froze all Iranian assets in the United States and appealed to American allies to organize a trade embargo of Iran. The trade restrictions were only partially effective—even America's most loyal European allies did not want to lose access to Iranian oil.

So a frustrated Carter, hounded by a public and press demanding "action," authorized a rescue attempt by U.S. commandos in April 1980. The raid was aborted in the Iranian desert because of helicopter malfunctions, however, and it ended with eight fatalities when a U.S. helicopter collided with a transport plane. Carter's presidency died with the failed raid. Secretary of State Cyrus Vance resigned in protest against the risky venture. Meanwhile, nightly television coverage of the taunting Iranian rebels generated a near obsession with the seeming impotence of the United States and the fate of the hostages. On January 20, 1981, the crisis ended after 444 days when Carter released several billion dollars of Iranian assets to ransom the kidnapped hostages. By then, however, Ronald Reagan had been elected president, and Carter was headed into retirement.

The turbulent and often tragic events of the 1970s—the Communist conquest of South Vietnam, the Watergate scandal and Nixon's resignation, the energy shortage and stagflation, and the Iranian hostage crisis—provoked among Americans what Carter labeled a "crisis of confidence." By 1980, U.S. power and prestige seemed to be declining, the economy remained in a shambles, and the social revolution launched in the 1960s, with the questions it raised for the family and other basic social and political institutions, had sparked a backlash of resentment in middle America. With theatrical timing, Ronald Reagan emerged to tap the growing reservoir of public frustration and transform his political career into a crusade to make America "stand tall again." He told his supporters that there was "a hunger in this land for a spiritual revival, a return to a belief in moral absolutes." The United States, he declared, remained the "greatest country in the world. We have the talent, we have the drive, we have the imagination. Now all we need is the leadership."

CHAPTER SUMMARY

- **Rebellion and Reaction** Civil rights activism was the catalyst for the heightened interest in social causes, especially among the young. Students for a Democratic Society launched the New Left. Other prominent causes of the era included the anti-war movement, the women's liberation movement, Native American rights, Hispanic rights, and gay rights. By 1970 a counterculture had emerged, featuring young people who used mind-altering drugs, lived on communes, and in other ways "dropped out" of the conventional world, which they viewed as corrupt.

- **End of the Vietnam War** Richard Nixon campaigned for the presidency pledging to secure a "peace with honor" in Vietnam, but years would pass before the war ended. His delays prompted an acceleration of anti-war protests. After the Kent State University shootings, the divisions between supporters and opponents of the war became especially contentious. The publication of the Pentagon Papers in 1971 and the heavy bombing of North Vietnam by the United States in December 1972 aroused intense worldwide protests. A month later North and South Vietnam agreed to end the war. The last U.S. troops left Vietnam in March 1973; two years later the government of South Vietnam collapsed, and the country was reunited under a Communist government.

- **Watergate** In an incident in 1972, burglars were caught breaking into the Democratic campaign headquarters at the Watergate complex in Washington, D.C. Eventually the Committee to Re-elect the President (CREEP) was implicated, and investigators probed the question of President Nixon's involvement. Nixon tried to block the judicial process, which led the public to call for the president to be impeached for obstruction of justice. In 1974, in *United States v. Richard M. Nixon*, the Supreme Court ruled that the president had to surrender the so-called Watergate tapes. Nixon resigned to avoid being impeached and removed from office.

- **Middle East Crisis** After the 1973 Yom Kippur War in the Middle East, the Organization of Petroleum Exporting Countries (OPEC) declined to sell oil to states supporting Israel until a cease-fire was reached. President Carter brokered the Camp David Accords of 1978, which laid the groundwork for a peace treaty between Israel and Egypt. The next year an Islamic revolution took place in Iran. Enraged militants stormed the U.S. embassy in Tehran and seized American diplomats and staff. In retaliation, President Carter froze all Iranian assets in the United States. Carter at last released several billlion dollars in Iranian assets to ransom the hostages. The Iranians released the hostages—but not until Ronald Reagan was in office.

CHRONOLOGY

1960	Students in Greensboro, North Carolina, stage a sit-in to demand service at a "whites-only" lunch counter
1960	Food and Drug Administration approves the birth-control pill
1963	Betty Friedan's *The Feminine Mystique* is published
March 1969	U.S. planes begin a fourteen-month-long bombing campaign aimed at Communist sanctuaries in Cambodia
July 1969	Neil Armstrong becomes the first person to walk on the moon
1971	Ratification of the Twenty-sixth Amendment gives eighteen-year-olds the right to vote in all elections
January 1973	In Paris, the United States, North and South Vietnam, and the Viet Cong agree to restore peace in Vietnam
1973	Congress passes the War Powers Act
April 1975	Saigon falls to the North Vietnamese
1978	Jimmy Carter brokers the Camp David Accords, an agreement between Israel and Egypt
1978	Supreme Court issues the *Bakke* decision
November 1979	Islamic militants storm the U.S. embassy in Tehran and take more than fifty Americans hostage

KEY TERMS & NAMES

36

A CONSERVATIVE INSURGENCY

FOCUS QUESTIONS wwnorton.com/studyspace

- What explains the rise of Ronald Reagan and Republican conservatism?

- What was the Iran-Contra incident, and what did it show about the nature of the executive branch of the government, even after Watergate?

- What factors led to the end of the cold war?

- What characterized the economy and society in the 1980s?

- What were the causes of the Gulf War?

President Jimmy Carter and his embattled Democratic administration hobbled through 1979. The economy remained sluggish, double-digit inflation continued unabated, and failed efforts to free the hostages in Iran made the administration appear indecisive. Carter's inability to persuade the nation to embrace his energy-conservation program revealed mortal flaws in his reading of the public mood and his understanding of legislative politics.

While the lackluster Carter administration was foundering, Republican conservatives were forging an aggressive plan to win the White House in 1980 and to assault "liberalism" in Washington. Those plans centered on the popularity and charisma of Ronald Reagan, the Hollywood actor turned California governor and prominent political commentator. Reagan was not a deep thinker, but he was a superb analyst of the public mood, an unabashed patriot, and a committed champion of conservative principles. He was also charming and cheerful, a likable politician renowned for his folksy anecdotes and optimistic outlook. Where the dour Carter denounced the evils of free-enterprise capitalism and scolded Americans to revive long-forgotten virtues of frugality, a sunny Reagan promised a "revolution of ideas" designed to unleash the capitalist spirit, restore national pride, and regain international respect.

Reagan promised to increase military spending, dismantle the "bloated" federal bureaucracy, reduce taxes and regulations, and in general shrink the role of the government. He also wanted to affirm old-time morality by banning abortions and reinstituting prayer in public schools. Reagan's appeal derived from his remarkable skill as a public speaker and his dogmatic commitment to a few overarching ideas and simple themes.

"The Great Communicator"

Ronald Reagan in 1980, shortly before his election.

As a true believer and an able compromiser, he combined the fervor of a revolutionary with the pragmatism of a diplomat.

Such attributes won Reagan two presidential terms, in 1980 and 1984, and ensured the election of his successor, George H. W. Bush, in 1988. Just how revolutionary the Reagan era was remains a subject of intense debate. What cannot be denied, however, is that Reagan's actions and beliefs set the tone for the decade's political and economic life.

THE REAGAN REVOLUTION

THE MAKING OF A PRESIDENT   Born in Illinois in 1911, Reagan graduated from Eureka College and then worked as a radio announcer and sportscaster before heading to Hollywood in 1937. In 1964 he entered the political limelight when he delivered a rousing speech on behalf of Barry Goldwater at the Republican Convention. During two terms as governor of California (1967–1975), he displayed a commitment to conservative principles as well as a political realism and an openness to compromise.

Nevertheless, by the middle 1970s Reagan's brand of free-enterprise conservatism still appeared too extreme for a national audience.

THE MOVE TO REAGAN By the eve of the 1980 election, however, Reagan had become the beneficiary of three developments that made his conservative vision of America much more viable. First, the 1980 census revealed that the population was aging, and large numbers of retirees were moving from the liberal Northeast to the conservative sunbelt states of the South and the West. This development meant that demographic forces were carrying the electorate toward Reagan's conservative position.

Second, in the 1970s the country experienced a massive revival of evangelical religion. No longer simply a local or provincial phenomenon, Catholic conservatives and Protestant evangelicals had bought television and radio stations and were operating schools and universities. The Reverend Jerry Falwell's grassroots organization, the Moral Majority, expressed the major political and social goals of the religious right wing: free enterprise should remain free, big government should be shrunk, abortion should be outlawed, prayer in public schools should be reinstated, Darwinian evolution should be

Anti-abortion movement

Anti-abortion demonstrators pass the Washington Monument on their way to the Capitol.

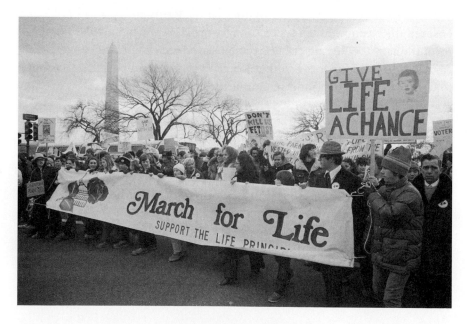

replaced in schoolbooks by the biblical story of creation, and Soviet communism should be opposed as a form of pagan totalitarianism. The moralistic zeal and financial resources of the religious right made its adherents effective opponents of liberal political candidates and programs. They rallied to Reagan's call for strengthening traditional values and local government.

A third factor contributing to the conservative resurgence was a well-organized and well-financed backlash against the feminist movement. During the 1970s, women who opposed the social goals of feminism formed counterorganizations with names like Women Who Want to Be Women and Females Opposed to Equality. Spearheading those efforts was Phyllis Schlafly, a right-wing Republican activist from Illinois. Schlafly orchestrated the campaign to defeat the equal-rights amendment and thereafter served as the galvanizing force behind a growing anti-feminist movement. She characterized feminists as a "bunch of bitter women seeking a constitutional cure for their personal problems," and she urged women to embrace their "God-given" roles as wives and mothers. Feminists, she charged, were "anti-family, anti-children, and pro-abortion."

Many of Schlafly's supporters also participated in a mushrooming anti-abortion, or "pro-life," movement. By 1980 the National Right to Life Committee, supported by the National Conference of Catholic Bishops, boasted 11 million members representing most religious denominations. The intensity of its members' commitment made it a powerful political force in its own right, and the Reagan campaign was quick to highlight its own support for traditional "family values," gender roles, and the "rights" of the unborn. Such hot-button cultural issues helped persuade many northern Democrats to support Reagan. Whites alienated by the increasingly liberal social agenda of the Democratic party became a crucial element in Reagan's electoral strategy.

THE ELECTION OF 1980 By 1980, voters were flocking to Reagan's cheery promises of less government, lower taxes, renewed prosperity, waning inflation, and revived military strength and national pride. His "supply-side" economics proposals, soon dubbed Reaganomics by supporters and voodoo economics by critics, suggested that the stagflation of the 1970s had resulted from excessive taxes, which weakened the incentive to work, save, and reinvest. The solution was to slash tax rates. For a long-suffering nation it was, in theory, an alluring economic panacea.

On election day, Reagan swept to a decisive victory, with 489 electoral votes to 49 for Carter, who carried only six states. The popular vote proved equally lopsided: 44 million (51 percent) to 35 million (41 percent), with

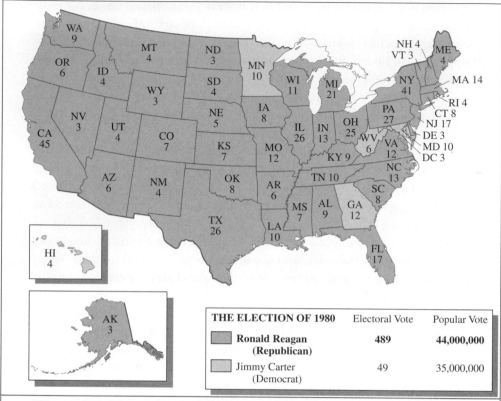

THE ELECTION OF 1980	Electoral Vote	Popular Vote
▓ Ronald Reagan **(Republican)**	**489**	**44,000,000**
░ Jimmy Carter (Democrat)	49	35,000,000

Why was Ronald Reagan such an appealing candidate in 1980? What was the impact of "nonvoting"? Why was there so much voter apathy?

7 percent going to John Anderson, a moderate Republican who bolted the party after Reagan's nomination and ran on an independent ticket.

In addition to affirming Reagan's conservative agenda, the 1980 election reflected the triumph of what one political scientist called the "largest mass movement of our time": nonvoting. Almost as striking as Reagan's one-sided victory was the fact that his total votes represented only 28 percent of registered voters. Only 53 percent of eligible voters cast ballots in the 1980 election. There were various explanations for the high level of voter apathy among working-class Americans. Some observers stressed the disillusionment with government that grew out of the Watergate affair. Others believed that the Democratic party had alienated its traditional blocs of support. Democratic leaders no longer spoke eloquently on behalf of those at the bottom of America's social scale. By embracing a fiscal conservatism indistinguishable from that of the Republicans, as Carter had done, Democrats had lost their appeal among blue-collar workers and the urban poor. When viewed in this light, Reagan's lopsided triumph represented both a resounding victory for conservative Republicans and a self-inflicted defeat by a fractured Democratic party. Flush with a sense of power and destiny, President-elect Ronald Reagan headed toward Washington with a blueprint for dismantling the welfare state.

REAGAN'S FIRST TERM

REAGANOMICS   Ronald Reagan brought to Washington a cheerful conservative philosophy with a simple premise. "Government is not the solution to our problem," he insisted; "government is the problem." Reagan credited Calvin Coolidge and Coolidge's Treasury secretary, Andrew Mellon, with demonstrating that by reducing taxes and easing government regulation of business, free-market capitalism would revive the economy. By cutting taxes and domestic federal spending and by following a supply-side economic program, he claimed, a surging economy would produce *more* government revenues, which in turn would help reduce the budget deficit.

Early on, Reagan focused on implementing his major campaign pledges: increased defense spending, reduced social spending, and a sweeping tax-reform package. Enough Democrats—mostly sympathetic southern conservatives dubbed boll weevils—supported the measures to pass them by overwhelming majorities. On August 1, 1981, Reagan signed the Economic Recovery Tax Act, which cut personal income taxes by 25 percent, lowered the maximum rate from 70 to 50 percent for 1982, cut the capital gains tax by a third, and offered a broad array of other tax concessions.

The new legislation embodied an idea that went back to Alexander Hamilton, George Washington's Treasury secretary: more money in the hands of the affluent would benefit society at large, since the wealthy would engage in productive consumption and investment. A closer parallel, as Reagan had pointed out, was Treasury Secretary Andrew Mellon's tax-reduction program of the 1920s. The difference was that the Reagan tax cuts were accompanied by massive increases in defense spending, which generated ever-mounting federal deficits. Reagan's advisers insisted that the unbalanced budgets were only temporary; the new tax plan would fuel economic growth and thereby boost tax revenues as personal income and corporate profits skyrocketed. But it did not work out that way. By the summer of 1983, a major economic recovery was under way, but the federal deficits had grown ever larger, so much so that the president, who in 1980 had pledged to balance the federal budget by 1983, had in fact run up debts larger than those of all his predecessors combined.

Bankers and investors feared that the rising federal debt would send interest rates soaring, a fear expressed in sagging bond and stock markets. A business slump and rising unemployment continued through most of 1982. That year the federal deficit doubled. Aides finally convinced Reagan that to reassure the public about deficits and the threat of inflation, the government needed "revenue enhancements," a euphemism for tax increases. With Reagan's support, Congress passed a new tax bill in 1982 that would raise almost $100 billion. During the midterm elections of 1982, Reagan urged voters to "stay the course" and appealed for more time to let his economic program take effect. Meanwhile, the economic slump persisted through that year, with unemployment standing at 10.4 percent, and the congressional Republicans experienced moderate losses in the elections.

THE DEFENSE BUILDUP   Reagan's conduct of foreign policy reflected his belief that trouble in the world stemmed mainly from Moscow. He charged that the Soviets were "prepared to commit any crime, to lie, to cheat" and do anything necessary to promote world communism. To thwart the advance of communism, Reagan and Secretary of Defense Caspar Weinberger embarked upon a major buildup of nuclear and conventional weapons to close the gap that they claimed had developed between Soviet and U.S. military forces.

In 1983, Reagan escalated the nuclear arms race by authorizing the Defense Department to develop a Strategic Defense Initiative, a complex defense system meant to destroy enemy missiles in outer space well before they reached their targets. Despite skepticism among the media and many scientists that such a "Star Wars" defense system could be built, the new initiative forced the Soviets to launch an expensive research and development program of their own to keep pace.

Reagan borrowed the rhetoric of Harry Truman, John Foster Dulles, and John F. Kennedy's inaugural address to express American resolve in the face of "Communist aggression anywhere in the world." Détente deteriorated even further when the Soviets imposed martial law in Poland during the winter of 1981. The crackdown came after Polish workers, united under the banner of an independent union called Solidarity, challenged the Communist monopoly of power. As with the Soviet interventions in Hungary in 1956 and Czechoslovakia in 1968, there was little the United States could do except register protest and impose economic sanctions against Poland's Communist government.

Strategic Defense Initiative

President Reagan addresses the nation on March 23, 1983, about the development of a space-age shield to intercept Soviet missiles.

THE AMERICAS   Reagan's foremost international concern, however, was in Central America, where he detected the most serious Communist threat. The tiny nation of El Salvador, caught up since 1980 in a brutal struggle between Communist-supported revolutionaries and right-wing extremists, received U.S. economic and military assistance. Reagan stopped short of sending troops, but he did increase the number of military advisers and the amount of financial aid sent to the Salvadoran government.

Even more troubling was the situation in Nicaragua. The State Department claimed that the Cuban-sponsored Sandinista government, which had only recently taken control of the country after ousting a corrupt dictator, was funneling Soviet and Cuban arms to leftist Salvadoran rebels. In response the Reagan administration ordered the CIA to train and supply guerrilla bands of disgruntled Nicaraguans, tagged Contras, who staged attacks on Sandinista bases and officials from sanctuaries in Honduras. In supporting these "freedom fighters," Reagan sought not only to impede the traffic in arms to Salvadoran rebels but also to overthrow the Communist Sandinistas.

Critics of Reagan's anti-Sandinista policy accused the Contras of being mostly right-wing fanatics who indiscriminately killed civilians as well as Sandinista soldiers. They also feared that the United States might eventually commit its own combat forces in a Vietnam-like intervention.

"Shhhhhh. It's Top Secret."

A comment on the Reagan administration's covert operations in Nicaragua.

THE MIDDLE EAST   The Middle East remained a tinderbox of geopolitical conflict throughout the 1980s. No peaceable end seemed possible in the bloody Iran-Iraq War, which had erupted in 1980, entangled as it was with the passions of Islamic fundamentalism. In 1984 both sides began to attack tankers in the Persian Gulf, a major source of the world's oil. Although the Reagan administration harbored no affection for either nation, it viewed Iranian fundamentalism as the greater threat and funneled aid to Iraq, a policy with unforeseen and grave consequences.

American diplomats continued to see Israel as the strongest ally in the volatile region, all the while seeking to encourage moderate Arab groups and anti-Communist governments. Continuing chaos in Lebanon, where ethnic and religious tensions erupted in near anarchy, threatened both Israel's borders and America's goals for the region. The capital, Beirut, became a battleground for rival Muslim and Christian factions, the army of the Palestine Liberation Organization (PLO), Syrian invaders cast as peacekeepers, and Israelis responding to PLO attacks.

French, Italian, and U.S. forces moved into Beirut as "peacekeepers," but in such small numbers as to become targets themselves. On October 23,

1983, an Islamic suicide bomber drove a truck laden with explosives into the U.S. Marine headquarters at the Beirut airport. The explosion left 241 Americans dead. On February 7, 1984, Reagan announced that the marines would be redeployed on warships offshore. The Israeli forces pulled back to southern Lebanon, while the Syrians remained in eastern Lebanon and imposed a tenuous peace upon the faction-ridden country.

GRENADA   In a fortunate turn for the Reagan administration, an easy military triumph closer to home eclipsed news of the debacle in Lebanon. On the tiny Caribbean island of Grenada, a leftist government had admitted Cuban workers to build a new airfield and had signed military agreements with several Communist-bloc countries. Appeals from the governments of neighboring islands led Reagan in 1983 to order 1,900 soldiers to invade the island, depose the radical regime, and evacuate a group of American students at Grenada's medical school. The UN General Assembly condemned the action, but most Grenadans and their neighbors applauded it, and the intervention was immensely popular in the United States.

REAGAN'S SECOND TERM

By 1983, prosperity had returned, and inflation had subsided; the Reagan "supply-side" economic program seemed to be working as touted. A dramatic fall in oil prices following the fragmentation of the OPEC cartel and Reagan's decision to remove price controls on oil and natural gas produced an economic expansion.

THE ELECTION OF 1984   By 1984, Reagan had restored strength and vitality to the White House and the nation. Reporters began to describe a "Reagan Revolution" in Washington. The president's prospects for reelection were bright. The Democratic nominee, former Minnesota senator and vice president Walter Mondale, faced an uphill struggle. Mondale won a lot of media attention by choosing as his running mate a woman, New York representative Geraldine Ferraro. Attention soon turned to Ferraro's husband's dubious business dealings, however. In any case, Reagan's skill and confidence at campaigning outshone Mondale, and the economic recovery made it difficult for the Democratic nominee to attract interest, much less generate enthusiasm. In the end, Reagan won almost 59 percent of the popular vote and lost only Minnesota and the District of Columbia. His coattails were not as long as they had been in 1980, however. Republicans gained only fifteen seats in the House, leaving them still greatly outnumbered by Democrats, 253 to 182. They also lost two Senate seats, creating a margin of only 53 to 47.

THE REAGAN DOCTRINE In his 1985 State of the Union message, the reelected president clarified what had come to be called the Reagan Doctrine in foreign affairs. The United States, he proclaimed, would support anti-Communist forces around the world seeking to "defy Soviet-supported aggression." In effect, he was challenging the isolationism that followed the nation's humbling experience in Vietnam. America, he promised, would not hesitate to intervene in the world's hot spots.

Yet for all his stern talk about the Soviet Union's being "an evil empire," Reagan was determined to reach an arms-control agreement with the Soviets. In Geneva in 1985, he met with Mikhail Gorbachev, the innovative new leader of the Soviet Union. The two signed several cultural and scientific agreements and issued a statement on arms-limitations talks, but no treaty was in the offing. Nearly a year after the Geneva summit, on sudden notice and with limited preparation, Gorbachev and Reagan met in Iceland for two days to discuss arms reductions. Early reports predicted a major breakthrough, including a total ban on nuclear weapons, but the talks collapsed over disagreement on

Foreign relations

A light moment at a meeting between U.S. president Ronald Reagan (left) and Soviet premier Mikhail Gorbachev (right).

Reagan's commitment to the Strategic Defense Initiative. After the Iceland meeting the two nations reduced the scope of their discussions in order to break the impasse.

The logjam impeding the arms negotiations suddenly broke when Gorbachev announced that he was willing to deal separately on a medium-range missile treaty. After nine months of strenuous negotiations, Reagan and Gorbachev met amid much fanfare in Washington on December 9, 1987, and signed a treaty to eliminate intermediate-range (300- to 3,000-mile) nuclear missiles. It was an epochal event, not only because it marked the first time that the two nations had agreed to destroy a whole class of weapons systems but also because it represented a key first step toward the eventual end of the arms race altogether. Under the terms of the treaty, the United States would destroy 859 missiles, and the Soviets would eliminate 1,752. Provision was also made for on-site inspections by each side to verify compliance. Still, this winnowing of weapons represented only 4 percent of the total number of nuclear missiles on both sides. Arms-control advocates thus looked toward a second and more comprehensive treaty that would eliminate long-range strategic missiles.

THE IRAN-CONTRA AFFAIR   During the fall of 1986, the Reagan administration suffered a double blow. In the midterm elections, Democrats regained control of the Senate by 55 to 45. For his final two years in office, Reagan would face an opposition Congress. What was worse, on election day reports surfaced that the United States, with Israeli assistance, had been secretly selling arms to Iran in the hope of securing the release of American hostages held in Lebanon by extremist Islamic groups with close ties to Iran. Such action contradicted Reagan's repeated public insistence that his administration would never negotiate with terrorists.

There was more to the story. Over the next several months, revelations reminiscent of the Watergate affair disclosed a more complicated series of covert activities carried out by administration officials. At the center of what came to be dubbed the Iran-Contra affair was the much-decorated marine lieutenant colonel Oliver North. An aide to the National Security Council who specialized in counterterrorism, North had been scheming to use the profits from the secret sale of military weapons to Iran to subsidize the Contra rebels fighting in Nicaragua even though Congress had voted to ban such aid.

Oliver North's activities, it turned out, had been approved by national security adviser Robert McFarlane; McFarlane's successor, Admiral John Poindexter; and CIA director William Casey. Both Secretary of State George Shultz and Secretary of Defense Caspar Weinberger criticized the arms sale

The Iran-Contra affair

National security adviser Robert McFarlane (left) tells reporters about his resignation. Vice Admiral John Poindexter (far right) succeeds him in the post.

to Iran, but their objections were ignored, and they were thereafter kept in the dark about what was going on. Later, on three occasions, Shultz threatened to resign over the continuing operation of the "pathetic" scheme. After information about the secret (and illegal) dealings surfaced in the press, McFarlane attempted suicide, Poindexter resigned, and North was fired Casey, who denied any connection, left the CIA for health reasons and died shortly thereafter from a brain tumor.

Under increasing criticism and amid growing doubts about his credibility and his ability, Reagan appointed both an independent counsel and a three-man commission, led by former Republican senator John Tower, to investigate the scandal. The Tower Commission issued a report early in 1987 that placed much of the responsibility for the bungled Iran-Contra affair on Reagan's loose management style. The president seemed unaware of what his staffers were doing.

The investigations of the independent counsel led to six indictments in 1988. A Washington jury found Oliver North guilty of three relatively minor charges but innocent of nine more serious counts, apparently reflecting the jury's reasoning that he had acted as an agent of higher-ups. His conviction was later overturned on appeal. The Iran-Contra affair left support for the

Nicaraguan Contras badly eroded in Congress, and it undermined much of Reagan's popularity.

THE POOR, THE HOMELESS, AND THE VICTIMS OF AIDS

The 1980s were years of vivid contrast. Despite unprecedented affluence, there were countless beggars in the streets and homeless people sleeping in doorways, in cardboard boxes, and on ventilation grates. A variety of factors caused the shortage of low-cost housing: the government had given up on building public housing, urban-renewal programs had demolished blighted areas but provided no housing for those they displaced, and owners had abandoned unprofitable buildings in poor neighborhoods or converted them into expensive condominiums, a process called gentrification.

In addition, after new medications enabled the deinstitutionalization of the mentally ill, many individuals ended up on the streets because the promised community mental-health services failed to materialize. By the summer of 1988, the *New York Times* estimated, more than 45 percent of New York's adults were living in poverty, totally outside the labor force, because of a lack of skills, drug use, and other problems.

Still another group cast aside was composed of people suffering from the frightening newly identified malady that had been named AIDS (acquired immunodeficiency syndrome). At the beginning of the decade, public health officials had begun to report that gay men and intravenous drug users were especially at risk for contracting AIDS. Those infected with the virus that causes AIDS showed signs of fatigue, developed a strange combination of infections, and soon died; people contracted the virus, HIV, by coming into contact with the blood or body fluids of an infected person.

The Reagan administration showed little interest in AIDS in part because it initially was viewed as a "gay" disease. Patrick Buchanan, the conservative spokesman who served as White House director of communications, said that homosexuals had "declared war on nature, and now nature is extracting an awful retribution."

THE REAGAN LEGACY

Although Ronald Reagan had declared in 1981 his intention to "curb the size and influence of the federal establishment," the welfare state remained intact when Reagan left office. Neither the Social Security system nor Medicare had been dismantled or overhauled, nor had any other major welfare programs. And the federal agencies that Reagan had threatened to abolish, such as the Department of Education, not only remained in place in 1989 but had seen their budgets grow. The federal budget as a percentage of the gross domestic product was higher when Reagan left office than when he had entered. Moreover, he did not try to push through Congress the incendiary social issues championed by the religious right, such as allowing prayer in public schools and a ban on abortions.

Yet Ronald Reagan succeeded in redefining the national political agenda and accelerated the conservative insurgency that had been developing for over twenty years. His greatest successes were in renewing America's soaring sense of possibilities, bringing inflation under control, stimulating the longest sustained period of peacetime prosperity in history, and helping to light the fuse of democratic freedom in Eastern Europe.

THE ELECTION OF 1988 As a new presidential election unfolded, eight Democratic presidential candidates engaged in a wild scramble for their party's nomination. As the primary season progressed, however, it soon

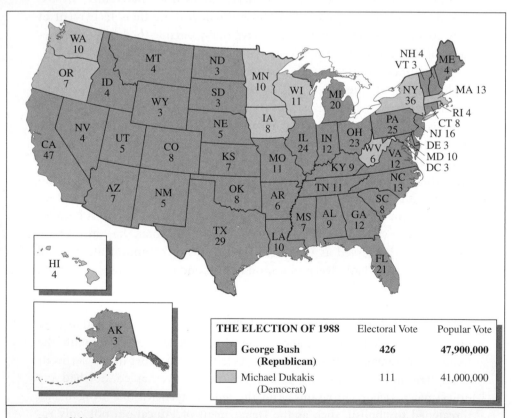

THE ELECTION OF 1988	Electoral Vote	Popular Vote
George Bush (Republican)	426	47,900,000
Michael Dukakis (Democrat)	111	41,000,000

How did George H. W. Bush overtake Michael Dukakis's lead in the polls? What was the role of race and class in the election results?

became a two-man race between Massachusetts governor Michael Dukakis and Jesse Jackson, an African American civil rights activist who had been one of Martin Luther King's chief lieutenants. Dukakis eventually won out and managed a difficult reconciliation with the Jackson forces that left the Democrats unified and confident as the fall campaign began.

The Republicans nominated Reagan's two-term vice president, George H. W. Bush, who after a bumpy start had easily cast aside his rivals in the primaries. As Reagan's handpicked heir, Bush claimed credit for the administration's successes, but like all vice presidents he also faced the challenge of defining his own political identity. Yet at the Republican Convention, Bush delivered a forceful address that sharply enhanced his stature. The most memorable line was a defiant statement on taxes: "Congress will push me to raise taxes, and I'll say no, and they'll push, and I'll say no, and they'll push again. And I'll say to them: Read my lips. No new taxes."

In a campaign given over to mudslinging, the Bush partisans attacked Dukakis as a camouflaged liberal who would increase federal spending, raise taxes, gut the defense budget, and refuse to intervene to prevent Communist aggression abroad. The Republican onslaught took its toll against the less organized, less focused Dukakis campaign. Moreover, the Republicans continued to benefit from the population growth in the sunbelt states, the shift of population from the Democratic cities to the Republican suburbs, and from the votes of many moderate and conservative Democrats and independents. Dukakis captured only ten states plus the District of Columbia, with clusters of support in the Northeast, Midwest, and Northwest. Bush carried the rest, with a margin of about 54 percent to 46 percent in the popular vote and 426 to 111 in the Electoral College.

THE BUSH ADMINISTRATION

George H. W. Bush viewed himself as a guardian president rather than an activist. He lacked Reagan's visionary outlook and skill as a speaker. Bush was a pragmatic caretaker eager to avoid "stupid mistakes" and find a way to get along with the Democratic majority in Congress. "We don't need to remake society," he announced. Bush therefore sought to consolidate the programs that Reagan had put in place rather than launch his own array of programs and policies.

THE DEMOCRACY MOVEMENT ABROAD   Bush entered the White House with more foreign-policy experience than most presidents, and he found the spotlight of the world stage more congenial than wrestling with the intractable problems of the inner cities and the deficit. Within two years of his inauguration, George Bush would lead the United States into two wars. Throughout most of 1989, however, he merely had to sit back and observe the dissolution of one totalitarian or authoritarian regime after another. For the first time in years, global democracy was on the march in a sequence of mostly bloodless revolutions that took the world by surprise.

Although in China a democracy movement came to a tragic end in 1989 when government forces mounted a deadly assault on demonstrators in Beijing's Tiananmen Square, Eastern Europe had an entirely different experience. Mikhail Gorbachev set events in motion by responding to Soviet economic problems with policies of perestroika (restructuring) and glasnost (openness), a loosening of centralized economic planning and censorship. His foreign policy sought rapprochement and trade with the West, and he aimed to relieve the Soviet economy of burdensome military costs.

Gorbachev backed off from Soviet imperial ambitions. Early in 1989, Soviet troops left Afghanistan after spending nine years bogged down in civil war there. Then in July in Paris, Gorbachev repudiated the Brezhnev Doctrine, which asserted the right of the Soviet Union to intervene in the internal affairs of other Communist countries. The days when Soviet tanks would roll through Warsaw and Prague were over, and leaders in the Eastern-bloc countries found themselves beset by demands for democratic reform. With opposition strength building, the old regimes fell with surprisingly little bloodshed. Communist party rule ended first in Poland and Hungary, then in Czechoslovakia and Bulgaria. In Romania the year of peaceful revolution ended in a bloodbath when the Romanian people were joined by the army in a bloody uprising against the brutal dictator Nicolae Ceaușescu. He and his wife were captured, tried, and then executed on Christmas Day.

The most spectacular event in the collapse of the Soviet Empire came on November 9, 1989, when the chief symbol of the cold war—the Berlin Wall—was torn down by Germans, and the East German government succumbed to popular pressures for change. With the borders to the West fully open, the Communist government of East Germany collapsed, a freely elected government came to power, and on October 3, 1990, the five states of East Germany were united with West Germany. The reunified German nation remained in NATO, and the Warsaw Pact alliance was dissolved.

The reform impulse that Gorbachev helped unleash in the Eastern-bloc countries careened out of control within the Soviet Union, however. Gorbachev proved unusually adept at political restructuring. While yielding to the Communist monopoly of government, he built a new presidential system that

Dissolution of the Soviet Empire

West Germans hacking away at the Berlin Wall on November 11, 1989, two days after all crossings between East Germany and West Germany were opened.

gave him, if anything, increased powers. His skills did not extend to an antiquated economy that resisted change, however. The revival of ethnic allegiances added to the instability. Although Russia proper included slightly more than half the Soviet Union's population, it was only one of fifteen constituent republics, most of which began to seek autonomy, if not independence.

Gorbachev's popularity in the Soviet Union shrank as it grew abroad. It especially eroded among the Communist hard-liners, who saw in his reforms the unraveling of their bureaucratic and political empire. On August 18, 1991, a cabal of political and military leaders tried to seize the reins of power in Russia. They accosted Gorbachev at his vacation retreat in the Crimea and demanded that he sign a decree proclaiming a state of emergency and transferring his powers to them. He replied, "Go to hell," whereupon he was placed under house arrest. Twelve hours later the Soviet news agency reported to the world that Gorbachev was "ill" and had temporarily transferred his powers to his vice president and an eight-member emergency committee. Political parties were suspended, newspapers were silenced, a

Action against Gorbachev

In August 1991, one day after Mikhail Gorbachev was placed under house arrest by Communists planning a coup, Russian president Boris Yeltsin (holding papers) makes a speech criticizing the plotters.

curfew was announced, and street demonstrations were banned. Tanks and armored vehicles surrounded government buildings in Moscow. The new leaders promised to end the "chaos and anarchy" they claimed were bedeviling the country.

But the coup was doomed from the start. Poorly planned and clumsily implemented, it lacked effective coordination. The plotters failed to arrest popular leaders such as Boris Yeltsin, the president of the Russian republic, and they neglected to close the airports or cut off telephone and television communications. Most important, the plotters failed to recognize the strength of the democratic idealism unleashed by Gorbachev's reforms.

As the political drama unfolded in the Soviet Union, foreign leaders denounced the coup. On August 20, President Bush responded favorably to Yeltsin's request for support and persuaded other leaders to join him in refusing to recognize the legitimacy of the new Soviet government. The next day, word began to seep out that the plotters had given up and were fleeing. Several committed suicide, and a newly released Gorbachev ordered the others arrested. But Gorbachev's freedom did not bring a restoration of his power. Boris Yeltsin emerged as the most popular political figure in the country. Gorbachev reclaimed the title of president of the Soviet Union, but he was forced to resign as head of the Communist party and admit that he had made a grave mistake in appointing the men who had turned against him.

So what had begun as a reactionary coup turned into a powerful accelerant for stunning changes in the Soviet Union. Most of the fifteen republics proclaimed their independence, with the Baltic republics of Latvia, Lithuania, and Estonia regaining the status of independent nations. The Communist party apparatus was dismantled, prompting celebrating crowds to topple statues of Lenin and other Communist heroes.

The aborted coup accelerated Soviet and American efforts to reduce the stockpiles of nuclear weapons. In 1991, President Bush announced that the United States would destroy all its tactical nuclear weapons on land and at sea in Europe and Asia, take its long-range bombers off twenty-four-hour-alert status, and initiate discussions with the Soviet Union for the purpose of instituting sharp cuts in nuclear missiles with multiple warheads. Bush explained that the prospect of a Soviet invasion of western Europe was "no longer a realistic threat," and this transformation presented an unprecedented opportunity for reducing the threat of nuclear holocaust. The Soviets responded by announcing reciprocal cutbacks. As Colin Powell, chairman of the Joint Chiefs of Staff, remarked, the cold war "has vaporized before our eyes."

By the end of 1991, the Soviet Union had dissolved into a new—and fragile—Commonwealth of Independent States made up of eleven autonomous republics (Georgia joined in 1993). Held together by little other than historic ties and contiguous borders, the federated republics soon suffered outbreaks of ethnic tensions and separatist movements. With the Communist party dissolved, the Soviet Union dismantled, and continuing economic woes creating obstacles to his leadership, Mikhail Gorbachev resigned as president at the end of 1991. Boris Yeltsin, now a national hero, replaced him.

The dilution of the Soviet military threat led the U.S. Defense Department in 1992 to withdraw large numbers of personnel from military bases in Asia and Europe. The Pentagon also announced a plan to shrink the armed forces by 500,000 troops over the next five years. In 1992, Bush and Yeltsin declared their intention to reduce their combined arsenals of nuclear weapons from about 22,500 to no more than 7,000 by 2003. All land-based multiple-warhead missiles were to be destroyed.

PANAMA   The end of the cold war did not spell the end of international tensions and conflicts, however. Indeed, in some respects the world became more unstable. Before the end of 1989, American troops were engaged in battle in Panama, where General Manuel Noriega, as chief of the

Panamanian Defense Forces since 1983, was head of the government in fact if not in title. Years earlier Noriega had worked secretly with the CIA, providing information about developments in Central America. At the same time, he got involved in the lucrative—and illegal—drug trade. In 1988 federal grand juries in Miami and Tampa indicted Noriega and fifteen others on charges of international drug smuggling, gunrunning, and laundering the profits through Panamanian banks.

In 1989, Panama's National Assembly named Noriega head of the government and proclaimed that Panama "is declared to be in a state of war" with the United States. The next day, December 16, 1989, a U.S. marine in Panama was killed. President Bush ordered an invasion of Panama in order to capture Noriega, bring him to the United States so that he could face the charges against him, and install a government headed by opposition leaders.

The 12,000 U.S. military personnel already in Panama were quickly joined by 12,000 more, and in the early morning of December 20 five military task forces struck at strategic targets in the country. Twenty-three U.S. servicemen were killed in the action, and estimates of Panamanians killed and wounded, including many civilians, were as high as 4,000. Noriega was captured, and he was detained in a U.S. federal prison for well over a year before his trial began in late 1991. He was convicted in 1992 on eight counts of racketeering and drug distribution.

THE GULF WAR Months after Panama had moved to the background of public attention, Saddam Hussein, dictator of Iraq, focused attention on the Middle East when his army suddenly invaded neighboring Kuwait on August 2, 1990. Kuwait had raised its production of oil, contrary to agreements with OPEC. The resulting drop in global oil prices offended the Iraqi regime, deep in debt and heavily dependent upon oil revenues. Saddam Hussein did not expect the firestorm of world indignation that his assault on Kuwait ignited. The UN Security Council unanimously condemned the invasion and demanded withdrawal. American secretary of state James Baker and Soviet foreign minister Eduard Shevardnadze issued a joint statement of condemnation. The Security Council then endorsed Resolution 661, an embargo on trade with Iraq.

President Bush condemned Iraq's "naked aggression" and dispatched planes and troops to Saudi Arabia on a "wholly defensive" mission: to protect Saudi Arabia. British forces soon joined in, as did troops from a half dozen Arab nations. On August 22, Bush ordered the mobilization of American reserve forces for the operation, now dubbed Operation Desert Shield. A flurry of peace efforts failed. Iraq refused to yield. On January 10, Congress began to

The Gulf War

U.S. soldiers adapt to desert conditions during Operation Desert Shield,
December 1990.

debate whether to authorize the use of U.S. armed forces. The outcome was
uncertain to the end, but on January 12 a resolution for the use of force passed
in the House, by a vote of 250 to 183, and in the Senate, by 52 to 47.

An allied force of over thirty nations was committed to Operation Desert
Storm by January 1991. The first missiles began to hit Iraq at about 2:30 A.M.
Baghdad time on January 17. Saddam Hussein, expecting an allied attack
northward into Kuwait, concentrated his forces in that country. But the
Iraqis were outflanked when 200,000 allied troops, largely American, British,
and French, turned up on the undefended Iraqi border with Saudi Arabia,
far to the west. The swift-moving allied ground assault began on February
24 and lasted only four days. Thousands of Iraqi soldiers surrendered, and
there was a quick breakthrough into Kuwait.

On February 28, six weeks after the fighting began, President Bush called
for a cease-fire, the Iraqis accepted, and the shooting ended. There were 137
American fatalities. The lowest estimate of Iraqi fatalities, civilian and military, was 100,000. The coalition forces occupied about a fifth of Iraq. The
consequences of the brief but intense Persian Gulf War, the "mother of all
battles" in Saddam Hussein's words, would be played out in the future in
ways no one predicted.

CHAPTER SUMMARY

- **Rise of Conservatism**   Ronald Reagan's charm, coupled with disillusionment over Jimmy Carter's presidency and the Republicans' call for a return to traditional values, won Reagan the presidency in 1980. The Republican insurgency was characterized by a cultural backlash against the feminist movement, and it was supported by Christian evangelicals and people who wanted lower taxes and a smaller, less intrusive federal government.

- **Iran-Contra Scandal**   Members of Reagan's administration secretly sold arms to Iran in the hopes of securing the release of American hostages held in Lebanon by extremists sympathetic to Iran. The deal contradicted the president's public claims that he would never deal with terrorists. Furthermore, profits from the arms sales were used to fund right-wing rebels in Nicaragua, known as Contras, despite Congress's having voted to ban any aid to the Contras. An independent commission appointed by the president determined that Reagan's loose management style was responsible for the illegal activities, and Reagan admitted that he had lied to the American people.

- **End of the Cold War**   Toward the end of the century, democratic movements exploded in China, where they failed, and in Eastern Europe, where they largely succeeded. In the Soviet Union, Mikhail Gorbachev's steps to restructure the economy and promote more open policies led to demands for further reform. Communist party rule collapsed in the Soviet satellite states. In November 1989, the Berlin Wall was torn down, and a year later Germany was reunified. Russia itself survived a coup by hard-liners, and by 1991 the cold war had ended.

- **Reaganomics**   Americans in the 1980s experienced unprecedented prosperity, yet beggars and homeless people were visible in most cities. The prevailing atmosphere was conservative, and AIDS was condemned as a "gay" disease. "Reaganomics" failed to reduce public spending, but the president nevertheless championed tax cuts for the rich. The result was massive public debt and the stock market collapse of 1987.

- **The Gulf War**   Saddam Hussein of Iraq invaded Kuwait in 1990. The United Nations condemned Hussein's action and authorized the use of force to dislodge Iraq from Kuwait, and over thirty nations committed themselves to Operation Desert Shield. When Hussein did not withdraw, the allied forces launched Operation Desert Storm, and the Iraqis surrendered within six weeks.

CHRONOLOGY

1982	Israeli troops invade Lebanon
1983	U.S. marines are killed in a suicide bombing in Beirut
1987	Tower Commission issues its report on the Iran-Contra affair
1987	Reagan delivers a speech at the Berlin Wall challenging the Soviet Union to tear down the wall
October 1987	Stock market experiences Black Monday
1989	China's government crushes the democracy movement at Tiananmen Square
November 1989	Berlin Wall is torn down
December 1989	U.S. troops invade Panama and capture Manuel Noriega
August 1991	Failure of a reactionary coup in Russia leads to the emergence of Boris Yeltsin
August 1990	Saddam Hussein invades Kuwait

KEY TERMS & NAMES

37

TRIUMPH AND TRAGEDY: AMERICA AT THE TURN OF THE CENTURY

FOCUS QUESTIONS wwnorton.com/studyspace

- How did the demographics of the United States change between 1980 and 2000?

- What led to the Democratic resurgence of the early 1990s and the surprising Republican landslide of 1994?

- What caused the surge and decline of the stock and financial markets in the 1990s and the early years of the twenty-first century?

- What were the consequences of the rise of global terrorism in the early twenty-first century?

- In what ways was the 2008 presidential election historic?

The United States entered the final decade of the twentieth century triumphant. American vigilance in the cold war had fueled the shocking collapse of the Soviet Union and the birth of democratic capitalism in eastern Europe. The United States was now the world's only superpower. By the mid-1990s the American economy would become the marvel of the world as remarkable gains in productivity afforded by new technologies created the greatest period of prosperity in modern history. Yet no sooner did the century come to an end than America's comfortable sense of physical and material security was shattered by a shocking terrorist assault that would kill thousands, plummet the economy into recession, and call into question conventional notions of national security and personal safety.

AMERICA'S CHANGING MOSAIC

DEMOGRAPHIC SHIFTS   The nation's population had grown to over 306 million by 2010. During the last quarter of the twentieth century, the sunbelt states of the South and the West continued to lure residents from the Midwest and the Northeast. Fully 90 percent of the nation's total population growth during the 1980s occurred in southern or western states. These population shifts forced a massive redistricting of the House of Representatives, with Florida, California, and Texas gaining seats and states such as New York losing them.

Women continued to enter the workforce in large numbers. In 1970, 38 percent of the workforce was female; in 2000 the figure was almost 50 percent. Women made up over a third of the new doctors (up from 4 percent in 1970), 40 percent of the new lawyers (up from 8 percent in 1970), and 23 percent of the new dentists (up from less than 1 percent in 1970).

The decline of the traditional family unit continued. In 2006 less than 65 percent of children lived with two parents, down from 85 percent in 1970. And more people were living alone than ever before, largely as a result of high divorce rates or a growing practice among young people of delaying marriage until well into their twenties. The number of single mothers increased 35 percent during the decade. The rate was much higher for African Americans: in 2000 fewer than 32 percent of African American children lived with both parents, down from 67 percent in 1960.

Young African Americans in particular faced shrinking economic opportunities at the start of the twenty-first century. The urban poor more than others were victimized by high rates of crime and violence, with young black men suffering the most. In 2000 the leading cause of death among African American men between the ages of fifteen and twenty-four was homicide. Over 25 percent of African American men aged twenty to twenty-nine were in prison, on parole, or on probation, while only 4 percent were enrolled in college. Nearly 40 percent of African American men were functionally illiterate.

THE NEW IMMIGRANTS   The racial and ethnic composition of the country was also changing rapidly during the early twenty-first century. By 2010 the United States had more foreign-born and first-generation residents than ever before. Over 30 percent of Americans claimed African, Asian, Hispanic, or American Indian ancestry. Hispanics represented 16 percent of the total population, African Americans 11 percent, Asians about 4 percent,

Illegal immigration

Increasing numbers of Chinese risked their savings and their lives to gain entry to the United States. These illegal immigrants are trying to keep warm after being forced to swim ashore when the freighter carrying them to the United States ran aground near Rockaway Beach in New York City in June 1993.

and American Indians almost 1 percent. The rate of increase among those four groups was twice as fast as it had been during the 1970s.

The primary cause of this dramatic change in the nation's ethnic mix was a surge of immigration. In 2000 the United States welcomed more than twice as many immigrants as all other countries in the world combined. For the first time in the nation's history, the majority of immigrants came not from Europe but from other parts of the world: Asia, Latin America, and Africa. Among the legal immigrants, Mexicans made up the largest share, averaging over 100,000 a year.

THE COMPUTER REVOLUTION   While demographic shifts and immigration were changing the nation's appearance, technological changes were transforming its behavior. A dramatic revolution in information technology produced a surge in productivity and prosperity during the 1980s and 1990s. Cellular phones, laser printers, VCRs and then DVDs, fax machines, personal computers, and iPods became commonplace. The computer age had arrived.

The idea of a programmable machine that would rapidly perform mental tasks had been around since the eighteenth century, but it took the crisis of World War II to gather the intellectual and financial resources needed to develop such a "computer." In 1946 a team of engineers at the University of Pennsylvania created ENIAC (electronic numerical integrator and computer), the first all-purpose, all-electronic digital computer.

With the invention in 1971 of the microprocessor—a computer on a silicon chip—the functions that had once been performed by computers taking up an entire room could be performed by a microchip circuit the size of a postage stamp. Engineers soon incorporated microchips into television sets, wristwatches, automobiles, kitchen appliances, and spacecraft.

The invention of the microchip made possible the personal computer. In 1975 an engineer named Ed Roberts developed the prototype of the so-called personal computer. The Altair 8800 was imperfect and cumbersome, with no display, no keyboard, and not enough memory to do anything useful. But its potential excited a Harvard sophomore named Bill Gates.

The computer age

Beginning with the cumbersome electronic numerical integrator and computer (ENIAC), pictured here in 1946, computer technology flourished, leading to the development of personal computers in the 1980s and the popularization of the Internet in the 1990s.

Gates improved the software of the Altair 8800, dropped out of college, and formed a company called Microsoft to market the new system. By 1977, Gates and others had helped transform the personal computer from a machine for hobbyists into a mass consumer product.

CULTURAL CONSERVATISM

Cultural conservatives helped elect Ronald Reagan and George Bush in the 1980s, but they were disappointed with the results. Once in office, neither president had, in the eyes of those conservatives, adequately addressed their moral agenda, including a complete ban on abortions and the restoration of prayer in public schools. By the 1990s a new generation of young conservative activists, mostly political independents or Republicans, had emerged as a major force in national affairs. They were more ideological, more libertarian, more partisan, and more impatient than their predecessors.

THE RELIGIOUS RIGHT   Although quite diverse, cultural conservatives tended to be evangelical Christians or orthodox Catholics, and they joined together to exert increasing religious pressure on the political process. In 1989 the television evangelist Pat Robertson organized the Christian Coalition to replace Jerry Falwell's Moral Majority as the flagship organization of the resurgent religious right. The Christian Coalition chose the Republican party as the best vehicle for promoting its pro–school prayer, anti-abortion, anti–gay rights positions. In addition to celebrating "traditional family values," it urged politicians to "radically downsize and delimit government." In many respects the religious right took control of the political and social agendas in the 1990s.

BUSH TO CLINTON

For months after the Persian Gulf War in 1991, George H. W. Bush seemed unbeatable. But the aftermath of Desert Storm was mixed, with Saddam Hussein's grip on Iraq still intact. Despite his image of strength abroad, Bush began to look weak even on foreign policy. The Soviet Union, meanwhile, stumbled on to its surprising end. On December 25, 1991, the Soviet flag over the Kremlin was replaced by the flag of the Russian Federation.

The Persian Gulf War

Iraqi soldiers surrender to the Allied forces in Kuwait.

The cold war had ended not just with the collapse of the Soviet Union but with the dismemberment of its fifteen constituent republics. As a result, the United States had become the world's only superpower.

"Containment" of the Soviet Union, the bedrock of American foreign policy for more than four decades, had lost its reason for being. Bush struggled to interpret the fluid new international scene. He spoke of a "new world order" but never defined it. By his own admission he had trouble with "the vision thing." By the end of 1991, a listless Bush faced a challenge in the Republican primary from the feisty television commentator and former White House aide Patrick Buchanan.

RECESSION AND DOWNSIZING   For the Bush administration and for the nation, the most devastating development in the early 1990s was a prolonged economic recession. The first major economic setback in more than eight years, it grew into the longest, if not the deepest, since the Great Depression. During 1991, 25 million workers—about 20 percent of the labor force—were unemployed at some point. The euphoria over the allied victory in the Gulf War quickly gave way to anxiety and to resentment generated by the depressed economy. At the end of 1991, *Time* magazine declared that "no one, not even George Bush" could deny "that the economy was sputtering." With his domestic policies in disarray and his foreign policy abandoned, George Bush tried a clumsy balancing act in addressing the recession, on the one hand acknowledging that "people are hurting" while on the other telling Americans that "this is a good time to buy a car."

TAX TURMOIL   President Bush had already set a political trap for himself when he declared at the 1988 Republican Convention: "Read my lips. No new taxes." Fourteen months into his presidency, he decided that the growing federal budget deficit was a greater risk than violation of his no-new-taxes pledge. After intense negotiations with congressional Democrats, Bush announced that reducing the federal deficit required "tax revenue increases." His backsliding set off a revolt among House Republicans, but a bipartisan majority (with most Republicans still opposed) finally approved a tax increase, raising the top personal rate from 28 to 31 percent, disallowing certain deductions in the upper brackets, and raising various excise taxes. Conservative Republicans would not let George Bush forget his abandoned pledge.

DEMOCRATIC RESURGENCE   As the Republicans divided over tax policy and social issues, the Democrats sought to present an image of centrist forces in control. For several years the Democratic Leadership Council, in which Arkansas governor William Jefferson Clinton figured prominently, had been pushing the party from the liberal left to the center of the political spectrum. Clinton strove to move the Democrats closer to the mainstream of political opinion. A graduate of Georgetown University, he had won a Rhodes scholarship to Oxford University and then earned a law degree from Yale, where he met his future wife, Hillary Rodham. By 1979, at age thirty-two, Bill Clinton was back in his native Arkansas, having been elected the youngest governor in the country. He served three more terms as governor and in the process emerged as a dynamic young leader committed to winning back the middle-class whites who had voted Republican during the 1980s. Democrats had grown so liberal, he argued, that they had alienated their key constituency, the "vital center."

A self-described moderate seeking the Democratic presidential nomination in 1992, Clinton promised to cut the defense budget, provide tax relief for the middle class, and create a massive economic-aid package for the former republics of the Soviet Union seeking to embrace democratic capitalism. Handsome, witty, intelligent, and a compelling speaker, Clinton projected an

The 1992 presidential campaign

Presidential candidate Bill Clinton and his running mate, Al Gore, brought youthful enthusiasm to the campaign trail.

image of youthful energy and optimism, reminding many political observers of John F. Kennedy. But underneath the veneer of Clinton's charisma were several flaws. He often seemed so determined to become president that he was willing to sacrifice consistency and principle. He made extensive use of polls to shape his stance on issues, pandered to special-interest groups, and flip-flopped on controversial subjects, leading critics to label him Slick Willie. Said one former opponent in Arkansas: "He'll be what people want him to be. He'll do or say what it will take to get elected." Even more enticing to the media and more embarrassing to Clinton were charges that he was a chronic adulterer and that he had manipulated the ROTC program during the Vietnam War to avoid the draft. Clinton's evasive denials of both allegations could not dispel a lingering distrust of his character.

Yet after a series of bruising party primaries, Clinton emerged as the front-runner at the Democratic nominating convention in the summer of 1992. Once nominated, Clinton chose Senator Albert Gore Jr. of Tennessee as his running mate. So the candidates were two southern Baptists from adjoining states.

Flushed with their convention victory and sporting a ten-point lead in the polls, the Clinton-Gore team stressed economic issues to win over working-class white and African American voters. Clinton won the election with

370 electoral votes and about 43 percent of the vote; Bush received 168 electoral votes and 39 percent of the vote; and off-and-on independent candidate H. Ross Perot of Texas garnered 18 percent of the popular vote but no electoral votes. A puckish billionaire, Perot found a large audience for his simplified explanations of public problems and his offers to just "get under the hood and fix them."

DOMESTIC POLICY IN CLINTON'S FIRST TERM

Clinton's inexperience in international affairs and congressional maneuvering led to several missteps in his first year as president. Like George Bush before him, he reneged on several campaign promises. He abandoned his proposed middle-class tax cut in order to keep down the federal deficit. Nine days into office he backed down when the Pentagon and Congress opposed his attempt to allow professed homosexuals to serve in the military; subsequently he announced an ambiguous policy concerning gays in the military that came to be known as "don't ask, don't tell." In Clinton's first two weeks in office, his approval rating dropped 20 percent.

THE ECONOMY   Clinton entered office determined to reduce the federal deficit without damaging the economy. To this end, on February 17, 1993, he proposed higher taxes for corporations and for individuals in higher tax brackets and called for an economic stimulus package for "investment" in public works (transportation, utilities, and the like) and "human capital" (education, skills, health, and welfare). Clinton's hotly contested deficit-reduction package passed by 218 to 216 in the House and 51 to 50 in the Senate, with Vice President Gore breaking the tie.

Equally contested was the North American Free Trade Agreement (NAFTA), which the Bush administration had negotiated with Canada and Mexico. The debate over its congressional approval revived old arguments on the tariff. Clinton stuck with his party's tradition of low tariffs and urged approval of NAFTA, which would make North America the largest free-trade area in the world. He and his supporters argued that tariff reductions would open up foreign markets to American industries. Opponents of the bill, including gadfly Ross Perot and organized labor, favored barriers that would discourage cheaper foreign products and believed that with NAFTA the country would hear the "giant sucking sound" of American jobs being drawn to Mexico. Yet Clinton prevailed, winning solid Republican support while losing a sizable minority of Democrats, mostly from the South, where executives predicted that textile mills would lose business to "cheap-labor" countries.

NAFTA protesters

Protesters going to a rally where House Majority Leader Richard Gephardt spoke to hundreds of opponents.

HEALTH-CARE REFORM

Clinton's major public-policy initiative was a federal health-care plan. Sentiment for health-care reform spread as annual medical costs skyrocketed and some 39 million Americans went without insurance either by choice or out of necessity. Universal medical coverage as proposed by Clinton would entitle every citizen and documented immigrant to health insurance. First Lady Hillary Clinton chaired the plan's task force and became the administration's lead witness on the plan before congressional committees. The bill aroused intense opposition from the pharmaceutical and insurance industries, and by the summer of 1994 Clinton's health-insurance plan was doomed. Lacking the votes to stop a filibuster by Senate Republicans, the Democrats acknowledged defeat and gave up the fight for universal medical coverage.

REPUBLICAN INSURGENCY

During 1994, Bill Clinton began to see his presidency unravel. Unable to get either health-care reform or welfare-reform bills through the Democratic Congress and having failed to carry out his campaign pledge for middle-class tax relief, he and his party found themselves on the defensive. In the midterm elections of 1994, the Democrats suffered a humbling defeat. It was the first election since 1952 in which Republicans captured both houses of Congress. Not a single Republican incumbent was defeated. Republicans also won a net gain of eleven governorships and fifteen state legislatures.

THE CONTRACT WITH AMERICA   A Georgian named Newton Leroy Gingrich led the Republican insurgency in Congress. Gingrich, a brilliant former history professor with an oversize ego, had helped mobilize religious and social conservatives associated with the Christian Coalition. In early 1995 he became the first Republican Speaker of the House in forty-two years. Gingrich announced that "we are at the end of an era." Liberalism, he claimed, was dead, and the Democratic party was dying. Gingrich pledged to start a new reign of congressional Republican dominance that would dismantle the "corrupt liberal welfare state." He was aided by freshman Republicans promoting what he called the Contract with America. The ten-point contract outlined an anti-big-government program with less regulation, less environmental conservation, term limits for members of Congress, a line-item veto for the president, welfare reform, and a balanced-budget amendment.

Yet the much-ballyhooed GOP revolution and the Contract with America fizzled out. The revolution that the imperious Gingrich touted was far too ambitious to be carried out in so limited a time with so slim a majority and so little sense of crisis. What is more, many of the Republican freshman representatives were scornful of compromise and were amateurs at legislative procedure; they limited Gingrich's ability to maneuver. The Senate, whose members were less spellbound by Gingrich and not party to the Contract with America anyway, rejected many of the bills that had been passed in the House. The "Republican revolution" of 1994 fizzled out, too, because Newt Gingrich became such an unpopular figure, both in Congress and among the electorate. He was too ambitious, too slick, too aggressive, too rambunctious. Clinton's lieutenants effectively portrayed him as an extremist.

LEGISLATIVE BREAKTHROUGH   In the late summer of 1996, as lawmakers were preparing to adjourn and participate in the presidential nominating conventions, the 104th Congress broke through its partisan gridlock and passed a flurry of important legislation that President Clinton quickly signed, including bills increasing the minimum wage and broadening access to health insurance.

Even more significant was a comprehensive welfare-reform measure that ended the federal government's open-ended guarantee of aid to the poor, a guarantee that had been in place since 1935. The Personal Responsibility and Work Opportunity Act of 1996 turned over the major federal welfare programs to the states, which would receive federal grants to fund them. The bill also limited the amount of time during which a person could receive welfare benefits funded by federal money and required that at least half of a state's welfare recipients have jobs or be enrolled in job-training programs by 2002. States failing to meet the deadline would have their federal funds cut.

The Republican-sponsored welfare-reform legislation passed the Senate by a vote of 74 to 24. When Clinton signed the bill, liberals charged that he was abdicating Democratic social principles in order to gain reelection amid the conservative climate of the times. Clinton and his centrist advisers dismissed the criticism, however. With his reelection bid at stake, the president was determined to live up to his 1992 campaign pledge to "end welfare as we know it." Clinton also knew that most voters in both parties were eager to see major cuts in federal entitlement programs.

THE 1996 CAMPAIGN   After clinching the Republican presidential nomination in 1996, Senate majority leader Bob Dole resigned his seat in order to devote himself to defeating Bill Clinton. As the 1996 presidential campaign unfolded, however, Clinton maintained a large lead in the polls. With an improving economy and no major foreign-policy crises to confront, personal and partisan issues surged into prominence. Concern about Dole's age (seventy-three) and his acerbic personality, as well as rifts in the Republican party between economic and social conservatives over issues such as abortion and gun control, hampered Dole's efforts to generate widespread support.

On November 5, 1996, Clinton won again, with an electoral vote of 379 to 159 and 49 percent of the popular vote. Dole received 41 percent of the popular vote, and independent candidate Ross Perot got 8 percent. The Republicans lost eight seats in the House but retained a 227 to 207 advantage over the Democrats in the House; in the Senate, Republicans gained two seats for a 55–45 majority.

THE CLINTON YEARS AT HOME

As the twentieth century came to a close, the United States benefited from a prolonged period of unprecedented prosperity. Buoyed by low inflation, high employment, declining federal budget deficits, dramatic improvements in productivity, the rapid globalization of economic life, and the leadership of Federal Reserve Board chairman Alan Greenspan, business and industry witnessed record profits.

THE "NEW ECONOMY"   During the late 1990s the stock market soared. In 1993 the Dow Jones Industrial Average hit 3,500. By 1996 it had topped 6,000. During 1998 it reached 9,000, defying the predictions of experts that the economy could not sustain such performance. In 1998, unemployment was only 4.3 percent, the lowest since 1970. Inflation was a measly 1.7 percent. People talked of the onset of a new economy, one that was centered on high-tech companies and would defy the boom-and-bust cycles of the previous hundred years. "It is possible," Greenspan suggested, "that we have moved 'beyond history.'"

In the 1990s much of the growth in the economy resulted from efforts to promote favored free markets on a world scale: global markets without tariffs and other barriers to free trade. More and more gigantic corporations such as IBM and General Electric had become international in scope. This phenomenon encouraged free-trade agreements such as NAFTA as well as most-favored-nation treatment for Communist China and other countries. With such agreements in place, American companies could easily "outsource" much of their production to plants in countries with lower labor costs. Increasingly, therefore, blue-collar labor lost ground to cheap foreign labor in assembly plants or "sweatshops" elsewhere in the world.

RACE INITIATIVES   After the triumphs of the civil rights movement in the 1960s, the momentum for minority advancement had run out—except for gains in college admissions and employment under the rubric of affirmative action. The conservative mood during the mid-1990s manifested itself in the Supreme Court. In 1995 the Court ruled against election districts redrawn to create African American or Hispanic majorities and narrowed federal affirmative-action programs.

In 1996 two major steps were taken against affirmative action in college admissions. In *Hopwood v. Texas*, a federal court ruled that considering race to achieve a diverse student body at the University of Texas was "not a compelling interest under the Fourteenth Amendment." Later that year the state of California passed Proposition 209, an initiative that ruled out race, sex, ethnicity, and national origin as criteria for preferring any group. These rulings eviscerated affirmative-action programs and drastically reduced African American enrollments, thereby prompting second thoughts. In addition, the nation still had not addressed intractable problems that lay beyond civil rights—that is, problems of dependency: illiteracy, poverty, unemployment, urban decay, and slums.

THE SCANDAL MACHINE   During his first term, President Clinton was dogged by allegations of improper involvement in the Whitewater Development Corporation. In 1978, as governor of Arkansas, he had invested in a resort to be built in northern Arkansas. The project turned out to be a fraud and a failure, and the Clintons took a loss on their investment. In 1994, Kenneth Starr, a Republican, was appointed to serve as independent counsel in an investigation of the Whitewater case. Starr's exhaustive investigation did not uncover evidence that the Clintons were directly involved in the fraud, although several of their close associates had been caught in the web and convicted of various charges, some related to Whitewater and some not.

Besides Whitewater, Starr's team of investigators looked into the allegations of Paula Jones that Clinton had sexually harassed her while he was governor of Arkansas and she was a state employee. In the course of the investigation, it surfaced that the president may have had a sexual affair with a former White House intern, Monica Lewinsky, and may have pressed her to lie about it under oath. Clinton publicly denied the affair, but the tawdry scandal would not disappear. In August 1998, President Clinton agreed to appear before a grand jury convened to investigate the sexual allegations. He was the first president in history to testify before a grand jury. On August 17, with the nation anxiously awaiting the results, Clinton recanted his earlier denials and acknowledged having had "inappropriate intimate physical contact" with Monica Lewinsky. Public reaction to Clinton's stunning about-face was mixed. A majority of Americans expressed sympathy for the president because of his public humiliation and wanted the matter dropped. Clinton's credibility had suffered a serious blow on account of his reckless lack of self-discipline and his efforts to deny and then cover up the sordid scandal.

Meanwhile, on September 9, 1998, Kenneth Starr submitted to Congress a 445-page report and eighteen boxes of supporting material. The Starr Report found "substantial and creditable" evidence of presidential wrongdoing. Drawing upon the evidence, the Republican-controlled House Judiciary Committee voted 21 to 16 to recommend a full impeachment inquiry into the allegations of perjury and obstruction of justice by the president. On October 8 the House of Representatives voted 258 to 176 to begin a wide-ranging impeachment inquiry of the president. Thirty-one Democrats joined the Republicans in supporting the investigation. On December 19, 1998, William Jefferson Clinton became the second president to be impeached by the House of Representatives. The House officially approved two articles of impeachment, charging Clinton with lying under oath to a federal grand jury and obstructing justice.

The Senate trial of President Clinton began on January 7, 1999. Five weeks later, on February 12, the Senate acquitted the president. Rejecting the first charge of perjury, 10 Republicans and all 45 Democrats voted "not guilty." On the charge of obstruction of justice, the Senate split 50–50 (which meant

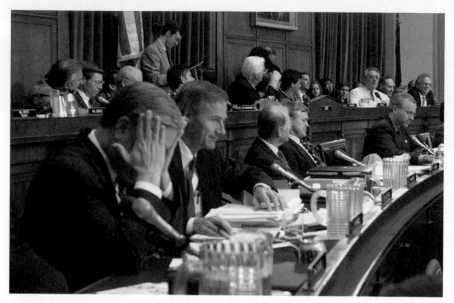

Impeachment

Representative Edward Pease, a member of the House Judiciary Committee, covers his face during the vote on the third of four articles of impeachment charging President Clinton with "high crimes and misdemeanors," December 1998.

acquittal, since 67 votes were needed for conviction). In both instances, senators had a hard time interpreting Clinton's philandering as constituting "high crimes and misdemeanors," the constitutional requirement for removal of a president from office. Clinton's supporters portrayed him as the victim of a puritanical special prosecutor and a partisan conspiracy run amok. His critics lambasted him as a lecherous man without honor or integrity. Both characterizations were incomplete. Politically astute, charismatic, and well-informed, Clinton had as much ability and potential as any president. Yet he was also shamelessly self-indulgent. The result was a scandalous presidency punctuated by dramatic achievements in welfare reform, economic growth, and foreign policy.

FOREIGN-POLICY CHALLENGES

Like Woodrow Wilson, Lyndon Johnson, and Jimmy Carter before him, Bill Clinton was a Democratic president who came into office determined to focus on the nation's domestic problems only to find himself mired in foreign

Clinton and the Middle East

President Clinton presides as Israeli prime minister Yitzhak Rabin (left) and PLO leader Yasir Arafat (right) agree to a peace accord between Israel and the Palestinians, September 1993.

entanglements. Clinton continued the Bush administration's intervention in Somalia, on the northeastern horn of Africa, where collapse of the government early in 1991 had left the country in anarchy, prey to tribal marauders. President Bush in 1992 had gained UN sanction for a military force led by American troops to relieve hunger and restore peace. In early 1993, U.S. troop levels peaked and began to shrink with the arrival of international forces. The Somalian operation proved successful at its primary mission, but it never solved the political problems that lay at the root of the population's starvation and civil strife.

THE MIDDLE EAST   Clinton also continued George Bush's policy of sponsoring patient negotiations between the Arabs and the Israelis. A new development was the inclusion of the PLO in the negotiations. In 1993 a draft agreement between Israel and the PLO provided for the restoration of Palestinian self-rule in the occupied Gaza Strip and in Jericho, on the West Bank of the Jordan River, in an exchange of land for peace as provided in UN Security Council resolutions. A formal signing occurred at the White House on September 13, 1993. With President Clinton presiding, Israeli prime minister Yitzhak Rabin and PLO leader Yasir Arafat exchanged handshakes, and their foreign ministers signed the agreement.

The Middle East peace process suffered a terrible blow in early November 1995, however, when Yitzhak Rabin was assassinated at a peace rally in Tel Aviv by an Israeli Jewish zealot who resented Rabin's efforts to negotiate with the Palestinians. Some observers feared that the assassin had killed the peace process as well when seven months later conservative hard-liner Benjamin Netanyahu narrowly defeated the U.S.-backed Shimon Peres in the Israeli elections. Yet in October 1998, Clinton brought Arafat, King Hussein of Jordan, and Netanyahu together at a conference center in Wye Mills, Maryland, where they reached an agreement. Under the Wye River Memorandum, Israel surrendered land in return for security guarantees by the Palestinians. As hard-liners attempted to derail the tenuous peace process, Netanyahu called elections early, and the Israeli public swept into power former general Ehud Barak, who promised to jump-start the peace process.

THE BALKANS   Clinton's foreign policy also addressed the chaotic transition in eastern Europe from Soviet domination to independence. When Yugoslavia imploded in 1991, fanatics and tyrants incited ethnic conflict as four of its six republics seceded. Serb minorities, backed by Serbia itself, stirred up civil wars in Croatia and Bosnia. In Bosnia especially, the war involved "ethnic cleansing"—driving Muslims from their homes and towns. In 1995, American negotiators finally persuaded the foreign ministers of Croatia, Bosnia, and the new Federal Republic of Yugoslavia to agree to a comprehensive peace plan. To enforce the agreement, 60,000 NATO troops would be dispatched to Bosnia as part of a peacekeeping operation. A cease-fire went into effect in October 1995.

In 1998 the Balkan tinderbox flared up again, this time in the Yugoslav province of Kosovo, a region long considered sacred by Christian Serbs. By 1989, however, over 90 percent of the 2 million Kosovars were ethnic Albanian Muslims. In that year, Yugoslav president Slobodan Milošević decided to reassert Serbian control over the province. He stripped Kosovo of its autonomy and established de facto martial law. When the Albanian Kosovars resisted and large numbers of Muslim men began to join the Kosovo Liberation Army, Serbian soldiers and state police ruthlessly suppressed them and launched another program of "ethnic cleansing," burning Albanian villages, murdering men, raping women, and displacing hundreds of thousands of Muslim Albanian Kosovars.

On March 24, 1999, NATO, relying heavily upon American military resources and leadership, launched air strikes against Yugoslavia. After seventy-two days of unrelenting bombardment, Milošević sued for peace on NATO's terms. An agreement was reached on June 3, 1999. As the Albanian Kosovars began to return to Kosovo, however, large numbers of Serbs, fearful of Muslim retribution, began to leave, and some of them were killed. Members of the Kosovo Liberation Army stepped into the vacuum left by the departing Serbs and began to take control of the province.

GLOBALIZATION   The deepening involvement of the United States in the complex affairs of eastern Europe symbolized the broadening scope of globalization. As the proliferation of globe-spanning information and communications technologies shrank time and distance, a cornucopia of consumer goods was produced, distributed, marketed, and sold by multinational companies all over the world, not just in the United States. As more nations entered the world economy and experienced prosperity, they benefited corporations in the United States by buying more American products and sending more and better goods to the United States. U.S. exports rose dramatically in the last twenty years of the twentieth century. By the end of the twentieth century, the American economy had become dependent on the global economy; foreign trade had become central to American prosperity—and to American politics. By 2000 over a third of the production of American multinational companies was occurring abroad, compared with only 9 percent in 1980. By the end of the twentieth century, the American economy had become internationalized to such a profound extent that global concerns exercised an overwhelming influence on American domestic and foreign policies.

THE ELECTION OF 2000

The election of 2000 revealed that American voters were split evenly along partisan lines. The two major-party candidates for president, Vice President Al Gore, the Democrat, and Texas governor George W. Bush, the Republican and son of the former president, presented sharply contrasting views on the role of the federal government, tax cuts, environmental policies, and the best way to preserve Social Security and Medicare. Gore, a Tennessee native and Harvard graduate whose father had been a senator, favored an active federal government that would preserve Social Security and subsidize prescription-medicine expenses for the elderly. He criticized proposed Republican tax cuts for catering to the wealthy. An environmental activist, Gore reaffirmed his support for the Environmental Protection Agency and the Interior Department.

Bush, on the other hand, proposed to transfer power from the federal government to the states, particularly in regard to the environment and education. He promoted more drilling for oil on federal land, and he endorsed the use of vouchers (cash grants) to enable parents to send their children to private schools. In international affairs, Bush questioned the need to maintain U.S. peacekeeping forces in Bosnia and the continuing expense of other global military commitments.

In the end the election was the one of the closest—and most controversial—in history. The television networks initially reported that Gore had narrowly won the state of Florida and its decisive twenty-five electoral votes. Later in the evening, however, the networks reversed themselves, saying that

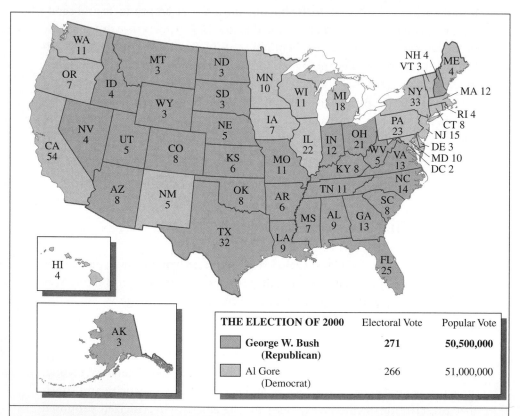

THE ELECTION OF 2000	Electoral Vote	Popular Vote
George W. Bush (Republican)	271	50,500,000
Al Gore (Democrat)	266	51,000,000

Why was the 2000 presidential election so close? How was the conflict over the election results resolved? How were differences between urban and rural voters key to the outcome of the election?

Florida was too close to call. The final tally in Florida showed Bush with a razor-thin lead, and state law required a recount. For the first time in 125 years, the results of a presidential election remained in doubt for weeks after the voting.

As a painstaking hand count of presidential ballots proceeded in Florida, supporters of Bush and Gore pursued victory through legal maneuvers in the Florida courts and the U.S. Supreme Court; each side accused the other of trying to steal the election. The political drama remained stalemated for five weeks. At last, on December 12, 2000, the Supreme Court halted the statewide manual recounts in Florida. In the case known as *Bush v. Gore,* a bare 5–4 majority ruled that any new recount would clash with existing Florida law. Bush was deemed the winner in Florida by the slimmest of margins: 537 votes. Although Gore amassed a 540,000-vote lead nationwide, he lost in the Electoral College by two votes when he lost Florida.

COMPASSIONATE CONSERVATISM

THE SECOND BUSH PRESIDENCY George W. Bush arrived in the White House amid the controversy of a disputed election to confront a sputtering economy and a falling stock market. By the spring of 2000, the high-tech companies that had led the soaring stock market during the 1990s had begun to stall. Many of the dazzling new dot-com businesses declared bankruptcy. Greed fed by record profits and speculative excesses had led businesses, investors, and consumers to take dangerous risks; many leading corporate executives, it turned out, had engaged in unethical practices that undermined the economy. The Internet bubble burst in 2001. Stock values collapsed, stealing over $2 trillion from household wealth. Consumer confidence and capital investment plummeted with the stock market. By March 2001 the economy was in recession for the first time in over a decade.

Yet Bush's disputed election and the political balance in Congress did not prevent the new president from launching an ambitious legislative agenda. Confident that he could win over Democrats, he promised within months of his inauguration to provide "an explosion of legislation" promoting his goal of "compassionate conservatism." The top item on Bush's wish list was a $1.6-trillion tax cut intended to stimulate the sagging economy. The Senate eventually trimmed the cut to $1.35 trillion over eleven years, and Bush signed it into law on June 7, 2001.

NO CHILD LEFT BEHIND   In addition to tax reduction, one of President Bush's top priorities was education reform. In late 2001, Congress passed a comprehensive education-improvement plan called No Child Left Behind, and the president signed the bill in early 2002. It required states to set new learning standards and ensure that all students were "proficient" at reading and math by 2014. It also mandated that all teachers be "highly qualified" in their subject area by 2005, allowed children in low-performing schools to transfer to other schools, and required states to submit annual reports of students' scores on standardized tests. Schools and school districts that fell short of the new standards were eligible for financial and technical assistance, but if progress did not occur, the federal government would issue a series of sanctions; ultimately a chronically failing school district would be taken over by the state. States soon criticized the program, noting that it provided insufficient funds for remedial programs and that poor school districts, many of them in blighted inner cities or rural areas, would be especially hard-pressed to meet the guidelines.

EXPLOITING THE ENVIRONMENT   The Bush administration's environmental policies ignited a firestorm of controversy. The president sought to roll back restrictions on economic development posed by long-standing environmental regulations. In addition, he allowed more logging in national forests and opened up more federal land, including wildlife sanctuaries, to exploration for energy sources in the face of dramatic increases in oil and gasoline prices. Like Ronald Reagan before him, Bush appointed former industry executives to federal agencies responsible for enforcing environmental regulations, and he exempted the Defense Department from many environmental restrictions. James Jeffords, a Republican turned independent and the ranking minority member of the Senate Environment and Public Works Committee, predicted that the Bush administration would "go down in history as the greatest disaster for public health and the environment in the history of the United States."

GLOBAL TERRORISM

With the collapse of the Soviet Union and the end of the cold war, world politics had grown more unstable during the 1990s. Where ideologies such as capitalism and communism had earlier been the cause of conflict and tension in foreign relations, issues of religion, ethnicity, and clashing cultural values now divided peoples. Nations were no longer the sole actors on the stage of world politics. Instead, nebulous multinational groups inspired by religious fanaticism and anti-American rage were using high-tech terrorism to gain notoriety and exact vengeance. Well-financed and well-armed terrorists flourished in the cracks of foundering nations such as Sudan, Somalia, Pakistan, Yemen, and Afghanistan. Throughout the 1990s the United States fought a losing secret war against global terrorism. The ineffectiveness of Western intelligence agencies in tracking the movements and intentions of militant extremists became tragically evident in the late summer of 2001.

SEPTEMBER 11, 2001: A DAY OF INFAMY   At 8:45 A.M. on September 11, 2001, the world watched in horror as a commercial airliner hijacked by Islamic terrorists slammed into the north tower of the World Trade Center in New York City. A second hijacked jumbo jet, traveling at 500 miles per hour, hit the south tower eighteen minutes later. The fuel-laden planes turned the majestic buildings into infernos. The iconic twin towers, both 110 stories tall and occupied by thousands of people, collapsed from the intense heat. Surrounding buildings also crumpled. The entire southern end of Manhattan—ground zero—became a hellish scene of twisted steel, suffocating smoke, and wailing sirens.

While the catastrophic drama in New York was unfolding, a third hijacked plane crashed into the Pentagon in Washington, D.C. A fourth commandeered airliner, thought to be headed for the White House, missed its mark when passengers, who had heard reports of the earlier incidents via cell phones, assaulted the hijackers to prevent the plane from being used as a weapon. During the struggle in the cockpit, the plane went out of control and plummeted into the Pennsylvania countryside, killing all on board.

The hijackings represented the costliest terrorist assault on the United States in the nation's history. There were 266 passengers and crew members aboard the crashed jets. More than 100 civilians and military personnel were killed at the Pentagon. The death toll at the World Trade Center was over 2,600, with many firefighters, police officers, and rescue workers among the dead. Hundreds of those killed were foreign nationals working in the financial district; some eighty nations lost citizens in the attacks. The terrorists also destroyed a powerful symbol of America: the World Trade Center towers were the central offices of global capitalism.

The terrorist attacks of September 11 created shock and chaos, grief and anger. They also prompted an unprecedented display of national unity and patriotism. People rushed to donate blood, food, and money. Volunteers clogged military-recruiting centers. American flags were in evidence everywhere. Citizens around the world held vigils at U.S. embassies. World leaders offered condolences and support. For the first time in its history, NATO invoked Article 5 of its charter, which states that an attack on any member will be considered an attack on all.

Within hours of the hijackings, officials had identified the nineteen terrorists as members of al Qaeda (the Base), a well-financed worldwide network of Islamic extremists led by a wealthy Saudi renegade, Osama bin Laden. Years before, bin Laden had declared holy war on the United States, Israel, and the Saudi monarchy. For several years he had been using remote bases in war-torn Afghanistan as terrorist training centers. Collaboring with bin Laden's terrorist network was Afghanistan's ruling Taliban, a coalition of radical Islamists that had emerged in the mid-1990s following the forced withdrawal of Soviet troops from Afghanistan. Taliban leaders provided bin Laden with a safe haven in exchange for his financial and military support

September 11, 2001

Smoke pours out of the north tower of the World Trade Center as the south tower bursts into flames after being struck by a second hijacked airplane. Both towers collapsed about an hour later.

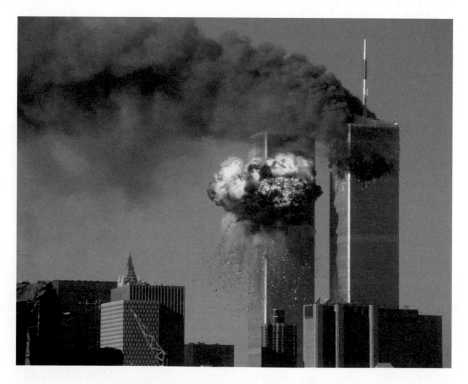

against the Northern Alliance, a cluster of rebel groups opposed to Taliban rule. Bin Laden sought to mobilize into a global army Muslim militants energized by local causes. As many as 20,000 recruits from twenty countries circulated through his Afghan training camps. Most of the terrorists received religious indoctrination and basic infantry training to prepare them to fight for the Taliban. A smaller group was selected by al Qaeda for elite training to organize secret cells around the world and engage in urban warfare, assassination, demolition, and sabotage, with Western Europe and the United States as the primary target.

WAR ON TERRORISM   The September 11 assault on the United States changed the course of the new presidency, the nation, and the world. The economy, already in decline, went into a free fall. President Bush, who had never professed to know much about international relations or world affairs and had shown only disdain for Bill Clinton's "multilateralism," was thrust onto center stage as commander in chief of a wounded nation eager for vengeance. The Bush administration immediately forged an international

Operation Enduring Freedom

Smoke rises from the Taliban village of Khanaqa, fifty-five miles from the Afghan capital Kabul, after a U.S. aircraft released bombs.

coalition to strike at terrorism worldwide. The coalition demanded that Afghanistan's Taliban government surrender the terrorists or risk military attack. In a televised address on September 20, Bush warned Americans that the war against terrorism would be a lengthy campaign involving covert action as well as conventional military forces, which would target not only terrorists but also the groups and governments that abet them. "Every nation in every region," he said, "now has a decision to make: either you are with us or you are with the terrorists."

On October 7, after the Taliban defiantly refused to turn over bin Laden, the United States and its allies launched a ferocious military campaign— Operation Enduring Freedom—to locate and punish terrorists or "those harboring terrorists." U.S. and British cruise missiles and bombers destroyed Afghan military installations and al Qaeda training camps. The coalition found key allies in neighboring Pakistan and in Afghanistan's Northern Alliance. On December 9, only two months after the American-led military campaign in Afghanistan had begun, the Taliban regime collapsed. With its collapse, the war in Afghanistan devolved into a high-stakes manhunt for the elusive Osama bin Laden and an international network of terrorists operating in sixty countries.

TERRORISM AT HOME While the military campaign continued in Afghanistan, officials in Washington worried that terrorists might launch additional attacks in the United States with biological, chemical, or even nuclear weapons. To address the threat and to help restore public confidence, President Bush created a new federal agency, the Office of Homeland Security. Another new federal agency, the Transportation Security Administration, assumed responsibility for screening airline passengers. At the same time, President Bush and a supportive Congress created new legislation, known as the USA Patriot Act, which gave government agencies the right to eavesdrop on confidential conversations between prison inmates and their lawyers and permitted suspected terrorists to be tried in secret military courts. Civil liberties groups voiced grave concerns that the measures jeopardized constitutional rights and protections. But the crisis atmosphere after September 11 caused most people to support these extraordinary steps.

THE BUSH DOCTRINE In the fall of 2002, President Bush unveiled a new national security doctrine that marked a distinct shift from that of previous administrations. Containment and deterrence had been the guiding strategic concepts of the cold war. Now, President Bush declared, the growing menace posed by "shadowy networks" of terrorist groups and unstable

Bush's defense policy

President George W. Bush addresses soldiers in July 2002 as part of an appeal to Congress to speed approval of increased defense spending after the September 11 terrorist attacks.

rogue nations with "weapons of mass destruction" required a new doctrine of preemptive military action. "If we wait for threats to fully materialize," he explained, "we will have waited too long. In the world we have entered, the only path to safety is the path of action. And this nation will act."

A SECOND PERSIAN GULF WAR During 2002 and 2003, Iraq emerged as the focus of the Bush administration's new policy of "preemptive" military action to prevent terrorism and destroy presumed weapons of mass destruction. In September 2002, President Bush urged the United Nations to confront the "grave and gathering danger" posed by Saddam Hussein's dictatorial regime in Iraq. He warned that the United States would act alone if the UN did not respond. In October, Congress approved a resolution proposed by Bush authorizing him to use "all means that he determines to be appropriate, including force," to defend the United States against the threat posed by Iraq's supposed possession of biological and chemical weapons. On November 8 the UN Security Council passed Resolution 1441 ordering Iraq to disarm immediately or face "serious consequences." Faced with growing international pressure, Hussein grudgingly allowed UN weapons inspectors to return to Iraq "without conditions."

On March 17, 2003, President Bush issued an ultimatum to Saddam Hussein: he and his sons must leave Iraq within forty-eight hours or face a U.S.-led invasion. Hussein refused. Two days later, on March 19, American and British forces, supported by what George Bush called the "coalition of the willing," attacked Iraq. Operation Iraqi Freedom involved a massive bombing campaign followed closely by a fast-moving invasion across the Iraqi desert from bases in Kuwait. Some 250,000 American soldiers, sailors, and marines were joined by 50,000 British troops as well as small contingents from other countries, including Australia and Poland. On April 9, after three weeks of intense fighting amid sweltering heat and blinding sandstorms, allied forces occupied Baghdad, the capital of Iraq. Saddam's Baathist regime and his inept army collapsed and fled a week later. On May 1, 2003, an exuberant President Bush declared that the war was essentially over. "The battle of Iraq," he said, "is one victory in a war on terror that began on September 11, 2001, and still goes on."

A continued presence in Iraq

U.S. military police patrol the market in Abu Ghraib, on the outskirts of Baghdad.

The complicated Iraqi military campaign was a brilliantly orchestrated demonstration of intense firepower, daring maneuver, and complex logistical support. No one had predicted such a quick and decisive victory—or so few casualties among the allied forces. The six-week war came at a cost of fewer than 200 combat deaths among the 300,000 coalition troops. Over 2,000 Iraqi soldiers were killed; civilian casualties numbered in the tens of thousands.

REBUILDING IRAQ It proved easier to win the war than to rebuild Iraq, however. Secretary of Defense Donald Rumsfeld saw the Iraq War as an opportunity to showcase America's new military strategy, with its focus on airpower, precision weaponry, sophisticated communications, and mobile ground forces adept at stealth and speed. Yet winning the peace proved far more difficult than winning the war. No sooner had Saddam Hussein's tyranny been destroyed than the allies faced the daunting task of restoring order and installing a democratic government in a chaotic Iraq torn by age-old religious feuds and ethnic tensions. Looting was rampant and basic services nonexistent. Saddam Hussein and many of his lieutenants evaded capture and organized insurgent attacks against the allied forces and the interim Iraqi government. Violence engulfed the war-torn country. Vengeful Islamic jihadists (holy warriors) from around the world streamed into Iraq to wage a merciless campaign of terror and sabotage against the coalition forces and their Iraqi allies.

Defense Department analysts had greatly underestimated the difficulty of pacifying and reconstructing postwar Iraq. As Secretary Rumsfeld told his staff in October 2003, the invasion of Iraq was the easy part. The allies now faced "a long, hard slog" in their effort to install a new Iraqi government and restore basic services in the midst of a growing guerrilla insurgency. By the fall of 2003, President Bush was forced to admit that substantial numbers of American troops (around 150,000) would remain in Iraq much longer than originally anticipated and that rebuilding the fractured nation would take much longer than expected. Victory on the battlefields of Iraq did not bring peace to the Middle East. Militant Islamic groups seething with hatred for the United States remained a constant global threat. In addition, the dispute over the Iraq War strained relations between the Anglo-American alliance and France, Germany, and Russia, all of which opposed the war.

Throughout 2003 and 2004 the Iraqi insurgency and its campaign of terror grew in scope and savagery. Near-daily suicide car bombings and roadside ambushes of U.S. military convoys wreaked havoc among Iraqi civilians and allied troops. Terrorists kidnapped foreign civilians and beheaded several of them in grisly rituals videotaped for the world to see. In the United States the euphoria of battlefield victory turned to dismay as the number of casualties and the expense of the occupation soared. In the face of mounting criticism, President Bush urged Americans to "stay the course," insisting that a democratic Iraq would bring stability to the volatile Middle East and thereby blunt the momentum of Islamic terrorism.

But the president's credibility suffered a sharp blow in January 2004 when administration officials admitted that no weapons of mass destruction—the primary reason for launching the invasion—had been found in Iraq. The chief weapons inspector told Congress that the intelligence reports about Hussein's supposed secret weapons were "almost all wrong." Furthermore, shocking revelations in April 2004 of American soldiers torturing Iraqi prisoners further eroded public confidence in Bush's handling of the war and its aftermath.

By September 2004, U.S. military deaths in Iraq had reached 1,000, and during 2006 the number was well over 2,500. Although Saddam Hussein had been captured in December 2003 and Iraqi citizens elected their first democratic government in January 2005 and approved a new constitution nine months later, Iraq seemed less secure than ever. The continuing guerrilla war in Afghanistan and the new one in Iraq strained American military resources and the federal budget.

THE ELECTION OF 2004   Growing public concern about the mayhem in Iraq complicated George Bush's campaign for a second presidential term. Throughout 2004 his approval rating plummeted. And in the new century the electorate had become deeply polarized. A ferocious partisanship dominated civic commentary in the early years of the century. Democrats still fumed over the contested election results of 2000. When asked about the intensity of his critics, a combative George Bush declared the furor "a compliment. It means I'm willing to take a stand." One of his advisers explained it more bluntly: "He likes being hated. It lets him know he's doing the right thing."

The 2004 presidential campaign was punctuated by negative attacks on each candidate as the two parties sought to galvanize their loyalists. The Democratic nominee, Senator John Kerry of Massachusetts, lambasted the Bush administration for misleading the nation on the issue of weapons of mass destruction in Iraq and for its inept handling of the Iraq occupation. Kerry also highlighted the record budget deficits occurring under the Republican leadership. Bush countered that the tortuous efforts to create a democratic government in Iraq would enhance America's long-term security.

The 2004 election

President George W. Bush (center) and Democratic candidate Senator John Kerry (left) participate in the second presidential debate, a town-hall-style exchange held at Washington University in St. Louis, Missouri.

On election day the exit polls suggested a Kerry victory, but in the end the election hinged on the crucial swing state of Ohio. No Republican had ever lost Ohio and still won the presidency. After an anxious night viewing returns from Ohio and even considering the contested ballots, Kerry conceded the election. "The outcome," he stressed, "should be decided by voters, not a protracted legal battle." By narrowly winning Ohio, Bush garnered 286 electoral votes to Kerry's 251. The 2004 election was remarkable for its high voter turnout. Almost 120 million people voted, some 15 million more than in the disputed 2000 election.

Bush won the popular vote by 50.73 to 48.27 percent, the narrowest margin won by any incumbent president. Yet in some respects the close election was not so close. Bush received 3.5 million more votes nationwide than Kerry, and Republicans increased their control of both the House and the Senate. Trumpeting "the will of the people at my back," Bush pledged to bring democracy to Iraq, overhaul the tax code and eliminate the estate tax, revamp Social Security, trim the federal deficit, limit financial awards for medical malpractice lawsuits, pass an energy bill, and create more jobs. "I earned capital in the campaign, political capital, and now I intend to spend it," he told reporters.

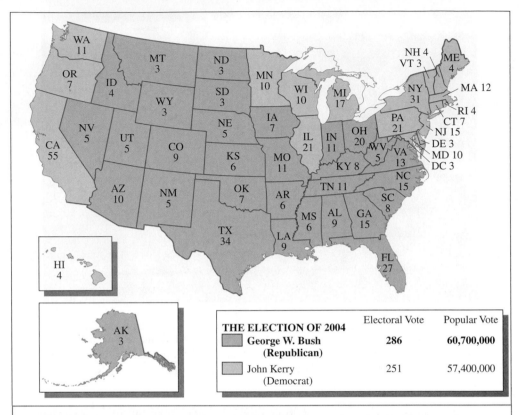

THE ELECTION OF 2004	Electoral Vote	Popular Vote
George W. Bush (Republican)	286	60,700,000
John Kerry (Democrat)	251	57,400,000

How did the war in Iraq polarize the electorate? In what ways did the election of 2004 give Republicans a mandate?

SECOND-TERM BLUES

Yet like many modern presidents, George Bush sputtered in his second term. In 2005 he pushed through Congress an energy bill and a Central American Free Trade Act. But his effort to privatize Social Security retirement accounts went nowhere, and soaring budget deficits made repeal of the estate tax politically impossible.

The retirement of Sandra Day O'Connor from the Supreme Court in July 2005 ignited a fierce political debate over combustible issues such as abortion, gay marriage, and affirmative action. Militants on the left and on the right exerted unrelenting pressure on the White House, but Bush's shrewd decision to nominate John G. Roberts Jr., a socially conservative circuit court judge, stalemated critics because Roberts's legal credentials were impeccable. Yet the fractious cultural debates did not subside. No sooner had the Senate overwhelmingly confirmed Roberts (78 to 22) than Chief Justice William Rehnquist died. Bush then named Roberts the new chief justice and nominated Harriet E. Miers, a longtime friend and former personal lawyer turned White House legal counsel, to replace O'Connor. Critics, many of them Republican conservatives, denounced Miers as a legal mediocrity and a presidential crony. The furor led Miers to withdraw her nomination in late October 2005, a humiliating development for President Bush that further hobbled his stalled legislative efforts. Her withdrawal coincided with the indictment of Vice President Richard Cheney's chief of staff, Lewis Libby, for perjury and obstruction of justice relating to an investigation of administration officials who purportedly revealed the identity of a covert CIA agent in a supposed act of political revenge. To address concerns that the Bush administration was sputtering in its second term and to heal the ruptures within the Republican coalition, Bush nominated to the Supreme Court Samuel Alito Jr., a federal judge and a favorite of conservatives.

HURRICANE KATRINA   In the summer of 2005, President Bush's eroding public support suffered another blow, this time when a natural disaster turned into a political crisis. In late August a killer hurricane named Katrina slammed into the Gulf coast, devastating large areas of Alabama, Mississippi, and Louisiana. The sultry metropolis of New Orleans was virtually destroyed as levees and flood walls holding back the Mississippi River and Lake Pontchartrain burst, inundating three quarters of the city. Katrina's awful wake left over 1,000 people dead in three states and millions homeless and hopeless.

Local political officials and the Federal Emergency Management Agency (FEMA) were caught unprepared as the catastrophe unfolded. Disaster plans were incomplete; confusion and incompetence abounded. A wave of public outrage crashed against the Bush administration. In the face of blistering criticism, President Bush accepted responsibility for the balky federal response to the disaster and accepted the resignation of the FEMA director. Rebuilding the Gulf coast would take a long time and a lot of money.

A STALLED PRESIDENCY   George Bush bore the brunt of public indignation over the federal response to the Katrina disaster. Thereafter,

Hurricane Katrina

Cars and buildings are partially submerged on Canal Street, a central thoroughfare in New Orleans, September 3, 2005.

his second presidential term was beset by political problems, a sputtering economy, and growing public dissatisfaction with performance and the continuing war in Iraq. Even his support among Republicans crumbled, and many social conservatives felt betrayed by his sporadic attention to their concerns. The editors of the *Economist*, an influential conservative newsmagazine, declared that Bush had become "the least popular re-elected president since Richard Nixon became embroiled in the Watergate fiasco." The skyrocketing gasoline prices and the federal budget deficit fueled public frustration. President Bush and Congress had overseen the largest increase in federal spending since Franklin Roosevelt. The president's efforts to reform the tax code, Social Security, and immigration laws languished during his second term, and the turmoil and violence in Iraq showed no signs of abating. Senator Chuck Hagel, a Nebraska Republican, declared in 2005 that "we're losing in Iraq." The drumbeat of disillusionment prompted President

Bush to acknowledge "setbacks" in Iraq and flaws in the intelligence reports that provided the rationale for going to war.

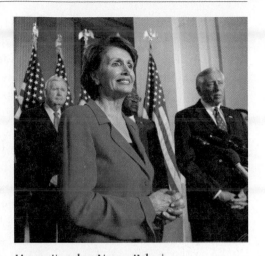

House Speaker Nancy Pelosi

At a news conference on Capitol Hill.

VOTER REBELLION In the November 2006 congressional elections the Democrats capitalized on the public disapproval of the Bush administration to win control of the House of Representatives, the Senate, and a majority of governorships and state legislatures. The election results were so lopsided that for the first time in history the victorious party (the Democrats) did not lose a single incumbent or open congressional seat or governorship. Former Republican congressman Dick Armey said that "the Republican Revolution of 1994 officially ended" with the 2006 election. "It was a rout." George Bush admitted that the voters had given him and his party a "thumpin'" that would require a "new era of cooperation" with the victorious Democrats. As it turned out, however, the Bush White House and the Democratic Congress became mired in partisan gridlock. Stalemate trumped bipartisanship.

The transformational election also included a significant milestone: Californian Nancy Pelosi, the leader of the Democrats in the House of Representatives, became the highest-ranking woman in the history of the U.S. Congress upon her election as House Speaker in January 2007.

THE "SURGE" IN IRAQ The 2006 election was largely a referendum on the lack of progress in the Iraq War. Throughout the fall the violence and casualties in Iraq had spiked. The newly elected Iraqi government remained unstable, and fighting among the various religious and ethnic factions grew more chaotic. Bush remained stubbornly "committed to victory" in Iraq. But he responded to declining public and political support by replacing Donald Rumsfeld, the combative secretary of defense, with Robert Gates, a former head of the CIA. The president also created the Iraq Study Group, a nonpartisan task force co-chaired by Lee H. Hamilton, a former Democratic congressman, and James A. Baker III, secretary of state under the first President Bush. The group's report recommended that the United States step up the training of Iraqi troops and withdraw virtually all U.S. combat forces from a "grave and deteriorating Iraq" by the spring of 2008.

President Bush disagreed with the findings of the Iraq Study Group and others, including key military leaders, who urged a phased withdrawal. On January 10, 2007, he announced that he was sending a "surge" of 20,000 (eventually 30,000) additional American troops to Iraq, bringing the ultimate total to almost 170,000. Most Democrats opposed the escalation and instead called for an exit strategy. Senate majority leader Harry Reid, a Nevada Democrat, proclaimed in April 2007 that the United States had "lost" the war in Iraq and should beat a hasty retreat. During the summer of 2007, congressional Democrats tried to force the withdrawal of U.S. forces from Iraq, but Bush held firm. The "surge" of additional soldiers, he explained,

General David Petraeus

General Petraeus salutes U.S. soldiers during his visit at the village of Jadihah northeast of Baghdad, Iraq.

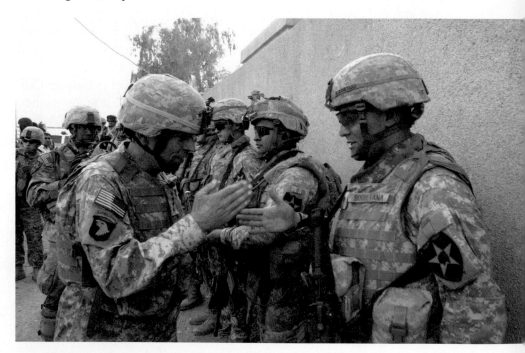

would involve a change in strategy as well as additional soldiers. The U.S. troops would shift their focus from offensive operations to the protection of Iraqi civilians from attacks by terrorist insurgents and sectarian militias. Bush hoped that the additional security would enable Iraqi leaders to promote political reconciliation among the war-torn country's major factions, the Shiites, Sunnis, and Kurds.

From a military perspective, the "surge" strategy succeeded. By the fall of 2008, the convulsive violence in Iraq had declined dramatically, and the U.S.-supported Iraqi government had grown in stature and confidence. But the financial expenses and human casualties of American involvement in Iraq continued to generate widespread criticism, and the "surge" failed to attain its political objectives. Iraqi leaders had yet to build a stable, self-sustaining democracy. The U.S. general who masterminded the "surge" strategy admitted that the gains remained "fragile and reversible." In 2008, as the number of U.S. combat deaths in Iraq passed 4,000, President Bush acknowledged that the conflict was "longer and harder and more costly than we anticipated." During 2008 over 60 percent of Americans said that going to war in Iraq had been a mistake.

The "surge"

An Iraqi reads a pamphlet asking for information on insurgents, handed to him by U.S. troops brought to Baghdad in an attempt to bring security to the city.

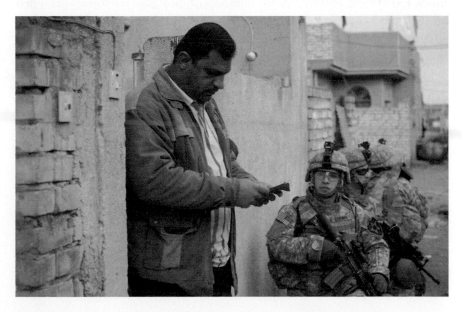

ECONOMIC WOES   After the intense but brief 2001 recession, the American economy had begun a period of prolonged expansion. Prosperity was fueled primarily by a prolonged housing boom, ultra-low interest and mortgage rates, easy credit, and reckless consumer spending. Home values across the nation had risen at rates that were unprecedented—and, as it turned out, unsustainable. Between 1997 and 2006, home prices in the United States, especially in the Sunbelt states, rose 85 percent, leading to a frenzy of irresponsible lending and building—and a debt-fueled consumer spending spree. Tens of millions of people bought houses that were more expensive than they could afford, refinanced their mortgages, or tapped home-equity loans to make discretionary purchases. The irrational confidence in soaring housing prices also led government regulatory agencies and mortgage lenders to ease credit restrictions so that more people could buy homes. Predatory lenders offered an array of so-called subprime loans with low initial "teaser" rates to home buyers with weak credit ratings and a low annual income. Investment banks and brokerage firms exacerbated the housing bubble by buying and selling bundles of home mortgages and other complex financial instruments, which they marketed as safe forms of "securitized" investments.

Such mortgage-backed securities were viable assets as long as home prices kept rising faster than personal income. In 2007, however, home values and housing sales began a precipitous decline. By the fall of 2007, the housing bubble had burst. Sales of new homes plummeted—as did asking prices. During 2008 the loss of trillions of dollars in home-equity value set off a seismic shock across the economy. Record numbers of mortgage borrowers defaulted on their payments. Foreclosures soared, adding to the glut of homes for sale and further reducing home prices. Banks lost billions, first on shaky subprime mortgages, then on most other categories of debt: credit cards, car loans, student loans, and an array of commercial mortgage-backed securities.

Capitalism depends on access to capital; short-term credit is the lifeblood of the economy. In 2008, however, the nation's credit supply froze up. Concerned about their own insolvency as well as their ability to gauge credit risks, banks essentially stopped lending—to the public and to each other. So people stopped buying; businesses stopped selling; industries slashed production and postponed investment. The sudden contraction of consumer credit, corporate spending, and consumer purchases triggered by the financial crisis pushed the economy into a deepening recession in 2008. The scale and suddenness of the slump caught economic experts and business leaders by surprise. Some of the nation's most prestigious banks, investment firms, and insurance companies went belly-up. The price of food and gasoline spiked. Unemployment soared. "Almost all businesses are in a survival mode," said one economist, "and they're slashing payrolls and investments. We're in store for some big job losses." Indeed, some two million jobs disappeared in 2008.

The high-flying stock market, itself fed by artificially low interest rates, began to tremble in September 2008; during October the bottom fell out. The Dow Jones Industrial Average lost a third of its value. Panic set in amid the turmoil. By late fall 2008 the United States was facing its greatest financial crisis since the Great Depression of the 1930s. What had begun as a decline in home prices had become a global economic meltdown—fed by the paralyzing fright of insecurity. No investment seemed safe. As people saw their retirement savings accounts gutted, they were left confused, anxious, and angry. A Missouri couple expressed a common concern: "We were always optimistic when we were young. We thought that every year, things would get better." Now the bubble had burst. Even Alan Greenspan, the former chairman of the Federal Reserve Board, found himself in a state of "shocked disbelief."

Amid what quickly became a global financial crisis, policy makers faced the challenge of shoring up the financial system and dealing with the social effects (panic) of a deepening recession. The crisis demanded decisive action.

The financial bailout

President Bush (left) and Treasury Secretary Henry Paulson speak to reporters from the steps of the Treasury Department after the House passed the $700 billion financial bailout bill (TARP).

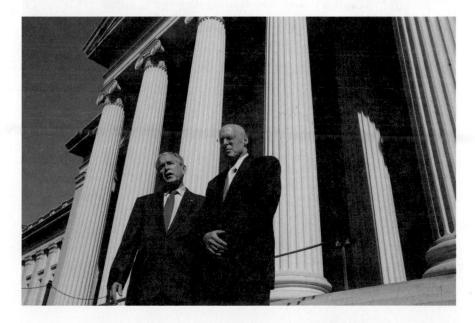

On October 3, 2008, after two weeks of contentious and often emotional congressional debate, President Bush signed into law a far-reaching historic bank bailout fund called the Troubled Asset Relief Program (TARP). The TARP called for the Treasury Department to spend $700 billion to keep banks and other financial institutions from collapsing. "By coming together on this legislation, we have acted boldly to prevent the crisis on Wall Street from becoming a crisis in communities across our country," Bush said after the House voted 263 to 171 to pass the TARP bill. Despite such unprecedented government investment in the private financial sector, the economy still sputtered. In early October, stock markets around the world began to crash. Economists warned that the world was at risk of careening into a depression.

A HISTORIC ELECTION

The economic crisis had potent political effects. As two preeminent economists noted, "In the eight years since George W. Bush took office, nearly every component of the U.S. economy has deteriorated." Budget

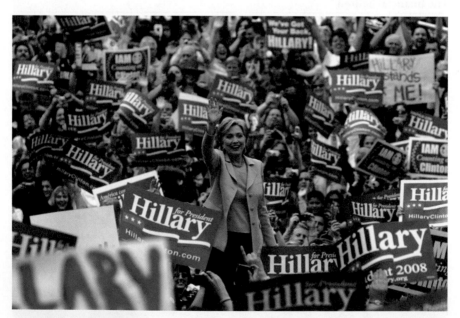

The Clinton campaign

Democratic presidential hopeful Senator Hillary Clinton speaks at the Fort Worth Stockyards.

deficits, trade deficits, and consumer debt had reached record levels, and the total expense of the American war in Iraq was projected to top $3 trillion. During the president's last year in office, just 29 percent of the voters "approved" of his leadership. And more than 80 percent said that the nation was headed in the "wrong direction." Even a prominent Republican strategist, Kevin Phillips, deemed Bush "perhaps the least competent president in modern history."

Bush's vulnerability excited Democrats about the possibility of regaining the White House in the 2008 election. As a journalist predicted in November 2007, "It looks highly likely that this will be the Democrats' year." Not only was the Bush presidency floundering, but the once-indomitable Republican party was in disarray, plagued by scandals, riven by factions, and lacking effective leadership. In 2004 the American electorate had been evenly divided by party identification: 43 percent for both the Democratic and the Republican parties. By 2008 the Democrats were leading the Republicans 50 percent to 35 percent.

The early front-runner for the Democratic nomination was New York senator Hillary Clinton, the highly visible spouse of ex-president Bill Clinton. Like her husband, she displayed an impressive command of policy issues and mobilized a well-funded campaign team. And as the first woman with a serious chance of gaining the presidency, she garnered widespread support among voters eager for female leadership. But in the end an overconfident Clinton was upset in the Democratic primaries and caucuses by little-known first-term senator Barack Obama of Illinois, an inspiring speaker who attracted huge crowds by promising a "politics of hope" and bolstering their

The Obama campaign

Democratic presidential hopeful, Senator Barack Obama waves to supporters at Waterfront Park in Portland, Oregon.

desire for "change." While the Clinton campaign courted the powerful members of the party establishment, Obama mounted an innovative Internet-based campaign directed at grassroots voters, donors, and volunteers. Obama was especially popular among young people. In early June, 2008, Obama gained enough delegates to secure the Democratic nomination.

Obama was the first African American presidential nominee of either party, the gifted biracial son of a white mother from Kansas and a black Kenyan father who left the household and returned to Africa when Barack was a toddler. The forty-seven-year-old Harvard Law School graduate and former professor, community organizer, and state legislator presented himself as a conciliator who could inspire and unite a diverse people and forge bipartisan collaborations.

Obama exuded poise, confidence, and energy. By contrast, his Republican opponent, seventy-two-year-old Arizona senator John McCain, was the oldest presidential candidate in history. The son and grandson of distinguished Navy admirals, McCain had graduated from the U.S. Naval Academy

The 2008 presidential debates

Republican presidential candidate John McCain (left) and Democratic presidential candidate Barack Obama (right) focused on foreign policy, national security, and the financial crisis at the first of three presidential debates.

before serving as a pilot in the Vietnam War. Captured after his plane was shot down, he spent over five years as a prisoner of war in Hanoi, suffering frequent torture. As a twenty-five-year veteran of Congress, a leading Republican senator, and a 2004 candidate for the Republican presidential nomination, he had developed a reputation as a bipartisan maverick willing to work with Democrats to achieve key legislative goals. McCain had voted against President Bush's tax cuts for the wealthy in 2001 and 2003, and he criticized the religious right for being "agents of intolerance."

Concerns about McCain's support among Republican conservatives led him to select Alaska governor Sarah Palin as his running mate, the first woman on a Republican ticket. Although hardly known outside party circles, Palin held the promise of winning over religious conservatives nervous about McCain's ideological purity. She opposed abortion, gay marriage (Obama opposed it too), and stem-cell research, and she endorsed the teaching of creationism in public schools. For his part, Barack Obama rejected calls to choose Hillary Clinton as his running mate. Instead, he selected veteran Delaware senator Joseph Biden.

THE 2008 ELECTION   The presidential campaign started in August 2008 with polls suggesting a very tight race. But the dramatic economic downturn in September and October gave Obama and the Democrats a powerful partisan weapon. Obama shrewdly capitalized on widespread dissatisfaction with the Republicans and centered his campaign on the echoing promise of "change." He repeatedly linked McCain with the unpopular George W. Bush. His pledge to avoid politics as usual and adopt a "post-partisan" approach resonated with voters tired of attack politics. Obama denounced the prevailing Republican "economic philosophy that says we should give more and more to those with the most and hope that prosperity trickles down to everyone else." He described the 2008 financial meltdown as the "final verdict on this failed philosophy."

While Obama's campaign projected a youthful, vibrant, energetic, disciplined, and consistent tone, John McCain struggled to define himself and his message. With each successive televised debate, the calm and confident Obama widened his lead. Meanwhile, as the editors of *Newsweek* magazine noted, the "U.S. economy went from being *an* issue in the presidential election to the *only* issue." With the country's finances in a tailspin, McCain made a clumsy statement in September—"the fundamentals of our economy are strong"—that would come back to haunt him. Within ten days, McCain reversed himself, announcing that the economic crisis was so serious that he needed to suspend his campaign in order to return to the Senate.

Election night rally

President-elect Barack Obama, his wife Michelle, and two daughters, Sasha and Malia wave to the crowd of supporters in Chicago's Grant Park.

Still floundering, he tried to refocus the campaign debate on his support for the Iraq War and the success of the "surge" strategy. Obama parried by promising a phased withdrawal of American forces. The Obama campaign also pledged to broaden health-insurance coverage, promote renewable energy, raise taxes on the wealthy, and get the economy growing again.

On November 4, 2008, Barack Obama made history by becoming the nation's first person of color elected president. "Change has come to America," he announced in his victory speech. His triumph was decisive and sweeping. The inspirational Obama won the popular vote by seven points: 53 percent to 46 percent. His margin in the electoral vote was even more impressive: 365 to 173. The president-elect won big among his core supporters—voters under age thirty, women, minorities, the very poor, and first-time voters. He collected 95 percent of the African American vote and 66 percent of voters aged eighteen to twenty-nine, and he won the Hispanic vote. Obama also helped the Democrats win solid majorities in the House and Senate races.

Within days of his electoral victory, Barack Obama had adopted a bipartisan approach in selecting his new cabinet members. He appointed Hillary

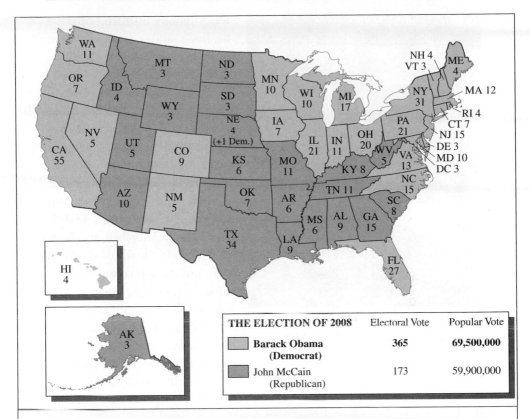

THE ELECTION OF 2008	Electoral Vote	Popular Vote
Barack Obama (Democrat)	**365**	**69,500,000**
John McCain (Republican)	173	59,900,000

How did the economic crisis affect the outcome of the election? What are the similarities and differences between the map of the 2004 election and the map of the 2008 election?

Clinton secretary of state, renewed Republican Robert Gates as secretary of defense, selected retired general James Jones, who had campaigned for McCain, as his national security adviser, and appointed Eric Holder as the nation's first African American attorney general.

THE FIRST ONE HUNDRED DAYS

On January 20, 2009, President Obama delivered a sobering inaugural address in frigid weather amid daunting challenges. The United States was embroiled in two wars, in Iraq and Afghanistan. The economy was in shambles, unemployment was soaring, and the national debt was hemorrhaging. Yet it

The Oath of Office

Barack Obama takes the oath as the forty-fourth President of the United States.

was Obama's inspiring promise of hope and change that led millions of spectators to crowd into Washington, D.C., to witness the historic swearing-in ceremony.

Like Franklin Roosevelt, a supremely self-confident Obama acted quickly—some said too quickly—to fulfill his campaign pledges. With a boldness and scope reminiscent of Ronald Reagan, Obama launched an audacious agenda. He would overhaul government regulations, reform education, energy, environmental, and health-care policies, restructure the tax code, invigorate the economy, and recast U.S. foreign policy. On his second day in office, he issued an executive order to begin a case-by-case review of all suspected terrorists being held at the U.S. detention center at the Guantánamo Bay Naval Base in Cuba. The prisoners were to be released or transferred to other prisons, and the detention center would be closed within a year. In March, Obama eased restrictions on the federal funding of human embryonic stem-cell research. His doing so outraged abortion opponents but pleased those who believe that stem-cell research can lead to medical cures for many diseases. Obama also lifted restrictions on American travel to Cuba that had been in place for nearly fifty years. And he offered to talk with the totalitarian leaders of Iran and North Korea, something his predecessors had refused to do.

REVIVING THE ECONOMY   The new Obama administration's main challenge was to keep the deepening recession from becoming a prolonged depression. Unemployment in early 2009 had passed 8 percent and was still rising. More than 5 million people had lost their jobs since 2007. The financial sector remained paralyzed. At the same time, U.S. military forces remained embroiled in the conflicts in Iraq and Afghanistan. Like Franklin Roosevelt, Obama wanted to be a "transformative" president. To do so, he needed to move swiftly to enact his ambitious agenda while still enjoying widespread public support. Like Roosevelt in 1933, the new president sought to restore public confidence during these "difficult and uncertain times" by acting "boldly and wisely" to fulfill his campaign pledges and stimulate the stagnant economy. He assured the nation that "we will rebuild, we will recover."

In mid-February, after a prolonged and often strident debate, Congress passed, and Obama signed, a $787-billion economic stimulus bill—the largest in history—called the American Recovery and Reinvestment Act. The gargantuan bill (over 1,000 pages long) included cash distributions to the states, funds for food stamps, unemployment benefits, construction projects to renew the nation's infrastructure (roads, bridges, levees, government buildings, and the electricity grid), funds for renewable-energy systems, and tax reductions. But the passage of the stimulus bill showed no evidence that Obama was successful in implementing a "bipartisan" presidency. Only three Senate Republicans voted for the bill. Not a single House Republican voted for it, and eleven House Democrats opposed it as well. In February, Obama continued his calibrated boldness by ordering the Treasury Department to implement tax cuts for 95 percent of Americans (all but the most wealthy), and he announced plans to let the tax cuts for the rich implemented by George W. Bush expire in 2010. During the summer of 2009, Congressional Democrats began working with the White House to develop the two largest and most controversial of Obama's proposals: health-care reform and climate-change legislation.

LEAVING IRAQ? President Obama announced on February 27, 2009, that all U.S. combat troops would be withdrawn from Iraq by the end of 2011. A "transitional force" of 35,000 to 50,000 troops would assist Iraqi security forces, protect Americans and fight terrorism, Obama said. "The drawdown of our military should send a clear signal that Iraq's future is now its own responsibility. The long-term success of the Iraqi nation will depend on decisions made by Iraq's leaders and the fortitude of the Iraqi people," Obama said. At the same time that he was reducing U.S. military involvement in Iraq, Obama dispatched 21,000 additional troops to Afghanistan, which he called "ground zero" in the battle against terrorism. Obama's Iraqi withdrawal plan prompted many hard questions: Did his timetable provide enough time for Iraqis to forge a self-reliant government and economy? Could the U.S. withdrawal trigger a civil war between Sunnis and Shiites? Only time would tell.

CHAPTER SUMMARY

- **Changing Demographics** From 1980 to 2009 the population of the United States grew by 20 percent to 290 million. The South and the West lured residents from the Midwest and the Northeast. The number of traditional family units continued to decline; the poverty rate was especially high among African Americans. A wave of immigrants caused Latinos to surpass African Americans as the nation's largest minority.

- **Divided Government** The popularity of President George H. W. Bush waned after the Gulf War an economic recession, and his decision to raise taxes. The election of William Jefferson Clinton and the Democratic victory was short-lived, however. Speaker Newt Gingrich mobilized the Christian Coalition against "liberalism" with his Contract with America to achieve the Republican landslide of 1994.

- **Economic Prosperity and Crises** The United States benefited from a period of unprecedented prosperity during the 1990s, fueled by the dramatic effect of the new computer-based industries on the economy. The collapse of high-tech companies in 2000 betrayed the underlying insecurity of the market. Economic growth soon surged again primarily because of consumers' ability to borrow against the skyrocketing value of their home mortgages. In 2007 the country experienced an unparalleled crisis when the global financial markets collapsed under the weight of "toxic" financial securities.

- **Global Terrorism** The September 11 attacks led President George W. Bush to declare a war on terrorism and enunciate the Bush Doctrine. In 2002 the Bush administration shifted its focus to Saddam Hussein. The American-led Operation Iraqi Freedom succeeded in removing Hussein from power but was fully unprepared to establish order in a country that was soon riven by sectarian violence. The American public became bitterly divided over the Iraq War.

- **2008 Presidential Election** The 2008 presidential campaigns included the first major female candidate, Senator Hillary Clinton; an African American, Senator Barack Obama; and Senator John McCain, the oldest candidate in history. Obama won the popular vote and a landslide victory in the Electoral College, becoming the nation's first African American president. His victory was fueled by the collapse of the economy, an unprecedented Internet- and grassroots-based campaign, and voters' weariness with President Bush and the Republican policies of the preceding eight years.

GLOSSARY

36°30' According to the Missouri Compromise, any part of the Louisiana Purchase north of this line (Missouri's southern border) was to be excluded from slavery.

54th Massachusetts Regiment After President Abraham Lincoln's Emancipation Proclamation, the Union army organized all black military units, which white officers led. The 54th Massachusetts Regiment was one of the first of such units to be organized.

Abigail Adams (1744–1818) As the wife of John Adams, she endured long periods of separation from him while he served in many political roles. During these times apart, she wrote often to her husband; and their correspondence has provided a detailed portrait of life during the Revolutionary War.

abolition In the early 1830s, the anti-slavery movement shifted its goal from the gradual end of slavery to the immediate end or abolition of slavery.

John Adams (1735–1826) He was a signer of the Declaration of Independence and a delegate to the First and Second Continental Congress. During the Revolutionary War, he worked as a diplomat in France and Holland and negotiated the peace treaty with Britain. After the Revolutionary War, he served as the minister to Britain as well as the vice president and the second president of the United States. As president, he passed the Alien and Sedition Acts and endured a stormy relationship with France, which included the XYZ affair.

John Quincy Adams (1767–1848) As secretary of state under President Monroe, he negotiated agreements to define the boundaries of the Oregon country and the Transcontinental Treaty. He urged President Monroe to issue the Monroe Doctrine, which incorporated Adams's views. As president, Adams envisioned an expanded federal government and a broader use of federal powers. Adams's nationalism and praise of European leaders caused a split in his party. Some Republicans suspected him of being a closet monarchist and left to form the Democrat party. In the presidential election 1828, Andrew Jackson claimed that Adams had gained the presidency through a "corrupt bargain" with Henry Clay, which helped Jackson win the election.

Samuel Adams (1722–1803) A genius of revolutionary agitation, he believed that English Parliament had no right to legislate for the colonies. He organized the Sons of Liberty as well as protests in Boston against the British.

Jane Addams (1860–1935) As the leader of one of the best known settlement houses, she rejected the "do-goodism" spirit of religious reformers. Instead, she focused on solving the practical problems of the poor and tried to avoid the assumption that she and other social workers knew what was best for poor immigrants. She established child care for working mothers, health clinics, job training, and other social programs. She was also active in the peace movement and was awarded the Noble Peace Prize in 1931 for her work on its behalf.

Agricultural Adjustment Act (1933) New Deal legislation that established the Agricultural Adjustment Administration (AAA) to improve agricultural prices by limiting market supplies; declared unconstitutional in *United States v. Butler* (1936).

Emilio Aguinaldo (1869?–1964) He was a leader in Filipino struggle for independence. During the war of 1898, Commodore George Dewey brought Aguinaldo back to the Philippines from exile to help fight the Spanish. However, after the Spanish surrendered to Americans, America annexed the Philippines and Aguinaldo fought against the American military until he was captured in 1901.

Alamo, Battle of the Siege in the Texas War for Independence of 1836, in which the San Antonio mission fell to the Mexicans. Davy Crockett and Jim Bowie were among the courageous defenders.

Alien and Sedition Acts (1798) Four measures passed during the undeclared war with France that limited the freedoms of speech and press and restricted the liberty of noncitizens.

American Federation of Labor Founded in 1881 as a federation of trade unions made up of skilled workers, the AFL under president Samuel Gompers successfully pushed for the eight-hour workday.

American Indian Movement Fed up with the poor conditions on Indian reservations and the federal government's unwillingness to help, Native Americans founded the American Indian Movement (AIM) in 1963. In 1973, AIM led 200 Sioux in the occupation of Wounded Knee. After a ten-week standoff with the federal authorities, the government agreed to reexamine Indian treaty rights and the occupation ended.

American Protective Association Nativist, anti-Catholic secret society founded in Iowa in 1887 and active until the end of the century.

American Recovery and Reinvestment Act Hoping to restart the weak economy, President Obama signed this $787-billion economic stimulus bill in February of 2009. The bill included cash distributions to states, funds for food stamps, unemployment benefits, construction projects to renew the nation's infrastructure, funds for renewable-energy systems, and tax reductions.

American System Program of internal improvements and protective tariffs promoted by Speaker of the House Henry Clay in his presidential campaign of 1824; his proposals formed the core of Whig ideology in the 1830s and 1840s.

anaconda strategy Union General Winfield Scott developed this three-pronged strategy to defeat the Confederacy. Like a snake strangling its prey, the Union army would crush its enemy through exerting pressure on Richmond, blockading Confederate ports, and dividing the South by invading its major waterways.

Annapolis Convention In 1786, all thirteen colonies were invited to a convention in Annapolis to discuss commercial problems, but only representatives from five states attended. However, the convention was not a complete failure because the delegates decided to have another convention in order to write the constitution.

anti-Federalists Forerunners of Thomas Jefferson's Democratic-Republican party; opposed the Constitution as a limitation on individual and states' rights, which led to the addition of a Bill of Rights to the document.

Anti-Masonic party This party grew out of popular hostility toward the Masonic fraternal order and entered the presidential election of 1832 as a third party. It was the first party to run as a third party in a presidential election as well as the first to hold a nomination convention and announce a party platform.

Benedict Arnold (1741–1801) A traitorous American commander who planned to sell out the American garrison at West Point to the British, but his plot was discovered before it could be executed and he joined the British army.

Atlanta Compromise Speech to the Cotton States and International Exposition in 1895 by educator Booker T. Washington, the leading black spokesman of the day; black scholar W. E. B. Du Bois gave the speech its derisive name and criticized Washington for encouraging blacks to accommodate segregation and disenfranchisement.

Atlantic Charter Issued August 12, 1941, following meetings in Newfoundland between President Franklin D. Roosevelt and British Prime Minister Winston Churchill, the charter signaled the allies' cooperation and stated their war aims.

Crispus Attucks (1723–1770) During the Boston Massacre, he was supposedly at the head of the crowd of hecklers who baited the British troops. He was killed when the British troops fired on the crowd.

Stephen F. Austin (1793–1836) He established the first colony of Americans in Texas, which eventually attracted 2,000 people.

Axis powers In World War II, the nations of Germany, Italy, and Japan.

Aztec Empire Mesoamerican people who were conquered by the Spanish under Hernando Cortés, 1519–1528.

baby boom Markedly higher birth rate in the years following World War II; led to the biggest demographic "bubble" in American history.

Bacon's Rebellion Unsuccessful 1676 revolt led by planter Nathaniel Bacon against Virginia governor William Berkeley's administration, because it had failed to protect settlers from Indian raids.

Bank of the United States Proposed by the first Secretary of the Treasury Alexander Hamilton, the bank opened in 1791 and operated until 1811 to issue a uniform currency, make business loans, and collect tax monies. The second Bank of the United States was chartered in 1816 but was not renewed by President Andrew Jackson twenty years later.

barbary pirates Plundering pirates off the Mediterranean coast of Africa; President Thomas Jefferson's refusal to pay them tribute to protect

American ships sparked an undeclared naval war with North African nations, 1801–1805.

Battle of the Bulge On December 16, 1944, the German army launched a counter attack against the Allied forces, which pushed them back. However, the Allies were eventually able to recover and breakthrough the German lines. This defeat was a great blow to the Nazi's morale and their army's strength. The battle used up the last of Hitler's reserve units and opened a route into Germany's heartland.

Bear Flag Republic On June 14, 1846, a group of Americans in California captured Sonoma from the Mexican army and declared it the Republic of California whose flag featured a grizzly bear. In July, the commodore of the U.S. Pacific Fleet landed troops on California's shores and declared it part of the United States.

Beats A group of writers, artists, and musicians whose central concern was the discarding of organizational constraints and traditional conventions in favor of liberated forms of self expression. They came out of the bohemian underground in New York's Greenwich Village in the 1950s and included the writers Jack Kerouac, Allen Ginsberg, and William Burroughs. Their attitudes and lifestyles had a major influence on the youth of the 1960s.

beatnik A name referring to almost any young rebel who openly dissented from the middle class life. The name itself stems from the Beats.

Nicholas Biddle (1786–1844) He was the president of the second Bank of the United States. In response to President Andrew Jackson's attacks on the bank, Biddle curtailed the bank's loans and exchanged its paper currency for gold and silver. He was hoping to provoke an economic crisis to prove the bank's importance. In response, state banks began printing paper without restraint and lent it to speculators, causing a binge in speculating and an enormous increase in debt.

Bill of Rights First ten amendments to the U.S. Constitution, adopted in 1791 to guarantee individual rights and to help secure ratification of the Constitution by the states.

Osama bin Laden (1957–) He is the leader of al Qaeda whose members attacked America on September 11, 2001. Years before the attack, he had declared *jihad* (holy war) on the United States, Israel, and the Saudi monarchy. In Afghanistan, the Taliban leaders gave Osama bin Laden a safe haven in exchange for aid in fighting the Northern Alliance, who were rebels opposed to the Taliban. After the 9/11 terrorist attacks, the United States asked the Taliban to turn over bin Laden. Following their refusal, America and multinational coalition invaded Afghanistan and overthrew the Taliban, but they did not capture bin Laden.

black codes Laws passed in southern states to restrict the rights of former slaves; to combat the codes, Congress passed the Civil Rights Act of 1866 and the Fourteenth Amendment and set up military governments in southern states that refused to ratify the amendment.

black power A more militant form of protest for civil rights that originated in urban communities, where nonviolent tactics were less effective than in the South. Black power encouraged African Americans to take pride in their racial heritage and forced black leaders and organizations to focus attention on the plight of poor inner-city blacks.

James Gillepsie Blaine (1830–1893) As a Republican congressman from Maine, he developed close ties with business leaders, which contributed to him losing the presidential election of 1884. He later opposed President Cleveland's efforts to reduce tariffs, which became a significant issue in the 1888 presidential election. Blaine served as secretary of state under President Benjamin Harrison and his flamboyant style often overshadowed the president.

"bleeding" Kansas Violence between pro- and antislavery settlers in the Kansas Territory, 1856.

blitzkrieg The German "lightening war" strategy used during World War II; the Germans invaded Poland, France, Russia, and other countries with fast-moving, well-coordinated attacks using aircraft, tanks, and other armored vehicles, followed by infantry.

Bolsheviks Under the leadership of Vladimir Lenin, this Marxist party led the November 1917 revolution against the newly formed provisional government in Russia. After seizing control, the Bolsheviks negotiated a peace treaty with Germany, the Treaty of Brest-Litovsk, and ended their participation in World War I.

Bonus Expeditionary Force Thousands of World War I veterans, who insisted on immediate payment of their bonus certificates, marched on Washington in 1932; violence ensued when President Herbert Hoover ordered their tent villages cleared.

Daniel Boone (1734–1820) He found and expanded a trail into Kentucky, which pioneers used to reach and settle the area.

John Wilkes Booth (1838?–1865) He assassinated President Abraham Lincoln at the Ford's Theater on April 14, 1865. He was pursued to Virginia and killed.

Bourbons In post–Civil War southern politics, the opponents of the Redeemers were called Bourbons. They were known for having forgotten nothing and learned nothing from the ordeal of the Civil War.

Joseph Brant (1742?–1807) He was the Mohawk leader who led the Iroquois against the Americans in the Revolutionary War.

brinkmanship Secretary of State John Foster Dulles believed that communism could be contained by bringing America to the brink of war with an aggressive communist nation. He believed that the aggressor would back down when confronted with the prospect of receiving a mass retaliation from a country with nuclear weapons.

John Brown (1800–1859) He was willing to use violence to further his antislavery beliefs. In 1856, a pro-slavery mob sacked the free-state town of Lawrence, Kansas. In response, John Brown went to the pro-slavery settlement of Pottawatomie, Kansas and hacked to death several people, which led to a guerrilla war in the Kansas territory. In 1859, he attempted to raid the federal arsenal at Harpers Ferry. He had hoped to use the stolen weapons to arm slaves, but he was captured and executed. His failed raid instilled panic throughout the South, and his execution turned him into a martyr for his cause.

***Brown v. Board of Education of Topeka* (1954)** U.S. Supreme Court decision that struck down racial segregation in public education and declared "separate but equal" unconstitutional.

William Jennings Bryan (1860–1925) He delivered the pro-silver "cross of gold" speech at the 1896 Democratic Convention and won his party's nomination for president. Disappointed pro-gold Democrats chose to walk out of the convention and nominate their own candidate, which split the Democratic party and cost them the White House. Bryan's loss also crippled the Populist movement that had endorsed him.

"Bull Moose" Progressive party In the 1912 election, Theodore Roosevelt was unable to secure the Republican nomination for president. He left the Republican party and formed his own party of progressive Republicans, called the "Bull Moose" party. Roosevelt and Taft split the Republican vote, which allowed Democrat Woodrow Wilson to win.

Bull Run, Battles of (First and Second Manassas) First land engagement of the Civil War took place on July 21, 1861, at Manassas Junction, Virginia, at which surprised Union troops quickly retreated; one year later, on August 29–30, Confederates captured the federal supply depot and forced Union troops back to Washington.

Martin Van Buren (1782–1862) During President Jackson's first term, he served as secretary of state and minister to London. He often politically fought Vice President John C. Calhoun for the position of Jackson's successor. A rift between Jackson and Calhoun led to Van Buren becoming vice president during Jackson's second term. In 1836, Van Buren was elected president, and he inherited a financial crisis. He believed that the government should not continue to keep its deposits in state banks and set up an independent Treasury, which was approved by Congress after several years of political maneuvering.

General John Burgoyne (1722–1792) He was the commander of Britain's northern forces during the Revolutionary War. He and most of his troops surrendered to the Americans at the Battle of Saratoga.

burned-over district Area of western New York strongly influenced by the revivalist fervor of the Second Great Awakening; Disciples of Christ and Mormons are among the many sects that trace their roots to the phenomenon.

Aaron Burr (1756–1836) Even though he was Thomas Jefferson's vice president, he lost favor with Jefferson's supporters who were Republicans. He sought to work with the Federalists and run as their candidate for the governor of New York. Alexander Hamilton opposed Burr's candidacy and his stinging remarks on the subject led to Burr challenging him to duel in which Hamilton was killed.

George H. W. Bush (1924–) He had served as vice president during the Reagan administration and then won the presidential election of 1988. During his presidential campaign, Bush promised not to raise taxes. However, the federal deficit had become so big that he had to raise taxes. Bush chose to make fighting illegal drugs a priority. He created the Office of National Drug Control Policy, but it was only moderately successful in stopping drug use. In 1989, Bush ordered the invasion of Panama and the capture of Panamanian leader Manuel Noriega, who was wanted in America on drug charges. He was captured, tried, and convicted. In 1990, Saddam Hussein invaded Kuwait; and Bush sent the American military to Saudi Arabia on a defensive mission. He assembled a multinational force and launched Operation Desert Storm, which took Kuwait back from Saddam in 1991. The euphoria over the victory in Kuwait was short lived as the country slid into a recession. He lost the 1992 presidential election to Bill Clinton.

George W. Bush (1946-) In the 2000 presidential election, Texas governor George W. Bush ran as the Republican nominee against Democratic nominee Vice President Al Gore. The election ended in controversy over the final vote tally in Florida. Bush had slightly more votes, but a recount was required by state law. However, it was stopped by Supreme Court and Bush was declared president. After the September 11 terrorist attacks, he launched his "war on terrorism." President George W. Bush adapted the Bush Doctrine, which claimed the right to launch preemptive military attacks against enemies. The United States invaded Afghanistan and Iraq with unclear outcomes leaving the countries divided. In the summer of 2006, Hurricane Katrina struck the Gulf Coast and left destruction across several states and three-quarters of New Orleans flooded. Bush was attacked for the unpreparedness of the federal government to handle the disaster as well as his own slowness to react. In September 2008, the nation's economy nosedived as a credit crunch spiraled into a global economic meltdown. Bush signed into law the bank bailout fund called Troubled Asset Relief Program (TARP), but the economy did not improve.

Bush Doctrine Believing that America's enemies were now terrorist groups and unstable rogue nations, President George W. Bush adapted a foreign policy that claimed the right to launch preemptive military attacks against enemies.

***Bush v. Gore* (2000)** The close 2000 presidential election came down to Florida's decisive twenty-five electoral votes. The final tally in Florida gave Bush a slight lead, but it was so small that a recount was required by state law. While the votes were being recounted, a legal battle was being waged to stop the recount. Finally, the case, *Bush v. Gore*, was present to the Supreme Court who ruled 5–4 to stop the recount and Bush was declared the winner.

buying (stock) on margin The investment practice of making a small down payment (the "margin") on a stock and borrowing the rest of money need for the purchase from a broker who held the stock as security against a down market. If the stock's value declined and the buyer failed to meet a margin call for more funds, the broker could sell the stock to cover his loan.

John C. Calhoun (1782–1850) He served in both the House of Representatives and the Senate for South Carolina before becoming secretary of war under President Monroe and then John Quincy Adams's vice president. He introduced the bill for the second national bank to Congress and led the minority of southerners who voted for the Tariff of 1816. However, he later chose to oppose tariffs. During his time as secretary of war under President Monroe, he authorized the use of federal troops against the Seminoles who were attacking settlers. As John Quincy Adams's vice president, he supported a new tariffs bill to win presidential candidate Andrew Jackson additional support. Jackson won the election, but the new tariffs bill passed and Calhoun had to explain why he had changed his opinion on tariffs.

Camp David Accords Peace agreement between Israeli Prime Minister Menachem Begin and Egyptian President Anwar Sadat, brokered by President Jimmy Carter in 1978.

"Scarface" Al Capone (1899–1947) He was the most successful gangster of the Prohibition era whose Chicago-based criminal empire included bootlegging, prostitution, and gambling.

Andrew Carnegie (1835–1919) He was a steel magnate who believed that the general public benefited from big business even if these companies employed harsh business practices. This philosophy became deeply ingrained in the conventional wisdom of some Americans. After retiring, he devoted himself to philanthropy in hopes of promoting social welfare and world peace.

carpetbaggers Northern emigrants who participated in the Republican governments of the reconstructed South.

Jimmy Carter (1924–) Jimmy Carter, an outsider to Washington, capitalized on the post-Watergate cynicism and won the 1976 presidential election. He created departments of Energy and Education and signed into law several environmental initiatives. However, his efforts to support the Panama Canal Treaties and his unwillingness to make deals with legislators caused other bills to be either gutted or stalled in Congress. Despite his efforts to improve the economy, the recession continued and inflation increased. In 1978, he successfully brokered a peace agreement between Israel and Egypt called the Camp David Accords. Then his administration was plagued with a series of crises. Fighting in the Middle East produced a fuel shortage in the United States. The Soviets invaded Afghanistan and Carter responded with the suspension of an arms-control treaty with the Soviets, the halting of grain shipments to the Soviet Union, and a call for a boycott of the Olympic Games in Moscow. In Iran, revolutionaries toppled the shah's government and seized the American embassy, taking hostage those inside. Carter struggled to get the hostages released and was unable to do so until after he lost the 1980 election to Ronald Reagan. He was awarded the Nobel Peace Prize in 2002 for his efforts to further peace and democratic elections around the world.

Jacques Cartier (1491–1557) He led the first French effort to colonize North America and explored the Gulf of St. Lawrence and reached as far as present day Montreal on the St. Lawrence River.

Bartolomé de Las Casas (1484–1566) A Catholic missionary who renounced the Spanish practice of coercively converting Indians and advocated the better treatment for them. In 1552, he wrote *A Brief Relation of the Destruction of the Indies*, which described the Spanish's cruel treatment of the Indians.

Fidel Castro (1926–) In 1959, his Communist regime came to power in Cuba after two years of guerrilla warfare against the dictator Fulgenico Batista. He enacted land redistribution programs and nationalized all foreign-owned property. The latter action as well as his political trials and summary executions damaged relations between Cuba and America. Castro was turned down when he asked for loans from the United States. However, he did receive aid from the Soviet Union.

Carrie Chapman Catt (1859–1947) She was a leader of a new generation of activists in the women's suffrage movement who carried on the work started by Elizabeth Cady Stanton and Susan B. Anthony.

Cesar Chavez (1927–1993) He founded the United Farm Workers (UFW) in 1962 and worked to organize migrant farm workers. In 1965, the UFW joined Filipino farm workers striking against corporate grape farmers in California's San Joaquin Valley. In 1970, the strike and a consumer boycott on grapes compelled the farmers to formally recognize the UFW. As the result of Chavez's efforts, wages and working conditions improved for migrant workers. In 1975, the California state legislature passed a bill that required growers to bargain collectively with representatives of the farm workers.

Chinese Exclusion Act (1882) The first federal law to restrict immigration on the basis of race and class. Passed in 1882, the act halted Chinese immigration for ten years, but it was periodically renewed and then indefinitely extended in 1902. Not until 1943 were the barriers to Chinese immigration finally removed.

Church of Jesus Christ of Latter-day Saints / Mormons Founded in 1830 by Joseph Smith, the sect was a product of the intense revivalism of the burned-over district of New York; Smith's successor Brigham Young led 15,000 followers to Utah in 1847 to escape persecution.

Winston Churchill (1874–1965) The British prime minister who led the country during World War II. Along with Roosevelt and Stalin, he helped shape the post-war world at the Yalta Conference. He also coined the term "iron curtain," which he used in his famous "The Sinews of Peace" speech.

"city machines" Local political party officials used these organizations to dispense patronage and favoritism amongst voters and businesses to ensure their loyal support to the political party.

Civil Rights Act of 1957 First federal civil rights law since Reconstruction; established the Civil Rights Commission and the Civil Rights Division of the Department of Justice.

Civil Rights Act of 1964 Outlawed discrimination in public accommodations and employment.

Henry Clay (1777–1852) In the first half of the nineteenth century, he was the foremost spokesman for the American system. As speaker of the House in the 1820s, he promoted economic nationalism, "market revolution," and the rapid development of western states and territories. He formulated the "second" Missouri Compromise, which denied the Missouri state legislature the power to exclude the rights of free blacks and mulattos. In the deadlocked presidential election of 1824, the House of Representatives decided the election. Clay supported John Quincy Adams, who won the presidency and appointed Clay to secretary of state. Andrew Jackson claimed that Clay had entered into a "corrupt bargain" with Adams for his own selfish gains.

Hillary Rodham Clinton (1947–) In the 2008 presidential election, Senator Hillary Clinton, the spouse of former President Bill Clinton, initially was the front-runner for the Democratic nomination, which made her the first woman with a serious chance to win the presidency. However,

Senator Barack Obama's Internet-based and grassroots-orientated campaign garnered him enough delegates to win the nomination. After Obama became president, she was appointed secretary of state.

William Jefferson Clinton (1946–) The governor of Arkansas won the 1992 presidential election against President George H. W. Bush. In his first term, he pushed through Congress a tax increase, an economic stimulus package, the adoption of the North America Free Trade Agreement, welfare reform, a raise in the minimum wage, and improved public access to health insurance. However, he failed to institute major health-care reform, which had been one of his major goals. In 1996, Clinton defeated Republican presidential candidate Bob Dole. Clinton was scrutinized for his investment in the fraudulent Whitewater Development Corporation, but no evidence was found of him being involved in any wrongdoing. In 1998, he was revealed to have had a sexual affair with a White House intern. Clinton had initially lied about the affair and tried to cover up it, which led to a vote in Congress on whether or not to begin an impeachment inquiry. The House of Representatives voted to impeach Clinton, but the Senate found him not guilty. Clinton's presidency faced several foreign policy challenges. In 1994, he used U.S. forces to restore Haiti's democratically elected president to power after he had been ousted during a coup. In 1995, the Clinton Administration negotiated the Dayton Accords, which stopped the ethnic strife in the former Yugoslavia and the Balkan region. Clinton sponsored peace talks between Arabs and Israelis, which culminated in Israeli Prime Minister Yitzhak Rabin and the Palestine Liberation Organization leader Yasir Arafat signing the Oslo Accords in 1993. This agreement provided for the restoration of Palestinian self-rule in specific areas in exchange for peace as provided in UN Security Council resolutions.

Coercive Acts / Intolerable Acts (1774) Four parliamentary measures in reaction to the Boston Tea Party that forced payment for the tea, disallowed colonial trials of British soldiers, forced their quartering in private homes, and set up a military government.

coffin ships Irish immigrants fleeing the potato famine had to endure a six-week journey across the Atlantic to reach America. During these voyages, thousands of passengers died of disease and starvation, which led to the ships being called "coffin ships."

Christopher Columbus (1451–1506) The Italian sailor who persuaded King Ferdinand and Queen Isabella of Spain to fund his expedition across the Atlantic to discover a new trade route to Asia. Instead of arriving at China or Japan, he reached the Bahamas in 1492.

Committee on Public Information During World War I, this committee produced war propaganda that conveyed the Allies' war aims to Americans as well as attempted to weaken the enemy's morale.

Committee to Re-elect the President (CREEP) During Nixon's presidency, his administration engaged in a number of immoral acts, such as attempting to steal information and falsely accusing political appointments of sexual improprieties. These acts were funded by money illegally collected through CREEP.

Thomas Paine's *Common Sense* This pamphlet refocused the blame for the colonies' problems on King George III rather than on Parliament and advocated a declaration of independence, which few colonialists had considered prior to its appearance.

Compromise of 1850 Complex compromise mediated by Senator Henry Clay that headed off southern secession over California statehood; to appease the South it included a stronger fugitive slave law and delayed determination of the slave status of the New Mexico and Utah territories.

Compromise of 1877 Deal made by a special congressional commission on March 2, 1877, to resolve the disputed presidential election of 1876; Republican Rutherford B. Hayes, who had lost the popular vote, was declared the winner in exchange for the withdrawal of federal troops from the South, marking the end of Reconstruction.

Conestoga wagons These large horse-drawn wagons were used to carry people or heavy freight long distances, including from the East to the western frontier settlements.

conquistadores Spanish term for "conqueror," applied to European leaders of campaigns against indigenous peoples in central and southern America.

consumer culture In the post-World War II era, affluence seemed to be forever increasing in America. At the same time, there was a boom in construction as well as products and appliances for Americans to buy. As a result, shopping became a major recreational activity. Americans started spending more, saving less, and building more shopping centers.

containment U.S. strategy in the cold war that called for containing Soviet expansion; originally devised in 1947 by U.S. diplomat George F. Kennan.

Continental army Army authorized by the Continental Congress, 1775–1784, to fight the British; commanded by General George Washington.

Contras The Reagan administration ordered the CIA to train and supply guerrilla bands of anti-Communist Nicaraguans called Contras. They were fighting the Sandinista government that had recently come to power in Nicaragua. The State Department believed that the Sandinista government was supplying the leftist Salvadoran rebels with Soviet and Cuban arms. A cease-fire agreement between the Contras and Sandinistas was signed in 1988.

Calvin Coolidge "Silent Cal" (1872–1933) After President Harding's death, his vice president, Calvin Coolidge, assumed the presidency. Coolidge believed that the nation's welfare was tied to the success of big business, and he worked to end government regulation of business and industry as well as reduce taxes. In particular, he focused on the nation's industrial development.

Hernán Cortés (1485–1547) The Spanish conquistador who conquered the Aztec Empire and set the precedent for other plundering conquistadores.

General Charles Cornwallis (1738–1805) He was in charge of British troops in the South during the Revolutionary War. His surrendering to George Washington at the Battle of Yorktown ended the Revolutionary War.

Corps of Discovery Meriwether Lewis and William Clark led this group of men on an expedition of the newly purchased Louisiana territory, which took them from Missouri to Oregon. As they traveled, they kept detailed journals and drew maps of the previously unexplored territory. Their reports attracted traders and trappers to the region and gave the United States a claim to the Oregon country by right of discovery and exploration.

"corrupt bargain" A vote in the House of Representatives decided the deadlocked presidential election of 1824 in favor of John Quincy Adams, who Speaker of the House Henry Clay had supported. Afterward, Adams appointed Clay secretary of state. Andrew Jackson charged Clay with having made a "corrupt bargain" with Adams that gave Adams the presidency and Clay a place in his administration. There was no evidence of such a deal, but it was widely believed.

the counterculture "Hippie" youth culture of the 1960s, which rejected the values of the dominant culture in favor of illicit drugs, communes, free sex, and rock music.

court-packing plan President Franklin D. Roosevelt's failed 1937 attempt to increase the number of U.S. Supreme Court justices from nine to fifteen in order to save his Second New Deal programs from constitutional challenges.

covenant theory A Puritan concept that believed true Christians could enter a voluntary union for the common worship of God. Taking the idea one step further, the union could also be used for the purposes of establishing governments.

Coxey's Army Jacob S. Coxey, a Populist, led this protest group that demanded the federal government provide the unemployed with meaningful employment. In 1894, Coxey's Army joined other protests groups in a march on Washington D.C. The combination of the march and the growing support of Populism scared many Americans.

Credit Mobilier scandal Construction company guilt of massive overcharges for building the Union Pacific Railroad were exposed; high officials of the Ulysses S. Grant administration were implicated but never charged.

George Creel (1876–1953) He convinced President Woodrow Wilson that the best approach to influencing public opinion was through propaganda rather than censorship. As the executive head of the Committee on Public Information, he produced propaganda that conveyed the Allies' war aims.

"Cross of Gold" Speech In the 1896 election, the Democratic party split over the issue of whether to use gold or silver to back American currency. Significant to this division was the "Cross of Gold" speech that William Jennings Bryan delivered at the Democratic convention. This pro-silver speech was so well received that Bryan won the nomination to be their presidential candidate. Disappointed pro-gold Democrats chose to walk out of the convention and nominate their own candidate.

Cuban missile crisis Caused when the United States discovered Soviet offensive missile sites in Cuba in October 1962; the U.S.–Soviet confrontation was the cold war's closest brush with nuclear war.

cult of domesticity The belief that women should stay at home to manage the household, educate their children with strong moral values, and please their husbands.

George A. Custer (1839–1876) He was a reckless and glory-seeking Lieutenant Colonel of the U.S. Army who fought the Sioux Indians in the Great Sioux War. In 1876, he and his detachment of soldiers were entirely wiped out in the Battle of Little Bighorn.

D-day June 6, 1944, when an Allied amphibious assault landed on the Normandy coast and established a foothold in Europe from which Hitler's defenses could not recover.

Jefferson Davis (1808–1889) He was the president of the Confederacy during the Civil War. When the Confederacy's defeat seemed invitable in early 1865, he refused to surrender. Union forces captured him in May of that year.

Eugene V. Debs (1855–1926) He founded the American Railway Union, which he organized against the Pullman Palace Car Company during the Pullman strike. Later he organized the Social Democratic party, which eventually became the Socialist Party of America. In the 1912 presidential election, he ran as the Socialist party's candidate and received more than 900,000 votes.

Declaratory Act Following the repeal of the Stamp Act in 1766, Parliament passed this act which asserted Parliament's full power to make laws binding the colonies "in all cases whatsoever."

deism Enlightenment thought applied to religion; emphasized reason, morality, and natural law.

détente In the 1970s, the United States and Soviet Union began working together to achieve a more orderly and restrained competition between each other. Both countries signed an agreement to limit the number of Intercontinental Long Range Ballistic Missiles (ICBMs) that each country could possess and to not construct antiballistic missiles systems. They also signed new trade agreements.

George Dewey (1837–1917) On April 30, 1898, Commodore George Dewey's small U.S. naval squadron defeated the Spanish warships in Manila Bay in the Philippines. This quick victory aroused expansionist fever in the United States.

John Dewey (1859–1952) He is an important philosopher of pragmatism. However, he preferred to use the term *instrumentalism*, because he saw ideas as instruments of action.

Ngo Dinh Diem (1901–1963) Following the Geneva Accords, the French, with the support of America, forced the Vietnamese emperor to accept Dinh Diem as the new premier of South Vietnam. President Eisenhower sent advisors to train Diem's police and army. In return, the United States expected Diem to enact democratic reforms and distribute land to the peasants. Instead, he suppressed his political opponents, did little or no land distribution, and let corruption grow. In 1956, he refused to participate in elections to reunify Vietnam. Eventually, he ousted the emperor and declared himself president.

Dorothea Dix (1802–1887) She was an important figure in increasing the public's awareness of the plight of the mentally ill. After a two-year investigation of the treatment of the mentally ill in Massachusetts, she presented her findings and won the support of leading reformers. She eventually convinced twenty states to reform their treatment of the mentally ill.

Dixiecrats Deep South delegates who walked out of the 1948 Democratic National Convention in protest of the party's support for civil rights legislation and later formed the States' Rights (Dixiecrat) party, which nominated Strom Thurmond of South Carolina for president.

dollar diplomacy The Taft administration's policy of encouraging American bankers to aid debt-plagued governments in Haiti, Guatemala, Honduras, and Nicaragua.

Donner party Forty-seven surviving members of a group of migrants to California were forced to resort to cannibalism to survive a brutal winter trapped in the Sierra Nevadas, 1846–1847; highest death toll of any group traveling the Overland Trail.

Stephen A. Douglas (1812–1861) As a senator from Illinois, he authored the Kansas-Nebraska Act. Once passed, the act led to violence in Kansas between pro- and antislavery factions and damaged the Whig party. These damages prevented Senator Douglas from being chosen as the presidential candidate of his party. Running for senatorial reelection in 1858, he engaged Abraham Lincoln in a series of public debates about slavery in the territories. Even though Douglas won the election, the debates gave Lincoln a national reputation.

Frederick Douglass (1818–1895) He escaped from slavery and become an eloquent speaker and writer against slavery. In 1845, he published his autobiography entitled *Narrative of the Life of Frederick Douglass* and two years later he founded an abolitionist newspaper for blacks called the *North Star*.

dot-coms In the late 1990s, the stock market soared to new heights and defied the predictions of experts that the economy could not sustain such a performance. Much of the economic success was based on dot-com enterprises, which were firms specializing in computers, software, telecommunications, and the internet. However, many of the companies' stock market values were driven higher and higher by speculation instead of financial success. Eventually the stock market bubble burst.

Dred Scott v. Sandford (1857) U.S. Supreme Court decision in which Chief Justice Roger B. Taney ruled that slaves could not sue for freedom and that Congress could not prohibit slavery in the territories, on the grounds that such a prohibition would violate the Fifth Amendment rights of slaveholders.

W. E. B. Du Bois (1868–1963) He criticized Booker T. Washington's views on civil rights as being accommodationist. He advocated "ceaseless agitation" for civil rights and the immediate end to segregation and an enforcement of laws to protect civil rights and equality. He promoted an education for African Americans that would nurture bold leaders who were willing to challenge discrimination in politics.

John Foster Dulles (1888–1959) As President Eisenhower's secretary of state, he institutionalized the policy of containment and introduced the strategy of deterrence. He believed in using brinkmanship to halt the spread of communism. He attempted to employ it in Indochina, which led to the United States' involvement in Vietnam.

dust bowl Great Plains counties where millions of tons of topsoil were blown away from parched farmland in the 1930s; massive migration of farm families followed.

Peggy Eaton (1796–1879) The wife of John Eaton, President Jackson's secretary of war, was the daughter of a tavern owner with an unsavory past. Supposedly her first husband had committed suicide after learning that she was having an affair with John Eaton. The wives of members of Jackson's cabinet snubbed her because of her lowly origins and past. The scandal that resulted was called the Eaton Affair.

Jonathan Edwards (1703–1758) New England Congregationalist minister, who began a religious revival in his Northampton church and was an important figure in the Great Awakening.

Election of 1912 The presidential election of 1912 featured four candidates: Wilson, Taft, Roosevelt, and Debs. Each candidate believed in the basic assumptions of progressive politics, but each had a different view on how progressive ideals should be implemented through policy. In the end, Taft and Roosevelt split the Republican party votes and Wilson emerged as the winner.

Queen Elizabeth I of England (1533–1603) The protestant daughter of Henry VIII, she was Queen of England from 1558-1603 and played a major role in the Protestant Reformation. During her long reign, the doctrines and services of the Church of England were defined and the Spanish Armada was defeated.

General Dwight D. Eisenhower (1890–1969) During World War II, he commanded the Allied Forces landing in Africa and was the supreme Allied commander as well as planner for Operation Overlord. In 1952, he was elected president on his popularity as a war hero and his promises to clean up Washington and find an honorable peace in the Korean War. His administration sought to cut the nation's domestic programs and budget, but he left the basic structure of the New Deal intact. In July of 1953, he announced the end of fighting in Korea. He appointed Earl Warren to the Supreme Court whose influence helped the court become an important force for social and political change. His secretary of state, John Foster Dulles, institutionalized the policies of containment and deterrence. Eisenhower supported the withdrawal of British forces from the Suez Canal and established the Eisenhower doctrine, which promised to aid any nation against aggression by a communist nation. Eisenhower preferred that state and local institutions to handle civil rights issues, and he refused to force states to comply with the Supreme Court's civil rights decisions. However, he did propose the legislation that became the Civil Rights Act of 1957.

Ellis Island Reception center in New York Harbor through which most European immigrants to America were processed from 1892 to 1954.

Emancipation Proclamation (1863) President Abraham Lincoln issued a preliminary proclamation on September 22, 1862, freeing the slaves in the Confederate states as of January 1, 1863, the date of the final proclamation.

Ralph Waldo Emerson (1803–1882) As a leader of the transcendentalist movement, he wrote poems, essays, and speeches that discussed the sacredness of nature, optimism, self-reliance, and the unlimited potential of the individual. He wanted to transcend the limitations of inherited conventions and rationalism to reach the inner recesses of the self.

encomienda System under which officers of the Spanish conquistadores gained ownership of Indian land.

Enlightenment Revolution in thought begun in the seventeenth century that emphasized reason and science over the authority of traditional religion.

enumerated goods According to the Navigation Act, these particular goods, like tobacco or cotton, could only be shipped to England or other English colonies.

Erie Canal Most important and profitable of the barge canals of the 1820s and 1830s; stretched from Buffalo to Albany, New York, connecting the Great Lakes to the East Coast and making New York City the nation's largest port.

ethnic cleansing The act of killing an entire group of people in a region or country because of its ethnic background. After the collapse of the former Yugoslavia in 1991, Serbs in Bosnia attacked communities of Muslims, which led to intervention by the United Nations. In 1998, fighting broke out again in the Balkans between Serbia and Kosovo. Serbian police and military attacked, killed, raped, or forced Muslim Albanian Kosovars to leave their homes.

Fair Employment Practices Commission Created in 1941 by executive order, the FEPC sought to eliminate racial discrimination in jobs; it possessed little power but represented a step toward civil rights for African Americans.

Farmers' Alliance Two separate organizations (Northwestern and Southern) of the 1880s and 1890s that took the place of the Grange, worked for similar causes, and attracted landless, as well as landed, farmers to their membership.

Federal Writers' Project During the Great Depression, this project provided writers, such as Ralph Ellison, Richard Wright, and Saul Bellow, with work, which gave them a chance to develop as artists and be employed.

The Federalist Collection of eighty-five essays that appeared in the New York press in 1787–1788 in support of the Constitution; written by Alexander Hamilton, James Madison, and John Jay but published under the pseudonym "Publius."

Geraldine Ferraro (1935–) In the 1984 presidential election, Democratic nominee, Walter Mondale, chose her as his running mate. As a member of the U.S. House of Representatives from New York, she was the first woman to be a vice-presidential nominee for a major political party. However, she was placed on the defensive because of her husband's complicated business dealings.

Fifteenth Amendment This amendment forbids states to deny any person the right to vote on grounds of "race, color or pervious condition of servitude." Former Confederate states were required to ratify this amendment before they could be readmitted to the Union.

the "final solution" The Nazi party's systematic murder of some 6 million Jews along with more than a million other people including, but not limited to, gypsies, homosexuals, and handicap individuals.

Food Administration After America's entry into World War I, the economy of the home front needed to be reorganized to provide the most efficient means of conducting the war. The Food Administration was a part of this effort. Under the leadership of Herbert Hoover, the organization sought to increase agricultural production while reducing civilian consumption of foodstuffs.

force bill During the nullification crisis between President Andrew Jackson and South Carolina, Jackson asked Congress to pass this bill, which authorized him to use the army to force South Carolina to comply with federal law.

Gerald Ford (1913–2006) He was President Nixon's vice president and assumed the presidency after Nixon resigned. President Ford issued Nixon a pardon for any crimes related to the Watergate scandal. The American public's reaction was largely negative; and Ford never regained the public's confidence. He resisted congressional pressure to both reduce taxes and increase federal spending, which sent the American economy into the deepest recession since the Great Depression. Ford retained Kissinger as his secretary of state and continued Nixon's foreign policy goals, which included the signing of another arms-control agreement with the Soviet Union. He was heavily criticized following the collapse of South Vietnam.

Fort Laramie Treaty (1851) Restricted the Plains Indians from using the Overland Trail and permitted the building of government forts.

Fort Necessity After attacking a group of French soldiers, George Washington constructed and took shelter in this fort from vengeful French troops. Washington eventually surrendered to them after a day-long battle. This conflict was a significant event in igniting the French and Indian War.

Fort Sumter First battle of the Civil War, in which the federal fort in Charleston (South Carolina) Harbor was captured by the Confederates on April 14, 1861, after two days of shelling.

"forty-niners" Speculators who went to northern California following the discovery of gold in 1848; the first of several years of large-scale migration was 1849.

Fourteen Points President Woodrow Wilson's 1918 plan for peace after World War I; at the Versailles peace conference, however, he failed to incorporate all of the points into the treaty.

Fourteenth Amendment (1868) Guaranteed rights of citizenship to former slaves, in words similar to those of the Civil Rights Act of 1866.

Franciscan Missions In 1769, Franciscan missioners accompanied Spanish soldiers to California and over the next fifty years established a chain of missions from San Diego to San Francisco. At these missions, friars sought to convert Indians to Catholicism and make them members of the Spanish empire. The friars stripped the Indians of their native heritage and used soldiers to enforce their will.

Benjamin Franklin (1706–1790) A Boston-born American, who epitomized the Enlightenment for many Americans and Europeans, Franklin's wide range of interests led him to become a publisher, inventor, and statesman. As the latter, he contributed to the writing of the Declaration of Independence, served as the minister to France during the Revolutionary War, and was a delegate to the Constitutional Convention.

Free-Soil party Formed in 1848 to oppose slavery in the territory acquired in the Mexican War; nominated Martin Van Buren for president in 1848, but by 1854, most of the party's members had joined the Republican party.

Freedmen's Bureau Reconstruction agency established in 1865 to protect the legal rights of former slaves and to assist with their education, jobs, health care, and landowning.

freedom riders In 1961, the Congress of Racial Equality had this group of black and white demonstrators ride buses to test the federal court ruling that had banned segregation on buses and trains and in terminals. Despite being attacked, they never gave up. Their actions drew national attention and generated respect and support for their cause.

John C. Frémont "the Pathfinder" (1813–1890) He was an explorer and surveyor who helped inspire Americans living in California to rebel against the Mexican government and declare independence.

French and Indian War Known in Europe as the Seven Years' War, the last (1755–1763) of four colonial wars fought between England and France for control of North America east of the Mississippi River.

Sigmund Freud (1865–1939) He was the founder of psychoanalysis, which suggested that human behavior was motivated by unconscious and irrational forces. By the 1920s, his ideas were being discussed more openly in America.

Fugitive Slave Act of 1850 Gave federal government authority in cases involving runaway slaves; so much more punitive and prejudiced in favor of slaveholders than the 1793 Fugitive Slave Act had been that Harriet Beecher Stowe was inspired to write *Uncle Tom's Cabin* in protest; the new law was part of the Compromise of 1850, included to appease the South over the admission of California as a free state.

fundamentalism Anti-modernist Protestant movement started in the early twentieth century that proclaimed the literal truth of the Bible; the name came from *The Fundamentals*, published by conservative leaders.

"gag rule" In 1831, the House of Representatives adopted this rule, which prevented the discussion and presentation of any petitions for the abolition of slavery to the House. John Quincy Adams, who was elected to the House after his presidency ended, fought the rule on the grounds that it violated the First Amendment. In 1844, he succeeded in having it repealed.

William Lloyd Garrison (1805–1879) In 1831, he started the anti-slavery newspaper *Liberator* and helped start the New England Anti-Slavery Society. Two years later, he assisted Arthur and Lewis Tappan in the founding of the American Anti-Slavery Society. He and his followers believed that America had been thoroughly corrupted and needed a wide range of reforms. He embraced every major reform movement of the day: abolition, temperance, pacifism, and women's rights. He wanted to go beyond just freeing slaves and grant them equal social and legal rights.

Marcus Garvey (1887–1940) He was the leading spokesman for Negro Nationalism, which exalted blackness, black cultural expression, and black exclusiveness. He called upon African Americans to liberate themselves from the surrounding white culture and create their own businesses, cultural centers, and newspapers. He was also the founder of the Universal Negro Improvement Association.

Citizen Genêt (1763–1834) As the ambassador to the United States from the new French Republic, he engaged American privateers to attack British ships and conspired with frontiersmen and land speculators to organize an attack on Spanish Florida and Louisiana. His actions and the French radicals excessive actions against their enemies in the new French Republic caused the French Revolution to lose support among Americans.

Geneva Accords In 1954, the Geneva Accords were signed, which ended French colonial rule in Indochina. The agreement created the independent nations of Laos and Cambodia and divided Vietnam along the 17th parallel until an election in 1956 would reunify the country.

German U-boat German submarines, or U-boats, were used to attack enemy merchant ships in the waters around the British Isles during World War I. The sinking of the ocean liner *Lusitania* by a German submarine caused a public outcry in America, which contributed to the demands to expand the United States' military.

Gettysburg, Battle of Fought in southern Pennsylvania, July 1–3, 1863; the Confederate defeat and the simultaneous loss at Vicksburg spelled the end of the South's chances in the Civil War.

Ghost Dance movement This spiritual and political movement came from a Paiute Indian named Wovoka (or Jack Wilson). He believed that a messiah would come and rescue the Indians and restore their lands. To hasten the arrival of the messiah, the Indians needed to take up a ceremonial dance at each new moon.

Newt Gingrich (1943–) He led the Republican insurgency in Congress in the mid 1990s through mobilizing religious and social conservatives. Along with other Republican congressmen, he created the Contract with America, which was a ten-point anti-big government program. However, the program fizzled out after many of its bills were not passed by Congress.

The Gilded Age Mark Twain and Charles Dudley Warner's 1873 novel, the title of which became the popular name for the period from the end of the Civil War to the turn of the century.

glasnost Soviet leader Mikhail Gorbachev instituted this reform, which brought about a loosening of censorship.

Glorious Revolution In 1688, the Protestant Queen Mary and her husband, William of Orange, took the British throne from King James II in a bloodless coup. Afterward, Parliament greatly expanded its power and passed the Bill of Rights and the Act of Toleration, both of which would influence attitudes and events in the colonies.

Barry Goldwater (1909–1998) He was a leader of the Republican right whose book, *The Conscience of a Conservative*, was highly influential to that segment of the party. He proposed eliminating the income tax and overhauling Social Security. In 1964, he ran as the Republican presidential candidate and lost to President Johnson. He campaigned against Johnson's war on poverty, the tradition of New Deal, the nuclear test ban and the Civil Rights Act of 1964. He advocated the wholesale bombing of North Vietnam.

Samuel Gompers (1850–1924) He served as the president of the American Federation of Labor from its inception until his death. He focused on achieving concrete economic gains such as higher wages, shorter hours, and better working conditions.

"good neighbor" policy Proclaimed by President Franklin D. Roosevelt in his first inaugural address in 1933, it sought improved diplomatic relations between the United States and its Latin American neighbors.

Mikhail Gorbachev (1931–) In the late 1980s, Soviet leader Mikhail Gorbachev attempted to reform the Soviet Union through his programs of *perestroika* and *glasnost*. He pursued a renewal of détente with America and signed new arms-control agreements with President Reagan. Gorbachev chose not to involve the Soviet Union in the internal affairs of other Communist countries, which removed the threat of armed Soviet crackdowns on reformers and protesters in Eastern Europe. Gorbachev's decision allowed the velvet revolutions of Eastern Europe to occur without outside interference. Eventually the political, social, and economic upheaval he had unleashed would lead to the break-up of the Soviet Union.

Al Gore (1948–) He served as a senator of Tennessee and then as President Clinton's vice president. In the 2000 presidential election, he was the Democratic candidate and campaigned on preserving Social Security, subsidizing prescription-medicine expenses for the elderly, and protecting the environment. His opponent was Governor George W. Bush, who promoted compassionate conservatism and the transferring of power from the federal government to the states. The election ended in controversy. The close election came down to Florida's electoral votes. The final tally in Florida gave Bush a slight lead, but it was so small that a recount was required by state law. While the votes were being recounted, a legal battle was being waged to stop the recount. Finally, the case, *Bush v. Gore*, was presented to the Supreme Court who ruled 5–4 to stop the recount and Bush was declared the winner.

Jay Gould (1836–1892) As one of the biggest railroad robber barons, he was infamous for buying rundown railroads, making cosmetic improvements and then reselling them for a profit. He used corporate funds for personal investments and to bribe politicians and judges.

gradualism This strategy for ending slavery involved promoting the banning of slavery in the new western territories and encouraging the release of slaves from slavery. Supporters of this method believed that it would bring about the gradual end of slavery.

Granger movement Political movement that grew out of the Patrons of Husbandry, an educational and social organization for farmers founded in 1867; the Grange had its greatest success in the Midwest of the 1870s, lobbying for government control of railroad and grain elevator rates and establishing farmers' cooperatives.

Ulysses S. Grant (1822–1885) After distinguishing himself in the western theater of the Civil War, he was appointed general in chief of the Union army in 1864. Afterward, he defeated General Robert E. Lee through a policy of aggressive attrition. He constantly attacked Lee's army until it was grind down. Lee surrendered to Grant on April 9th, 1865 at the Appomattox Court House. In 1868, he was elected President and his tenure suffered from scandals and fiscal problems including the debate on whether or not greenbacks, paper money, should be removed from circulation.

Great Awakening Fervent religious revival movement in the 1720s through the 1740s that was spread throughout the colonies by ministers like

New England Congregationalist Jonathan Edwards and English revivalist George Whitefield.

great black migration After World War II, rural southern blacks began moving to the urban North and Midwest in large numbers in search of better jobs, housing, and greater social equality. The massive influx of African American migrants overwhelmed the resources of urban governments and sparked racial conflicts. In order to cope with the new migrants and alleviate racial tension, cities constructed massive public-housing projects that segregated African Americans into overcrowded and poor neighborhoods.

Great Compromise (Connecticut Compromise) Mediated the differences between the New Jersey and Virginia delegations to the Constitutional Convention by providing for a bicameral legislature, the upper house of which would have equal representation and the lower house of which would be apportioned by population.

Great Depression Worst economic depression in American history; it was spurred by the stock market crash of 1929 and lasted until World War II.

Great Sioux War In 1874, Lieutenant Colonel Custard led an exploratory expedition into the Black Hills, which the United States government had promised to the Sioux Indians. Miners soon followed and the army did nothing to keep them out. Eventually, the army attacked the Sioux Indians and the fight against them lasted for fifteen months before the Sioux Indians were forced to give up their land and move onto a reservation.

Great Society Term coined by President Lyndon B. Johnson in his 1965 State of the Union address, in which he proposed legislation to address problems of voting rights, poverty, diseases, education, immigration, and the environment.

Horace Greeley (1811–1872) In reaction to Radical Reconstruction and corruption in President Ulysses S. Grant's administration, a group of Republicans broke from the party to form the Liberal Republicans. In 1872, the Liberal Republicans chose Horace Greeley as their presidential candidate who ran on a platform of favoring civil service reform and condemning the Republican's Reconstruction policy.

greenbacks Paper money issued during the Civil War. After the war ended, a debate emerged on whether or not to remove the paper currency from circulation and revert back to hard-money currency (gold coins).

Opponents of hard-money feared that eliminating the greenbacks would shrink the money supply, which would lower crop prices and make it more difficult to repay long-term debts. President Ulysses S. Grant, as well as hard-currency advocates, believed that gold coins were morally preferable to paper currency.

Greenback party Formed in 1876 in reaction to economic depression, the party favored issuance of unsecured paper money to help farmers repay debts; the movement for free coinage of silver took the place of the greenback movement by the 1880s.

Nathanael Greene (1742–1786) He was appointed by Congress to command the American army fighting in the South during the Revolutionary War. Using his patience and his skills of managing men, saving supplies, and avoiding needless risks, he waged a successful war of attrition against the British.

Sarah Grimké (1792–1873) and **Angelina Grimké (1805–1879)** These two sisters gave anti-slavery speeches to crowds of mixed gender that caused some people to condemn them for engaging in unfeminine activities. The sisters rejected this opinion and made the role of women in the anti-slavery movement a prominent issue. In 1840, William Lloyd Garrison convinced the Anti-Slavery Society to allow women equal participation in the organization. A group of members that did not agree with this decision left the Anti-Slavery Society to form the American and Foreign Anti-Slavery Society.

Half-Way Covenant Allowed baptized children of church members to be admitted to a "halfway" membership in the church and secure baptism for their own children in turn, but allowed them neither a vote in the church, nor communion.

Alexander Hamilton (1755–1804) His belief in a strong federal government led him to become a contributor to *The Federalist* and leader of the Federalists. As the first secretary of the Treasury, he laid the foundation for American capitalism through his creation of a federal budget, funded debt, a federal tax system, a national bank, a customs service, and a coast guard. His "Reports on Public Credit" and "Reports on Manufactures" outlined his vision for economic development and government finances in America. He died in a duel against Aaron Burr.

Warren Harding (1865–1923) In the 1920 presidential election, he was the Republican nominee who promised Americans a "return to normalcy," which would mean a return to conservative values and a turning away from President Wilson's internationalism. His message resonated with voters' conservative postwar mood; and he won the election. Once in office, Harding's administration dismantled many of the social and economic components of progressivism and pursued a pro-business agenda. Harding appointed four pro-business Supreme Court Justices and his administration cut taxes, increased tariffs and promoted a lenient attitude towards government regulation of corporations. However, he did speak out against racism and ended the exclusion of African Americans from federal positions. His administration did suffer from a series of scandals as the result of him appointing members of the Ohio gang to government positions.

Harlem Renaissance African American literary and artistic movement of the 1920s and 1930s centered in New York City's Harlem district; writers Langston Hughes, Jean Toomer, Zora Neale Hurston, and Countee Cullen were among those active in the movement.

Hartford Convention Meeting of New England Federalists on December 15, 1814, to protest the War of 1812; proposed seven constitutional amendments (limiting embargoes and changing requirements for officeholding, declaration of war, and admission of new states), but the war ended before Congress could respond.

Patrick Henry (1736–1799) He inspired the Virginia Resolves, which declared that Englishmen could only be taxed by their elected representatives. In March of 1775, he met with other colonial leaders to discuss the goals of the upcoming Continental Congress and famously declared "Give me liberty or give me death." During the ratification process of the U.S. Constitution, he became one of the leaders of the anti-federalists.

Hideki Tōjō (1884–1948) He was Japan's war minister and later prime minister during World War II.

Alger Hiss (1904–1996) During the second Red Scare, Alger Hiss, who had served in several government departments, was accused of being a spy for the Soviet Union and was convicted of lying about espionage. The case was politically damaging to the Truman administration because the president called the charges against Hiss a "red herring." Richard

Nixon, then a California congressman, used his persistent pursuit of the case and his anti-Communist rhetoric to raise his national profile and to win election to the Senate.

Adolph Hitler "Führer" (1889–1945) The leader of the Nazis who advocated a violent anti-Semitic, anti-Marxist, pan-German ideology. He started World War II in Europe and orchestrated the systematic murder of some 6 million Jews along with more than a million others.

HIV/AIDS Human Immunodeficiency Virus (HIV) is a virus that attacks the body's T-cells, which are necessary to help the immune system fight off infection and disease. Acquired Immunodeficiency Syndrome (AIDS) occurs after the HIV virus has destroyed the body's immune system. HIV is transferred when body fluids, such as blood or semen, which carry the virus, enter the body of an uninfected person. The virus appeared in America in the early 1980s. The Reagan administration was slow to respond to the "AIDS Epidemic," because effects of the virus were not fully understood and they deemed the spread of the disease as the result of immoral behavior.

Homestead Act (1862) Authorized Congress to grant 160 acres of public land to a western settler, who had only to live on the land for five years to establish title.

Herbert Hoover (1874–1964) Prior to becoming president, Hoover served as the secretary of commerce in both the Harding and Coolidge administrations. During his tenure at the Commerce Department, he pursued new markets for business and encouraged business leaders to share information as part of the trade-association movement. The Great Depression hit while he was president. Hoover believed that the nation's business structure was sound and sought to revive the economy through boosting the nation's confidence. He also tried to restart the economy with government constructions projects, lower taxes and new federal loan programs, but nothing worked.

House Un-American Activities Committee (HUAC) Formed in 1938 to investigate subversives in the government; best-known investigations were of Hollywood notables and of former State Department official Alger Hiss, who was accused in 1948 of espionage and Communist party membership.

Sam Houston (1793–1863) During Texas's fight for independence from Mexico, Sam Houston was the commander in chief of the Texas forces, and he led the attack that captured General Antonio López de Santa Anna. After Texas gained its independence, he was name its first president.

Jacob Riis' *How the Other Half Lives* Jacob Riis was an early muckraking journalist who exposed the slum conditions in New York City in his book *How the Other Half Lives.*

General William Howe (1729–1814) As the commander of the British army in the Revolutionary War, he seized New York City from Washington's army, but failed to capture it. He missed several more opportunities to quickly end the rebellion, and he resigned his command after the British defeat at Saratoga.

Saddam Hussein (1937–2006) The former dictator of Iraq who became the head of state in 1979. In 1980, he invaded Iran and started the eight-year-long Iran-Iraq War. In 1990, he invaded Kuwait, which caused the Gulf War of 1991. In 2003, he was overthrown and captured when the United States invaded. He was sentenced to death by hanging in 2006.

Anne Hutchinson (1591–1643) The articulate, strong-willed, and intelligent wife of a prominent Boston merchant, who espoused her belief in direct divine revelation. She quarreled with Puritan leaders over her beliefs; and they banished her from the colony.

impressment The British navy used press-gangs to kidnap men in British and colonial ports who were then forced to serve in the British navy.

indentured servant Settler who signed on for a temporary period of servitude to a master in exchange for passage to the New World; Virginia and Pennsylvania were largely peopled in the seventeenth and eighteenth centuries by English indentured servants.

"Indian New Deal" This phrase refers to the reforms implemented for Native Americans during the New Deal era. John Collier, the commissioner of the Bureau of Indian Affairs (BIA), increased the access Native Americans had to relief programs and employed more Native Americans at the BIA. He worked to pass the Indian Reorganization Act. However, the version of the act passed by Congress was a much-diluted version of

Collier's original proposal and did not greatly improve the lives of Native Americans.

Indian Removal Act (1830) Signed by President Andrew Jackson, the law permitted the negotiation of treaties to obtain the Indians' lands in exchange for their relocation to what became Oklahoma.

Indochina This area of Southeast Asian consists of Laos, Cambodia, became and Vietnam and was once controlled by France as a colony. After the Viet Minh defeated the French, the Geneva Accords were signed, which ended French colonial rule. The agreement created the independent nations of Laos and Cambodia and divided Vietnam along the 17th parallel until an election would reunify the country. Fearing a communist take over, the United States government began intervening in the region during the Truman administration, which led to President Johnson's full-scale military involvement in Vietnam.

Industrial Workers of the World A radical union organized in Chicago in 1905, nicknamed the Wobblies; its opposition to World War I led to its destruction by the federal government under the Espionage Act.

internationalists Prior to the United States' entry in World War II, internationalists believed that America's national security depended on aiding Britain in its struggle against Germany.

internment of Japanese Americans In 1942, President Roosevelt issued an executive order to have all Japanese Americans forcibly relocated to relocation camps. More than 60 percent of the more than 100,000 internees were American citizens.

interstate highway system In the late 1950s, construction began on a national network of interstate superhighways for the purpose of commerce and defense. The interstate highways would enable the rapid movement of military convoys and the evacuation of cities after a nuclear attack.

Iranian Hostage Crisis In 1979, a revolution in Iran placed the Ayatollah Ruhollah Khomeini, a fundamental religious leader, in power. In November 1979, revolutionaries seized the American embassy in Tehran and held those inside hostage. President Carter struggled to get the hostages. He tried pressuring Iran through appeals to the United Nations, freezing Iranian assets in the United States and imposing a trade embargo. During an aborted rescue operation, a helicopter collided with a transport plane and killed eight U.S. soldiers. Finally, Carter un-froze several billion dollars in Iranian assets, and the hostages were re-leased after being held for 444 days; but not until Ronald Reagan had become president of the United States.

Iran-Contra affair Scandal of the second Reagan administration involving sale of arms to Iran in partial exchange for release of hostages in Lebanon and use of the arms money to aid the Contras in Nicaragua, which had been expressly forbidden by Congress.

Irish Potato Famine In 1845, an epidemic of potato rot brought a famine to rural Ireland that killed over 1 million peasants and instigated a huge increase in the number or Irish immigrating to America. By 1850, the Irish made up 43 percent of the foreign-born population in the United States; and in the 1850s, they made up over half the population of New York City and Boston.

iron curtain Term coined by Winston Churchill to describe the cold war di-vide between western Europe and the Soviet Union's Eastern European satellites.

Iroquois League An alliance of the Iroquois tribes that used their strength to force Europeans to work with them in the fur trade and to wage war across what is today eastern North America.

Andrew Jackson (1767–1837) As a major general in the Tennessee militia, he defeated the Creek Indians, invaded the panhandle of Spanish Florida and won the Battle of New Orleans. In 1818, his successful campaign against Spanish forces in Florida gave the United States the upper hand in negotiating for Florida with Spain. As president, he ve-toed bills for the federal funding of internal improvements and the re-chartering of the Second National Bank. When South Carolina nul-lified the Tariffs of 1828 and 1832, Jackson requested that Congress pass a "force bill" that would authorize him to use the army to compel the state to comply with the tariffs. He forced eastern Indians to move west of the Mississippi River so their lands could be used by white set-tlers. Groups of those who opposed Jackson come together to form a new political part called the Whigs.

Jesse Jackson (1941–) An African American civil rights activist who had been one of Martin Luther King Jr.'s chief lieutenants. He is most famous for founding the social justice organization the Rainbow

Coalition. In 1988, he ran for the Democratic presidential nomination, which became a race primarily between him and Michael Dukakis. Dukakis won the nomination, but lost the election to Republican nominee Vice President George H. W. Bush.

Thomas "Stonewall" Jackson (1824–1863) He was a Confederate general who was known for his fearlessness in leading rapid marches, bold flanking movements, and furious assaults. He earned his nickname at the Battle of the First Bull Run for standing courageously against Union fire. During the battle of Chancellorsville, his own men accidently mortally wounded him.

William James (1842–1910) He was the founder of Pragmatism and one of the fathers of modern psychology. He believed that ideas gained their validity not from their inherent truth, but from their social consequences and practical application.

Jay's Treaty Treaty with Britain negotiated in 1794 by Chief Justice John Jay; Britain agreed to vacate forts in the Northwest Territories, and festering disagreements (border with Canada, prewar debts, shipping claims) would be settled by commission.

Thomas Jefferson (1743–1826) He was a plantation owner, author, the drafter of the Declaration Independence, ambassador to France, leader of the Republican party, secretary of state, and the third president of the United States. As president, he purchased the Louisiana territory from France, withheld appointments made by President Adams leading to *Marybury v. Madison*, outlawed foreign slave trade, and was committed to a "wise and frugal" government.

Jesuits A religious order founded in 1540 by Ignatius Loyola. They sought to counter the spread of Protestantism during the Protestant Reformation and spread the Catholic faith through work as missionaries. Roughly 3,500 served in New Spain and New France.

"Jim Crow" laws In the New South, these laws mandated the separation of races in various public places that served as a way for the ruling whites to impose their will on all areas of black life.

Andrew Johnson (1808–1875) As President Abraham Lincoln's vice president, he was elevated to the presidency after Lincoln's assassination. In order to restore the Union after the Civil War, he issued an amnesty proclamation and required former Confederate states to ratify the Thirteenth Amendment. He fought Radical Republicans in Congress over whether he or Congress had the authority to restore states rights to the former Confederate states. This fight weakened both his political and public support. In 1868, the Radical Republicans attempted to impeach Johnson but fell short on the required number of votes needed to remove him from office.

Lyndon B. Johnson (1908–1973) Former member of the United States House of Representatives and the former Majority Leader of the United States Senate, Vice President Lyndon Johnson, assumed the presidency after President Kennedy's assassination. He was able to push through Congress several pieces of Kennedy's legislation that had been stalled including the Civil Rights Act of 1964. He declared "war on poverty" and promoted his own social program called the Great Society, which sought to end poverty and racial injustice. In 1965, he signed the Immigration and Nationality Service Act, which abolished the discriminatory quotas system that had been the immigration policy since the 1920s. Johnson greatly increased America's role in Vietnam. By 1969, there were 542,000 U.S. troops fighting in Vietnam and a massive anti-war movement had developed in America. In 1968, Johnson announced that he would not run for re-election.

Kansas-Nebraska Act (1854) Law sponsored by Illinois senator Stephen A. Douglas to allow settlers in newly organized territories north of the Missouri border to decide the slavery issue for themselves; fury over the resulting nullification of the Missouri Compromise of 1820 led to violence in Kansas and to the formation of the Republican party.

Florence Kelley (1859–1932) As the head of the National Consumer's League, she led the crusade to promote state laws to regulate the number of working hours imposed on women who were wives and mothers.

George F. Kennan (1904–2005) While working as an American diplomat, he devised the strategy of containment, which called for the halting of Soviet expansion. It became America's choice strategy throughout the cold war.

John F. Kennedy (1917–1963) Elected president in 1960, he was interested in bringing new ideas to the White House. Despite the difficulties he had in getting his legislation through Congress, he did establish the Alliance for Progress programs to help Latin America, the Peace Corps, the Trade

Expansion Act of 1962, and funding for urban renewal projects and the space program. He mistakenly proceeded with the Bay of Pigs invasion, but he successfully handled the Cuban missile crisis. In Indochina, his administration became increasingly involved in supporting local governments through aid, advisors, and covert operations. In 1963, he was assassinated by Lee Harvey Oswald in Dallas, Texas.

Kent State During the spring of 1970, students on college campuses across the country protested the expansion of the Vietnam War into Cambodia. At Kent State University, the National Guard attempted to quell the rioting students. The guardsmen panicked and shot at rock-throwing demonstrators. Four student bystanders were killed.

Kentucky and Virginia Resolutions (1798–1799) Passed in response to the Alien and Sedition Acts, the resolutions advanced the state-compact theory that held states could nullify an act of Congress if they deemed it unconstitutional.

Francis Scott Key (1779–1843) During the War of 1812, he watched British forces bombard Fort McHenry, but fail to take it. Seeing the American flag still flying over the fort at dawn inspired him to write "The Star-Spangled Banner," which became the American national anthem.

Keynesian economics A theory of economics developed by John Maynard Keynes. He argued that increased government spending, even if it increased the nation's deficit, during an economic downturn was necessary to reinvigorate a nation's economy. This view was held by Harry Hopkins and Harold Ickes who advised President Franklin Roosevelt during the Great Depression.

Martin Luther King Jr. (1929–1968) As an important leader of the civil rights movement, he urged people to use nonviolent civil disobedience to demand their rights and bring about change. He successfully led the Montgomery bus boycott. While in jail for his role in demonstrations, he wrote his famous "Letter from Birmingham City Jail," in which he defended his strategy of nonviolent protest. In 1963, he delivered his famous "I Have a Dream Speech" from the steps of the Lincoln Memorial as a part of the March on Washington. A year later, he was awarded the Nobel Peace Prize. In 1968, he was assassinated.

King William's War (War of the League of Augsburg) First (1689–1697) of four colonial wars between England and France.

King Philip (?–1676) or Metacomet The chief of the Wampanoages, who the colonists called King Philip. He resented English efforts to convert Indians to Christianity and waged a war against the English colonists in which he was killed.

Henry Kissinger (1923–) He served as the secretary of state and national security advisor in the Nixon administration. He negotiated with North Vietnam for an end to the Vietnam War. In 1973, an agreement was signed between America, North and South Vietnam, and the Viet Cong to end the war. The cease-fire did not last; and South Vietnam fell to North Vietnam. He helped organize Nixon's historic trips to China and the Soviet Union. In the Middle East, he negotiated a cease-fire between Israel and its neighbors following the Yom Kippur War and solidified Israel's promise to return to Egypt most of the land it had taken during the 1967 war.

Knights of Labor Founded in 1869, the first national union picked up many members after the disastrous 1877 railroad strike, but lasted under the leadership of Terence V. Powderly, only into the 1890s; supplanted by the American Federation of Labor.

Know-Nothing party Nativist, anti-Catholic third party organized in 1854 in reaction to large-scale German and Irish immigration; the party's only presidential candidate was Millard Fillmore in 1856.

Ku Klux Klan Organized in Pulaski, Tennessee, in 1866 to terrorize former slaves who voted and held political offices during Reconstruction; a revived organization in the 1910s and 1920s stressed white, Anglo-Saxon, fundamentalist Protestant supremacy; the Klan revived a third time to fight the civil rights movement of the 1950s and 1960s in the South.

Marquis de Lafayette (1757–1834) A wealthy French idealist excited by the American cause, he offered to serve in Washington's army for free in exchange for being named a major general. He overcame Washington's initial skepticism to become one of his most trusted aides.

Land Ordinance of 1785 Directed surveying of the Northwest Territory into townships of thirty-six sections (square miles) each, the sale of the sixteenth section of which was to be used to finance public education.

Bartolomé de Las Casas (1484–1566) A Catholic missionary who renounced the Spanish practice of coercively converting Indians and advocated the better treatment for them. In 1552, he wrote *A Brief Relation of the Destruction of the Indies*, which described the Spanish's cruel treatment of the Indians.

League of Nations Organization of nations to mediate disputes and avoid war established after World War I as part of the Treaty of Versailles; President Woodrow Wilson's "Fourteen Points" speech to Congress in 1918 proposed the formation of the league.

Mary Elizabeth Lease (1850–1933) She was a leader of the farm protest movement who advocated violence if change could not be obtained at the ballot box. She believed that the urban-industrial East was the enemy of the working class.

Robert E. Lee (1807–1870) Even though he had served in the United States Army for thirty years, he chose to fight on the side of the Confederacy and took command of the Army of North Virginia. Lee was excellent at using his field commanders; and his soldiers respected him. However, General Ulysses S. Grant eventually wore down his army, and Lee surrendered to Grant at the Appomattox Court House on April 9, 1865.

Lend-Lease Act (1941) Permitted the United States to lend or lease arms and other supplies to the Allies, signifying increasing likelihood of American involvement in World War II.

John Dickinson's "Letters from a Farmer in Pennsylvania" These twelve letters appeared in the *Pennsylvania Chronicle* and argued that Parliament could regulate colonial commerce and collect duties that related to that purpose, but it did not have the right to levy taxes for revenue.

Levittown First low-cost, mass-produced development of suburban tract housing built by William Levitt on Long Island, New York, in 1947.

Lexington and Concord, Battle of The first shots fired in the Revolutionary War, on April 19, 1775, near Boston; approximately 100 Minutemen and 250 British soldiers were killed.

Liberator William Lloyd Garrison started this anti-slavery newspaper in 1831 in which he renounced gradualism and called for abolition.

Queen Liliuokalani (1838–1917) In 1891, she ascended to the throne of the Hawaiian royal family and tried to eliminate white control of the Hawaiian government. Two years later, Hawaii's white population revolted and seized power with the support of American marines.

Abraham Lincoln (1809–1865) His participation in the Lincoln-Douglas debates gave him a national reputation and he was nominated as the Republican party candidate for president in 1860. Shortly after he was elected president, southern states began succeeding from the Union and in April of 1861 he declared war on the succeeding states. On January 1, 1863, Lincoln signed the Emancipation Proclamation, which freed all slaves. At the end of the war, he favored a reconstruction strategy for the former Confederate states that did not radically alter southern social and economic life. However, before his plans could be finalized, John Wilkes Booth assassinated Lincoln at Ford's Theater on April 14, 1865.

Lincoln-Douglas debates Series of senatorial campaign debates in 1858 focusing on the issue of slavery in the territories; held in Illinois between Republican Abraham Lincoln, who made a national reputation for himself, and incumbent Democratic senator Stephen A. Douglas, who managed to hold onto his seat.

John Locke (1632–1704) An English philosopher whose ideas were influential during the Enlightenment. He argued in his *Essay on Human Understanding* (1690) that humanity is largely the product of the environment, the mind being a blank tablet, *tabula rasa*, on which experience is written.

Henry Cabot Lodge (1850–1924) He was the chairman of the Senate Foreign Relations Committee who favored limiting America's involvement in the League of Nations' covenant and sought to amend the Treaty of Versailles.

de Lôme letter Spanish ambassador Depuy de Lôme wrote a letter to a friend in Havana in which he described President McKinley as "weak" and a seeker of public admiration. This letter was stolen and published in the *New York Journal*, which increased the American public's dislike of Spain and moved the two countries closer to war.

Lone Star Republic After winning independence from Mexico, Texas became its own nation that was called the Lone Star Republic. In 1836, Texans drafted themselves a constitution, legalized slavery, banned free blacks, named Sam Houston president, and voted for the annexation to the United States. However, quarrels over adding a slave state and fears of instigating a war with Mexico delayed Texas's entrance into the Union until December 29, 1845.

Huey Long (1893–1935) He began his political career in Louisiana where he developed a reputation for being an unscrupulous reformer. As a U.S. senator, he became a critic of President Roosevelt's New Deal Plan and offered his alternative called the Share-the-Wealth program. He was assassinated in 1935.

Lords Commissioners of Trade and Plantations (the Board of Trade) William III created this organization in 1696 to investigate the enforcement of the Navigations Act, recommend ways to limit colonial manufactures, and encourage the production of raw materials in the colonies that were needed in Britain.

Louisiana Purchase President Thomas Jefferson's 1803 purchase from France of the important port of New Orleans and 828,000 square miles west of the Mississippi River to the Rocky Mountains; it more than doubled the territory of the United States at a cost of only $15 million.

Lowell System Lowell mills were the first to bring all the processes of spinning and weaving cloth together under one roof and have every aspect of the production mechanized. In addition, the Lowell mills were designed to be model factory communities that provided the young women employees with meals, a boardinghouse, moral discipline, and educational and cultural opportunities.

Martin Luther (1483–1546) A German monk who founded the Lutheran church. He protested abuses in the Catholic Church by posting his Ninety-five Theses, which began the Protestant Reformation.

General Douglas MacArthur (1880–1964) During World War II, he and Admiral Chester Nimitz dislodged the Japanese military from the Pacific Islands they had occupied. Following the war, he was in charge of the occupation of Japan. After North Korea invaded South Korea, Truman sent the U.S. military to defend South Korea under the command of MacArthur. Later in the war, Truman expressed his willingness to negotiate the restoration of prewar boundaries which MacArthur attempted to undermine. Truman fired MacArthur for his open insubordination.

James Madison (1751–1836) He participated in the Constitutional Convention during which he proposed the Virginia Plan. He believed in a strong federal government and was a leader of the Federalists and a contributor to *The Federalist*. However, he also presented to Congress the Bill of Rights and drafted the Virginia Resolutions. As the secretary of state, he withheld a commission for William Marbury, which led to the landmark *Marbury v. Madison* decision. During his presidency, he declared war on Britain in response to violations of American shipping rights, which started the War of 1812.

Alfred Thayer Mahan's *The Influence of Sea Power Upon History, 1660–1783* Alfred Thayer Mahan was an advocate for sea power and Western imperialism. In 1890, he published *The Influence of Sea Power Upon History*, 1660–1783 in which he argued that a nation's greatness and prosperity comes from maritime power. He believed that America's "destiny" was to control the Caribbean, build the Panama Canal, and spread Western civilization across the Pacific.

Malcolm X (1925–1964) The most articulate spokesman for black power. Originally, the chief disciple of Elijah Muhammad, the black Muslim leader in the United States, Malcolm X broke away from him and founded his own organization committed to establishing relations between African Americans and the nonwhite peoples of the world. Near the end of his life, he began to preach a biracial message of social change. In 1964, he was assassinated by members of a rival group of black Muslims.

Manchuria incident The northeast region of Manchuria was an area contested between China and Russia. In 1931, the Japanese claimed that they needed to protect their extensive investments in the area and moved their army into Manchuria. They quickly conquered the region and set up their own puppet empire. China asked both the United States and the League of Nations for help and neither responded.

Manifest Destiny Imperialist phrase first used in 1845 to urge annexation of Texas; used thereafter to encourage American settlement of European colonial and Indian lands in the Great Plains and Far West.

Horace Mann (1796–1859) He believed the public school system was the best way to achieve social stability and equal opportunity. As a reformer of education, he sponsored a state board of education, the first state-supported "normal" school for training teachers, a state association for teachers, the minimum school year of six months, and led the drive for a statewide school system.

***Marbury v. Madison* (1803)** First U.S. Supreme Court decision to declare a federal law—the Judiciary Act of 1801—unconstitutional; President John Adams's "midnight appointment" of Federalist judges prompted the suit.

March on Washington Civil rights demonstration on August 28, 1963, where the Reverend Martin Luther King Jr. gave his "I Have a Dream" speech on the steps of the Lincoln Memorial.

George C. Marshall (1880–1959) As the chairman of the Joint Chiefs of Staff, he orchestrated the Allied victories over Germany and Japan in World War II. In 1947, he became President Truman's secretary of state and proposed the massive reconstruction program for western Europe called the Marshall Plan.

Chief Justice John Marshall (1755–1835) During his long tenure as chief justice of the supreme court (1801–1835), he established the foundations for American jurisprudence, the authority of the Supreme Court, and the constitutional supremacy of the national government over states.

Marshall Plan U.S. program for the reconstruction of post–World War II Europe through massive aid to former enemy nations as well as allies; proposed by General George C. Marshall in 1947.

massive resistance In reaction to the *Brown v. Board of Education* decision of 1954, U.S. Senator Harry Byrd encouraged southern states to defy federally mandated school integration.

Senator Joseph R. McCarthy (1908–1957) In 1950, this senator became the shrewdest and most ruthless exploiter of America's anxiety of communism. He claimed that the United States government was full of Communists and led a witch hunt to find them, but he was never able to uncover a single communist agent.

George B. McClellan (1826–1885) In 1861, President Abraham Lincoln appointed him head of the Army of the Potomac and, later, general in chief of the U.S. Army. He built his army into well trained and powerful force. However, he often delayed taking action against the enemy even though Lincoln wanted him to attack. After failing to achieve a decisive victory against the Confederacy, Lincoln removed McClellan from command in 1862.

Cyrus Hall McCormick (1809–1884) In 1831, he invented a mechanical reaper to harvest wheat, which transformed the scale of agriculture. By hand a farmer could only harvest a half an acre a day, while the McCormick reaper allowed two people to harvest twelve acres of wheat a day.

William McKinley (1843–1901) As a congressman, he was responsible for the McKinley Tariff of 1890, which raised the duties on manufactured products to their highest level ever. Voters disliked the tariff and McKinley, as well as other Republicans, lost their seats in Congress the next election. However, he won the presidential election of 1896 and raised the tariffs again. In 1898, he annexed Hawaii and declared war on Spain. The war concluded with the Treaty of Paris, which gave America control over Puerto Rico, Guam, and the Philippines. Soon America was fighting Filipinos, who were seeking independence for their country. In 1901, McKinley was assassinated.

Robert McNamara (1916–) He was the secretary of defense for both President Kennedy and President Johnson and a supporter of America's involvement in Vietnam.

McNary-Haugen Bill Vetoed by President Calvin Coolidge in 1927 and 1928, the bill to aid farmers would have artificially raised agricultural prices by selling surpluses overseas for low prices and selling the reduced supply in the United States for higher prices.

Andrew Mellon (1855–1937) As President Harding's secretary of the Treasury, he sought to generate economic growth through reducing government spending and lowering taxes. However, he insisted that the tax reductions mainly go to the rich because he believed the wealthy would reinvest their money and spur economic growth. In order to bring greater efficiency and nonpartisanship to the government's budget process, he persuaded Congress to pass the Budget and Accounting Act of 1921, which created a new Bureau of the Budget and a General Accounting Office.

mercantile system A nationalistic program that assumed that the total amount of the world's gold and silver remained essentially fixed with only a nation's share of that wealth subject to change.

James Meredith (1933–) In 1962, the governor of Mississippi defied a Supreme Court ruling and refused to allow James Meredith, an African American, to enroll at the University of Mississippi. Federal marshals were sent to enforce the law which led to clashes between a white mob and the marshals. Federal troops intervened and two people were killed and many others were injured. A few days later, Meredith was able to register at the university.

Merrimack* (ship renamed the *Virginia*) and the *Monitor First engagement between ironclad ships; fought at Hampton Roads, Virginia, on March 9, 1862.

Metacomet (?–1676) or King Philip The chief of the Wampanoages, who the colonists called King Philip. He resented English efforts to convert Indians to Christianity and waged a war against the English colonists in which he was killed.

militant nonviolence After the success of the Montgomery bus boycott, people were inspired by Martin Luther King Jr.'s use of this nonviolent form of protest. Throughout the civil rights movement, demonstrators used this method of protest to challenge racial segregation in the South.

Ho Chi Minh (1890–1969) He was the Vietnamese communist resistance leader who drove the French and the United States out of Vietnam. After the Geneva Accords divided the region into four countries, he controlled North Vietnam, and ultimately became the leader of all of Vietnam at the conclusion of the Vietnam War.

minstrelsy A form of entertainment that was popular from the 1830s to the 1870s. The performances featured white performers who were made up as African Americans or blackface. They performed banjo and fiddle music, "shuffle" dances and lowbrow humor that reinforced racial stereotypes.

Minutemen Special units organized by the militia to be ready for quick mobilization.

Miranda v. Arizona **(1966)** U.S. Supreme Court decision required police to advise persons in custody of their rights to legal counsel and against self-incrimination.

Mississippi Plan In 1890, Mississippi instituted policies that led to a near-total loss of voting rights for blacks and many poor whites. In order to vote, the state required that citizens pay all their taxes first, be literate, and have been residents of the state for two years and one year in an electoral district. Convicts were banned from voting. Seven other states followed this strategy of disenfranchisement.

Missouri Compromise Deal proposed by Kentucky senator Henry Clay to resolve the slave/free imbalance in Congress that would result from Missouri's admission as a slave state; in the compromise of March 20, 1820, Maine's admission as a free state offset Missouri, and slavery was prohibited in the remainder of the Louisiana Territory north of the southern border of Missouri.

Model T Ford Henry Ford developed this model of car so that it was affordable for everyone. Its success led to an increase in the production of automobiles which stimulated other related industries such steel, oil, and rubber. The mass use of automobiles increased the speed goods could be transported, encouraged urban sprawl, and sparked real estate booms in California and Florida.

modernism As both a mood and movement, modernism recognized that Western civilization had entered an era of change. Traditional ways of thinking and creating art were being rejected and replaced with new understandings and forms of expression.

Molly Maguires Secret organization of Irish coal miners that used violence to intimidate mine officials in the 1870s.

Monroe Doctrine President James Monroe's declaration to Congress on December 2, 1823, that the American continents would be thenceforth closed to colonization but that the United States would honor existing colonies of European nations.

Montgomery bus boycott Sparked by Rosa Parks's arrest on December 1, 1955, a successful year-long boycott protesting segregation on city buses; led by the Reverend Martin Luther King Jr.

Moral Majority Televangelist Jerry Falwell's political lobbying organization, the name of which became synonymous with the religious right— conservative evangelical Protestants who helped ensure President Ronald Reagan's 1980 victory.

J. Pierpont Morgan (1837–1913) As a powerful investment banker, he would acquire, reorganize, and consolidate companies into giant trusts. His biggest achievement was the consolidation of the steel industry into the United States Steel Corporation, which was the first billion-dollar corporation.

James Monroe (1758–1831) He served as secretary of state and war under President Madison and was elected president. As the latter, he signed the Transcontinental Treaty with Spain which gave the United States Florida and expanded the Louisiana territory's western border to the Pacific coast. In 1823, he established the Monroe Doctrine. This foreign policy proclaimed the American continents were no longer open to colonization and America would be neutral in European affairs.

Robert Morris (1734–1806) He was the superintendent of finance for the Congress of the Confederation during the final years of the Revolutionary War. He envisioned a national finance plan of taxation and debt management, but the states did not approve the necessary amendments to the Articles of Confederation need to implement the plan.

Samuel B. Morse (1791–1872) In 1832, he invented the telegraph and revolutionized the speed of communication.

mountain men Inspired by the fur trade, these men left civilization to work as trappers and reverted to a primitive existence in the wilderness. They were the first whites to find routes through the Rocky Mountains, and they pioneered trails that settlers later used to reach the Oregon country and California in the 1840s.

muckrakers Writers who exposed corruption and abuses in politics, business, meat-packing, child labor, and more, primarily in the first decade of the twentieth century; their popular books and magazine articles spurred public interest in progressive reform.

Mugwumps Reform wing of the Republican party that supported Democrat Grover Cleveland for president in 1884 over Republican James G. Blaine, whose influence peddling had been revealed in the Mulligan letters of 1876.

Benito Mussolini "Il Duce" (1883–1945) The Italian founder of the Fascist party who came to power in Italy in 1922 and allied himself with Adolf Hitler and the Axis powers during World War II.

My Lai Massacre In 1968, Lieutenant William Calley and his soldiers massacred 347 Vietnamese civilians in the village of My Lai. Twenty-five army officers were charged with complicity in the massacre and its cover-up but only Calley was convicted. Later, President Nixon granted him parole.

NAFTA Approved in 1993, the North American Free Trade Agreement with Canada and Mexico allowed goods to travel across their borders free of tariffs; critics argued that American workers would lose their jobs to cheaper Mexican labor.

National Industrial Recovery Act (1933) Passed on the last of the Hundred Days; it created public-works jobs through the Federal Emergency Relief Administration and established a system of self-regulation for industry through the National Recovery Administration, which was ruled unconstitutional in 1935.

National Recovery Administration This organization's two goals were to stabilize business and generate purchasing power for consumers. The first goal was to be achieved through the implementation industry-wide codes that set wages and prices, which would reduce the chaotic competition. To provide consumers with purchasing power, the administration would provide jobs, define workplace standards, and raise wages.

National Socialist German Workers' (Nazi) party Founded in the 1920s, this party gained control over Germany under the leadership of Adolf Hitler in 1933 and continued in power until Germany's defeat at the end of World War II. It advocated a violent anti-Semitic, anti-Marxist, pan-German ideology. The Nazi party systematically murdered some 6 million Jews along with more than a million others.

nativism Anti-immigrant and anti-Catholic feeling in the 1830s through the 1850s; the largest group was New York's Order of the Star-Spangled Banner, which expanded into the American, or Know-Nothing party in 1854. In the 1920, there was a surge in nativism as Americans grew to fear immigrants who might be political radicals. In response, new strict immigration regulations were established.

nativist A native-born American who saw immigrants as a threat to his way of life and employment. During the 1880s, nativist groups worked to stop the flow of immigrates into the United States. Of these groups, the most successful was the American Protective Association who promoted government restrictions on immigration, tougher naturalization requirements, the teaching of English in schools and workplaces that refused to employ foreigners or Catholics.

Navigation Acts Passed by the English Parliament to control colonial trade and bolster the mercantile system, 1650–1775; enforcement of the acts led to growing resentment by colonists.

new conservatism The political philosophy of those who led the conservative insurgency of the early 1980s. This brand of conservatism was personified in Ronald Reagan who believed in less government, supply-side economics, and "family values."

New Deal Franklin D. Roosevelt's campaign promise, in his speech to the Democratic National Convention of 1932, to combat the Great Depression with a "new deal for the American people;" the phrase became a catchword for his ambitious plan of economic programs.

New France The name used for the area of North America that was colonized by the French. Unlike Spanish or English colonies, New France had a small number of colonists, which forced them to initially seek good relations with the indigenous people they encountered.

New Freedom Democrat Woodrow Wilson's political slogan in the presidential campaign of 1912; Wilson wanted to improve the banking system, lower tariffs, and, by breaking up monopolies, give small businesses freedom to compete.

New Frontier John F. Kennedy's program, stymied by a Republican Congress and his abbreviated term; his successor Lyndon B. Johnson had greater success with many of the same concepts.

New Jersey Plan The delegations to the Constitutional Convention were divided between two plans on how to structure the government: New Jersey wanted one legislative body with equal representation for each state.

New Nationalism Platform of the Progressive party and slogan of former President Theodore Roosevelt in the presidential campaign of 1912; stressed government activism, including regulation of trusts, conservation, and recall of state court decisions that had nullified progressive programs.

"new Negro" In the 1920s, a slow and steady growth of black political influence occurred in northern cities where African Americans were freer to speak and act. This political activity created a spirit of protest that expressed itself culturally in the Harlem Renaissance and politically in "new Negro" nationalism.

New Netherlands Dutch colony conquered by the English to become four new colonies New York, New Jersey, Pennsylvania, and Delaware.

New South *Atlanta Constitution* editor Henry W. Grady's 1886 term for the prosperous post–Civil War South: democratic, industrial, urban, and free of nostalgia for the defeated plantation South.

William Randolph Hearst's *New York Journal* In the late 1890s, the *New York Journal* and its rival, the *New York World*, printed sensationalism on the Cuban revolution as part of their heated competition for readership. The *New York Journal* printed a negative letter from the Spanish ambassador about President McKinley and inflammatory coverage of the sinking of the *Maine* in Havana Harbor. These two events roused the American public's outcry against Spain.

Joseph Pulitzer's *New York World* In the late 1890s, the *New York World* and its rival, *New York Journal*, printed sensationalism on the Cuban revolution as part of their heated competition for readership.

Admiral Chester Nimitz (1885–1966) During World War II, he was the commander of central Pacific. Along with General Douglas MacArthur, he dislodged the Japanese military from the Pacific Islands they had occupied.

Nineteenth Amendment (1920) Granted women the right to vote.

Richard Nixon (1913–1994) He first came to national prominence as a congressman involved in the investigation of Alger Hiss. Later he served as vice president during the Eisenhower administration. In 1960, he ran as the Republican nominee for president and lost to John Kennedy. In 1968, he ran and won the presidency against Democratic nominee Hubert Humphrey. During his campaign, he promised to bring about "peace with honor" in Vietnam. He told southern conservatives that he would slow the federal enforcement of civil rights laws and appoint pro-southern justices to the Supreme Court. After being elected, he fulfilled the latter promise attempted to keep the former. He opened talks with the North Vietnamese and began a program of Vietnamization of the war. He also bombed Cambodia. In 1973, America, North and South Vietnam, and the Viet Cong agreed to end the war and the United States withdrew. However, the cease-fire was broken, and the South Vietnam fell to North Vietnam. In 1970, Nixon changed U.S. foreign policy. He declared that the America was no longer the world's policemen and he would seek some partnerships with Communist countries. With his historic visit to China, he ended twenty years of diplomatically isolating China and he began taking steps towards cultural exchanges and trade. In 1972, Nixon travelled to Moscow and signed agreements with the Soviet Union on arms control and trade. That same year, Nixon was reelected, but the Watergate scandal erupted shortly after his victory. When his knowledge of the break-in and subsequent cover-up was revealed, Nixon resigned the presidency under threat of impeachment.

No Child Left Behind President George W. Bush's education reform plan that required states to set and meet learning standards for students and make sure that all students were "proficient" in reading and writing by 2014. States had to submit annual reports of students' standardized test scores. Teachers were required to be "proficient" in their subject area.

Schools who failed to show progress would face sanctions. States criticized the lack of funding for remedial programs and noted that poor school districts would find it very difficult to meet the new guidelines.

Lord North (1732–1792) The first minister of King George III's cabinet whose efforts to subdue the colonies only brought them closer to revolution. He helped bring about the Tea Act of 1773, which led to the Boston Tea Party. In an effort to discipline Boston, he wrote, and Parliament passed, four acts that galvanized colonial resistance.

North Atlantic Treaty Organization (NATO) Defensive alliance founded in 1949 by ten western European nations, the United States, and Canada to deter Soviet expansion in Europe.

Northwest Ordinance Created the Northwest Territory (area north of the Ohio River and west of Pennsylvania), established conditions for self-government and statehood, included a Bill of Rights, and permanently prohibited slavery.

nullification Concept of invalidation of a federal law within the borders of a state; first expounded in the Kentucky and Virginia Resolutions (1798), cited by South Carolina in its Ordinance of Nullification (1832) of the Tariff of Abominations, used by southern states to explain their secession from the Union (1861), and cited again by southern states to oppose the *Brown v. Board of Education* decision (1954).

Nuremberg trials At the site of the annual Nazi party rallies, twenty-one major German offenders faced an international military tribunal for Nazi atrocities. After a ten-month trial, the court acquitted three and sentenced eleven to death, three to life imprisonment, and four to shorter terms.

Barack Obama (1961–) In the 2008 presidential election, Senator Barack Obama mounted an innovative Internet based and grassroots orientated campaign that garnered him enough delegates to win the Democratic nomination. As the nation's economy nosedived in the fall of 2008, Obama linked the Republican economic philosophy with the country's dismal financial state and promoted a message of "change" and "politics of hope," which resonated with voters. He decisively won the presidency and became America's first person of colored to be elected president.

Sandra Day O'Connor (1930–) She was the first woman to serve on the Supreme Court of the United States and was appointed by President Reagan. Reagan's critics charged that her appointment was a token gesture and not a sign of any real commitment to gender equality.

Ohio gang In order to escape the pressures of the White House, President Harding met with a group of people, called the "Ohio gang," in a house on K Street in Washington D.C. Members of this gang were given low-level positions in the American government and they used their White House connection to "line their pockets" by granting government contracts without bidding, which led to a series of scandals, most notably the Teapot Dome Scandal.

Frederick Law Olmsted (1822–1903) In 1858, he constructed New York's Central Park, which led to a growth in the movement to create urban parks. He went on to design parks for Boston, Brooklyn, Chicago, Philadelphia, San Francisco, and many other cities.

Opechancanough (?–1644) The brother and successor of Powhatan who led his tribe in an attempt to repel the English settlers in Virginia in 1622.

Open Door Policy In hopes of protecting the Chinese market for U.S. exports, Secretary of State John Hay unilaterally announced in 1899 that Chinese trade would be open to all nations.

Operation Desert Shield After Saddam Hussein invaded Kuwait in 1990, President George H. W. Bush sent American military forces to Saudi Arabia on a strictly defensive mission. They were soon joined by a multinational coalition. When the coalition's mission changed to the retaking of Kuwait, the operation was renamed Desert Storm.

Operation Desert Storm Multinational allied force that defeated Iraq in the Gulf War of January 1991.

Operation Overlord The Allies' assault on Hitler's "Atlantic Wall," a seemingly impregnable series of fortifications and minefields along the French coastline that German forces had created using captive Europeans for laborers.

J. Robert Oppenheimer (1904–1967) He led the group of physicists at the laboratory in Los Alamos, New Mexico, who constructed the first atomic bomb.

Oregon Country The Convention of 1818 between Britain and the United States established the Oregon Country as being west of the crest of the

Rocky Mountains and the two countries were to jointly occupy it. In 1824, the United States and Russia signed a treaty that established the line of 54°40′ as the southern boundary of Russia's territorial claim in North America. A similar agreement between Britain and Russia finally gave the Oregon Country clearly defined boarders, but it remained under joint British and American control.

Oregon fever Enthusiasm for emigration to the Oregon Country in the late 1830s and early 1840s.

Osceola (1804?–1838) He was the leader of the Seminole nation who resisted the federal Indian removal policy through a protracted guerilla war. In 1837, he was treacherously seized under a flag of truce and imprisoned at Fort Moultrie, where he was left to die.

Overland (Oregon) Trail Route of wagon trains bearing settlers from Independence, Missouri, to the Oregon Country in the 1840s to 1860s.

A. Mitchell Palmer (1872–1936) As the attorney general, he played an active role in government's response to the Red Scare. After several bombings across America, including one at Palmer's home, he and other Americans became convinced that there was a well-organized Communist terror campaign at work. The federal government launched a campaign of raids, deportations, and collecting files on radical individuals.

Panic of 1819 Financial collapse brought on by sharply falling cotton prices, declining demand for American exports, and reckless western land speculation.

panning A method of mining that used a large metal pan to sift gold dust and nuggets from riverbeds during the California gold rush of 1849.

Rosa Parks (1913–2005) In 1955, she refused to give up her seat to a white man on a city bus in Montgomery, Alabama, which a local ordinance required of blacks. She was arrested for disobeying the ordinance. In response, black community leaders organized the Montgomery bus boycott.

Alice Paul (1885–1977) She was a leader of the women's suffrage movement and head of the Congressional Committee of National Women Suffrage Association. She instructed female suffrage activists to use more militant tactics, such as picketing state legislatures, chaining themselves to public buildings, inciting police to arrest them, and undertaking hunger strikes.

Norman Vincent Peale (1898–1993) He was a champion of the upbeat and feel-good theology that was popular in the 1950s religious revival. He advocated getting rid of any depressing or negative thoughts and replacing them with "faith, enthusiasm and joy," which would make an individual popular and well liked.

"peculiar institution" This term was used to describe slavery in America because slavery so fragrantly violated the principle of individual freedom that served as the basis for the Declaration of Independence.

Pentagon papers Informal name for the Defense Department's secret history of the Vietnam conflict; leaked to the press by former official Daniel Ellsberg and published in the *New York Times* in 1971.

Pequot War Massacre in 1637 and subsequent dissolution of the Pequot Nation by Puritan settlers, who seized the Indians' lands.

perestroika Soviet leader Mikhail Gorbachev introduced these political and economic reforms, which included reconstructing the state bureaucracy, reducing the privileges of the political elite, and shifting from a centrally planned economy to a mixed economy.

Commodore Matthew Perry (1794–1858) In 1854, he negotiated the Treaty of Kanagawa, which was the first step in starting a political and commercial relationship between the United States and Japan.

John J. Pershing (1860–1948) After Pancho Villa had conducted several raids into Texas and New Mexico, President Woodrow Wilson sent troops under the command of General John J. Pershing into Mexico to stop Villa. However, after a year of chasing Villa and not being able to catch him, they returned to the United States. During World War I, Pershing commanded the first contingent of U.S. soldiers sent to Europe and advised the War Department to send additional American forces.

"pet banks" During President Andrew Jackson's fight with the national bank, Jackson resolved to remove all federal deposits from it. To comply with Jackson's demands, Secretary of Treasury Taney continued to draw on government's accounts in the national bank, but deposit all new federal receipts in state banks. The state banks that received these deposits were called "pet banks."

Dien Bien Phu The defining battle in the war between French colonialists and the Viet Minh. The Viet Minh's victory secured North Vietnam for

Ho Chi Minh and was crucial in compelling the French to give up Indochina as a colony.

Pilgrims Puritan Separatists who broke completely with the Church of England and sailed to the New World aboard the *Mayflower*, founding Plymouth Colony on Cape Cod in 1620.

Gifford Pinchot (1865–1946) As the head of the Division of Forestry, he implemented a conservation policy that entailed the scientific management of natural resources to serve the public interest. His work helped start the conservation movement. In 1910, he exposed to the public the decision of Richard A. Ballinger's, President Taft's secretary of the interior, to open up previously protected land for commercial use. Pinchot was fired, but the damage to Taft's public image resulted in the loss of many pro-Taft candidates in 1910 congressional election.

Elizabeth Lucas Pinckney (1722? –1793) One of the most enterprising horticulturists in colonial America, she began managing her family's three plantations in South Carolina at the age of sixteen. She had tremendous success growing indigo, which led to many other plantations growing the crop as well.

Pinckney's Treaty Treaty with Spain negotiated by Thomas Pinckney in 1795; established United States boundaries at the Mississippi River and the 31st parallel and allowed open transportation on the Mississippi.

Francisco Pizarro (1478?–1541) In 1531, he lead his Spanish soldiers to Peru and conquered the Inca Empire.

planters In the antebellum South, the owner of a large farm worked by twenty or more slaves.

James Knox Polk "Young Hickory" (1795–1849) As President, his chief concern was the expansion of the United States. In 1846, his administration resolved the dispute with Britain over the Oregon Country border. Shortly, after taking office, Mexico broke off relations with the United States over the annexation of Texas. Polk declared war on Mexico and sought to subvert Mexican authority in California. The United States defeated Mexico; and the two nations signed the Treaty of Guadalupe Hidalgo in which Mexico gave up any claims on Texas north of the Rio Grande River and ceded New Mexico and California to the United States.

Pontiac's Rebellion The Peace Treaty of 1763 gave the British all French land east of the Mississippi River. This area included the territory of

France's Indian allies who were not consulted about the transfer of their lands to British control. In an effort to recover their autonomy, Indians captured British forts around the Great Lakes and in the Ohio Valley as well as attacked settlements in Pennsylvania, Maryland, and Virginia.

popular sovereignty Allowed settlers in a disputed territory to decide the slavery issue for themselves.

Populist / the People's party Political success of Farmers' Alliance candidates encouraged the formation in 1892 of the People's party (later renamed the Populist party); active until 1912, it advocated a variety of reform issues, including free coinage of silver, income tax, postal savings, regulation of railroads, and direct election of U.S. senators.

Chief Powhatan Wahunsonacock He was called Powhatan by the English after the name of his tribe, and was the powerful, charismatic chief of numerous Algonquian-speaking towns in eastern Virginia representing over 10,000 Indians.

pragmatism William James founded this philosophy in the early 1900s. Pragmatists believed that ideas gained their validity not from their inherent truth, but from their social consequences and practical application.

Proclamation of 1763 Royal directive issued after the French and Indian War prohibiting settlement, surveys, and land grants west of the Appalachian Mountains; although it was soon over-ridden by treaties, colonists continued to harbor resentment.

proprietary colonies A colony owned by an individual, rather than a joint-stock company.

pueblos The Spanish term for the adobe cliff dwellings of the indigenous people of the southwestern United States.

Pullman Strike Strike against the Pullman Palace Car Company in the company town of Pullman, Illinois, on May 11, 1894, by the American Railway Union under Eugene V. Debs; the strike was crushed by court injunctions and federal troops two months later.

Puritans English religious group that sought to purify the Church of England; founded the Massachusetts Bay Colony under John Winthrop in 1630.

Quakers George Fox founded the Quaker religion in 1647. They rejected the use of formal sacraments and ministry, refused to take oaths and embraced pacifism. Fleeing persecution, they settled and established the colony of Pennsylvania.

Radical Republicans Senators and congressmen who, strictly identifying the Civil War with the abolitionist cause, sought swift emancipation of the slaves, punishment of the rebels, and tight controls over the former Confederate states after the war.

Raleigh's Roanoke Island Colony English expedition of 117 settlers, including Virginia Dare, the first English child born in the New World; colony disappeared from Roanoke Island in the Outer Banks sometime between 1587 and 1590.

A. Philip Randolph (1889–1979) He was the head of the Brotherhood of Sleeping Car Porters who planned a march on Washington D.C. to demand an end to racial discrimination in the defense industries. To stop the march, Roosevelt administration negotiated an agreement with the Randolph group. The demonstration would be called off and an executive order would be issued that forbid discrimination in defense work and training programs and set up the Fair Employment Practices Committee.

range wars In the late 1800s, conflicting claims over land and water rights triggered violent disputes between farmers and ranchers in parts of the western United States.

Ronald Reagan (1911–2004) In 1980, the former actor and governor of California was elected president. In office, he reduced social spending, cut taxes, and increased defense spending. He was criticized for cutting important programs, such as housing and school lunches and increasing the federal deficit. By 1983, prosperity had returned to America and Reagan's economic reforms appeared to be working, but in October of 1987 the stock market crashed. Some blamed the federal debt, which had tripled in size since Reagan had taken office. In the early 1980s, HIV/AIDS cases were beginning to be reported in America, but the Reagan administration chose to do little about the growing epidemic. Reagan believed that most of the world's problems came from the Soviet Union, which he called the "evil empire." In response, he conducted a major arms build up. Then in 1987, he signed an arms-control treaty with the Soviet Union. He authorized covert CIA operations in Central America. In 1986, the Iran-Contra scandal came to light which revealed arms sales were being conducted with Iran in a partial exchange for the release of hostages in Lebanon. The arms money was being used to aid the Contras.

Reaganomics Popular name for President Ronald Reagan's philosophy of "supply side" economics, which combined tax cuts, less government spending, and a balanced budget with an unregulated marketplace.

Reconstruction Finance Corporation Federal program established in 1932 under President Herbert Hoover to loan money to banks and other institutions to help them avert bankruptcy.

Red Scare Fear among many Americans after World War I of Communists in particular and noncitizens in general, a reaction to the Russian Revolution, mail bombs, strikes, and riots.

Redeemers In post–Civil War southern politics, redeemers were supporters of postwar Democratic leaders who supposedly saved the South from Yankee domination and the constraints of a purely rural economy.

Dr. Walter Reed (1851–1902) His work on yellow fever in Cuba led to the discovery that the fever was carried by mosquitoes. This understanding helped develop more effective controls of the worldwide disease.

Reformation European religious movement that challenged the Catholic Church and resulted in the beginnings of Protestant Christianity. During this period, Catholics and Protestants persecuted, imprisoned, tortured, and killed each other in large numbers.

reparations As a part of the Treaty of Versailles, Germany was required to confess its responsibility for World War I and make payments to the victors for the entire expense of the war. These two requirements created a deep bitterness among Germans.

Alexander Hamilton's Report on Manufactures First Secretary of the Treasury Alexander Hamilton's 1791 analysis that accurately foretold the future of American industry and proposed tariffs and subsidies to promote it.

"return to normalcy" In the 1920 presidential election, Republican nominee Warren G. Harding campaigned on the promise of a "return to normalcy," which would mean a return to conservative values and a turning away from President Wilson's internationalism.

Paul Revere (1735–1818) On the night of April 18, 1775, British soldiers marched towards Concord to arrest American Revolutionary leaders and seize their depot of supplies. Paul Revere famously rode through the night and raised the alarm about the approaching British troops.

Roaring Twenties In 1920s, urban America experienced an era of social and intellectual revolution. Young people experimented with new forms of recreation and sexuality as well as embraced jazz music. Leading young urban intellectuals expressed a disdain for old-fashioned rural and small-town values. The Eastern, urban cultural shift clashed with conservative and insular midwestern America, which increased the tensions between the two regions.

Jackie Robinson (1919–1972) In 1947, he became the first African American to play major league baseball. He won over fans and players and stimulated the integration of other professional sports.

rock-and-roll music Alan Freed, a disc jockey, noticed white teenagers were buying rhythm and blues records that had been only purchased by African Americans and Hispanic Americans. Freed began playing these records, but called them rock-and-roll records as a way to overcome the racial barrier. As the popularity of the music genre increased, it helped bridge the gap between "white" and "black" music.

John D. Rockefeller (1839–1937) In 1870, he founded the Standard Oil Company of Ohio, which was his first step in creating his vast oil empire. Eventually, he perfected the idea of a holding company: a company that controlled other companies by holding all or at least a majority of their stock. During his lifetime, he donated over $500 million in charitable contributions.

Romanticism Philosophical, literary, and artistic movement of the nineteenth century that was largely a reaction to the rationalism of the previous century; Romantics valued emotion, mysticism, and individualism.

Eleanor Roosevelt (1884–1962) She redefined the role of the presidential spouse and was the first woman to address a national political convention, write a nationally syndicated column and hold regular press conferences. She travelled throughout the nation to promote the New Deal, women's causes, organized labor, and meet with African American leaders. She was her husband's liaison to liberal groups and brought women activists and African American and labor leaders to the White House.

Franklin D. Roosevelt (1882–1945) Elected during the Great Depression, Roosevelt sought to help struggling Americans through his New Deal programs that created employment and social programs, such as Social Security. Prior to American's entry into World War II, he supported Britain's fight against Germany through the lend-lease program. After the bombing of Pearl Harbor, he declared war on Japan and Germany and led the country through most of World War II before dying of cerebral hemorrhage. In 1945, he met with Winston Churchill and Joseph Stalin at the Yalta Conference to determine the shape of the post-War world.

Theodore Roosevelt (1858–1919) As the assistant secretary of the navy, he supported expansionism, American imperialism and war with Spain. He led the First Volunteer Cavalry, or Rough Riders, in Cuba during the war of 1898 and used the notoriety of this military campaign for political gain. As President McKinley's vice president, he succeeded McKinley after his assassination. His forceful foreign policy became known as "big stick diplomacy." Domestically, his policies on natural resources helped start the conversation movement. Unable to win the Republican nomination for president in 1912, he formed his own party of progressive Republicans called the "Bull Moose" party.

Roosevelt Corollary to the Monroe Doctrine (1904) President Theodore Roosevelt announced in what was essentially a corollary to the Monroe Doctrine that the United States could intervene militarily to prevent interference from European powers in the Western Hemisphere.

Rough Riders The First U.S. Volunteer Cavalry, led in battle in the Spanish-American War by Theodore Roosevelt; they were victorious in their only battle near Santiago, Cuba; and Roosevelt used the notoriety to aid his political career.

Nicola Sacco (1891–1927) In 1920, he and Bartolomeo Vanzetti were Italian immigrants who were arrested for stealing $16,000 and killing a paymaster and his guard. Their trial took place during a time of numerous bombings by anarchists and their judge was openly prejudicial. Many liberals and radicals believe that the conviction of Sacco and Vanzetti was based on their political ideas and ethnic origin rather than the evidence against them.

"salutary neglect" Edward Burke's description of Robert Walpole's relaxed policy towards the American colonies, which gave them greater independence in pursuing both their economic and political interests.

Sandinista Cuban-sponsored government that came to power in Nicaragua after toppling a corrupt dictator. The State Department believed that the Sandinistas were supplying the leftist Salvadoran rebels with Cuban and Soviet arms. In response, the Reagan administration ordered the CIA to train and supply guerrilla bands of anti-Communist Nicaraguans called Contras. A cease-fire agreement between the Contras and Sandinistas was signed in 1988.

Margaret Sanger (1883–1966) As a birth-control activist, she worked to distribute birth control information to working-class women and opened the nation's first family-planning clinic in 1916. She organized the American Birth Control League, which eventually changed its name to Planned Parenthood.

General Antonio López de Santa Anna (1794–1876) In 1834, he seized political power in Mexico and became a dictator. In 1835, Texans rebelled against him and he led his army to Texas to crush their rebellion. He captured the missionary called the Alamo and killed all of its defenders, which inspired Texans to continue to resistance and Americans to volunteer to fight for Texas. The Texans captured Santa Anna during a surprise attack and he bought his freedom by signing a treaty recognizing Texas's independence.

Saratoga, Battle of Major defeat of British general John Burgoyne and more than 5,000 British troops at Saratoga, New York, on October 17, 1777.

scalawags White southern Republicans—some former Unionists—who served in Reconstruction governments.

Phyllis Schlafly (1924–) She was a right-wing Republican activist who spearheaded the anti-feminism movement. She believed feminist were "anti-family, anti-children, and pro-abortion." She worked against the equal-rights amendment for women and civil rights protection for gays.

Winfield Scott (1786–1866) During the Mexican War, he was the American general who captured Mexico City, which ended the war. Using his popularity from his military success, he ran as a Whig party candidate for President.

Sears Roebuck and Company By the end of the nineteenth century, this company dominated the mail-order industry and helped create a truly national market. Its mail-order catalog and low prices allowed people living in rural areas and small towns to buy products that were previously too expensive or available only to city dwellers.

secession Shortly after President Abraham Lincoln was elected, southern states began dissolving their ties with the United States because they believed Lincoln and the Republican party were a threat to slavery.

second Bank of the United States In 1816, the second Bank of the United States was established in order to bring stability to the national economy, serve as the depository for national funds, and provide the government with the means of floating loans and transferring money across the country.

Second Great Awakening Religious revival movement of the early decades of the nineteenth century, in reaction to the growth of secularism and rationalist religion; began the predominance of the Baptist and Methodist churches.

Second New Deal To rescue his New Deal program form judicial and political challenges, President Roosevelt launched a second phase of the New Deal in 1935. He was able to convince Congress to pass key pieces of legislation including the National Labor Relations act and Social Security Act. Roosevelt called the latter the New Deal's "supreme achievement" and pensioners started receiving monthly checks in 1940.

Seneca Falls Convention First women's rights meeting and the genesis of the women's suffrage movement; held in July 1848 in a church in Seneca Falls, New York, by Elizabeth Cady Stanton and Lucretia Coffin Mott.

"separate but equal" Principle underlying legal racial segregation, which was upheld in *Plessy v. Ferguson* (1896) and struck down in *Brown v. Board of Education* (1954).

separation of powers The powers of government are split between three separate branches (executive, legislative, and judicial) who check and balance each other.

September 11 On September 11, 2001, Islamic terrorists, who were members of al Qaeda terrorist organization, hijacked four commercial airliners. Two were flown into the World Trade Center and a third into the Pentagon. A fourth plane was brought down in Shanksville, Pennsylvania, when its passengers attacked the cockpit. In response, President George W. Bush launched his "war on terrorism." His administration assembled an international coalition to fight terrorism, and they invaded Afghanistan after the country's government would not turn over al Qaeda's leader, Osama bin Laden. However, bin Laden evaded capture. Fearful of new attacks, Bush created the Office of Homeland Security and the Transportation Security Administration.

Bush and Congress passed the U.S.A. Patriot Act, which allowed government agencies to try suspected terrorists in secret military courts and eavesdrop on confidential conversations.

settlement houses Product of the late nineteenth-century movement to offer a broad array of social services in urban immigrant neighborhoods; Chicago's Hull House was one of hundreds of settlement houses that operated by the early twentieth century.

Shakers Founded by Mother Ann Lee Stanley in England, the United Society of Believers in Christ's Second Appearing settled in Watervliet, New York, in 1774 and subsequently established eighteen additional communes in the Northeast, Indiana, and Kentucky.

sharecropping Type of farm tenancy that developed after the Civil War in which landless workers—often former slaves—farmed land in exchange for farm supplies and a share of the crop; differed from tenancy in that the terms were generally less favorable.

Share-the-Wealth program Huey Long, a critic of President Roosevelt, offered this program as an alternative to the New Deal. The program proposed to confiscate large personal fortunes, which would be used to guarantee every poor family a cash grant of $5,000 and every worker an annual income of $2,500. Under this program, Long promised to provide pensions, reduce working hours, pay veterans' bonuses, and ensures a college education to every qualified student.

Shays's Rebellion Massachusetts farmer Daniel Shays and 1,200 compatriots, seeking debt relief through issuance of paper currency and lower taxes, stormed the federal arsenal at Springfield in the winter of 1787 but were quickly repulsed.

William T. Sherman's March through Georgia Union General William T. Sherman believed that there was a connection between the South's economy, morale, and ability to wage war. During his March through Georgia, he wanted to demoralize the civilian populace and destroy the resources they needed to fight. His army seized food and livestock that the Confederate Army might have used as well as wrecked railroads and mills and burned plantations.

Sixteenth Amendment (1913) Legalized the federal income tax.

Alfred E. Smith (1873–1944) In the 1928 presidential election, he won the Democratic nomination, but failed to win the presidency. Rural voters distrusted him for being Catholic and the son of Irish immigrants as well as his anti-Prohibition stance.

Captain John Smith (1580–1631) A swashbuckling soldier of fortune with rare powers of leadership and self-promotion, he was appointed to the resident council to manage Jamestown.

Joseph Smith (1805–1844) In 1823, he claimed that the Angel Moroni showed him the location of several gold tablets on which the Book of Mormon was written. Using the Book of Mormon as his gospel, he founded the Church of Jesus Christ of Latter-day Saints, or Mormons. Joseph and his followers upset non-Mormons living near them so they began looking for a refuge from persecution. In 1839, they settled in Commerce, Illinois, which they renamed Nauvoo. In 1844, Joseph and his brother were arrested and jailed for ordering the destruction of a newspaper that opposed them. While in jail, an anti-Mormon mob stormed the jail and killed both of them.

social Darwinism Application of Charles Darwin's theory of natural selection to society; used the concept of the "survival of the fittest" to justify class distinctions and to explain poverty.

social gospel Preached by liberal Protestant clergymen in the late nineteenth and early twentieth centuries; advocated the application of Christian principles to social problems generated by industrialization.

social justice An important part of the Progressive's agenda, social justice sought to solve social problems through reform and regulation. Methods used to bring about social justice ranged from the founding of charities to the legislation of a ban on child labor.

Sons of Liberty Organized by Samuel Adams, they were colonialists with a militant view against the British government's control of the colonies.

Hernando de Soto (1500?–1542) A conquistador who explored the west coast of Florida, western North Carolina and along the Arkansas river from 1539 till his death in 1542.

Southern Christian Leadership Conference (SCLC) Civil rights organization founded in 1957 by the Reverend Martin Luther King Jr., and other civil rights leaders.

"southern strategy" This strategy was a major reason for Richard Nixon's victory in the 1968 presidential election. To gain support in the South, Nixon assured southern conservatives that he would slow the federal enforcement of civil rights laws and appoint pro-southern justices to the Supreme Court. As president, Nixon fulfilled these promises.

Spanish flu Unprecedentedly lethal influenza epidemic of 1918 that killed more than 22 million people worldwide.

Herbert Spencer (1820–1903) As the first major proponent of social Darwinism, he argued that human society and institutions are subject to the process of natural selection and that society naturally evolves for the better. Therefore, he was against any form of government interference with the evolution of society, like business regulations, because it would help the "unfit" to survive.

spoils system The term—meaning the filling of federal government jobs with persons loyal to the party of the president—originated in Andrew Jackson's first term; the system was replaced in the Progressive Era by civil service.

stagflation During the Nixon administration, the economy experienced inflation and a recession at the same time, which is syndrome that defies the orthodox laws of economics. Economists named this phenomenon "stagflation."

Joseph Stalin (1879–1953) The Bolshevik leader who succeeded Lenin as the leader of the Soviet Union in 1924 and ruled the country until his death. During his totalitarian rule of the Soviet Union, he used purges and a system of forced labor camps to maintain control over the country. During the Yalta Conference, he claimed vast areas of Eastern Europe for Soviet domination. After the end of World War II, the alliance between the Soviet Union and the Western powers altered into the tension of the cold war and Stalin erected the "iron curtain" between Eastern and Western Europe.

Stalwarts Conservative Republican party faction during the presidency of Rutherford B. Hayes, 1877–1881; led by Senator Roscoe B. Conkling of New York, Stalwarts opposed civil service reform and favored a third term for President Ulysses S. Grant.

Stamp Act Congress Twenty-seven delegates from nine of the colonies met from October 7 to 25, 1765 and wrote a Declaration of the Rights and Grievances of the Colonies, a petition to the King and a petition to Parliament for the repeal of the Stamp Act.

Standard Oil Company of Ohio John D. Rockefeller found this company in 1870, which grew to monopolize 90 to 95 percent of all the oil refineries in the country. It was also a "vertical monopoly" in that the company controlled all aspects of production and the services it needed to conduct business. For example, Standard Oil produced their own oil barrels and cans as well as owned their own pipelines, railroad tank cars, and oil-storage facilities.

Elizabeth Cady Stanton (1815–1902) She was a prominent reformer and advocate for the rights of women, and she helped organize the Seneca Falls Convention to discuss women's rights. The convention was the first of its kind and produced the Declaration of Sentiments, which proclaimed the equality of men and women.

staple crop, or cash crop A profitable market crop, such as cotton or tobacco.

Thaddeus Stevens (1792–1868) As one of the leaders of the Radical Republicans, he argued that the former Confederate states should be viewed as conquered provinces, which were subject to the demands of the conquerors. He believed that all of southern society needed to be changed, and he supported the abolition of slavery and racial equality.

Adlai E. Stevenson (1900–1965) In the 1952 and 1956 presidential elections, he was the Democratic nominee who lost to Dwight Eisenhower. He was also the U.S. Ambassador to the United Nations and is remembered for his famous speech in 1962 before the UN Security Council that unequivocally demonstrated that the Soviet Union had built nuclear missile bases in Cuba.

Strategic Defense Initiative ("Star Wars") Defense Department's plan during the Reagan administration to build a system to destroy incoming missiles in space.

Levi Strauss (1829–1902) A Jewish tailor who followed miners to California during the gold rush and began making durable work pants that were later dubbed blue jeans or Levi's.

Students for a Democratic Society (SDS) Major organization of the New Left, founded at the University of Michigan in 1960 by Tom Hayden and Al Haber.

suburbia The postwar era witnessed a mass migration to the suburbs. As the population in cities areas grew, people began to spread further out within the urban areas, which created new suburban communities. By 1970 more people lived in the suburbs (76 million) than in central cities (64 million).

sunbelt The label for an arc that stretched from the Carolinas to California. During the postwar era, much of the urban population growth occurred in this area.

the "surge" In early 2007, President Bush decided he would send a "surge" of new troops to Iraq and implement a new strategy. U.S. forces would shift their focus from offensive operations to the protection of Iraqi civilians from attacks by terrorist insurgents and sectarian militias. While the "surge" reduced the violence in Iraq, Iraqi leaders were still unable to develop a self-sustaining democracy.

Taliban A coalition of ultraconservative Islamists who rose to power in Afghanistan after the Soviets withdrew. The Taliban leaders gave Osama bin Laden a safe haven in their country in exchange for aid in fighting the Northern Alliance, who were rebels opposed to the Taliban. After September 11 terrorist attacks, the United States asked the Taliban to turn over bin Laden. After they refused, America invaded Afghanistan, but bin Laden evaded capture.

Tammany Hall The "city machine" used by "Boss" Tweed to dominate politics in New York City until his arrest in 1871.

Tariff of 1816 First true protective tariff, intended strictly to protect American goods against foreign competition.

Tariff of 1832 This tariff act reduced the duties on many items, but the tariffs on cloth and iron remained high. South Carolina nullified it along with the tariff of 1828. President Andrew Jackson sent federal troops to the state and asked Congress to grant him the authority to enforce the tariffs. Henry Clay presented a plan of gradually reducing the tariffs until 1842, which Congress passed and ended the crisis.

TARP In 2008 President George W. Bush signed into law the bank bailout fund called Troubled Asset Relief Program (TARP), which required the Treasury Department to spend $700 billion to keep banks and other financial institutions from collapsing.

Zachary Taylor (1784–1850) During the Mexican War, he scored two quick victories against Mexico, which made him very popular in America. President Polk chose him as the commander in charge of the war. However, after he was not put in charge of the campaign to capture Mexico City, he chose to return home. Later he used his popularity from his military victories to be elected the president as a member of the Whig party.

Taylorism In his book *The Principles of Scientific Management*, Frederick W. Taylor explained a management system that claimed to be able to reduce waste through the scientific analysis of the labor process. This system called Taylorism, promised to find the optimum technique for the average worker and establish detailed performance standards for each job classification.

Teapot Dome Harding administration scandal in which Secretary of the Interior Albert B. Fall profited from secret leasing to private oil companies of government oil reserves at Teapot Dome, Wyoming, and Elk Hills, California.

Tecumseh (1768–1813) He was a leader of the Shawnee tribe who tried to unite all Indians into a confederation that could defend their hunting grounds. He believed that no land cessions could be made without the consent of all the tribes since they held the land in common. His beliefs and leadership made him seem dangerous to the American government and they waged war on him and his tribe. He was killed at the Battle of the Thames.

Tejanos Texas settlers of Spanish or Mexican descent.

Teller Amendment On April 20, 1898, a joint resolution of Congress declared Cuba independent and demanded the withdrawal of Spanish forces. The Teller amendment was added to this resolution, and it declaimed any designs the United States had on Cuban territory.

Tenochtitlán The capital city of the Aztec Empire. The city was built on marshy islands on the western side of Lake Tetzcoco, which is the site of present-day Mexico City.

Tet offensive Surprise attack by the Viet Cong and North Vietnamese during the Vietnamese New Year of 1968; turned American public opinion strongly against the war in Vietnam.

Thirteenth Amendment This amendment to the U.S. Constitution freed all slaves in the United States. After the Civil War ended, the former confederate states were required to ratify this amendment before they could be readmitted to the Union.

Gulf of Tonkin incident On August 2 and 4 of 1964, North Vietnamese vessels attacked two American destroyers in Gulf of Tonkin off the coast of North Vietnam. President Johnson described the attacks as unprovoked. In reality, the U.S. ships were monitoring South Vietnamese attacks on North Vietnamese islands that America advisors had planned. The incident spurred the Tonkin Gulf resolution.

Tonkin Gulf resolution (1964) Passed by Congress in reaction to supposedly unprovoked attacks on American warships off the coast of North Vietnam; it gave the president unlimited authority to defend U.S. forces and members of SEATO.

Tories Term used by Patriots to refer to Loyalists, or colonists who supported the Crown after the Declaration of Independence.

Trail of Tears Cherokees' own term for their forced march, 1838–1839, from the southern Appalachians to Indian lands (later Oklahoma); of 15,000 forced to march, 4,000 died on the way.

Transcendentalism Philosophy of a small group of mid-nineteenth-century New England writers and thinkers, including Ralph Waldo Emerson, Henry David Thoreau, and Margaret Fuller; they stressed "plain living and high thinking."

Transcontinental railroad First line across the continent from Omaha, Nebraska, to Sacramento, California, established in 1869 with the linkage of the Union Pacific and Central Pacific railroads at Promontory, Utah.

triangular trade Means by which exports to one country or colony provided the means for imports from another country or colony. For example, merchants from colonial New England shipped rum to West Africa and used it to barter for slaves who were then taken to the West Indies. The slaves were sold or traded for materials that the ships brought back to New England including molasses which is need to make rum.

Treaty of Ghent The signing of this treaty in 1814 ended the War of 1812 without solving any of the disputes between Britain and the United States.

Harry S. Truman (1884–1972) As President Roosevelt's vice president, he succeeded him after his death near the end of World War II. After the war, Truman wrestled with the inflation of both prices and wages, and his attempts to bring them both under control led to clashes with organized labor and Republicans. He did work with Congress to pass the National Security Act, which made the Joint Chiefs of Staff a permanent position and created the National Military Establishment and the Central Intelligence Agency. He banned racial discrimination in the hiring of federal employees and ended racial segregation in the armed forces. In foreign affairs, he established the Truman Doctrine to contain communism and the Marshall Plan to rebuild Europe. After North Korea invaded South Korea, Truman sent the U.S. military to defend

South Korea under the command of General Douglas MacArthur. Later in the war, Truman expressed his willingness to negotiate the restoration of prewar boundaries which MacArthur attempted to undermine. Truman fired MacArthur for his open insubordination.

Truman Doctrine President Harry S. Truman's program of post–World War II aid to European countries—particularly Greece and Turkey—in danger of being undermined by communism.

Sojourner Truth (1797? –1883) She was born into slavery, but New York State freed her in 1827. She spent the 1840s and 1850s travelling across the country and speaking to audiences about her experiences as slave and asking them to support abolition and women's rights.

Harriet Tubman (1820–1913) She was born a slave, but escaped to the North. Then she returned to the South nineteen times and guided 300 slaves to freedom.

Nat Turner (1800–1831) He was the leader of the only slave revolt to get past the planning stages. In August of 1831, the revolt began with the slaves killing the members of Turner's master's household. Then they attacked other neighboring farmhouses and recruited more slaves until the militia crushed the revolt. At least fifty-five whites were killed during the uprising and seventeen slaves were hanged afterwards.

Tuskegee Airmen During World War II, African Americans in the armed forces usually served in segregated units. African American pilots were trained at a separate flight school in Tuskegee, Alabama, and were known as Tuskegee Airmen.

Mark Twain (1835–1910) Born Samuel Langhorne Clemens in Missouri, he became a popular humorous writer and lecturer and established himself as one of the great American authors. Like other authors of the local-color movement, his stories expressed the nostalgia people had for rural culture and old folkways as America became increasingly urban. His two greatest books, *The Adventures of Tom Sawyer* and *The Adventures of Huckleberry Finn*, drew heavily on his childhood in Missouri.

"Boss" Tweed (1823–1878) An infamous political boss in New York City, Tweed used his "city machine," the Tammany Hall ring, to rule, plunder and sometimes improve the city's government. His political domination of New York City ended with his arrest in 1871 and conviction in 1873.

Twenty-first Amendment (1933) Repealed prohibition on the manufacture, sale, and transportation of alcoholic beverages, effectively nullifying the Eighteenth Amendment.

Underground Railroad Operating in the decades before the Civil War, the "railroad" was a clandestine system of routes and safehouses through which slaves were led to freedom in the North.

Unitarianism Late eighteenth-century liberal offshoot of the New England Congregationalist church; Unitarianism professed the oneness of God and the goodness of rational man.

United Nations Security Council A major agency within the United Nations which remains in permanent session and has the responsibility of maintaining international peace and security. Originally, it consisted of five permanent members, (United States, Soviet Union, Britain, France, and the Republic of China), and six members elected to two-year terms. After 1965, the number of rotating members was increased to ten. In 1971, the Republic of China was replaced with the People's Republic of China and the Soviet Union was replaced by the Russian Federation in 1991.

Utopian communities These communities flourished during the Jacksonian era and were attempts to create the ideal community. They were social experiments conducted in relative isolation, so they had little impact on the world outside of their communities. In most cases, the communities quickly ran out of steam and ended.

Cornelius Vanderbilt (1794–1877) In the 1860s, he consolidated several separate railroad companies into one vast entity, New York Central Railroad.

Bartolomeo Vanzetti (1888–1927) In 1920, he and Nicola Sacco were Italian immigrants who were arrested for stealing $16,000 and killing a paymaster and his guard. Their trial took place during a time of numerous bombings by anarchists and their judge was openly prejudicial. Many liberals and radicals believe that the conviction of Sacco and Vanzetti was based on their political ideas and ethnic origin rather than the evidence against them.

Amerigo Vespucci (1455–1512) Italian explorer who reached the New World in 1499 and was the first to suggest that South America was a new continent. Afterward, European mapmakers used a variant of his first name, America, to label the New World.

Viet Cong In 1956, these guerrilla forces began attacking South Vietnam's government and in 1960 the resistance groups coalesced as the National Liberation Front.

Vietnamization President Nixon's policy of equipping and training the South Vietnamese so that they could assume ground combat operations in the place of American soldiers. Nixon hoped that a reduction in U.S. forces in Vietnam would defuse the anti-war movement.

Vikings Norse people from Scandinavia who sailed to Newfoundland about A.D. 1001.

Pancho Villa (1877–1923) While the leader of one of the competing factions in the Mexican civil war, he provoked the United States into intervening. He hoped attacking the United States would help him build a reputation as an opponent of the United States, which would increase his popularity and discredit Mexican President Carranza.

Virginia Company A joint stock enterprise that King James I chartered in 1606. The company was to spread Christianity in the New World as well as find ways to make a profit in it.

Virginia Plan The delegations to the Constitutional Convention were divided between two plans on how to structure the government: Virginia called for a strong central government and a two-house legislature apportioned by population.

George Wallace (1919–1998) An outspoken defender of segregation. As the governor of Alabama, he once attempted to block African American students from enrolling at the University of Alabama. He ran as the presidential candidate for the American Independent party in 1968. He appealed to voters who were concerned about rioting anti-war protestors, the welfare system, and the growth of the federal government.

War Hawks In 1811, congressional members from the southern and western districts who clamored for a war to seize Canada and Florida were dubbed "war hawks."

Warren Court The U.S. Supreme Court under Chief Justice Earl Warren, 1953–1969, decided such landmark cases as *Brown v. Board of Education* (school desegregation), *Baker v. Carr* (legislative redistricting), and *Gideon v. Wainwright* and *Miranda v. Arizona* (rights of criminal defendants).

Booker T. Washington (1856–1915) He founded a leading college for African Americans in Tuskegee, Alabama, and become the foremost black educator in America by the 1890s. He believed that the African American community should establish an economic base for its advancement before striving for social equality. His critics charged that his philosophy sacrificed educational and civil rights for dubious social acceptance and economic opportunities.

George Washington (1732–1799) In 1775, the Continental Congress named him the commander in chief of the Continental Army. He had previously served as an officer in the French and Indian War, but had never commanded a large unit. Initially, his army was poorly supplied and inexperienced, which led to repeated defeats. Washington realized that he could only defeat the British through wearing them down, and he implemented a strategy of evasion and selective confrontations. Gradually, the army developed into an effective force and, with the aid of the French, defeated the British. In 1787, he was the presiding officer over the Constitutional Convention, but participated little in the debates. In 1789, the Electoral College chose Washington to be the nation's first president. He assembled a cabinet of brilliant minds, which included Thomas Jefferson, James Madison, and Alexander Hamilton. Together, they would lay the foundations of American government and capitalism. Washington faced the nation's first foreign and domestic crises. In 1793, the British and French were at war. Washington chose to keep America neutral in the conflict even though France and the United States had signed a treaty of alliance. A year later, the Whiskey Rebellion erupted in Pennsylvania, and Washington sent militiamen to suppress the rebels. After two terms in office, Washington chose to step down; and the power of the presidency was peacefully passed to John Adams.

Watergate Washington office and apartment complex that lent its name to the 1972–1974 scandal of the Nixon administration; when his knowledge of the break-in at the Watergate and subsequent cover-up was revealed, Nixon resigned the presidency under threat of impeachment.

Daniel Webster (1782–1852) As a representative from New Hampshire, he led the New Federalists in opposition to the moving of the second national bank from Boston to Philadelphia. Later, he served as representative and a senator for Massachusetts and emerged as a champion of a stronger national government. He also switched from opposing to supporting tariffs because New England had built up its manufactures with the understanding tariffs would protect them from foreign competitors.

Webster-Ashburton Treaty Settlement in 1842 of U.S.–Canadian border disputes in Maine, New York, Vermont, and in the Wisconsin Territory (now northern Minnesota).

Webster-Hayne debate U.S. Senate debate of January 1830 between Daniel Webster of Massachusetts and Robert Hayne of South Carolina over nullification and states' rights.

Ida B. Wells (1862–1931) After being denied a seat on a railroad car because she was black, she became the first African American to file a suit against such discrimination. As a journalist, she criticized Jim Crow laws, demanded that blacks have their voting rights restored and crusaded against lynching. In 1909, she helped found the National Association for the Advancement of Colored People (NAACP).

western front The military front that stretched from the English Channel through Belgium and France to the Alps during World War I.

Whig party Founded in 1834 to unite factions opposed to President Andrew Jackson, the party favored federal responsibility for internal improvements; the party ceased to exist by the late 1850s, when party members divided over the slavery issue.

Whigs Another name for revolutionary Patriots.

Whiskey Rebellion Violent protest by western Pennsylvania farmers against the federal excise tax on corn whiskey, 1794.

George Whitefield (1714–1770) A true catalyst of the Great Awakening, he sought to reignite religious fervor in the American congregations. During his tour of the American Colonies in 1739, he gave spellbinding sermons and preached the notion of "new birth"—a sudden, emotional moment of conversion and salvation.

Eli Whitney (1765–1825) He invented the cotton gin which could separate cotton from its seeds. One machine operator could separate fifty times more cotton than worker could by hand, which led to an increase in cotton production and prices. These increases gave planters a new profitable use for slavery and a lucrative slave trade emerged from the coastal South to the Southwest.

Wilderness Road Originally an Indian path through the Cumberland Gap, it was used by over 300,000 settlers who migrated westward to Kentucky in the last quarter of the eighteenth century.

Roger Williams (1603–1683) Puritan who believed that the purity of the church required a complete separation between church and state and freedom from coercion in matters of faith. In 1636, he established the town of Providence, the first permanent settlement in Rhode Island and the first to allow religious freedom in America.

Wendell L. Willkie (1892–1944) In the 1940 presidential election, he was the Republican nominee who ran against President Roosevelt. He supported aid to the Allies and criticized the New Deal programs. Voters looked at the increasingly dangerous world situation and chose to keep President Roosevelt in office for a third term.

Wilmot Proviso Proposal to prohibit slavery in any land acquired in the Mexican War, but southern senators, led by John C. Calhoun of South Carolina, defeated the measure in 1846 and 1847.

Woodrow Wilson (1856–1924) In the 1912 presidential election, Woodrow Wilson ran under the slogan of New Freedom, which promised to improve of the banking system, lower tariffs, and break up monopolies. He sought to deliver on these promises through passage of the Underwood-Simmons Tariff, the Federal Reserve Act of 1913, and new antitrust laws. Though he was weak on implementing social change and showed a little interest in the plight of African Americans, he did eventually support some labor reform. At the beginning of World War I, Wilson kept America neutral, but provided the Allies with credit for purchases of supplies. However, the sinking of U.S. merchant ships and the news of Germany encouraging Mexico to attack America caused Wilson to ask Congress to declare war on Germany. Following the war, Wilson supported the entry of America into the League of Nations and the ratification of the Treaty of Versailles; but Congress would not approve the entry or ratification.

John Winthrop Puritan leader and Governor of the Massachusetts Bay Colony who resolved to use the colony as a refuge for persecuted Puritans and as an instrument of building a "wilderness Zion" in America.

Women Accepted for Voluntary Emergency Services (WAVES) During World War II, the increased demand for labor shook up old prejudices about gender roles in workplace and in the military. Nearly 200,000 women served in the Women's Army Corps or its naval equivalent, Women Accepted for Volunteer Emergency Service (WAVES).

Women's Army Corps (WAC) During World War II, the increased demand for labor shook up old prejudices about gender roles in workplace and in the military. Nearly 200,000 women served in the Women's Army

Corps or its naval equivalent, Women Accepted for Volunteer Emergency Service (WAVES).

Woodstock In 1969, roughly a half a million young people converged on a farm near Bethel, New York, for a three-day music festival that was an expression of the flower children's free spirit.

Wounded Knee, Battle of Last incident of the Indians Wars took place in 1890 in the Dakota Territory, where the U.S. Cavalry killed over 200 Sioux men, women, and children who were in the process of surrender.

XYZ affair French foreign minister Tallyrand's three anonymous agents demanded payments to stop French plundering of American ships in 1797; refusal to pay the bribe led to two years of sea war with France (1798–1800).

Yalta Conference Meeting of Franklin D. Roosevelt, Winston Churchill, and Joseph Stalin at a Crimean resort to discuss the postwar world on February 4–11, 1945; Soviet leader Joseph Stalin claimed large areas in eastern Europe for Soviet domination.

yeomen Small landowners (the majority of white families in the South) who farmed their own land and usually did not own slaves.

surrender at Yorktown Last battle of the Revolutionary War; General Lord Charles Cornwallis along with over 7,000 British troops surrendered at Yorktown, Virginia, on October 17, 1781.

Brigham Young (1801–1877) Following Joseph Smith's death, he became the leader of the Mormons and promised Illinois officials that the Mormons would leave the state. In 1846, he led the Mormons to Utah and settled near the Salt Lake. After the United States gained Utah as part of the Treaty of Guadalupe Hidalgo, he became the governor of the territory and kept the Mormons virtually independent of federal authority.

youth culture The youth of the 1950s had more money and free time than any previous generation which allowed a distinct youth culture to emerge. A market emerged for products and activities that were specifically for young people such as transistor radios, rock records, *Seventeen* magazine, and Pat Boone movies.

APPENDIX

THE DECLARATION OF
INDEPENDENCE (1776)

WHEN IN THE COURSE OF HUMAN EVENTS, it becomes necessary for one people to dissolve the political bands which have connected them with another, and to assume the Powers of the earth, the separate and equal station to which the Laws of Nature and of Nature's God entitle them, a decent respect to the opinions of mankind requires that they should declare the causes which impel them to the separation.

We hold these truths to be self-evident, that all men are created equal, that they are endowed by their Creator with certain unalienable rights, that among these are Life, Liberty, and the pursuit of Happiness. That to secure these rights, Governments are instituted among Men, deriving their just powers from the consent of the governed. That whenever any Form of Government becomes destructive of these ends, it is the Right of the People to alter or to abolish it, and to institute new Government, laying its foundation on such principles and organizing its powers in such form, as to them shall seem most likely to effect their Safety and Happiness. Prudence, indeed, will dictate that Governments long established should not be changed for light and transient causes; and accordingly all experience hath shown, that mankind are more disposed to suffer, while evils are sufferable, than to right themselves by abolishing the forms to which they are accustomed. But when a long train of abuses and usurpations, pursuing invariably the same Object evinces a design to reduce them under absolute Despotism, it is their right, it is their duty, to throw off such Government, and to provide new Guards for their future security.—Such has been the patient sufferance of these Colonies; and such is now the necessity which constrains them to alter their former Systems of Government. The history of the present King of Great Britain is a history of repeated injuries and usurpations, all having in direct object the establishment of an absolute Tyranny over these States. To prove this, let Facts be submitted to a candid world.

He has refused his Assent to Laws, the most wholesome and necessary for the public good.

He has forbidden his Governors to pass Laws of immediate and pressing importance, unless suspended in their operation till his Assent should be obtained; and when so suspended, he has utterly neglected to attend to them.

He has refused to pass other Laws for the accommodation of large districts of people, unless those people would relinquish the right of Representation in the Legislature, a right inestimable to them and formidable to tyrants only.

He has called together legislative bodies at places unusual, uncomfortable, and distant from the depository of their public Records, for the sole purpose of fatiguing them into compliance with his measures.

He has dissolved Representative Houses repeatedly, for opposing with manly firmness his invasions on the rights of the people.

He has refused for a long time, after such dissolutions, to cause others to be elected; whereby the Legislative powers, incapable of Annihilation, have returned to the People at large for their exercise; the State remaining in the mean time exposed to all dangers of invasion from without, and convulsions within.

He has endeavoured to prevent the population of these States; for that purpose obstructing the Laws of Naturalization of Foreigners; refusing to pass others to encourage their migrations hither, and raising the conditions of new Appropriations of Lands.

He has obstructed the Administration of Justice, by refusing his Assent to Laws for establishing Judiciary powers.

He has made Judges dependent on his Will alone, for the tenure of their offices, and the amount and payment of their salaries.

He has erected a multitude of New Offices, and sent hither swarms of Officers to harass our People, and eat out their substance.

He has kept among us, in times of peace, Standing Armies without the Consent of our legislatures.

He has affected to render the Military independent of and superior to the Civil Power.

He has combined with others to subject us to a jurisdiction foreign to our constitution, and unacknowledged by our laws; giving his Assent to their Acts of pretended Legislation:

For quartering large bodies of armed troops among us:

For protecting them, by a mock Trial, from Punishment for any Murders which they should commit on the Inhabitants of these States:

For cutting off our Trade with all parts of the world:

For imposing taxes on us without our Consent:

For depriving us of many cases, of the benefits of Trial by jury:

For transporting us beyond Seas to be tried for pretended offences:

For abolishing the free System of English Laws in a neighbouring Province, establishing therein an Arbitrary government, and enlarging its

Boundaries so as to render it at once an example and fit instrument for introducing the same absolute rule into these Colonies:

For taking away our Charters, abolishing our most valuable Laws, and altering fundamentally the Forms of our Governments:

For suspending our own Legislatures, and declaring themselves in vested with Power to legislate for us in all cases whatsoever.

He has abdicated Government here, by declaring us out of his Protection and waging War against us.

He has plundered our seas, ravaged our Coasts, burnt our towns, and destroyed the lives of our people.

He is at this time transporting large armies of foreign mercenaries to compleat the works of death, desolation, and tyranny, already begun with circumstances of Cruelty & perfidy scarcely paralleled in the most barbarous ages, and totally unworthy the Head of a civilized nation.

He has constrained our fellow Citizens taken Captive on the high Seas to bear Arms against their Country, to become the executioners of their friends and Brethren, or to fall themselves by their Hands.

He has excited domestic insurrections amongst us, and has endeavoured to bring on the inhabitants of our frontiers, the merciless Indian Savages, whose known rule of warfare, is an undistinguished destruction of all ages, sexes, and conditions.

In every stage of these Oppressions We have Petitioned for Redress in the most humble terms: Our repeated Petitions have been answered only by repeated injury. A Prince, whose character is thus marked by every act which may define a Tyrant, is unfit to be the ruler of a free people.

Nor have We been wanting in attention to our British brethren. We have warned them from time to time of attempts by their legislature to extend an unwarrantable jurisdiction over us. We have reminded them of the circumstances of our emigration and settlement here. We have appealed to their native justice and magnanimity, and we have conjured them by the ties of our common kindred to disavow these usurpations, which, would inevitably interrupt our connections and correspondence. They too must have been deaf to the voice of justice and of consanguinity. We must, therefore, acquiesce in the necessity, which denounces our Separation, and hold them, as we hold the rest of mankind, Enemies in War, in Peace Friends.

WE, THEREFORE, the Representatives of the UNITED STATES OF AMERICA, in General Congress, Assembled, appealing to the Supreme Judge of the world for the rectitude of our intentions, do, in the Name, and by Authority of the good People of these Colonies, solemnly publish and declare, That these United Colonies are, and of Right ought to be FREE AND INDEPENDENT STATES; that they are Absolved from all Allegiance to the

British Crown, and that all political connection between them and the State of Great Britain, is and ought to be totally dissolved; and that as Free and Independent States, they have full Power to levy War, conclude Peace, contract Alliances, establish Commerce, and to do all other Acts and Things which Independent States may of right do. And for the support of this Declaration, with a firm reliance on the Protection of Divine Providence, we mutually pledge to each other our Lives, our Fortunes, and our sacred Honor.

The foregoing Declaration was, by order of Congress, engrossed, and signed by the following members:

John Hancock

NEW HAMPSHIRE
Josiah Bartlett
William Whipple
Matthew Thornton

MASSACHUSETTS BAY
Samuel Adams
John Adams
Robert Treat Paine
Elbridge Gerry

RHODE ISLAND
Stephen Hopkins
William Ellery

CONNECTICUT
Roger Sherman
Samuel Huntington
William Williams
Oliver Wolcott

NEW YORK
William Floyd
Philip Livingston
Francis Lewis
Lewis Morris

NEW JERSEY
Richard Stockton
John Witherspoon
Francis Hopkinson
John Hart
Abraham Clark

PENNSYLVANIA
Robert Morris
Benjamin Rush
Benjamin Franklin
John Morton
George Clymer
James Smith
George Taylor
James Wilson
George Ross

DELAWARE
Caesar Rodney
George Read
Thomas M'Kean

MARYLAND
Samuel Chase
William Paca
Thomas Stone
Charles Carroll, of Carrollton

VIRGINIA
George Wythe
Richard Henry Lee
Thomas Jefferson
Benjamin Harrison
Thomas Nelson, Jr.
Francis Lightfoot Lee
Carter Braxton

NORTH CAROLINA
William Hooper
Joseph Hewes
John Penn

SOUTH CAROLINA
Edward Rutledge
Thomas Heyward, Jr.
Thomas Lynch, Jr.
Arthur Middleton

GEORGIA
Button Gwinnett
Lyman Hall
George Walton

Resolved, that copies of the declaration be sent to the several assemblies, conventions, and committees, or councils of safety, and to the several commanding officers of the continental troops; that it be proclaimed in each of the united states, at the head of the army.

ARTICLES OF
CONFEDERATION (1778)

To all to whom these Presents shall come, we the undersigned Delegates of the States affixed to our Names send greeting.

Whereas the Delegates of the United States of America in Congress assembled did on the fifteenth day of November in the Year of our Lord One Thousand Seven Hundred and Seventy-seven, and in the Second Year of the Independence of America agree to certain articles of Confederation and perpetual Union between the States of Newhampshire, Massachusetts-bay, Rhodeisland and Providence Plantations, Connecticut, New York, New Jersey, Pennsylvania, Delaware, Maryland, Virginia, North-Carolina, South-Carolina and Georgia in the Words following, viz.

Articles of Confederation and perpetual Union between the States of Newhampshire, Massachusetts-bay, Rhodeisland and Providence Plantations, Connecticut, New-York, New-Jersey, Pennsylvania, Delaware, Maryland, Virginia, North-Carolina, South-Carolina and Georgia.

ARTICLE I. The stile of this confederacy shall be "The United States of America."

ARTICLE II. Each State retains its sovereignty, freedom and independence, and every power, jurisdiction and right, which is not by this confederation expressly delegated to the United States, in Congress assembled.

ARTICLE III. The said States hereby severally enter into a firm league of friendship with each other, for their common defence, the security of their liberties, and their mutual and general welfare, binding themselves to assist each other, against all force offered to, or attacks made upon them, or any of them, on account of religion, sovereignty, trade or any other pretence whatever.

ARTICLE IV. The better to secure and perpetuate mutual friendship and intercourse among the people of the different States in this Union, the free inhabitants of each of these States, paupers, vagabonds and fugitives from justice excepted, shall be entitled to all privileges and immunities of free citizens in the several States; and the people of each State shall have free ingress and regress to and from any other State, and shall enjoy therein all the privileges of trade and commerce, subject to the same duties, impositions and restrictions as the inhabitants thereof respectively, provided that such restrictions shall not extend so far as to prevent the removal of property imported into any State, to any other State of which the owner is an inhabitant; provided also that no imposition, duties or restriction shall be laid by any State, on the property of the United States, or either of them.

If any person guilty of, or charged with treason, felony, or other high misdemeanor in any State, shall flee from justice, and be found in any of the United States, he shall upon demand of the Governor or Executive power, of the State from which he fled, be delivered up and removed to the State having jurisdiction of his offence.

Full faith and credit shall be given in each of these States to the records, acts and judicial proceedings of the courts and magistrates of every other State.

ARTICLE V. For the more convenient management of the general interests of the United States, delegates shall be annually appointed in such manner as the legislature of each State shall direct, to meet in Congress on the first Monday in November, in every year, with a power reserved to each State, to recall its delegates, or any of them, at any time within the year, and to send others in their stead, for the remainder of the year.

No State shall be represented in Congress by less than two, nor by more than seven members; and no person shall be capable of being a delegate for more than three years in any term of six years; nor shall any person, being a delegate, be capable of holding any office under the United States, for which he, or another for his benefit receives any salary, fees or emolument of any kind.

Each State shall maintain its own delegates in a meeting of the States, and while they act as members of the committee of the States.

In determining questions in the United States, in Congress assembled, each State shall have one vote.

Freedom of speech and debate in Congress shall not be impeached or questioned in any court, or place out of Congress, and the members of Congress shall be protected in their persons from arrests and imprisonments, during the time of their going to and from, and attendance on Congress, except for treason, felony, or breach of the peace.

ARTICLE VI. No State without the consent of the United States in Congress assembled, shall send any embassy to, or receive any embassy from, or enter into any conference, agreement, alliance or treaty with any king, prince or state; nor shall any person holding any office of profit or trust under the United States, or any of them, accept of any present, emolument, office or title of any kind whatever from any king, prince or foreign state; nor shall the United States in Congress assembled, or any of them, grant any title of nobility.

No two or more States shall enter into any treaty, confederation or alliance whatever between them, without the consent of the United States in Congress assembled, specifying accurately the purposes for which the same is to be entered into, and how long it shall continue.

No State shall lay any imposts or duties, which may interfere with any stipulations in treaties, entered into by the United States in Congress assembled, with any king, prince or state, in pursuance of any treaties already proposed by Congress, to the courts of France and Spain.

No vessels of war shall be kept up in time of peace by any State, except such number only, as shall be deemed necessary by the United States in Congress assembled, for the defence of such State, or its trade; nor shall any body of forces be kept up by any State, in time of peace, except such number only, as in the judgment of the United States, in Congress assembled, shall be deemed requisite to garrison the forts necessary for the defence of such State; but every State shall always keep up a well regulated and disciplined militia, sufficiently armed and accoutred, and shall provide and constantly have ready for use, in public stores, a due number of field pieces and tents, and a proper quantity of arms, ammunition and camp equipage.

No State shall engage in any war without the consent of the United States in Congress assembled, unless such State be actually invaded by enemies, or shall have received certain advice of a resolution being formed by some nation of Indians to invade such State, and the danger is so imminent as not to admit of a delay, till the United States in Congress assembled can be consulted: nor shall any State grant commissions to any ships or vessels of war, nor letters of marque or reprisal, except it be after a declaration of war by the United States in Congress assembled, and then only against the kingdom or state and the subjects thereof, against which war has been so declared, and under such regulations as shall be established by the United States in Congress assembled, unless such State be infested by pirates, in which case vessels of war may be fitted out for that occasion, and kept so long as the danger shall continue, or until the United States in Congress assembled shall determine otherwise.

ARTICLE VII. When land-forces are raised by any State of the common defence, all officers of or under the rank of colonel, shall be appointed by the Legislature of each State respectively by whom such forces shall be raised, or in such manner as such State shall direct, and all vacancies shall be filled up by the State which first made the appointment.

ARTICLE VIII. All charges of war, and all other expenses that shall be incurred for the common defence or general welfare, and allowed by the United States in Congress assembled, shall be defrayed out of a common treasury, which shall be supplied by the several States, in proportion to the value of all land within each State, granted to or surveyed for any person, as such land and the buildings and improvements thereon shall be estimated according to such mode as the United States in Congress assembled, shall from time to time direct and appoint.

The taxes for paying that proportion shall be laid and levied by the authority and direction of the Legislatures of the several States within the time agreed upon by the United States in Congress assembled.

ARTICLE IX. The United States in Congress assembled, shall have the sole and exclusive right and power of determining on peace and war, except in the cases mentioned in the sixth article—of sending and receiving ambassadors—entering into treaties and alliances, provided that no treaty of commerce shall be made whereby the legislative power of the respective States shall be restrained from imposing such imposts and duties on foreigners, as their own people are subjected to, or from prohibiting the exportation or importation of and species of goods or commodities whatsoever—of establishing rules for deciding in all cases, what captures on land or water shall be legal, and in what manner prizes taken by land or naval forces in the service of the United States shall be divided or appropriated—of granting letters of marque and reprisal in times of peace—appointing courts for the trial of piracies and felonies committed on the high seas and establishing courts for receiving and determining finally appeals in all cases of captures, provided that no member of Congress shall be appointed a judge of any of the said courts.

The United States in Congress assembled shall also be the last resort on appeal in all disputes and differences now subsisting or that hereafter may arise between two or more States concerning boundary, jurisdiction or any other cause whatever; which authority shall always be exercised in the manner following. Whenever the legislative or executive authority or lawful agent of any State in controversy with another shall present a petition to Congress, stating the matter in question and praying for a hearing, notice thereof shall be given by order of Congress to the legislative or executive authority of the other State in controversy, and a day assigned for the appearance of the parties by their lawful agents, who shall then be directed to appoint by joint consent, commissioners or judges to constitute a court for hearing and determining the matter in question: but if they cannot agree, Congress shall name three persons out of each of the United States, and from the list of such persons each party shall alternately strike out one, the petitioners beginning, until the number shall be reduced to thirteen; and from that number not less than seven, nor more than nine names as Congress shall direct, shall in the presence of Congress be drawn out by lot, and the persons whose names shall be so drawn or any five of them, shall be commissioners or judges, to hear and finally determine the controversy, so always as a major part of the judges who shall hear the cause shall agree in the determination: and if either party shall neglect to attend at the day appointed, without reasons, which Congress shall judge sufficient, or being present shall refuse to strike, the Congress shall proceed to nominate three persons out of each State, and the Secretary of Congress shall strike in behalf of such party absent or refusing; and the judgment and sentence of the court to be appointed, in the manner before prescribed, shall be final and conclusive; and if any of the parties shall refuse to submit to the authority of such court, or to appear or defend their claim or cause, the court shall nevertheless proceed to pronounce sentence, or judgment, which shall in like manner be final and decisive, the judgment or sentence and other proceedings being in either case transmitted to Congress, and lodged among the acts of Congress for the security of the parties concerned: provided that every commissioner, before he sits in judgment, shall take an oath to be administered by one of the judges of the supreme or superior court of the State where the case shall be tried, "well and truly to hear and determine the matter in question, according to the best of his judgment, without favour, affection or hope of reward:" provided also that no State shall be deprived of territory for the benefit of the United States.

All controversies concerning the private right of soil claimed under different grants of two or more States, whose jurisdiction as they may respect such lands, and the states which passed such grants are adjusted, the said grants or either of them being at the same time claimed to have originated antecedent to such settlement of jurisdiction, shall on the petition of either party to the Congress of the United States, be finally determined as near as may be in the same manner as is before prescribed for deciding disputes respecting territorial jurisdiction between different States.

The United States in Congress assembled shall also have the sole and exclusive right and power of regulating the alloy and value of coin struck by their own authority, or by that of the respective States—fixing the standard of weights and measures throughout the United States—regulating the trade and managing all affairs with the Indians, not members of any of the States, provided that the legislative right of any State within its own limits be not infringed or violated—establishing and regulating post-offices from one State to another, throughout all of the United States, and exacting such postage on the papers passing thro' the same as may be requisite to defray the expenses of the said office—appointing all officers of the land forces, in the service of the United States, excepting regimental officers—appointing all the officers of the naval forces, and commissioning all officers whatever in the service of the United States—making rules for the government and regulation of the said land and naval forces, and directing their operations.

The United States in Congress assembled shall have authority to appoint a committee, to sit in the recess of Congress, to be denominated "a Committee of the States," and to consist of one delegate from each State; and to appoint such other committees and civil officers as may be necessary for managing the general affairs of the United States under their direction—to appoint one of their number to preside, provided that no person be allowed to serve in the office of president more than one year in any term of three years; to ascertain the necessary sums of money to be raised for the service of the United States, and to appropriate and apply the same for defraying the public expenses—to borrow money, or emit bills on the credit of the United States, transmitting every half year to the respective States an account of the sums of money so borrowed or emitted,—to build and equip a navy—to agree upon the number of land forces, and to make requisitions from each State for its quota, in proportion to the number of white inhabitants in such State; which requisition shall be binding, and thereupon the Legislature of each State shall appoint the regimental officers, raise the men and cloath, arm and equip them in a soldier like manner, at the expense of the United States; and the officers and men so cloathed, armed and equipped shall march to the place appointed, and within the time agreed on by the United States in Congress assembled: but if the United States in Congress assembled shall, on consideration of circumstances judge proper that any State should not raise men, or should raise a smaller number of men than the quota thereof, such extra number shall be raised, officered, cloathed, armed and equipped in the same manner as the quota of such State, unless the legislature of such State shall judge that such extra number cannot be safely spared out of the same, in which case they shall raise officer, cloath, arm and equip as many of such extra number as they judge can be safely spared. And the officers and men so cloathed, armed and equipped, shall march to the place appointed, and within the time agreed on by the United States in Congress assembled.

The United States in Congress assembled shall never engage in a war, nor grant letters of marque and reprisal in time of peace, nor enter into any treaties or alliances, nor coin money, nor regulate the value thereof, nor ascertain the sums and expenses necessary for the defence and welfare of the United States, or any of them, nor emit bills, nor borrow money on the credit of the United States, nor appropriate money, nor agree upon the number of vessels to be built or purchased, or the number of land or sea forces to be raised, nor appoint a commander in chief of the army or navy, unless nine States assent to the same: nor shall a question on any other point, except for adjourning from day to day be determined, unless by the votes of a majority of the United States in Congress assembled.

The Congress of the United States shall have power to adjourn to any time within the year, and to any place within the United States, so that no period of adjournment be for a longer duration than the space of six months, and shall publish the journal of their proceedings monthly, except such parts thereof relating to treaties, alliances or military operations, as in their judgment require secresy; and the yeas and nays of the delegates of each State on any question shall be entered on the Journal, when it is desired by any delegate; and the delegates of a State, or any of them, at his or their request shall be furnished with a transcript of the said journal, except such parts as are above excepted, to lay before the Legislatures of the several States.

ARTICLE X. The committee of the States, or any nine of them, shall be authorized to execute, in the recess of Congress, such of the powers of Congress as the United States in Congress assembled, by the consent of nine States, shall from time to time think expedient to vest them with; provided that no power be delegated to the said committee, for the exercise of which, by the articles of confederation, the voice of nine States in the Congress of the United States assembled is requisite.

ARTICLE XI. Canada acceding to this confederation, and joining in the measures of the United States, shall be admitted into, and entitled to all the advantages of this Union: but no other colony shall be admitted into the same, unless such admission be agreed to by nine States.

ARTICLE XII. All bills of credit emitted, monies borrowed and debts contracted by, or under the authority of Congress, before the assembling of the United States, in pursuance of the present confederation, shall be deemed and considered as a charge against the United States, for payment and satisfaction whereof the said United States, and the public faith are hereby solemnly pledged.

ARTICLE XIII. Every State shall abide by the determinations of the United States in Congress assembled, on all questions which by this confederation are submitted to them. And the articles of this confederation shall be inviolably observed by every State, and the Union shall be perpetual; nor shall any alteration at any time hereafter be made in any of them; unless such alteration be agreed to in a Congress of the United States, and be afterwards confirmed by the Legislatures of every State.

And whereas it has pleased the Great Governor of the world to incline the hearts of the Legislatures we respectively represent in Congress, to approve of, and to authorize us to ratify the said articles of confederation and perpetual union. Know ye that we the undersigned delegates, by virtue of the power and authority to us given for that purpose, do by these presents, in the name and in behalf of our respective constituents, fully and entirely ratify and confirm each and every of the said articles of confederation and perpetual union, and all and singular the matters and things therein contained: and we do further solemnly plight and engage the faith of our respective constituents, that they shall abide by the determinations of the United States in Congress assembled, on all questions, which by the said confederation are submitted to them. And that the articles thereof shall be inviolably observed by the States we respectively represent, and that the Union shall be perpetual.

In witness thereof we have hereunto set our hands in Congress. Done at Philadelphia in the State of Pennsylvania the ninth day of July in the year of our Lord one thousand seven hundred and seventy-eight, and in the third year of the independence of America.

THE CONSTITUTION OF THE UNITED STATES (1787)

WE THE PEOPLE OF THE UNITED STATES, in order to form a more perfect Union, establish Justice, insure domestic Tranquility, provide for the common defence, promote the general Welfare, and secure the Blessings of Liberty to ourselves and our Posterity, do ordain and establish this Constitution for the United States of America.

ARTICLE. I.

Section. 1. All legislative Powers herein granted shall be vested in a Congress of the United States, which shall consist of a Senate and House of Representatives.

Section. 2. The House of Representatives shall be composed of Members chosen every second Year by the People of the several States, and the Electors in each State shall have the Qualifications requisite for Electors of the most numerous Branch of the State Legislature.

No Person shall be a Representative who shall not have attained to the Age of twenty five Years, and been seven Years a Citizen of the United States, and who shall not, when elected, be an Inhabitant of that State in which he shall be chosen.

Representatives and direct Taxes shall be apportioned among the several States which may be included within this Union, according to their respective Numbers, which shall be determined by adding to the whole Number of free Persons, including those bound to Service for a Term of Years, and excluding Indians not taxed, three fifths of all other Persons. The actual Enumeration shall be made within three Years after the first Meeting of the Congress of the United States, and within every subsequent Term of ten Years, in such

Manner as they shall by Law direct. The Number of Representatives shall not exceed one for every thirty Thousand, but each State shall have at Least one Representative; and until such enumeration shall be made, the State of New Hampshire shall be entitled to chuse three, Massachusetts eight, Rhode-Island and Providence Plantations one, Connecticut five, New-York six, New Jersey four, Pennsylvania eight, Delaware one, Maryland six, Virginia ten, North Carolina five, South Carolina five, and Georgia three.

When vacancies happen in the Representation from any state, the Executive Authority thereof shall issue Writs of Election to fill such Vacancies.

The House of Representatives shall chuse their Speaker and other Officers; and shall have the sole Power of Impeachment.

Section. 3. The Senate of the United States shall be composed of two Senators from each State, chosen by the legislature thereof, for six Years; and each Senator shall have one Vote.

Immediately after they shall be assembled in Consequence of the first Election, they shall be divided as equally as may be into three Classes. The Seats of the Senators of the first Class shall be vacated at the Expiration of the second Year, of the second Class at the Expiration of the fourth Year, and of the third Class at the Expiration of the sixth Year, so that one third maybe chosen every second Year; and if Vacancies happen by Resignation, or otherwise, during the Recess of the Legislature of any State, the Executive thereof may make temporary Appointments until the next Meeting of the Legislature, which shall then fill such Vacancies.

No Person shall be a Senator who shall not have attained to the Age of thirty Years, and been nine Years a Citizen of the United States, and who shall not, when elected, be an Inhabitant of that State for which he shall be chosen.

The Vice President of the United States shall be President of the Senate, but shall have no Vote, unless they be equally divided.

The Senate shall chuse their other Officers, and also a President pro tempore, in the Absence of the Vice President, or when he shall exercise the Office of President of the United States.

The Senate shall have the sole Power to try all Impeachments. When sitting for that Purpose, they shall be on Oath or Affirmation. When the President of the United States is tried, the Chief Justice shall preside: And no Person shall be convicted without the Concurrence of two thirds of the Members present.

Judgment in Cases of Impeachment shall not extend further than to removal from Office, and disqualification to hold and enjoy any Office of honor, Trust or Profit under the United States: but the Party convicted shall nevertheless be liable and subject to Indictment, Trial, Judgment and Punishment, according to Law.

Section. 4. The Times, Places and Manner of holding Elections for Senators and Representatives, shall be prescribed in each State by the Legislature thereof; but the Congress may at any time by Law make or alter such Regulations, except as to the Places of chusing Senators.

The Congress shall assemble at least once in every Year, and such Meeting shall be on the first Monday in December, unless they shall by Law appoint a different Day.

Section. 5. Each House shall be the Judge of the Elections, Returns and Qualifications of its own Members, and a Majority of each shall constitute a Quorum to do Business; but a smaller Number may adjourn from day to day, and may be authorized to compel the Attendance of absent Members, in such Manner, and under such Penalties as each House may provide.

Each House may determine the Rules of its Proceedings, punish its Members for disorderly Behaviour, and, with the Concurrence of two thirds, expel a Member.

Each House shall keep a Journal of its Proceedings, and from time to time publish the same, excepting such Parts as may in their Judgment require Secrecy; and the Yeas and Nays of the Members of either House on any question shall, at the Desire of one fifth of those Present, be entered on the Journal.

Neither House, during the Session of Congress, shall, without the Consent of the other, adjourn for more than three days, not to any other Place than that in which the two Houses shall be sitting.

Section. 6. The Senators and Representatives shall receive a Compensation for their Services, to be ascertained by Law, and paid out of the Treasury of the United States. They shall in all Cases, except Treason, Felony and Breach of the Peace, be privileged from Arrest during their Attendance at the Session of their respective Houses, and in going to and returning from the same; and for any Speech or Debate in either House, they shall not be questioned in any other Place.

No Senator or Representative shall, during the Time for which he was elected, be appointed to any civil Office under the Authority of the United States, which shall have been created, or the Emoluments whereof shall have been encreased during such time; and no Person holding any Office under the United States, shall be a Member of either House during his Continuance in Office.

Section. 7. All Bills for raising Revenue shall originate in the House of Representatives; but the Senate may propose or concur with Amendments as on other Bills.

Every Bill which shall have passed the House of Representatives and the Senate shall, before it become a Law, be presented to the President of the United States; If he approve he shall sign it, but if not he shall return it, with his Objections to that House in which it shall have originated, who shall enter the Objections at large on their Journal, and proceed to reconsider it. If after such Reconsideration two thirds of that House shall agree to pass the Bill, it shall be sent, together with the Objections, to the other House, by which it shall likewise be reconsidered, and if approved by two thirds of that House, it shall become a Law. But in all such Cases the Votes of both Houses shall be determined by yeas and Nays, and the Names of the Persons voting for and against the Bill shall be entered on the Journal of each House respectively. If any Bill shall not be returned by the President within ten Days (Sundays excepted) after it shall have been presented to him, the Same shall be a Law, in like Manner as if he had signed it, unless the Congress by their Adjournment prevent its Return, in which Case it shall not be a Law.

Every Order, Resolution, or Vote to which the Concurrence of the Senate and House of Representatives may be necessary (except on a question of Adjournment) shall be presented to the President of the United States; and before the Same shall take Effect, shall be approved by him, or being disapproved by him, shall be repassed by two thirds of the Senate and House of Representatives, according to the Rules and Limitations prescribed in the Case of a Bill.

Section. 8. The Congress shall have Power To lay and collect Taxes, Duties, Imposts and Excises, to pay the Debts and provide for the common Defence and general Welfare of the United States; but all Duties, Imposts and Excises shall be uniform throughout the United States;

To borrow Money on the credit of the United States;

To regulate Commerce with foreign Nations, and among the several States, and with the Indian Tribes;

To establish an uniform Rule of Naturalization, and uniform Laws on the subject of Bankruptcies throughout the United States;

To coin Money, regulate the Value thereof, and of foreign Coin, and fix the Standard of Weights and Measures;

To provide for the Punishment of counterfeiting the Securities and current Coin of the United States;

To establish Post Offices and Post Roads;

To promote the Progress of Science and useful Arts, by securing for limited Times to Authors and Inventors the exclusive Right to their respective Writings and Discoveries;

To constitute Tribunals inferior to the supreme Court;

To define and punish Piracies and Felonies committed on the high Seas, and Offences against the Law of Nations;

To declare War, grant Letters of Marque and Reprisal, and make Rules concerning Captures on land and Water;

To raise and support Armies, but no Appropriation of Money to that Use shall be for a longer Term than two Years;

To provide and maintain a Navy;

To make Rules for the Government and Regulation of the land and naval Forces;

To provide for calling forth the Militia to execute the Laws of the Union, suppress Insurrections and repel Invasions;

To provide for organizing, arming, and disciplining, the Militia, and for governing such Part of them as may be employed in the Service of the United States, reserving to the States respectively, the Appointment of the Officers, and the Authority of training the Militia according to the discipline prescribed by Congress.

To exercise exclusive Legislation in all Cases whatsoever, over such District (not exceeding ten Miles square) as may, by Cession of Particular States, and the Acceptance of Congress, become the Seat of the Government of the United States, and to exercise like Authority over all Places purchased by the Consent of the Legislature of the State in which the Same shall be, for the Erection of Forts, Magazines, Arsenals, dock-Yards, and other needful Buildings;—And

To make all Laws which shall be necessary and proper for carrying into Execution the foregoing Powers, and all other Powers vested by this Constitution in the Government of the United States, or in any Department or Officer thereof.

Section. 9. The Migration or Importation of such Persons as any of the States now existing shall think proper to admit, shall not be prohibited by the Congress prior to the Year one thousand eight hundred and eight, but a Tax or duty may be imposed on such Importation, not exceeding ten dollars for each Person.

The Privilege of the Writ of Habeas Corpus shall not be suspended, unless when in Cases of Rebellion or Invasion the public Safety may require it.

No Bill of Attainder or ex post facto Law shall be passed.

No Capitation, or other direct, Tax shall be laid, unless in Proportion to the Census or Enumeration herein before directed to be taken.

No Tax or Duty shall be laid on Articles exported from any State.

No Preference shall be given by any Regulation of Commerce or Revenue to the Ports of one State over those of another: nor shall Vessels bound to, or from, one State, be obliged to enter, clear, or pay Duties in another.

No Money shall be drawn from the Treasury, but in Consequence of Appropriations made by Law; and a regular Statement and Account of the Receipts and Expenditures of all public Money shall be published from time to time.

No Title of Nobility shall be granted by the United States: And no Person holding any Office of Profit or trust under them, shall, without the Consent of the Congress, accept of any present, Emolument, Office, or Title, of any kind whatever, from any King, Prince, or foreign State.

Section 10. No State shall enter into any Treaty, Alliance, or Confederation; grant Letters of Marque and Reprisal; coin Money; emit Bills of Credit; make any Thing but gold and silver Coin a Tender in Payment of Debts; pass any Bill of Attainder, ex post facto Law, or Law impairing the Obligation of Contracts, or grant any Title of Nobility.

No State shall, without the Consent of the Congress, lay any Imposts or Duties on Imports or Exports, except what may be absolutely necessary for executing its inspection Laws: and the net Produce of all Duties and Imposts, laid by any State on Imports or Exports, shall be for the Use of the Treasury of the United States; and all such Laws shall be subject to the Revision and Controul of the Congress.

No State shall, without the Consent of Congress, lay any Duty of Tonnage, keep Troops, or Ships of War in time of Peace, enter into any Agreement or Compact with another State, or with a foreign Power, or engage in War, unless actually invaded, or in such imminent Danger as will not admit of delay.

ARTICLE. II.

Section. 1. The executive Power shall be vested in a President of the United States of America. He shall hold his Office during the term of four Years, and, together with the Vice President, chosen for the same Term, be elected, as follows:

Each State shall appoint, in such Manner as the Legislature thereof may direct, a Number of Electors, equal to the whole Number of Senators and Representatives to which the State may be entitled in the Congress: but no Senator or Representative, or Person holding an Office of Trust or Profit under the United States, shall be appointed an Elector.

The Electors shall meet in their respective States, and vote by Ballot for two Persons, of whom one at least shall not be an Inhabitant of the same State with themselves. And they shall make a List of all the Persons voted for, and of the Number of Votes for each; which List they shall sign and certify, and transmit sealed to the Seat of the Government of the United States, directed to the President of the Senate. The President of the Senate shall, in the Presence of the Senate and House of Representatives, open all the Certificates, and the Votes shall then be counted. The Person having the greatest Number of Votes shall be the President, if such Number be a Majority of the whole Number of Electors appointed; and if there be more than one who have such Majority, and have an equal Number of Votes, then the House of Representatives shall immediately chuse by Ballot one of them for President; and if no Person have a Majority, then from the five highest on the List the said House shall in like Manner chuse the President. But in chusing the President, the Votes shall be taken by States, the Representation from each State having one Vote; A quorum for this Purpose shall consist of a Member or Members from two thirds of the States, and a Majority of all the States shall be necessary to a Choice. In every Case, after the Choice of the President, the Person having the greatest Number of Votes of the Electors shall be the Vice President. But if there should remain two or more who have equal Votes, the Senate shall chuse from them by Ballot the Vice President.

The Congress may determine the Time of chusing the Electors, and the Day on which they shall give their Votes; which Day shall be the same throughout the United States.

No Person except a natural born Citizen, or a Citizen of the United States, at the time of the Adoption of this Constitution, shall be eligible to the Office of President; neither shall any Person be eligible to that Office who shall not have attained to the Age of thirty five Years, and been fourteen Years a Resident within the United States.

In Case of the Removal of the President from Office, or of his Death, Resignation, or Inability to discharge the Powers and Duties of the said Office, the Same shall devolve on the Vice President, and the Congress may by Law provide for the Case of Removal, Death, Resignation or Inability, both of the President and Vice President, declaring what Officer shall then

act as President, and such Officer shall act accordingly, until the Disability be removed, or a President shall be elected.

The President shall, at stated Times, receive for his Services, a Compensation, which shall neither be encreased or diminished during the Period for which he shall have been elected, and he shall not receive within that Period any other Emolument from the United States, or any of them.

Before he enters on the Execution of his Office, he shall take the following Oath or Affirmation:—"I do solemnly swear (or affirm) that I will faithfully execute the Office of President of the United States, and will to the best of my Ability, preserve, protect and defend the Constitution of the United States."

Section. 2. The President shall be Commander in Chief of the Army and Navy of the United States, and of the Militia of the several States, when called into the actual Service of the United States; he may require the Opinion, in writing, of the principal Officer in each of the executive Departments, upon any Subject relating to the Duties of their respective Offices, and he shall have Power to grant Reprieves and Pardons for Offences against the United States, except in Cases of Impeachment.

He shall have Power, by and with the Advice and Consent of the Senate, to make Treaties, provided two thirds of the Senators present concur; and he shall nominate, and by and with the Advice and Consent of the Senate, shall appoint Ambassadors, other public Ministers and Consuls, Judges of the supreme Court, and all other Officers of the United States, whose Appointments are not herein otherwise provided for, and which shall be established by Law; but the Congress may by Law vest the Appointment of such inferior Officers, as they think proper, in the President alone, in the Courts of Law, or in the Heads of Departments.

The President shall have Power to fill up all Vacancies that may happen during the Recess of the Senate, by granting Commissions which shall expire at the End of their next Session.

Section. 3. He shall from time to time give to the Congress Information of the State of the Union, and recommend to their Consideration such Measures as he shall judge necessary and expedient; he may, on extraordinary Occasions, convene both Houses, or either of them, and in Case of Disagreement between them, with Respect to the Time of Adjournment, he may adjourn them to such Time as he shall think proper; he shall receive Ambassadors and other public Ministers; he shall take Care that the Laws be faithfully executed, and shall Commission all the Officers of the United States.

Section. 4. The President, Vice President and all civil Officers of the United States, shall be removed from Office on Impeachment for, and Conviction of, Treason, Bribery, or other high Crimes and Misdemeanors.

ARTICLE. III.

Section. 1. The judicial Power of the United States, shall be vested in one supreme Court, and in such inferior Courts as the Congress may from time to time ordain and establish. The Judges, both of the supreme and inferior Courts, shall hold their Offices during good Behavior, and shall, at stated Times, receive for their Services, a Compensation, which shall not be diminished during their Continuance in Office.

Section. 2. The judicial Power shall extend to all Cases, in Law and Equity, arising under this Constitution, the Laws of the United States, and Treaties made, or which shall be made, under their Authority;—to all Cases affecting Ambassadors, other public Ministers and Consuls;—to all Cases of admiralty and maritime Jurisdiction;—the Controversies to which the United States shall be a Party;—to Controversies between two or more States;—between a State and Citizens of another State;—between Citizens of different States;—between Citizens of the same State claiming Lands under Grants of different States, and between a State, or the Citizens thereof, and foreign States, Citizens or Subjects.

In all cases affecting Ambassadors, other public Ministers and Consuls, and those in which a State shall be Party, the supreme Court shall have original Jurisdiction. In all the other Cases before mentioned, the supreme Court shall have appellate Jurisdiction, both as to Law and Fact, with such Exceptions, and under such Regulations as the Congress shall make.

The Trial of all Crimes, except in Cases of Impeachment, shall be by Jury; and such Trial shall be held in the State where the said Crimes shall have been committed; but when not committed within any State, the Trial shall be at such Place or Places as the Congress may by Law have directed.

Section. 3. Treason against the United States, shall consist only in levying War against them, or in adhering to their Enemies, giving them Aid and Comfort. No Person shall be convicted of Treason unless on the Testimony of two Witnesses to the same overt Act, or on Confession in open Court.

The Congress shall have Power to declare the Punishment of Treason, but no Attainder of Treason shall work Corruption of Blood, or Forfeiture except during the Life of the Person attainted.

ARTICLE. IV.

Section. 1. Full Faith and Credit shall be given in each State to the public Acts, Records, and judicial Proceedings of every other State. And the Congress may by general Laws prescribe the Manner in which such Acts, Records and Proceedings shall be proved, and the Effect thereof.

Section. 2. The Citizens of each State shall be entitled to all Privileges and Immunities of Citizens in the several States.

A Person charged in any State with Treason, Felony, or other Crime, who shall flee from Justice, and be found in another State, shall on Demand of the executive Authority of the State from which he fled, be delivered up, to be removed to the State having Jurisdiction of the Crime.

No Person held to Service or Labour in one State, under the Laws thereof, escaping into another, shall, in Consequence of any Law or Regulation therein, be discharged from such Service or Labour, but shall be delivered up on Claim of the Party to whom such Service or Labour may be due.

Section. 3. New States may be admitted by the Congress into this Union; but no new State shall be formed or erected within the Jurisdiction of any other State; nor any State be formed by the Junction of two or more States, or Parts of States, without the consent of the Legislatures of the States concerned as well as of the Congress.

The Congress shall have Power to dispose of and make all needful Rules and Regulations respecting the Territory or other Property belonging to the United States; and nothing in this Constitution shall be so construed as to Prejudice any Claims of the United States, or of any particular States.

Section. 4. The United States shall guarantee to every State in this Union a Republican Form of Government, and shall protect each of them against Invasion; and on Application of the Legislature, or of the Executive (when the Legislature cannot be convened) against domestic Violence.

ARTICLE. V.

The Congress, whenever two thirds of both Houses shall deem it necessary, shall propose Amendments to this Constitution, or, on the Application of the

Legislatures of two thirds of the several States, shall call a Convention for proposing Amendments, which, in either Case, shall be valid to all Intents and Purposes, as Part of this Constitution, when ratified by the Legislatures of three fourths of the several States, or by Conventions in three fourths thereof, as the one or the other Mode of Ratification may be proposed by the Congress; Provided that no Amendment which may be made prior to the Year One thousand eight hundred and eight shall in any Manner affect the first and fourth Clauses in the Ninth Section of the first Article; and that no State, without its Consent, shall be deprived of its equal Suffrage in the Senate.

ARTICLE. VI.

All Debts contracted and Engagements entered into, before the Adoption of this Constitution, shall be as valid against the United States under this Constitution, as under the Confederation.

This Constitution, and the Laws of the United States which shall be made in Pursuance thereof; and all Treaties made, or which shall be made, under the Authority of the United States, shall be the supreme Law of the Land; and the Judges in every State shall be bound thereby, any Thing in the Constitution or Laws of any State to the Contrary notwithstanding.

The Senators and Representatives before mentioned, and the Members of the several State Legislatures, and all executive and judicial Officers, both of the United States and of the several States, shall be bound by Oath or Affirmation, to support this Constitution; but no religious Test shall ever be required as a Qualification to any Office or public Trust under the United States.

ARTICLE. VII.

The Ratification of the Conventions of nine States, shall be sufficient for the Establishment of this Constitution between the States so ratifying the Same.

Done in Convention by the Unanimous Consent of the States present the Seventeenth Day of September in the Year of our Lord one thousand seven hundred and Eighty seven and of the Independence of the United States of America the Twelfth. In witness thereof We have hereunto subscribed our Names,

Go. WASHINGTON—Presdt.
and deputy from Virginia.

New Hampshire	{ John Langdon Nicholas Gilman	Delaware	{ Geo: Read Gunning Bedford jun John Dickinson Richard Bassett Jaco: Broom
Massachusetts	{ Nathaniel Gorham Rufus King		
Connecticut	{ Wm Saml Johnson Roger Sherman	Maryland	{ James McHenry Dan of St Thos Jenifer Danl Carroll
New York: ...	Alexander Hamilton		
New Jersey	{ Wil: Livingston David A. Brearley. Wm Paterson. Jona: Dayton	Virginia	{ John Blair— James Madison Jr.
		North Carolina	{ Wm Blount Richd Dobbs Spaight. Hu Williamson
Pennsylvania	{ B Franklin Thomas Mifflin Robt Morris Geo. Clymer Thos FitzSimons Jared Ingersoll James Wilson Gouv Morris	South Carolina	{ J. Rutledge Charles Cotesworth Pinckney Charles Pinckney Pierce Butler.
		Georgia	{ William Few Abr Baldwin

AMENDMENTS TO THE CONSTITUTION

Articles in Addition to, and Amendment of the Constitution of the United States of America, proposed by Congress, and ratified by the Legislatures of the several States, pursuant to the fifth Article of the original Constitution.

AMENDMENT I.

Congress shall make no law respecting an establishment of religion, or prohibiting the free exercise thereof; or abridging the freedom of speech, or of the press; or the right of the people peaceably to assemble, and to petition the Government for a redress of grievances.

AMENDMENT II.

A well regulated Militia, being necessary to the security of a free State, the right of the people to keep and bear Arms, shall not be infringed.

AMENDMENT III.

No Soldier shall, in time of peace be quartered in any house, without the consent of the Owner, nor in time of war, but in a manner to be prescribed by law.

AMENDMENT IV.

The right of the people to be secure in their persons, houses, papers, and effects, against unreasonable searches and seizures, shall not be violated, and no Warrants shall issue, but upon probable cause, supported by Oath or affirmation, and particularly describing the place to be searched, and the persons or things to be seized.

AMENDMENT V.

No person shall be held to answer for a capital, or otherwise infamous crime, unless on a presentment or indictment of a Grand Jury, except in cases arising in the land or naval forces, or in the Militia, when in actual service in time of War or public danger; nor shall any person be subject for the same offence to be twice put in jeopardy of life or limb; nor shall be compelled in any criminal case to be a witness against himself, nor be deprived of life, liberty, or property, without due process of law; nor shall private property be taken for public use, without just compensation.

AMENDMENT VI.

In all criminal prosecutions, the accused shall enjoy the right to a speedy and public trial, by an impartial jury of the State and district wherein the crime shall have been committed, which district shall have been previously ascertained by law, and to be informed of the nature and cause of the accusation; to be confronted with the witnesses against him; to have compulsory process for obtaining witnesses in his favor, and to have the Assistance of Counsel for his defence.

AMENDMENT VII.

In Suits at common law, where the value in controversy shall exceed twenty dollars, the right of trial by jury shall be preserved, and no fact tried by a jury, shall be otherwise re-examined in any Court of the United States, than according to the rules of the common law.

AMENDMENT VIII.

Excessive bail shall not be required, nor excessive fines imposed, nor cruel and unusual punishments inflicted.

AMENDMENT IX.

The enumeration in the Constitution, of certain rights, shall not be construed to deny or disparage others retained by the people.

AMENDMENT X.

The powers not delegated to the United States by the Constitution, nor prohibited by it to the States, are reserved to the States respectively, or to the people. [The first ten amendments went into effect December 15, 1791.]

AMENDMENT XI.

The Judicial power of the United States shall not be construed to extend to any suit in law or equity, commenced or prosecuted against one of the United States by Citizens of another State, or by Citizens or Subjects of any Foreign State. [January 8, 1798.]

AMENDMENT XII.

The Electors shall meet in their respective states, and vote by ballot for President and Vice-President, one of whom, at least, shall not be an inhabitant of the same state with themselves; they shall name in their ballots the person voted for as President, and in distinct ballots the person voted for as Vice-President, and they shall make distinct lists of all persons voted for as President, and of all persons voted for as Vice President, and of the number of votes for each, which lists they shall sign and certify, and transmit sealed to the seat of the government of the United States, directed to the President of the Senate;—The President of the Senate shall, in the presence of the Senate and House of Representatives, open all the certificates and the votes shall then be counted;—The person having the greatest number of votes for President, shall be the President, if such number be a majority of the whole number of Electors appointed; and if no person have such majority, then from the persons having the highest numbers not exceeding three on the list of those voted for as President, the House of Representatives shall choose immediately, by ballot, the President. But in choosing the President, the votes shall be taken by states, the representation from each state having one vote; a quorum for this purpose shall consist of a member or members from two-thirds of the states, and a majority of all the states shall be necessary to a choice. And if the House of Representatives shall not choose a President whenever the right of choice shall devolve upon them, before the fourth day of March next following, then the Vice-President shall act as President, as in the case of the death or other constitutional disability of the President.— The person having the greatest number of votes as Vice-President, shall be the Vice-President, if such number be a majority of the whole number of Electors appointed, and if no person have a majority, then from the two highest numbers on the list, the Senate shall choose the Vice-President; a quorum for the purpose shall consist of two-thirds of the whole number of Senators, and a majority of the whole number shall be necessary to a choice. But no person constitutionally ineligible to the office of President shall be eligible to that of Vice-President of the United States. [September 25, 1804.]

AMENDMENT XIII.

Section 1. Neither slavery nor involuntary servitude, except as a punishment for crime whereof the party shall have been duly convicted, shall exist within the United States, or any place subject to their jurisdiction.

Section 2. Congress shall have power to enforce this article by appropriate legislation. [December 18, 1865.]

AMENDMENT XIV.

Section 1. All persons born or naturalized in the United States, and subject to the jurisdiction thereof, are citizens of the United States and of the State wherein they reside. No State shall make or enforce any law which shall abridge the privileges or immunities of citizens of the United States; nor shall any State deprive any person of life, liberty, or property, without due process of law; nor deny to any person within its jurisdiction the equal protection of the laws.

Section 2. Representatives shall be apportioned among the several States according to their respective numbers, counting the whole number of persons in each State, excluding Indians not taxed. But when the right to vote at any election for the choice of electors for President and Vice President of the United States, Representatives in Congress, the Executive and Judicial officers of a State, or the members of the Legislature thereof, is denied to any of the male inhabitants of such State, being twenty-one years of age, and citizens of the United States, or in any way abridged, except for participation in rebellion, or other crime, the basis of representation therein shall be reduced in the proportion which the number of such male citizens shall bear to the whole number of male citizens twenty-one years of age in such State.

Section 3. No person shall be a Senator or Representative in Congress, or elector of President and Vice President, or hold any office, civil or military, under the United States, or under any State, who, having previously taken an oath, as a member of Congress, or as an officer of the United States, or as a member of any State legislature, or as an executive or judicial officer of any State, to support the Constitution of the United States, shall have engaged in insurrection or rebellion against the same, or given aid or comfort to the enemies thereof. But Congress may by a vote of two-thirds of each House, remove such disability.

Section 4. The validity of the public debt of the United States, authorized by law, including debts incurred for payment of pensions and bounties for services in suppressing insurrection or rebellion, shall not be questioned. But neither the United States nor any State shall assume or pay any debt or obligation incurred in aid of insurrection or rebellion against the United States, or any claim for the loss or emancipation of any slave; but all such debts, obligations and claims shall be held illegal and void.

Section 5. The Congress shall have power to enforce, by appropriate legislation, the provisions of this article. [July 28, 1868.]

AMENDMENT XV.

Section 1. The right of citizens of the United States to vote shall not be denied or abridged by the United States or by any State on account of race, color, or previous condition of servitude—

Section 2. The Congress shall have power to enforce this article by appropriate legislation.—[March 30, 1870.]

AMENDMENT XVI.

The Congress shall have power to lay and collect taxes on incomes, from whatever source derived, without apportionment among the several

States, and without regard to any census or enumeration. [February 25, 1913.]

Amendment XVII.

The Senate of the United States shall be composed of two senators from each State, elected by the people thereof, for six years; and each Senator shall have one vote. The electors in each State shall have the qualifications requisite for electors of the most numerous branch of the State legislature.

When vacancies happen in the representation of any State in the Senate, the executive authority of such State shall issue writs of election to fill such vacancies: *Provided,* That the legislature of any State may empower the executive thereof to make temporary appointments until the people fill the vacancies by election as the legislature may direct.

This amendment shall not be so construed as to affect the election or term of any senator chosen before it becomes valid as part of the Constitution. [May 31, 1913.]

Amendment XVIII.

After one year from the ratification of this article, the manufacture, sale, or transportation of intoxicating liquors within, the importation thereof into, or the exportation thereof from the United States and all territory subject to the jurisdiction thereof for beverage purposes is hereby prohibited.

The Congress and the several States shall have concurrent power to enforce this article by appropriate legislation.

This article shall be inoperative unless it shall have been ratified as an amendment to the Constitution by the legislatures of the several States, as provided in the Constitution, within seven years from the date of the submission thereof to the States by Congress. [January 29, 1919.]

Amendment XIX.

The right of citizens of the United States to vote shall not be denied or abridged by the United States or by any State on account of sex.

The Congress shall have power by appropriate legislation to enforce the provisions of this article. [August 26, 1920.]

AMENDMENT XX.

Section 1. The terms of the President and Vice-President shall end at noon on the twentieth day of January, and the terms of Senators and Representatives at noon on the third day of January, of the years in which such terms would have ended if this article had not been ratified; and the terms of their successors shall then begin.

Section 2. The Congress shall assemble at least once in every year, and such meeting shall begin at noon on the third day of January, unless they shall by law appoint a different day.

Section 3. If, at the time fixed for the beginning of the term of the President, the President-elect shall have died, the Vice-President-elect shall become President. If a President shall not have been chosen before the time fixed for the beginning of his term, or if the President-elect shall have failed to qualify, then the Vice-President-elect shall act as President until a President shall have qualified; and the Congress may by law provide for the case wherein neither a President-elect nor a Vice-President-elect shall have qualified, declaring who shall then act as President, or the manner in which one who is to act shall be selected, and such person shall act accordingly until a President or Vice-President shall have qualified.

Section 4. The Congress may by law provide for the case of the death of any of the persons from whom the House of Representatives may choose a President whenever the right of choice shall have devolved upon them, and for the case of the death of any of the persons from whom the Senate may choose a Vice-President whenever the right of choice shall have devolved upon them.

Section 5. Sections 1 and 2 shall take effect on the 15th day of October following the ratification of this article.

Section 6. This article shall be inoperative unless it shall have been ratified as an amendment to the Constitution by the legislatures of three-fourths of the several States within seven years from the date of its submission. [February 6, 1933.]

Amendment XXI.

Section 1. The eighteenth article of amendment to the Constitution of the United States is hereby repealed.

Section 2. The transportation or importation into any State, Territory or possession of the United States for delivery or use therein of intoxicating liquors, in violation of the laws thereof, is hereby prohibited.

Section 3. This article shall be inoperative unless it shall have been ratified as an amendment to the Constitution by convention in the several States, as provided in the Constitution, within seven years from the date of the submission thereof to the States by the Congress. [December 5, 1933.]

Amendment XXII.

Section 1. No person shall be elected to the office of the President more than twice, and no person who has held the office of President, or acted as President, for more than two years of a term to which some other person was elected President shall be elected to the office of the President more than once. But this Article shall not apply to any person holding the office of President when this Article was proposed by the Congress, and shall not prevent any person who may be holding the office of President, or acting as President, during the term within which this Article becomes operative from holding the office of President or acting as President during the remainder of such term.

Section 2. This article shall be inoperative unless it shall have been ratified as an amendment to the Constitution by the legislatures of three-fourths of the several states within seven years from the date of its submission to the States by the Congress. [February 27, 1951.]

Amendment XXIII.

Section 1. The District constituting the seat of government of the United States shall appoint in such manner as the Congress may direct:

A number of electors of President and Vice-President equal to the whole number of Senators and Representatives in Congress to which the District would be entitled if it were a State, but in no event more than the least populous State; they shall be in addition to those appointed by the States, but they shall be considered, for the purposes of the election of President and Vice-President, to be electors appointed by a State; and they shall meet in the District and perform such duties as provided by the twelfth article of amendment.

Section 2. The Congress shall have the power to enforce this article by appropriate legislation. [March 29, 1961.]

AMENDMENT XXIV.

Section 1. The right of citizens of the United States to vote in any primary or other election for President or Vice President, for electors for President or Vice President, or for Senator or Representative in Congress, shall not be denied or abridged by the United States or any State by reason of failure to pay any poll tax or other tax.

Section 2. The Congress shall have power to enforce this article by appropriate legislation. [January 23, 1964.]

AMENDMENT XXV.

Section 1. In case of the removal of the President from office or of his death or resignation, the Vice President shall become President.

Section 2. Whenever there is a vacancy in the office of Vice President, the President shall nominate a Vice President who shall take office upon confirmation by a majority vote of both Houses of Congress.

Section 3. Whenever the President transmits to the President pro tempore of the Senate and the Speaker of the House of Representatives his written declaration that he is unable to discharge the powers and duties of his office, and until he transmits to them a written declaration to the contrary, such powers and duties shall be discharged by the Vice President as Acting President.

Section 4. Whenever the Vice President and a majority of either the principal officers of the executive departments or of such other body as Congress may by law provide, transmit to the President pro tempore of the Senate and the Speaker of the House of Representatives their written declaration that the President is unable to discharge the powers and duties of his office, the Vice President shall immediately assume the powers and duties of the office as Acting President.

Thereafter, when the President transmits to the President pro tempore of the Senate and the Speaker of the House of Representatives his written declaration that no inability exists, he shall resume the powers and duties of his office unless the Vice President and a majority of either the principal officers of the executive departments or of such other body as Congress may by law provide, transmit within four days to the President pro tempore of the Senate and the Speaker of the House of Representatives their written declaration that the President is unable to discharge the powers and duties of his office. Thereupon Congress shall decide the issue, assembling within forty-eight hours for that purpose if not in session. If the Congress, within twenty-one days after receipt of the latter written declaration, or, if Congress is not in session, within twenty-one days after Congress is required to assemble, determines by two-thirds vote of both Houses that the President is unable to discharge the powers and duties of his office, the Vice President shall continue to discharge the same as Acting President; otherwise, the President shall resume the powers and duties of his office. [February 10, 1967.]

AMENDMENT XXVI.

Section 1. The right of citizens of the United States, who are eighteen years of age or older, to vote shall not be denied or abridged by the United States or by any State on account of age.

Section 2. The Congress shall have power to enforce this article by appropriate legislation [June 30, 1971.]

AMENDMENT XXVII.

No law, varying the compensation for the services of the Senators and Representatives shall take effect, until an election of Representatives shall have intervened. [May 8, 1992.]

PRESIDENTIAL ELECTIONS

Year	Number of States	Candidates	Parties	Popular Vote	% of Popular Vote	Electoral Vote	% Voter Participation
1789	11	**GEORGE WASHINGTON**	No party designations			69	
		John Adams				34	
		Other candidates				35	
1792	15	**GEORGE WASHINGTON**	No party designations			132	
		John Adams				77	
		George Clinton				50	
		Other candidates				5	
1796	16	**JOHN ADAMS**	Federalist			71	
		Thomas Jefferson	Democratic-Republican			68	
		Thomas Pinckney	Federalist			59	
		Aaron Burr	Democratic-Republican			30	
		Other candidates				48	
1800	16	**THOMAS JEFFERSON**	Democratic-Republican			73	
		Aaron Burr	Democratic-Republican			73	
		John Adams	Federalist			65	
		Charles C. Pinckney	Federalist			64	
		John Jay	Federalist			1	
1804	17	**THOMAS JEFFERSON**	Democratic-Republican			162	
		Charles C. Pinckney	Federalist			14	

Year	Number of States	Candidates	Parties	Popular Vote	% of Popular Vote	Electoral Vote	% Voter Participation
1808	17	**JAMES MADISON**	Democratic-Republican			122	
		Charles C. Pinckney	Federalist			47	
		George Clinton	Democratic-Republican			6	
1812	18	**JAMES MADISON**	Democratic-Republican			128	
		DeWitt Clinton	Federalist			89	
1816	19	**JAMES MONROE**	Democratic-Republican			183	
		Rufus King	Federalist			34	
1820	24	**JAMES MONROE**	Democratic-Republican			231	
		John Quincy Adams	Independent			1	
1824	24	**JOHN QUINCY ADAMS**	Democratic-Republican	108,740	30.5	84	26.9
		Andrew Jackson	Democratic-Republican	153,544	43.1	99	
		Henry Clay	Democratic-Republican	47,136	13.2	37	
		William H. Crawford	Democratic-Republican	46,618	13.1	41	
1828	24	**ANDREW JACKSON**	Democratic	647,286	56.0	178	57.6
		John Quincy Adams	National-Republican	508,064	44.0	83	

Year	Number of States	Candidates	Parties	Popular Vote	% of Popular Vote	Electoral Vote	% Voter Participation
1832	24	**ANDREW JACKSON**	Democratic	688,242	54.5	219	55.4
		Henry Clay	National-Republican	473,462	37.5	49	
		William Wirt	Anti-Masonic ⎤	101,051	8.0	7	
		John Floyd	Democratic ⎦			11	
1836	26	**MARTIN VAN BUREN**	Democratic	765,483	50.9	170	57.8
		William H. Harrison	Whig ⎤			73	
		Hugh L. White	Whig	739,795	49.1	26	
		Daniel Webster	Whig			14	
		W. P. Mangum	Whig ⎦			11	
1840	26	**WILLIAM H. HARRISON**	Whig	1,274,624	53.1	234	80.2
		Martin Van Buren	Democratic	1,127,781	46.9	60	
1844	26	**JAMES K. POLK**	Democratic	1,338,464	49.6	170	78.9
		Henry Clay	Whig	1,300,097	48.1	105	
		James G. Birney	Liberty	62,300	2.3		
1848	30	**ZACHARY TAYLOR**	Whig	1,360,967	47.4	163	72.7
		Lewis Cass	Democratic	1,222,342	42.5	127	
		Martin Van Buren	Free Soil	291,263	10.1		
1852	31	**FRANKLIN PIERCE**	Democratic	1,601,117	50.9	254	69.6
		Winfield Scott	Whig	1,385,453	44.1	42	
		John P. Hale	Free Soil	155,825	5.0		
1856	31	**JAMES BUCHANAN**	Democratic	1,832,955	45.3	174	78.9
		John C. Frémont	Republican	1,339,932	33.1	114	
		Millard Fillmore	American	871,731	21.6	8	

Year	Number of States	Candidates	Parties	Popular Vote	% of Popular Vote	Electoral Vote	% Voter Participation
1860	33	**ABRAHAM LINCOLN**	Republican	1,865,593	39.8	180	81.2
		Stephen A. Douglas	Democratic	1,382,713	29.5	12	
		John C. Breckinridge	Democratic	848,356	18.1	72	
		John Bell	Constitutional Union	592,906	12.6	39	
1864	36	**ABRAHAM LINCOLN**	Republican	2,206,938	55.0	212	73.8
		George B. McClellan	Democratic	1,803,787	45.0	21	
1868	37	**ULYSSES S. GRANT**	Republican	3,013,421	52.7	214	78.1
		Horatio Seymour	Democratic	2,706,829	47.3	80	
1872	37	**ULYSSES S. GRANT**	Republican	3,596,745	55.6	286	71.3
		Horace Greeley	Democratic	2,843,446	43.9	66	
1876	38	Rutherford B. Hayes	Republican	4,036,572	48.0	185	81.8
		Samuel J. Tilden	Democratic	4,284,020	51.0	184	
1880	38	**JAMES A. GARFIELD**	Republican	4,453,295	48.5	214	79.4
		Winfield S. Hancock	Democratic	4,414,082	48.1	155	
		James B. Weaver	Greenback-Labor	308,578	3.4		
1884	38	**GROVER CLEVELAND**	Democratic	4,879,507	48.5	219	77.5
		James G. Blaine	Republican	4,850,293	48.2	182	
		Benjamin F. Butler	Greenback-Labor	175,370	1.8		
		John P. St. John	Prohibition	150,369	1.5		
1888	38	**BENJAMIN HARRISON**	Republican	5,477,129	47.9	233	79.3
		Grover Cleveland	Democratic	5,537,857	48.6	168	
		Clinton B. Fisk	Prohibition	249,506	2.2		
		Anson J. Streeter	Union Labor	146,935	1.3		

Year	Number of States	Candidates	Parties	Popular Vote	% of Popular Vote	Electoral Vote	% Voter Participation
1892	44	**GROVER CLEVELAND**	Democratic	5,555,426	46.1	277	74.7
		Benjamin Harrison	Republican	5,182,690	43.0	145	
		James B. Weaver	People's	1,029,846	8.5	22	
		John Bidwell	Prohibition	264,133	2.2		
1896	45	**WILLIAM MCKINLEY**	Republican	7,102,246	51.1	271	79.3
		William J. Bryan	Democratic	6,492,559	47.7	176	
1900	45	**WILLIAM MCKINLEY**	Republican	7,218,491	51.7	292	73.2
		William J. Bryan	Democratic; Populist	6,356,734	45.5	155	
		John C. Wooley	Prohibition	208,914	1.5		
1904	45	**THEODORE ROOSEVELT**	Republican	7,628,461	57.4	336	65.2
		Alton B. Parker	Democratic	5,084,223	37.6	140	
		Eugene V. Debs	Socialist	402,283	3.0		
		Silas C. Swallow	Prohibition	258,536	1.9		
1908	46	**WILLIAM H. TAFT**	Republican	7,675,320	51.6	321	65.4
		William J. Bryan	Democratic	6,412,294	43.1	162	
		Eugene V. Debs	Socialist	420,793	2.8		
		Eugene W. Chafin	Prohibition	253,840	1.7		
1912	48	**WOODROW WILSON**	Democratic	6,296,547	41.9	435	58.8
		Theodore Roosevelt	Progressive	4,118,571	27.4	88	
		William H. Taft	Republican	3,486,720	23.2	8	
		Eugene V. Debs	Socialist	900,672	6.0		
		Eugene W. Chafin	Prohibition	206,275	1.4		

Year	Number of States	Candidates	Parties	Popular Vote	% of Popular Vote	Electoral Vote	% Voter Participation
1916	48	WOODROW WILSON	Democratic	9,127,695	49.4	277	61.6
		Charles E. Hughes	Republican	8,533,507	46.2	254	
		A. L. Benson	Socialist	585,113	3.2		
		J. Frank Hanly	Prohibition	220,506	1.2		
1920	48	WARREN G. HARDING	Republican	16,143,407	60.4	404	49.2
		James M. Cox	Democratic	9,130,328	34.2	127	
		Eugene V. Debs	Socialist	919,799	3.4		
		P. P. Christensen	Farmer-Labor	265,411	1.0		
1924	48	CALVIN COOLIDGE	Republican	15,718,211	54.0	382	48.9
		John W. Davis	Democratic	8,385,283	28.8	136	
		Robert M. La Follette	Progressive	4,831,289	16.6	13	
1928	48	HERBERT C. HOOVER	Republican	21,391,993	58.2	444	56.9
		Alfred E. Smith	Democratic	15,016,169	40.9	87	
1932	48	FRANKLIN D. ROOSEVELT	Democratic	22,809,638	57.4	472	56.9
		Herbert C. Hoover	Republican	15,758,901	39.7	59	
		Norman Thomas	Socialist	881,951	2.2		
1936	48	FRANKLIN D. ROOSEVELT	Democratic	27,752,869	60.8	523	61.0
		Alfred M. Landon	Republican	16,674,665	36.5	8	
		William Lemke	Union	882,479	1.9		
1940	48	FRANKLIN D. ROOSEVELT	Democratic	27,307,819	54.8	449	62.5
		Wendell L. Willkie	Republican	22,321,018	44.8	82	
1944	48	FRANKLIN D. ROOSEVELT	Democratic	25,606,585	53.5	432	55.9
		Thomas E. Dewey	Republican	22,014,745	46.0	99	

Year	Number of States	Candidates	Parties	Popular Vote	% of Popular Vote	Electoral Vote	% Voter Participation
1948	48	**HARRY S. TRUMAN**	Democratic	24,179,345	49.6	303	53.0
		Thomas E. Dewey	Republican	21,991,291	45.1	189	
		J. Strom Thurmond	States' Rights	1,176,125	2.4	39	
		Henry A. Wallace	Progressive	1,157,326	2.4		
1952	48	**DWIGHT D. EISENHOWER**	Republican	33,936,234	55.1	442	63.3
		Adlai E. Stevenson	Democratic	27,314,992	44.4	89	
1956	48	**DWIGHT D. EISENHOWER**	Republican	35,590,472	57.6	457	60.6
		Adlai E. Stevenson	Democratic	26,022,752	42.1	73	
1960	50	**JOHN F. KENNEDY**	Democratic	34,226,731	49.7	303	62.8
		Richard M. Nixon	Republican	34,108,157	49.5	219	
1964	50	**LYNDON B. JOHNSON**	Democratic	43,129,566	61.1	486	61.9
		Barry M. Goldwater	Republican	27,178,188	38.5	52	
1968	50	**RICHARD M. NIXON**	Republican	31,785,480	43.4	301	60.9
		Hubert H. Humphrey	Democratic	31,275,166	42.7	191	
		George C. Wallace	American Independent	9,906,473	13.5	46	
1972	50	**RICHARD M. NIXON**	Republican	47,169,911	60.7	520	55.2
		George S. McGovern	Democratic	29,170,383	37.5	17	
		John G. Schmitz	American	1,099,482	1.4		

Year	Number of States	Candidates	Parties	Popular Vote	% of Popular Vote	Electoral Vote	% Voter Participation
1976	50	**JIMMY CARTER** Gerald R. Ford	Democratic Republican	40,830,763 39,147,793	50.1 48.0	297 240	53.5
1980	50	**RONALD REAGAN** Jimmy Carter John B. Anderson Ed Clark	Republican Democratic Independent Libertarian	43,901,812 35,483,820 5,719,437 921,188	50.7 41.0 6.6 1.1	489 49	52.6
1984	50	**RONALD REAGAN** Walter F. Mondale	Republican Democratic	54,451,521 37,565,334	58.8 40.6	525 13	53.1
1988	50	**GEORGE H. W. BUSH** Michael Dukakis	Republican Democratic	47,917,341 41,013,030	53.4 45.6	426 111	50.1
1992	50	**BILL CLINTON** George H. W. Bush H. Ross Perot	Democratic Republican Independent	44,908,254 39,102,343 19,741,065	43.0 37.4 18.9	370 168	55.0
1996	50	**BILL CLINTON** Bob Dole H. Ross Perot	Democratic Republican Independent	47,401,185 39,197,469 8,085,295	49.0 41.0 8.0	379 159	49.0
2000	50	**GEORGE W. BUSH** Al Gore Ralph Nader	Republican Democrat Green	50,455,156 50,997,335 2,882,897	47.9 48.4 2.7	271 266	50.4
2004	50	**GEORGE W. BUSH** John F. Kerry	Republican Democrat	62,040,610 59,028,444	50.7 48.3	286 251	60.7
2008	50	**BARACK OBAMA** John McCain	Democrat Republican	69,456,897 59,934,814	52.92% 45.66%	365 173	63.0

Candidates receiving less than 1 percent of the popular vote have been omitted. Thus the percentage of popular vote given for any election year may not total 100 percent.

Before the passage of the Twelfth Amendment in 1804, the electoral college voted for two presidential candidates; the runner-up became vice president.

ADMISSION OF STATES

Order of Admission	State	Date of Admission	Order of Admission	State	Date of Admission
1	Delaware	December 7, 1787	26	Michigan	January 26, 1837
2	Pennsylvania	December 12, 1787	27	Florida	March 3, 1845
3	New Jersey	December 18, 1787	28	Texas	December 29, 1845
4	Georgia	January 2, 1788	29	Iowa	December 28, 1846
5	Connecticut	January 9, 1788	30	Wisconsin	May 29, 1848
6	Massachusetts	February 7, 1788	31	California	September 9, 1850
7	Maryland	April 28, 1788	32	Minnesota	May 11, 1858
8	South Carolina	May 23, 1788	33	Oregon	February 14, 1859
9	New Hampshire	June 21, 1788	34	Kansas	January 29, 1861
10	Virginia	June 25, 1788	35	West Virginia	June 30, 1863
11	New York	July 26, 1788	36	Nevada	October 31, 1864
12	North Carolina	November 21, 1789	37	Nebraska	March 1, 1867
13	Rhode Island	May 29, 1790	38	Colorado	August 1, 1876
14	Vermont	March 4, 1791	39	North Dakota	November 2, 1889
15	Kentucky	June 1, 1792	40	South Dakota	November 2, 1889
16	Tennessee	June 1, 1796	41	Montana	November 8, 1889
17	Ohio	March 1, 1803	42	Washington	November 11, 1889
18	Louisiana	April 30, 1812	43	Idaho	July 3, 1890
19	Indiana	December 11, 1816	44	Wyoming	July 10, 1890
20	Mississippi	December 10, 1817	45	Utah	January 4, 1896
21	Illinois	December 3, 1818	46	Oklahoma	November 16, 1907
22	Alabama	December 14, 1819	47	New Mexico	January 6, 1912
23	Maine	March 15, 1820	48	Arizona	February 14, 1912
24	Missouri	August 10, 1821	49	Alaska	January 3, 1959
25	Arkansas	June 15, 1836	50	Hawaii	August 21, 1959

POPULATION OF THE UNITED STATES

Year	Number of States	Population	% Increase	Population per Square Mile
1790	13	3,929,214		4.5
1800	16	5,308,483	35.1	6.1
1810	17	7,239,881	36.4	4.3
1820	23	9,638,453	33.1	5.5
1830	24	12,866,020	33.5	7.4
1840	26	17,069,453	32.7	9.8
1850	31	23,191,876	35.9	7.9
1860	33	31,443,321	35.6	10.6
1870	37	39,818,449	26.6	13.4
1880	38	50,155,783	26.0	16.9
1890	44	62,947,714	25.5	21.1
1900	45	75,994,575	20.7	25.6
1910	46	91,972,266	21.0	31.0
1920	48	105,710,620	14.9	35.6
1930	48	122,775,046	16.1	41.2
1940	48	131,669,275	7.2	44.2
1950	48	150,697,361	14.5	50.7
1960	50	179,323,175	19.0	50.6
1970	50	203,235,298	13.3	57.5
1980	50	226,504,825	11.4	64.0
1985	50	237,839,000	5.0	67.2
1990	50	250,122,000	5.2	70.6
1995	50	263,411,707	5.3	74.4
2000	50	281,421,906	6.8	77.0
2008	50	304,059,724	8.0	79.6

IMMIGRATION TO THE UNITED STATES, FISCAL YEARS 1820–2008

Year	Number	Year	Number	Year	Number	Year	Number
1820–1989	**55,457,531**	**1871–80**	**2,812,191**	**1921–30**	**4,107,209**	**1971–80**	**4,493,314**
1820	8,385	1871	321,350	1921	805,228	1971	370,478
1821–30	**143,439**	1872	404,806	1922	309,556	1972	384,685
1821	9,127	1873	459,803	1923	522,919	1973	400,063
1822	6,911	1874	313,339	1924	706,896	1974	394,861
1823	6,354	1875	227,498	1925	294,314	1975	386,914
1824	7,912	1876	169,986	1926	304,488	1976	398,613
1825	10,199	1877	141,857	1927	335,175	1976 TQ	103,676
1826	10,837	1878	138,469	1928	307,255	1977	462,315
1827	18,875	1879	177,826	1929	279,678	1978	601,442
1828	27,382	1880	457,257	1930	241,700	1979	460,348
1829	22,520	**1881–90**	**5,246,613**	**1931–40**	**528,431**	1980	530,639
1830	23,322	1881	669,431	1931	97,139	**1981–90**	**7,338,062**
1831–40	**599,125**	1882	788,992	1932	35,576	1981	596,600
1831	22,633	1883	603,322	1933	23,068	1982	594,131
1832	60,482	1884	518,592	1934	29,470	1983	559,763
1833	58,640	1885	395,346	1935	34,956	1984	543,903
1834	65,365	1886	334,203	1936	36,329	1985	570,009
1835	45,374	1887	490,109	1937	50,244	1986	601,708
1836	76,242	1888	546,889	1938	67,895	1987	601,516
1837	79,340	1889	444,427	1939	82,998	1988	643,025
1838	38,914	1890	455,302	1940	70,756	1989	1,090,924
1839	68,069	**1891–1900**	**3,687,564**	**1941–50**	**1,035,039**	1990	1,536,483
1840	84,066	1891	560,319	1941	51,776	**1991–2000**	**9,090,857**
1841–50	**1,713,251**	1892	579,663	1942	28,781	1991	1,827,167
1841	80,289	1893	439,730	1943	23,725	1992	973,977
1842	104,565	1894	285,631	1944	28,551	1993	904,292
		1895	258,536	1945	38,119	1994	804,416
		1896	343,267	1946	108,721		

Year	Number	Year	Number	Year	Number	Year	Number
1843	52,496						
1844	78,615						
1845	114,371					1995	720,461
1846	154,416					1996	915,900
1847	234,968	1897	230,832	1947	147,292	1997	798,378
1848	226,527	1898	229,299	1948	170,570	1998	660,477
1849	297,024	1899	311,715	1949	188,317	1999	644,787
1850	369,980	1900	448,572	1950	249,187	2000	841,002
1851–60	**2,598,214**	**1901–10**	**8,795,386**	**1951–60**	**2,515,479**	**2001–8**	**8,330,011**
1851	379,466	1901	487,918	1951	205,717	2001	1,058,902
1852	371,603	1902	648,743	1952	265,520	2002	1,059,356
1853	368,645	1903	857,046	1953	170,434	2003	705,827
1854	427,833	1904	812,870	1954	208,177	2004	957,883
1855	200,877	1905	1,026,499	1955	237,790	2005	1,122,373
1856	200,436	1906	1,100,735	1956	321,625	2006	1,266,129
1857	251,306	1907	1,285,349	1957	326,867	2007	1,052,415
1858	123,126	1908	782,870	1958	253,265	2008	1,107,126
1859	121,282	1909	751,786	1959	260,686		
1860	153,640	1910	1,041,570	1960	265,398		
1861–70	**2,314,824**	**1911–20**	**5,735,811**	**1961–70**	**3,321,677**		
1861	91,918	1911	878,587	1961	271,344		
1862	91,985	1912	838,172	1962	283,763		
1863	176,282	1913	1,197,892	1963	306,260		
1864	193,418	1914	1,218,480	1964	292,248		
1865	248,120	1915	326,700	1965	296,697		
1866	318,568	1916	298,826	1966	323,040		
1867	315,722	1917	295,403	1967	361,972		
1868	138,840	1918	110,618	1968	454,448		
1869	352,768	1919	141,132	1969	358,579		
1870	387,203	1920	430,001	1970	373,326		

Source: U.S. Department of Homeland Security.

IMMIGRATION BY REGION AND SELECTED COUNTRY OF LAST RESIDENCE, FISCAL YEARS 1820–2008

Region and country of last residence	1820 to 1829	1830 to 1839	1840 to 1849	1850 to 1859	1860 to 1869	1870 to 1879	1880 to 1889	1890 to 1899
Total	128,502	538,381	1,427,337	2,814,554	2,081,261	2,742,137	5,248,568	3,694,294
Europe	99,272	422,771	1,369,259	2,619,680	1,877,726	2,251,878	4,638,677	3,576,411
Austria-Hungary	—	—	—	—	3,375	60,127	314,787	534,059
Austria	—	—	—	—	2,700	54,529	204,805	268,218
Hungary	—	—	—	—	483	5,598	109,982	203,350
Belgium	28	20	3,996	5,765	5,785	6,991	18,738	19,642
Bulgaria	—	—	—	—	—	—	—	52
Czechoslovakia	—	—	—	—	—	—	—	—
Denmark	173	927	671	3,227	13,553	29,278	85,342	56,671
Finland	—	—	—	—	—	—	—	—
France	7,694	39,330	75,300	81,778	35,938	71,901	48,193	35,616
Germany	5,753	124,726	385,434	976,072	723,734	751,769	1,445,181	579,072
Greece	17	49	17	32	51	209	1,807	12,732
Ireland	51,617	170,672	656,145	1,029,486	427,419	422,264	674,061	405,710
Italy	430	2,225	1,476	8,643	9,853	46,296	267,660	603,761
Netherlands	1,105	1,377	7,624	11,122	8,387	14,267	52,715	29,349
Norway-Sweden	91	1,149	12,389	22,202	82,937	178,823	586,441	334,058
Norway	—	—	—	—	16,068	88,644	185,111	96,810
Sweden	—	—	—	—	24,224	90,179	401,330	237,248
Poland	19	366	105	1,087	1,886	11,016	42,910	107,793
Portugal	177	820	196	1,299	2,083	13,971	15,186	25,874
Romania	—	—	—	—	—	—	5,842	6,808
Russia	86	280	520	423	1,670	35,177	182,698	450,101
Spain	2,595	2,010	1,916	8,795	6,966	5,540	3,995	9,189
Switzerland	3,148	4,430	4,819	24,423	21,124	25,212	81,151	37,020
United Kingdom	26,336	74,350	218,572	445,322	532,956	578,447	810,900	328,759
Yugoslavia	—	—	—	—	—	—	—	—
Other Europe	3	40	79	4	9	590	1,070	145

Region / Country								
Asia	34	55	121	36,080	54,408	134,128	71,151	61,285
China	3	8	32	35,933	54,028	133,139	65,797	15,268
Hong Kong	9	38	33	42	50	166	247	102
India	—	—	—	—	—	—	—	102
Iran	—	—	—	—	—	—	—	—
Israel	—	—	—	—	—	—	—	—
Japan	—	—	—	—	138	193	1,583	13,998
Jordan	—	—	—	—	—	—	—	—
Korea	—	—	—	—	—	—	—	—
Philippines	—	—	—	—	—	—	—	—
Syria	—	—	—	—	—	—	—	—
Taiwan	19	8	45	94	129	382	2,478	27,510
Turkey	—	—	—	—	—	—	—	—
Vietnam	—	—	—	—	—	—	—	—
Other Asia	3	1	11	11	63	248	1,046	4,407
America	9,655	31,905	50,516	84,145	130,292	345,010	524,826	37,350
Canada and Newfoundland	2,297	11,875	34,285	64,171	117,978	324,310	492,865	3,098
Mexico	3,835	7,187	3,069	3,446	1,957	5,133	2,405	734
Caribbean	3,061	11,792	11,803	12,447	8,751	14,285	27,323	31,480
Cuba	—	—	—	—	—	—	—	—
Dominican Republic	—	—	—	—	—	—	—	—
Haiti	—	—	—	—	—	—	—	—
Jamaica	—	—	—	—	—	—	—	—
Other Caribbean	3,061	11,792	11,803	12,447	8,751	14,285	27,323	31,480
Central America	57	94	297	512	70	173	279	649
Belize	—	—	—	—	—	—	—	—
Costa Rica	—	—	—	—	—	—	—	—
El Salvador	—	—	—	—	—	—	—	—
Guatemala	—	—	—	—	—	—	—	—
Honduras	—	—	—	—	—	—	—	—
Nicaragua	—	—	—	—	—	—	—	—
Panama	—	—	—	—	—	—	—	—
Other Central America	57	94	297	512	70	173	279	649
South America	405	957	1,062	3,569	1,536	1,109	1,954	1,389
Argentina	—	—	—	—	—	—	—	—
Bolivia	—	—	—	—	—	—	—	—

Region and country of last residence	1820 to 1829	1830 to 1839	1840 to 1849	1850 to 1859	1860 to 1869	1870 to 1879	1880 to 1889	1890 to 1899
Brazil	—	—	—	—	—	—	—	—
Chile	—	—	—	—	—	—	—	—
Colombia	—	—	—	—	—	—	—	—
Ecuador	—	—	—	—	—	—	—	—
Guyana	—	—	—	—	—	—	—	—
Paraguay	—	—	—	—	—	—	—	—
Peru	—	—	—	—	—	—	—	—
Suriname	—	—	—	—	—	—	—	—
Uruguay	—	—	—	—	—	—	—	—
Venezuela	—	—	—	—	—	—	—	—
Other South America	405	957	1,062	3,569	1,536	1,109	1,954	1,389
Other America	—	—	—	—	—	—	—	—
Africa	15	50	61	84	407	371	763	432
Egypt	—	—	—	—	4	29	145	51
Ethiopia	—	—	—	—	—	—	—	—
Liberia	1	8	5	7	43	52	21	9
Morocco	—	—	—	—	—	—	—	—
South Africa	—	—	—	—	35	48	23	9
Other Africa	14	42	56	77	325	242	574	363
Oceania	3	7	14	166	187	9,996	12,361	4,704
Australia	2	1	2	15	—	8,930	7,250	3,098
New Zealand	—	—	—	—	—	39	21	12
Other Oceania	1	6	12	151	187	1,027	5,090	1,594
Not Specified	19,523	83,593	7,366	74,399	18,241	754	790	14,112

Total	8,202,388	6,347,380	4,295,510	699,375	856,608	2,499,268	3,213,749	6,244,379
Europe	7,572,569	4,985,411	2,560,340	444,399	472,524	1,404,973	1,133,443	668,866
Austria-Hungary	2,001,376	1,154,727	60,891	12,531	13,574	113,015	27,590	20,437
Austria	532,416	589,174	31,392	5,307	8,393	81,354	17,571	15,374
Hungary	685,567	565,553	29,499	7,224	5,181	31,661	10,019	5,063
Belgium	37,429	32,574	21,511	4,013	12,473	18,885	9,647	7,028
Bulgaria	34,651	27,180	2,824	1,062	449	97	598	1,124
Czechoslovakia	—	—	101,182	17,757	8,475	1,624	2,758	5,678
Denmark	61,227	45,830	34,406	3,470	4,549	10,918	9,797	4,847
Finland	—	—	16,922	2,438	2,230	4,923	4,310	2,569
France	67,735	60,335	54,842	13,761	36,954	50,113	46,975	32,066
Germany	328,722	174,227	386,634	119,107	119,506	576,905	209,616	85,752
Greece	145,402	198,108	60,774	10,599	8,605	45,153	74,173	37,729
Ireland	344,940	166,445	202,854	28,195	15,701	47,189	37,788	22,210
Italy	1,930,475	1,229,916	528,133	85,053	50,509	184,576	200,111	55,562
Netherlands	42,463	46,065	29,397	7,791	13,877	46,703	37,918	11,234
Norway-Sweden	426,981	192,445	170,329	13,452	17,326	44,224	36,150	13,941
Norway	182,542	79,488	70,327	6,901	8,326	22,806	17,371	3,835
Sweden	244,439	112,957	100,002	6,551	9,000	21,418	18,779	10,106
Poland	—	—	223,316	25,555	7,577	6,465	55,742	63,483
Portugal	65,154	82,489	44,829	3,518	6,765	13,928	70,568	42,685
Romania	57,322	13,566	67,810	5,264	1,254	914	2,339	24,753
Russia	1,501,301	1,106,998	61,604	2,463	605	453	2,329	33,311
Spain	24,818	53,262	47,109	3,669	2,774	6,880	40,793	22,783
Switzerland	32,541	22,839	31,772	5,990	9,904	17,577	19,193	8,316
United Kingdom	469,518	371,878	341,552	61,813	131,794	195,709	220,213	153,644
Yugoslavia	—	—	49,215	6,920	2,039	6,966	17,990	16,267
Other Europe	514	6,527	22,434	9,978	5,584	11,756	6,845	3,447
Asia	299,836	269,736	126,740	19,231	34,532	135,844	358,605	2,391,356
China	19,884	20,916	30,648	5,874	16,072	8,836	14,060	170,897
Hong Kong	—	—	—	—	—	13,781	67,047	112,132
India	3,026	3,478	2,076	554	1,692	1,850	18,638	231,649
Iran	—	—	208	198	1,144	3,195	9,059	98,141
Israel	—	—	—	—	98	21,376	30,911	43,669

Region and country of last residence	1900 to 1909	1910 to 1919	1920 to 1929	1930 to 1939	1940 to 1949	1950 to 1959	1960 to 1969	1980 to 1989
Japan	139,712	77,125	42,057	2,683	1,557	40,651	40,956	44,150
Jordan	—	—	—	—	—	4,899	9,230	28,928
Korea	—	—	—	—	83	4,845	27,048	322,708
Philippines	—	—	—	391	4,099	17,245	70,660	502,056
Syria	—	—	5,307	2,188	1,179	1,091	2,432	14,534
Taiwan	—	—	—	—	—	721	15,657	119,051
Turkey	127,999	160,717	40,450	1,327	754	2,980	9,464	19,208
Vietnam	—	—	—	—	—	290	2,949	200,632
Other Asia	9,215	7,500	5,994	6,016	7,854	14,084	40,494	483,601
America	277,809	1,070,539	1,591,278	230,319	328,435	921,610	1,674,172	2,695,329
Canada and Newfoundland	123,067	708,715	949,286	162,703	160,911	353,169	433,128	156,313
Mexico	31,188	185,334	498,945	32,709	56,158	273,847	441,824	1,009,586
Caribbean	100,960	120,860	83,482	18,052	46,194	115,661	427,235	790,109
Cuba	—	—	12,769	10,641	25,976	73,221	202,030	132,552
Dominican Republic	—	—	—	1,026	4,802	10,219	83,552	221,552
Haiti	—	—	—	156	823	3,787	28,992	121,406
Jamaica	—	—	—	—	—	7,397	62,218	193,874
Other Caribbean	100,960	120,860	70,713	6,229	14,593	21,037	50,443	120,725
Central America	7,341	15,692	16,511	6,840	20,135	40,201	98,560	339,376
Belize	77	40	285	193	433	1,133	4,185	14,964
Costa Rica	—	—	—	431	1,965	4,044	17,975	25,017
El Salvador	—	—	—	597	4,885	5,094	14,405	137,418
Guatemala	—	—	—	423	1,303	4,197	14,357	58,847
Honduras	—	—	—	679	1,874	5,320	15,078	39,071
Nicaragua	—	—	—	405	4,393	7,812	10,383	31,102
Panama	—	—	—	1,452	5,282	12,601	22,177	32,957
Other Central America	7,264	15,652	16,226	2,660	—	—	—	—

Region / Country							
South America	359,862	250,754	78,418	19,662	9,990	43,025	39,938	15,253
Argentina	23,442	49,384	16,346	3,108	1,067	—	—	—
Bolivia	9,798	6,205	2,759	893	50	—	—	—
Brazil	22,944	29,238	11,547	3,653	1,468	4,627	—	—
Chile	19,749	12,384	4,669	1,320	347	—	—	—
Colombia	105,494	68,371	15,567	3,454	1,027	—	—	—
Ecuador	48,015	34,107	8,574	2,207	244	—	—	—
Guyana	85,886	4,546	1,131	596	131	—	—	—
Paraguay	3,518	1,249	576	85	33	—	—	—
Peru	49,958	19,783	5,980	1,273	321	—	—	—
Suriname	1,357	612	299	130	25	—	—	—
Uruguay	7,235	4,089	1,026	754	112	—	—	—
Venezuela	22,405	20,758	9,927	2,182	1,155	—	—	—
Other South America	61	28	17	7	4,010	38,398	39,938	15,253
Other America	83	22,671	60,314	25,375	25	29	—	—
Africa	141,990	23,780	13,016	6,720	2,120	6,362	8,867	6,326
Egypt	26,744	5,581	1,996	1,613	781	1,063	—	—
Ethiopia	12,927	804	302	28	10	—	—	—
Liberia	6,420	841	289	37	35	—	—	—
Morocco	3,471	2,880	2,703	879	73	—	—	—
South Africa	15,505	4,360	2,278	1,022	312	—	—	—
Other Africa	76,923	9,314	5,448	3,141	909	5,299	8,867	6,326
Oceania	41,432	23,630	11,353	14,262	3,306	9,860	12,339	12,355
Australia	16,901	14,986	8,275	11,201	2,260	8,404	11,280	11,191
New Zealand	6,129	3,775	1,799	2,351	790	935	—	—
Other Oceania	18,402	4,869	1,279	710	256	521	1,059	1,164
Not Specified	305,406	119	12,472	135	—	930	488	33,493

Region and country of last residence	1990 to 1999	2000	2001	2002	2003	2004	2005	2006	2007	2008
Total	9,775,398	841,002	1,058,902	1,059,356	703,542	957,883	1,122,257	1,266,129	1,052,415	1,107,126
Europe	1,348,612	131,920	176,892	177,059	102,546	135,663	180,396	169,156	120,759	121,146
Austria-Hungary	27,529	2,009	2,303	4,004	2,176	3,689	4,569	2,991	2,057	2,576
Austria	18,234	986	996	2,650	1,160	2,442	3,002	1,301	849	1,505
Hungary	9,295	1,023	1,307	1,354	1,016	1,247	1,567	1,690	1,208	1,071
Belgium	7,077	817	997	834	515	746	1,031	891	733	829
Bulgaria	16,948	4,779	4,273	3,476	3,706	4,042	5,451	4,690	3,766	2,805
Czechoslovakia	8,970	1,407	1,911	1,854	1,472	1,871	2,182	2,844	1,851	1,650
Denmark	6,189	549	732	651	435	568	714	738	505	551
Finland	3,970	377	497	365	230	346	549	513	385	287
France	35,945	4,063	5,379	4,567	2,926	4,209	5,035	4,945	3,680	5,246
Germany	92,207	12,230	21,992	20,977	8,061	10,270	12,864	10,271	8,640	8,456
Greece	25,403	5,113	1,941	1,486	900	1,213	1,473	1,544	1,152	943
Ireland	65,384	1,264	1,531	1,400	1,002	1,518	2,083	2,038	1,599	1,499
Italy	75,992	2,652	3,332	2,812	1,890	2,495	3,179	3,406	2,682	2,738
Netherlands	13,345	1,455	1,888	2,296	1,321	1,713	2,150	1,928	1,482	1,423
Norway-Sweden	17,825	1,967	2,544	2,082	1,516	2,011	2,264	2,111	1,604	1,557
Norway	5,211	508	582	460	385	457	472	532	388	386
Sweden	12,614	1,459	1,962	1,622	1,131	1,554	1,792	1,579	1,216	1,171
Poland	172,249	9,750	12,308	13,274	11,004	14,048	14,836	16,704	9,717	7,896
Portugal	25,497	1,373	1,611	1,301	808	1,062	1,084	1,439	1,054	781
Romania	48,136	6,506	6,206	4,515	3,305	4,078	6,431	6,753	5,240	4,563
Russia	433,427	43,156	54,838	55,370	33,513	41,959	60,344	59,720	41,593	45,092
Spain	18,443	1,390	1,875	1,588	1,102	1,453	2,002	2,387	1,810	1,970
Switzerland	11,768	1,339	1,786	1,493	862	1,193	1,465	1,199	885	936
United Kingdom	156,182	14,427	20,118	17,940	11,155	16,680	21,956	19,984	16,113	16,189
Yugoslavia	57,039	11,960	21,854	28,051	8,270	13,213	19,249	11,066	6,364	5,812
Other Europe	29,087	3,337	6,976	6,723	6,377	7,286	9,485	10,994	7,847	7,347

Asia	2,859,899	254,932	326,112	325,749	235,339	319,025	382,707	411,746	359,387	369,339
China	342,058	41,804	50,677	55,901	37,342	50,280	64,887	83,590	70,924	75,410
Hong Kong	116,894	7,181	10,282	7,938	5,015	5,421	5,004	4,514	4,450	4,389
India	352,528	38,938	65,673	66,644	47,032	65,507	79,139	58,072	55,371	59,728
Iran	76,899	6,481	8,003	7,684	4,696	5,898	7,306	9,829	8,098	9,920
Israel	41,340	3,871	4,892	4,907	3,686	5,206	6,963	6,667	4,999	6,682
Japan	66,582	7,688	10,424	9,106	6,702	3,655	9,929	9,107	7,213	7,510
Jordan	42,755	4,476	5,106	4,774	4,008	5,186	5,430	5,512	5,516	5,692
Korea	179,770	15,107	19,728	19,917	12,076	19,441	26,002	24,472	21,278	26,155
Philippines	534,338	40,465	50,644	48,493	43,133	54,651	57,654	71,133	68,792	52,391
Syria	22,906	2,255	3,542	3,350	2,046	2,549	3,350	3,080	2,550	3,310
Taiwan	132,647	9,457	12,457	9,932	7,168	9,314	9,389	8,545	9,053	9,237
Turkey	38,687	2,702	3,463	3,914	3,318	4,491	6,449	6,433	4,728	4,953
Vietnam	275,379	25,159	34,537	32,372	21,227	30,074	30,832	29,701	27,510	29,807
Other Asia	637,116	49,348	56,684	50,817	37,890	52,352	70,373	91,091	68,905	74,155
America	5,137,743	392,461	470,794	477,363	305,936	408,972	432,726	548,812	434,272	491,045
Canada and Newfoundland	194,788	21,289	29,991	27,142	16,447	22,439	29,930	23,913	20,324	22,366
Mexico	2,757,418	171,445	204,032	216,924	114,758	173,711	157,992	170,042	143,180	188,015
Caribbean	1,004,687	84,250	96,384	93,914	67,498	82,116	91,371	144,477	114,318	134,744
Cuba	159,037	17,897	25,832	27,435	8,685	15,385	20,651	44,248	25,441	48,057
Dominican Republic	359,818	17,373	21,139	22,386	26,112	30,063	27,365	37,997	27,875	31,801
Haiti	177,446	21,977	22,470	19,151	11,924	13,695	13,491	21,625	29,978	25,522
Jamaica	181,243	15,603	15,031	14,507	13,045	13,581	17,774	24,538	18,873	18,077
Other Caribbean		11,400	11,912	10,435	7,732	9,392	12,090	16,069	12,151	11,287
Central America	610,189	60,331	72,504	66,298	53,283	61,253	52,629	74,244	53,834	49,741
Belize	12,600	774	982	983	616	888	901	1,263	1,089	1,113
Costa Rica	17,054	1,390	1,863	1,686	1,322	1,811	2,479	3,459	2,722	2,287
El Salvador	273,017	22,301	30,876	30,472	27,854	29,297	20,891	31,258	20,009	18,937
Guatemala	126,043	9,861	13,399	15,870	14,195	18,655	16,466	23,674	17,198	15,791
Honduras	72,830	5,851	6,546	6,355	4,582	5,339	6,825	8,036	7,300	6,389

Region and country of last residence	1990 to 1999	2000	2001	2002	2003	2004	2005	2006	2007	2008
Nicaragua	80,446	18,258	16,908	9,171	3,503	3,842	3,196	4,035	3,587	3,486
Panama	28,149	1,896	1,930	1,761	1,211	1,421	1,869	2,519	1,929	1,738
Other Central America	—	—	—	—				—		
South America	570,624	55,143	67,880	73,082	53,946	69,452	100,803	136,134	102,616	96,178
Argentina	30,065	2,472	3,426	3,791	3,193	4,672	6,945	7,239	5,375	5,170
Bolivia	18,111	1,744	1,804	1,660	1,365	1,719	2,164	4,000	2,326	2,350
Brazil	50,744	6,767	9,391	9,034	6,108	10,247	16,329	17,741	13,546	11,813
Chile	18,200	1,660	1,881	1,766	1,255	1,719	2,354	2,727	2,202	1,988
Colombia	137,985	14,125	16,234	18,409	14,400	18,055	24,705	42,017	32,055	29,349
Ecuador	81,358	7,624	9,654	10,524	7,022	8,366	11,528	17,624	12,011	11,541
Guyana	74,407	5,255	7,835	9,492	6,373	5,721	8,771	9,010	5,288	6,302
Paraguay	6,082	394	464	413	222	324	523	725	518	489
Peru	110,117	9,361	10,838	11,737	9,169	11,369	15,205	21,300	17,056	14,873
Suriname	2,285	281	254	223	175	170	287	341	193	225
Uruguay	6,062	396	516	499	470	750	1,110	1,639	1,340	1,380
Venezuela	35,180	5,052	5,576	5,529	4,190	6,335	10,870	11,758	10,696	10,689
Other South America	28	12	7	5	4	5	12	13	10	
Other America	37	3	3	3	4	1	1	2	—	1
Africa	346,416	40,790	50,009	56,002	45,559	62,623	79,697	112,100	89,277	100,881
Egypt	44,604	4,323	5,333	6,215	3,928	6,590	10,296	13,163	10,178	10,728
Ethiopia	40,097	3,645	4,620	6,308	5,969	7,180	8,378	13,390	11,340	11,703
Liberia	13,587	1,225	1,477	1,467	1,081	1,540	1,846	3,736	3,771	3,478
Morocco	15,768	3,423	4,752	3,188	2,969	3,910	4,165	4,704	4,311	4,187
South Africa	21,964	2,814	4,046	3,685	2,088	3,335	4,425	3,173	2,842	2,638
Other Africa	210,396	25,360	29,781	35,139	29,524	40,068	50,587	73,934	56,835	68,147
Oceania	56,800	5,928	7,201	6,495	5,076	6,954	7,432	8,000	6,639	5,926
Australia	24,288	2,694	3,714	3,420	2,488	3,397	4,090	3,770	3,026	3,031
New Zealand	8,600	1,080	1,347	1,364	1,030	1,420	1,457	1,344	1,234	1,092
Other Oceania	23,912	2,154	2,140	1,711	1,558	2,137	1,885	2,886	2,379	1,803
Not Specified	25,928	14,971	17,894	16,688	9,086	24,646	39,299	16,315	42,081	18,789

— Represents zero or not available.

PRESIDENTS, VICE PRESIDENTS,
AND SECRETARIES OF STATE

	President	Vice President	Secretary of State
1.	George Washington, Federalist 1789	John Adams, Federalist 1789	Thomas Jefferson 1789 Edmund Randolph 1794 Timothy Pickering 1795
2.	John Adams, Federalist 1797	Thomas Jefferson, Dem.-Rep. 1797	Timothy Pickering 1797 John Marshall 1800
3.	Thomas Jefferson, Dem.-Rep. 1801	Aaron Burr, Dem.-Rep. 1801 George Clinton, Dem.-Rep. 1805	James Madison 1801
4.	James Madison, Dem.-Rep. 1809	George Clinton, Dem.-Rep. 1809 Elbridge Gerry, Dem.-Rep. 1813	Robert Smith 1809 James Monroe 1811
5.	James Monroe, Dem.-Rep. 1817	Daniel D. Tompkins, Dem.-Rep. 1817	John Q. Adams 1817
6.	John Quincy Adams, Dem.-Rep. 1825	John C. Calhoun, Dem.-Rep. 1825	Henry Clay 1825
7.	Andrew Jackson, Democratic 1829	John C. Calhoun, Democratic 1829 Martin Van Buren, Democratic 1833	Martin Van Buren 1829 Edward Livingston 1831 Louis McLane 1833 John Forsyth 1834
8.	Martin Van Buren, Democratic 1837	Richard M. Johnson, Democratic 1837	John Forsyth 1837
9.	William H. Harrison, Whig 1841	John Tyler, Whig 1841	Daniel Webster 1841

President	Vice President	Secretary of State
10. John Tyler, Whig and Democratic 1841	None	Daniel Webster 1841 Hugh S. Legaré 1843 Abel P. Upshur 1843 John C. Calhoun 1844
11. James K. Polk, Democratic 1845	George M. Dallas, Democratic 1845	James Buchanan 1845
12. Zachary Taylor, Whig 1849	Millard Fillmore, Whig 1848	John M. Clayton 1849
13. Millard Fillmore, Whig 1850	None	Daniel Webster 1850 Edward Everett 1852
14. Franklin Pierce, Democratic 1853	William R. King, Democratic 1853	William L. Marcy 1853
15. James Buchanan, Democratic 1857	John C. Breckinridge, Democratic 1857	Lewis Cass 1857 Jeremiah S. Black 1860
16. Abraham Lincoln, Republican 1861	Hannibal Hamlin, Republican 1861 Andrew Johnson, Unionist 1865	William H. Seward 1861
17. Andrew Johnson, Unionist 1865	None	William H. Seward 1865
18. Ulysses S. Grant, Republican 1869	Schuyler Colfax, Republican 1869 Henry Wilson, Republican 1873	Elihu B. Washburne 1869 Hamilton Fish 1869
19. Rutherford B. Hayes, Republican 1877	William A. Wheeler, Republican 1877	William M. Evarts 1877

	President	Vice President	Secretary of State
20.	James A. Garfield, Republican 1881	Chester A. Arthur, Republican 1881	James G. Blaine 1881
21.	Chester A. Arthur, Republican 1881	None	Frederick T. Frelinghuysen 1881
22.	Grover Cleveland, Democratic 1885	Thomas A. Hendricks, Democratic 1885	Thomas F. Bayard 1885
23.	Benjamin Harrison, Republican 1889	Levi P. Morton, Republican 1889	James G. Blaine 1889 John W. Foster 1892
24.	Grover Cleveland, Democratic 1893	Adlai E. Stevenson, Democratic 1893	Walter Q. Gresham 1893 Richard Olney 1895
25.	William McKinley, Republican 1897	Garret A. Hobart, Republican 1897 Theodore Roosevelt, Republican 1901	John Sherman 1897 William R. Day 1898 John Hay 1898
26.	Theodore Roosevelt, Republican 1901	Charles Fairbanks, Republican 1905	John Hay 1901 Elihu Root 1905 Robert Bacon 1909
27.	William H. Taft, Republican 1909	James S. Sherman, Republican 1909	Philander C. Knox 1909
28.	Woodrow Wilson, Democratic 1913	Thomas R. Marshall, Democratic 1913	William J. Bryan 1913 Robert Lansing 1915 Bainbridge Colby 1920
29.	Warren G. Harding, Republican 1921	Calvin Coolidge, Republican 1921	Charles E. Hughes 1921
30.	Calvin Coolidge, Republican 1923	Charles G. Dawes, Republican 1925	Charles E. Hughes 1923 Frank B. Kellogg 1925

	President	Vice President	Secretary of State
31.	Herbert Hoover, Republican 1929	Charles Curtis, Republican 1929	Henry L. Stimson 1929
32.	Franklin D. Roosevelt, Democratic 1933	John Nance Garner, Democratic 1933 Henry A. Wallace, Democratic 1941 Harry S. Truman, Democratic 1945	Cordell Hull 1933 Edward R. Stettinius, Jr. 1944
33.	Harry S. Truman, Democratic 1945	Alben W. Barkley, Democratic 1949	Edward R. Stettinius, Jr. 1945 James F. Byrnes 1945 George C. Marshall 1947 Dean G. Acheson 1949
34.	Dwight D. Eisenhower, Republican 1953	Richard M. Nixon, Republican 1953	John F. Dulles 1953 Christian A. Herter 1959
35.	John F. Kennedy, Democratic 1961	Lyndon B. Johnson, Democratic 1961	Dean Rusk 1961
36.	Lyndon B. Johnson, Democratic 1963	Hubert H. Humphrey, Democratic 1965	Dean Rusk 1963
37.	Richard M. Nixon, Republican 1969	Spiro T. Agnew, Republican 1969 Gerald R. Ford, Republican 1973	William P. Rogers 1969 Henry Kissinger 1973
38.	Gerald R. Ford, Republican 1974	Nelson Rockefeller, Republican 1974	Henry Kissinger 1974
39.	Jimmy Carter, Democratic 1977	Walter Mondale, Democratic 1977	Cyrus Vance 1977 Edmund Muskie 1980

	President	Vice President	Secretary of State
40.	Ronald Reagan, Republican 1981	George H. W. Bush, Republican 1981	Alexander Haig 1981 George Schultz 1982
41.	George H. W. Bush, Republican 1989	J. Danforth Quayle, Republican 1989	James A. Baker 1989 Lawrence Eagleburger 1992
42.	William J. Clinton, Democratic 1993	Albert Gore, Jr., Democratic 1993	Warren Christopher 1993 Madeleine Albright 1997
43.	George W. Bush, Republican 2001	Richard B. Cheney, Republican 2001	Colin L. Powell 2001 Condoleezza Rice 2005
44.	Barack Obama, Democratic 2009	Joseph R. Biden, Democratic 2009	Hillary Rodham Clinton 2009

FURTHER READINGS

CHAPTER 18

The most comprehensive treatment of Reconstruction is Eric Foner's *Reconstruction: America's Unfinished Revolution, 1863–1877* (1988). On Andrew Johnson, see Hans L. Trefousse's *Andrew Johnson: A Biography* (1989). An excellent brief biography of Grant is Josiah Bunting III's *Ulysses S. Grant* (2004).

Scholars have been sympathetic to the aims and motives of the Radical Republicans. See, for instance, Herman Belz's *Reconstructing the Union: Theory and Policy during the Civil War* (1969) and Richard Nelson Current's *Those Terrible Carpetbaggers: A Reinterpretation* (1988). The ideology of the Radicals is explored in Michael Les Benedict's *A Compromise of Principle: Congressional Republicans and Reconstruction, 1863–1869* (1974). On the black political leaders, see Phillip Dray's *Capitol Men: The Epic Story of Reconstruction through the Lives of the First Black Congressmen* (2008).

The intransigence of southern white attitudes is examined in Michael Perman's *Reunion without Compromise: The South and Reconstruction, 1865–1868* (1973) and Dan T. Carter's *When the War Was Over: The Failure of Self-Reconstruction in the South, 1865–1867* (1985). Allen W. Trelease's *White Terror: The Ku Klux Klan Conspiracy and Southern Reconstruction* (1971) covers the various organizations that practiced vigilante tactics. On the massacre of African Americans, see Charles Lane's *The Day Freedom Died: The Colfax Massacre, the Supreme Court, and the Betrayal of Reconstruction* (2008). The difficulties former slaves had in adjusting to the new labor system are documented in James L. Roark's *Masters without Slaves: Southern Planters in the Civil War and Reconstruction* (1977). Books on southern politics during Reconstruction include Michael Perman's *The Road to Redemption: Southern Politics, 1869–1879* (1984), Terry L. Seip's *The South Returns to Congress: Men, Economic Measures, and Intersectional Relationships, 1868–1879* (1983), and Mark W. Summers's *Railroads, Reconstruction, and the Gospel of Prosperity: Aid under the Radical Republicans, 1865–1877* (1984).

Numerous works study the freed blacks' experience in the South. Start with Leon F. Litwack's *Been in the Storm So Long: The Aftermath of Slavery* (1979). Joel Williamson's *After Slavery: The Negro in South Carolina during Reconstruction, 1861–1877* (1965) argues that South Carolina blacks took an active role in pursuing their political and economic rights. The Freedmen's Bureau is explored in William S. McFeely's *Yankee Stepfather: General O. O. Howard and the Freedmen* (1968). The situation of freed slave women is discussed in Jacqueline Jones's *Labor of Love, Labor of Sorrow: Black Women, Work and the Family, from Slavery to the Present* (1985).

The politics of corruption outside the South is depicted in William S. McFeely's *Grant: A Biography* (1981). The political maneuvers of the election of 1876 and the resultant crisis and compromise are explained in C. Vann Woodward's *Reunion and Reaction: The Compromise of 1877 and the End of Reconstruction* (1951) and in William Gillette's *Retreat from Reconstruction, 1869–1879* (1979). The role of religion in determining the fate of Reconstruction is the focus of Edward J. Blum's *Reforging the White Republic: Race, Religion, and American Nationalism, 1865–1898* (2005).

CHAPTER 19

The classic study of the emergence of the New South remains C. Vann Woodward's *Origins of the New South, 1877–1913* (1951). A more recent treatment of southern society after the end of Reconstruction is Edward L. Ayers's *Southern Crossing: A History of the American South, 1877–1906* (1995). A good survey of industrialization in the South is James C. Cobb's *Industrialization and Southern Society, 1877–1984* (1984).

C. Vann Woodward's *The Strange Career of Jim Crow,* commemorative ed. (2002), remains the standard on southern race relations. Some of Woodward's points are challenged in Howard N. Rabinowitz's *Race Relations in the Urban South, 1865–1890* (1978). Leon F. Litwack's *Trouble in Mind: Black Southerners in the Age of Jim Crow* (1998) treats the rise of legal segregation, while Michael Perman's *Struggle for Mastery: Disfranchisement in the South, 1888–1908* (2001) surveys efforts to keep African Americans from voting. An award-winning study of white women and the race issue is Glenda Elizabeth Gilmore's *Gender and Jim Crow: Women and the Politics of White Supremacy in North Carolina, 1896–1920* (1996). On W. E. B. Du Bois, see David Levering Lewis's *W. E. B. Du Bois: Biography of a Race, 1868–1919* (1993).

For stimulating reinterpretations of the frontier and the development of the West, see William Cronon's *Nature's Metropolis: Chicago and the Great*

West (1991), Patricia Nelson Limerick's *The Legacy of Conquest: The Unbroken Past of the American West* (1987), Richard White's *"It's Your Misfortune and None of My Own": A New History of the American West* (1991), and Walter Nugent's *Into the West: The Story of Its People* (1999). An excellent overview is James M. McPherson's *Into the West: From Reconstruction to the Final Days of the American Frontier* (2006).

The role of African Americans in western settlement is the focus of William Loren Katz's *The Black West: A Documentary and Pictorial History of the African American Role in the Westward Expansion of the United States,* rev. ed. (2005), and Nell Irvin Painter's *Exodusters: Black Migration to Kansas after Reconstruction* (1977). The best account of the conflicts between Indians and whites is Robert M. Utley's *The Indian Frontier of the American West, 1846–1890* (1984). On Sitting Bull, see Utley's *The Lance and the Shield: The Life and Times of Sitting Bull* (1993). For a presentation of the Native American side of the story, see Peter Nabokov's *Native American Testimony: A Chronicle of Indian-White Relations from Prophecy to the Present, 1492–2000,* rev. ed. (1999). On the demise of the buffalo herds, see Andrew C. Isenberg's *The Destruction of the Bison: An Environmental History, 1750–1920* (2000).

CHAPTER 20

For masterly syntheses of post–Civil War industrial development, see Walter Licht's *Industrializing America: The Nineteenth Century* (1995) and Maury Klein's *The Genesis of Industrial America, 1870–1920* (2007). On the growth of railroads, see Albro Martin's *Railroad Triumphant: The Growth, Rejection, and Rebirth of a Vital American Force* (1992). A monumental study of the transcontinental railroad is David Haward Bain's *Empire Express: Building the First Transcontinental Railroad* (1999). On the 1877 railroad strike, see David O. Stowell's *Streets, Railroad, and the Great Strike of 1877* (1999).

On entrepreneurship in the iron and steel sector, and Thomas J. Misa's *A Nation of Steel: The Making of Modern America, 1865–1925* (1995). The best biographies of the leading business tycoons are Ron Chernow's *Titan: The Life of John D. Rockefeller, Sr.* (1998), David Nasaw's *Andrew Carnegie* (2006), and Jean Strouse's *Morgan: American Financier* (1999). Nathan Rosenberg's *Technology and American Economic Growth* (1972) documents the growth of invention during the period.

Much of the scholarship on labor stresses the traditional values and the culture of work that people brought to the factory, Hebert G. Gutman's *Work, Culture, and Society in Industrializing America: Essays in American*

Working-Class and Social History (1975) best introduces these themes. The leading survey remains David Montgomery's *The Fall of the House of Labor: The Workplace, the State, and American Labor Activism, 1865–1925* (1987).

For the role of women in the changing workplace, see Alice Kessler-Harris's *Out to Work: A History of Wage-Earning Women in the United States* (1982) and Susan E. Kennedy's *If All We Did Was to Weep at Home: A History of White Working-Class Women in American* (1979).

As for the labor unions, Gerald N. Grob's *Workers and Utopia: A Study of Ideological Conflict in the American Labor Movement, 1865–1900* (1961) examines the difference in outlook between the Knights of Labor and the American Federation of Labor. For the Knights, see Leon Fink's *Workingmen's Democracy: The Knights of Labor and American Politics* (1983). Also useful is Susan Levine's *Labor's True Woman: Carpet Weavers, Industrialization, and Labor Reform in the Gilded Age* (1984), on the role of women in the Knights. On Mother Jones, see Elliott J. Gorn's *Mother Jones: The Most Dangerous Woman in America* (2001). To trace the rise of socialism among organized workers, see Nick Salvatore's *Eugene V. Debs: Citizen and Socialist* (1982). The key strikes are discussed in Paul Arvich's *The Haymarket Tragedy* (1984) and Paul Krause's *The Battle for Homestead, 1880–1892: Politics, Culture, and Steel* (1992).

CHAPTER 21

For a survey of urbanization, see David R. Goldfield's *Urban America: A History*, 2nd ed. (1989). Gunther Barth discusses the emergence of a new urban culture in *City People: The Rise of Modern City Culture in Nineteenth-Century America* (1980). John Bodnar offers a synthesis of the urban immigrant experience in *The Transplanted: A History of Immigrants in Urban America* (1985). See also Roger Daniels's *Guarding the Golden Door: American Immigration Policy and Immigrants since 1882* (2004). Walter Nugent's *Crossings: The Great Transatlantic Migrations, 1870–1914* (1992) provides a wealth of demographic information and insight. Efforts to stop Chinese immigration are described in Erika Lee's *At America's Gates: Chinese Immigration during the Exclusion Era* (2003).

On urban environments and sanitary reforms, see Martin V. Melosi's *The Sanitary City: Urban Infrastructure in America from Colonial Times to the Present* (2000), Joel A. Tarr's *The Search for the Ultimate Sink: Urban Pollution in Historical Perspective* (1996), and Suellen Hoy's *Chasing Dirt: The American Pursuit of Cleanliness* (1995).

For the growth of urban leisure and sports, see Roy Rosenzweig's *Eight Hours for What We Will: Workers and Leisure in an Industrial City, 1870–1920*

(1983) and Steven A. Riess's *City Games: The Evolution of American Urban Society and the Rise of Sports* (1989). Saloon culture is examined in Madelon Powers's *Faces along the Bar: Lore and Order in the Workingman's Saloon, 1870–1920* (1998).

Richard Hofstadter's *Social Darwinism in American Thought,* rev. ed. (1969), and Cynthia Eagle Russett's *Darwin in America: The Intellectual Response, 1865–1912* (1976) examine the impact of the theory of evolution. On the rise of realism in thought and the arts during the second half of the nineteenth century, see David E. Shi's *Facing Facts: Realism in American Thought and Culture, 1850–1920* (1995). Pragmatism is the focus of Louis Menand's *The Metaphysical Club: A Story of Ideas in America* (2001).

Eleanor Flexner and Ellen Fitzpatrick's *Century of Struggle: The Woman's Rights Movement in the United States,* enl. ed. (1996), surveys the condition of women in the late nineteenth century. The best study of the settlement house movement is Jean Bethke Elshtain's *Jane Addams and the Dream of American Democracy: A Life* (2002).

CHAPTER 22

A good overview of the Gilded Age is Vincent P. De Santis's *The Shaping of Modern America, 1877–1916* (1973). Nell Irvin Painter's *Standing at Armageddon: The United States, 1877–1919* (1987) focuses on the experience of the working class. For a stimulating overview of the political, social, and economic trends during the Gilded Age, see Jack Beatty's *Age of Betrayal: The Triumph of Money in America, 1865–1900* (2007). On the development of city rings and bosses, see Kenneth D. Ackerman's *Boss Tweed: The Rise and Fall of the Corrupt Pol Who Conceived the Soul of Modern New York* (2005). Excellent presidential biographies include Hans L. Trefousse's *Rutherford B. Hayes* (2002), Zachary Karabell's *Chester Alan Arthur* (2004), Henry F. Graff's *Grover Cleveland* (2002), and Kevin Phillips's *William McKinley* (2003).

Scholars have also examined various Gilded Age issues and interest groups. Gerald W. McFarland's *Mugwumps, Morals, and Politics, 1884–1920* (1975) examines the issue of reforming government service. Tom E. Terrill's *The Tariff, Politics, and American Foreign Policy, 1874–1901* (1973) lends clarity to that complex issue. The finances of the Gilded Age are covered in Walter T. K. Nugent's *Money and American Society, 1865–1880* (1968).

One of the most controversial works on populism is Lawrence Goodwyn's *The Populist Movement: A Short History of the Agrarian Revolt in America*

(1978). A more balanced account is Robert C. McMath Jr.'s *American Populism: A Social History, 1877–1898* (1992). On the role of religion in the agrarian protest movements, see Joe Creech's *Righteous Indignation: Religion and the Populist Revolution* (2006). The best biography of Bryan is Michael Kazin's *A Godly Hero: The Life of William Jennings Bryan* (2006).

CHAPTER 23

An excellent survey of the diplomacy of the era is Charles S. Campbell's *The Transformation of American Foreign Relations, 1865–1900* (1976). For background on the events of the 1890s, see Walter LaFeber's *The American Search for Opportunity, 1865–1913* (1993) and David Healy's *U.S. Expansionism: The Imperialist Urge in the 1890s* (1970). The dispute over American policy in Hawaii is covered in Thomas J. Osborne's *"Empire Can Wait": American Opposition to Hawaiian Annexation, 1893–1898* (1981).

Ivan Musicant's *Empire by Default: The Spanish-American War and the Dawn of the American Century* (1998) is the most comprehensive volume on the conflict. For the war's aftermath in the Philippines, see Stuart Creighton Miller's *"Benevolent Assimilation": The American Conquest of the Philippines, 1899–1903* (1982). Robert L. Beisner's *Twelve against Empire: The Anti-Imperialists, 1898–1900* (1968) handles the debate over annexation. On the Philippine-American War, see David J. Silbey's *A War of Frontier and Empire: The Philippine-American War, 1899–1902* (2007).

A good introduction to American interest in China is Michael H. Hunt's *The Making of a Special Relationship: The United States and China to 1914* (1983). Kenton J. Clymer's *John Hay: The Gentleman as Diplomat* (1975) examines the role of this key secretary of state in forming policy.

For U.S. policy in the Caribbean and Central America, see Walter LaFeber's *Inevitable Revolutions: The United States in Central America*, 2nd ed. (1993). David McCullough's *The Path between the Seas: The Creation of the Panama Canal, 1870–1914* (1977) presents the fullest account of how the United States secured the Panama Canal.

CHAPTER 24

A splendid analysis of progressivism is John Whiteclay Chambers II's *The Tyranny of Change: America in the Progressive Era, 1890–1920*, rev. ed. (2000). On Ida Tarbell and the muckrakers, see Steve Weinberg's *Taking on* the Trust: The Epic Battle of Ida Tarbell and John D. Rockefeller (2008). The evolution of government policy toward business is examined in Martin J. Sklar's The Corporate Reconstruction of American Capitalism, 1890–1916: The Market, the Law, and Politics (1988). Mina Carson's Settlement Folk: Social Thought and the American Settlement Movement, 1885–1930 (1990) and Jack M. Holl's Juvenile Reform in the Progressive Era: William R. George and the Junior Republic Movement (1971) examine the social problems in the cities. An excellent study of the role of women in progressivism's emphasis on social justice is Kathryn Kish Sklar's Florence Kelley and the Nation's Work: The Rise of Women's Political Culture, 1830–1900 (1995). On the tragic fire at the Triangle Shirtwaist Company, see David Von Drehle's Triangle: The Fire That Changed America (2003).

There is a rich body of scholarship focused on the conservation movement. See especially Rebecca Conard's Places of Quiet Beauty: Parks, Preserves, and Environmentalism (1997), Samuel P. Hays's Conservation and the Gospel of Efficiency: The Progressive Conservation Movement, 1890–1920 (1959), Karl Jacoby's Crimes against Nature: Squatters, Poachers, Thieves, and the Hidden History of American Conservation (2001), John F. Reiger's American Sportsmen and the Origins of Conservation (1975), and Ted Steinberg's Down to Earth: Nature's Role in American History (2002). Robert Kanigel's The One Best Way: Frederick Winslow Taylor and the Enigma of Efficiency (1997) highlights the role of efficiency in the Progressive Era.

On the pivotal election of 1912, see James Chace's 1912: Wilson, Roosevelt, Taft, and Debs—The Election That Changed the Country (2004). Excellent biographies include Kathleen Dalton's Theodore Roosevelt: A Strenuous Life (2002) and H. W. Brands's Woodrow Wilson (2003). For banking developments, see Allan H. Meltzer's A History of the Federal Reserve, vol. 1, 1913–1951 (2003).

CHAPTER 25

A lucid overview of international events covered in this chapter is Robert H. Ferrell's Woodrow Wilson and World War I, 1917–1921 (1985). On Wilson's stance toward war, see Ross Gregory's The Origins of American Intervention in the First World War (1971). An excellent brief biography is H. W. Brands's Woodrow Wilson (2003).

Edward M. Coffman's The War to End All Wars: The American Military Experience in World War I (1968) is a detailed presentation of America's military involvement. See also Gary Mead's The Doughboys: America and the First World War (2000). David M. Kennedy's Over Here: The First World War *and American Society* (1980) surveys the impact of the war on the home front, as does Meirion Harries and Susie Harries's *The Last Days of Innocence: America at War, 1917–1918* (1997). One of the best overviews of the European context of the war is John Keegan, *The First World War* (1998). Maurine Weiner Greenwald's *Women, War, and Work: The Impact of World War I on Women Workers in the United States* (1980) discusses the role of women. Ronald Schaffer's *America in the Great War: The Rise of the War Welfare State* (1991) shows the effect of war mobilization on business organization. Richard Polenberg's *Fighting Faiths: The Abrams Case, the Supreme Court, and Free Speech* (1987) examines the prosecution of a case under the 1918 Sedition Act.

How American diplomacy fared in the making of peace has received considerable attention. Thomas J. Knock interrelates domestic affairs and foreign relations in his explanation of Wilson's peacemaking in *To End All Wars: Woodrow Wilson and the Quest for a New World Order* (1992).

The problems of the immediate postwar years are chronicled by a number of historians. The best overview is Ann Hagedorn's *Savage Peace: Hope and Fear in America, 1919* (2007). On the Spanish flu, see John M. Barry's *The Great Influenza: The Epic Story of the Deadliest Plague in History* (2004). Labor tensions are examined in David E. Brody's *Labor in Crisis: The Steel Strike of 1919* (1965) and Francis Russell's *A City in Terror: Calvin Coolidge and the 1919 Boston Police Strike* (1975). On racial strife, see William M. Tuttle Jr.'s *Race Riot: Chicago in the Red Summer of 1919* (1970). The fear of Communists is analyzed in Robert K. Murray's *Red Scare: A Study in National Hysteria, 1919–1920* (1955).

CHAPTER 26

For a lively survey of the social and cultural changes during the interwar period, start with William E. Leuchtenburg's *The Perils of Prosperity, 1914–32*, 2nd ed. (1993). The best introduction to the culture of the 1920s remains Loren Baritz's *The Culture of the Twenties* (1970). See also Lynn Dumenil's *The Modern Temper: American Culture and Society in the 1920s* (1995).

John Higham's *Strangers in the Land: Patterns of American Nativism, 1860–1925*, 2nd ed. (2002) details the story of immigration restriction. The controversial Sacco and Vanzetti case is thoroughly explored in *Kill Now, Talk Forever: Debating Sacco and Vanzetti*, edited by Richard Newby (2001). For analysis of the revival of Klan activity, see Nancy MacLean's *Behind the Mask of Chivalry: The Making of the Second Ku Klux Klan* (1994). The best analysis of the Scopes trial is Edward J. Larson's *Summer for the Gods: The Scopes Trial and America's*

Continuing Debate over Science and Religion (1997). On Prohibition, see Michael A. Lerner's *Dry Manhattan: Prohibition in New York City* (2007).

Women's suffrage is treated extensively in Eleanor Flexner and Ellen Fitzpatrick's *Century of Struggle: The Woman's Rights Movement in the United States,* enlarged ed. (1996). The best study of the birth-control movement is Ellen Chesler's *Woman of Valor: Margaret Sanger and the Birth Control Movement in America* (1992). See Charles Flint Kellogg's *NAACP: A History of the National Association for the Advancement of Colored People* (1967) for his analysis of the pioneering court cases against racial discrimination. Nathan Irvin Huggins's *Harlem Renaissance* (1971) assesses the cultural impact of the Great Migration on New York City. The emergence of jazz is ably documented in Burton W. Peretti's *The Creation of Jazz: Music, Race, and Culture in Urban America* (1992). On the African American migration to Chicago, see James R. Grossman's *Land of Hope: Chicago, Black Southerners, and the Great Migration* (1989). Nicholas Lemann's *The Promised Land: The Great Black Migration and How It Changed America* (1991) is a fine exposition of the changes brought about by the migration in both the South and the North.

On southern modernism, see Daniel Joseph Singal's *The War Within: From Victorian to Modernist Thought in the South, 1919–1945* (1982). Stanley Coben's *Rebellion against Victorianism: The Impetus for Cultural Change in 1920s America* (1991) surveys the appeal of modernism among writers, artists, and intellectuals.

CHAPTER 27

A fine synthesis of events immediately following the First World War is Ellis W. Hawley's *The Great War and the Search for a Modern Order: A History of the American People and Their Institutions, 1917–1933,* 2nd ed. (1992). On the election of 1920, see David Pietrusza, *1920: The Year of the Six Presidents* (2006).

On Harding, see Robert K. Murray's *The Harding Era: Warren G. Harding and His Administration* (1969). On Coolidge, see Robert H. Ferrell's *The Presidency of Calvin Coolidge* (1998). On Hoover, see Martin L. Fausold's *The Presidency of Herbert C. Hoover* (1985). The Democratic candidate for president in 1928 is explored in Robert A. Slayton's *Empire Statesman: The Rise and Redemption of Al Smith* (2001). The influential secretary of the Treasury during the 1920s is ably analyzed in David Cannadine's *Mellon: An American Life* (2006).

Overviews of the depressed economy are found in Charles P. Kindle-berger's *The World in Depression, 1929–1939,* rev. and enlarged ed. (1986) and Peter Fearon's *War, Prosperity, and Depression: The U.S. Economy, 1917–1945* (1987). John A. Garraty's *The Great Depression: An Inquiry into the Causes, Course, and Consequences of the Worldwide Depression of the Nineteen-Thirties* (1986) describes how people survived the Depression. On the removal of the Bonus Army, see Paul Dickson and Thomas B. Allen's *The Bonus Army: An American Epic* (2004).

CHAPTER 28

A comprehensive overview of the New Deal is David M. Kennedy's *Freedom from Fear: The American People in Depression and War, 1929–1945* (1999). On the critics of the New Deal, see Alan Brinkley's *Voices of Protest: Huey Long, Father Coughlin, and the Great Depression* (1982).

James N. Gregory's *American Exodus: The Dust Bowl Migration and Okie Culture in California* (1989) describes the migratory movement's effect on American culture. On the environmental and human causes of the dust bowl, see Donald Worster, *Dust Bowl: The Southern Plains in the 1930s* (1979).

CHAPTER 29

The best overview of interwar diplomacy remains Selig Adler's *The Uncertain Giant, 1921–1941: American Foreign Policy between the Wars* (1965). Joan Hoff's *American Business and Foreign Policy, 1920–1933* (1971) highlights the efforts of Republican administrations during the 1920s to promote international commerce. Robert Dallek's *Franklin D. Roosevelt and American Foreign Policy, 1932–1945* (1979) provides a judicious assessment of Roosevelt's foreign policy during the 1930s.

A noteworthy study is Waldo Heinrichs's *Threshold of War: Franklin D. Roosevelt and American Entry into World War II* (1988). See also David Reynolds's *From Munich to Pearl Harbor: Roosevelt's America and the Origins of the Second World War* (2001). Bruce M. Russett's *No Clear and Present Danger: A Skeptical View of the United States Entry into World War II,* 25th anniversary ed. (1997), provides a critical account of American actions.

On Pearl Harbor, see Gordon W. Prange's *Pearl Harbor: The Verdict of History* (1986). Japan's perspective is described in Akira Iriye's *The Origins of the Second World War in Asia and the Pacific* (1987).

Chapter 30

John Keegan's *The Second World War* (1989) surveys the European conflict, while Charles B. MacDonald's *The Mighty Endeavor: The American War in Europe* (1986) concentrates on U.S. involvement. Roosevelt's wartime leadership is analyzed in Eric Larrabee's *Commander in Chief: Franklin Delano Roosevelt, His Lieutenants, and Their War* (1987).

Books on specific European campaigns include Stephen E. Ambrose's *D-Day, June 6, 1944: The Climactic Battle of World War II* (1994) and Charles B. MacDonald's *A Time for Trumpets: The Untold Story of the Battle of the Bulge* (1985). On the Allied commander, see Carlo D'Este's *Eisenhower: A Soldier's Life* (2002).

For the war in the Far East, see John Costello's *The Pacific War, 1941–1945* (1981), Ronald H. Spector's *Eagle against the Sun: The American War with Japan* (1985), John W. Dower's award-winning *War without Mercy: Race and Power in the Pacific War* (1986), and Dan van der Vat's *The Pacific Campaign: The U.S.-Japanese Naval War, 1941–1945* (1991).

An excellent overview of the war's effects on the home front is Michael C. C. Adams's *The Best War Ever: America and World War II* (1994). On economic effects, see Harold G. Vatter's *The U.S. Economy in World War II* (1985).

Susan M. Hartmann's *The Home Front and Beyond: American Women in the 1940s* (1982) treats the new working environment for women. Neil A. Wynn looks at the participation of blacks in *The Afro-American and the Second World War* (1976). The story of the oppression of Japanese Americans is told in Peter Irons's *Justice at War: The Story of the Japanese American Internment Cases* (1983).

A sound introduction to U.S. diplomacy during the conflict can be found in Gaddis Smith's *American Diplomacy during the Second World War, 1941–1945* (1965). To understand the role that Roosevelt played in policy making, consult Warren F. Kimball's *The Juggler: Franklin Roosevelt as Wartime Statesman* (1991).

The issues and events that led to the deployment of atomic weapons are addressed in Martin J. Sherwin's *A World Destroyed: The Atomic Bomb and the Grand Alliance* (1975).

Chapter 31

The cold war remains a hotly debated topic. The traditional interpretation is best reflected in John Lewis Gaddis's *The United States and the Origins of the Cold War, 1941–1947* (1972) and *We Now Know: Rethinking Cold War History* (1997). Both superpowers, Gaddis argues, were responsible for causing the cold war, but the Soviet Union was more culpable. The revisionist perspective is represented by Gar Alperovitz's *Atomic Diplomacy: Hiroshima and Potsdam: The Use of the Atomic Bomb and the American Confrontation with Soviet Power*, 2nd ed. (1994). Alperovitz places primary responsibility for the conflict on the United States. Also see H. W. Brands's *The Devil We Knew: Americans and the Cold War* (1993) and Melvyn P. Leffler's *A Preponderance of Power: National Security, the Truman Administration, and the Cold War* (1992). On the architect of containment, see David Mayers's *George Kennan and the Dilemmas of U.S. Foreign Policy* (1988).

Arnold A. Offner indicts Truman for clumsy statesmanship in *Another Such Victory: President Truman and the Cold War, 1945–1953* (2002). For a positive assessment of Truman's leadership, see Alonzo L. Hamby's *Beyond the New Deal: Harry S. Truman and American Liberalism* (1973). The domestic policies of the Fair Deal are treated in William C. Berman's *The Politics of Civil Rights in the Truman Administration* (1970), Richard M. Dalfiume's *Desegregation of the U.S. Armed Forces: Fighting on Two Fronts, 1939–1953* (1969), and Maeva Marcus's *Truman and the Steel Seizure Case: The Limits of Presidential Power* (1977). The most comprehensive biography of Truman is David McCullough's *Truman* (1992).

For an introduction to the tensions in Asia, see Akira Iriye's *The Cold War in Asia: A Historical Introduction* (1974). For the Korean conflict, see Callum A. MacDonald's *Korea: The War before Vietnam* (1986) and Max Hasting's *The Korean War* (1987).

The anti-Communist syndrome is surveyed in David Caute's *The Great Fear: The Anti-Communist Purge under Truman and Eisenhower* (1978). Arthur Herman's *Joseph McCarthy: Reexamining the Life and Legacy of America's Most Hated Senator* (2000) covers McCarthy himself. For a well-documented account of how the cold war was sustained by superpatriotism, intolerance, and suspicion, see Stephen J. Whitfield's *The Culture of the Cold War*, 2nd ed. (1996).

CHAPTER 32

Two excellent overviews of social and cultural trends in the postwar era are William H. Chafe's *The Unfinished Journey: America since World War II*, 6th ed. (2006), and William E. Leuchtenburg's *A Troubled Feast: America since 1945*, rev. ed. (1979). For insights into the cultural life of the

1950s, see Jeffrey Hart's *When the Going Was Good! American Life in the Fifties* (1982) and David Halberstam's *The Fifties* (1993).

The baby boom generation and its impact are vividly described in Paul C. Light's *Baby Boomers* (1988). The emergence of the television industry is discussed in Erik Barnouw's *Tube of Plenty: The Evolution of American Television,* 2nd rev. ed. (1990), and Ella Taylor's *Prime-Time Families: Television Culture in Postwar America* (1989).

A comprehensive account of the process of suburban development is Kenneth T. Jackson's *Crabgrass Frontier: The Suburbanization of the United States* (1985). Equally good is Tom Martinson's *American Dreamscape: The Pursuit of Happiness in Postwar Suburbia* (2000).

The middle-class ideal of family life in the 1950s is examined in Elaine Tyler May's *Homeward Bound: American Families in the Cold War Era,* rev. ed. (2008). Thorough accounts of women's issues are found in Wini Breines's *Young, White, and Miserable: Growing Up Female in the Fifties* (1992). For an overview of the resurgence of religion in the 1950s, see George M. Marsden's *Religion and American Culture,* 2nd ed. (2000).

A lively discussion of movies of the 1950s can be found in Peter Biskind's *Seeing Is Believing: How Hollywood Taught Us to Stop Worrying and Love the Fifties* (1983). The origins and growth of rock and roll are surveyed in Carl Belz's *The Story of Rock,* 2nd ed. (1972). Thoughtful interpretive surveys of postwar literature include Josephine Hendin's *Vulnerable People: A View of American Fiction since 1945* (1978) and Malcolm Bradbury's *The Modern American Novel* (1983). The colorful Beats are brought to life in Steven Watson's *The Birth of the Beat Generation: Visionaries, Rebels, and Hipsters, 1944–1960* (1995).

CHAPTER 33

Scholarship on the Eisenhower years is extensive. A carefully balanced overview of the period is Chester J. Pach, Jr. and Elmo Richardson's *The Presidency of Dwight D. Eisenhower,* rev. ed. (1991). For the manner in which Eisenhower conducted foreign policy, see Robert A. Divine's *Eisenhower and the Cold War* (1981). Tom Wicker deems Eisenhower a better person than a president in *Dwight D. Eisenhower* (2002).

For the buildup of U.S. involvement in Indochina, consult Lloyd C. Gardner's *Approaching Vietnam: From World War II through Dienbienphu, 1941–1954* (1988) and David L. Anderson's *Trapped by Success: The Eisenhower Administration and Vietnam, 1953–61* (1991). How the Eisenhower Doctrine came to be implemented is traced in Stephen E. Ambrose and Douglas G. Brinkley's *Rise to Globalism: American Foreign Policy since 1938*, 8th ed. (1997).

The impact of the Supreme Court during the 1950s is the focus of Archibald Cox's *The Warren Court: Constitutional Decision as an Instrument of Reform* (1968). A masterly study of the important Warren Court decision on school desegregation is James T. Patterson's *Brown v. Board of Education: A Civil Rights Milestone and Its Troubled Legacy* (2001).

For the story of the early years of the civil rights movement, see Taylor Branch's *Parting the Waters: America in the King Years, 1954–1963* (1988) and Robert Weisbrot's *Freedom Bound: A History of America's Civil Rights Movement* (1990).

CHAPTER 34

A dispassionate analysis of John Kennedy's life is Thomas C. Reeves's *A Question of Character: A Life of John F. Kennedy* (1991). The best study of the Kennedy administration's domestic policies is Irving Bernstein's *Promises Kept: John F. Kennedy's New Frontier* (1991). For details on the still swirling conspiracy theories about the assassination, see David W. Belin's *Final Disclosure: The Full Truth about the Assassination of President Kennedy* (1988).

The most comprehensive biography of Johnson is Robert Dallek's two-volume work, *Lone Star Rising: Lyndon Johnson and His Times, 1908–1960* (1991) and *Flawed Giant: Lyndon Johnson and His Times, 1961–1973* (1998). On the Johnson administration, see Vaughn Davis Bornet's *The Presidency of Lyndon B. Johnson* (1984).

Among the works that interpret liberal social policy during the 1960s, John E. Schwarz's *America's Hidden Success: A Reassessment of Twenty Years of Public Policy* (1983) offers a glowing endorsement of Democratic programs. For a contrasting perspective, see Charles Murray's *Losing Ground: American Social Policy, 1950–1980*, rev. ed. (1994).

On foreign policy, see *Kennedy's Quest for Victory: American Foreign Policy, 1961–1963* (1989), edited by Thomas G. Paterson. To learn more about Kennedy's problems in Cuba, see Mark J. White's *Missiles in Cuba: Kennedy, Khrushchev, Castro and the 1962 Crisis* (1997). See also Aleksandr Fursenko and Timothy Naftali's *"One Hell of a Gamble": Khrushchev, Castro and Kennedy, 1958–1964* (1997).

American involvement in Vietnam has received voluminous treatment from all political perspectives. For an excellent overview, see Larry Berman's *Planning a Tragedy: The Americanization of the War in Vietnam* (1983) and

Lyndon Johnson's War: The Road to Stalemate in Vietnam (1989), as well as Stanley Karnow's *Vietnam: A History,* 2nd rev. ed. (1997). An analysis of policy making concerning the Vietnam War is David M. Barrett's *Uncertain Warriors: Lyndon Johnson and His Vietnam Advisors* (1993). A fine account of the military involvement is Robert D. Schulzinger's *A Time for War: The United States and Vietnam, 1941–1975* (1997). On the legacy of the Vietnam War, see Arnold R. Isaacs's *Vietnam Shadows: The War, Its Ghosts, and Its Legacy* (1997).

Many scholars have dealt with various aspects of the civil rights movement and race relations in the 1960s. See especially Carl M. Brauer's *John F. Kennedy and the Second Reconstruction* (1977), David J. Garrow's *Bearing the Cross: Martin Luther King, Jr., and the Southern Christian Leadership Conference* (1986), and Adam Fairclough's *To Redeem the Soul of America: The Southern Christian Leadership Conference and Martin Luther King, Jr.* (1987). William H. Chafe's *Civilities and Civil Rights: Greensboro, North Carolina, and the Black Struggle for Freedom* (1980) details the original sit-ins. An award-winning study of racial and economic inequality in a representative American city is Thomas J. Sugrue's *The Origins of the Urban Crisis: Race and Inequality in Postwar Detroit* (1996).

CHAPTER 35

An engaging overview of the cultural trends of the 1960s is Maurice Isserman and Michael Kazin's *America Divided: The Civil War of the 1960s,* 3rd ed. (2007). The New Left is assessed in Irwin Unger's *The Movement: A History of the American New Left, 1959–1972* (1974). On the Students for a Democratic Society, see Kirkpatrick Sale's *SDS* (1973) and Allen J. Matusow's *The Unraveling of America: A History of Liberalism in the 1960s* (1984). Also useful is Todd Gitlin's *The Sixties: Years of Hope, Days of Rage,* rev. ed. (1993).

Two influential assessments of the counterculture by sympathetic commentators are Theodore Roszak's *The Making of a Counter-culture: Reflections on the Technocratic Society and Its Youthful Opposition* (1969) and Charles A. Reich's *The Greening of America: How the Youth Revolution Is Trying to Make America Livable* (1970). A good scholarly analysis that takes the hippies seriously is Timothy Miller's *The Hippies and American Values* (1991).

The best study of the women's liberation movement is Ruth Rosen's *The World Split Open: How the Modern Women's Movement Changed America,* rev. ed. (2006). The organizing efforts of Cesar Chavez are detailed in Ronald B. Taylor's *Chavez and the Farm Workers* (1975). The struggles of Native

Americans for recognition and power are sympathetically described in Stan Steiner's *The New Indians* (1968).

On Nixon, see Melvin Small's *The Presidency of Richard Nixon* (1999). For a solid overview of the Watergate scandal, see Stanley I. Kutler's *The Wars of Watergate: The Last Crisis of Richard Nixon* (1990). For the way the Republicans handled foreign affairs, consult Tad Szulc's *The Illusion of Peace: Foreign Policy in the Nixon Years* (1978).

The loss of Vietnam and the end of American involvement there are traced in Larry Berman's *No Peace, No Honor: Nixon, Kissinger, and Betrayal in Vietnam* (2001). William Shawcross's *Sideshow: Kissinger, Nixon and the Destruction of Cambodia*, rev. ed. (2002), deals with the broadening of the war, while Larry Berman's *Planning a Tragedy: The Americanization of the War in Vietnam* (1982) assesses the final impact of U.S. involvement. The most comprehensive treatment of the anti-war movement is Tom Wells's *The War Within: America's Battle over Vietnam* (1994).

A comprehensive treatment of the Ford administration is contained in John Robert Greene's *The Presidency of Gerald R. Ford* (1995). The best overview of the Carter administration is Burton I. Kaufman's *The Presidency of James Earl Carter, Jr.*, 2nd rev. ed. (2006). A work more sympathetic to the Carter administration is John Dumbrell's *The Carter Presidency: A Re-evaluation*, 2nd ed. (1995). Gaddis Smith's *Morality, Reason, and Power: American Diplomacy in the Carter Years* (1986) provides an overview. Background on how the Middle East came to dominate much of American policy is found in William B. Quandt's *Decade of Decisions: American Policy toward the Arab-Israeli Conflict, 1967–1976* (1977).

CHAPTER 36

Two brief accounts of Reagan's presidency are David Mervin's *Ronald Reagan and the American Presidency* (1990) and Michael Schaller's *Reckoning with Reagan: America and Its President in the 1980s* (1992). A more substantial biography is John Patrick Diggins's *Ronald Reagan: Fate, Freedom, and the Making of History* (2007). An excellent analysis of the 1980 election is Andrew E. Busch's *Reagan's Victory: The Presidential Election of 1980 and the Rise of the Right* (2005). A more comprehensive summary of the Reagan years is Sean Wilentz's *The Age of Reagan: A History, 1974–2008* (2008).

On Reaganomics, see David A. Stockman's *The Triumph of Politics: Why the Reagan Revolution Failed* (1986) and Robert Lekachman's *Greed Is Not*

Enough: Reaganomics (1982). On the issue of arms control, see Strobe Talbott's *Deadly Gambits: The Reagan Administration and the Stalemate in Nuclear Arms Control* (1984).

For Reagan's foreign policy in Central America, see James Chace's *Endless War: How We Got Involved in Central America—and What Can Be Done* (1984) and Walter LaFeber's *Inevitable Revolutions: The United States in Central America*, 2nd ed. (1993). Insider views of Reagan's foreign policy are offered in Alexander M. Haig Jr.'s *Caveat: Realism, Reagan, and Foreign Policy* (1984) and Caspar W. Weinberger's *Fighting for Peace: Seven Critical Years in the Pentagon* (1990).

On Reagan's second term, see Jane Mayer and Doyle McManus's *Landslide: The Unmaking of the President, 1984–1988* (1988). For a masterly work on the Iran-Contra affair, see Theodore Draper's *A Very Thin Line: The Iran Contra Affairs* (1991). Several collections of essays include varying assessments of the Reagan years. Among these are *The Reagan Revolution?* (1988), edited by B. B. Kymlicka and Jean V. Matthews; *The Reagan Presidency: An Incomplete Revolution?* (1990), edited by Dilys M. Hill, Raymond A. Moore, and Phil Williams, and *Looking Back on the Reagan Presidency* (1990), edited by Larry Berman.

On the 1988 campaign, see Jack W. Germond and Jules Witcover's *Whose Broad Stripes and Bright Stars? The Trivial Pursuit of the Presidency, 1988* (1989) and Sidney Blumenthal's *Pledging Allegiance: The Last Campaign of the Cold War* (1990). For a social history of the decade, see John Ehrman's *The Eighties: America in the Age of Reagan* (2005).

Chapter 37

On George H. W. Bush's presidency, see *Leadership and the Bush Presidency: Prudence or Drift in an Era of Change?*, edited by Ryan J. Barilleaux and Mary E. Stuckey (1992), and Charles Tiefer's *The Semi-Sovereign Presidency: The Bush Administration's Strategy for Governing without Congress* (1994). Among the journalistic accounts of the presidential election of 1992, the best narrative is Jack W. Germond and Jules Witcover's *Mad as Hell: Revolt at the Ballot Box, 1992* (1993). The best scholarly study is Theodore J. Lowi and Benjamin Ginsberg's *Democrats Return to Power: Politics and Policy in the Clinton Era* (1994).

Analysis of the Clinton years can be found in Joe Klein's *The Natural: The Misunderstood Presidency of Bill Clinton* (2002). Clinton's impeachment is assessed in Richard A. Posner's *An Affair of State: The Investigation, Impeachment, and Trial of President Clinton* (1999).

On changing demographic trends, see Sam Roberts's *Who We Are Now: The Changing Face of America in the Twenty-First Century* (2004). On social and cultural life in the 1990s, see Haynes Johnson's *The Best of Times: America in the Clinton Years* (2001). The onset and growth of the AIDS epidemic are traced in *And the Band Played On: Politics, People, and the AIDS Epidemic,* 20th anniversary ed. (2007), by Randy Shilts.

Aspects of fundamentalist and apocalyptic movements are the subject of Paul Boyer's *When Time Shall Be No More: Prophecy Belief in Modern American Culture* (1992), George M. Marsden's *Understanding Fundamentalism and Evangelicalism,* new ed. (2006), and Ralph E. Reed's *Politically Incorrect: The Emerging Faith Factor in American Politics* (1994).

On the invention of the computer and the Internet, see Paul E. Ceruzzi's *A History of Modern Computing,* 2nd ed. (2003), and Janet Abbate's *Inventing the Internet* (1999). The booming economy of the 1990s is well analyzed in Joseph E. Stiglitz's *The Roaring Nineties: A New History of the World's Most Prosperous Decade* (2003). On the rising stress within the workplace, see Jill Andresky Fraser's *White-Collar Sweatshop: The Deterioration of Work and Its Rewards in Corporate America* (2001). Aspects of corporate restructuring and downsizing are the subject of Bennett Harrison's *Lean and Mean: The Changing Landscape of Corporate Power in the Age of Flexibility* (1994).

For further treatment of the end of the cold war, see Michael R. Beschloss and Strobe Talbott's *At the Highest Levels: The Inside Story of the End of the Cold War* (1993) and Richard Crockatt's *The Fifty Years War: The United States and the Soviet Union in World Politics, 1941–1991* (1995). On the Persian Gulf conflict, see Lester H. Brune's *America and the Iraqi Crisis, 1990–1992: Origins and Aftermath* (1993). On the transformation of American foreign policy, see James Mann's *Rise of the Vulcans: The History of Bush's War Cabinet* (2004), Claes G. Ryn's *America the Virtuous: The Crisis of Democracy and the Quest for Empire* (2003), and Stephen M. Walt's *Taming American Power: The Global Response to U.S. Primacy* (2005).

The disputed 2000 presidential election is the focus of Jeffrey Toobin's *Too Close to Call: The Thirty-Six-Day Battle to Decide the 2000 Election* (2001). On the attacks of September 11, 2001, and their aftermath, see *The Age of Terror: America and the World after September 11,* edited by Strobe Talbott and Nayan Chanda (2001).

On the environmental history of New Orleans, see Craig E. Colten's *An Unnatural Metropolis: Wresting New Orleans from Nature* (2004). For a devastating account of the Bush administration by a White House insider, see Scott McClellan's *What Happened: Inside the Bush White House and Washington's Culture of Deception* (2008). On the historic 2008 election, see Michael Nelson's *The Elections of 2008* (2009).

CREDITS

CHAPTER 18: p. 520, Library of Congress; **p. 522,** Library of Congress; **p. 523,** Library of Congress; **p. 527,** Library of Congress; **p. 530,** Library of Congress; **p. 537,** Bettmann/Corbis; **p. 540,** Library of Congress; **p. 544,** Library of Congress; **p. 545,** Library of Congress; **p. 549,** Library of Congress.

PART 5: p. 555, Granger Collection; **p. 556,** Granger Collection.

CHAPTER 19: p. 559, Library of Congress; **p. 565,** Granger Collection; **p. 567,** Library of Congress; **p. 570,** Special Collections, University of Chicago Library; **p. 571,** Library of Congress; **p. 572,** Warder Collection; **p. 574,** Kansas State Historical Society; **p. 579,** Warder Collection; **p. 582,** Bettmann/Corbis; **p. 585,** Corbis; **p. 587,** Western Historical Collections University of Oklahoma Library.

CHAPTER 20: p. 590, Library of Congress; **p. 592,** Alfred Stieglitz, The Hand of Man 1902, hotogravure, P.1978.112, Amon Carter Museum; **p. 593,** Bettmann/Corbis; **p. 595** Union Pacific Museum; **p. 599,** Warder Collection; **p. 607,** American Petroleum Institute Historical Photo Collection; **p. 601,** Carnegie Library of Pittsburgh; **p. 602,** Pierpont Morgan Library; **p. 603,** Granger Collection; **p. 609,** T. V. Powderly Photographic Collection, The American Catholic History Research Center University Archives, The Catholic University of America, Washington, D.C.; **p. 613,** Walter P. Reuther Library, Wayne State University.

CHAPTER 21: p. 618, Library of Congress; **p. 622,** The Art Archive/Culver Pictures; **p. 623,** Bettmann/Corbis; **p. 626,** The Bryon Collection, Museum of the City of New York; **p. 627,** William Williams Papers, Manuscripts and Archives Division, The New York Public Library, Astor, Lenox and Tilden Foundations; **p. 630,** Bettmann/Corbis; **p. 632,** Brown Brothers; **p. 633,** Old York Library; **p. 634,** Library of Congress; **p. 636,** Special Collections, Vassar College Libraries; **p. 638,** American Museum of Natural History; **p. 640,** Time Life Pictures/Getty Images; **p. 643,** The Salvation Army National Archives; **p. 644,** University of Illinois at Chicago.

CHAPTER 22: p. 650, Library of Congress; **p. 651,** Library of Congress; **p. 655,** Library of Congress; **p. 658,** Warder Collection; **p. 660,** Bettmann/Corbis; **p. 662,**

Bettmann/Corbis; **p. 665,** Library of Congress; **p. 666,** Library of Congress; **p. 669,** Kansas State Historical Society; **p. 672,** Library of Congress; **p. 674,** Library of Congress.

PART 6: **p. 681,** Library of Congress; **p. 683,** Library of Congress.

CHAPTER 23: **p. 685,** Bettmann/Corbis; **p. 689,** Hawaii State Archives; **p. 692,** Library of Congress; **p. 693,** Bettmann/Corbis; **p. 699,** National Archives; **p. 698,** Photo: Corporal George J. Vennage; Courtesy of OSU Rare Books & Manuscripts Library; **p. 696,** Library of Congress; **p. 702,** Granger Collection; **p. 706,** Bettmann/Corbis; **p. 707,** Bettmann/Corbis.

CHAPTER 24: **p. 712,** Library of Congress; **p. 715,** Granger Collection; **p. 717,** Library of Congress; **p. 718,** Bettmann/Corbis; **p. 719,** Corbis; **p. 722 (top),** Collection of The New York Historical Society; **p. 722 (bottom),** Library of Congress; **p. 725,** Library of Congress; **p. 728,** Library of Congress; **p. 729,** Library of Congress; **p. 730,** Granger Collection; **p. 731,** Library of Congress; **p. 734,** Warder Collection; **p. 737,** Warder Collection; **p. 739,** Corbis.

CHAPTER 25: **p. 744,** Library of Congress; **p. 746,** Bettmann/Corbis; **p. 749,** Alamy; **p. 753,** The New York Times; **p. 755,** Bettmann/Corbis; **p. 757,** Swim Ink 2, LLC/Corbis; **p. 760,** Everett Collection; **p. 750,** National Archives; **p. 762,** Bettmann/Corbis; **p. 766,** Mary Evans Picture Library; **p. 769,** Courtesy of the Ding Darling Wildlife Society.

CHAPTER 26: **p. 776,** Bettmann/Corbis; **p. 778,** Bettmann/Corbis; **p. 780,** Bettmann/Corbis; **p. 782,** Bettmann/Corbis; **p. 784,** Ramsey Archive; **p. 785,** Bettmann/Corbis; **p. 786,** Bettmann/Corbis; **p. 789,** AP Photos.

CHAPTER 27: **p. 798,** Bettmann/Corbis; **p. 800,** Hulton Archive/Getty Images; **p. 803,** The Washington Post. Reprinted with permission; **p. 805,** Hulton Archive/Getty Images; **p. 807,** Bettmann/Corbis; **p. 809,** From the Collections of The Henry Ford Museum; **p. 812,** Bettmann/Corbis; **p. 813,** David J. & Janice L. Frent Collection/Corbis; **p. 814,** Herbert Hoover Presidential Library; **p. 819,** Bettmann/Corbis; **p. 821,** New York Daily News.

CHAPTER 28: **p. 824,** Bettmann/Corbis; **p. 827,** AP Photos; **p. 830,** National Archives; **p. 835,** Library of Congress; **p. 838,** National Archives; **p. 840,** Library of Congress; **p. 843,** Bettmann/Corbis; **p. 844,** Hulton Archives/Getty Images; **p. 845,** Bettmann/Corbis; **p. 846,** Bettmann/Corbis; **p. 848,** Library of Congress; **p. 851,** Corbis; **p. 856,** Granger Collection; **p. 857,** Bettmann/Corbis.

CHAPTER 29: **p. 862,** Bettmann/Corbis; **p. 864,** AP Photo; **p. 868,** National Archives; **p. 872,** 1938, The Washington Post; **p. 874,** British Information Services; **p. 875,** Granger Collection; **p. 878,** Bettmann/Corbis, **p. 882,** Library of Congress.

CHAPTER 30: **p. 886,** Bettmann/Corbis; **p. 888,** Warder Collection; **p. 890,** Swim Ink 2, LLC/Corbis; **p. 892,** Library of Congress; **p. 893,** AP Photo; **p. 895,** Bettmann/Corbis; **p. 903,** Eisenhower Presidential Library; **p. 904,** National Archives; **p. 910,** National Archives; **p. 913,** National Archives; **p. 915,** Bettmann/Corbis; **p. 917,** Hulton Archives/Getty Images.

PART 7: p. 923, Bill Eppridge/Getty Images; **p. 925,** Peter Turnley/Corbis.

CHAPTER 31: p. 927, Bettmann/Corbis; **p. 929,** University of Louisville; **p. 931,** Granger Collection; **p. 935,** Library of Congress; **p. 937,** Hartford Courant; **p. 939,** Hy Peskin/Getty Images; **p. 940,** 1948, Washington Post; **p. 941,** Bettmann/Corbis; **p. 948,** Bettmann/Corbis; **p. 950,** Yale Joel/Getty Images.

CHAPTER 32: p. 954, Hulton Archives/Getty Images; **p. 956,** William Joseph O'Keefe Collection, Veterans History Project, Library of Congress; **p. 958,** AP Photo; **p. 959,** AP Photo; **p. 961,** Library of Congress; **p. 963,** Fogg Art Museum, Harvard University; **p. 964,** PNI/Archive Museum of Art; **p. 960,** William Gottlieb/Corbis; **p. 971,** AP Photos; **p. 966,** Art Shay/Time Life Pictures/Getty Images; **p. 968,** Hulton/Getty Images; **p. 969,** AP Photos.

CHAPTER 33: p. 976, Bettmann/Corbis; **p. 981,** Bettmann/Corbis; **p. 982,** AP Photo; **p. 983,** "Don't Be Afraid—I Can Always Pull You Back" from Herblock's *Special for Today* (Simon & Schuster 1958); **p. 984,** Photoworld; **p. 985,** AP Photo; **p. 993,** AP Photo; **p. 995,** University of Louisville; **p. 997,** Black Star/Stock Photo; **p. 998,** Joseph Scherschel/Time Life Pictures/Getty Images.

CHAPTER 34: p. 1004, Bettmann/Corbis; **p. 1008,** National Archives; **p. 1010,** National Archives; **p. 1012,** Hulton Archives/Getty Images; **p. 1016,** Time Life Pictures/Getty Images; **p. 1017,** AP Photo; **p. 1021,** Bettmann/Corbis; **p. 1024,** National Archives; **p. 1028,** Newark Star-Ledger; **p. 1027,** Bettmann/Corbis.

CHAPTER 35: p. 1036, Bettmann/Corbis; **p. 1037,** Ted Streshinsky/Corbis; **p. 1039,** Magnum Photos; **p. 1041,** John Dominis/Getty Images; **p. 1042,** Bettmann/Corbis; **p. 1045,** AP Photos; **p. 1050,** Howard Ruffner/Time Life Pictures/Getty Images; **p. 1055,** Bettmann/Corbis; **p. 1056,** NASA Kennedy Space Center; **p. 1057,** John Dominis/Getty Images; **p. 1058,** AP Photo; **p. 1061,** AP Photo; **p. 1063,** Wally McNamee/Corbis; **p. 1066,** AP Photo.

CHAPTER 36: p. 1070, Bettmann/Corbis; **p. 1071,** Bettmann/Corbis; **p. 1072,** Bettmann/Corbis; **p. 1077,** Bettmann/Corbis; **p. 1078,** Los Angeles Times Syndicate; **p. 1082,** Bettmann/Corbis; **p. 1080,** AP Photo; **p. 1087,** Woodfin Camp; **p. 1088,** AP Photo; **p. 1091,** Bettmann/Corbis.

CHAPTER 37: p. 1094, Smiley N. Pool/Dallas Morning News/Corbis; **p. 1096,** AP Photo; **p. 1097,** Library of Congress; **p. 1099,** Durand-Hudson-Langevin-Orban/Sygma/Corbis; **p. 1101,** Chris Wilkins/Getty Images; **p. 1103,** AP Photo; **p. 1108,** AP Photo; **p. 1109,** AP Photo; **p. 1116,** Sean Adair/Reuters/Corbis; **p. 1117,** AP Photo; **p. 1119,** Reuters/Corbis; **p. 1120,** Bettmann/Corbis, **p. 1123,** Brooks Kraft/Corbis; **p. 1126,** Reuters/Corbis; **p. 1127,** AP Photo; **p. 1128,** AP Photo; **p. 1129,** AP Photo; **p. 1131,** AP Photo; **p. 1132,** Michael Ainsworth/Dallas Morning News/Corbis; **p. 1133,** AP Photo; **p. 1134,** Shawn Thew/epa/Corbis; **p. 1136,** AP Photo; **p. 1138,** Jim Young/Reuters/Corbis.

INDEX

Page numbers in *italics* refer to illustrations.

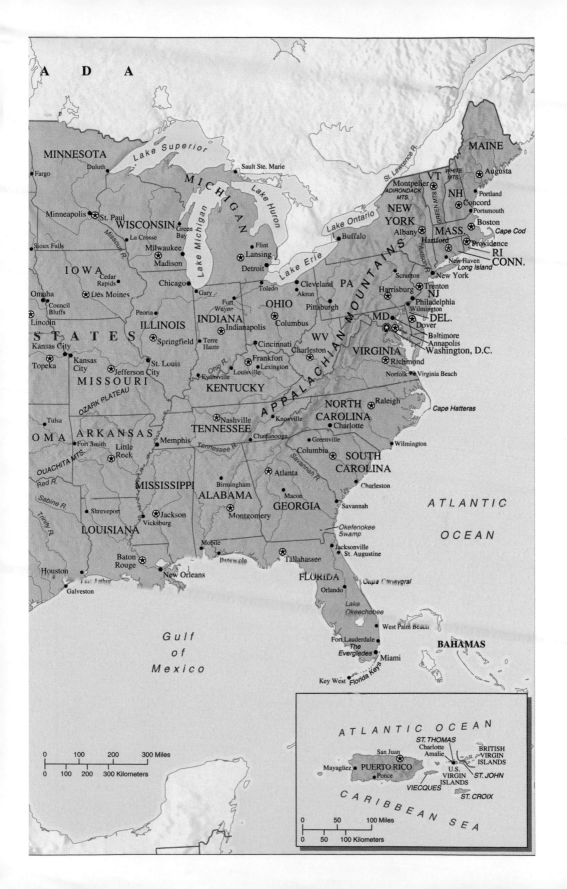

A D A

MINNESOTA
Fargo
Duluth
Lake Superior
Sault Ste. Marie
MICHIGAN
Lake Huron

Minneapolis ⊛ St. Paul
WISCONSIN
Green Bay
La Crosse
Sioux Falls
Milwaukee
Madison
Lake Michigan

IOWA
Cedar Rapids
Des Moines
Chicago
Gary
Fort Wayne
INDIANA
OHIO
Columbus
Flint
⊛ Lansing
Detroit
Lake Erie
Cleveland
Akron
Pittsburgh

Omaha
Council Bluffs
Lincoln
STATES
Peoria
ILLINOIS
⊛ Springfield
⊛ Indianapolis
Terre Haute
Cincinnati
Ohio R.
Louisville
Frankfort
Lexington
Evansville

Lake Ontario
Buffalo

MAINE
WHITE MTS.
⊛ Augusta
VT
Montpelier
ADIRONDACK MTS.
NH
⊛ Concord
Portland
Portsmouth
NEW YORK
Albany ⊛
GREEN MTS.
MASS.
Boston
Cape Cod
Hartford
⊛ Providence
RI
New Haven
CONN.
Long Island
New York
Scranton
PA
Harrisburg
Trenton
NJ
Philadelphia
Wilmington
DEL.
MD
Dover
Baltimore
Annapolis
Washington, D.C.

Kansas City
Topeka
Kansas City
⊛ Jefferson City
MISSOURI
OZARK PLATEAU

St. Louis
WV
Charleston
VIRGINIA
⊛ Richmond
Norfolk Virginia Beach

Tulsa
OMA
ARKANSAS
Fort Smith
Little Rock ⊛
OUACHITA MTS.
Red R.
Sabine R.
Trinity R.

KENTUCKY
⊛ Nashville
Knoxville
TENNESSEE
Chattanooga
Tennessee R.
Memphis

APPALACHIAN MOUNTAINS

NORTH CAROLINA
⊛ Raleigh
Charlotte
Greenville
Columbia
SOUTH CAROLINA
Charleston
Wilmington
Cape Hatteras

ATLANTIC
OCEAN

Shreveport
LOUISIANA
Houston
Port Arthur
Galveston
Baton Rouge
New Orleans

MISSISSIPPI
⊛ Jackson
Vicksburg
Birmingham
ALABAMA
⊛ Montgomery
Mobile
Pensacola

Atlanta ⊛
Macon
GEORGIA
Savannah
Okefenokee Swamp
Jacksonville
St. Augustine
Tallahassee

FLORIDA
Orlando
Cape Canaveral
Lake Okeechobee

Gulf
of
Mexico

West Palm Beach
Fort Lauderdale
The Everglades
Miami
Key West
Florida Keys

BAHAMAS

0   100   200   300 Miles
0   100   200   300 Kilometers

ATLANTIC OCEAN
ST. THOMAS
Charlotte Amalie
San Juan
BRITISH VIRGIN ISLANDS
Mayagüez ⊛ PUERTO RICO
Ponce
U.S. VIRGIN ISLANDS
ST. JOHN
VIEQUES
ST. CROIX

CARIBBEAN SEA

0   50   100 Miles
0   50   100 Kilometers